The SAGE Handbook of Nonverbal Communication

The SAGE
Handbook of
Nonverbal
Communication

Editors

Valerie Manusov **&** Miles L. Patterson
University of Washington   *University of Missouri, St. Louis*

SAGE Publications
Thousand Oaks ▪ London ▪ New Delhi

For information:

Sage Publications, Inc.
2455 Teller Road
Thousand Oaks, California 91320
E-mail: order@sagepub.com

Sage Publications Ltd.
1 Oliver's Yard
55 City Road
London EC1Y 1SP
United Kingdom

Sage Publications India Pvt. Ltd.
B-42, Panchsheel Enclave
Post Box 4109
New Delhi 110 017 India

Printed in the United States of America

Library of Congress Cataloging-in-Publication Data

The SAGE handbook of nonverbal communication / [edited by] Valerie Manusov, Miles L. Patterson.
   p. cm.
Includes bibliographical references and index.
ISBN 1-4129-0404-8 (cloth)
   1. Nonverbal communication. I. Title: Handbook of nonverbal communication.
II. Manusov, Valerie Lynn. III. Patterson, Miles L.
BF637.N66S24 2006
302.2′22—dc22

                                        2006004826

This book is printed on acid-free paper.

06   07   08   09   10   10 9 8 7 6 5 4 3 2 1

Acquiring Editor:	Todd R. Armstrong
Editorial Assistant:	Camille Herrera
Project Editor:	Astrid Virding
Copyeditor:	Quads/Linda Gray
Typesetter:	C&M Digitals (P) Ltd.
Indexer:	Juniee Oneida
Cover Designer:	Edgar Abarca

CONTENTS

PART IV: CONTEXTS AND CONSEQUENCES

PART V: FINAL THOUGHTS

ACKNOWLEDGMENTS

This volume would not exist if not for the encouragement and direction of Todd Armstrong, Editor from Sage Publications. Along with help from Deya Saoud and Camille Herrera, we had an easy time bringing the *The SAGE Handbook of Nonverbal Communication* into being. We are grateful for the careful copy editing work of Linda Gray and to the always diligent Astrid Virding for guiding the manuscript through production. We also thank our wonderful authors for their extensive work on these chapters. Authors provided several drafts of their chapters, responding wonderfully to our often demanding feedback. Because there is such demand for their expertise in contributing to a wide variety of publications, we appreciate their efforts even more. Valerie and Miles would like to thank our respective departments—Communication at the University of Washington and Psychology at the University of Missouri, St. Louis—for their support throughout this process. More important, we would like to thank our respective families for their constant support and patience: Chuck and Cameron McSween and Dianne and Kevin Patterson.

SAGE Publications gratefully thanks the following reviewers: Mark L. Knapp, Jesse H. Jones Centennial Professor in Communication and UT Distinguished Teaching Professor, University of Texas at Austin; Susanne M. Jones, University of Minnesota, Twin Cities; Ross Buck, University of Connecticut; and Peter A. Andersen, San Diego State University.

PREFACE

◆ Valerie Manusov
University of Washington

◆ Miles L. Patterson
University of Missouri, St. Louis

Putting together any *Handbook* is daunting. The challenge of creating an edited volume is enhanced further when the research area is interdisciplinary, as is the study of nonverbal cues. We decided that the focus should be on *communication* and not the entire spectrum of research concerned with nonverbal behavior. Over the years, scholars have argued over where to draw the line between communicative and noncommunicative events. In some cases, this led to a very restricted view of communication, including only those behaviors that were sent intentionally and had a consistent meaning, at least within a particular culture. Our preference is to assume a broader definition of nonverbal communication, encompassing the sending and receiving of information through appearance, objects, the environment, and behavior in social settings.

Choosing topics and authors to represent the breadth of the field and, at the same time, provide a discriminating analysis of research and theory, presented another challenge. There was a large range of expertise and issues that merited consideration. Although not fully inclusive, we were fortunate in enlisting scholars who have devoted much of their academic life to understanding better the processes involved in the give-and-take of nonverbal communication. This helped us in our goal for the *Handbook* to provide a path to understanding the subtleties of our social interactions and our relationships with one another. The chapters in the *Handbook* emphasize the primacy of nonverbal channels in facilitating interpersonal contact and regulating our social worlds.

Unlike other *Handbooks,* the current volume's chapters are not meant to be exhaustive of the research in the area. Rather, authors were given the charge of *making an argument for what is important in their respective areas.* Thus, for example, Fridlund and Russell call for a move away from thinking about emotions as the primary function of facial displays. Robinson, in his chapter on physician-patient nonverbal interaction argues for the importance of a situated, focused microanalytic assessment of the cues that occur in such interactions. Walther argues that computer- mediated communication is not devoid of nonverbal cues as is often asserted but, rather, that chronemics have always been a source of message value for people communicating online. As readers work through this *Handbook,* they will see a range of expertise and perspective that reflects the amazing sophistication of current scholarship on nonverbal communication.

To organize the large and diverse set of arguments about nonverbal communication, we placed the chapters into four primary categories. This first section, "foundations," provides an array of issues that underlie all conceptualizations of and research into nonverbal communication. Specifically, chapters include the broad history of nonverbal communication (Knapp), parallel processes in nonverbal communication (Patterson), methods (Gray & Ambady), cognitive bases (Lakin), skills (Riggio), and coordination with language (Bavelas & Chovil). These issues are essential for understanding how nonverbal

communication works and how it has been studied. Our second section, "factors of influence," brings together work on the myriad forces that help shape our use of nonverbal communication. This section emphasizes the importance of biology (Buck & Renfro Powers), evolution (Floyd), personality (Gifford), age (Feldman & Tyler), sex and gender (Hall), culture (Matsumoto), and the media (Manusov & Jaworski). Each of these chapters argues for the ways in which the particular factors work to shape the practice and meaning of nonverbal communication.

The third section of the handbook, "functions," follows the premise that nonverbal communication serves a variety of different purposes. That is, nonverbal communication facilitates short-term and long-term ends in our social world. These functions include sending relational messages of intimacy (Andersen, Guerrero, & Jones) and dominance (Burgoon & Dunbar), expressing intentions and, to a lesser degree, emotions (Fridlund & Russell), creating and managing impressions (Keating), deceiving others or helping us detect deception (Vrij), regulating interaction (Cappella & Schreiber), and building and reflecting rapport (Tickle-Degnen). These chapters discuss the complexity of these communicative functions and suggest the importance of nonverbal cues for the communication of fundamental human endeavors.

An awareness of the importance of nonverbal cues is reflected again in our fourth section, "contexts and consequences." In this set of chapters, the authors work to reveal the ways in which particular contexts shape and make salient certain nonverbal processes. They also discuss the very real implications of nonverbal behavior within these contexts. The contexts we have focused on for this *Handbook* are close relationships (Noller), education (McCroskey, Richmond, & McCroskey), physician-patient interaction (Robinson), computer-mediated communication (Walther), groups (Dovidio, Hebl, Richeson, & Shelton), and organizations (Remland). The implications and importance of nonverbal cues are also made clear in Giles and Le Poire's engaging Introduction.

Although we have worked to organize this *Handbook* into a larger frame, two caveats are important to note. First, reading across chapters shows a range of places where debate exists in the research community about the best ways to conceptualize and measure certain nonverbal phenomena. In our final chapter, Patterson and Manusov work to make these debates—about the role of learning and inheritance, about the nature and "privilege" of certain processes such as emotional expression over others—even more apparent. Second, readers will see that the chapters cross-reference one another, showing—sometimes despite areas of difference—the important connection between many of the lines of research highlighted in this volume. They also reflect just how far research on nonverbal cues and processes has come.

Ours is an interdisciplinary field, creating opportunities to see the myriad factors involved in nonverbal communication and sometimes adding blinders to what we choose to investigate. It is our hope that the current *Handbook* encourages the former and discourages the latter, working to develop a full and integrated set of future nonverbal scholarship.

INTRODUCTION

The Ubiquity and Social Meaningfulness of Nonverbal Communication

◆ Howard Giles
University of California, Santa Barbara

◆ Beth A. Le Poire
California Lutheran University

Nonverbal communication—in all its impressive manifestations—is central to the communication process by being "an inherent and essential part of message creation (production) and interpretation (processing)" (Burgoon, 1994, p. 239). It also generates enormous interest among academics and the general public. Evidence of this interest comes in myriad forms and practices that people find instrumental to their daily lives. Our goal in this prologue is to excite readers' understandings about the ubiquity of nonverbal communication and the ways it is developed from our very earliest of days to its instrumental role in maintaining lifelong partnerships (see Driver & Gottman, 2004, for a larger discussion of nonverbal communication in long-term relationships; Feldman & Tyler, this volume, for a discussion of nonverbal communication across the lifespan). Moreover, as an introductory chapter to a larger set of issues including the foundations, functions, contexts, and consequences of nonverbal cues, we explore the particular influence nonverbal communication has on important health, developmental, and marital outcomes.

◆ *The Ubiquity of Nonverbal Communication*

That nonverbal communication is integral to communicative interactions is indisputable. Indeed, when verbal and nonverbal cues are incongruent, Burgoon (1994) contends that individuals often accord greater credence to the latter than to the former features (see also Remland, this volume). Her argument is based on ample evidence. For example, Argyle, Salter, Nicholson, Williams, and Burgess (1970) created videotapes of a performer reflecting superior, neutral, or inferior attitudes toward participants in their psychological experiments. This presentation of attitudes was accomplished in a design where verbal and nonverbal were congruent or incongruent with each other. In one of the conditions, a superior statement was accompanied by nervous smiling, a lowered head, and a tone of voice expressing eagerness to please. The authors found the nonverbal cues were three to four times more important in attributing superiority-inferiority to the actor than were the verbal statements.

Repeating the study, but this time using a friend-hostile dimensions, nonverbal cues were found to be six times more important than what was said verbally (Argyle, Alkema, & Gilmour, 1971). This finding may indicate that nonverbal communication is especially important when relational messages are of paramount importance. Even in interactions where verbal communication accounts for more of the variance in meaning acquisition (e.g., persuasion, information transmission), nonverbal communication still contributes to communicative

outcomes significantly (van Swol, 2003). So important is the interaction of nonverbal communication with verbal communication that numerous scholars caution against separating nonverbal and verbal communication for analysis (e.g., Cappella & Street, 1985; see also Bavelas & Chovil, this volume).

Furthermore, nonverbal communication is central to socially meaningful outcomes of communication interactions across all relationship types. In addition to the processes mentioned previously, nonverbal cues can affect deception detection and its outcomes (e.g., Forrest & Feldman, 2000; Vrij, this volume), conflict management (e.g., Beaumont & Wagner, 2004), the communication of stigma (e.g., Le Poire, 1994), information transmission (e.g., Frick-Horbury, 2002), and interactional management (e.g., Jones, Gallois, Callan, & Barker, 1999; see Cappella & Schreiber, this volume). Nonverbal communication is also central to the establishment, maintenance, and dissolution of relationships (see Noller, this volume). Nonverbal communication is valued as so important—and beyond the scope of our quest here—as to garner the attention of scholars in thousands of studies across communication, linguistics, sociology, psychology, psychiatry, education, biology, physiology, and anthropology. Many of these studies are referenced across this *Handbook's* chapters.

◆ *The Social Impact of Nonverbal Communication*

Perhaps most important for the present volume, nonverbal communication can be valued for the very real impacts it has in day-to-day living. One area where this can be seen regards health. Nonverbal communication affects health outcomes in formal health care settings, and it can also be seen to have an effect in interpersonal relationships. Specifically, parents can affect mental and physical health outcomes in their children through their nonverbal behavior (e.g., Miller, Benson, & Galbraith, 2001). In addition, marital partners can also affect each other's physical and mental health through their nonverbal interaction behaviors (e.g., Kiecolt-Glaser, McGuire, Robles, & Glaser, 2002).

In addition to health, however, we focus in this section on nonverbal communication and development, making the argument that nonverbal communication from parents to children and teachers to children also affects the development of children physically, socially, and intellectually (see also, Feldman & Tyler, this volume). Also, we look at some of the ample research focusing on the role of nonverbal communication in close relationships, centering on the impact of nonverbal communication with relational satisfaction. Finally, whereas these important outcomes are all housed within important relationships, nonverbal communication can have important ramifications in nonpersonal relationships as well (see also Dovidio, Hebl, Richeson, & Shelton, this volume; Remland, this volume). We focus here primarily on the ways in which nonverbal cues affect people's judgments of one another.

HEALTH OUTCOMES

The role of nonverbal communication in health care has been studied extensively within physician-patient interactions (e.g., Aruguete & Roberts, 2002; Rosenthal, 2002; see Robinson, this volume), and physical health outcomes of older patients have been linked to the nonverbal communication of physical therapists (e.g., Ambady, Koo, Rosenthal, & Winograd,

2002). Additionally, because nonverbal behavior deficits are central to autism, nonverbal behaviors are often used as an early diagnostic tool for detecting this condition in children (Bristol-Power & Spinella, 1999). Partners' use of nonverbal communication has also been linked to better recidivism outcomes for substance abusers (e.g., Le Poire, Dailey, & Duggan, 2002; Le Poire, Duggan, & Dailey, 2001).

Nonverbal communication from caregivers toward their children has also been associated with better health outcomes for children. Specifically, as up to half of all parents are not likely to talk directly with their children about sex (Jaccard, Dittus, & Gordon, 2000), it is reassuring to realize that parenting style can reduce the incidence of sexually risky behavior. A summary of more than 20 studies indicates that parent-child closeness (which is enhanced through nonverbal expressions of warmth) is associated with reduced adolescent pregnancy risk through sexual abstinence, postponement of intercourse, having fewer sexual partners, and using contraception consistently (see Miller et al., 2001, for a review). Thus, authoritative parents seem to provide the right mix of nonverbal warmth and parental control necessary to provide their children with the tools necessary to reduce their risk of pregnancy, regardless of whether or not they are talking directly with their adolescent children about sex and the potential outcomes of risky sex.

This relationship of greater warmth and better health outcomes holds for substance use as well. For instance, adolescents' substance use is associated with both family affection and parental control (Hall, Henggeler, Ferreira, & East, 1992). Consistently, moderate amounts of parental control and parental support are related to decreased illicit drug use, whereas higher amounts of control and support were both predictive of decreased alcohol use (Stice, Barrera, & Chassin, 1993). These results provide evidence for the contention that the nonverbal communication of warmth, in combination with higher amounts ofcontrol, is associated with better health outcomes among adolescents.

Nonverbal expressions of negative emotions within marriages may actually be related to mental and physical health outcomes as well. Supportive nonverbal and verbal communication is one of the resources associated with close personal relationships. Such supportive communication diminishes the expression of negative emotions and enhances health in part through its positive impact on immune and endocrine regulation (e.g., Kiecolt-Glaser et al., 2002). If spouses evoke greater amounts of negative emotional expression, their actions can stimulate immune dysregulation, which may be one of the core mechanisms underlying conditions such as cardiovascular disease, osteroporosis, arthritis, Type 2 diabetes, and certain cancers (Kiecolt-Glaser et al., 2002). Unhappy marriages, then, may be rife with negative emotional expression, which can explain the poorer mental and physical health of unhappily married individuals. Supportive communication may facilitate greater physical health through its ability to ameliorate negative emotions. Alternatively, less supportive communication and the resulting negative emotions may actually be a detriment to physical health.

NONVERBAL COMMUNICATION AND DEVELOPMENTAL OUTCOMES

In addition to specific health outcomes, the influence of nonverbal communication between parents and children also reaches to better developmental outcomes for children. For instance, infants rely almost exclusively on vocalics and touch as a basis for forming secure attachments to caregivers. Specifically, infants' sensitivities to vocal cues appear to be rooted in the need for security in that infants perceive up and down glides in pitch as providing important information about affect and security (Papousek, Bornstein, Nuzzo, Papousek, & Symmes, 1990). Soon thereafter, infants use vocalizations to establish communication with their caregivers. By 8 to 12 weeks, they can coo, and by around 6 months, infants can babble (Oller, 1986). These vocalizations seem to be aimed specifically at others. Infants actually vocalize more when their parents are around than when they are alone (Masataka, 1993). Moreover, when parents respond to these vocalizations, infants engage in even more vocalizations (Legerstee, 1991).

In addition, infants' distress vocalizations occur in the first 4 to 5 months (Stark, Rose, & McLagen, 1975) and are highly potent and arousing signals for caregivers (Van Egeren & Barratt, 2004). In this way, distress cries may be the most adaptive form of communication that infants possess. Work comparing mothers with fathers, women with men, and parents with nonparents show that, across groups, people can interpret the earliest distress cries correctly (Papousek, 1989). Mothers are better at distinguishing distress cries for food as opposed to those of discomfort, however (Stallings, Fleming, Corter, Worthman, & Steiner, 2001). In general, parents (regardless of culture) respond to distress cries by holding, rocking/bouncing, singing, or talking in melodic rhythms (Keller et al., 1996; Papousek & Papousek, 1991). If the child is out of a parent's reach momentarily, the parent will begin rapid-fire, high-pitched verbalizations with a pitch that falls by the end (Papousek, Papousek, & Bornstein, 1985).

Besides vocalizations, infants rely on other forms of nonverbal communication.

Increased gaze between mothers and infants is related to more frequent vocalizations by both, but especially by mothers (Stevenson, Ver Hoeve, Roach, & Leavitt, 1986). Because infants often avoid eye contact when they are distressed, mothers of distressed infants usually attempt to reestablish eye contact through increased touch, smiling, and social play (Beebe & Stern, 1977). In addition, infants who use gestures more frequently may actually acquire language more quickly (Van Egeren & Barratt, 2004). Likewise, children who use their hands to point relatively early (some as early as 3 months) use more gestures overall and have better speech comprehension (Butterworth & Morissette, 1996) than children who point later in their development.

Although we would caution against elevating nonverbal communication to primary or even causal status in what follows, nonverbal cues are, arguably, central to the disciplinary styles that parents enact. Specifically, parents who exhibit greater warmth and responsivity toward their children (in combination with moderate to high control attempts) have children who generally exhibit higher achievement (e.g., authoritative parenting; Baumrind, 1996). This communicative manifestation of warmth is composed primarily of nonverbal signals (see Andersen, Guerrero, & Jones, this volume). Furthermore, nonverbal warmth is related to better outcomes in children. In one study, for example, children of authoritative parents (i.e., those showing high warmth and high demandingness) were the most cognitively motivated, competent, and achievement oriented (Baumrind, 1991). In another study, they were also the most intrinsically motivated (Ginsburg & Bronstein, 1993). Further, they attained the highest math and verbal achievement (Baumrind, 1991). Parents with authoritative styles of parenting also had children with higher self-esteem (Buri,

Louiselle, Misukanis, & Mueller, 1988) and self-actualization (Dominguez & Carton, 1997).

Children are likewise influenced by the nonverbal communication of their teachers (see McCroskey, Richmond, & McCroskey, this volume). In a now famous study, Rosenthal and Jacobsen (1968) compared the expectancy effects of teachers who had been given high expectations for students to teachers who had not been afforded them. In this study, and the 400 or so follow-up studies (for a review, see Rosenthal & Rubin, 1978), teachers communicated their expectancies to students in the classrooms through a whole host of nonverbal and verbal behaviors. Most relevant to nonverbal communication, however, teachers communicated in ways that foster a more positive climate with students for whom they have high expectations. In a follow-up meta-analytic study examining interpersonal expectancy effects in the classroom across 31 meta-analyses, Harris and Rosenthal (1985) found significant effects for nonverbal behaviors communicating expectancies. Among them, eye contact, wait time, gestures, distance, smiles, duration of interactions, and speech rate were all significant in predicting positive outcomes. Of the nonverbal behaviors included in the analyses on which Harris and Rosenthal's analysis was based, only touch and lean were not related to outcomes.

MARITAL NONVERBAL PROCESSES AND OUTCOMES

Nonverbal communication does not, however, relate only to the successful development of children. The valence of nonverbal communication has also been associated with marital satisfaction and marital stability. Gottman and Levinson (1992) argue, based on numerous behavioral investigations, that successful marriages have a 5:1 ratio in terms of positive to negative behaviors. They found that couples who displayed more positivity than negativity when they spoke to each other were more satisfied, less likely to have thought about divorce, and less likely to have actually separated. This ratio is especially important to marriages in which one or both partners are distressed (i.e., less satisfied). Individuals in distressed relationships tend to display more negative and less positive affect, and they are more likely to reciprocate negative affect (e.g., Noller, 1984, this volume). Negative behaviors may be the most predictive of marital satisfaction (e.g., Gottman & Levinson, 1986; Huston & Vangelisti, 1991), with negative behaviors being more predictive of marital satisfaction than positive ones (e.g., Broderick & O'Leary, 1986). This is the case, despite the fact that happier partners display more positive behaviors than do their unhappier counterparts (e.g., Cutrona, 1996).

Negative nonverbal communication behaviors may also predict divorce. Gottman (1994) argues that the consistent use of what he calls the "Four Horsemen of the Apocalypse" can portend the destruction of the marriage and tends to mark distressed couples (i.e., those with low amounts of marital satisfaction and high amounts of marital instability). Gottman and his colleagues found that couples in distress display greater expressions of criticism, contempt, defensiveness, and stonewalling consistently. Whereas all these displays include combinations of verbal and nonverbal behavior, contempt and stonewalling, in particular, are typically potent and negative nonverbal messages. According to Gottman, contempt and stonewalling, including their nonverbal manifestations, are particularly predictive of divorce.

To be more specific, contempt includes expressions of extremely negative affect toward a partner and can often include psychological abuse and intentional insults. Nonverbal indicators of contempt include eye rolling, disgust facial expressions, sneers, and hostile humor. It is likely that the intentional use of insults within conflict in marital relationships will result in distress as hurtful messages from romantic partners and other family members elicit greater negative feelings than those from other people (Vangelisti & Crumley, 1998). Such hurt, as part of a larger pattern of negative communication, can be destructive to family relationships in that negative communication (e.g., attacking the other, defensiveness, crying, ignoring the message), greater distancing behavior, and lower relationship satisfaction can ensue (e.g., Vangelisti, 1994, 2001; Vangelisti & Crumley, 1998; Vangelisti & Young, 2000). Stonewalling, on the other hand, includes responding to an onslaught of negative affect with withdrawal including flat facial affect. Its use implies that the issue is not worth addressing (strategically or not) and is not worthy of an emotional response. Gottman (1994) notes that men are more likely to respond by stonewalling, because they tend to be more physiologically reactive during conflict and thus may feel more of an intense pressure to withdraw from conflict situations (Gottman & Levinson, 1988). Stonewalling is one mechanism used to withdraw.

In tandem with this work is research on demand-withdrawal patterns during marital conflict (e.g., Caughlin & Vangelisti, 1999). A large amount of research illustrates that when wives want changes in a relationship, they are likely to make demands that are followed by the husbands' tendency to withdraw verbally and nonverbally (e.g., Baucom, Notarius, Burnett, & Haefner, 1990; Christensen & Shenk, 1991; Gottman & Levinson, 1988). This pattern of conflict is destructive in that dissatisfied marriages often evidence the demand-withdraw pattern of conflict, and these marriages frequently end in divorce (e.g., Heavey, Christensen, & Malamuth, 1995; Noller, Feeney, Bonnell, & Callan, 1994; Schaap, Buunk, & Kerkstra, 1988). One of the reasons why these marriages may end is that this particular destructive conflict pattern is not easily alterable (e.g., Jacobson, Follette, & Pagle, 1986).

We have shown some means through which nonverbal behaviors are an integral component of the communication and meaning acquisition processes through the child-rearing process on to marital dynamics and even divorce. These highly personal communication situations highlight some of the many meaningful ways in which nonverbal communication influences personal relationship and developmental outcomes. Nonverbal communication can also be highly influential across more nonpersonal relationships, however, and it is to this impact that we now turn our attention.

THE NATURE OF NONVERBAL COMMUNICATION IN NON-INTERPERSONAL RELATIONSHIPS

One of the most frequently studied parameters of nonverbal communication (as we have just discussed and as can be seen throughout this *Handbook*) is *immediacy*, defined as those communication behaviors, some visual others vocal, that "enhance closeness to and nonverbal interaction with another" (Mehrabian, 1969, p. 213). Signaling (consciously or unconsciously) feelings of, or the intent to become, relationally closer to another comes in various guises and sizes, including gaze and eye contact, smiling, forward body, and vocal warmth (Andersen, 1979). Such stances can also be processed vis-à-vis inanimate objects, as witnessed in some people's

responses to others who do not nonverbally position themselves "correctly" when the national anthem is being performed when pledging allegiance to the flag.

Immediacy displays may also reflect social distance and avoidance (Burgoon & Hale, 1984). For example, backward lean and frowning, are inferentially rich to the extent they are mined by us to attribute the actor as likeable, respected, committed, credible, persuasive, dynamic, and so on (e.g., see Zhou et al., 2002). So important is the use of nonverbal immediacy to convey closeness (or distance) that expressions of intimacy and closeness differentiate between marriages that are simply enduring and those that are enduring *and* the ideal happy marriage (e.g., Cuber & Haroff, 1965; Gottman & Levinson, 1988). Attributional work like this can be just as easily invoked watching soap operas or TV news interviews as it is in face-to-face interactions (see Manusov & Jaworski, this volume).

Nonverbal cues also have their optimal levels and latitudes of acceptance, however, and, as such, can be overaccommodated as in the case where some older people become the unwanted recipients of patronizing talk through exaggerated intonations, oversmiling, and slowed-down speech rates (Ryan, Hummert, & Boich, 1995). Being the recipient of such communications with patronizers representing different people in different contexts over time is not easily discountable. It can eventually imply a debilitating message for the receiver that he or she is cognitively and communicatively now much older and "past it." In other words, not only can nonverbal cues engender social support and relational harmony, they can also be part and parcel of the social construction of aging and even demise (Giles, 1999).

The social meanings of these and other immediacy cues (e.g., the timing of events, touch, proximity, body movements) vary in their interpretive potential rather dramatically between cultures (Burgoon, 1995; see also, Matsumoto, this volume) and often appear as essential ingredients of cross-cultural training programs and etiquette books. Indeed, the *absence* of such cues, such as a lack of nonverbal expressiveness or neutrality, can influence important social decisions by teachers, medical personnel, law enforcement, and so forth. In his discussion of the performative nature of preaching, for example, Robinson (1980) remarked that "a pastor's words may insist, 'This is important,' but if his voice sounds flat and expressionless and his body stands limp, the congregation will not believe him" (cited in Mikkelson & Floyd, 2005, p. 194). Often, reactions to the presence or the absence of nonverbal cues are stereotypic, leading to inaccurate presumptions and even irresponsible actions.

There are, of course, many other nonverbal cues including accent that people use to categorize others into social groups, often triggering allied trait attributions and their associated affect (Giles & Billings, 2004). Indeed, not a day goes by for one of us (HG) when his non-North American accent is not commented upon by strangers. Speech rate, pitch, timing, rhythm, and intonation are (paralinguistic) nonverbal cues people can manipulate to manage impressions or in forming impressions of others (Pittam, 2000; see also Keating, this volume). Paramount among these are historically sensitive dress styles and fashion, which sometimes elicit evaluative comments among (and subsequent affirmation from) older males about certain young women's dress modes, such as "I'm glad *I* don't have a daughter these days!" Wearing a tie, jacket, or suit can signal formality and professionalism in some work and leisure contexts yet be construed as irreverently Western in some Muslim contexts. Furthermore, being under- or overdressed can cause observational concern or lament.

The use of spectacles or even sunglasses in some contexts, watches, designer-labeled clothing, jewelry, and men's gold neck chains; the plethora of possible hairstyles (buzz-cuts, braids, bob); and a ball-cap turned backward all have their unique social meanings and, again, sometimes stimulate passionate reactions, deep-seated emotions, and intense comment from third parties. Facial rings, lipstick colors, eye makeup, hairstyles, body size, gang graffiti and gang signs, and cosmetics are but a few of the myriad ways we can send messages out (again more or less strategically) about our ideologies, aspirations, and group memberships, be they ethnic, sexual orientation, political, or whatever (see Harwood & Giles, 2005).

Given the recent fascination with physical beauty as evidenced by current American television programs focusing on cosmetic surgery (e.g., the *Swan, Makeover*), and the current emphasis on physical beauty and youth evidenced by such trends as Botox and breast augmentation, it is not that surprising that nonverbal communication emphasizing physical attraction has received a great amount of research attention. Finally, the use of other possessions transported or in the workplace and home—certain kinds of cell phones; books, newspapers, or magazines read and or displayed; suitcase style; music and movies played; new technological artifacts; cars; residence location and architecture; remodels; decorations and artwork; and so on—can communicate status and trait attributions (cultured, pretentious, lifespan crisis, macho, cheap, etc.). They can also influence encounters, even those with strangers, through the type of messages they convey.

◆ Conclusions

Nonverbal communication is of considerable consequence in many aspects of social life. Numerous investigations place nonverbal communication as central to meaning acquisition (Birdwhistell, 1970), especially in communication interactions where relational communication (Burgoon & Le Poire, 1999), emotional expressions (Boone & Buck, 2003), and impression management (Xin, 2004) are concerned. Moreover, nonverbal communication can be influential in the relationships surrounding health care, and they can also have a significant impact on important familial relationships. Children and their nurturers display nonverbal behavior that facilitates the safety and development of infants, children, and adolescents. The use of nonverbal warmth (in combination with moderate to high control attempts), for example, appears to ensure better health outcomes for adolescents by reducing risky sexual behavior and substance use and abuse. In addition, teachers' use of nonverbal behavior communicates important expectancies to students and affects the student's performance on a variety of academic indicators. Moreover, nonverbal communication facilitates the "health" of marriages as well in that more positive nonverbal communication and less negative destructive nonverbal communication (e.g., contempt, stonewalling, withdrawal, expression of negative emotions) predict greater marital stability and satisfaction and even better physical health outcomes.

Clearly, nonverbal communication functions in important socially meaningful ways across a variety of relationships. With this backdrop accessed, we trust readers will have a more informed springboard with which to access specific chapters and the various theoretical models discussed in them. Along with the *Handbook*'s editors, we hope that readers will see the complexities of this communication system, the many foundational issues into which it is embedded, the myriad functions that it serves for

communicators, and the ways in which the context influences nonverbal meaning and process and creates relevant, and often problematic, consequences, which a more complete understanding of nonverbal communication can help to address.

◆ References

Ambady, N., Koo, J., Rosenthal, R., & Winograd, C. H. (2002). Physical therapists' nonverbal communication predicts geriatric patients' health outcomes. *Psychology and Aging, 17,* 443–452.

Andersen, J. F. (1979). Teacher immediacy as a predictor of teaching effectiveness. In D. Nimmo (Ed.), *Communication yearbook 3* (pp. 543–559). New Brunswick, NJ: Prentice Hall.

Argyle, M., Alkema, F., & Gilmour, R. (1971). The communication of friendly and hostile attitudes by verbal and nonverbal signals. *European Journal of Social Psychology, 2,* 385–402.

Argyle, M., Salter, V., Nicholson, H., Williams, M., & Burgess, P. (1970). The communication of inferior and superior attitudes by verbal and nonverbal signals. *British Journal of Social and Clinical Psychology, 9,* 222–231.

Aruguete, M. S., & Roberts, C. A. (2002). Participants' ratings of male physicians who vary in race and communication style. *Psychological Reports, 91,* 793–806.

Baucom, D. H., Notarius, C. I., Burnett, C. K., & Haefner, P. (1990). Gender differences and sex-role identity in marriage. In F. D. Fincham & T. N. Bradbury (Eds.), *The psychology of marriage* (pp. 150–171). New York: Guilford.

Baumrind, D. (1991). The influence of parenting style on adolescent competence and substance use. *Journal of Early Adolescence, 11,* 56–95.

Baumrind, D. (1996). Parenting: The discipline controversy revisited. *Family Relations, 45,* 405–414.

Beaumont, S. L., & Wagner, S. L. (2004). Adolescent-parent verbal conflict: The roles of conversational styles and disgust emotions. *Journal of Language and Social Psychology, 23,* 338–368.

Beebe, B., & Stern, D. N. (1977). Engagement-disengagement and early object experiences. In N. Freedman & S. Granel (Eds.), *Communicative structures and psychic structures* (pp. 35–55). New York: Plenum Press.

Birdwhistell, R. L. (1970). *Kinesics and context.* Philadelphia: University of Pennsylvania Press.

Boone, R. T., & Buck, R. (2003). Emotional expressivity and trustworthiness: The role of nonverbal behavior in the evolution of cooperation. *Journal of Nonverbal Behavior, 27,* 163–182.

Bristol-Power, M. M., & Spinella, G. (1999). Research on screening and diagnosis in autism: A work in progress. *Journal of Autism and Developmental Disorders, 29,* 435–438.

Broderick, J. E., & O'Leary, K. D. (1986). Contributions to affect, attitudes, and behavior to marital satisfaction. *Journal of Consulting and Clinical Psychology, 54,* 514–517.

Burgoon, J. K. (1994). Nonverbal signals. In M. L. Knapp & G. R. Miller (Eds.), *Handbook of interpersonal communication* (2nd ed., pp. 229–285). Thousand Oaks, CA: Sage.

Burgoon, J. K. (1995). Cross-cultural and intercultural applications of expectancy violations theory. In R. L. Wiseman (Ed.), *Intercultural communication theory* (pp. 194–215). Thousand Oaks: Sage.

Burgoon, J. K., & Hale, J. L. (1984). The fundamental topoi of relational communication. *Communication Monographs, 51,* 193–214.

Burgoon, J. K., & Le Poire, B. A. (1999). Nonverbal cues and interpersonal judgments: Participant and observer perceptions of intimacy, dominance, composure, and formality. *Communication Monographs, 66,* 105–124.

Buri, J. R., Louiselle, P. A., Misukanis, T. M., & Mueller, R. A. (1988). Effects of parental authoritarianism and authoritativeness on self-esteem. *Personality and Social Psychology Bulletin, 14,* 271–282.

Butterworth, G., & Morissette, P. (1996). Onset of pointing and the acquisition of language in infancy. *Journal of Reproductive and Infant Psychology, 14,* 219–231.

Cappella, J. N., & Street, R. L., Jr. (1985). Introduction: A functional approach to the structure of communication behavior. In R. L. Street Jr. & J. N. Cappella (Eds.), *Sequence and pattern in communicative behavior* (pp. 1–29). London: Edward Arnold.

Caughlin, J. P., & Vangelisti, A. L. (1999). Desire for change in one's partner as predictor of the demand/withdraw pattern of marital communication. *Communication Monographs, 66,* 66–89.

Christensen, A., & Shenk, J. L. (1991). Communication, conflict, and psychological distance in nondistressed, clinic, and divorcing couples. *Journal of Consulting and Clinical Psychology, 59,* 458–463.

Cuber, J. F., & Haroff, P. (1965). *Sex and the significant Americans.* Baltimore: Penguin.

Cutrona, C. E. (1996). *Social support in couples.* Thousand Oaks, CA: Sage.

Dominguez, M. M., & Carton, J. S. (1997). The relationship between self-actualization and parenting style. *Journal of Social Behavior and Personality, 12,* 1093–1100.

Driver, J. L., & Gottman, J. M. (2004). Daily marital interactions and positive affect during marital conflict among newlywed couples. *Family Process, 43,* 301–314.

Forrest, J. A., & Feldman, R. S. (2000). Detecting deception and judge's involvement: Lower task involvement leads to better lie detection. *Personality and Social Psychology Bulletin, 26,* 118–125.

Frick-Horbury, D. (2002). The effects of hand gestures on verbal recall as a function of high- and low-verbal-skill levels. *Journal of General Psychology, 129,* 137–147.

Giles, H. (1999). Managing dilemmas in the "silent revolution": A call to arms! *Journal of Communication, 49,* 170–182.

Giles, H., & Billings, A. (2004). Language attitudes. In A. Davies & E. Elder (Eds.),

Handbook of applied linguistics (pp. 187–209). Oxford, UK: Blackwell.

Ginsburg, G., & Bronstein, P. (1993). Family factors related to children's intrinsic/extrinsic motivational orientation and academic performance. *Child Development, 64,* 1461–1471.

Gottman, J. M. (1994). *What predicts divorce? The relationship between marital processes and marital outcomes.* Hillsdale, NJ: Lawrence Erlbaum.

Gottman, J. M., & Levinson, R. W. (1986). Assessing the role of emotion in marriage. *Behavioral Assessment, 8,* 31–48.

Gottman, J. M., & Levinson, R. W. (1988). The social psychophysiology of marriage. In P. Noller & M. A. Fitzpatrick (Eds.), *Perspectives on marital interaction* (pp. 182–200). Philadelphia: Multilingual Matters.

Gottman, J. M., & Levinson, R. W. (1992). Marital processes predictive of later dissolution: Behavior, physiology, and health. *Journal of Personality and Social Psychology, 63,* 221–233.

Hall, J. A., Henggeler, S. W., Ferreira, D. K., & East, P. L. (1992). Sibling relations and substance use in high-risk female adolescents. *Family Dynamics of Addiction Quarterly, 2,* 44–51.

Harris, M. J., & Rosenthal, R. (1985). Mediation of interpersonal expectancy effects: 31 meta-analyses. *Psychological Bulletin, 97,* 363–386.

Harwood, J., & Giles, H. (2005). *Intergroup communication: Multiple perspectives.* Berlin: Peter Lang.

Heavey, C. L., Christensen, A., & Malamuth, N. M. (1995). The longitudinal impact of demand and withdrawal during marital conflict. *Journal of Consulting and Clinical Psychology, 63,* 797–801.

Huston, T. L., & Vangelisti, A. L. (1991). Socioemotional behavior and satisfaction in marital relationships. *Journal of Personality and Social Psychology, 61,* 721–733.

Jaccard, J., Dittus, P. J., & Gordon, V. V. (2000). Parent-teen communication about premarital sex: Factors associated with the extent of communication. *Journal of Adolescent Research, 15,* 187–208.

Jacobson, N. S., Follette, W. C., & Pagel, M. (1986). Predicting who will benefit from behavioral marital therapy. *Journal of Consulting and Clinical Psychology, 54,* 518–522.

Jones, E., Gallois, C., Callan, V., & Barker, M. (1999). Strategies of accommodation: Development of a coding system for conversational interaction. *Journal of Language and Social Interaction, 18,* 123–152.

Keller, H., Chasiotis, A., Risau Peters, J., Voelker, S., Zach, U., & Restemeier, R. (1996). Psychobiological aspects of infant crying. *Early Development and Parenting, 5,* 1–13.

Kiecolt-Glaser, J. K., McGuire, L., Robles, T. F., & Glaser, R. (2002). Psychoneuroimmunology: Psychological influences on immune function and health. *Journal of Consulting and Clinical Psychology, 70,* 537–547.

Legerstee, M. (1991). Changes in the quality of infant sounds as a function of social and nonsocial stimulation. *First Language, 11,* 327–343.

Le Poire, B. A. (1994). Attraction toward and nonverbal stigmatization of gays and persons with AIDS: Evidence of instrumentally symbolic attitudinal structures. *Human Communication Research, 21,* 241–279.

Le Poire, B. A., Dailey, R., & Duggan, A. (2002, November). *Nonverbal reinforcement and punishment of substance abuse: A conversational test of INC.* Paper presented to the National Communication Association, New Orleans, LA.

Le Poire, B. A., Duggan, A., & Dailey, R. (2001, November). *The influence of nonverbal communication on continued substance abuse.* Paper presented to the National Communication Association, Atlanta, GA.

Masataka, N. (1993). Effects of contingent and noncontingent maternal stimulation on the vocal behaviour of three- to four-month-old Japanese infants. *Journal of Child Language, 20,* 303–312.

Mehrabian, A. (1969). Some referents and measures of nonverbal behavior. *Behavioral Research Methods and Instruments, 1,* 213–217.

Mikkelson, A. C., & Floyd, K. (2005, February). *Effective preaching: How nonverbal immediacy influences motivation, affective learning, and perceptions of credibility.* Paper presented at the Western States Communication Association Annual Meeting, San Francisco.

Miller, B. C., Benson, B., & Galbraith, K. A. (2001). Family relationships and adolescent pregnancy risk: A research synthesis. *Developmental Review, 21,* 1–38.

Noller, P. (1984). *Nonverbal communication and marital interaction.* Oxford, UK: Penguin.

Noller, P., Feeney, J. A., Bonnell, D., & Callan, V. (1994). A longitudinal study of conflict in early marriage. *Journal of Social and Personal Relationships, 11,* 233–253.

Oller, D. K. (1986). Metaphonology and infant vocalizations. In R. A. B. Lindblom (Ed.), *Precursors of early speech* (pp. 21–35). New York: Stockton.

Papousek, M. (1989). Determinants of responsiveness to infant vocal expression of emotional state. *Infant Behavior and Development, 12,* 507–524.

Papousek, M., Bornstein, M. H., Nuzzo, C., Papousek, H., & Symmes, D. (1990). Infant responses to prototypical melodic contours in parental speech. *Infant Behavior and Development, 13,* 539–545.

Papousek, M., & Papousek, H. (1991). Early verbalizations as precursors of language development. In M. E. Lamb & H. Keller (Eds.), *Infant development: Perspectives from German speaking countries* (pp. 299–328). Hillsdale, NJ: Lawrence Erlbaum.

Papousek, M., Papousek, H., & Bornstein, M. H. (1985). The naturalistic vocal environment of young infants: On the significance of homogeneity and variability in parent speech. In T. Field & N. Fox (Eds.), *Social perception in infants* (pp. 269–297). Norwood, NJ: Ablex.

Pittam, J. (2000). *Voice and social identity.* Thousand Oaks, CA: Sage.

Robinson, H. (1980). *Biblical preaching: The development and delivery of expository messages.* Grand Rapids, MI: Baker Books.

Rosenthal, R. (2002). Covert communication in classrooms, clinics, courtrooms, and cubicles. *American Psychologist, 57,* 839–849.

Rosenthal, R., & Jacobsen, L. (1968). *Pygmalion in the classroom.* New York: Holt, Rinehart, & Winston.

Rosenthal, R., & Rubin, D. B. (1978). Interpersonal expectancy effects: The first 345 studies. *Behavioral and Brain Sciences, 3,* 377–386.

Ryan, E. B., Hummert, M. L., & Boich, L. (1995). Communication predicaments of aging: Patronizing behavior toward older adults. *Journal of Language and Social Psychology, 14,* 144–166.

Schaap, C., Buunk, B., & Kerkstra, A. (1988). Marital conflict resolution. In P. Noller & M. A. Fitzpatrick (Eds.), *Perspectives on marital interaction* (pp. 245–270). Clevedon, UK: Multilingual Matters.

Stallings, J., Fleming, A. S., Corter, C., Worthman, C., & Steiner, M. (2001). The effects of infant cries and odors on sympathy, cortisol, and autonomic responses in new mothers and nonpostpartum women. *Parenting: Science and Practice, 1,* 71–100.

Stark, R. E., Rose, S. N., & McLagen, M. (1975). Features of infant sounds: The first eight weeks of life. *Journal of Child Language, 2,* 205–221.

Stevenson, M. B., Ver Hoeve, J. N., Roach, M. A., & Leavitt, L. A. (1986). The beginning of conversation: Early patterns of mother-infant vocal responsiveness. *Infant Behavior and Development, 9,* 423–440.

Stice, E., Barrera, M., & Chassin, L. (1993). Relation of parental support and control to adolescents' externalizing symptomatology and substance use: A longitudinal examination of curvilinear effects. *Journal of Abnormal Child Psychology, 21,* 609–629.

Van Egeren, L. A., & Barratt, M. S. (2004). The developmental origins of communication: Interactional systems in infancy. In A. Vangelisti (Ed.), *Handbook of family communication* (pp. 287–310). Mahwah, NJ: Lawrence Erlbaum.

van Swol, L. M. (2003). The effects of nonverbal mirroring on perceived persuasiveness, agreement with an imitator, and reciprocity in a group discussion. *Communication Research, 30,* 461–480.

Vangelisti, A. L. (1994). Messages that hurt. In W. R Cupach & B. H. Spitzberg (Eds.), *The dark side of interpersonal communication* (pp. 53–82). Hillsdale, NJ: Lawrence Erlbaum.

Vangelisti, A. L. (2001). Making sense of hurtful interactions in close relationships: When hurt feelings create distance. In V. Manusov & J. H. Harvey (Eds.), *Attributions, communication behavior, and close relationships* (pp. 38–58). Cambridge, UK: Cambridge University Press.

Vangelisti, A. L., & Crumley, L. P. (1998). Reactions to messages that hurt: The influence of relational contexts. *Communication Monographs, 65,* 173–196.

Vangelisti, A. L., & Young, S. L. (2000). When words hurt: The effects of perceived intentionality on interpersonal relationships.

Journal of Social and Personal Relationships, 17, 393–424.

Xin, K. R. (2004). Asian American managers: An impression gap?: An investigation of impression management and supervisor-subordinate relationships. *Journal of Applied Behavioral Science, 40,* 160–181.

Zhou, Q., Eisenberg, N., Losoya, S. H., Fabes, R. A., Reiser, M., Guthrie, I. K., Murphy, B. C., Cumberland, A. J., & Shepard, S. A. (2002). The relations of parental warmth and positive expressiveness to children's empathy-related responding and social functioning: A longitudinal study. *Child Development, 73,* 893–915.

PART I

FOUNDATIONS

1

AN HISTORICAL OVERVIEW
OF NONVERBAL RESEARCH

◆ Mark L. Knapp
University of Texas at Austin

One faces the future with one's past.

—Pearl S. Buck

Long before there were written records, painters, pottery makers, sculptors, dancers, philosophers, leaders, and others, whose work necessitated an understanding of how and why human beings use (or should use) their bodies and with what effect, "researched" nonverbal communication. Walking styles, gestures, forms of handshaking, and other nonverbal behavior practiced centuries ago can be pieced together by examining a variety of written documents, including diaries, plays, histories, folklore, legal codes, and traveler's accounts (Bremmer & Roodenburg, 1991). In this chapter, I focus only on those written works or scholarly movements that have had widespread influence and/or key issues associated with nonverbal studies that serve as important links in a chain leading to the modern study of nonverbal behavior and non-verbal communication.

◆ *Rhetoric and the Delivery Canon*

The words of the philosopher Confucius (1951/ca. 500 BCE), who expounded on the ways to lead a good life, aesthetics, politics, etiquette, and other topics more than 2,500 years ago, have been preserved. In these records, we find his commentary on communicating without words:

1. He said: I'd like to do without words.

2. Tze-Kung said: But, boss, if you don't say it, how can we little guys pass it on?

3. He said: Sky, how does that talk? The four seasons go on, everything gets born. Sky, what words does the sky use? (p. 87, Book 17, XIX).

Confucius also made observations repeatedly on what, today, we would refer to as the coordination of verbal and nonverbal signals: for example, "3. There are three things a gentleman honors in his way of life: . . . that his facial expression come near to corresponding with what he says" (p. 35, Book 8, IV), and

1. He said: elaborate phrases and expression to fit [insinuating, pious appearance] self-satisfied deference; Tso Ch'iuming was ashamed of; I also am ashamed of 'em. To conceal resentment while shaking hands in a friendly manner, Tso-Ch'iuming was ashamed to; I also am ashamed to. (p. 22–23, Book 5, XXIV)

At about the same time Confucius was proffering his advice in China, philosophers and scholars in Athens and Sicily initiated the publication of the first handbooks on oral rhetoric. The study of oral rhetoric or persuasive speaking is an important tributary of nonverbal knowledge because an understanding of a speaker's gestures, posture, and voice are central to an understanding of their effectiveness. Aristotle and other Greek rhetoricians thought of rhetoric as having five canons: invention, arrangement, style, memory, and delivery (Kennedy, 1963). In offering these canons, Aristotle (1991/ca. 350 BCE) established the importance of the nonverbal behaviors involved in delivering a speech, saying that sometimes delivery exerts more influence than the substance of the speech.

But it was the Roman orators and teachers who refined, clarified, categorized, and expanded on the behaviors involved in speech delivery (Kennedy, 1972). Cicero (1942/ca. 55 BCE) established a connection between nonverbal behavior and emotion: "For nature has assigned to every emotion a particular look and tone of voice and bearing of its own" (Section 216). He also addressed the relative influence of various channels when he said, "In the matter of delivery which we are now considering the face is next in importance to the voice; and the eyes are the dominant feature of the face" (Section 222). And like Confucius, Cicero underlined the need for congruence of verbal and nonverbal signals: "For by action the body talks, so it is all the more necessary to make it agree with the thought" (Section 222).

Another Roman rhetorician, whose influence on later rhetorical scholars extended hundreds of years after his death, was Quintilian (1922/90 CE). Quintilian, like those before him, argued for the "harmony" of speech, gesture, and face, but he justified his recommendation by saying that incongruent signals will "not only lack weight, but will fail to carry conviction" (chap. III, 67). He also discussed the role of an orator's dress (chap. III, 137ff) and made an attempt to classify gestures into two broad categories:

The gestures of which I have thus far spoken are such as naturally proceed from us simultaneously with our words. But there are others which indicate things by means of mimicry. For example, you may suggest a sick man by mimicking the gesture of a doctor feeling the pulse, or a harpist by a movement of the hands as though they were plucking the strings. (chap. III, 88)

An early attempt to ascribe meaning to various nonverbal signals is also found in Quintilian's *Institutio Oratoria*. In this text, for example, throwing the head back was a behavior that was believed to assist in expressing arrogance and the eyebrows were depicted as showing "anger by contraction . . . cheerfulness by expansion" (chap. III, 69, 80).

Attention to nonverbal behavior associated typically with the delivery canon virtually disappeared during the Middle Ages and the Renaissance when a concern for style predominated. There was, however, a brief treatment of delivery in Thomas Wilson's *The Arte of Rhetorique* in 1553. In this book, Wilson discusses "how to speak in a pleasing tone, how to gesture well, and how to pronounce correctly" (cited in Bizzell & Herzberg, 1990, p. 587). In the mid-to-late 1600s, both Wilkins and Fenelon complained about the quality of pulpit oratory, whereas "others offered advice on delivery for preachers and lawyers, with discussions of acting, facial expression, posture, movement, gesture, projection, tone, pace, and modulation" (Bizzell & Herzberg, 1990, p. 649).

But it was the elocution movement that comprised the next major milestone linking nonverbal behavior and the rhetorical canon of delivery. This movement, which began around 1750 and extended into the early 20th century, is not associated normally with important advances in rhetorical thought. But the elocutionists were keenly interested in body movements and vocalizations, and they developed detailed lists of the many ways a body and voice can be used to deliver written speeches and literary works. In his effort to improve British education, Irish actor Thomas Sheridan sought to restore the stature of delivery in rhetorical study. His published lectures on the subject from 1756 to 1762 discuss

> what is now standard speech-text material on oral interpretation, vocal expressiveness, and gestures. Words, Sheridan argues, are not the only constituent of language. Expressions and gestures also communicate. Indeed, they are more primitive than words, more natural where words are artificial, more universal where words are national, and more expressive of emotion than the sophisticated language of words. (Bizzell & Herzberg, 1990, p. 650)

Gilbert Austin (1753–1837), another well-known elocutionist, developed an elaborate notation system with symbols for recording voice speed, force, variety, pausing, over 50 foot movements, over 100 arm positions, and thousands of hand positions, not to mention arm elevation and motion, among other behaviors (Bizzell & Herzberg, 1990). His illustrations from *Chironomia* (1806) are still reproduced widely (see Figure 1.1). The exceedingly detailed notations represent a significant early contribution toward recording and analyzing nonverbal behavior. But Austin's approach was not widely accepted as an effective method for learning how to perform while delivering a speech because of the stilted and unnatural behavior it effected.

Elocutionist François Delsarte (1811–1871) also created a system of oratory that

Figure 1.1   Illustrations from Austin's *Chironomia*

detailed body movements (Shawn, 1954). Delsarte's observation about shoulders is less noteworthy for its accuracy than it is for the implication that nonverbal behavior has a multimeaning potential:

> Now the shoulder is limited, in its proper domain, to proving, first, that the emotion expressed by the face is or is not true. Then, afterward, to marking, with mathematical rigor, the degree of intensity to which the emotion rises. (Delaumosne, 1893, pp. 438–439)

Gradually, however, the formal and detailed instruction of the elocutionists gave way to a less formal and research-based approach to delivery in 20th-century public speaking texts. Speech delivery in modern public speaking textbooks is girded with theories, findings, and citations from scholars whose work is viewed as central to the study of nonverbal communication (Gronbeck, McKerrow, Ehninger, & Monroe, 1990).

◆ The 19th Century: Two Influential Works

Contemporary scholarship focusing on gestures and facial expressions owes a huge debt to two works published in the 19th century: de Jorio's (1832) *Gestural Expression of the Ancients in the Light of Neapolitan Gesturing* and Darwin's (1872/1998) *The Expression of the Emotions in Man and Animals*. Kendon (1982b, 2004), who has researched thoroughly the development of gestural study throughout history, says this about de Jorio's work: "It remains one of the most complex treatises on the subject ever published and it is the first ever to present a study of gesture from what today would be called an ethnographic point of view" (Kendon, 2000, p. xx).

De Jorio believed that his analysis of the everyday gestural behavior of ordinary people in Naples would help archeologists and others to better understand the gestures depicted on Greco-Roman vases, frescos, and sculptures that were being discovered. In the process, however, he provided much more. Among other contributions, Kendon credits de Jorio for (1) establishing the importance of context in understanding gestures (e.g., the same gesture may take on a different meaning with variations in accompanying facial and bodily activity); (2) identifying ways that gestures function with words and as substitutes for words; (3) treating gesture for the first time "as if it is a culturally established communicative code analogous to language" (Kendon, 2000, p. xx); and (4) an approach to making a gesture dictionary that even today shows more promise than many extant efforts.

Charles Darwin, like de Jorio, was extremely skilled at amassing, describing, and interpreting a wealth of observations. Ekman (1998a) said, "Almost everyone now studying the facial expressions of emotion acknowledges that the field began with Darwin's *Expression*" (p. xxviii). One hundred years after Darwin's observations from largely anecdotal data, scholars using more systematic and rigorous research methods confirmed the validity of many of his observations about the facial expressions of emotion in adult human beings, infants, and other animals (Ekman, 1973; Ekman & Friesen, 1971; Ekman, Friesen, & Ellsworth, 1972).

Darwin was one of the first to study facial expressions in the context of evolutionary principles and one of the first to use photographs to illustrate expressions (see Floyd, this volume). His idea that there was a pan-cultural morphology for certain expressions stimulated controversy among scholars, but it also stimulated research that enabled us to understand better what aspects of an expression are common to our species, the morphology of facial expressions, and how certain aspects of facial expressions of emotion can be modified by cultural teachings (Ekman, 1998b). And whereas he did not discuss the issue of

deception at length, contemporary efforts by scholars to study nonverbal expressive behavior during deception are quite compatible with his ideas (Ekman, 2001).

◆ The Early 20th Century

At least four key developments during the first half of the 20th century set the stage for what was to be the blossoming of nonverbal studies at midcentury. First, there was a growing interest in human interaction and communication by prominent scholars from many disciplines (Delia, 1987). Symbolic interactionists (e.g., George Herbert Mead), researchers interested in group dynamics (e.g., Kurt Lewin, Elton Mayo), propaganda (e.g., Harold Lasswell), cybernetics (e.g., Norbert Wiener), and information theory (e.g., Claude Shannon and Warren Weaver) all took different approaches to communication, but together they made social interaction a key to understanding social life at all levels. This not only opened the door for the examination of myriad behaviors affecting human transactions but also made understanding of human interaction an important and respectable area for disciplines, such as sociology, psychology, anthropology, linguistics, psychiatry, ethology, and speech.

This focus on human interaction occurred at a time when the concern for more scientific approaches to social issues was also gaining strength. Thus, nonverbal research during this period is characterized by the use of more sophisticated and precise procedures for studying and recording behavior, the use of film, and an increasingly innovative variety of methods. According to DePaulo and Friedman (1998), the experimental study of nonverbal behavior by psychologists grew rapidly during this period and by the 1920s "a very active group of researchers was studying spontaneous versus posed facial expression of emotion, vocal expression, and gestures" (p. 6). Anthropologist Eliot Chapple (1940, 1949), for example, began using a mechanical device, called an interaction chronograph, which produced an ongoing graphic record of who talked, when, and for how long. Among other uses, data from this device provided an early glimpse at response matching and interaction synchrony.

In 1930, anthropologist Franz Boas was perhaps the first social scientist to use the motion picture camera to generate data in natural settings with the goal of studying human gestures, motor habits, and dance. Davis (1979) attributes the first microscopic frame-by-frame analysis of filmed movement patterns to Halverson (1931), a child psychologist. During the 1920s, an extremely detailed system for annotating the movements of dancers quantitatively and qualitatively was devised by Rudolf Laban (1926; Hutchinson, 1970). Although nonverbal researchers have not embraced Labanotation (or any other comprehensive whole-body coding system) as a way of recording ongoing human behavior, coding and notational methods are common in nonverbal research.

Given the preceding trends, it is not surprising that David Efron's (1941) landmark study of gestures employed a variety of innovative methods, including (1) direct observation of natural interaction; (2) filmed interactions, which he studied and from which he elicited perceptions of naive observers; (3) frequency counts, graphs, and charts; and (4) sketches of interactant gesturing made by a professional painter. As Ekman noted in his preface to the reissue of Efron's (1972) book, "Efron's methods are unique for his time and exemplary for ours. Rarely has such a diversity of investigatory techniques been utilized in a single study of body movement" (p. 8).

Efron's (1941) study is also significant as an illustration of how nonverbal behavior is a product of the environment in which people live and the cultural context with which they identify. This idea was credited with rebutting Hitler and others who wanted to persecute people for styles of body movement and gesture that were believed to be inferior and unchangeable because of their race, culture, or ethnic group. It also served, however, to delay the search for behaviors that may be common to human beings throughout the world (Ekman, 1998b). Franz Boas, Efron's advisor and mentor to many of the anthropologists who made seminal contributions to the study of nonverbal behavior in the 1950s, went so far as to say this in the preface to Efron's (1941) book: "The environment has such a fundamental influence that in larger groups, particularly in sub-divisions of the White race, the genetic element may be ruled out entirely or almost entirely as a determining factor" (p. 20).

The belief that one might learn a lot about a person's internal states by observing his or her behavior was another early 20th-century conception that fits the study of nonverbal behavior well. Allport and Vernon (1933), for example, provided experimental evidence that certain movement patterns were congruent with certain personality traits. German expression psychology during the 1930s was also studying movement patterns and their linkage to personality as well as various aspects of facial expressions of emotion (e.g., Asendorpf, 1982; Wallbott, 1982). But because this research was sometimes transformed into Nazi racist ideology (Asendorpf & Wallbott, 1982) and was not associated with rigorous research standards (Ellgring, 1981), few German emigrants to the United States pursued this work.

The relationship of more static features of body shape and appearance to personality traits was also of interest during this time. Kretschmer (1925), a psychiatrist, coded the dimensions of many body parts in an effort to identify human form with certain abnormal personality characteristics and disorders. Sheldon (1940) also believed that body measurements would tell us a lot about a person's temperament, intelligence, moral worth, and future achievement. Much of his work used three broad classifications of body types: the thin ectomorph, the muscular mesomorph, and the fatty endomorph. He gathered data for his catalog of body types by photographing freshman students in the nude at various colleges and universities. Subsequent analysis of his personal notes showed that he drew racist conclusions from his work (Rosenbaum, 1995). Although studies of characteristics associated with body shape stereotypes persisted in nonverbal research, the validity of these perceptions has not been established.

◆ *The 1950s: Laying
   a Foundation*

For nonverbal behavior studies, the 1950s was a decade of significant events and scholarship. The works of scholars like Trager (1958), Birdwhistell (1952, 1970), and E. T. Hall (1959) are considered fundamental to those who later specialized in paralanguage, body movement/posture, and space. Ironically, some of these pioneers were not as much interested in understanding nonverbal behavior per se as they were in understanding the structure and organization of interaction as a whole. Kendon and Sigman (1996) point out, "Birdwhistell used to say that the study of nonverbal communication would be like the study of non-cardiac physiology" (p. 231). Lyons (1972) is more direct: "The fact that there is such a complete and intimate interpenetration of language and non-language should always be borne in mind in considering the relationship between verbal and non-verbal communication" (p. 54).

Language was very much a part of the academic background of Birdwhistell,

Trager, and Hall and they, like Goffman, Scheflen, and Ruesch, believed an understanding of the structure and organization of interaction depended on observations of co-occurring verbal and nonverbal behavior (see also Bavelas & Chovil, this volume; Robinson, this volume). The tendency of researchers to develop a program of research around a single nonverbal behavior, which occurred with some frequency during the 1960s and 1970s, was probably not what these "structuralists" had in mind.

The study of nonverbal behavior as a part of the overall structure and organization of human interaction gained considerable momentum as a result of a 1955 collaboration at the Center for Advanced Behavioral Studies at Stanford University (see reviews by Kendon, 1990; Leeds-Hurwitz, 1987). Among others, this group included psychiatrists (e.g., Fromm-Reichman, Brosin), anthropological linguists (e.g., McQuown, Hockett), and anthropologists (e.g., G. Bateson, Birdwhistell). Using a brief film of "Doris," one of Gregory Bateson's patients in family therapy, efforts were made to develop a detailed frame-by-frame analysis of both verbal and nonverbal behavior. Ironically, the film showed a lot of Doris' behavior and little of Bateson's, and the analysis of mutual influence, so critical to the structural approach, was restricted severely. The results of this collaboration were never published, but the approach and its application can be found in the work of Pittinger, Hockett, and Danehy (1960), Kendon (1982a), Birdwhistell (1970, pp. 227–250), and in what Scheflen (1973) called "context analysis."

The use of the terms *kinesics* (Birdwhistell, 1952) and *proxemics* (Hall, 1959) for body movement/posture and spatial relations, respectively, illustrated the belief that nonverbal codes had a structure similar to a linguistic code. About 1968, Birdwhistell modified his approach, going beyond a purely linguistic analysis and maintaining that some, but not all, nonverbal behavior had an organization like language (Kendon & Sigman, 1996, p. 16). Birdwhistell's place in the history of nonverbal studies lies not so much with whether he was right or wrong about the way nonverbal behavior is coded, but in the fact that his work energized scholars in several disciplines to examine body movement and posture systematically from various perspectives.

Birdwhistell's ideas also seem to have resonated with Erving Goffman, who took one of his courses at the University of Toronto in the 1940s. Later, Goffman (1963, 1967, 1971) made it clear that his observations associated with "interaction order" involved the dynamic interplay of the totality of behavior, including eye gaze, body movement, gestures, positioning, verbalizations, and the like. Goffman identified his approach to studying interaction with the way ethologists studied animal behavior even though he had little use for their Darwinian interpretations (Kendon, 1988).

Although the animal studies of ethologists Konrad Lorenz and Niko Tinbergen were well known in the 1950s, it was not until the 1960s that human ethology and the work of scholars like Eibl-Eibesfeldt (1970, pp. 442–534) found their place within the nonverbal literature and reinvigorated the discussion of biological bases for human behavior. For many years after World War II, human behavior was commonly believed to be almost totally malleable by culture, and any data that suggested otherwise were considered "politically loaded" and fodder for racist actions. For example, Ekman (1998b) reports the stiff opposition he received in the late 1960s from Birdwhistell, Gregory Bateson, and Margaret Mead when he reported research supporting a pan-cultural morphology for certain facial expressions (Ekman & Friesen, 1971; Ekman, Sorenson, & Friesen, 1969).

The 1950s were also a fertile time for psychological approaches. Mahl (1987) and

Goldman-Eisler (1968) were exploring spontaneous speech, pauses, hesitations, and speech disturbances and their relation to anxiety, emotion, and cognition.[1] Frank (1957) published a seminal monograph on the role of touching in human interaction in which he said, "in many interpersonal relations, tactile 'language' functions most effectively and communicates more fully than vocal language" (p. 214). At about the same time, Harlow's (1958) work was receiving widespread attention because it suggested that touching was so powerful that it may sometimes be preferred to nursing for young primates. A cornerstone for later studies of how environments affect human interaction was established in the "beautiful and ugly room" studies (Maslow & Mintz, 1956).

It was also during the mid-1950s that Rosenthal (2002) felt he had unwittingly directed the participants in his doctoral dissertation to behave in accord with his hypotheses. After establishing the existence of these expectancy effects in various arenas of human behavior, he then examined the way these expectancies were communicated by subtle (out of awareness) nonverbal signals (Rosenthal, 1966; Rosenthal & Jacobson, 1968). Ekman, whose later work exerted a powerful influence on the modern study of nonverbal communication, published his first article on the subject in 1957: A proposal for a method of sampling and recording nonverbal behavior.

An early reference to the label, "nonverbal communication," is also found in the work of interpersonal psychiatrist Jurgen Ruesch (1953) when he refers to its multimeaning potential:

Silent actions . . . always have a potentially twofold function: they are an implementation in their own right and they may stand for something else, or both. This double meaning of actions introduces great difficulties into the evaluation of nonverbal communication inasmuch as a perceiver can never be quite sure when action is intended to convey a message and when it is intended for other purposes. (p. 233)

Ruesch's later collaboration with photographer Weldon Kees may be the first book with "nonverbal communication" in the title (Ruesch & Kees, 1956).

◆ The Tipping Point

As an outgrowth of the pioneering work put forth in the 1950s, scholars with interests in paralanguage, kinesics, and proxemics continued their research. But the late 1960s and early 1970s was the period of emergence for a broadly visible, respectable, and sustainable field of nonverbal studies. One cannot fully understand the emergence of nonverbal studies during this period without considering the climate of the times. It was an era that favored a concern for personal relationships and the kind of revelations about informal interaction that arose out of "consciousness-raising" and "sensitivity" groups. Davis (1971) said,

The enormous public interest in nonverbal communications seems to be part of the spirit of the times, the need that many people feel to get back in touch with their own emotions—the search for the emotional truth that perhaps gets expressed nonverbally. (p. 2)

Larger societal issues and trends also affected specific areas of nonverbal study. For example, worries about world overpopulation (Erlich, 1971), and the fear that crowded humans might act like the aberrant rats in Calhoun's (1962) widely publicized studies spurred the interest in space, density, and territory. Soon after, the women's movement raised questions about nonverbal signals as subtle manifestations of power

(Henley, 1977; and later, Hall, 1984 and this volume; Mayo & Henley, 1981).

In 1969, a thorough review of nonverbal research (Duncan, 1969) and what was to become a highly influential theoretical treatise on the origins, usage, coding, and categorization of nonverbal behavior (Ekman & Friesen, 1969; updated in Ekman, 1999) appeared. This was a time when theoretical issues like awareness, intent, coding, meaning, classification, and units of measurement were very much on the academic table. Even questions about whether the term *nonverbal* described the emerging field of research adequately (Harrison & Knapp, 1972; Kendon, 1981) and questions about when nonverbal behavior should be considered "communicative" and when it should not were debated (e.g., Wiener, Devoe, Rubinow, & Geller, 1972; and later, Russell & Fernández-Dols, 1997).

In 1970, a freelance journalist, Julius Fast, wrote a best-selling book that went a long way toward making the subject of "body language" a topic of national interest and recognition. Other popular books followed (Montagu, 1971; Morris, 1971; 1977, 1985). Some of the less academic popular accounts portrayed the "reading" of body language in misleading ways (Koivumaki, 1975), but these books continued to arouse the public's interest in the subject. By 1970, courses in nonverbal communication were being offered at Purdue, Michigan State, the University of California, and a few other universities (see McCroskey, Richmond, & McCroskey, this volume). Textbooks for nonverbal courses also appeared suddenly in social psychology (e.g., Argyle, 1975; Mehrabian, 1971; Weitz, 1974) and in communication (Eisenberg & Smith, 1971; Harrison, 1974; Knapp, 1972).

On top of this growing interest in the study of nonverbal behavior was the increasing availability of affordable videotape recorders. In 1972, Harrison, Cohen,

Crouch, Genova, and Steinberg summarized this period by saying,

> Sharp changes have taken place in the nonverbal communication literature in the past decade, and in particular, in the last two years. A decade ago, few books existed; and the early works tended to be speculative, anecdotal, and tentative. . . . Major works are now emerging which, on the one hand, organize and synthesize the existing data from a variety of fields. Research programs extending over a number of years are now culminating and the results are becoming available. Theoretical issues have become clarified, and a range of active theories vie for support. Finally, methodological problems are being examined and, frequently, they are being solved. . . . The amount of knowledge has now reached a "critical mass"—and a general availability—so that even more exciting things may be ahead. (pp. 473–474)

More exciting things were ahead. In 1979, Davis said, "In the past five years alone more books have been published on body language than in the preceding 95. It is an idea that has found its time" (p. 51). The first issue of the *Journal of Environmental Psychology and Nonverbal Behavior* appeared in 1976, and in 1980 the name was changed to the *Journal of Nonverbal Behavior*. As the output of research has grown, articles and books devoted to the special demands of conducting nonverbal research and measuring nonverbal phenomena have also been published (e.g., Kulp, Cornetto, & Knapp, 2005; Manusov, 2005; Scherer & Ekman, 1982).

◆ An Outpouring of Research

Myriad studies bearing on the structure, organization, and effects of nonverbal behavior were published during the last four decades of the 20th century. The breadth and depth of the literature today is too massive for the kind of broad-based literature reviews that characterized the research done prior to 1980 (e.g., Burgoon, 1980; Knapp, Wiemann, & Daly, 1978).[2] But two general approaches can be said to have characterized the research during this period: The *structural and ethological* researchers tended to emphasize descriptions of how interactions are organized, whereas others emphasized the manipulation of *psychological* variables and/or nonverbal behavior to observe the effects. Within each of these two broad approaches, some scholars focused on a particular body part, some examined multiple nonverbal signals, and some studies went beyond body movements per se and focused on "related non-word phenomena" like physical appearance, environmental factors, and the use of space.

In the tradition of those who laid the foundation for scrutinizing the way interactants structure and organize their behavior, Kendon (1977) showed how interactants use their faces, eyes, and spatial formations for various interaction functions, including kissing and greeting rituals. Kendon's (2004) analysis of gestures may be the most thorough work available on the subject. In like manner, the detailed analyses of facial expressions of emotion by Ekman and his colleagues are unmatched (Ekman & Friesen, 1975; Ekman, Friesen, & Hager, 2002). Duncan and Fiske (1977) and Goodwin (1981) illustrated how speakers and listeners coordinate their verbal and nonverbal behavior during the exchange of speaking turns, whereas Condon and Ogston (1971) described a form of interdependent behavior between interactants as *synchrony*. Subsequent studies examined a variety of ways interactants coordinate their behavior through matching and synchrony (Bernieri & Rosenthal, 1999; see

Tickle-Degnen, this volume). Eibl-Eibesfeldt (1970) compared the facial expressions of children born blind and deaf with those of others born with hearing and sight, whereas other ethologists described patterns of eye gaze, body movement, and paralinguistic phenomena (Hinde, 1972; von Cranach & Vine, 1978).

In the "variable analytic" tradition, some research programs have focused on specific body areas, such as eye gaze and mutual gaze (Argyle & Cook, 1976; Fehr & Exline, 1987), pupil dilation (Hess, 1975), vocal signals (Davitz, 1964; Scherer, 1986), and touch (Field, 1995). Four decades of work on the face by Ekman and his colleagues are the basis of a substantial body of literature on the production and perception of expressions of emotion (Ekman et al., 1972; Ekman & Rosenberg, 1997; see Matsumoto, this volume). Even though most studies have examined the face and voice as spontaneous emotional expressions, the work of some scholars (e.g., Fridlund, 1994) views these expressions as social displays that are purposefully enacted to communicate. As noted earlier, research in "related" areas like physical appearance (Berscheid & Walster, 1974; Rhodes & Zebrowitz, 2002), space (Burgoon, 1978; Sommer, 1969, 2002), and the environment (Mehrabian, 1976) has been sufficient to establish an academic niche within the larger field of nonverbal studies.

Typical of multivariable approaches are studies that focus on (1) interaction *processes* like the reciprocity and compensation of nonverbal behavior (Argyle & Dean, 1965; Patterson, 1984) and incongruent verbal and nonverbal signals (Bavelas, Black, Chovil, & Mullett 1990; Volkmar & Siegel, 1982) and (2) interaction *outcomes* or goals like deception (Ekman, 2001; see also Vrij, this volume), power and dominance (Ellyson & Dovidio, 1985; see also Burgoon & Dunbar, this volume), expectancies (Blanck, 1993), and immediacy (Andersen, 1985; Mehrabian, 1972; see also Andersen, Guerrero, & Jones, this volume). Multivariable studies are also common in studies that give special attention to context (Feldman, 1982; Philippot, Feldman, & Coats, 1999), such as those detailed later in this volume.

◆ *Moving On*

At different points in the 2,500-year history of nonverbal research, studies have varied in terms of subject matter, methods, and frequency. But the disciplinary breadth of interest and the number of studies conducted during the past 40 years have provided unparalleled insights. Of course, not all subareas of nonverbal research flourish at the same time. Areas of study like the human use of space and territory, pupil dilation, and some others popular in the 1960s and 1970s, are currently at low ebb, whereas the study of gestures, as one example, is currently at high tide. The recent interest in and proliferation of gesture research necessitated the establishment of a separate academic journal called *Gesture* in 2001. The extent to which communicators can encode and decode nonverbal behavior accurately is another area of considerable interest (Hall & Bernieri, 2001; see Riggio, this volume). Ambady, LaPlante, and Johnson (2001), for example, have shown that decoders often use very brief excerpts of another person's ongoing nonverbal behavior to make judgments. These "thin slices" have also been shown to be reliable predictors of behavior. Other scholars are exploring the conditions under which nonverbal behavior is "automatically" (with little or no awareness and/or intent) encoded and decoded (Patterson, 1999; Spitz, 1997; Wegner & Bargh, 1998; see also Lakin, this volume).

The application of nonverbal research to particular settings like classrooms, courtrooms, marriages, political speeches, medical interviews, marketing, and cross-cultural encounters is also considered a worthy target for current nonverbal research (Riggio & Feldman, 2005).

Coexisting with this current tendency to value things on the basis of their utility in important arenas of everyday life is a widespread interest in the management of close relationships. This trend has set the stage for more studies of nonverbal communication among friends, family, and lovers (Feeney, Noller, Sheehan, & Peterson, 1999; Knapp, 1983; Manusov, 1995; Noller, 1984 and this volume), even though the preponderance of nonverbal research to date has been conducted with interactants who are strangers or acquaintances.

Despite a current surge of interest in the biological foundations of human behavior in all the behavioral sciences, we seem to be circumspect in attributing any given behavior exclusively to either culture or biology. Unlike the past, there appears to be a greater acceptance that both may play a role in the manifestation of nonverbal behavior (Segerstråle & Molnár, 1997). Paradoxically, nonverbal behavior seems to be thought of and studied as both a subarea that complements the study of human interaction and a way of approaching the study of human interaction per se. Those who study gestures, for example, view the interdependence of verbal behavior and gestures as natural and integral to their studies (e.g., Feyereisen & de Lannoy, 1991; Kendon, 2004; McNeill, 1992, 2000; see also, Bavelas & Chovil, this volume). Other nonverbal scholars not only examine the interrelationship of verbal and nonverbal behavior but also embrace the role of appearance, environmental factors, space, and time as parts of the nonverbal domain. In short, nonverbal studies leave no element of social interaction untouched.

In one sense, therefore, the term *nonverbal* suggests a separate piece of the interaction puzzle, but in another sense it is a term that identifies a starting point for describing the total interactive situation. Patterson (1983), Knapp (1984), and others have argued for multisignal, multimeaning, interactive, and processual approaches to nonverbal research. These are all elements that characterize natural, human interaction. To the extent that future nonverbal research assumes these features, the study of nonverbal signals may become what Birdwhistell, Scheflen, Goffman, and others envisioned in the mid-20th century.

◆ Notes

1. The Mahl and Goldman-Eisler volumes cited here summarize their research programs, both of which were initiated in the early 1950s.
2. This review is similarly constrained. Not all important research contributions could be noted. See Knapp and Hall (2005) for a more complete review of nonverbal research.

◆ References

Allport, G. W., & Vernon, P. E. (1933). *Studies in expressive movement.* New York: Macmillan.

Ambady, N., LaPlante, D., & Johnson, E. (2001). Thin-slice judgments as a measure of interpersonal sensitivity. In J. A. Hall & F. J. Bernieri (Eds.), *Interpersonal sensitivity: Theory and measurement* (pp. 89–101). Mahwah, NJ: Erlbaum.

Andersen, P. A. (1985). Nonverbal immediacy in interpersonal communication. In A. W. Siegman & S. Feldstein (Eds.), *Multichannel integrations of nonverbal behavior* (pp. 1–36). Hillsdale, NJ: Erlbaum.

Argyle, M. (1975). *Bodily communication.* New York: International Universities Press.

Argyle, M., & Cook, M. (1976). *Gaze and mutual gaze.* New York: Cambridge University Press.

Argyle, M., & Dean, J. (1965). Eye contact, distance and affiliation. *Sociometry, 28,* 289–304.

Aristotle. (1991/ca.350 BCE). *On rhetoric* (trans. G. A. Kennedy). New York: Oxford University Press.

Asendorpf, J. (1982). Contributions of the German "Expression Psychology" to nonverbal communication research: Part II. The face. *Journal of Nonverbal Behavior, 6,* 199–219.

Asendorpf, J., & Wallbott, H. G. (1982). Contributions of the German "Expression Psychology" to nonverbal communication research. Part I: Theories and concepts. *Journal of Nonverbal Behavior, 6,* 135–147.

Bavelas, J. B., Black, A., Chovil, N., & Mullett, J. (1990*)*. *Equivocal communication.* Newbury Park, CA: Sage.

Bernieri, F. J., & Rosenthal, R. (1999). Interpersonal coordination: Behavior matching and interactional synchrony. In R. S. Feldman & B. Rimé (Eds.), *Fundamentals of nonverbal behavior* (pp. 401–432). New York: Cambridge University Press.

Berscheid, E., & Walster, E. H. (1974). Physical attractiveness. In L. Berkowitz (Ed.), *Advances in experimental social psychology* (Vol. 7, pp. 157–215). New York: Academic Press.

Birdwhistell, R. L. (1952). *Introduction to kinesics: An annotation system for analysis of body motion and gesture.* Washington, DC: U.S. Department of State Foreign Service Institute.

Birdwhistell, R. L. (1970). *Kinesics and context.* Philadelphia: University of Pennsylvania Press.

Bizzell, P., & Herzberg, B. (Eds.). (1990). *The rhetorical tradition: Readings from classical times to the present.* Boston: Bedford Books.

Blanck, P. D. (Ed.). (1993). *Interpersonal expectations: Theory, research, and applications.* New York: Cambridge University Press.

Bremmer, J., & Roodenburg, H. (Eds.). (1991). *A cultural history of gesture.* Ithaca, NY: Cornell University Press.

Burgoon, J. K. (1978). A communication model of personal space violations: Explication and an initial test. *Human Communication Research, 4,* 129–142.

Burgoon, J. K. (1980). Nonverbal communication research in the 1970s: An overview. In D. K. Nimmo (Ed.), *Communication yearbook 4* (pp. 179–197). New Brunswick, NJ: Transaction Books.

Calhoun, J. B. (1962). Population density and social pathology. *Scientific American, 206,* 139–148.

Chapple, E. D. (1940). Measuring human relations: An introduction to the study of interaction of individuals. *Genetic Psychology Monographs, 22,* 3–147.

Chapple, E. D. (1949). The interaction chronograph: Its evolution and present application. *Personnel, 25,* 295–307.

Cicero, M. T. (1942/ca. 55 BCE). *De oratore, book III* (H. Rackham, Trans.). Cambridge, MA: Harvard University Press.

Condon, W. S., & Ogston, W. D. (1971). Speech and body motion synchrony of the speaker-hearer. In D. L. Horton & J. J. Jenkins (Eds.), *Perception of language.* Columbus, OH: Merrill.

Confucius, K. (1951/ca. 500 BCE). *Confucian analects* (E. Pound, Trans.). New York: Kasper & Horton.

Cranach, M. von, & Vine, I. (Eds.). (1978). *Social communication and movement.* New York: Academic Press.

Darwin, C. (1998). *The expression of the emotions in man and animals.* New York: Oxford University Press. (Original work published 1872)

Davis, F. (1971). *Inside intuition.* New York: McGraw-Hill.

Davis, M. (1979). The state of the art: Past and present trends in body movement research. In A. Wolfgang (Ed.), *Nonverbal behavior: Applications and cultural implications* (pp. 51–66). New York: Academic Press.

Davitz, J. R. (1964). *The communication of emotional meaning.* New York: McGraw-Hill.

Delaumosne, A. (Ed.). (1893). *Delsarte system of oratory* (4th ed.). New York: Edgar S. Werner.

Delia, J. G. (1987). Communication research: A history. In C. R. Berger & S. H. Chaffee (Eds.), *Handbook of communication science* (pp. 20–98). Newbury Park, CA: Sage.

DePaulo, B. M., & Friedman, H. S. (1998). Nonverbal communication. In D. T. Gilbert, S. T. Fiske, & G. Lindzey (Eds.),

The handbook of social psychology (Vol. 2, 4th ed.). New York: McGraw-Hill.

Duncan, S., Jr. (1969). Nonverbal communication. *Psychological Bulletin, 72,* 118–137.

Duncan, S., Jr., & Fiske, D. W. (1977). *Face-to-face interaction: Research, methods, and theory.* Hillsdale, NJ: Erlbaum.

Efron, D. (1941). *Gesture and environment.* New York: King's Crown Press. (Republished as *Gesture, race and culture,* 1972. The Hague: Mouton)

Efron, D. (1972). *Gesture, race and culture.* The Hague: Mouton.

Eibl-Eibesfeldt, I. (1970). *Ethology: The biology of behavior* (2nd ed.). New York: Holt, Rinehart & Winston.

Eisenberg, A. M., & Smith, R. R. (1971). *Nonverbal communication.* New York: Bobbs-Merrill.

Ekman, P. (1957). A methodological study of nonverbal behavior. *Journal of Psychology, 43,* 141–149.

Ekman, P. (Ed.). (1973). *Darwin and facial expression: A century of research in review.* New York: Academic Press.

Ekman, P. (1998a). Introduction to the third edition. In C. Darwin, *The expression of the emotions of man and animals* (3rd ed., pp. xxi–xxxvi). New York: Oxford University Press.

Ekman, P. (1998b). Afterword: Universality of emotional expression? A personal history of the dispute. In C. Darwin, *The expression of the emotions in man and animals* (3rd ed., pp. 363–393). New York: Oxford University Press.

Ekman, P. (1999). Emotional and conversational nonverbal signals. In L. Messing & R. Campbell (Eds.), *Gesture, speech and sign* (pp. 45–55). New York: Oxford University Press.

Ekman, P. (2001). *Telling lies.* New York: Norton.

Ekman, P., & Friesen, W. V. (1969). The repertoire of nonverbal behavior: Categories, origins, usage, and coding. *Semiotica, 1,* 49–98.

Ekman, P., & Friesen, W. V. (1971). Constants across cultures in the face and emotion. *Journal of Personality and Social Psychology, 17,* 124–129.

Ekman, P., & Friesen, W. V. (1975). *Unmasking the face.* Englewood Cliffs, NJ: Prentice Hall.

Ekman, P., Friesen, W. V., & Ellsworth, P. (1972). *Emotion in the human face.* Elmsford, NY: Pergamon Press.

Ekman, P., Friesen, W. V., & Hager, J. C. (2002). *The facial action coding system* (2nd ed.). Salt Lake City, UT: Research Nexus eBook.

Ekman, P., & Rosenberg, E. (Eds.). (1997). *What the face reveals: Basic and applied studies of spontaneous expression using the facial action coding system (FACS).* New York: Oxford University Press.

Ekman, P., Sorenson, E. R., & Friesen, W. V. (1969). Pan-cultural elements of facial displays of emotions. *Science, 164,* 86–88.

Ellgring, H. (1981). Nonverbal communication: A review of research in Germany. *German Journal of Psychology, 5,* 59–84.

Ellyson, S. L., & Dovidio, J. F. (1985). *Power, dominance and nonverbal behavior.* New York: Springer.

Erlich, P. R. (1971). *The population bomb.* New York: Ballantine Books.

Fast, J. (1970). *Body language.* New York: Evans.

Feeney, J. A., Noller, P., Sheehan, G., & Peterson, C. (1999). Conflict issues and conflict strategies as contexts for nonverbal behavior in close relationships. In P. Philippot, R. S. Feldman, & E. J. Coats (Eds.), *The social context of nonverbal behavior* (pp. 348–371). New York: Cambridge University Press.

Fehr, B. J., & Exline, R. V. (1987). Social visual interaction: A conceptual and literature review. In A. W. Siegman & S. Feldstein (Eds.), *Nonverbal behavior and communication* (pp. 225–326). Hillsdale, NJ: Erlbaum.

Feldman, R. S. (Ed.). (1982). *Development of nonverbal behavior in children.* New York: Springer.

Feyereisen, P., & de Lannoy, J-D. (1991). *Gestures and speech: Psychological investigations.* New York: Cambridge University Press.

Field, T. M. (Ed.). (1995). *Touch in early development.* Mahwah, NJ: Erlbaum.

Frank, L. K. (1957). Tactile communication. *Genetic Psychology Monographs, 56,* 209–255.

Fridlund, A. J. (1994). *Human facial expression: An evolutionary view*. San Diego, CA: Academic Press.

Goffman, E. (1963). *Behavior in public places: Notes on the social organization of gatherings*. New York: Free Press.

Goffman, E. (1967). *Interaction ritual: Essays on face-to-face behavior*. New York: Doubleday Anchor.

Goffman, E. (1971). *Relations in public*. New York: Basic Books.

Goldman-Eisler, F. (1968). *Psycholinguistics: Experiments in spontaneous speech*. New York: Academic Press.

Goodwin, C. (1981). *Conversational organization*. New York: Academic Press.

Gronbeck, B. E., McKerrow, R. E., Ehninger, D., & Monroe, A. H. (1990). *Principles and types of speech communication*. Glenview, IL: Scott, Foresman/Little Brown.

Hall, E. T. (1959). *The silent language*. Garden City, NY: Doubleday.

Hall, J. A. (1984). *Nonverbal sex differences*. Baltimore: Johns Hopkins University Press.

Hall, J. A. & Bernieri, F. (Eds.). (2001). *Interpersonal sensitivity: Theory and measurement*. Mahwah, NJ: Erlbaum.

Halverson, H. M. (1931). An experimental study of prehension of infants by means of systematic cinema records. *Genetic Psychology Monographs, 10*, 107–286.

Harlow, H. F. (1958). The nature of love. *American Psychologist, 13, 678–685.*

Harrison, R. P. (1974). *Beyond words*. Englewood Cliffs, NJ: Prentice Hall.

Harrison, R. P., Cohen, A. A., Crouch, W. W., Genova, K. L., & Steinberg, M. (1972). The nonverbal communication literature. *Journal of Communication, 22, 460–476.*

Harrison, R. P., & Knapp, M. L. (1972). Toward an understanding of nonverbal communication systems. *Journal of Communication, 22, 339–352.*

Henley, N. M. (1977). *Body politics: Power, sex, and nonverbal communication*. Englewood Cliffs, NJ: Prentice Hall.

Hess, E. H. (1975). *The tell-tale eye*. New York: Van Nostrand Reinhold.

Hinde, R. A. (Ed.). (1972). *Non-verbal communication*. New York: Cambridge University Press.

Hutchinson, A. (1970). *Labanotation: The system of analyzing and recording movement*. New York: Theater Arts Books.

de Jorio, A. (1832). *La mimica degli antichi investigata nel gestire napolitano* [Gestural expression of the ancients in the light of Neapolitan gesturing]. Naples, Italy: Stamperia del Fibreno.

Kendon, A. (1977). *Studies in the behavior of social interaction*. Bloomington: University of Indiana Press.

Kendon, A. (1981). Introduction: Current issues in the study of "nonverbal communication." In A. Kendon (Ed.), *Nonverbal communication, interaction, and gesture* (pp. 1–53). New York: Mouton.

Kendon, A. (1982a). The organization of behavior in face-to-face interaction: Observations on the development of a methodology. In K. R. Scherer & P. Ekman (Eds.), *Handbook of methods in nonverbal research* (pp. 440–505). New York: Cambridge University Press.

Kendon, A. (1982b). The study of gesture: Some observations on its history. *Recherches Sémiotiques/Semiotic Inquiry, 2*, 45–62.

Kendon, A. (1988). Goffman's approach to face-to-face interaction. In P. Drew & A. Wootton (Eds.), *Erving Goffman: Exploring the interaction order* (pp. 14–40). Cambridge, UK: Polity Press.

Kendon, A. (1990). Some context for context analysis: A view of the origins of structural studies of face-to-face interaction. In A. Kendon (Ed.), *Conducting interaction: Patterns of focused encounters* (pp. 15–49). New York: Cambridge University Press.

Kendon, A. (2000). Introduction: Andrea de Jorio and his work on gesture. In A. de Jorio (Ed.), *Gesture in Naples and gesture in classical antiquity* (pp. xix–cvii). Bloomington: Indiana University Press.

Kendon, A. (2004). *Gesture: Visible action as utterance*. New York: Cambridge University Press.

Kendon, A., & Sigman, S. J. (1996). Ray L. Birdwhistell (1918–1994). *Semiotica, 112*, 231–261.

Kennedy, G. (1963). *The art of persuasion in Greece*. Princeton, NJ: Princeton University Press.

Kennedy, G. (1972). *The art of rhetoric in the Roman world*. Princeton, NJ: Princeton University Press.

Knapp, M. L. (1972). *Nonverbal communication in human interaction*. New York: Holt, Rinehart & Winston.

Knapp, M. L. (1983). Dyadic relationship development. In J. M. Wiemann & R. P. Harrison (Eds.), *Nonverbal interaction* (pp. 179–207). Beverly Hills, CA: Sage.

Knapp, M. L. (1984). The study of nonverbal behavior vis-á-vis human communication theory. In A. Wolfgang (Ed.), *Nonverbal behavior: Perspectives, applications, intercultural insights* (pp. 15–40). New York: C. J. Hogrefe.

Knapp, M. L., & Hall, J. A. (2005). *Nonverbal communication in human interaction* (6th ed.). Belmont, CA: Wadsworth.

Knapp, M. L., Wiemann, J. M., & Daly, J. A. (1978). Nonverbal communication: Issues and appraisal. *Human Communication Research, 4,* 271–280.

Koivumaki, J. H. (1975). Body language taught here. *Journal of Communication, 25,* 26–30.

Kretschmer, E. (1925). *Physique and character: An investigation of the nature of constitution and the theory of temperament*. New York: Harcourt Brace Jovanovich.

Kulp, C., Cornetto, K., & Knapp, M. L. (2005). The description of nonverbal behavior. In U. Ammon, N. Dittmar, K. J. Mattheier, & P. Trudgill (Eds.), *An international handbook of the science of language and society* (Vol. 2, pp. xx–xx). New York: Walter De Gruyter.

Laban, R. (1926). *Choreographic*. Jena, Germany: Eugen Diederichs.

Leeds-Hurwitz, W. (1987). The social history of *The natural history of an interview*: A multidisciplinary investigation of social communication. *Research on Language and Social Interaction, 20,* 1–51.

Lyons, J. (1972). Human language. In R. A. Hinde (Ed.), *Non-verbal communication* (pp. 49–85). New York: Cambridge University Press.

Mahl, G. F. (1987). *Explorations in nonverbal and vocal behavior*. Hillside, NJ: Erlbaum.

Manusov, V. (1995). Reacting to changes in nonverbal behavior: Relational satisfaction and adaptation patterns in romantic dyads. *Human Communication Research, 21,* 456–477.

Manusov, V. (Ed.). (2005). *The sourcebook of nonverbal measures*. Mahwah, NJ: Erlbaum.

Maslow, A. H., & Mintz, N. L. (1956). Effects of esthetic surroundings: I. Initial effects of three esthetic conditions upon perceiving "energy" and "well-being" in faces. *Journal of Psychology, 41,* 247–254.

Mayo, C., & Henley, N. M. (Eds.). (1981). *Gender and nonverbal behavior*. New York: Springer.

McNeill, D. (1992). *Hand and mind: What gestures reveal about thought*. Chicago: University of Chicago Press.

McNeill, D. (2000). *Language and gesture*. New York: Cambridge University Press.

Mehrabian, A. (1971). *Silent messages*. Belmont, CA: Wadsworth.

Mehrabian, A. (1972). *Nonverbal communication*. Chicago: Aldine-Atherton.

Mehrabian, A. (1976). *Public places and private spaces*. New York: Basic Books.

Montagu, M. F. A. (1971). *Touching: The human significance of the skin*. New York: Columbia University Press.

Morris, D. (1971). *Intimate behavior*. New York: Random House.

Morris, D. (1977). *Manwatching: A field guide to human behavior*. New York: Abrams.

Morris, D. (1985). *Bodywatching*. New York: Crown.

Noller, P. (1984). *Nonverbal communication and marital interaction*. New York: Pergamon Press.

Patterson, M. L. (1983). *Nonverbal behavior: A functional perspective*. New York: Springer.

Patterson, M. L. (1984). Nonverbal exchange: Past, present, and future. *Journal of Nonverbal Behavior, 8,* 350–359.

Patterson, M. L. (1999). The evolution of a parallel process model of nonverbal communication. In P. Philippot, R. S. Feldman, & E. J. Coats (Eds.), *The social context of nonverbal behavior* (pp. 317–347). New York: Cambridge University Press.

Philippot, P., Feldman, R. S., & Coats, E. J. (Eds.). (1999). *The social context of nonverbal behavior*. New York: Cambridge University Press.

Pittinger, R. E., Hockett, C. F., & Danehy, J. J. (1960). *The first five minutes: A sample of microscopic interview analysis.* Ithaca, NY: Paul Martineau.

Quintilian, M. F. (1922/ca. 90 CE). *The institutio oratoria, book XI* (H. E. Butler, Trans.). Cambridge, MA: Harvard University Press.

Rhodes, G., & Zebrowitz, L. A. (Eds.). (2002). *Facial attractiveness: Evolutionary, cognitive, and social perspectives.* Westport, CT: Ablex.

Riggio, R. E., & Feldman, R. S. (Eds.). (2005). *Applications of nonverbal communication.* Mahwah, NJ: Erlbaum.

Rosenbaum, R. (1995, January 15). The posture photo scandal. *New York Times Magazine,* pp. 26–31, 40, 46, 55–56.

Rosenthal, R. (1966). *Experimenter effects in behavioral research.* New York: Appleton-Century-Crofts.

Rosenthal, R. (2002). Covert communication in classrooms, clinics, courtrooms, and cubicles. *American Psychologist, 57,* 839–849.

Rosenthal, R., & Jacobson, L. (1968). *Pygmalion in the classroom.* New York: Holt, Rinehart & Winston.

Ruesch, J. (1953). Synopsis of the theory of human communication. *Psychiatry, 16,* 215–243.

Ruesch, J., & Kees, W. (1956). *Nonverbal communication: Notes on the visual perception of human relations.* Los Angeles: University of California Press.

Russell, J. A., & Fernández-Dols, J. M. (1997). *The psychology of facial expression.* New York: Cambridge University Press.

Scheflen, A. E. (1973). *Communicational structure: Analysis of a psychotherapy transaction.* Bloomington: University of Indiana Press.

Scherer, K. R. (1986). Vocal affect expression: A review and a model for future research. *Psychological Bulletin, 99,* 143–165.

Scherer, K. R., & Ekman, P. (Eds.). (1982). *Handbook of nonverbal behavior research.* New York: Cambridge University Press.

Segerstråle, U., & Molnár, P. (Eds.). (1997). *Nonverbal communication: Where nature meets culture.* Mahwah, NJ: Erlbaum.

Shawn, T. (1954). *Every little movement: A book about Francois Delsarte.* Pittsfield, MA: Eagle Print & Binding.

Sheldon, W. H. (1940). *The varieties of human physique: An introduction to constitutional psychology.* New York: Harper & Row.

Sommer, R. (1969). *Personal space.* Englewood Cliffs, NJ: Prentice Hall.

Sommer, R. (2002). Personal space in a digital age. In R. B. Bechtel & A. Churchman (Eds.), *Handbook of environmental psychology* (pp. 647–660). New York: Wiley.

Spitz, H. H. (1997). *Nonconscious movements: From mystical messages to facilitated communication.* Mahwah, NJ: Erlbaum.

Trager, G. L. (1958). Paralanguage: A first approximation. *Studies in Linguistics, 13,* 1–12.

Volkmar, F. R., & Siegel, A. E. (1982). Responses to consistent and discrepant social communications. In R. S. Feldman (Ed.), *Development of nonverbal behavior in children* (pp. 231–255). New York: Springer.

Wallbott, H. G. (1982). Contributions of the German "Expression Psychology" to nonverbal communication research: Part III. Gait, gestures, and body movement. *Journal of Nonverbal Behavior, 7,* 20–32.

Wegner, D. M., & Bargh, J. A. (1998). Control and automaticity in social life. In D. T. Gilbert, S. T. Fiske, & G. Lindzey (Eds.), *The handbook of social psychology* (Vol. 1, 4th ed., pp. 446–496). New York: McGraw-Hill.

Weitz, S. (Ed.). (1974). *Nonverbal communication: Readings with commentary.* New York: Oxford University Press.

Wiener, M., Devoe, S., Rubinow, S., & Geller, J. (1972). Nonverbal behavior and nonverbal communication. *Psychological Review, 79,* 185–214.

2

THE EVOLUTION OF THEORIES OF INTERACTIVE BEHAVIOR

◆ Miles L. Patterson

University of Missouri, St. Louis

S peculation about the role and impact of nonverbal behavior in the human condition has been present for centuries in philosophy, science, and literature (see Knapp, this volume). Nevertheless, the development of systematic and focused empirical research on nonverbal behavior is a relatively recent phenomenon, growing rapidly from the late 1950s through the present day. Although the vast majority of this work consists of empirical research, theoretical scholarship has also been important, not only in developing a broader understanding of nonverbal communication but also in shaping subsequent empirical work. This chapter focuses on some of this theoretical development. In particular, I discuss *theories of interactional nonverbal behavior* (i.e., patterned cues in face-to-face contexts).

Although nonverbal communication operates in a wide variety of contexts, it is especially important in face-to-face interactions. In such interactions, patterns of behavior are "negotiated" subtly and move typically toward some degree of stability. Partners' behavior patterns might converge and be similar in form, or they might diverge and be dissimilar. Simultaneously, interactants make a wide variety of judgments about their partners and the interaction. So, how do we explain the complex cognitive and behavioral adjustments in a wide range of face-to-face encounters? This is the central question underlying the theories discussed in this chapter. The purposes of this chapter are (1) to trace the development of theories of interactive behavior and (2) to discuss, in some detail, a more comprehensive, *parallel process model* of nonverbal communication (see also Patterson, 2001). Although this chapter focuses specifically on the behavioral give-and-take between people, these theories have important implications for a wide variety of topics in nonverbal communication, including emotions, deception, influence, impression management, and intimacy.

Even though this chapter highlights the parallel process model of nonverbal communication, it is important to appreciate the how and why of the changing theoretical landscape over time. Because newer theories build necessarily on earlier theories and on the research stimulated by them, it is useful to consider the course of these developments. As a participant in these efforts over the last 30 years, I cannot claim an absence of bias regarding the merits of particular theories. Nevertheless, perhaps I can provide an insider's perspective on the evolution of theories of interactive behavior.

◆ Early Theories

With few exceptions, the advent of systematic empirical research on nonverbal communication was marked by a focus on one behavior or channel at a time (e.g., Exline, 1963; Sommer, 1959). For example, researchers studying spatial behavior did not generally concern themselves with the simultaneous changes in gaze or facial expressions. Instead, investigators often examined how culture, gender, personality, or the specific situation affected the behavior of interest.

Although these were all interesting issues, this line of research provided little insight into the dynamic relationships across nonverbal behaviors as people interacted with one another. The landscape changed dramatically, however, with the publication of a 1965 article by Argyle and Dean.

EQUILIBRIUM THEORY

In their equilibrium theory, Argyle and Dean (1965) focused on how individuals maintain a comfortable or appropriate level of behavioral intimacy or involvement in interactions. They proposed that a small set of behaviors, including distance, gaze, smiling, and verbal intimacy (self-disclosure) determines the overall level of involvement in an interaction. As the underlying intimacy in a relationship increased, for example, from initial strangers to acquaintances to good friends or lovers, the comfortable level of involvement also increased. Over the course of any specific interaction, there was pressure to maintain a balance, or equilibrium, in the level of involvement. For example, if a stranger approached too closely, one might turn away and avoid eye contact. This kind of adjustment was termed *compensation* because the reduction in gaze compensated for the too close approach.

Equilibrium theory was especially important because it was the first attempt to explain the momentary behavioral adjustments that people make over the course of an interaction. Early empirical research not only supported equilibrium theory, but it also expanded the range of relevant behaviors (for a review, see Patterson, 1973. In addition to the behaviors Argyle and Dean (1965) proposed, body orientation, lean, touch, posture, and expressiveness also contributed to the overall involvement between interaction partners (see Andersen, Guerrero, & Jones, this volume).

Over time, however, two distinct limitations to equilibrium theory became evident. First, the results of a few studies directly contradicted the predictions of equilibrium theory (e.g., Breed, 1972; Chapman, 1975). Instead of compensating for increased involvement, individuals in these studies increased, or *reciprocated,* the higher involvement of a partner. Second, the majority of the empirical research supporting equilibrium theory involved confederates who acted in a relatively extreme fashion toward their unsuspecting partners in settings where the research participants had little control over their immediate environments. Examples of this research included studies of spatial invasion, staring, or the initiation of unexpected touch. Under these circumstances, it is not surprising that most people compensated. That is, they left the setting, turned away, or avoided gaze in response to the confederate's increased involvement. This kind of pattern might not be expected between good friends interacting on their own territories. In fact, reciprocation might be more common in interactions between friends, family member, or lovers. A different approach was needed to explain both compensation and reciprocation between strangers and intimate partners.

AFFECT-BASED THEORIES

From the mid-1970s to the mid-1980s, a number of different theories were advanced to explain compensation and reciprocation across a wide range of relationships. Because there was research linking arousal to increased levels of nonverbal involvement (e.g., Gale, Lucas, Nissim, & Harpham, 1972; McBride, King, & James, 1965), arousal seemed a likely mediator of nonverbal adjustments. Although several theories shared a common emphasis on arousal in explaining patterns of compensation and reciprocation, important differences were also evident.

My own *arousal-labeling theory* proposed that the experience of arousal in response to a change in the partner's nonverbal behavior precipitated a labeling or self-attribution process (Patterson, 1976). This process was the mechanism at the core of Schachter and Singer's (1962) two-factor theory of emotions. The arousal-labeling theory predicted that if the partner's change in nonverbal involvement (e.g., a close approach, touch, and a high level of gaze) was sufficient to produce arousal, individuals initiated the labeling process. Next, if the resulting emotional state was positive (e.g., liking, love, comfort), then the individual would reciprocate the partner's increased involvement. Thus, a close approach, smile, and touch from a good friend would increase arousal, be labeled as liking, and lead to reciprocating the friend's high involvement. This reciprocation might take the form of smiling back at the friend and increasing gaze. If similar behavior was initiated unexpectedly by a stranger, arousal would also be increased, but it would be more often labeled as discomfort and lead to compensation. Thus, the recipient might turn away and avoid gaze in attempting to reestablish some degree of comfort and control in the setting.

Around the same time, Burgoon proposed an *expectancy-violations model of personal space* (Burgoon, 1978; Burgoon & Jones, 1976). Although this theory focused originally on the effects of preferred interaction distances on communication outcomes, such as communicator credibility and attractiveness (Hale & Burgoon, 1984), its extension to effects on nonverbal involvement was fairly direct. Specifically, when expectations about preferred levels of involvement are violated, arousal is increased, and a labeling or interpretation of the arousal is made, as in the arousal-labeling model. In general, the expectancy-violations model predicts a compensatory adjustment to more extreme violations of expectancies and a reciprocal adjustment to low-level violations of expectancies. This pattern is qualified, however, by the reward value of the partner. For example, the same moderate level violation of increased involvement initiated by a high- versus low-valued partner would produce very different adjustments. Specifically, the violation by the high-valued partner would be labeled positively and lead to reciprocation, whereas the same violation by the low-valued partner would be labeled negatively and lead to compensation (Hale & Burgoon, 1984).

Another theory focusing on the central role of arousal and how it is labeled was the *cognitive valence model* (Andersen, 1985). In this theory, reactions to a partner's change in nonverbal involvement were a product, first, of the intensity of the arousal change and, second, of how moderate levels of arousal change might be labeled. Specifically, if a partner's behavior precipitated little or no change in one's arousal, no behavioral adjustment (compensation or reciprocation) was required. In contrast, if the partner's behavior precipitated a large increase or decrease in arousal, then that would be experienced negatively and result in compensation. It was only when the arousal change was in a moderate range that several valencing factors determined the affective experience of an individual. Specifically, social norms, relationships, perceptions of the partner, the environmental context, and other personal characteristics of the individual shaped the experience of the arousal. Like the other theories, negatively labeled or valenced arousal led to compensation, and positively labeled or valenced arousal led to reciprocation.

These three theories predict that an individual's affective state following a partner's change in nonverbal involvement is the proximate determinant of behavioral adjustments. In each case, the labeling or attribution of one's arousal is critical. The fourth affect-based approach, *discrepancy-arousal theory* (Cappella & Greene, 1982), however, proposed a very different explanation. Although Cappella and Greene suggested several distinguishing characteristics of their approach, the one that set it apart from other affect-based theories most clearly was its emphasis on arousal alone as the critical mediator of nonverbal adjustments. Cappella and Greene argued that in the course of interaction, adjustments happen so quickly that there is literally not enough time for a labeling, or attribution, process to mediate the behavioral changes. In other words, behavioral adjustments to a partner's change in involvement are more rapid than the presumed cognitive mediating processes. Consequently, they proposed that arousal alone, which could be activated very rapidly, was the critical mediator of nonverbal adjustments (Cappella & Greene, 1982).

According to discrepancy-arousal theory, as an interaction starts, there is a more or less automatic comparison between the actual and the expected levels of involvement. In general, as the discrepancy between the expected and the actual level of involvement increases, so does arousal. A critical link in this theory is the relationship between the intensity of arousal and a person's resulting affect. Specifically, Cappella and Greene (1982) suggested that the valence and intensity of affect follow a curvilinear relationship with arousal. That is, low to moderate levels of arousal produce increasingly positive affect, but as arousal increases beyond moderate levels, affect becomes less positive. With increasingly high levels of arousal, affect becomes increasingly negative. At this point in the sequence, one that happens very rapidly, the predicted behavioral adjustments parallel those in the other affect-based theories. That is, the greater the positive affect that one experiences, the greater the reciprocation of the partner's nonverbal involvement, and the greater the negative affect that one experiences, the greater the compensation for the partner's nonverbal involvement.

Although these four theories propose distinct processes mediating behavioral adjustments, it is very difficult to structure a critical test of their relative merits (but see Andersen, Guerrero, Buller, & Jorgensen, 1998). In most cases, the theories make similar predictions for a specific set of circumstances. For example, each of the theories predicts that *substantially increased involvement* (close approach, sustained gaze, a smile, and touch) *from a disliked other precipitates compensation* (turning away and gaze avoidance). Each of the theories also predicts that *similar increased involvement from a well-liked other precipitates reciprocation* (increased gaze, a smile, and touch).

Actually measuring the hypothesized mediating processes (arousal change and cognitions) as they occur in interactions, however, is demanding. Although the monitoring of physiological arousal in structured interactions has been done occasionally (e.g., Coutts, Schneider, & Montgomery, 1980; Whitcher & Fisher, 1979), most of the research on interactive behavior does not include physiological measures. In two studies in our own laboratory that did employ physiological measures, we found only very limited support for the predicted increase in arousal following confederates' increased nonverbal involvement toward a subject (Ickes, Patterson, Rajecki, & Tanford, 1982, study 2; Patterson, Jordan, Hogan, & Frerker, 1981). In addition, the intrusive nature of physiological measures also reduces the external validity of the results. It is probably fair to say that arousal *can* mediate nonverbal adjustments, especially when a partner's behavior is extreme,

but the few studies actually employing physiological measures have not demonstrated that arousal is a necessary mediator.

Assessing the role of cognitions in this kind of research is difficult because these measures have to be taken after the interactions. Thus, it is only after the interaction is completed that individuals might rate what they think about their partners, themselves, and the interaction. Alternatively, research participants might list the specific thoughts they recall from the interaction, sometimes prompted by a videotape replay of the interaction (Ickes, Bissonnette, Garcia, & Stinson, 1990; Patterson, 1983, p. 170). Such measures can provide some insight into what people might have been thinking during the interaction, but it is not the same as being able to assess those cognitions as they happen.

Assessment is further complicated by the fact that reported cognitions and attributions are often the product of the behavior, not the cause of the behavior (Bem, 1972). Thus, positive ratings of a confederate after an interaction do not necessarily mean that positive cognitions mediated a reciprocation pattern. Rather, behavioral adjustments could have happened for other reasons and, in turn, precipitated the cognitions. That is, the reported evaluations might not be present at the time of the actual behavior, but when participants are queried, they can provide such judgments based on their behavior. Such a sequence would be inconsistent with the predictions of these early theories. Of course, the sequencing issue would not apply to Cappella and Greene's (1982) discrepancy-arousal theory, because it excludes the role of cognitions in mediating adjustments specifically.

Although these issues are important concerns regarding these early theories, there were more basic limitations to all the theories. First, all the theories were *reactive* in nature. That is, they provided a kind of mechanistic explanation for predicting one person's reaction, given a particular behavior pattern from a partner. Even if the proposed mechanisms captured adequately the processes involved in nonverbal adjustments to partner's behavior, they were mute about the initiation of a particular interaction. That is, what is the reason behind the initial behavior in an interaction? Furthermore, once started, some sequences may not actually be reactive anyway. That is, sometimes individuals are not simply responding to their partner's immediately preceding behavior; rather, both parties are sometimes acting out a common script. An example of this kind of occurrence is the scripted routine in greetings.

The second major limitation to all the early theories was that they were all *affect driven*. Although the theories differed in just how individuals arrived at a particular affective state following a partner's behavior, the common prediction across the theories was that negative affect (e.g., anxiety or fear) precipitated compensation and positive affect (e.g., liking or love) precipitated reciprocation. Common sense and empirical results (Ickes et al., 1982) indicate that this is often not the case. For very practical reasons, there are times when we cannot let our feelings determine our behavior. In a similar fashion, it may be inappropriate, or at least risky, to respond with a high level of involvement to someone we like very much. In both cases, we manage our behavior to create a desirable impression in spite of our underlying feelings (for more on impression management, see Keating, this volume). That is, there is disconnect between what a person feels and the person's overt behavior. These limitations in the early theories prompted me to develop a different perspective on interactive behavior, one grounded in the functions served by particular behavior patterns.

◆ A Functional Perspective on Nonverbal Exchange

The basic assumption of the functional model is that interactive behavior is pragmatic. That is, nonverbal behavior can serve a number of different functions in social settings (Patterson, 1982, 1983). In the pursuit of particular goals, we not only react to our partners; we also initiate behavioral patterns to influence them. The pursuit of specific goals may also require behavior inconsistent with its underlying affect, contrary to the assumption of the theories reviewed in the last section. Affect in the functional model still provides a critical role in the initiation of, and reaction to, patterns of nonverbal behavior as a kind of "default" setting in interactions. The initiation of particular goals, however, such as gaining compliance from another person or deceiving someone, can override the role of affect in determining nonverbal behavior. Of course, this does not mean that these goal-oriented patterns are necessarily well done or successful.

Interactive behavior is, however, constrained by several determinants (Patterson, 1991). Specifically, as emphasized in this handbook, biology, culture, gender, and personality shape habitual patterns of interaction. The combination of genetic hardwiring, the social and cultural environments, and experience over time determines our behavioral predispositions, physiological reactivity to the social environment, and cognitive expectancies about others. In effect, this is the "baggage" that each of us brings to social settings and affects both the functions directing the interaction and the modal patterns of nonverbal involvement shown. That is, some of what we are as individuals is common in the hardwiring selected over the course of evolution, but culture, gender, and personality increase variability in the way we view our social worlds and relate to others (see chapters by Floyd, Hall, Gifford, and Matsumoto, this volume). The proposed linkages among the various determinants, mediating processes, and interaction outcomes can be seen in Figure 2.1.

Because this approach emphasizes the functions of interaction and recognizes that affect alone cannot determine particular patterns of nonverbal involvement, the focus moves away from simply predicting either compensation or reciprocation. Although people sometimes make reactive adjustments of compensation and reciprocation, in the functional approach, individuals are portrayed as more proactive in initiating specific patterns of behavior in the service of different goals. Because it is inappropriate to characterize such goal-driven patterns as simply compensation or reciprocation, a different kind of outcome metric was proposed for the functional model: the stability of nonverbal exchange.

When the perceived function of a given interaction is shared by the partners, interactions will tend to proceed in a relatively stable and predictable manner. As partners' similarity in culture and personality increases, the probability that expectancies and behavioral predispositions will be more compatible also increases. In turn, this increases the likelihood that nonverbal exchange will be more stable and predictable. Of course, there are exceptions to this generalization. For example, individuals who are complementary on the dominance-submissiveness dimension will typically have more stable interactions than those who are similar (see Burgoon & Dunbar, this volume, for more on the dominance-submissiveness dimension). When individuals have a sense of instability in the interaction, the model proposes that they are likely to experience arousal change and initiate a cognitive-affective assessment of the situation (see Figure 2.1, right half). Depending on the level of arousal change and the cognitive-affective

assessment, individuals may reevaluate the purpose (perceived function) of the interaction as they are also making nonverbal adjustments. Over time, these covert and overt adjustments promote stability in the interaction; but if they do not work, an early termination of the interaction is likely.

The functional approach emphasizes the utility of nonverbal communication in serving several general functions including (1) providing information, (2) regulating interaction, (3) expressing intimacy, (4) exercising influence, and (5) managing impressions (Patterson, 1991). Furthermore, similar patterns of behavior may be driven by different functions. For example, the same close approach, smile, and touch might reflect intimacy or simply be an attempt to manipulate the partner. Although the functional perspective captures the complex nature of nonverbal communication better than the affect-based theories, it does come at a cost. Specifically, the functional model does not attempt straightforward, directional predictions of behavioral adjustments, like those made by the affect-based theories. As a result, it falls short on an important quality of a good theory: being easily testable. On the other hand, because individuals can be proactive in meeting their goals and act independently of their underlying feelings, the task of framing specific predictions will necessarily be difficult. An interesting application and extension of the functional model can be seen in the area of social stigma and intergroup interactions (Hebl & Dovidio, 2005; see also Dovidio, Hebl, Richeson, & Shelton, this volume).

◆ Interaction Adaptation Theory

In an ambitious attempt to resolve the inconsistencies between empirical results and various theoretical explanations, Burgoon

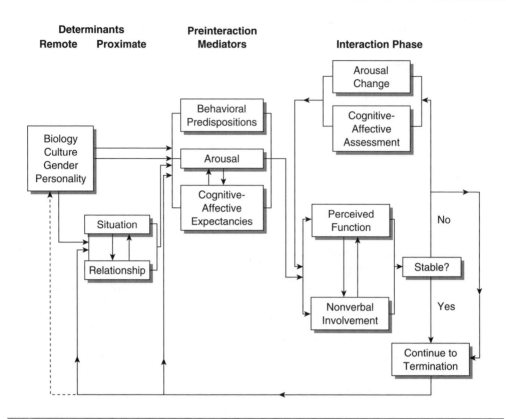

Figure 2.1   An Illustration of the Functional Model of Nonverbal Communication

and her colleagues (Burgoon et al., 1998; Burgoon, Stern, & Dillman, 1995) proposed the interaction adaptation theory (IAT). In this theory, several basic concepts are proposed as the major determinants of behavioral adjustments in interactions. The first three are the required (R), expected (E), and desired (D) levels of functionally driven behavior patterns. The R component refers to biological needs and drives, often operating outside of awareness, that influence interactive behavior. The E component refers to social factors, including knowledge of the setting, social norms, and the partner's typical behavior in the setting, that combine to determine behavioral expectancies. The D component refers to a range of individual factors, including personality characteristics, attitudes, and moods unique to a particular individual. These three factors, in turn, combine to

determine a person's interaction position (IP)—that is, the dominant behavioral predisposition likely for a given setting with a particular partner. In other words, one's IP is an estimate of the actor's likely behavior shaped by biology, experience, individual characteristics, and expectancies about a partner.

The particular valence and level of involvement represented in a person's IP are highly variable and dependent on the weight of the contributing R-E-D components. For example, if a particular interaction has implications for a person's safety and welfare, R will influence the final IP. If the setting and interaction are constrained by social norms—for example, in a job interview—the effect of E will be primary in determining IP. Likewise, if the situation is less structured and social norms are minimized, the personality characteristics and momentary affect will result in D being more important than R and E. Predictions about the course of interaction adaptation are possible only when the partner's actual interactive behavior (A) is known and compared to the actor's IP.

In general, IAT predicts that when A matches or is only slightly discrepant from IP, an actor should match or reciprocate the partner's behavior. As the discrepancy between A and IP gets larger, actors are more likely to engage in cognitive assessment and behavioral adjustment. According to IAT, there is pressure to minimize the discrepancy between A and IP to stabilize the interaction. The predicted behavioral adaptation is toward the factor (either A or IP) that is more positively valenced. For example, suppose the actor expects a high level of involvement (IP) from a partner, but the partner initiates a much lower level of involvement (A). In this case, the actor should compensate by trying to enlist greater involvement from the partner and, in the process, reduce the discrepancy between A and IP. If the actor expects a lower level of involvement (IP) from the partner, but the partner initiates a much higher level of involvement (A), then the actor should converge with or reciprocate the partner's high involvement. In the latter case, as in the former, the discrepancy between A and IP is reduced with the actor's behavioral adjustment.

In an experiment involving interactions among same- or cross-culture dyads, mixed support was found for the predictions of interpersonal adaptation theory (Burgoon et al., 1998). In general, partners adapted to one another as a function of their individual and cultural characteristics as predicted by interpersonal adaptation theory and by other theories reviewed here. Perhaps the most important contribution of interpersonal adaptation theory, however, is its emphasis on the pervasive pressure for behavioral adjustments, typically in the form of matching and reciprocity, which promote coordination and similarity across interactants.

◆ Parallel Process Model of Nonverbal Communication

SETTING THE CONTEXT

The theories discussed thus far have focused primarily on how individuals *behave* in interactions. Specifically, they address how we can explain, and potentially predict, patterns of nonverbal involvement in social settings. Early theories were primarily reactive in nature and stressed the importance of affect in precipitating nonverbal adjustments. The functional model and IAT recognized the necessity of trying to explain not only reactive adjustments but also behavior initiated by actors. Although individual actors engage necessarily in some cognitive activity in the process of managing nonverbal involvement, the focus in both the earlier and the later theories was clearly on *behavior*—that is, the encoding or sending of nonverbal communication.

Whereas the decoding or receiving of nonverbal behavior had been generally neglected in theories of interactive behavior, the opposite was the case in developing research and theory in social cognition (see, e.g., Fiske & Taylor, 1995; Kunda, 1999). This work, conducted primarily by social psychologists who were part of the "cognitive revolution" in psychology, provided a new perspective on the old issues of person perception and social judgment. For example, information-processing theories (e.g., Brewer, 1988; Fiske & Neuberg, 1990) focused largely on how a perceiver might attend to and process a person's characteristics, appearance, and category membership in forming an impression. These theories recognized that these processes sometimes operate relatively automatically and sometimes require effort (see Lakin, this volume).

A similar view of combined automatic and effortful (controlled) processes was pivotal in a theory of how perceivers move from behavioral observations to attributions (Gilbert & Krull, 1988; Gilbert, Pelham, & Krull, 1988). Specifically, Gilbert and his colleagues proposed that the first two stages of judgment, categorizing the behavior (e.g., friendly behavior) and next drawing a dispositional inference (e.g., friendly person), happen more or less automatically with little or no cognitive effort. Perceivers might, however, initiate an additional correction stage if they are sufficiently motivated and have the cognitive resources necessary to do the correction (Gilbert & Krull; Gilbert et al.). Around the same time, Bargh (1989, 1990) was making a strong case for automatic social judgments being the norm, not the exception, in forming impressions. Such automatic judgments were not, however, without purpose. For example, Fiske (1992) emphasized the pragmatic link of social cognition to interactive behavior in a reprise of William James's (1890/1983) observation from a century earlier that "thinking is for doing" (pp. 959–960). In a similar fashion, the ecological theory of social perception (McArthur & Baron, 1983) proposed that people are attuned particularly to perceiving the social affordances of others (e.g., Is this person good or bad for me?) quickly and accurately.

Although these researchers did not frame their mechanisms as part of a "communication" process, they were actually addressing the receiving side of communication. The parallel process model is an attempt to integrate the two sides of communication— social behavior and social judgment—into a single framework. Communicators send and receive nonverbal messages simultaneously in the service of specific goals. Just as changing our behavior (and often our appearance) to influence others is adaptive, attending selectively to and processing nonverbal information from others is also adaptive. Although much of our sending and receiving is relatively automatic, not all of it is, and changing circumstances can require considerable cognitive effort in social settings. The parallel process model frames the encoding and decoding processes of nonverbal communication in a single system, driven by a common set of determinants and mediating processes. The next section discusses the basic structure of the model and Figure 2.2 provides an illustration of the linkages among the determinants and processes in the model.

OVERVIEW OF THE PARALLEL PROCESS MODEL

Determinants. The determinants in Figure 2.2 (left side) identify the most important, though not the only, factors affecting the sending and receiving of nonverbal communication. These determinants constrain our habitual ways of communicating. That is, the effects of biology, culture, gender, and personality predispose us to communicate in a relatively consistent fashion over time. *Biology* also reflects the role of evolutionary pressures in shaping adaptive, hardwired patterns of communicating with others (see Buck & Renfro Powers, this volume, this volume; Floyd, this volume). For example, the positive, nurturing response to the baby-face appearance of infants is advantageous to their survival (Zebrowitz, 1997, chap. 4). Special sensitivity to facial expressions as signals of interpersonal intent may also be the product of natural selection (Fridlund, 1994; Fridlund & Russell, this volume).

Although natural selection has left us with some common, adaptive patterns of communication, culture, gender, and

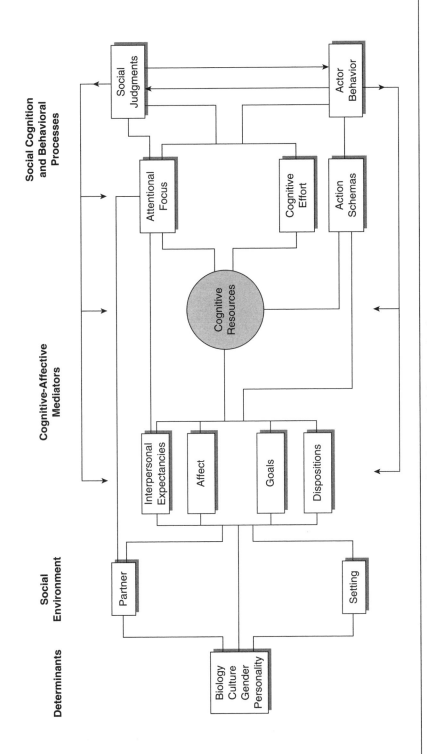

Figure 2.2   An Illustration of the Parallel Process Model of Nonverbal Communication

personality introduce increased variability in communication. For example, even though there is some degree of universality in expressive reactions, differences across *culture* are also evident (Elfenbein & Ambady, 2002; Russell, 1994; see also Matsumoto, this volume). Next, the effect of *gender* might be seen as the joint product of biology (the hardwired patterns) and culture (societal norms) in shaping patterns of nonverbal communication (see Hall, this volume). Finally, individual differences in *personality* also contribute to contrasting styles of nonverbal communication (see Gifford, this volume). Thus, the combined effects of the determinants produce both basic commonalities and differences in nonverbal communication.

Social Environment. Because the determinants also affect our choices of social environments, they have another, indirect influence on nonverbal communication, as seen in the second stage of the model. Interactions occur with specific partners in particular social settings. Because we interact differently with different people and in different settings, the social environment constrains our patterns of nonverbal communication. Just as we select settings, so do settings select us: I like to play golf, but the exclusive country clubs in St. Louis have little interest in having me as a member, even if I could afford to join them. The combined effect of self- and setting-selection processes results in greater homogeneity among people in most settings (Barker, 1968; Wicker, 1979). In turn, this increased similarity among people in specific settings not only facilitates greater accuracy in making social judgments of others (Funder, 1987; Swann, 1984) but also facilitates behavioral coordination in interactions.

Cognitive-Affective Mediators. The determinants and the social environment set the

context for interaction, but the cognitive-affective mediators are the processes that guide the course of communication. *Interpersonal expectancies* affect the social judgment and behavioral processes in nonverbal communication simultaneously. For example, expectancies can create a self-fulfilling prophecy in which actors' own behavior facilitates the behavior expected of a partner, without the actors' awareness of their role in the process (Rosenthal, 1974). Nevertheless, a partner's subtle appearance cues or behavior can also signal underlying dispositions (Jussim, 1991; Zebrowitz & Collins, 1997), resulting in an accurate judgment and not a self-fulfilling prophecy. *Affect* is a product of an individual's momentary disposition and goals, his or her relationship to the partner, and the setting constraints. Affect can influence both the formation of social judgments (e.g., Alloy & Abramson, 1988) and the patterns of nonverbal involvement, as seen in the early theories reviewed in this chapter. *Dispositions* refer to actor states precipitated in a specific social environment. The more obvious dispositions are linked to actors' personality characteristics (see Gifford, this volume). For example, the experience of social anxiety in a particular interaction can lead to decreased involvement (larger interpersonal distances and decreased gaze) and can affect social judgments adversely (Patterson & Ritts, 1997). *Goals* may be the most important of the mediators because they are the cognitive representations of desired states for which people strive (Berger, Knowlton, & Abrahams, 1996). Furthermore, goal-directed behavior, and even the goals themselves, can be activated automatically (Bargh & Chartrand, 1999).

The final mediator in the model, *cognitive resources,* refers to the total cognitive capacity available for managing our everyday activities. In social interactions, cognitive resources may be focused on a wide variety of concerns. For example, people might be preoccupied with personal problems, financial difficulties, or looming deadlines even as they are having a conversation at work. Because the total pool of cognitive resources is limited, the investment of substantial resources in matters outside of the interaction necessarily means that there is less that can be applied to the sending and receiving of nonverbal messages. In addition, whatever resources are committed to the immediate social situation can be variously distributed toward the self, the partner, the setting, or the topic of conversation.

Social Judgment and Behavioral Processes. The interaction processes are in the final stage of the model, with the social judgments represented in the top of Figure 2.2 and behaviors in the bottom half. Consistent with a functional approach, both social judgments and behaviors operate in concert for a common goal. Although each "track" can engage substantial cognitive effort, they typically operate on automatic. For example, on the social judgment "side," simply noticing an outgroup person may be sufficient to activate a stereotypic judgment (Bargh, 1989). On the behavioral "side," the cognitive representation of a particular goal, such as trying to impress another person, can be sufficient to trigger an automatic behavioral script. A particular goal, however, not only directs an actor's behavior but also directs the kinds of judgments made about the partner. For example, an actor trying to make a positive impression is more focused on metaperspective judgments (e.g., What does she think of me?) than on direct perspective judgments (e.g., What kind of person is she?). Thus, social judgment and behavioral processes operate typically on automatic as they complement each other in the pursuit of particular goals. The next section takes a closer look at the conditional links among selected component processes in this model.

DYNAMICS OF PARALLEL PROCESSING

Goals. A basic assumption underlying the parallel process model, and one consistent with the earlier functional model, is that communication is adaptive and goal oriented. In social settings, people read their social environments (decoding) and send nonverbal messages (encoding) simultaneously to others around them in the pursuit of particular goals. Although specific goals guide the operation of the parallel encoding and decoding processes, this does not mean that people must be consciously aware of the goals they are pursuing. Sometimes goals are triggered automatically and outside of awareness by the social environment (Bargh, 1997).

The relationship between the social judgment and behavioral processes in securing a particular goal is a complex one. Although it is assumed commonly that an actor's social judgments at Time 1 direct the actor's behavior at Time 2, specific goals can alter this sequence. Sometimes behavioral strategies may be initiated to test social judgments. That is, an individual might "float a trial balloon" to get a reading of a partner's sentiment on a particular issue without making a direct inquiry. For example, in dating relationships, one person might escalate behavioral intimacy to determine the partner's readiness for a romantic relationship. Another behavioral strategy might be playing hard to get as a means of testing a partner's interest and commitment. In addition, actors' scripted behavioral routines may operate independently of their social judgments of their partners (e.g., being pleasant to the disliked boss), consistent with a functional view of nonverbal communication.

Although the specific goals that drive nonverbal communication can vary widely, most people are also constrained by two broader metagoals (Berger, 1997, chap. 2).

First, we tend to pursue our communication goals in an *efficient* manner, minimizing effort. Fiske and Taylor (1995, chaps. 4–7) characterize perceivers as "cognitive misers" as they make judgments of others. Second, most people employ the behavioral strategies that are *appropriate* and follow social norms and customs (Berger, 1997, chap. 2). Thus, people typically take the path of least resistance and avoid calling undue negative attention to themselves.

Social Judgments. In general, research indicates that most initial social judgments happen more or less automatically, often outside of conscious awareness (e.g., Bargh, 1994; Brewer, 1988; see also Lakin, this volume). When the information about others (i.e., appearance and behavior) is ambiguous or inconsistent, considerable cognitive effort might be engaged in resolving a final judgment, but only if the perceiver is motivated to do so (Gilbert et al., 1988). Nevertheless, more is not always better when it comes to cognitive effort in making judgments. Rapid judgments from "thin slices of behavior" are, more often than not, accurate (Ambady & Rosenthal, 1992), and increased cognitive effort can even lead to more errors in judgment (Patterson & Stockbridge, 1998; Wilson & Schooler, 1991). When additional reflection is needed in making a judgment, it is possible only when there are sufficient cognitive resources available to the individual. If a person is distracted, worried, tired, or investing considerable effort in managing behavior, then corrections to an initial judgment are unlikely. Thus, the initial automatic judgment will dominate.

Social Behavior. Sending nonverbal communication, like receiving it, engages a variety of processes (from relatively automatic to more controlled). On the automatic end, our behavioral repertoire encompasses a wide range of basic, hardwired patterns of approach and avoidance that have undoubtedly been selected over the course of evolution. These would include expressive reactions that signal a person's intended course of action (Fridlund, 1994; see also Fridlund & Russell, this volume). Automatic patterns of increased involvement (e.g., close approach, gaze, and touch) might be activated in response to increased attraction or a need for comforting and supporting another person. In contrast, decreased involvement or behavioral avoidance may be precipitated by dislike, fear, or embarrassment. Besides the hardwired, affect-driven patterns, other patterns become automatic over time as a function of experience and learning. For example, most of us learn over time how to "make a good impression" when there is a lot at stake. The cognitive representations of these automatic sequences may be described as action schemata (see Figure 2.2, bottom) and can be initiated with little or no cognitive effort (Abelson, 1981; Vallacher & Wegner, 1987).

Another way to conceptualize the dynamics of behavioral processes is in terms of potentially competing response systems—that is, automatic versus controlled. Metcalfe and Mischel (1999) proposed such an approach in their "hot/cool system analysis" of the conflict involved in the delay of gratification. The "hot" response is the automatic approach to immediate gratification, which is initially under stimulus control (Metcalfe & Mischel, 1999), like Bargh's (1997) automatic actions. The hot system develops early and is simple, reflexive, and emotional in nature, like the affect-driven reactions discussed in the early theories in this chapter. In contrast, the "cool" response is a product of self-control. The cool system develops later and is more complex, reflective, and cognitive in nature. Strack and Deutsch (2004) proposed a model similar to the hot/cool system that engages both reflective and impulsive processes as determinants of social behavior. Specifically, the reflective system is based on knowledge about facts and values, whereas the impulsive system is based on associative links and motivational orientations (Strack & Deutsch, 2004). The predictions of both theories are consistent with the dynamics of the parallel process model—that is, stress and the lack of cognitive resources increases the probability of automatic actions and decreases the probability of controlled or effortful actions.

Coordinating Parallel Processes. The dynamic relationship between the parallel social judgment and behavior processes is constrained first by the influence of the determinants (biology, culture, gender, and personality) and the social environment (see Figure 2.2). Thus, we all come into particular settings with some stable tendencies in social judgments and social behavior. Automaticity in social judgments and behavior usually works well enough in navigating our social environments (Bargh, 1997), but it also provides another advantage: cognitive efficiency. Automatic processes do not, however, always work. When more controlled judgments and behavior are required, an individual needs to have the available cognitive resources and be motivated to apply those resources. If a person is stressed, cognitive resources are minimal, and controlled judgments and behaviors have low strength, then automatic judgments and behaviors will still tend to dominate.

What happens when we fail to achieve our specific goals? If we are sufficiently motivated, the feedback process can lead to adjustments in expectancies, affect, dispositions, and even the goals themselves (see Figure 2.2). Unless appropriate automatic adjustments are accessible, the subsequent recycling through the parallel processes requires additional resources and effort to activate more controlled processes.

Although the application of cognitive resources in reconsidering a faulty judgment, or in monitoring and managing behavior, may be effective, there is no guarantee that this will be the case. Additional adjustments may be required or individuals may simply terminate the interaction. Across interactions, the residual and cumulative effects of previous encounters shape subsequent goals, expectancies, affect, and dispositions.

◆ Conclusion

This chapter has traced the evolution of interaction theories from Argyle and Dean's (1965) equilibrium theory to the parallel process model of nonverbal communication (Patterson, 2001). As someone invested in these developments for more than three decades, it seems to me that there are some discernible trends over time. The early theories were reactive in nature, explaining and predicting behavioral adjustments given a partner's initial behavior. These theories differed in terms of the specific mediating processes, but they all emphasized a person's affective reaction as the proximate determinant of compensatory or reciprocal adjustments to a partner's nonverbal behavior. Although the early theories dealt only with reactive adjustments and did not appreciate that strategic adjustments may well be inconsistent with the underlying affect, they did offer specific, testable predictions.

In contrast, the functional model (Patterson, 1982) and interpersonal adaptation theory (Burgoon et al., 1995) moved away from simple reactive processes and emphasized that nonverbal adjustments are adaptive. That is, nonverbal patterns are shaped by different functions in different settings. Thus, people are agents not only reacting to others but also initiating behavior with specific ends in mind. Both theories also recognized that determinants such as biology, culture, gender, and personality shaped the course of interactive behavior. Although these theories painted a more representative picture of the complexity of interpersonal behavior, they did so at the expense of specific, testable predictions, characteristic of the earlier theories. Around the same time—that is, during the 1980s and 1990s—the burgeoning research in social cognition provided new and interesting insights into the dynamics of social judgments. Although their perspective was different, social cognition researchers were actually studying the decoding or receiving side of nonverbal communication.

I developed the parallel process model as a means of integrating two separate research paradigms—one focusing primarily on the behavioral processes and the other on the social judgment processes of nonverbal communication—into a unified theoretical framework (Patterson, 2001). Consistent with the increased appreciation of automatic behavioral and social judgment processes (Bargh, 1997), the parallel process model emphasizes the efficiency and utility of automatic processes in negotiating our social environments. Some interactions, however, require the initiation of controlled processes, possible only when there are adequate cognitive resources and the motivation to apply them. Thus, the actor in the parallel process model maintains a delicate balance between behavioral and social judgment processes, typically operating on automatic, in the service of specific goals. I think that the dynamics of the parallel process model are a closer approximation of the complexity of interactive behavior than those in previous theories, but I have no illusion that this is the final word on the topic.

◆ References

Abelson, R. P. (1981). The psychological status of the script concept. *American Psychologist, 36*, 715–729.

Alloy, L. B., & Abramson, L. Y. (1988). Depressive realism: Four theoretical perspectives. In L. B. Alloy (Ed.), *Cognitive processes in depression* (pp. 223–265). New York: Guilford Press.

Ambady, N., & Rosenthal, R. (1992). Thin slices of behavior as predictors of interpersonal consequences: A meta-analysis. *Psychological Bulletin, 111*, 256–274.

Andersen, P. A. (1985). Nonverbal immediacy in interpersonal communication. In A. W. Siegman & S. Feldstein (Eds.), *Multichannel integrations of nonverbal behavior* (pp. 1–36). Hillsdale, NJ: Erlbaum.

Andersen, P. A., Guerrero, L. K., Buller, D. B., & Jorgensen, P. F. (1998). An empirical comparison of three theories of nonverbal immediacy exchange. *Human Communication Research, 24*, 501–535.

Argyle, M., & Dean, J. (1965). Eye-contact, distance and affiliation. *Sociometry, 28*, 289–304.

Bargh, J. A. (1989). Conditional automaticity: Varieties of automatic influence in social perception and cognition. In J. S. Uleman & J. A. Bargh (Eds.), *Unintended thought* (pp. 3–51). New York: Guilford Press.

Bargh, J. A. (1990). Auto-motives: Preconscious determinants of thought and behavior. In E. T. Higgins & R. M. Sorrentino (Eds.), *Handbook of motivation and cognition* (2nd ed., pp. 93–130). New York: Guilford Press.

Bargh, J. A. (1994). The four horsemen of automaticity: Awareness, intention, efficiency, and control in social cognition. In R. S. Wyer & T. K. Srull (Eds.), *Handbook of social cognition* (2nd ed., pp. 1–40). Hillsdale, NJ: Erlbaum.

Bargh, J. A. (1997). The automaticity of everyday life. In R. S. Wyer (Ed.), *Advances in social cognition* (pp. 1–61). Mahwah, NJ: Erlbaum.

Bargh, J. A., & Chartrand, T. L. (1999). The unbearable automaticity of being. *American Psychologist, 54,* 462–479.

Barker, R. G. (1968). *Ecological psychology: Concepts and methods for studying the environment of human behavior.* Stanford, CA: Stanford University Press.

Bem, D. J. (1972). Self-perception theory. In L. Berkowitz (Ed.), *Advances in experimental social psychology* (Vol. 6, pp. 1–62). New York: Academic Press.

Berger, C. B. (1997). *Planning strategic interaction.* Mahwah, NJ: Erlbaum.

Berger, C. B., Knowlton, S. W., & Abrahams, M. F. (1996). The hierarchy principle in strategic communication. *Communication Theory, 6,* 111–142.

Breed, G. (1972). The effect of intimacy: Reciprocity or retreat? *British Journal of Social and Clinical Psychology, 11,* 135–142.

Brewer, M. B. (1988). A dual process model of impression formation. In T. K. Srull & R. S. Wyer Jr. (Eds.) *Advances in social cognition* (Vol. 1, pp. 1–36). Hillsdale, NJ: Erlbaum.

Burgoon, J. K. (1978). A communication model of personal space violations: Explication and an initial test. *Human Communication Research, 4,* 129–142.

Burgoon, J. K., Ebesu, A. S., White, C. H., Koch, P., Alvaro, E. M., & Kikuchi, T. (1998). The many faces of interaction adaptation. In M. T. Palmer & G. A. Barnett (Eds.), *Progress in communication sciences* (Vol. 14, pp. 191–220). Stamford, CT: Ablex.

Burgoon, J. K., & Jones, S. B. (1976). Toward a theory of personal space expectations and their violations. *Human Communication Research, 2,* 131–146.

Burgoon, J. K., Stern, L. A., & Dillman, L. (1995). *Interpersonal adaptation: Dyadic interaction patterns.* Cambridge, UK: Cambridge University Press.

Cappella, J. N., & Greene, J. O. (1982). A discrepancy-arousal explanation of mutual influence in expressive behavior for adult and infant-adult interaction. *Communication Monographs, 49,* 89–114.

Chapman, A. J. (1975). Eye contact, physical proximity and laughter: A reexamination of the equilibrium model of social intimacy. *Social Behavior and Personality, 3,* 143–155.

Coutts, L. M., Schneider, F. W., & Montgomery, S. (1980). An investigation of the arousal model of interpersonal intimacy. *Journal of Experimental Social Psychology, 16,* 545–561.

Elfenbein, H. A., & Ambady, N. (2002). On the universality and cultural specificity of emotion recognition: A meta-analysis. *Psychological Bulletin, 128,* 203–235.

Exline, R. V. (1963). Explorations in the process of person perception: Visual interaction in relation to competition, sex, and need for affiliation. *Journal of Personality, 31,* 1–20.

Fiske, S. T. (1992). Thinking is for doing: Portraits of social cognition from daguerreotype to laserphoto. *Journal of Personality and Social Psychology, 63,* 877–889.

Fiske, S. T., & Neuberg, S. L. (1990). A continuum of impression formation, from category-based to individuating processes: Influences of information and motivation on attention and interpretation. In M. Zanna (Ed.), *Advances in experimental social psychology* (Vol. 23, pp. 1–74). New York: Academic Press.

Fiske, S. T., & Taylor, S. E. (1995). *Social cognition* (2nd ed.). New York: McGraw-Hill.

Fridlund, A. J. (1994). *Human facial expression: An evolutionary view.* San Diego: Academic Press.

Funder, D. C. (1987). Errors and mistakes: Evaluating the accuracy of social judgment. *Psychological Bulletin, 101,* 75–90.

Gale, A., Lucas, B., Nissim, R., & Harpham, B. (1972). Some EEG correlates of face-to-face contact. *British Journal of Social and Clinical Psychology, 11,* 326–332.

Gilbert, D. T., & Krull, D. S. (1988). Seeing less and knowing more: The benefits of perceptual ignorance. *Journal of Personality and Social Psychology, 54,* 193–202.

Gilbert, D. T., Pelham, B. W., & Krull, D. S. (1988). On cognitive busyness: When person perceivers meet persons perceived. *Journal of Personality and Social Psychology, 54,* 733–740.

Hale, J. L., & Burgoon, J. K. (1984). Models of reactions to changes in nonverbal immediacy. *Journal of Nonverbal Behavior, 8,* 287–314.

Hebl, M. R., & Dovidio, J. F. (2005). Promoting the "social" in the examination of social stigmas. *Personality and Social Psychology Review, 9,* 156–182.

Ickes, W., Bissonnette, V., Garcia, S., & Stinson, L. L. (1990). Implementing and using the dyadic interaction paradigm. In C. Hendrick & M. S. Clark (Eds.), *Research methods in personality and social psychology* (pp. 16–44). Newbury Park, CA: Sage.

Ickes, W., Patterson, M. L., Rajecki, D. W., & Tanford, S. (1982). Behavioral and cognitive consequences of reciprocal versus compensatory responses to preinteraction expectancies. *Social Cognition, 1,* 160–190.

James, W. (1983). *The principles of psychology.* Cambridge, MA: Harvard University Press. (Original work published 1890)

Jussim, L. (1991). Social perception and social reality: A reflection-construction model. *Psychological Review, 98,* 54–73.

Kunda, Z. (1999). *Social cognition: Making sense of people.* Cambridge, MA: MIT Press.

McArthur, L. Z., & Baron, R. M. (1983). Toward an ecological theory of social perception. *Psychological Review, 90,* 215–238.

McBride, G., King, M. C., & James, J. W. (1965). Social proximity effects of galvanic skin responses in adult humans. *Journal of Psychology, 61,* 153–157.

Metcalfe, J., & Mischel, W. (1999). A hot/cool system analysis of delay of gratification: Dynamics of willpower. *Psychological Review, 106,* 3–19.

Patterson, M. L. (1973). Compensation in nonverbal immediacy behaviors: A review. *Sociometry, 36,* 237–252.

Patterson, M. L. (1976). An arousal model of interpersonal intimacy. *Psychological Review, 83,* 235–245.

Patterson, M. L. (1982). A sequential functional model of nonverbal exchange. *Psychological Review, 89,* 231–249.

Patterson, M. L. (1983). *Nonverbal behavior: A functional perspective.* New York: Springer-Verlag.

Patterson, M. L. (1991). A functional approach to nonverbal exchange. In R. S. Feldman & B. Rime (Eds.), *Fundamentals of nonverbal behavior* (pp. 458–495). Cambridge, UK: Cambridge University Press.

Patterson, M. L. (2001). Toward a comprehensive model of nonverbal communication. In W. P. Robinson & H. Giles (Eds.), *The new handbook of language and social psychology* (pp. 159–176). Chichester, UK: Wiley.

Patterson, M. L., Jordan, A., Hogan, M. B., & Frerker, D. (1981). Effects of nonverbal intimacy on arousal and behavioral adjustment. *Journal of Nonverbal Behavior, 5,* 184–198.

Patterson, M. L., & Ritts, V. (1997). Social and communicative anxiety: A review and meta-analysis. In B. R. Burleson (Ed.), *Communication yearbook 20* (pp. 262–303). Thousand Oaks, CA: Sage.

Patterson, M. L., & Stockbridge, E. (1998). Effects of cognitive demand and judgment strategy on person perception accuracy. *Journal of Nonverbal Behavior, 22,* 253–263.

Rosenthal, R. (1974). *On the social psychology of the self-fulfilling prophecy: Further evidence for Pygmalion effects and their mediating mechanisms.* New York: M.S.S. Information Corporation Modular Publication.

Russell, J. A. (1994). Is there a universal recognition of emotion from facial expression? A review of the cross-cultural studies. *Psychological Bulletin, 115,* 102–141.

Schachter, S., & Singer, J. E. (1962). Cognitive, social, and physiological determinants of emotional state. *Psychological Review, 69,* 379–399.

Sommer, R. (1959). Studies in personal space. *Sociometry, 22,* 247–260.

Strack, F., & Deutsch, R. (2004). Reflective and impulsive determinants of social behavior. *Personality and Social Psychology Review, 8,* 220–247.

Swann, W. B., Jr. (1984). Quest for accuracy in person perception: A matter of pragmatics. *Psychological Review, 91,* 457–477.

Vallacher, R. R., & Wegner, D. M. (1987). What do people think they're doing? Action identification and human behavior. *Psychological Review, 94,* 3–15.

Whitcher, S. J., & Fisher, J. D. (1979). Mulitdimensional reactions to therapeutic touch in a hospital setting. *Journal of Personality and Social Psychology, 37,* 87–96.

Wicker, A. W. (1979*). An introduction to ecological psychology.* Monterey, CA: Brooks/ Cole.

Wilson, T. D., & Schooler, J. W. (1991). Thinking too much: Introspection can reduce the quality of preferences and decisions. *Journal of Personality and Social Psychology, 60,* 181–192.

Zebrowitz, L. A. (1997). *Reading faces: Window to the soul?* Boulder, CO: Westview Press.

Zebrowitz, L. A., & Collins, M. A. (1997). Accurate social perception at zero acquaintance: The affordances of a Gibsonian approach. *Personality and Social Psychology Review, 1,* 204–223.

3

METHODS FOR THE STUDY OF NONVERBAL COMMUNICATION

◆ Heather M. Gray
Harvard University

◆ Nalini Ambady
Tufts University

A glance at the chapters in this volume reveals the wide range of questions researchers are asking about nonverbal communication. Whereas many are interested in how the nonverbal communication system has been shaped by biological, evolutionary, and cultural forces, others focus on the influence of the modern environment. Whereas some are curious about the social consequences of nonverbal displays, others attempt to catalog the constructs conveyed through facial expressions, bodily movements, vocal cues, and other ways of communicating without words. We can begin to understand these issues thanks in part to methods that capitalize on the widespread availability of visual and auditory media. The purpose of this chapter is to provide a survey of some of these methods.

The breadth of research questions about nonverbal communication is due in large part to the fact that nonverbal displays can be conceptualized as both independent and dependent variables. They are used as *independent* variables by researchers who want to understand the cognitive, affective, or behavioral consequences of nonverbal displays. For instance, to understand how first impressions regulate interpersonal processes, researchers can present nonverbal cues and measure subsequent attitudes and decisions (e.g., Ambady & Rosenthal, 1993; Harris & Rosenthal, 2005; Zebrowitz & Rhodes, 2004). Nonverbal cues are viewed as *dependent* variables when the cue is manipulated to infer subsequent cognitive or affective changes by observing nonverbal behavior (e.g., Dimberg, Thunberg, & Elmehed, 2000; Richeson & Shelton, 2005). At other times, nonverbal displays are studied as both independent and dependent variables, such as when researchers assess emotional responses to emotional displays or investigate behaviors co-occurring during interaction between people (see, e.g., Bavelas & Chovil, this volume). The survey of methods that follows is organized according to these two primary design considerations (i.e., nonverbal cues as independent and dependent variables).

Although many researchers who focus on interaction would not define their work according to these criteria but, rather, define nonverbal communication within a larger set of interactional processes (e.g., adaptation), we believe that the current approach can encapsulate some of what occurs in those studies as well. Following this contention, we first review some ways in which nonverbal behavior is used as an independent variable; such methods are useful in uncovering the perceptual, affective, and cognitive consequences of behavior communicated in a range of nonverbal channels. Next, we describe the ways in which nonverbal behavior is assessed as a dependent variable, organized according to the channel of communication used to infer the underlying subjective experience. For each method within these larger areas, we provide examples of the kinds of research

questions that can be addressed and highlight some issues that await further exploration. We then discuss major design considerations and the relative merits and limitations of each approach.

◆ Nonverbal Behavior as an Independent Variable

We begin this section with a summary of the ways in which nonverbal behavior can be used as an independent variable, with a focus on its widespread application of photographs, vocal clips, video clips, and interaction paradigms to the study of interpersonal communication.

PHOTOGRAPHS

Some Appropriate Uses. Still photographs can be used to study a wide range of processes, including the perception of fleeting states and enduring traits. One particularly active line of research asks whether emotions are recognized universally in static faces. The first studies to explore this question revealed that the six "basic" emotions (anger, disgust, fear, happiness, sadness, and surprise) are recognized at above-chance levels across cultures (e.g., Ekman, 1972); in these studies, participants viewed posed expressions and were asked to identify the emotion being expressed from a list of predetermined labels. Recognition of the intended category at accuracy rates greater than that expected by chance provided evidence for the universality of emotion recognition.

Current work extends this initial inquiry by focusing on a number of questions that may have implications for our understanding of the form and function of emotional displays: What are the social functions of these displays (Marsh, Adams, & Kleck, 2004), and do more "self-conscious" emotions—embarrassment, shame, and pride—also have universally recognizable displays (Tracy & Robins, 2004)? Although even the more basic question of universality in recognition is hotly debated (Ekman, 1994; Russell, 1994), some new evidence suggests that although emotional displays can be recognized across cultures, they may be better understood by members of the encoder's own national, ethnic, or regional group (Elfenbein & Ambady, 2002).

Other scholars attempt to understand how the ability to recognize emotions is related to long-term psychological adjustment. Results demonstrate consistently that the ability to recognize emotion from static faces is linked with both personal and social adjustment (e.g., Nowicki & Duke, 1994). Several standardized sets of emotional faces are useful in addressing these questions, particularly the Diagnostic Analysis of Nonverbal Accuracy (DANVA; Nowicki & Duke, 1994). The DANVA contains 24 emotional expressions (six each of anger, fear, happiness, and sadness), and it has been validated extensively and is used widely. An updated version, the DANVA-2, includes stimuli that vary in their intensity and represent encoders of different racial groups (Baum & Nowicki, 1998).

Still other researchers use photographs to gauge people's ability to understand others' mental lives. For example, Baron-Cohen and his colleagues have devised a task consisting of black-and-white photographs of the eye region of faces (the "Reading the Mind in the Eyes" test; Baron-Cohen, Wheelwright, & Hill, 2001). These stimuli have been used to investigate the extent to which people with autism or Asperger's syndrome show a selective impairment in the ability to use nonverbal behavior to infer mental states (Baron-Cohen et al., 2001).

In addition to using photographs to study the communication of relatively short-lived characteristics, particularly emotional and mental states, photography can also be used to study how aspects of identity, such as gender, age, and ethnicity, are perceived and interpreted. Social psychologists, for instance, have learned a great deal about prejudice and stereotypes by measuring cognitive and affective responses to still photographs representing people of different ethnic groups (e.g., Greenwald, Nosek, & Banaji, 2003). Static facial cues also form, albeit inaccurately, the basis for impressions of enduring psychological traits. For instance, considerable research demonstrates that people who have facial features that resemble those of infants (e.g., large eyes, round faces, small chins) are perceived to have childlike traits, such as submissiveness, dependence, honesty, and weakness (for a review, see Zebrowitz, 1997).

Design Considerations. Although the basic procedure for testing many of these phenomena involves a relatively invariable set of steps, the researcher is faced with important decisions at nearly every stage. The first decision to be made is whether to construct a new set of stimuli or to use a preexisting set. Some sets have been developed primarily for the study of individual differences in emotion recognition (e.g., Baum & Nowicki, 1998; Buck, 2005), and others are useful in exploring cultural factors in this process (e.g., Ekman & Friesen, 1976; Matsumoto & Ekman, 1988). Preexisting sets involve less work because they have already been validated and include normative data against which special populations can be compared. On the other hand, these sets provide less control over important issues such as the states being expressed and the selection of encoders and may not meet the needs of a particular research question.

If the decision is made to construct a new set of stimuli, a number of additional issues arise. For research on the recognition of emotions, as an example, should the expressions be spontaneous, induced, or posed? Spontaneous expressions can be sampled from a wide range of naturalistic situations; however, they provide little control over the qualities being communicated, the encoders, and the quality of the stimuli. Another, more controllable, option involves inducing emotions in encoders. Like spontaneous displays, induced displays have the advantage of being naturalistic; their primary drawbacks include their diminished intensity and the ethical issues associated with induced emotion. Given these issues, the preferred method involves obtaining posed displays from professional or lay actors. Encoders can be asked to relax and imagine the scenario vividly before performing it; this tends to increase the intensity of expressions (Banse & Scherer, 1996). For an extended discussion of these issues, see Archer, Akert, and Costanzo (1993) and Scherer (2003).

Emotional expressions can also be either "pure" or "blended" (consisting of a mix of emotions, such as happiness and surprise). Although most preexisting sets contain relatively pure expressions, perceivers appear to process blended expressions more efficiently, possibly because they are more likely to encounter them in real life (LaPlante & Ambady, 2000). It is now possible to create blended expressions artificially using software such as Adobe Photoshop (e.g., Marsh, Elfenbein, & Ambady, 2003). New digital editing techniques allowed Jones, Little, Burt, and Perrett (2004) to establish that the apparent health of the skin surface influences perceived attractiveness independently of face shape. Digital editing software also permitted Adams and Kleck (2003) to manipulate the direction of eye gaze in targets expressing a range of emotions, which was essential in documenting the joint contribution of eye gaze and emotional cues in the processing of facial displays.

These assessments are all meant to capture accuracy, but defining accuracy is itself a challenging process (see Riggio, this volume). As outlined by Kruglanski (1989),

there are at least three ways to define accuracy in this measurement context: (a) the degree of correspondence between a judgment and a criterion, (b) interpersonal consensus, and (c) the degree of a judgment's utility to the perceiver. Many researchers choose the first definition, using the display intended by the encoder (or the experimenter) as the criterion against which responses are compared. Because multiple criteria tend to overcome the inherent weaknesses of any single criterion, one option is to use more than one criterion in a single study.

There are several methods for validating stimuli for recognizability and authenticity before presenting them to study participants. One commonly used procedure involves presenting stimuli to an independent group of raters and computing the "effective" reliability of their judgments (of emotion or any other construct) using the Spearman-Brown formula with modified notations, as described by Rosenthal and Rosnow (1991). The formula is $R = nr/(1 + (n - 1)r)$, where R = the effective reliability, n = the number of raters, and r = the mean reliability of all the raters (i.e., mean of the correlations).

More pragmatic decisions must also be made regarding the manner in which responses are provided. The majority of studies in this area have used forced-choice or dimensional response formats. Alternatively, participants can use a free-response format and provide any label they choose. The relative merits of these response formats have been hotly debated (for a review, see Elfenbein, Mandal, Ambady, Harizuka, & Kumar, 2002). Briefly, although many scholars believe that emotions are categorical in nature, Russell (1993, 1994) and others argue that emotions should not be construed as mutually exclusive categories and that forced-choice formats inflate agreement artificially. Nevertheless, forced-choice designs are more convenient, obviating the time-consuming and often ambiguous task of analyzing open-ended responses. In addition, modifying forced-choice designs by adding a "none-of-the-above" option appears to reduce artifactual agreement (Frank & Stennett, 2001; Haidt & Keltner, 1999).

Although some scholars believe that all humans are motivated naturally to decode nonverbal cues (McArthur & Baron, 1983), steps can still be taken to increase the participants' desire to take the perceptual tasks seriously (such as limiting the length of the study and making it as interesting as possible). Also, it is important to consider the relative advantages and disadvantages of this method of stimulus presentation. The hallmark advantages of photographs are their ease of use and high degree of experimental control. Whereas control is achieved most prominently by the selection of a specific channel of nonverbal behavior to be displayed (e.g., the face, the torso, the entire body), it is also achieved in the choice of encoders, the nature of the displays, and the context in which the display arises. Researchers should also consider how the gender, age, socioeconomic status, and ethnicity of their encoders and perceivers might affect the generalizability of results.

At each step, the investigator can make decisions necessary for addressing lingering questions and advancing theory. With this high level of control comes an inevitable trade-off in ecological validity. As discussed by Elfenbein, Marsh, and Ambady (2002), the nonverbal displays encountered in everyday life "are subtle, embedded in a particular context, spontaneous, dynamic, fleeting, and exist in combination with other expressions, words and behaviors" (p. 44). Standardized stimuli generally fail to meet at least some of these criteria, but photographs often fail to meet all of them. Only static stimuli can be presented, a drawback given that perceived motion often plays a critically important role in social judgment (Ambady, Hallahan, & Connor, 1999; Heider & Simmel, 1944; Knight & Johnston, 1997). These limitations should be taken into account when considering how results may generalize to other kinds of viewing conditions.

VOCAL CLIPS

Some Appropriate Uses. When we hear someone speak, we discern meaning not only from the words they choose but also from how those words are spoken. Prosodic cues such as volume, pitch, and speech rate can play a more important role than speech content in our social inferences, perhaps because we implicitly understand that it is difficult for a speaker to control these signals (Ekman & Friesen, 1969). As a result, vocal cues have powerful effects on social interaction (e.g., Hummert, Mazloff, & Henry, 1999; Neumann & Strack, 2000; Noller, 2005). For instance, new research reveals that prosody (i.e., vocal qualities) may be as important as facial displays in communicating emotion (for a review, see Johnstone & Scherer, 2000). Several related issues await further investigation. As in the case of facial expressions, there is some evidence for the universal recognition of emotions based on language-free voice samples (see Scherer, 2003). At the same time, there appear to be culture-specific patterns in vocal emotion expression, similar to the nonverbal "accents" in facial display of emotion across cultures (Marsh et al., 2003; Scherer, 2003).

Some scholars in this area have focused on the link between psychological well-being and the ability to understand subtle vocal cues to emotion (e.g., Baum & Nowicki, 1998; Rosenthal, Hall, DiMatteo, Rogers, & Archer, 1979). This research has been aided by standardized sets of vocal cues, particularly the Profile of Nonverbal Sensitivity

(PONS; Rosenthal et al., 1979). The PONS assesses the ability to identify the meaning of nonverbal utterances presented in a range of bodily channels including the tone of voice. More recently, Baum and Nowicki (1998) developed a subtest of the DANVA to measure the ability to infer emotion from the voice (Rothman & Nowicki, 2004).

Design Considerations. When the decision is made to employ auditory samples in research, one option is to use a previously developed set of stimuli, such as the PONS or the DANVA. If the decision is made to construct a new set of stimuli, the resulting series of pragmatic and theoretical decisions parallel those used in photograph-based research.

A unique concern here involves removing the content of the spoken messages, which is necessary for isolating the prosodic features. One option involves editing spoken samples by content filtering (which removes the higher frequencies on which word recognition depends) or by randomized splicing (which rearranges segments of the voice in a random manner), as is done in the PONS test. Both can now be accomplished quite easily using sound editing software; however, they produce sound patterns that are not normally encountered in everyday life.

The other option is to provide encoders with standardized content such as the alphabet (Berry, 1991) or a basic neutral sentence (Baum & Nowicki, 1998). This strategy retains the verbal content but standardizes it so that only differences in nonverbal features remain (see also Noller, 2005). With the advent of analog and digital recording and playback devices, it is a relatively simple matter to record, manipulate, and present vocal cues to study participants (for more details, see Scherer, 2003). Another advantage of this approach is that unlike still photographs, vocal cues are inherently dynamic. To explore the role of nonverbal features in communication, however, it is important to isolate these features not only from their verbal content but also from the visual displays and contextual background that accompany them in everyday life.

VISUAL CLIPS

Some Appropriate Uses. Visual clips combine the visual nature of still photographs with the dynamic nature of vocal clips. In doing so, visual clips have been vital in documenting the remarkable accuracy with which perceivers can infer enduring and fleeting characteristics from brief glimpses of behavior. In a fascinating line of early research, for example, Johansson (1973) affixed lights to the major joints of actors and recorded high-contrast images of the actors moving in space, such that perceivers could only see a field of point lights. Perceivers could only identify the encoders in these displays as human when exposed to moving point-light displays; in static form, they appeared as a random series of dots. Subsequent work revealed that age and gender are also apparent in point-light movements (Koslowski & Cutting, 1977). Current work is exploring the extent to which perceivers can recover other socially relevant information, such as "Big Five" factors of personality (Heberlein, Adolphs, Tranel, & Damasio, 2004), from these highly impoverished displays.

Visual displays can be impoverished in several other ways. One approach involves sampling very brief samples, or "thin slices," of ongoing movement. Even the "thinnest" of slices capture the rich information on which social judgments are made (for a review, see Ambady, Bernieri, & Richeson, 2000). Ambady and colleagues (1999), for instance, asked perceivers to identify the sexual orientation of encoders on the basis of silent, very brief (1 or 10 seconds) video clips. Impressions of sexual orientation conformed to encoders' self-reports at greater-than-chance levels, suggesting that sexual orientation is conveyed reliably by dynamic nonverbal behavior.

An exciting frontier of research is cataloguing the mental processes we are able to accomplish automatically, without intention, deliberation, and conscious awareness. In our own work, we studied the connection between induced mood and the validity of social judgments based on thin slices of behavior. Induced sadness impaired accuracy consistently, perhaps because it evoked a more reasoned, careful analysis of available information (Ambady & Gray, 2002). This finding is consistent with work by Patterson and Stockbridge (1998), who found that under some conditions, perceivers made more accurate social inferences when they were prevented from deliberating carefully. Together, these results suggest that first impressions may result from a relatively automatic form of cognitive processing (Choi, Gray, & Ambady, 2004; Lakin, this volume).

Design Considerations. Several important construction and design decisions should seem familiar at this point, because they are common to research using photographs, vocal clips, and video clips. Options for using preexisting sets of stimuli include the PONS, described earlier, and an easily administered measure called the interpersonal perception task (IPT; Costanzo & Archer, 1989). The original IPT contains 30 short scenes and the shortened version contains 15 of those scenes (Costanzo & Archer, 1993). Both tap the ability to infer kinship, deception, competition, status, and intimacy. These scenes are naturalistic rather than posed, so there is an objectively correct answer to each question. Because the PONS and the IPT have already been normed on healthy populations, they are useful for studying the effects of psychological or physical trauma on nonverbal sensitivity. They can also be used to relate individual differences in nonverbal sensitivity to any number of skills, including workplace performance. Constructing a new set of video clips "in-house" can also be advantageous, particularly if one is interested in defining accuracy as the ability to predict a novel criterion, such as student evaluations (Ambady & Rosenthal, 1993), therapeutic outcomes (Ambady et al., 2002), or testosterone level (Dabbs, Bernieri, & Strong, 2001). A more detailed summary of the issues involved in such research can be found in Ambady et al. (2000).

A notable advantage of the visual-clip approach is its flexibility. Depending on one's theoretical orientation, behavior can be sampled from any channel of expressive communication. The central trade-off in ecological validity concerns the extent to which impressions formed on the basis of video clips differ from those made in everyday life. Because perceivers do not have contact with the encoders they are viewing, they do not experience the interaction demands ubiquitous to real encounters (e.g., Gilbert, Pelham, & Krull, 1988; Swann, 1984). Additionally, relatively artificial settings tend to heighten participants' awareness that their judgments are under scrutiny and therefore increase the extent to which inference processes are consciously monitored (Forgas, 1999). These limitations should be kept in mind when considering how the results obtained in these studies would generalize to other situations.

INTERACTIONS

Some Appropriate Uses. An alternative to presenting standardized nonverbal displays is to allow them to emerge more naturally by constructing brief interactions between study participants. Interaction paradigms have proved useful for furthering our understanding of complex interpersonal processes, such as interpersonal adaptation (i.e., the tendency for interaction partners to adjust spontaneously to or mutually influence one another; see Cappella & Schreiber, this volume). A long history of research in this area has demonstrated that adaptation is a ubiquitous feature of human social exchange (for a review, see Burgoon, Stern, & Dillman, 1995). In some of this research, nonverbal signs of adaptation are manipulated to investigate their consequences for relationship quality (Burgoon et al., 1995). Alternatively, as will be discussed in later sections, these signals can be observed naturalistically to draw inferences about preexisting relationships.

Interaction paradigms can also be used to better understand how people in relationships come to understand one another. For instance, Ickes and his colleagues devised an interaction paradigm for studying empathic accuracy, the ability to read mental and emotional states (for a review, see Ickes, 2001). In their *unstructured dyadic interaction paradigm*, two participants are left alone together for a brief time and their spontaneous conversation is videotaped. Later, the participants view the videotapes independently and complete written reports detailing the thoughts and feelings they experienced during the interaction. They also attempt to infer the thoughts and feelings their partners experienced during the interaction. Greater empathic accuracy is evidenced by greater correspondence between inferred and self-reported experience.

Even less exposure to another person can be sufficient for drawing surprisingly accurate inferences of personality, however. In the *zero-acquaintance* paradigm (e.g., Albright, Kenny, & Malloy, 1988), unacquainted peers assemble in small groups and rate themselves and each other on a variety of personality dimensions. These ratings are then averaged and correlated with self-ratings of personality. Although the accuracy of such ratings improves with acquaintanceship (e.g., Funder & Colvin, 1988), the convergence of strangers' ratings with self-ratings is surprisingly high (e.g., Albright et al., 1988).

Design Considerations. When photographs, vocal clips, or visual clips are chosen, one must accept a trade-off in realism in exchange for high experimental control. With interactions, the trade-off is reversed: Realism is achieved in all the ways it is limited when standardized stimuli are presented. Limiting the extent to which participants feel they are being watched and studied, using hidden cameras and microphones or one-way mirrors, further heightens the realism of interaction situations. Of course, less precision is achieved over the interpersonal processes under investigation in the interaction paradigm than occurs in controlled experiments. Precision concerns are especially salient in research on social perception, given that forming impressions is a serial process; the encoder must display the relevant cues, these cues must be made available to the perceiver, the perceiver must detect these cues, and finally, the perceiver must interpret these cues in light of previously stored knowledge (Funder, 1999). When standardized stimuli are presented, the experimenter can control the first three steps and study how information is processed once it has been displayed, made available, and detected. When interaction paradigms are used, however, all the stages are free to vary.

Interaction paradigms present some idiosyncratic methodological concerns. For instance, should a confederate be used? Confederates are helpful in standardizing interaction patterns, although very tightly controlling the conversation between a confederate and a participant will likely result in awkward, halting interactions. If confederates are to be used, care should be taken to ensure that they are unaware of the study's hypothesis or at least the condition assignment of their partners. In addition, it is generally preferable to use more than one confederate to increase the generalizability of results. For an extended discussion of these issues, see Guerrero and Le Poire (2005). In addition to these methodological concerns, the investigation must also decide what the participants will do during the interaction. Commonly, participants are asked to discuss a relatively neutral topic or to jointly complete a simple task (Chartrand & Bargh, 1999). To study how people resolve conflict, one can ask participants to discuss a disagreement they have had recently (Roberts, 2005).

It is usually necessary to have a videotaped or audiotaped record of the interaction. In such cases, the researcher faces another decision: whether to inform participants that they will be recorded. In making this decision, it is helpful to weigh the potential effects of increased self-awareness against the ethical and practical concerns of secretly recording people. One compromise is to inform participants that they will (or may) be recorded, and then minimize the salience of the recording devices in the hope that participants will forget they are being recorded. In any case, during debriefing it is essential to obtain informed consent for the future use of the recordings and to give participants the right to have their tapes erased.

◆ *Nonverbal Behavior as a Dependent Variable*

As was just seen, a range of methods is available for treating nonverbal behavior as an independent variable. A researcher can,

for example, manipulate nonverbal displays flexibly by presenting standardized stimuli or constructing brief interactions and then measure the reactions these displays evoke. In the current section, we turn our attention to the use of nonverbal behavior as a dependent variable. This strategy capitalizes on the connection between nonverbal behavior and the underlying subjective experience to study the effects of manipulated variables on cognition, affect, and behavior.

FACIAL CUES

Some Appropriate Uses. When we want to understand and describe subjective experience, asking people directly can be unsatisfactory for a number of reasons. Ongoing experiences may not be reportable because they are not consciously accessible, or they may be skewed by self-presentation demands or retrospective biases (e.g., Nisbett & Wilson, 1977). Nonverbal cues, including facial behavior, are an excellent alternative in many cases because their emergence requires little or no conscious awareness and is less controllable than verbal reports (DePaulo, 1992; Ekman & Friesen, 1969).

These advantages are well illustrated by a study conducted by Bonanno and colleagues (2002). These researchers hypothesized that facial expressions of positive and negative emotions may be informative about the ways in which survivors of childhood sexual assault respond to situations in which they might disclose the abuse. To that end, the researchers coded participants' facial cues to emotion during a narrative interview. Results indicated that survivors who did not disclose their abuse voluntarily when given the opportunity to do so were most likely to show facial displays of shame. This pattern suggests that facial displays of emotion may be used indirectly to communicate aspects of experience that may be too painful to be disclosed directly. This study also demonstrates the usefulness of examining facial displays of emotion in relation to a complex social problem, particularly one for which previous investigators have relied almost solely on verbal self-report.

Because facial cues to emotion can be too subtle to be recognized, researchers often turn to psychophysiological measures such as facial electromyography (EMG), which involves the placement of small surface electrodes over facial muscles. Dimberg et al. (2000), for example, used EMG recording to test the hypothesis that humans are predisposed to react to emotional facial stimuli spontaneously, quickly, and independently of conscious cognitive processes. The researchers focused on two major muscles: the zygomatic, which elevates the lips to form a smile, and the corrugator, which knits the eyebrows to form a frown. These muscles have long been associated with positive and negative affect, respectively. While their muscle movements were recorded, participants were exposed to happy, neutral, or angry faces at exposure times too short to be translated into conscious awareness. As predicted, happy faces evoked larger zygomatic activity and lower corrugator activity, and angry faces evoked larger corrugator activity and lower zygomatic activity, as early as half a second after the presentation of the faces, demonstrating that emotional reactions may be evoked unconsciously.

Like emotions, cognitive operations can be inferred from behavior. Eye movements are quite useful, given that they index several aspects of cognition reliably. Shifts in gaze direction, for example, can reflect the allocation of attention toward stimuli in the environment. Mogg, Millar, and Bradley (2000) took advantage of this connection to test the hypothesis that clinical anxiety is associated with hypervigilance toward threatening cues. They measured hypervigilance by assessing the direction and latency of eye movements toward emotional faces. As predicted, anxious participants were more likely than healthy controls to quickly shift their gaze toward angry faces. These results add to the growing body of research on the role of social cognitive processes in some emotional disorders.

Observing eye behavior to infer mental processes is particularly useful when dealing with participants who are unable to vocalize their thoughts. For example, a number of experimental methods have been developed that use infants' eye movements as an index of what they notice, perceive, and understand. In the *visual preference method,* experimenters show infants two displays, either side by side or sequentially, and monitor their looking time at each display. Preferential looking toward one of the objects indicates that the infant is noticing a difference between the two stimuli (e.g., Wilcox & Clayton, 1968). The *visual habituation procedure* can also be used to assess discrimination (Caron, Caron, & MacLean, 1988).

Design Considerations. Several well-developed methods have been employed for coding facial cues to emotion. The Emotion Facial Affect Coding Scheme (EMFACS; Ekman & Friesen, 1984) specifies the patterns of facial movement believed to be associated with the six basic emotions. This theoretically derived, anatomically based coding scheme describes facial activity in terms of 44 unique action units (AUs). Coders describe all visible muscular movement in terms of AUs or AU combinations. The Maximally Descriptive Facial Movement Coding System (MAX; Izard, 1979) is a similar technique used primarily with infants and children. Such detailed coding schemes are not without their disadvantages. They are relatively laborious and time-consuming, and they require extensive training. In addition, they necessitate that muscle movements be visible to the human eye. This problem is solved by EMG recording, in which detected muscle movements are filtered, amplified, and smoothed before being subjected to traditional data-analysis procedures (see Tassinary & Cacioppo, 2000, for more details). Like other psychophysiological techniques, EMG recording is relatively expensive and requires some additional training and equipment. An additional drawback is that the application of facial sensors is relatively intrusive.

VOCAL CUES

Some Appropriate Uses. Like facial displays, the voice can be an excellent index of emotional experience. For instance, faster speech rates are associated with more pleasant emotions, whereas sadness is consistently associated with the tendency to speak at a very slow rate and take longer pauses between words (see review by Siegman, 1987). Ellgring and Scherer (1996) capitalized on this association in their attempt to obtain a behavior-based measure of progress in therapy for major depression. In the early course of therapy, and again during remission, patients provided speech samples during standardized interviews. Remission from depression was marked by an increase in speech rate and a decrease in pause duration. On a broader note, the authors speculate that observations of nonverbal behavior may be a useful tool in charting therapeutic progress, particularly given the limitations of patients' ability and willingness to communicate some aspects of experience verbally.

Vocal cues can be used to index a broad range of emotional and cognitive states, a point illustrated by their application to the study of deception. When telling a lie, deceivers often experience fear, excitement, guilt, and increased mental load. In an attempt to discern how these emotional and cognitive changes are reflected in the voice, Vrij, Edward, Roberts, and Bull (2000) analyzed vocal cues and verbal behavior during deception and truth telling. Two reliable vocal indicators of deception emerged: (1) a longer latency period (the time between a question and its answer) and (2) more speech disturbances (instances of saying "ah" or "mm" between words; for a more detailed discussion, see Vrij, this volume).

Vocal cues also index interpersonal qualities reliably. For instance, *speech accommodation theory* proposes that a speaker's need for affiliation is reflected in a tendency to match a conversation partner's speech cues (Giles & Smith, 1979). According to this perspective, people match their partner's vocal cues spontaneously when they want to gain approval (for a review, see Buller, 2005). Gregory and Webster (1996) tested this hypothesis using naturalistic samples obtained from conversations between a talk show host (Larry King) and several of his guests. Lower status guests tended to accommodate their voices to King's, whereas King tended to accommodate his voice to match those of higher status guests (e.g., sitting presidents). Other vocal forms of accommodation, such as matching accent patterns, response latencies, and utterance durations, have been identified (Buller, 2005).

Design Considerations. Quantifying vocal cues involves a number of steps, beginning with the recording of voice samples and the isolation of specific segments for analysis. For speech rate analysis, trained coders can be asked to listen to each segment and count the number of syllables spoken. Alternatively, coders can simply rate speakers' voices on a continuous scale from relatively slow to relatively fast. Perceived similarity in speech rate can be measured by asking participants to rate whether their conversation partners spoke slower, faster, or at about the same pace as them. These methods are reviewed in more detail by Buller (2005).

BODILY MOVEMENTS

Some Appropriate Uses. Some bodily movements, when observed carefully, can paint a portrait of complex interpersonal processes that would otherwise lie beyond awareness, not only to an experimenter but also to the interactants. Gottman's (1979) work on married couples illustrates this point. In his *conflict interaction paradigm*, spouses are observed in the laboratory discussing an area of disagreement in their lives. Systematic review of the videotapes taken from these sessions reveals patterns of verbal and nonverbal behavior that can be surprisingly predictive of couples' long-term outcomes, including the likelihood and timing of divorce (e.g., Carrère & Gottman, 1999).

Subtle bodily movements also reveal relational qualities among nonintimates. For instance, in the *chameleon effect*, people unintentionally adopt the postures, gestures, and mannerisms of their interaction partners, particularly when they are more motivated to affiliate (Chartrand & Bargh, 1999; Lakin & Chartrand, 2003). An alternative to such mimicry is complementarity: the tendency to respond to nonverbal displays with contrasting behaviors. Tiedens and Fragale (2003) demonstrated recently that complementarity is particularly likely to emerge in displays of dominance and submission. In other words, we tend to display submissive postures in response to a partner's dominant postures, and vice versa.

Synchrony, mimicry, and complementarity are all patterns of interpersonal adaptation observed in relatively *focused situations*, when people share a common focus of attention. In *unfocused situations*, to use Goffman's (1963) distinction, people are simply "mutually present"; common examples include riding in an elevator or standing in line at the grocery store. Some scholars have been interested in the patterns of nonverbal adaptation that emerge in these common situations. Patterson (2005), for instance, developed the *passing encounters paradigm* to study how strangers mutually regulate their distance and contact when walking toward one another in public spaces. This nonreactive, structured paradigm is being used to better understand not only general tendencies in the behavior of strangers on the street but also the manner in which these behaviors are influenced by cultural and situational factors. Results from these studies may speak to larger issues about how strangers negotiate their behavior so as to maintain comfort and predictability.

Design Considerations. The first step in operationalizing the outcome measures highlighted in this section is building on prior theory and research to decide which bodily movements should theoretically be related to the variables of interest. In the case of marital communication, for instance, past research has indicated that marital satisfaction is reflected in spouses' reciprocation of negative affect (Gottman, 1994; see Noller, this volume). Researchers interested in marital satisfaction, therefore, might decide to look for escalations of negative behavior (e.g., crying in response to yelling). In the passing encounters paradigm, observers are interested in how participants respond to different types of confederate behavior (Patterson, 2005).

Once the behavioral categories have been defined, the researcher must choose a level of measurement. Behaviors can be coded categorically (as present or absent) or on a more continuous scale (e.g., rating the negativity of a given behavior on a 1–7 scale). Behaviors can also be rated in terms of both frequency and duration. Bakeman (2005) and White and Sargent (2005) provide detailed suggestions regarding the development and use of coding schemes in general, and Cappella (2005) discusses coding specifically for adaptation in dyadic interactions. As in other coding schemes, raters should be well trained and blind to experimental conditions, and their reliability must be sufficiently high. Although it is possible to code behavior in real time, video recordings provide the opportunity for multiple viewings and greater automation of some measurements (e.g., time).

◆ Conclusion

A central goal of this review has been to survey the application of contemporary methods in nonverbal behavior research to a variety of research questions. The examples provided are not intended to convey the full range of issues that can be addressed using nonverbal behavior methods; rather, they are meant to illustrate the diversity of topics that can benefit from the use of these methods. In the interest of brevity, we have limited our review to methods that involve the presentation or sampling of nonverbal behavior. Self-report measures tapping nonverbal expressiveness (Riggio & Riggio, 2005), explicit knowledge of nonverbal cue meaning (e.g., Rosip & Hall, 2004), and other constructs can be used to explore many of the issues we have discussed.

In the coming years, the study of nonverbal communication will likely be marked

by new advancements in methodology made possible primarily through interdisciplinary collaborations. For instance, explorations of the brain's response to social stimuli are becoming more common and refined, thanks to the expanded use of techniques previously consigned to cognitive psychology and cognitive neuroscience (e.g., Chiao, Bordeaux, & Ambady, 2004; Chiu, Ambady, & Deldin, 2004; Heberlein, Adolphs, Tranel, & Damasio, 2004). Along the same lines, paradigms originally developed to study social cognition are being used to expand our understanding of a range of psychological disorders, including depression and social anxiety (e.g., Gotlib et al., 2004). Increased knowledge of information technology is making it possible to study affective and cognitive responses to nonverbal stimuli on a very large scale using the World Wide Web (e.g., Nosek, Banaji, & Greenwald, 2002).

The future of nonverbal communication research may also be marked by advancements in the application of research findings to a variety of important real-world settings, including the workplace and government, courtrooms and police stations, hospitals and clinics, the classroom, and many others. Some of the findings discussed in this review are being applied to these settings. For instance, some are attempting to improve law enforcement officers' ability to detect lies by educating them on the nonverbal indices of deception (Vrij & Mann, 2005). Ambady and colleagues (2002) applied nonverbal research methods to study the interpersonal communication factors that predict the likelihood of malpractice claims, an important marker of health care satisfaction. These and other approaches bring together a diverse group of practitioners and researchers who can benefit from expanded knowledge of nonverbal communication.

◆ References

Adams, R. B., & Kleck, R. E. (2003). Perceived gaze direction and the processing of facial displays of emotion. *Psychological Science, 14,* 644–647.

Albright, L., Kenny, D. A., & Malloy, T. E. (1988). Consensus in personality judgments at zero acquaintance. *Journal of Personality and Social Psychology, 55,* 387–395.

Ambady, N., Bernieri, F. J., & Richeson, J. A. (2000). Toward a histology of social behavior: Judgmental accuracy from thin slices of the behavioral stream. *Advances in Experimental Social Psychology, 32,* 201–271.

Ambady, N., & Gray, H. M. (2002). On being sad and mistaken: Mood effects on the accuracy of thin-slice judgment. *Journal of Personality and Social Psychology, 83,* 947–961.

Ambady, N., Hallahan, M., & Connor, B. (1999). Accuracy of judgments of sexual orientation from thin slices of behavior. *Journal of Personality and Social Psychology, 77,* 538–547.

Ambady, N., LaPlante, D., Nguyen, T., Rosenthal, R., Chaumeton, N., & Levinson, W. (2002). Surgeon's tone of voice: A clue to malpractice history. *Surgery, 132,* 5–9.

Ambady, N., & Rosenthal, R. (1993). Half a minute: Predicting teacher evaluations from thin slices of nonverbal behavior and physical attractiveness. *Journal of Personality and Social Psychology, 64,* 431–441.

Archer, D., Akert, R., & Costanzo, M. (1993). The accurate perception of nonverbal behavior: Questions of theory and research design. In P. D. Blank (Ed.), *Interpersonal expectations: Theory, research, and applications* (pp. 242–260). New York: Cambridge University Press.

Bakeman, R. (2005). Analysis of coded nonverbal behavior. In V. Manusov (Ed.), *The sourcebook of nonverbal measures: Going beyond words* (pp. 375–382). Mahwah, NJ: Erlbaum.

Banse, R., & Scherer, K. R. (1996). Acoustic profiles in vocal emotion expression. *Journal of Personality and Social Psychology, 70,* 614–636.

Baron-Cohen, S., Wheelwright, S., & Hill, J. (2001). The "Reading the Mind in the Eyes" test revised version: A study with normal adults, and adults with Asperger syndrome or high-functioning autism. *Journal of Child Psychology and Psychiatry, 42,* 241–252.

Baum, K. M., & Nowicki, S. (1998). Perception of emotion: Measuring decoding accuracy of adult prosodic cues varying in intensity. *Journal of Nonverbal Behavior, 22,* 89–107.

Berry, D. S. (1991). Accuracy in social perception: Contribution of facial and vocal information. *Journal of Personality and Social Psychology, 61,* 298–307.

Bonanno, G. A., Keltner, D., Noll, J. G., Putnam, F. W., Trickett, P. K., LeJeune, J., et al. (2002). When the face reveals what words do not: Facial expressions of emotion, smiling, and the willingness to disclose childhood sexual abuse. *Journal of Personality and Social Psychology, 83,* 94–110.

Buck, R. (2005). Measuring emotional experience, expression, and communication: The slide-viewing technique. In V. Manusov (Ed.), *The sourcebook of nonverbal measures: Going beyond words* (pp. 457–470). Mahwah, NJ: Erlbaum.

Buller, D. B. (2005). Methods for measuring speech rate. In V. Manusov (Ed.), *The sourcebook of nonverbal measures: Going beyond words* (pp. 317–324). Mahwah, NJ: Erlbaum.

Burgoon, J. K., Stern, L. A., & Dillman, L. (1995). *Interpersonal adaptation: Dyadic interaction patterns.* New York, NY: Cambridge University Press.

Cappella, J. N. (2005). Coding mutual adaptation in dyadic nonverbal interaction. In V. Manusov (Ed.), *The sourcebook of nonverbal measures: Going beyond words* (pp. 383–392). Mahwah, NJ: Erlbaum.

Caron, A. J., Caron, R. F., & MacLean, D. J.(1988). Infant discrimination of naturalistic emotional expressions: The role of face and voice. *Child Development, 59,* 604–616.

Carrère, S., & Gottman, J. M. (1999). Predicting divorce among newlyweds from the first three minutes of a marital conflict discussion. *Family Process, 38,* 293–301.

Chartrand, T. L., & Bargh, J. A. (1999). The chameleon effect: The perception-behavior link and social interaction. *Journal of Personality and Social Psychology, 76,* 893–910.

Chiao, J. Y., Bordeaux, A. R., & Ambady, N. (2004). Mental representations of social status. *Cognition, 93,* B49–B57.

Chiu, P., Ambady, N., & Deldin, P. (2004). Contingent negative variation to emotional in- and out-group stimuli differentiates high- and low-prejudiced individuals. *Journal of Cognitive Neuroscience, 6,* 1830–1839.

Choi, Y. S., Gray, H. M., & Ambady, N. (2004). The glimpsed world: Unintended communication and unintended perception. In R. Hassin, J. Bargh, & J. Uleman (Eds.), *The new unconscious* (pp. 309–333). New York: Oxford University Press.

Costanzo, M., & Archer, D. (1989). Interpreting the expressive behavior of others: The Interpersonal Perception Task. *Journal of Nonverbal Behavior, 13,* 225–245.

Costanzo, M., & Archer, D. (Producers). (1993). *Interpersonal Perception Task-15* [Videotape]. (Available from the University of California, 2000 Center Street, Berkeley, CA 94704)

Dabbs, J. M., Bernieri, F. J., & Strong, R. K. (2001). Going on stage: Testosterone in greetings and meetings. *Journal of Research in Personality, 35,* 27–40.

DePaulo, B. M. (1992). Nonverbal behavior and self-presentation. *Psychological Bulletin, 11,* 203–243.

Dimberg, U., Thunberg, M., & Elmehed, K. (2000). Unconscious facial reactions to emotional facial expressions. *Psychological Science, 11,* 86–89.

Ekman, P. (1972). Universals and cultural differences in facial expressions of emotion. In J. Cole (Ed.), *Nebraska Symposium on Motivation* (pp. 207–283). Lincoln: University of Nebraska Press.

Ekman, P. (1994). Strong evidence for universals in facial expressions: A reply to Russell's mistaken critique. *Psychological Bulletin, 115,* 268–287.

Ekman, P., & Friesen, W. V. (1969). Nonverbal leakage and cues to deception. *Psychiatry, 32,* 88–106.

Ekman, P., & Friesen, W. V. (1976). *Pictures of facial affect.* Palo Alto, CA: Consulting Psychologists Press.

Ekman, P., & Friesen, W. V. (1984). *Emotion Facial Action Coding System (EMFACS).* San Francisco: University of California Press.

Elfenbein, H. A., & Ambady, N. (2002). On the universality and cultural specificity of emotion recognition: A meta-analysis. *Psychological Bulletin, 128,* 203–235.

Elfenbein, H. A., Mandal, M. K., Ambady, N., Harizuka, S., & Kumar, S. (2002). Cross-cultural patterns in emotion recognition: Highlighting design and analytical techniques. *Emotion, 2,* 75–84.

Elfenbein, H. A., Marsh, A. A., & Ambady, N. (2002). Emotional intelligence and the recognition of emotion from facial expressions. In L. F. Barrett & P. Salovey (Eds.), *The wisdom in feeling* (pp. 37–59). New York: Guilford.

Ellgring, H., & Scherer, K. R. (1996). Vocal indicators of mood change in depression. *Journal of Nonverbal Behavior, 20,* 83–110.

Forgas, J. P. (1999). Feeling and speaking: Mood effects on verbal communication strategies. *Personality and Social Psychology Bulletin, 25,* 850–863.

Frank, M. G., & Stennett, J. (2001). The forced-choice paradigm and the perception of facial expressions of emotion. *Journal of Personality and Social Psychology, 80,* 75–85.

Funder, D. C. (1999). *Personality judgment: A realistic approach to person perception.* San Diego, CA: Academic Press.

Funder, D. C., & Colvin, C. R. (1988). Friends and strangers: Acquaintanceship, agreement, and the accuracy of personality judgment. *Journal of Personality and Social Psychology, 55,* 149–158.

Gilbert, D. T., Pelham, B. W., & Krull, D. S. (1988). On cognitive busyness: When person perceivers meet persons perceived. *Journal of Personality and Social Psychology, 54,* 733–740.

Giles, H., & Smith, P. M. (1979). Accommodation theory: Optimal levels of convergence. In H. Giles & R. St. Clair (Eds.), *Language and social psychology* (pp. 45–65). Baltimore: University Park Press.

Goffman, E. (1963). *Behavior in public places.* New York: Free Press.

Gotlib, I. H., Kasch, K. L., Trail, S., Joorman, J., Arnow, B., & Johnson, S. L. (2004). Coherence and specificity of information-processing biases in depression and social phobia. *Journal of Abnormal Psychology, 113,* 386–398.

Gottman, J. M. (1979). *Marital interaction: Empirical investigations.* New York: Academic Press.

Gottman, J. M. (1994). *What predicts divorce?* Hillsdale, NJ: Erlbaum.

Greenwald, A. G., Nosek, B. A., & Banaji, M. R. (2003). Understanding and using the Implicit Association Test: I. An improved scoring algorithm. *Journal of Personality and Social Psychology, 85,* 197–216.

Gregory, S. W., & Webster, S. (1996). A nonverbal signal in voices of interview partners effectively predicts communication accommodation and social status perceptions. *Journal of Personality and Social Psychology, 70,* 1231–1240.

Guerrero, L. K., & Le Poire, B. A. (2005). Nonverbal research involving experimental manipulations by confederates. In V. Manusov (Ed.), *The sourcebook of nonverbal measures; Going beyond words* (pp. 507–522). Mahwah, NJ: Erlbaum.

Haidt, J., & Keltner, D. (1999). Culture and facial expression: Open-ended methods find more expressions and a gradient of recognition. *Cognition and Emotion, 13,* 225–266.

Harris, M., & Rosenthal, R. (2005). No more teachers' dirty looks: Effects of teacher nonverbal behavior on student outcomes. In R. E. Riggio & R. S. Feldman (Eds.), *Applications of nonverbal communication* (pp. 157–192). Mahwah, NJ: Erlbaum.

Heberlein, A. S, Adolphs, R., Tranel, D., & Damasio, H. (2004). Cortical regions for judgments of emotions and personality traits from point-light walkers. *Journal of Cognitive Neuroscience, 16,* 1143–1158.

Heider, F., & Simmel, M. (1944). An experimental study of apparent behavior. *American Journal of Psychology, 57,* 43–259.

Hummert, M. L., Mazloff, D., & Henry, C. (1999). Vocal characteristics of older adults and stereotyping. *Journal of Nonverbal Behavior, 23,* 111–132.

Ickes, W. (2001). Measuring empathic accuracy. In J. A. Hall & F. J. Bernieri (Eds.), *Interpersonal sensitivity: Theory and measurement* (pp. 219–241). Mahwah, NJ: Erlbaum.

Izard, C. E. (1979). *The Maximally Discriminative Facial Movement Coding System (MAX).* Newark: University of Delaware, Information Technologies and University Media Services.

Johansson, G. (1973). Visual perception of biological motion and a model for its analysis. *Perception and Psychophysics, 14,* 201–211.

Johnstone, T., & Scherer, K. R. (2000). Vocal communication of emotion. In M. Lewis & J. Haviland (Eds.), *Handbook of emotion* (2nd ed., pp. 220–235). New York: Guilford.

Jones, B. C., Little, A. C., Burt, D. M., & Perrett, D. I. (2004). When facial attractiveness is only skin deep. *Perception, 33,* 569–576.

Knight, B., & Johnston, A. (1997). The role of movement in face recognition. *Visual Cognition, 4,* 265–273.

Kozlowski, L. T., & Cutting, J. E. (1977). Recognizing the sex of a walker from a dynamic point-light display. *Perception and Psychophysics, 21,* 575–580.

Kruglanski, A. W. (1989). The psychology of being "right": The problem of accuracy in social perception and cognition. *Psychological Bulletin, 106,* 395–409.

Lakin, J. L., & Chartrand, T. L. (2003). Using nonconscious behavioral mimicry to create affiliation and rapport. *Psychological Science, 14,* 334–339.

LaPlante, D., & Ambady, N. (2000). Multiple messages: Facial recognition advantage for compound expressions. *Journal of Nonverbal Behavior, 24,* 211–224.

Marsh, A. A., Adams, R. B., & Kleck, R. E. (2004). Why do fear and anger look the way they do? Form and social function in facial expression. *Personality and Social Psychology Bulletin, 31,* 73–86.

Marsh, A. A., Elfenbein, H. A., & Ambady, N. (2003). Nonverbal "accents": Cultural differences in facial expressions of emotion. *Psychological Science, 14,* 373–376.

Matsumoto, D., & Ekman, P. (1988). *Japanese and Caucasian facial expressions of emotion (JACFEE)* [Slides]. San Francisco: San Francisco State University, Department of Psychology, Intercultural and Emotion Research Laboratory.

McArthur, L. Z., & Baron, R. M. (1983). Toward an ecological theory of social perception. *Psychological Review, 90,* 215–238.

Mogg, K., Millar, N., & Bradley, B. P. (2000). Biases in eye movements to threatening facial expressions in generalized anxiety disorder and depressive disorder. *Journal of Abnormal Psychology, 109,* 695–704.

Neumann, R., & Strack, F. (2000). "Mood contagion": The automatic transfer of mood between persons. *Journal of Personality and Social Psychology, 79,* 211–223.

Nisbett, R., & Wilson, T. (1977). Telling more than we can know: Verbal reports on mental processes. *Psychological Review, 84,* 231–259.

Noller, P. (2005). Standard content methodology: Controlling the verbal channel. In V. Manusov (Ed.), *The sourcebook of nonverbal measures: Going beyond words* (pp. 417–430). Mahwah, NJ: Erlbaum.

Nosek, B. A., Banaji, M. R., & Greenwald, A. G. (2002). E-research: Ethics, security, design, and control in psychological research on the Internet. *Journal of Social Issues, 58,* 161–176.

Nowicki, S., & Duke, M. (1994). Individual differences in the nonverbal communication of affect: The Diagnostic Analysis of Nonverbal Accuracy Scale. *Journal of Nonverbal Behavior,* 789–735.

Patterson, M. L. (2005). The passing encounters paradigm: Monitoring microinteractions between pedestrians. In V. Manusov (Ed.), *The sourcebook of nonverbal measures: Going beyond words* (pp. 431–440). Mahwah, NJ: Erlbaum.

Patterson, M. L., & Stockbridge, E. (1998). Effects of cognitive demand and judgment strategy on person perception accuracy. *Journal of Nonverbal Behavior, 22,* 253–263.

Richeson, J. A., & Shelton, J. N. (2005). Thin slices of racial bias. *Journal of Nonverbal Behavior, 29,* 75–86.

Riggio, R. E., & Riggio, H. R. (2005). Self-report measures of emotional and nonverbal expressiveness. In V. Manusov (Ed.), *The sourcebook of nonverbal measures: Going beyond words* (pp. 105–112). Mahwah, NJ: Erlbaum.

Roberts, L. J. (2005). Conflict, real life, and videotape: Procedures for eliciting naturalistic couple interactions. In V. Manusov (Ed.), *The sourcebook of nonverbal measures: Going beyond words* (pp. 471–481). Mahwah, NJ: Erlbaum.

Rosenthal, R., Hall, J. A., DiMatteo, M. R., Rogers, P. L., & Archer, D. (1979). *Sensitivity to nonverbal communication: The PONS Test.* Baltimore: Johns Hopkins University Press.

Rosenthal, R., & Rosnow, R. L. (1991). *Essentials of behavioral research: Methods and data analysis* (2nd ed.). Boston: McGraw-Hill.

Rosip, J. C., & Hall, J. A. (2004). Knowledge of nonverbal cues, gender, and nonverbal decoding accuracy. *Journal of Nonverbal Behavior, 28,* 264–286.

Rothman, A. D., & Nowicki, S. (2004). A measure of the ability to identify emotion in children's tone of voice. *Journal of Nonverbal Behavior, 29,* 67–92.

Russell, J. A. (1993). Forced-choice response format in the study of facial expression. *Motivation and Emotion, 17,* 41–51.

Russell, J. A. (1994). Is there universal recognition of emotion from facial expressions? A review of the cross-cultural studies. *Psychological Bulletin, 115,* 102–141.

Scherer, K. R. (2003). Vocal communication of emotion: A review of research paradigms. *Speech Communication, 40,* 227–256.

Siegman, A. W. (1987). The telltale voice: Nonverbal messages of verbal communication. In W. Siegman & S. Feldstein (Eds.), *Nonverbal behavior and communication*

(2nd ed., pp. 351–433). Hillsdale, NJ: Erlbaum.

Swann, W. B., Jr. (1984). Quest for accuracy in person perception: A matter of pragmatics. *Psychological Review, 91,* 457–477.

Tassinary, L. G., & Cacioppo, J. T. (2000). The skeletomotor system: Surface electromyography. In J. T. Cacioppo, L. G. Tassinary, & G. Berntson (Eds.), *Handbook of psychophysiology* (2nd ed., pp. 163–199). New York: Cambridge University Press.

Tiedens, L. Z., & Fragale, A. R. (2003). Power moves: Complementarity in dominant and submissive nonverbal behavior. *Journal of Personality and Social Psychology, 84,* 558–568.

Tracy, J. L., & Robins, R. W. (2004). Show your pride: Evidence for a discrete emotion expression. *Psychological Science, 15,* 194–197.

Vrij, A., Edward, K., Roberts, K. P., & Bull, R. (2000). Detecting deceit via analysis of verbal and nonverbal behavior. *Journal of Nonverbal Behavior, 24,* 239–263.

Vrij, A., & Mann, S. (2005). Police use of nonverbal behaviors as indicators of deception. In R. E. Riggio & R. S Feldman. (Eds.), *Applications of nonverbal communication* (pp. 63–94). Mahwah, NJ: Erlbaum.

White, C. H., & Sargent, J. (2005). Researcher choices and practices in the study of nonverbal communication. In V. Manusov (Ed.), *The sourcebook of nonverbal measures: Going beyond words* (pp. 3–21). Mahwah, NJ: Erlbaum.

Wilcox, B., & Clayton, F. (1968). Infant visual fixation on motion pictures of the human face. *Journal of Experimental Child Psychology, 6,* 22–32.

Zebrowitz, L.A. (1997). *Reading faces: Window to the soul?* Boulder, CO: Westview Press.

Zebrowitz, L. A., & Rhodes, G. (2004). Sensitivity to "bad genes" and the anomalous face overgeneralization effect: Cue validity, cue utilization, and accuracy in judging intelligence and health. *Journal of Nonverbal Behavior, 28,* 167–185.

4

AUTOMATIC COGNITIVE PROCESSES AND NONVERBAL COMMUNICATION

◆ Jessica L. Lakin
Drew University

Nonverbal behavior is arguably one of the most powerful methods of communication; it conveys important information about a person's likes and dislikes, emotions, personal characteristics, and relationships (e.g., intimacy, dominance, trust, similarity). Whereas no one would be surprised that *verbal* communication of this type of information has a cognitive basis, messages conveyed and received *nonverbally* also have their basis in cognitive processes, although not always in conscious, controlled ones. Thus, understanding nonverbal communication relies, to some extent, on appreciating its cognitive foundation. This cognition refers to the mental activities and processes in which humans (and other animals) engage. Cognitive activities include, but are not limited to, learning, receiving, storing, processing, judging, and using information (Neisser, 1967).

The cognitive processes associated with nonverbal communication can occur with awareness, but they are also likely to, and in fact often do, occur without conscious awareness (for a review, see Hassin, Uleman, & Bargh, 2005). The purpose of this chapter is to review the automatic cognitive bases of nonverbal behaviors. To accomplish this objective, I first discuss what it means for a cognitive process to be (relatively) automatic or (relatively) controlled. This is followed by specific examples of nonverbal communication that appear to be relatively automatic. I then conclude with a discussion of important issues and future directions, including methodological considerations, the role of controlled processes, and the importance of cognitive resources.

◆ Automatic and Controlled Processes

In 1975, Posner and Snyder considered a basic question of human existence: How much control do people have over their thoughts, behaviors, and decisions? Since they posed their question, researchers have demonstrated that much of what we do cognitively happens without intention, awareness, or conscious control (Hassin et al., 2005). Although the history of automaticity and automatic processes has been reviewed in extensive detail elsewhere (Bargh, 1994, 1996, 1997; Bargh & Chartrand, 1999), a basic discussion of what it means for a process to be more controlled or more automatic seems necessary before turning attention to specific examples of nonverbal communication and their relationship to automatic cognitive processes.

Controlled processes are characterized by awareness, intentionality, controllability, and cognitive effort (Bargh, 1994, 1996; Posner & Snyder, 1975; Shiffrin & Schneider, 1977). Aspects of *awareness* include recognizing the cognitive process or stimulus consciously, but they also involve an acknowledged recognition of the influence that the process or stimulus is having. *Intentionality* refers to the necessity of an act

of will to start the process, whereas *controllability* refers to the fact that an act of will can stop the process once it has been started (i.e., it does not run to conclusion autonomously). Finally, and despite the limited amount of cognitive resources that people have and the already high demands on these resources, controlled processes require a share of these limited attentional resources (i.e., they require *cognitive effort*).

Automatic processes are more difficult to define. Because the four characteristics associated with controlled processes do not occur in an all-or-none fashion, it is not correct to assume that automatic processes are, by default, characterized by unawareness, unintentionality, and uncontrollability and require no cognitive effort. Although a process that has these four characteristics would certainly be considered automatic, processes that are characterized by one, two, or even three of these features have also been referred to historically as automatic (Bargh, 1994, 1996, 1997). It is also possible for various combinations of these four basic characteristics to occur. For example, experienced drivers intend to get in a car and go somewhere, even if when they arrive, they have no conscious awareness of anything that occurred during the trip. This example demonstrates that there are several types of automatic processes, resulting in a *continuum of automaticity* (ranging from completely automatic to completely controlled) rather than a simple dichotomy (Bargh, 1996, 1997; Bargh & Chartrand, 1999).

Specifically, *preconscious automaticity* represents the completely automatic end of the continuum, because it corresponds to the initial unconscious processing of incoming environmental information. This analysis occurs without intention, control, or awareness, and it is largely effortless. *Goal-directed automaticity*, however, represents a point somewhere in the middle of the continuum, because it corresponds to intentional, controllable processes that become automatic and effortless over time. Both preconscious and goal-dependent automatic effects are autonomous: Once the processes are started, they operate by themselves without awareness and conscious guidance. Regardless of whether an automatic effect is preconscious or goal dependent, it is possible for it to become controlled if a person becomes aware of the process. Conscious processes that are effortful, intentional, and controllable represent the completely *controlled* end of the continuum (Bargh, 1996, 1997; Bargh & Chartrand, 1999).

Recent research from the cognitive, social, comparative, and neuroscience literatures has demonstrated a strong associative link between perceptions from the environment and the brain regions associated with producing the observed behavior (i.e., a perception-behavior link; Bargh & Chartrand, 1999; Bargh, Chen, & Burrows, 1996; see Dijksterhuis & Bargh, 2001, for a review). This memory-based link results in relevant, associated behaviors becoming activated automatically on perception of a stimulus. Although the perception-behavior link posits an unmediated relationship between perception and behavior, the existence of this link is dependent on the fact that ideas are represented mentally (i.e., cognitively). Therefore, in a sense, some type of minimal cognitive mediation is involved (Dijksterhuis & Bargh, 2001).

◆ Automatic Effects in Social Evaluation and Behavior

There is an impressive abundance of automatic preconscious and goal-dependent effects relevant to nonverbal communication demonstrated in the social cognition literature. Some of these effects have been argued explicitly to be a result of the perception-behavior link. As with the historical conception of automaticity, there are quite a few reviews of these effects (Bargh & Chartrand, 1999; Wheeler & Petty, 2001), but I begin with a brief review here to place automatic nonverbal communication effects in context.

IMPRESSIONS

Impressions of other people can be affected automatically by activation of relevant knowledge structures. Srull and Wyer (1979) demonstrated this when they made traits related to "hostility" or "kindness" accessible to participants and then asked them, in an ostensibly unrelated task, to form an impression of a person whose behaviors were ambiguously hostile or ambiguously kind. Their results indicated that participants were likely to interpret the ambiguous behaviors in a manner consistent with the traits that had been made accessible previously. Higgins, Rholes, and Jones (1977) demonstrated a similar effect with the activation of either positive (e.g., adventurous) or negative (e.g., reckless) traits relevant to a person's behaviors (e.g., crossing the Atlantic in a sailboat). Participants evaluated the target person more positively when the activated traits had positive connotations than when they had negative connotations. People's impressions were affected by accessible constructs without intention or awareness.

From these two classic demonstrations, an entire literature on spontaneous trait inferences grew (Uleman, 1999; Uleman, Newman, & Moskowitz, 1996; Winter & Uleman, 1984). It also became clear that impressions are based on traits that are chronically accessible (i.e., personally important; Higgins, 1996) as well as traits that are temporarily accessible (i.e., primed; as in the work by Higgins et al., 1977; Srull & Wyer, 1979) and that salient physical cues (e.g., sex, race) can automatically activate stereotypes associated with particular groups of people (Brewer, 1988; Devine, 1989; Fiske & Neuberg, 1990). Together, this work demonstrates that people make inferences about the behaviors of others, without intention, control, effort, or awareness of having done so. Many of these behaviors are nonverbal cues.

BEHAVIOR

Behavior is also affected automatically by external stimuli. In the first demonstration of this idea, Bargh et al. (1996) showed that activating the trait "rude" caused people to interrupt an experimenter who was ostensibly helping a confederate more quickly than did participants who had the trait "polite" activated. This finding has been replicated in a number of behavioral domains: Activating "politicians" causes long-windedness (Dijksterhuis & van Knippenberg, 2000), and activating "supermodels" causes poor performance on a trivia test, whereas activating "professors" causes better performance (Dijksterhuis & van Knippenberg, 1998).

Likewise, activating traits associated with conformity causes people to agree more with a group of confederates (Epley & Gilovich, 1999); activating helpfulness traits causes people to be more helpful (Macrae & Johnston, 1998); activating aggression-related ideas causes people to give longer "shocks" to another participant (Carver, Ganellen, Froming, & Chambers, 1983); activating the elderly stereotype causes people to walk more slowly (Bargh et al., 1996), increases slowness on a lexical decision task (Dijksterhuis, Spears, & Lepinasse, 2001), and promotes poor memory (Dijksterhuis, Aarts, Bargh, & van Knippenberg, 2000; Levy, 1996); and

activating stereotypes for African Americans causes hostility (Bargh et al., 1996) and decreased intellectual performance (Steele & Aronson, 1995; Wheeler, Jarvis, & Petty, 2000). As evidenced by the social inappropriateness of many of these behavioral effects, participants are not aware that they are occurring and are not being affected intentionally, nor do they seem to be able to control the effects that the activation of the various constructs is having.

ATTITUDES

Just as impressions are formed automatically when traits are accessible, either chronically or temporarily, evaluations of stimuli are activated automatically when the stimuli are presented. This automatic evaluation work can be traced back to Zajonc (1980), who argued that the evaluation of a stimulus is connected closely to the representation of the stimulus itself. That is, when the stimulus is presented, a positive or negative evaluation of that stimulus becomes activated without awareness, effort, or intention. In support of this idea, research has demonstrated that attitudes are activated automatically when a stimulus is presented (Bargh, Chaiken, Govender, & Pratto, 1992; Fazio, Sanbonmatsu, Powell, & Kardes, 1986).

Using a procedure similar to the activation of impressions and behaviors, Kawakami, Dovidio, and Dijksterhuis (2003) have even found that when a stereotype is made accessible, people report attitudes consistent with the stereotypical attitudes of that group. For example, when the category of "elderly" is accessible, people report more conservative attitudes, and when the category "skinhead" is accessible, people report more prejudiced attitudes. These effects occur even when the categories were made accessible to participants with a subliminal priming procedure, again suggesting that this effect occurs without conscious awareness.

GOALS

In addition to impressions, behaviors, and attitudes, it has been proposed that goals can become active automatically. Because goal-related information and behaviors are represented mentally, if a goal is pursued frequently and consistently in a particular context or with a particular person, the context or person alone will eventually be able to activate the goal without intention or awareness. The goal is then pursued just as it would be if it had been instigated consciously (Bargh, 1990; Shah, 2005). In support of this argument, Chartrand and Bargh (1996) replicated two well-known information-processing goal studies, but they instigated the goals in participants without their awareness; the results were identical to those obtained when participants had been pursuing the goals consciously.

Other work has shown that participants who had achievement goals activated outside of awareness performed better on a task, and persisted on the task even when a more attractive alternative was introduced, than participants who did not have an active achievement goal (Bargh, Gollwitzer, Lee-Chai, Barndollar, & Trötschel, 2001). Cooperation goals (Bargh et al., 2001) and affiliation goals (Lakin & Chartrand, 2003) can also be pursued without conscious awareness or guidance. Significant others can even be a source of automatic goal activation. For example, Shah (2003) has found that performance on an experimental task increases when close significant others who would want participants to do well are made accessible to them.

SUMMARY

The research reviewed in these sections has demonstrated that people's impressions, behaviors, attitudes, and goal pursuits can be affected by automatically activated concepts. In other words, what people think, do, and feel can be influenced without conscious awareness, intention, or control. In the next section of this chapter, I turn to evidence for this contention specifically within the domain of nonverbal communication.

◆ Automatic Nonverbal Communication

There are several general pieces of evidence to suggest that at least some nonverbal communication is automatic. First, and as noted, there are numerous demands on relatively limited conscious cognitive resources; the sheer amount of these resources needed to process all nonverbal communication in a controlled manner makes this possibility exceedingly unlikely. Second, because the basis of verbal communication is largely conscious, humans have a tendency to direct their focus to what is said and not to focus consciously on the nonverbal cues that are, by definition, unsaid (DePaulo & Friedman, 1998). Yet it is clear that this information is still being processed cognitively because it regulates interactions effectively (see Cappella & Schreiber, this volume). Third, some nonverbal cues cannot be controlled easily, and when efforts to control those behaviors are exerted, they are not usually successful (see later sections in this chapter). Finally, although some researchers have argued that nonverbal communication is deliberate and strategic, there is recent evidence that even strategic behaviors can occur automatically (Lakin & Chartrand, 2003; Lakin, Chartrand, & Arkin, 2005); consciousness is not required for behavior to be either strategic or adaptive.

The empirical work reviewed in this chapter so far has focused on automaticity generally. I turn attention now to the subcategory of these effects that is relevant to nonverbal communication directly (for another review, see Choi, Gray, & Ambady, 2005). Very little research on nonverbal communication, however, has been conducted in such a way as to show definitive evidence that the effects are occurring automatically (i.e., by reducing the likelihood of consciousness being involved, by using funneled-debriefing procedures, by having awareness checks, etc.). Nevertheless, there are several programs of research that demonstrate automatic nonverbal communication indirectly. A sensitive reader will no doubt note that the subcategories listed below correspond with some of the chapters in the Contexts and Functions sections of this *Handbook*. A brief, noncomprehensive review of these topics is covered here to demonstrate that some of these effects occur automatically.

SOCIAL RELATIONSHIPS

Information about social relationships is relatively easy to infer from people's nonverbal behaviors. In terms of social status, dominant people tend to stand taller, use more personal space, interrupt more, and talk louder than less dominant people (Henley, 1977; Burgoon & Dunbar, this volume; but see Hall, 2005). Powerful people look at others the same amount when speaking as when listening, but less powerful people look more when listening than when they are speaking (Fehr & Exline, 1987). Relationship status can also be inferred from nonverbal behaviors. Research using the Interpersonal Perception Task (IPT) (Costanzo & Archer, 1989; see Riggio, this volume), which contains video clips of less than a minute, has demonstrated that one can accurately identify when people are related and when they are in significant relationships (Smith, Archer, & Costanzo, 1991). Rapport can also be determined from watching people interact, at least partially because rapport is related to interactional synchrony,

interpersonal distance, and eye contact (Bernieri, 1988; Bernieri, Davis, Rosenthal, & Knee, 1994; Grahe & Bernieri, 1999; see Tickle-Degnen, this volume). Marital status can even be determined via nonverbal means, given the surprising finding that the longer people have been married, the more similar they look (Zajonc, Adelmann, Murphy, & Neidenthal, 1987).

Is the encoding and decoding of this social relationship information occurring automatically? As the majority of this research has not been conducted with an eye toward answering this specific question, the answer must be inferred from the methodologies that have been used, as well as some of the research findings. This information suggests several reasons to accept the argument that these processes are occurring automatically. First, decoding of social relationship information, as evidenced by research using the IPT, often occurs quickly; clips from the task are less than one minute, suggesting that people's decoding of this information must also occur very quickly (reducing the likelihood of conscious involvement). Second, certain types of conscious instructions interfere with the accuracy of decoding relationship information (e.g., Patterson & Stockbridge, 1998; Patterson, this volume). When this type of interference happens, it suggests that people have developed automatic and efficient strategies for processing the information, and conscious attention interferes with the use of the strategies on which people typically rely.

Third, participants in studies such as the ones reviewed above can rarely identify the factors that influenced their judgments (e.g., Bernieri et al., 1994). One study even found that confederates who were instructed to create liking with a partner could not identify accurately the behaviors they used and how they used them, even though they were successful at their goal (Palmer & Simmons, 1995). Research on nonconscious behavioral mimicry (reviewed in the Rapport section below) has also demonstrated that people are not consciously aware that they mimic the behaviors of others or that other people might be mimicking their behaviors or that this mimicry creates liking (Chartrand & Bargh, 1999; Chartrand, Maddux, & Lakin, 2005). This lack of conscious awareness is the hallmark of an automatic process.

Finally, an interesting line of research has demonstrated recently that postural complementarity, with regard to dominant and submissive nonverbal behaviors, occurs without conscious intention or control (Tiedens & Fragale, 2003). In these studies, confederates were instructed to engage in dominant (i.e., postural expansion) or constricted (i.e., postural constriction) nonverbal behaviors, and the nonverbal behaviors of participants were measured. Results indicated that participants exhibited complementary behaviors to those of the confederate and that interactions where complementarity occurred were reported to be more comfortable. Importantly, extensive debriefing of all participants, using a funneled debriefing procedure (see Bargh & Chartrand, 2000), revealed that they were not aware that complementarity had occurred or that it had affected the comfort level of the interaction (Tiedens & Fragale, 2003).

EMOTIONAL EXPRESSION

In addition to relationship information, people may encode information automatically about their own emotions and decode the emotions of others. In *Emotional Contagion*, Hatfield, Cacioppo, and Rapson (1994) synthesize a wealth of data from a variety of research subareas supporting the idea that emotions are communicated automatically and spread to other people. More often than not, this contagion occurs through nonverbal cues, such as facial expressions, tone of voice, and gestures. One particular piece of evidence that supports the idea that emotions can be encoded automatically is the fact that some emotional expressions are instantaneous and cannot be controlled (Ekman & Davidson, 1994), two defining characteristics of automatic processes. Certain emotional facial expressions, like the Duchenne smile (Frank, Ekman, & Friesen, 1993) or blushing (Leary, Britt, Cutlip, & Templeton, 1992), are argued to be spontaneous depictions of enjoyment or embarrassment, respectively. The spontaneity associated with these emotional expressions could be a result of an evolutionarily developed automatic link between experiencing an emotion and nonverbal indicators of that emotion (Buck, 1984; Ekman, 1992, see Floyd, this volume), similar to the perception-behavior link idea reviewed earlier.

An alternative approach to understanding the spontaneity associated with emotional expressions is the behavioral ecology view (Fridlund, 1994; Fridlund & Russell, this volume). This perspective suggests that facial displays do not reflect expressions of discrete, internal, emotional states but rather are messages that signal people's intentions within a particular context. Fridlund (1994) argues that displays of facial expressions have evolved to meet specific selection pressures and that because they reveal information about people's intentions, they are displayed to serve people's social motives. Although this approach offers a different explanation for what "emotional" facial expressions mean, this perspective also suggests that facial expressions have evolved to serve specific purposes, can occur quickly within a particular context, and often occur without conscious intention or awareness.

Some emotional facial expressions are also difficult to create consciously, suggesting that when these expressions occur, they do so automatically. For example, expressions of fear are almost impossible to re-create without truly being fearful (Ekman, 1985). Finally, a recent meta-analysis suggests that observers can detect accurately the state and trait anxiety of others, although the magnitude of these effects depends on the communication channel (Harrigan, Wilson, & Rosenthal, 2004). Because anxiety is a negative emotional state that most people would not want to convey to others, this information is probably being encoded without intention or awareness.

Tone of voice may also convey information automatically about a speaker's emotional state. Neumann and Strack (2000) had participants listen to a speech that was delivered in either a slightly happy or a slightly sad voice. After hearing the text, participants rated their own mood. People's moods were affected by the tone in which the passage was read and, consistent with emotional contagion, participants automatically encoded this emotional information. When they repeated the text that they heard, they imitated the tone of the original reading spontaneously. This encoding occurred despite the fact that participants were not consciously aware of the original tone of the message and were not given instructions to mimic the original tone.

The automaticity of encoding of emotional expressions is demonstrated most clearly in research by Ulf Dimberg and colleagues (Dimberg 1982, 1997; Dimberg, Thunberg, & Elmehed, 2000). In his work, Dimberg had participants look at pictures of people displaying happy or angry facial expressions. He then measured their subtle facial movements with electromyographic (EMG) technology. The results showed that participants moved the muscles associated with smiling when looking at the happy pictures and the muscles associated with frowning when looking at the angry pictures. This effect occurred even when the facial expressions were presented outside of conscious awareness (i.e., subliminally),

suggesting that this decoding can occur automatically.

PREJUDICE

Prejudice, or negative feelings about groups of people, can also be communicated automatically through nonverbal cues (see Dovidio, Hebl, Richeson, & Shelton, this volume). Because categorical information (e.g., race, sex; Brewer, 1988; Fiske & Neuberg, 1990) is processed automatically in most cases, simply seeing a member of a stereotyped group can activate, without awareness, thoughts and feelings about that group (Blair, 2002; Devine, 1989; Fiske, 1998). It has been argued that a dissociation often exists between people's conscious and unconscious attitudes toward minority groups; therefore, researchers have been able to measure both and determine the effects that each has on social interactions.

This work has shown that nonverbal behaviors like gaze, blinking, body posture, and interpersonal distance can indicate prejudiced feelings toward interaction partners (Crosby, Bromley, & Saxe, 1980; McConnell & Liebold, 2001; Towles-Schwen & Fazio, 2003). In one demonstration, people who indicated negative feelings toward Blacks on an implicit measure of prejudice also blinked more (a sign of uncomfortableness) and made less eye contact during an interaction with an African American partner (Dovidio, Kawakami, Johnson, Johnson, & Howard, 1997). Dovidio, Kawakami, and Gaertner (2002) replicated this effect and showed that the less positive nonverbal behaviors of participants who had implicit racial biases led the African American partners of these participants to feel that the interaction had been less friendly.

Likewise, Vanman, Saltz, Nathan, and Warren (2004) have also shown that facial EMG activity can be related to another person's race; participants who had cheek EMG activity (i.e., activity that would be associated with smiling) when viewing pictures of White targets were more likely to nominate a White applicant for a prestigious award than a Black applicant. Participants in these studies were not aware of the negative nonverbal behaviors they encoded or the fact that these nonverbal behaviors were affecting their interactions negatively. This work therefore provides evidence that both encoding and decoding of prejudicial feelings can occur automatically. In fact, as Dovidio et al. (2002) have discussed, researchers first turned to nonverbal behaviors as indicators of prejudice because of their hypothesized "leakiness" (i.e., uncontrollability) and spontaneity.

IMPRESSION MANAGEMENT AND PERSONALITY EXPRESSION

Although impression management and self-presentation can certainly be conscious (see Keating, this volume), these communicative functions can also occur relatively effortlessly and without conscious guidance, particularly in cases where people are not particularly motivated to convey a desired identity. Moreover, it is also clear that people may infer traits and make attributions from the nonverbal behaviors of others automatically and that these judgments can be quite accurate. Together, this literature suggests that people often express their personality and decode personality information about others automatically through nonverbal behaviors.

People tend to use different self-presentational strategies in different situations and with different types of people. For example, when people are instructed to make an interaction partner like them, they nod, smile, and make more eye contact than do people who did not receive these

instructions (Godfrey, Jones, & Lord, 1986). People copy the postures of interaction partners more when they are told those partners might be helpful than when opportunities to get help from the partners are not available (La France, 1985). Nonverbal behaviors are also dependent on the people for whom the display occurs (see DePaulo & Friedman, 1998, for a review). Finally, the ecological theory of perception suggests that people are able to gain, relatively automatically, information about other people from their appearances and movements, information that Gibson (1979) calls *affordances*. This information is able to be gathered easily because appearance and behavior express some personality characteristics accurately (Zebrowitz & Collins, 1997).

Nonverbal communication is therefore sensitive to conscious goals and situational constraints. Although this strategic use of nonverbal behaviors suggests that their cognitive basis is conscious, being strategic does not demand consciousness. There are several lines of research that suggest that people alter their nonverbal behaviors automatically. Tice, Butler, Muraven, and Stillwell (1995) hypothesized that people's default self-presentational strategy with strangers is to present a positive image, whereas people's default self-presentational strategy with friends is to present a modest image. Consistent with this proposition, when participants behaved consistently with their default tendencies, their self-presentations used few cognitive resources, which led to increased memory of the details of the interaction. Participants who used nondefault self-presentational strategies (e.g., modesty with strangers) were not able to pursue these strategies automatically and used conscious cognitive resources to accomplish their goals (see also Patterson, Churchill, Farag, & Borden, 1991/1992). Other research has also demonstrated that self-presenting in a way that is inconsistent with personality is cognitively taxing and requires attentional resources (Pontari & Schlenker, 2000).

Attributional processes, whereby people infer traits and make dispositional or situational attributions, can also happen automatically. An extensive literature on spontaneous trait inferences has demonstrated that simply presenting people with descriptions of other people's behaviors results in inferring traits from them (Uleman, 1999; Uleman et al., 1996). Participants in these studies were not instructed to infer traits and typically even denied that they had done so (Winter & Uleman, 1984). Related research has found that people might also make emotion inferences when reading descriptions of other's behavior automatically (Gernsbacher, Goldsmith, & Robertson, 1992). Finally, people make both dispositional and situational attributions without the use of limited cognitive resources or conscious intention (Gilbert, Pelham, & Krull, 1988; Krull, 1993). Thus, when people perceive the behaviors of others, they seem to decode this information effortlessly and unintentionally, at least in most circumstances.

Automatic self-presentation, impression management, trait inferences, and attributions are likely to be beneficial to most people in most situations but only to the extent that these relatively effortless categorizations are correct. Ambady and her colleagues have demonstrated that people's automatic decodings of the behaviors of others are remarkably accurate (Ambady, Bernieri, & Richeson, 2000; Gray & Ambady, this volume). In one empirical demonstration, participants watched video clips of teachers' nonverbal behaviors, some as short as six seconds, and then judged teacher effectiveness. Participants' ratings were strongly correlated with students' end-of-semester ratings (Ambady & Rosenthal, 1993).

A meta-analysis has revealed a medium to large effect size for accuracy of predictions from nonverbal presentations and that length of observation time did not significantly affect accuracy; accuracy was just as good when people observed behavior for 30 seconds as it was when people observed behavior for five minutes (Ambady & Rosenthal, 1992). The fact that people can be so accurate at decoding in such short time frames suggests that the process is likely not occurring with much conscious intention or guidance. Moreover, when conscious attention is devoted to this type of task, decoding accuracy decreases (Gilbert & Krull, 1988; Patterson & Stockbridge, 1998).

EXPECTANCIES

Just as people convey personality through their nonverbal behaviors, expectancies that a person holds for others are also conveyed through nonverbal behaviors, seemingly without intention or awareness (see Remland, this volume). Communication of these expectancies—in certain contexts and under certain conditions—results in a self-fulfilling prophecy, whereby perceivers elicit behaviors that are consistent with their original ideas and then conclude that their expectancies were truthful, without realizing the role that they have played in confirming them (Rosenthal, 2003). For example, researchers' behaviors can affect the responses of their participants (Rosenthal, 1976), and the expectations of teachers have been found to affect the behaviors of their students (Rosenthal & Jacobson, 1968). That people are unaware that they have elicited the behavior they expected suggests that these expectancies are being conveyed automatically. This is particularly the case when *negative* expectancies are conveyed, which would likely be controlled if people were aware of them (e.g., Word, Zanna, & Cooper, 1974).

There is also evidence that people are affected automatically by the expectancies that others have for them (i.e., automatic decoding of expectancies). Word et al. (1974) showed that when White participants in a second study were treated as Black participants had been treated in a first study (e.g., abrupt questioning, lack of eye contact), the quality of the interaction decreased. The White participants stuttered more and made less eye contact as a result of the expectancies for a less successful interview that the interviewer was conveying. Chen and Bargh (1997) found a similar result: When stereotypes of African Americans were activated outside of conscious awareness, participants treated an interaction partner in a way that was consistent with this stereotype, eliciting more hostility. Participants were unaware that the stereotype had been activated and were unaware that their own behavior was influencing the behavior of their interaction partner. The results of this study are consistent with many other research findings that stereotype activation results in stereotype-consistent behaviors (see Wheeler & Petty, 2001, for a review). Again, these studies demonstrate consistently that people are not aware that their behavior is affected or is being affected by the expectancies of others.

RAPPORT

Not all behaviors that occur outside of awareness are problematic. For example, many people have been interested in the relationship between posture sharing (either mimicking or mirroring) and the development and maintenance of rapport (for a review, see Tickle-Degnen, this volume). The fact that people mimic the nonverbal behaviors of others (both significant others and strangers) has long been established (Chartrand et al., 2005). Further work has demonstrated that people tend to mimic others and thereby demonstrate or develop rapport without intention, control, or

conscious awareness (e.g., Bavelas, Black, Lemery, & Mullett, 1986; Bernieri, 1988; Bernieri, Reznick, & Rosenthal, 1988; La France, 1979, 1982; La France & Broadbent, 1976). Because this research does not typically include awareness checks or attempts to rule out conscious involvement, the automaticity of these effects is, again, inferred from participants' apparent lack of awareness.

There is more definitive evidence that behavioral mimicry can occur nonconsciously, however, and that this automatic mimicry results in smoother interactions and the development of liking. Chartrand and Bargh (1999) found that participants mimicked the nonverbal behaviors of a confederate without conscious awareness. In a second study, they found that mimicry leads to increased liking for the mimicker and smoother interactions. Thus, mimicking others and being mimicked can communicate rapport automatically. This finding is consistent with the work of Lakin and Chartrand (2003), who found that participants who pursue an unconscious affiliation goal are more likely to mimic the behaviors of an interaction partner than participants who do not have an active affiliation goal (see also Lakin, Jefferis, Cheng, & Chartrand, 2003).

A second study expanded on this finding by giving participants who had a nonconsciously activated affiliation goal a success or failure experience (Lakin & Chartrand, 2003). Participants either succeeded (i.e., had a pleasant interaction with a confederate) or failed at their goal (i.e., had a relatively less pleasant interaction with a confederate). In a subsequent interaction with a different confederate, participants who still had affiliation goals (i.e., those who initially failed) mimicked the nonverbal behaviors of their interaction partner more than participants who had been successful. This effect occurred despite the fact that participants did not consciously know they were pursuing an affiliation goal and did not consciously acknowledge the confederate's behaviors or how the confederate's behaviors were affecting their own behaviors.

A recent social exclusion experience may also lead to increases in behavioral mimicry (Lakin et al., 2005; Lakin & Chartrand, 2005). The need to belong is one of the strongest core motivations, and it affects people's thoughts, feelings, and behaviors frequently (Williams, Forgas, & von Hippel, 2005). It is therefore not surprising that when people have been excluded from a social group, they will engage in behaviors that help them to create liking and allow them to reenter the group. Recent research has shown that mimicking the nonverbal behaviors of group members may be one such strategy (Lakin et al., 2005). When participants were excluded from a computerized ball-tossing game and then interacted with a confederate in a different context, they mimicked the behaviors of the confederate more than when they had not been excluded during the ball-toss game. In other words, participants who were trying to create liking and affiliation were able to pursue this goal through mimicking another person. Together with the findings from Lakin and Chartrand (2003), this work suggests that people can pursue a goal to develop rapport or liking by mimicking the behaviors of others automatically.

Finally, paradigms that involve having a confederate mimic the behaviors of participants have demonstrated that being mimicked causes people to be more interdependent (van Baaren, Maddux, Chartrand, de Bouter, & van Knippenberg, 2003), be more helpful (van Baaren, Holland, Kawakami, & van Knippenberg, 2004), and provide bigger tips (van Baaren, Holland, Steenaert, & van Knippenberg, 2003; for an overview, see Tickle-Degnen, this volume). Mimicry also leads to greater persuasion (Bailenson & Yee, 2005). Because work on mimicry

typically compares participants who are mimicked with participants who are not mimicked, these effects occur arguably as a direct result of the positive feelings that occur automatically with mimicry. The majority of this work includes awareness checks and other methodological strategies that reduce the role of consciousness in these effects (Bargh & Chartrand, 2000).

◆ Discussion and Future Directions

As the literatures reviewed above demonstrate, nonverbal behaviors can communicate information automatically about social relationships, emotions, prejudice, personality, and expectations, as well as indicate relationship status and rapport. As a whole, this research compellingly argues that nonverbal communication has, at least in part, its basis in automatic processes. There are, however, several important topics that deserve research attention.

METHODOLOGICAL CONCERNS

Whereas not all the research reviewed here has provided definitive evidence that the processes are occurring without awareness, intention, control, or cognitive effort, the several lines of research that do provide this evidence demonstrate that nonverbal communication can and does occur automatically. Moreover, the research that does not contain definitive evidence often has methodological characteristics suggesting that people are not aware of what their nonverbal behaviors are communicating or the extent to which their own thoughts, feelings, and behaviors are being affected by the nonverbal communications of others.

Although this suggests that a significant component of nonverbal communication is occurring automatically, to determine definitively the role that automatic processes play in nonverbal communication, researchers should consider including methodological strategies in future research that would reduce the role of controlled processes. For example, participants could be encouraged to make judgments and decisions quickly to reduce their reliance on conscious processes, or they could be put under cognitive load so that their available cognitive resources would be split among several tasks. Researchers could also include awareness checks or funneled debriefings to determine how aware people are of their cognitive processes (Bargh & Chartrand, 2000). By using these sorts of methodologies, future research will be better able to determine the relative contribution of automatic processes to nonverbal communication.

ROLE OF CONTROLLED PROCESSES

Even though I have argued that much of nonverbal communication appears to occur automatically, it would be a mistake to assume that there is no controlled cognitive basis to nonverbal communication as well. We may be unaware of the nonverbal cues that we encode typically, but we can direct our "internal eye" easily onto these behaviors and therefore become more aware of them. People may not process the nonverbal messages they receive from others consciously, but if something causes a disruption in their automatic processing (e.g., an unusual event), or if people are motivated to learn about another person, that process can easily become conscious. Finally, people may even try to control (i.e., with intention and awareness, and with varying degrees of success) their nonverbal behaviors (although even control can become automatized with enough practice; see Kawakami, Dovidio, Moll, Hermsen, & Russin, 2000).

Future work in nonverbal communication would benefit from explicit acknowledgment of the role that both automatic and controlled processes play in the encoding and decoding of nonverbal behaviors. For example, Patterson (2001, this volume) has taken this approach in his parallel process model. He integrated encoding and decoding of nonverbal communication into a single framework by suggesting that these processes occur in parallel and that they both can be more or less controlled cognitive processes. In addition, he argued that factors like biology, culture, personality, situational constraints, interpersonal expectancies, affect, and goals can affect people's social cognition. The parallel process model therefore synthesizes much of the work that social psychologists, communication scholars, and others were conducting on nonverbal communication already (see Patterson, 2001, for a review), which is an important first step in creating a more complete understanding of nonverbal communication processes.

This model also has several interesting implications for the study of the cognitive processes related to nonverbal communication. First, the parallel process model implies that people are sophisticated users and consumers of nonverbal cues. The fact that encoding and decoding occur in parallel demonstrates that neither process requires extensive cognitive resources (i.e., that neither process is particularly effortful). This implication is consistent with my argument that much of nonverbal communication occurs automatically, perhaps even that which appears to be used relatively strategically. Arguably, we have evolved automatic strategies to deal with the incredible amounts of social information that we must process and to help us accomplish our important objectives and goals. Given the importance of nonverbal cues, it is not surprising that automatic nonverbal communication would also be evolutionarily adaptive.

IMPORTANCE OF COGNITIVE RESOURCES

Another interesting area for future research to explore is the role of cognitive resources in nonverbal communication. Because cognitive resources are limited, the amount of cognitive resources that a person has will be a crucial factor determining whether a person is able to use controlled processes to decode nonverbal communication. For example, the parallel process model would predict that when cognitive resources are devoted to encoding or decoding for whatever reason (i.e., we are particularly motivated to convey an impression, we are interested in an interaction partner's intentions), they will be less available to the other process (because they occur in parallel). In other words, if we have to think about encoding, fewer resources can be devoted to decoding. This could have important implications for situations where people need to be focused specifically on one process or the other. Alternatively, because both the sending and the receiving of nonverbal cues can be relatively automatic, one could argue that devoting resources to one process would not necessarily cause the other to deteriorate (because it would be relatively automatic). Future research on nonverbal communication will need to explore these different possibilities; determining how cognitive resources affect nonverbal communication will provide important insight into how automatic these processes really are.

◆ Conclusion

Nonverbal communication conveys information automatically about our social relationships, emotions, prejudices, personalities, and expectations, as well as indicates existing levels of rapport or the desire to create rapport. The cognitive processes that underlie this important source of information, however, are not always automatic. Parallel process models, or other models that recognize explicitly the role for both automatic and controlled processes in nonverbal communication, will likely represent the future of research in this area. Ironically, with more awareness of automatic processes, we should have a greater appreciation of the importance of nonverbal communication.

◆ References

Ambady, N., Bernieri, F. J., & Richeson, J. A. (2000). Toward a histology of social behavior: Judgmental accuracy from thin slices of the behavioral stream. In M. P. Zanna (Ed.), *Advances in experimental social psychology* (Vol. 32, pp. 201–271). San Diego, CA: Academic Press.

Ambady, N., & Rosenthal, R. (1992). Thin slices of expressive behavior as predictors of interpersonal consequences: A meta-analysis. *Psychological Bulletin, 111,* 256–274.

Ambady, N., & Rosenthal, R. (1993). Half a minute: Predicting teacher evaluations from thin slices of nonverbal behavior and physical attractiveness. *Journal of Personality and Social Psychology, 64,* 431–441.

Bailenson, J. N., & Yee, N. (2005). Digital chameleons: Automatic assimilation of nonverbal gestures in immersive virtual environments. *Psychological Science, 16,* 814–819.

Bargh, J. A. (1990). Auto-motives: Preconscious determinants of social interaction. In E. T. Higgins & R. Sorrentino (Eds.), *Handbook of motivation and cognition* (Vol. 2, pp. 93–130). New York: Guilford Press.

Bargh, J. A. (1994). The four horsemen of automaticity: Awareness, intention, efficiency, and control in social cognition. In R. S. Wyer & T. K. Srull (Eds.), *Handbook of social cognition* (2nd ed., pp. 1–40). Hillsdale, NJ: Erlbaum.

Bargh, J. A. (1996). Automaticity in social psychology. In E. T. Higgins & A. W. Kruglanski (Eds.), *Social psychology: Handbook of basic principles* (pp. 169–183). New York: Guilford Press.

Bargh, J. A. (1997). The automaticity of everyday life. In R. S. Wyer (Ed.), *The automaticity of everyday life: Advances in social cognition* (Vol. 10, pp. 1–61). Mahwah, NJ: Erlbaum.

Bargh, J. A., Chaiken, S., Govender, R., & Pratto, F. (1992). The generality of the automatic attitude activation effect. *Journal of Personality and Social Psychology, 62,* 893–912.

Bargh, J. A., & Chartrand, T. L. (1999). The unbearable automaticity of being. *American Psychologist, 54,* 462–479.

Bargh, J. A., & Chartrand, T. L. (2000). The mind in the middle: A practical guide to priming and automaticity research. In H. T. Reis & C. M. Judd (Eds.), *Handbook of research methods in social and personality psychology* (pp. 253–285). New York: Cambridge University Press.

Bargh, J. A., Chen, M., & Burrows, L. (1996). Automaticity of social behavior: Direct effects of trait construct and stereotype activation on action. *Journal of Personality and Social Psychology, 71,* 230–244.

Bargh, J. A., Gollwitzer, P. M., Lee-Chai, A., Barndollar, K., & Trötschel, R. (2001). The automated will: Nonconscious activation and pursuit of behavioral goals. *Journal of Personality and Social Psychology, 81,* 1014–1027.

Bavelas, J. B., Black, A., Lemery, C. R., & Mullett, J. (1986). "I show how you feel": Motor mimicry as a communicative act. *Journal of Personality and Social Psychology, 50,* 322–329.

Bernieri, F. J. (1988). Coordinated movement and rapport in teacher-student interactions. *Journal of Nonverbal Behavior, 12,* 120–138.

Bernieri, F. J., Davis, J. M., Rosenthal, R., & Knee, C. R. (1994). Interactional synchrony and rapport: Measuring synchrony in displays devoid of sound and facial affect. *Personality and Social Psychology Bulletin, 20,* 303–311.

Bernieri, F. J., Reznick, J. S., & Rosenthal, R. (1988). Synchrony, pseudosynchrony, and dissynchrony: Measuring the entertainment process in mother–infant interactions. *Journal of Personality and Social Psychology, 54,* 243–253.

Blair, I. V. (2002). The malleability of automatic stereotypes and prejudice. *Personality and Social Psychology Review, 6,* 242–261.

Brewer, M. B. (1988). A dual process model of impression formation. In T. K. Srull & R. S. Wyer (Eds.), *Advances in social cognition* (Vol. 1, pp. 1–36). Hillsdale, NJ: Erlbaum Associates.

Buck, R. (1984). *The communication of emotion.* New York: Guilford.

Carver, C. S., Ganellen, R. J., Froming, W. J., & Chambers, W. (1983). Modeling: An analysis in terms of category accessibility. *Journal of Experimental Social Psychology, 19,* 403–421.

Chartrand, T. L., & Bargh, J. A. (1996). Automatic activation of impression formation and memorization goals: Nonconscious goal priming reproduces effects of explicit task instructions. *Journal of Personality and Social Psychology, 71,* 464–478.

Chartrand, T. L., & Bargh, J. A. (1999). The chameleon effect: The perception–behavior link and social interaction. *Journal of Personality and Social Psychology, 76,* 893–910.

Chartrand, T. L., Maddux, W. W., & Lakin, J. L. (2005). Beyond the perception–behavior link: The ubiquitous utility and motivational moderators of nonconscious mimicry. In R. R. Hassin, J. S. Uleman, & J. A. Bargh (Eds.), *The new unconscious* (pp. 334–361). New York: Oxford University Press.

Chen, M., & Bargh, J. A. (1997). Nonconscious behavioral confirmation processes: The self-fulfilling nature of automatically-activated stereotypes. *Journal of Experimental Social Psychology, 33,* 541–560.

Choi, Y. S., Gray, H. M., & Ambady, N. (2005). The glimpsed world: Unintended communication and unintended perception. In

R. R. Hassin, J. S. Uleman, & J. A. Bargh (Eds.), *The new unconscious* (pp. 309–333). New York: Oxford University Press.

Costanzo, M., & Archer, D. (1989). Interpreting the expressive behavior of others: The Interpersonal Perception Task. *Journal of Nonverbal Behavior, 13,* 225–245.

Crosby, F., Bromley, S., & Saxe, L. (1980). Recent unobtrusive studies of Black and White discrimination and prejudice: A literature review. *Psychological Bulletin, 87,* 546–563.

DePaulo, B. M., & Friedman, H. S. (1998). Nonverbal communication. In D. T. Gilbert, S. T. Fiske, & G. Lindzey (Eds.), *The handbook of social psychology* (4th ed., pp. 3–40). New York: Oxford University Press.

Devine, P. G. (1989). Stereotypes and prejudice: Their automatic and controlled components. *Journal of Personality and Social Psychology, 56,* 5–18.

Dijksterhuis, A., Aarts, H., Bargh, J. A., & van Knippenberg, A. (2000). On the relation between associative strength and automatic behavior. *Journal of Experimental Social Psychology, 36,* 531–544.

Dijksterhuis, A., & Bargh, J. A. (2001). The perception–behavior expressway: Automatic effects of social perception on social behavior. In M. P. Zanna (Ed.), *Advances in Experimental Social Psychology* (Vol. 33, pp. 1–40). San Diego, CA: Academic Press.

Dijksterhuis, A., & van Knippenberg, A. (1998). The relation between perception and behavior or how to win a game of Trivial Pursuit. *Journal of Personality and Social Psychology, 74,* 865–877.

Dijksterhuis, A., & van Knippenberg, A. (2000). Behavioral indecision: Effects of self-focus on automatic behavior. *Social Cognition, 18,* 55–74.

Dijksterhuis, A., Spears, R., & Lepinasse, V. (2001). Reflecting and deflecting stereotypes: Assimilation and contrast in impression formation and automatic behavior. *Journal of Experimental Social Psychology, 37,* 286–299.

Dimberg, U. (1982). Facial reactions to facial expressions. *Psychophysiology, 19,* 643–647.

Dimberg, U. (1997). Psychophysiological reactions to facial expressions. In U. Segerstrale & P. Molnar (Eds.), *Nonverbal communication: Where nature meets culture* (pp. 47–60). Mahwah, NJ: Erlbaum.

Dimberg, U., Thunberg, M., & Elmehed, K. (2000). Unconscious facial reactions to emotional facial expressions. *Psychological Science, 11,* 86–89.

Dovidio, J. F., Kawakami, K., & Gaertner, S. L. (2002). Implicit and explicit prejudice and interracial interaction. *Journal of Personality and Social Psychology, 82,* 62–68.

Dovidio, J. F., Kawakami, K., Johnson, C., Johnson, B., & Howard, A. (1997). On the nature of prejudice: Automatic and controlled processes. *Journal of Experimental Social Psychology, 33,* 510–540.

Ekman, P. (1985). *Telling lies.* New York: Norton.

Ekman, P. (1992). An argument for basic emotions. *Cognition and Emotion, 6,* 169–200.

Ekman, P., & Davidson, R. J. (Eds.). (1994). *The nature of emotion.* New York: Oxford University Press.

Epley, N., & Gilovich, T. (1999). Just going along: Nonconscious priming and conformity to social pressure. *Journal of Personality and Social Psychology, 35,* 578–589.

Fazio, R. H., Sanbonmatsu, D. M., Powell, M. C., & Kardes, F. R. (1986). On the automatic activation of attitudes. *Journal of Personality and Social Psychology, 50,* 229–238.

Fehr, B. J., & Exline, R. V. (1987). Social visual interaction: A conceptual and literature review. In S. Feldstein & A. W. Siegman (Eds.), *Nonverbal behavior and communication* (2nd ed., pp. 225–325). Hillsdale, NJ: Erlbaum.

Fiske, S. T. (1998). Stereotyping, prejudice, and discrimination. In D. T. Gilbert, S. T. Fiske, & G. Lindzey (Eds.), *The handbook of social psychology* (4th ed., pp. 357–411). New York: Oxford University Press.

Fiske, S. T., & Neuberg, S. L. (1990). A continuum of impression formation, from category-based to individuating processes: Influences of information and motivation on attention and interpretation. In M. P. Zanna (Ed.), *Advances in Experimental Social Psychology* (Vol. 23, pp. 1–74). San Diego, CA: Academic Press.

Frank, M. G., Ekman, P., & Friesen, W. V. (1993). Behavioral markers and recognizability of the smile of enjoyment. *Journal of Personality and Social Psychology, 64,* 83–93.

Fridlund, A. J. (1994). *Human facial expression.* San Diego, CA: Academic Press.

Gernsbacher, M. A., Goldsmith, H. H., & Robertson, R. R. (1992). Do readers mentally represent characters' emotional states? *Cognition and Emotion, 6,* 89–111.

Gibson, J. J. (1979). *The ecological approach to visual perception.* Boston: Houghton Mifflin.

Gilbert, D. T., & Krull, D. S. (1988). Seeing less and knowing more: The benefits of perceptual ignorance. *Journal of Personality and Social Psychology, 54,* 193–202.

Gilbert, D. T., Pelham, B. W., & Krull, D. S. (1988). On cognitive busyness: When person perceivers meet persons perceived. *Journal of Personality and Social Psychology, 54,* 733–740.

Godfrey, D. K., Jones, E. E., & Lord, C. G. (1986). Self-promotion is not ingratiating. *Journal of Personality and Social Psychology, 50,* 106–115.

Grahe, J. E., & Bernieri, F. J. (1999). The importance of nonverbal cues in judging rapport. *Journal of Nonverbal Behavior, 23,* 253–269.

Hall, J. A. (2005). Meta-analysis of nonverbal behavior. In V. Manusov (Ed.), *The sourcebook of nonverbal measures: Going beyond words* (pp. 483–492). Mahwah, NJ: Erlbaum Associates.

Harrigan, J. A., Wilson, K., & Rosenthal, R. (2004). Detecting state and trait anxiety from auditory and visual cues: A meta-analysis. *Personality and Social Psychology Bulletin, 30,* 56–66.

Hassin, R. R., Uleman, J. S., & Bargh, J. A. (Eds.). (2005). *The new unconscious.* New York: Oxford University Press.

Hatfield, E., Cacioppo, J. T., & Rapson, R. L. (1994). *Emotional contagion.* Cambridge: Cambridge University Press.

Henley, N. M. (1977). *Body politics: Power, sex and nonverbal communication.* Englewood Cliffs, NJ: Prentice Hall.

Higgins, E. T. (1996). Knowledge activation: Accessibility, applicability, and salience. In E. T. Higgins & A. W. Kruglanski (Eds.), *Social psychology: Handbook of basic principles* (pp. 133–168). New York: Guilford Press.

Higgins, E. T., Rholes, W. S., & Jones, C. R. (1977). Category accessibility and impression formation. *Journal of Experimental Social Psychology, 13,* 141–154.

Krull, D. S. (1993). Does the grist change the mill? The effect of the perceiver's inferential goal on the process of social inference. *Personality and Social Psychology Bulletin, 19,* 340–348.

Kawakami, K., Dovidio, J. F., & Dijksterhuis, A. (2003). Effect of social category priming on personal attitudes. *Psychological Science, 14,* 315–319.

Kawakami, K., Dovidio, J. F., Moll, J., Hermsen, S., & Russin, A. (2000). Just say no (to stereotyping): Effects of training in the negation of stereotypic associations on stereotype activation. *Journal of Personality and Social Psychology, 78,* 871–888.

La France, M. (1979). Nonverbal synchrony and rapport: Analysis by the cross-lag panel technique. *Social Psychology Quarterly, 42,* 66–70.

La France, M. (1982). Posture mirroring and rapport. In M. Davis (Ed.), *Interaction rhythms: Periodicity in communicative behavior* (pp. 279–298). New York: Human Sciences Press.

La France, M. (1985). Postural mirroring and intergroup relations. *Personality and Social Psychology Bulletin, 11,* 207–217.

La France, M., & Broadbent, M. (1976). Group rapport: Posture sharing as a nonverbal indicator. *Group and Organization Studies, 1,* 328–333.

Lakin, J. L., & Chartrand, T. L. (2003). Using nonconscious behavioral mimicry to create affiliation and rapport. *Psychological Science, 14,* 334–339.

Lakin, J. L., & Chartrand, T. L. (2005). Exclusion and nonconscious behavioral mimicry. In

K. D. Williams, J. P. Forgas, & W. von Hippel (Eds.), *The social outcast: Ostracism, social exclusion, rejection, and bullying* (pp. 279–295). New York: Psychology Press.

Lakin, J. L., Chartrand, T. L., & Arkin, R. M. (2005). *I am too just like you: Nonconscious mimicry as a behavioral response to social exclusion.* Unpublished manuscript.

Lakin, J. L., Jefferis, V. E., Cheng, C. M., & Chartrand, T. L. (2003). The chameleon effect as social glue: Evidence for the evolutionary significance of nonconscious mimicry. *Journal of Nonverbal Behavior, 27,* 145–162.

Leary, M. R., Britt, T. W., Cutlip, W. D., II., & Templeton, J. L. (1992). Social blushing. *Psychological Bulletin, 112,* 446–460.

Levy, B. (1996). Improving memory in old age through implicit self-stereotyping. *Journal of Personality and Social Psychology, 71,* 1092–1107.

Macrae, C. N., & Johnston, L. (1998). Help, I need somebody: Automatic action and inaction. *Social Cognition, 16,* 400–417.

McConnell, A. R., & Liebold, J. M. (2001). Relations among the Implicit Association Test, discriminatory behavior, and explicit measures of racial attitudes. *Journal of Experimental Social Psychology, 37,* 435–442.

Neisser, U. (1967). *Cognitive psychology.* Englewood Cliffs, NJ: Prentice Hall.

Neumann, R., & Strack, F. (2000). "Mood contagion": The automatic transfer of mood between persons. *Journal of Personality and Social Psychology, 79,* 211–223.

Palmer, M. T., & Simmons, K. B. (1995). Communicating intentions through nonverbal behaviors: Conscious and nonconscious encoding of liking. *Human Communication Research, 22,* 128–160.

Patterson, M. L. (2001). Toward a comprehensive model of nonverbal communication. In W. P. Robinson & H. Giles (Eds.), *The new handbook of language and social psychology* (pp. 159–176). New York: Wiley.

Patterson, M. L., Churchill, M. E., Farag, F., & Borden, E. (1991/1992). Impression management, cognitive demand, and interpersonal sensitivity. *Current Psychology: Research & Reviews, 10,* 263–271.

Patterson, M. L., & Stockbridge, E. (1998). Effects of cognitive demand and judgment strategy on person perception accuracy. *Journal of Nonverbal Behavior, 22,* 253–263.

Pontari, B. A., & Schlenker, B. R. (2000). The influence of cognitive load on self-presentation: Can cognitive busyness help as well as harm social performance? *Journal of Personality and Social Psychology, 78,* 1092–1108.

Posner, M. I., & Snyder, C. R. R. (1975). Attention and cognitive control. In R. L. Solso (Ed.), *Information processing and cognition: The Loyola symposium* (pp. 55–85). Hillsdale, NJ: Erlbaum.

Rosenthal, R. (1976). *Experimenter effects in behavioral research.* New York: Irvington.

Rosenthal, R. (2003). Covert communication in laboratories, classrooms, and the truly real world. *Current Directions in Psychological Science, 12,* 151–154.

Rosenthal, R., & Jacobson, L. (1968). *Pygmalion in the classroom.* New York: Holt, Rinehart, & Winston.

Shah, J. Y. (2003). Automatic for the people: How representations of significant others implicitly affect goal pursuit. *Journal of Personality and Social Psychology, 84,* 661–681.

Shah, J. Y. (2005). The automatic pursuit and management of goals. *Current Directions in Psychological Science, 14,* 10–13.

Shiffrin, R. M., & Schneider, W. (1977). Controlled and automatic human information processing: II. Perceptual learning, automatic attending and a general theory. *Psychological Review, 84,* 127–190.

Smith, H. J., Archer, D., & Costanzo, M. (1991). "Just a hunch": Accuracy and awareness in person perception. *Journal of Nonverbal Behavior, 15,* 3–18.

Srull, T. K., & Wyer, R. S. (1979). The role of category accessibility in the interpretation of information about persons: Some determinants and implications. *Journal of Personality and Social Psychology, 37,* 1660–1672.

Steele, C. M., & Aronson, J. (1995). Stereotype threat and the intellectual test performance of African Americans. *Journal of*

Personality and Social Psychology, 69, 797–811.

Tice, D. M., Butler, J. L., Muraven, M. B., & Stillwell, A. M. (1995). When modesty prevails: Differential favorability of self-presentation to friends and strangers. *Journal of Personality and Social Psychology, 69,* 1120–1138.

Tiedens, L. Z., & Fragale, A. R. (2003). Power moves: Complementarity in dominant and submissive nonverbal behavior. *Journal of Personality and Social Psychology, 84,* 558–568.

Towles-Schwen, T., & Fazio, R. H. (2003). Choosing social situations: The relation between automatically activated racial attitudes and anticipated comfort interacting with African Americans. *Personality and Social Psychology Bulletin, 29,* 170–182.

Uleman, J. S. (1999). Spontaneous versus intentional inferences in impression formation. In S. Chaiken & Y. Trope (Eds.), *Dual-process theories in social psychology* (pp. 141–160). New York: Guilford Press.

Uleman, J. S., Newman, L. S., & Moskowitz, G. B. (1996). People as flexible interpreters: Evidence and issues from spontaneous trait inference. In M. P. Zanna (Ed.), *Advances in Experimental Social Psychology* (Vol. 28, pp. 179–211). San Diego, CA: Academic Press.

van Baaren, R. B., Holland, R. W., Kawakami, K., & van Knippenberg, A. (2004). Mimicry and prosocial behavior. *Psychological Science, 15,* 71–74.

van Baaren, R. B., Holland, R. W., Steenaert, B., & van Knippenberg, A. (2003). Mimicry for money: Behavioral consequences of imitation. *Journal of Experimental Social Psychology, 39,* 393–398.

van Baaren, R. B., Maddux, W. W., Chartrand, T. L., de Bouter, C., & van Knippenberg, A. (2003). It takes two to mimic: Behavioral consequences of self-construals. *Journal*

of Personality and Social Psychology, 84, 1093–1102.

Vanman, E. J., Saltz, J. L., Nathan, L. R., & Warren, J. A. (2004). Racial discrimination by low-prejudiced Whites facial movements as implicit measures of attitudes related to behavior. *Psychological Science, 15,* 711–714.

Wheeler, S. C., Jarvis, W. B. G., & Petty, R. E. (2000). Think unto others: The self-destructive impact of negative racial stereotypes. *Journal of Experimental Social Psychology, 37,* 173–180.

Wheeler, S. C., & Petty, R. E. (2001). The effects of stereotype activation on behavior: A review of possible mechanisms. *Psychological Bulletin, 127,* 797–826.

Williams, K. D., Forgas, J. P., & von Hippel, W. (Eds.). (2005). *The social outcast: Ostracism, social exclusion, rejection, and bullying.* New York: Psychology Press.

Winter, L., & Uleman, J. S. (1984). When are social judgments made? Evidence for the spontaneousness of trait inferences. *Journal of Personality and Social Psychology, 47,* 237–252.

Word, C. O., Zanna, M. P., & Cooper, J. (1974). The nonverbal mediation of self-fulfilling prophecies in interracial interaction. *Journal of Experimental Social Psychology, 10,* 109–120.

Zajonc, R. B. (1980). Feeling and thinking: Preferences need no inferences. *American Psychologist, 35,* 151–175.

Zajonc, R. B., Adelmann, P. K., Murphy, S. T., & Neidenthal, P. M. (1987). Convergence in the physical appearance of spouses. *Motivation and Emotion, 11,* 335–346.

Zebrowitz, L. A., & Collins, M. A. (1997). Accurate social perception at zero acquaintance: The affordances of a Gibsonian approach. *Personality and Social Psychology Review, 1,* 204–223.

5

NONVERBAL SKILLS AND ABILITIES

◆ Ronald E. Riggio
Kravis Leadership Institute,
Claremont McKenna College

The practice of nonverbal communication relies on a range of innate and developed foundational processes. One foundation underlying the use of nonverbal communication focuses on individual differences in the abilities to communicate nonverbally. This ability, or skill, approach is akin to a personality perspective in that it focuses on individual differences in the sending (encoding), receiving (decoding), and regulation (management) of nonverbal communication (for more on personality, see Gifford, this volume). In other words, people vary in their abilities to convey nonverbal messages to others accurately, "read" others' nonverbal communications, and monitor and control their nonverbal displays.

The skill approach to nonverbal communication was advanced in a 1979 book edited by Robert Rosenthal, *Skill in Nonverbal Communication: Individual Differences*, and by the work of Rosenthal and colleagues (1979) on the Profile of Nonverbal Sensitivity (PONS), a measure of individual differences in the ability to decode nonverbal messages. In Rosenthal's *Skill* volume, Friedman (1979) argued that the skill approach to nonverbal communication represented three important shifts in conceptualizing the study of human social interaction. The first was a shift from an emphasis on cognitive processes (e.g., attitudes, cognitive attributions) in interpersonal relations to a focus on emotional processes. The second shift moved the focus from abstract traits to more concrete abilities. The third shifts the concept of nonverbal skill from a study of inferred states to the study of process. A clear example of this last shift is illustrated by research on expectancy effects (Harris & Rosenthal, 2005; Rosenthal & Jacobson, 1968) that prompted scholars to try to understand the "process" of how positive (and negative) expectations are conveyed.

The work by researchers who were focusing on individual differences in nonverbal communication skill represented the groundwork for the highly popular concept of *emotional intelligence* (Goleman, 1995, 1998; Mayer & Salovey, 1997; Salovey & Mayer, 1990). Indeed, Friedman (1979) used the analogy of an intelligence test, with its "right" and "wrong" answers, when discussing the measurement advantages of a nonverbal skill approach to personality over traditional traitlike measures. The same measurement distinction divides the emotional intelligence research community with its distinction between the "abilities model" and the "mixed model" (Caruso, Mayer, & Salovey, 2002; Mayer, Salovey, & Caruso, 2000) for explaining and describing emotional intelligence. The abilities model of emotional intelligence focuses on abilities to perceive, understand, use, and manage emotions, and it is represented by the Multifactor Emotional Intelligence Scale (MEIS) and the Mayer, Salovey, Caruso, Emotional Intelligence Test (MSCEIT) (Mayer, Salovey, & Caruso, 1997, 2002) measures.

Both these instruments are performance-based assessments of emotional abilities, many of which are central to skill in nonverbal communication and, like most measures of emotional intelligence ability, have correct and incorrect answers. The mixed model of emotional intelligence combines emotional skills and abilities with traitlike notions of personality, which are represented by Goleman's (1995, 1998) work and instruments like the Bar-On Emotional Quotient

Inventory (EQI; Bar-On, 1997). Its measures of emotional intelligence resemble self-report personality assessments typically.

Not unlike emotional intelligence, nonverbal skills are important for success in various aspects of social life. Specifically, there is evidence that nonverbal skills and abilities are important in initiating and maintaining social interaction, developing interpersonal relationships, and managing impressions. Nonverbal skills and abilities are also linked to stress management and to success in careers in various business settings (Riggio, 1992a, 2005). Importantly, nonverbal skills, unlike personality traits, can be learned and improved. For example, research on deception detection suggests that this decoding ability improves by providing feedback concerning performance accuracy and with practice (Zuckerman, Koestner, & Alton, 1984; Zuckerman, Koestner, & Colella, 1985), as well as by providing decoders information concerning more accurate nonverbal clues to deception (de Turck, Harszlak, Bodhorn, & Texter, 1990; see also Patterson, Foster, & Bellmer, 2001). There is also evidence that nonverbal expressiveness can be improved through training (Taylor, 2002; see also Vrij, this volume).

Following the belief in the importance of nonverbal skills for an array of outcomes, this chapter reviews theory and research on the skill approach to nonverbal communication by focusing on three general domains of nonverbal skills and abilities: (1) nonverbal decoding skill, (2) nonverbal encoding skill, and (3) skill in regulating nonverbal communication. In addition to defining these skill domains, the means of measuring these nonverbal skills will be reviewed, as will research on the impact of each specific nonverbal skill domain on outcomes in human social interaction. Finally, the research and application potentials of the nonverbal skills and abilities perspective will be discussed.

◆ *Skill in Nonverbal Decoding*

Skill in nonverbal decoding involves sensitivity to the nonverbal messages of others as well as the ability to interpret those messages accurately. For the most part, others' nonverbal messages involve the communication of emotions, attitudes (e.g., liking or disliking), and cues of status or dominance (Mast, 2002). Skill in nonverbal decoding is a subset of the broader construct of interpersonal sensitivity, which is defined as "the ability to sense, perceive accurately, and respond appropriately to one's personal, interpersonal, and social environment" (Bernieri, 2001, p. 3).

A number of assessment instruments have been designed to measure individual differences in nonverbal decoding skill. An examination of the properties of these various skill instruments can help illustrate the conceptual and methodological issues involved in studying nonverbal skills and abilities. The earliest and simplest instruments consisted of having respondents attempt to decode photographs of basic facial expressions of emotions. The Brief Affect Recognition Test (BART), developed by Ekman and Friesen (1974), is an example of this type of measure. Using a tachistoscope, test takers are presented with a brief presentation (a fraction of a second) of individuals posing "basic" emotional expressions (happiness, sadness, surprise, disgust, fear, and anger) and must choose the correct emotion. A total accuracy score represents the measure of nonverbal or emotional decoding skill. Matsumoto and colleagues (2000) developed an improved version of this instrument, the Japanese and Caucasian Brief Affect Recognition Test (JACBART). A limitation of these instruments, however, is the focus on measuring accuracy in decoding only static, visual cues of distinct facial expressions of emotions, devoid of context.

Similarly, Buck and colleagues (Buck, 1978, 2005; Buck, Miller, & Caul, 1974; Buck, Savin, Miller, & Caul, 1972) developed a technique to assess individual differences in the ability to read subtle, natural (unposed) emotional expressions. Using this "slide-viewing technique" (SVT), the faces of stimulus subjects are videotaped while watching emotion-evoking slides and talking about them. Some of the slides are meant to evoke positive emotions (a group of laughing children, sleeping baby); others evoke negative emotions (severe facial injury, crying child with crutch). Others are simply unusual or scenic slides. Respondents view the silent video segments of stimulus subjects' faces and try to determine which slide the stimulus subject was viewing. Again, a total accuracy score is the measure of emotional or nonverbal decoding skill, but scores can also be obtained for accuracy at decoding specific emotions. Buck (1976) also developed a standardized instrument, the Communication of Affect Receiving Ability Test (CARAT), from some of the video sequences. The slide-viewing technique measures spontaneous, natural, dynamic emotional expressions and relies on videotape segments rather than still photographs, providing more of the available nonverbal information.

The Diagnostic Analysis of Nonverbal Accuracy (DANVA) assesses both visual cues of basic emotional expressions and auditory nonverbal cues (i.e., paralanguage) of emotion (Nowicki & Duke, 1994). The DANVA is actually a collection of several instruments that includes both posed and spontaneous photographs of emotional expressions (including subtests measuring facial expressions of emotions, emotions expressed via hand gestures, and emotions expressed via body posture). In addition, there are subtests that measure decoding of vocal cues, with audio segments of emotions being expressed while using the same content-standard sentence ("I am going out of the room now but I'll be back later."). In all cases, respondents choose the correct emotional expression ("happy," "sad," "angry," or "fearful"). Scores are the number of correct choices on each subtest. There are both adult and child versions of the DANVA (Nowicki & Duke, 2001) as well as a modified version of both measures useful in the field (Duke & Nowicki, 2005). The DANVA assesses sensitivity to both visual and auditory cues and increases the range of nonverbal expressions by including the ability to decode both posed and spontaneous expressions of emotions. Research shows that scores on the DANVA correlate with greater overall social competence and better psychosocial adjustment (Nowicki & Duke, 2001).

Perhaps the most well-known measure of nonverbal decoding skill is the aforementioned PONS (Rosenthal et al., 1979). The PONS consists of 220 brief, two-second audio and video clips of a woman enacting multiple, emotionally laden scenes (e.g., expressing jealous rage, asking for a favor, talking about the death of a friend). By masking the spoken words via electronic content filtering or randomized splicing of the audio track, only nonverbal cues are presented. Eleven different channels (e.g., face only, body only, audio only, and all possible combinations) are used to assess specific aspects of nonverbal decoding. After each clip, respondents are presented with a multiple-choice item and instructed to choose the correct portrayal. A total accuracy score represents general sensitivity to nonverbal cues (Hall, 2001). There are also brief versions of the PONS that use only the audio or visual cues. The full-length PONS has been used widely in research and has demonstrated good psychometric properties (Hall, 2001; Rosenthal, 1979). Not surprisingly, research with the PONS suggests that persons receiving high scores are more interpersonally

aware than those receiving low scores (e.g., Ambady, Hallahan, & Rosenthal, 1995; Hall & Carter, 1999). In addition, physicians receiving higher scores on the PONS had more satisfied patients than their colleagues with low-sensitivity scores (DiMatteo, Friedman, & Taranta, 1979).

The PONS assesses a wide range of sensitivity to different channels of nonverbal communication: audio versus visual, the relatively "rich" nonverbal cues provided by facial expressions versus the more limited range of cues emitted by the body channel. It also involves nonverbal cues displayed in a number of enacted scenarios, such as "helping a customer" or "talking about one's divorce," sometimes combining the nonverbal display of emotion with cues of dominance-submission (e.g., "talking to a lost child" or "asking forgiveness"). Other items involve reading cues that represent complex blendings of emotions and circumstances (e.g., "returning a faulty item to a store," "talking about one's wedding"), whereas some are seemingly devoid of emotional content (e.g., "ordering food in a restaurant"). The breadth of the PONS's sampling of enacted scenes and the multiple channels of nonverbal cue displays seem to capture the diversity of nonverbal behavior, but this has led to low internal consistency (see Hall, 2001) and can be time-consuming to implement. Other limitations of the PONS are its reliance on a lone sender and the fact that the scenarios are posed rather than genuine enactments of emotions.

The Interpersonal Perception Task (IPT; Archer & Costanzo, 1988; Costanzo & Archer, 1989) is another measure of nonverbal decoding skill but one that focuses more on reading nonverbal, verbal, and situational cues to assess the ability to decode the relationships among video interactants, their status or dominance in relationship to one another, their level of intimacy in the relationship, and whether they are truth telling or deceiving. Scenes include trying to determine a child's parent (relationship), identifying the person of higher status or the winner of a sporting event (status or dominance), or trying to determine the length of a couple's dating relationship (intimacy). The IPT consists of 30 brief video (with full audio) scenes of one, two, or more stimulus persons, communicating with an interviewer, communicating with another person on the telephone, or in face-to-face communication. After watching the scene, respondents choose the correct interpretation via a multiple-choice question. There is also a brief version of the IPT (IPT-15, Costanzo & Archer, 1993) that removed some of the problematic items from the longer version (e.g., items that were decoded at about chance or less than chance accuracy).

The IPT goes beyond nonverbal decoding and presents individuals being assessed with both the audio and the video interaction between or among participants. Most other measures of nonverbal decoding skill eliminate the verbal content to focus solely on nonverbal (visual and paralinguistic) cues. The authors of the IPT suggest that it is more closely aligned with the construct of "social intelligence" than with emotional intelligence (Archer, Costanzo, & Akert, 2001). Research with the IPT has been primarily focused on psychometric issues, although there is evidence that persons scoring high on the IPT are more socially aware and socially competent (Archer et al., 2001). In a study of college roommates, high scorers on the IPT had higher-quality and more supportive relationships with one another than did low IPT scorers (Hodgins & Zuckerman, 1990).

The IPT has the advantage of using naturalistic interactions as opposed to the posed communications used in most other measures of nonverbal decoding skill. Moreover, rather than presenting a single communicator, the IPT has many segments with two or more interactants, requiring a more sophisticated level of decoding skill, such as the ability to notice inconsistencies between verbal and nonverbal channels or to use cues of dyadic rapport (Bernieri & Gillis, 2001; Bernieri & Rosenthal, 1991). It is also likely that correct decoding of IPT scenes requires not just recognition of specific cues, as in decoding facial expressions of emotion, but also sophisticated interpretation of complex verbal, nonverbal, and social cues. For example, one study found that whereas Japanese and American participants scored about the same in the visual-only condition of the IPT-15, Japanese participants' accuracy in relation to Americans dropped off considerably when the vocal and verbal cues were added (Iizuka, Patterson, & Matchen, 2002). Furthermore, respondents who rely on "common sense" heuristics tend to make systematic errors on the IPT, such as assuming that the older interactant (or the male interactant) has the higher status (Archer & Costanzo, 1988). An individual who has great skill in nonverbal and situational decoding should be more likely to avoid these errors.

A limitation of all the performance measures of nonverbal decoding skill is the relatively small sampling of what is obviously a vast domain of nonverbal behavior. For instance, the BART and DANVA focus exclusively on emotional communication. Although the PONS assesses skill in decoding an array of nonverbal messages involving cues of emotion, status, and relationship, it is limited to one sender; the IPT has multiple senders, but it is brief (15 or 30 items) and suffers from low internal consistency (Hall, 2001). The extremely low internal consistency coefficients (KR20s of .38 and .52 for the brief and long versions of the IPT) suggest that the IPT may indeed be assessing a broad domain of interpersonal skills. Finally, performance measures of nonverbal skill are time-consuming to develop and often difficult to administer.

Another approach to measuring nonverbal skill involves the use of self-report methods. Self-report methods offer the advantages of sampling across a broad range of nonverbal skill-related areas, and they are relatively easy to administer (Riggio & Riggio, 2001). The earliest published attempt to assess nonverbal decoding skill via self-reports was by Zuckerman and Larrance (1979) with their Perceived Decoding Ability (PDA) and Perceived Encoding Ability (PEA) tests. As part of a larger "social skill" model, Riggio's Social Skills Inventory (SSI; Riggio, 1986, 1989, 2005; Riggio & Carney, 2003) uses self-report techniques to measure two decoding abilities, emotional sensitivity (the ability to decode emotions and other nonverbal cues) and social sensitivity (the ability to decode and understand social situations, social roles, and social scripts). Unfortunately, measuring nonverbal decoding skill via self-reports has demonstrated only limited success. For example, correlations between self-report measures of decoding skill and performance measures have been positive but low (typically below .20). The emotional sensitivity subscale of the SSI, however, has had a slightly stronger relationship with decoding scores on the DANVA (decoding faces) and a similar decoding facial expressions subtest of the Multifactor Emotional Intelligence Test (correlations of .22 and .26, respectively; Riggio & Carney, 2003). In addition, self-reported emotional sensitivity is correlated substantially with relevant self-reported social behaviors, including the size and closeness of social networks (Riggio, 1986; Riggio, Watring, & Throckmorton, 1993).

Skill in decoding nonverbal communication is considered a very important component of nonverbal ability. It is aligned closely with important personality characteristics,

particularly empathy and being other-oriented (Losoya & Eisenberg, 2001). Nonverbally sensitive individuals may also be more prone to emotional contagion effects, vicariously experiencing others' emotions (Hatfield, Cacioppo, & Rapson, 1994). Indeed, there is a .48 correlation between the emotional sensitivity scale of the SSI and a self-report measure of emotional contagion (Riggio & Carney, 2003). This suggests that although nonverbal sensitivity is considered to be an important component of global nonverbal skill or competence, it is possible to be *too* nonverbally sensitive. Davis (1983, 1994), in his multidimensional model of empathy, conceptualizes one aspect of other-oriented sensitivity as taking another's perspective or showing some empathic concern with others' emotional states. A different form of empathy, however, is labeled "personal distress," suggesting emotional contagion effects. Taken to an extreme, nonverbal sensitivity may cause people to experience some personal distress. It is important to emphasize that when considering global skill or competence in nonverbal and emotional communication, an individual needs to also possess skills in decoding, encoding, and regulating communication and emotional processes (see Riggio, 1986; Riggio & Carney, 2003).

DETECTION OF DECEPTION

The ability to detect deception accurately is a particular nonverbal decoding skill. Because of its complexity, the ability to detect deception is rare, with a very small percentage of the general population able to detect deception much above chance levels (Ekman, O'Sullivan, & Frank, 1999; Malone & DePaulo, 2001; Vrij, this volume). Yet some individuals seem to be particularly successful at detecting deception and are labeled "wizards" (O'Sullivan, 2005). These rare individuals are particularly skilled at reading nonverbal cues, although they also possess a number of other skills and qualities critical for detecting deception. These include the ability to notice inconsistencies in and between nonverbal and verbal cues, a strong motivation to both observe and analyze human behavior, and an ability to avoid the systematic cognitive biases that hamper the ability to detect deception successfully in the general population (O'Sullivan, 2005).

A great deal of research suggests why decoding of deception is such a difficult skill. First, there is a trusting bias: a tendency to believe that others' communications are more likely to be truthful than deceptive (Ekman, 1985; Riggio, 1992b). This manifests itself in proportionately more judgments of "truth" as opposed to "lie" in most experimental investigations of deception detection. Second, people may not be able to hone their deception detection skills if they receive inadequate feedback concerning whether someone was lying or telling the truth (i.e., in everyday life, we may never find out for sure if a friend or relation was lying to us or not). People may also rely too much on stereotypical cues of deception, such as an inability to maintain eye contact, nervous fidgeting, and slow, staccato speech patterns, cues that may be unrelated to actual deception (DePaulo et al., 2003). Furthermore, because deceivers are also aware of these stereotypical deception cues, they may take steps to ensure that they monitor and control these "known" clues to deception. For example, in one study, participants engaged in significantly greater eye contact when deceiving as compared with truth telling, presumably in an effort to look more honest (Riggio & Friedman, 1983).

There is some evidence that nonverbal decoding abilities, including deception detection, are correlated, although the magnitude of relationships is modest. For example, the ability to detect one kind of lie is related to detecting the accuracy of another form of lie (Frank & Ekman, 1997). In addition, the ability to detect deception is slightly positively related to the ability to decode nonverbal cues of emotion (Buller & Burgoon, 1994; Malone & DePaulo, 2001). Likewise, a review of intercorrelations among standardized performance measures of decoding skill (e.g., PONS, IPT, CARAT) shows that there are positive relationships among the tests, but they are quite modest (Hall, 2001). This result suggests, perhaps, that nonverbal decoding skill is complex and multifaceted, consisting of multiple abilities that are somewhat related to, but considerably independent from, one another.

◆ Skill in Nonverbal Encoding

Nonverbal encoding skill, also referred to as *nonverbal expressiveness*, involves the ability to send nonverbal messages to others accurately. Typically, performance measures of individual differences in nonverbal encoding consist of videotaping participants while they are sending emotional expressions spontaneously or while posing them on cue. For example, Buck's (2005) slide-viewing technique was reviewed earlier as a method of assessing nonverbal decoding skill. But the slide-viewing technique can also be used to measure individual differences in the spontaneous *encoding* of emotions: A measure of spontaneous encoding ability consists of the percentage of judges who can identify the emotion being portrayed correctly via facial expressions while the sender is viewing or discussing the emotion-evoking slide. More frequently, however, participants are asked to pose an emotion with either a facial expression or facially and vocally while reciting some content-standard sentence or phrase. In other instances, encoders may be asked to pose a positive or negative affect (i.e., liking or disliking) toward a person or object. Scores of nonverbal encoding ability consist of the percentage of judges who identify correctly the posed emotion or affect (e.g., Zaidel & Mehrabian, 1969; Zuckerman, Lipets, Koivumaki, & Rosenthal, 1975).

Unlike measures of nonverbal decoding ability, there are no standardized observation-based tests of nonverbal encoding ability readily available. Instead, researchers have either used the slide-viewing technique or created some form of posed nonverbal encoding task to measure individual differences. For example, in a series of studies, nonverbal encoding ability was measured by having participants pose each of six basic emotional expressions to a video camera while saying content-standard sentences (Friedman, Prince, Riggio, & DiMatteo, 1980). Persons scoring high on posed emotional encoding were evaluated as better speakers and were viewed as more likable than individuals scoring low on encoding ability (Riggio & Friedman, 1986). Good encoders of emotion were also more successful deceivers than were poor encoders (Riggio & Friedman, 1983).

Assessment of nonverbal or emotional encoding ability is a costly and time-consuming procedure that involves the use of multiple judges to obtain reliable scores concerning the individual senders' accuracy. As a result, researchers have turned to other methods to measure emotional encoding skill and have had good success using self-report means to assess nonverbal or emotional expressiveness. Zuckerman and Larrance's (1979) PEA measure, mentioned earlier, was the first such published measure. The Affective Communication Test (ACT; Friedman et al., 1980) has been used widely

as a measure of nonverbal encoding skill, although it is related more to spontaneous emotional encoding than to posed sending of emotions (Riggio & Riggio, 2005). Personality scholars have shown renewed interest in emotional expressiveness in the past decade, and several newer self-report measures have been developed, including the Berkeley Expressivity Questionnaire (BEQ; Gross & John, 1995) and the Emotional Expressivity Scale (EES; Kring, Smith, & Neale, 1994). All these measures are relatively brief, self-report instruments ranging from 13 to 17 items. For a review of these measures, see Riggio and Riggio (2005).

Whereas the PEA did not correlate significantly with either posed or spontaneous emotional encoding tasks (Zuckerman & Larrance, 1979), the other self-report measures (ACT, BEQ, and EES) have all correlated positively and significantly with emotional encoding tasks (Friedman & Riggio, 1999; Friedman et al., 1980; Gross & John, 1995; Kring et al., 1994). Moreover, persons scoring high on self-report measures of nonverbal or emotional encoding ability make more positive first impressions (Friedman, Riggio, & Casella, 1988), appear more attractive to others (DePaulo, Blank, Swaim, & Hairfield, 1992), are more socially self-confident and less lonely and shy (Friedman et al., 1980; Riggio, 1986), and report larger and more supportive social networks (Friedman et al., 1980; Riggio, 1992a) than do individuals scoring low on self-report measures of emotional or nonverbal expressiveness.

There is specific evidence of the tie between encoding abilities. In one of the earliest studies of the emotional contagion process, for instance, Friedman and Riggio (1981) found that nonverbally expressive individuals, as measured by the ACT, were able to "infect" others with their emotions through purely nonverbal channels. Nonverbal expressiveness has also been implicated in the ability to deceive successfully, but the relationship is complex. Nonverbally expressive individuals, as measured by a posed emotional encoding task, were somewhat more successful at deceiving others, but much of their success was related to a "demeanor bias." That is, they simply looked more honest and truthful than nonexpressive persons regardless of whether they were truth telling or lying. Presumably, this was due to their tendency to be animated and expressive and to avoid "nervous" cues that are stereotypically associated with deception (Riggio & Friedman, 1983).

Nonverbal or emotional expressiveness has often been either equated with the personality trait of extraversion or considered a component of it. Consistent evidence suggests, however, that although expressiveness and extraversion are related, they are different constructs (Friedman, 1983; Riggio & Riggio, 2002). The fact that nonverbal expressive ability is most often measured via self-report instruments (with shared method variance inflating the correlations between measures of expressiveness and measures of extraversion) further drives the misconception that expressiveness is "just extraversion."

The ability to convey nonverbal messages to others, particularly the sending of emotional messages, is a critical skill for social success, and a fundamental component of the larger construct of communication competence (see Greene & Burleson, 2003). Performance-based measurement of nonverbal encoding skill is a difficult task; therefore, it has not received as much attention as nonverbal decoding ability. Instead, researchers have relied on self-report measures of nonverbal expressiveness. Whereas evidence suggests that the ability to express positive emotions creates more favorable impressions and can positively influence others' moods, the expression of negative

affect, such as the spontaneous expression of anger or dislike, can have equally negative outcomes (see Burgoon & Bacue, 2003). Therefore, it is important to consider the monitoring and regulation of expressive displays when discussing competence in nonverbal skills and abilities.

◆ Skill in Nonverbal Regulation and Control

Skill in nonverbal communication involves more than just encoding and decoding abilities. The ability to regulate and control one's nonverbal communication is also a key component of what it means to be "nonverbally skilled" (Riggio, 1986). Specifically, the ability to regulate both the experience of emotions and the expression of those emotions has received a great deal of attention (e.g., Eisenberg, Champion, & Ma, 2004; Gross, 1998). People learn to suppress the expression of emotions, which is likely responsible for the consistent differences in emotional expressiveness due to culture (Ekman & Friesen, 1969; Matsumoto, 2001, this volume; Matsumoto & Yoo, 2005; but see Fridlund, 1994, this volume, for an alternative view) and gender (Hall, Carter, & Horgan, 2000; Riggio & Carney, 2003). Regulating or managing emotions is also one of the core elements in the abilities model of emotional intelligence (Mayer et al., 2000). Gross (2001) suggests that regulation of emotion can involve two processes: reappraisal and suppression. Reappraisal involves altering both the experience and the expression of an emotion, whereas suppression involves the inhibition of emotionally expressive behavior. In either case, the nonverbal communication of emotion can be controlled and can thus be considered an "ability."

Snyder's (1974, 1987) research on self-monitoring represents some of the earliest work attempting to measure control over nonverbal communication. By definition, self-monitoring is, in part, the ability to monitor, regulate, and control one's nonverbal displays. Yet self-monitoring also involves being attentive to others' nonverbal cues and an ability to adjust one's own expressive behavior to try to "fit in" to social situations. It has been argued, based on factor analyses of Snyder's (1974) self-monitoring scale, that the SMS also measures elements of nonverbal encoding and decoding skill (Riggio & Friedman, 1982). Indeed, a key validation study conducted by Snyder (1974) involved correlating SMS scores with posed emotional encoding and decoding tasks. Positive relationships between SMS and emotional encoding and decoding success suggest that self-monitoring could represent a measure of global social skill or competence. Factor analyses of the original SMS demonstrated separate factors that measured *other-directedness*, a tendency to focus on others' behavior, likely a prerequisite for nonverbal decoding skill, and *extraversion-acting*, a factor that involves not only control or communication but also a form of social acting skill that would be related to posed nonverbal encoding skill (Briggs & Cheek, 1988; Briggs, Cheek, & Buss, 1980). These results suggest that global nonverbal and social skills or competence is composed of encoding, decoding, and regulatory skills, inspiring a more general, multidimensional model of nonverbal and social skills (Riggio, 1986, 1989; Riggio & Carney, 2003).

In this multidimensional nonverbal and social skill model, *emotional control* (EC) is one of three core elements of nonverbal skill that involves the ability to control and regulate emotional and nonverbal displays. The other two elements in this model, discussed earlier, are emotional or nonverbal encoding (labeled *emotional expressivity*) and decoding (labeled *emotional sensitivity*).

Individuals scoring high on EC, for example, are able to stifle the expression of felt emotions or cover the display of the felt emotion with another emotional "mask." Tucker and Riggio (1988) found that individuals scoring high on EC were more difficult to decode in a spontaneous emotional sending using the slide-viewing technique, suggesting that they monitor and stifle their emotional expressions. Research also suggests that persons with high levels of EC have greater comfort speaking before large audiences, performed better in a discussion-oriented problem-solving group, and had more formal acting experience than persons lacking EC (Riggio, 1986; Riggio, Riggio, Salinas, & Cole, 2003).

Another measure of the ability to control nonverbal and emotional communication is the Emotion Regulation Questionnaire (ERQ), a 10-item self-report instrument with subscales measuring the ability to regulate emotions via reappraisal or suppression (Gross & John, 2003). Research using the ERQ suggests that there are psychologically "healthy" and "unhealthy" means to regulate and control the expression of emotion. For example, reappraisal-based EC or regulation leads to more positive outcomes (e.g., positive emotions, well-being), whereas controlling the expression of emotion via suppression leads to more negative outcomes. Riggio and Zimmerman (1991) found that persons scoring high on SSI-EC reported using social support strategies less to cope with stress, whereas persons scoring high on emotional expressiveness and sensitivity reported having larger supportive social networks and making greater use of social support strategies to cope with stress.

The ability to control strong emotions can be an asset in formal social settings, such as in public speaking, in the workplace, and in positions of authority when under crisis or stress, where an individual would not want to arouse others' anxiety levels further by nonverbally conveying his or her own anxiety and fears. Similarly, regulation and suppression of anxiety should lead high-control individuals to be more effective deceivers, although this was not the case in a study of deception that did not involve strong emotions or arousal (Riggio, Tucker, & Throckmorton, 1988). Bonanno and colleagues (2004) argue that abilities to both enhance and suppress emotional expression lead to greater flexibility and positive psychosocial outcomes. This suggests that having a broad repertoire of nonverbal skills is most important for social effectiveness and psychosocial well-being.

Riggio and colleagues (Perez & Riggio, 2003; Riggio, 1986; Riggio & Carney, 2003) have argued, however, that whereas possession of high levels of nonverbal and social skills is important for social success and personal adjustment, there needs to be a "balance" among the skills. For example, being overly emotionally expressive without possessing the ability to regulate and control that expressiveness is typically maladaptive. Emotionally expressive individuals who lack the ability to regulate these displays may appear emotionally unstable and "out of control." Similarly, being overly sensitive to nonverbal cues can make one susceptible to emotional contagion processes as discussed earlier. Perez, Riggio, and Kopelowicz (in press) found a connection between lack of balance among nonverbal and social skills and poor psychological adjustment in clinical patients.

◆ **The Skill Approach to Nonverbal Communication: Unrealized Potential**

There is more to nonverbal skill than just the ability to encode and decode nonverbal messages. Monitoring, regulation, and

control of nonverbal communication represent a set of complex skills that are particularly important for effective interpersonal communication. Indeed, each of the three areas of nonverbal skill just reviewed—decoding, encoding, and control—are each internally complex and multifaceted. There is still a great deal of research to be done to understand the domain of nonverbal communication skills fully.

The study of nonverbal communication has been dominated by the study of functions and process. Early research focused primarily on the meaning of various nonverbal behaviors, such as the communicative function of facial expressions (e.g., Ekman, Friesen, & Ellsworth, 1972), gestures (Birdwhistell, 1970), posture (e.g., Mehrabian, 1969), touch (e.g., Henley, 1977), and vocalics (e.g., Argyle, 1999). Later research used the "lens model" perspective (Brunswik, 1956) to try to understand the process by which, for example, a sender uses nonverbal cues to affect, persuade, or influence others or to understand the person perception process (see DePaulo & Friedman, 1998).

There has been comparatively little attention given to individual differences in the ability to communicate nonverbally. Friedman (1979) saw great potential in using the concept of skill in nonverbal communication to reframe thinking about individual differences from the traditional trait approach to more objectively measured skills and abilities. More than 25 years ago, he predicted that "the next few years will likely see a proliferation of measures of nonverbal sensitivity, nonverbal expressiveness, deceptive abilities, rhythm, expressive style, channel preference, self-monitoring, and the like" (Friedman, 1979, p. 23). In actuality, there have been relatively few measures of nonverbal skill (most of which are reviewed in this chapter), and these are not used widely. Research on individual differences is still dominated by traditional personality measures, with Big Five measures used in the majority of investigations. Indeed, a literature search turned up more than 1,000 publications with either "Big Five" or "NEO" (the primary Big Five scale) in the title as opposed to 35 publications with "nonverbal skill" or "nonverbal ability."

Admittedly, performance measures of nonverbal skill are extremely costly to develop, are time-consuming to administer, and sample only a limited "slice" of nonverbal behavior. The last characteristic may not be much of a problem, however, because thin slices can be quite informative (Ambady, LaPlante, & Johnson, 2001; Ambady & Rosenthal, 1992). It was, in fact, the time and costs issue that led this author to the development of self-report measures of nonverbal and social skill. These measures were supposed to be a "stopgap" until we could develop a battery of performance-based measures assessing the broad range of nonverbal skills and abilities suggested by nonverbal communication research. Because the self-report measures seemed to do the job and took on a life of their own, the standardized performance measures were never pursued fully. The technology exists, however, to have persons pose or spontaneously express emotions while being videotaped and then to have those videotaped expressions compared with templates of "correct" prototype emotional expressions. Similar technology could be used to assess performance-based abilities to regulate and control emotional expressions.

A similar situation exists in personnel selection. Assessment centers offer a performance-based alternative to traditional pencil-and-paper testing in evaluating job applicants (usually for managerial positions). The assessment center requires applicants to engage in a variety of work-related simulations, such as making a formal presentation, coaching a subordinate, participating in a group discussion, and other exercises, many of which are designed to assess, in part, communication and "people" skills (Howard, 1997; Thornton, 1992). Trained observers then evaluate the participants' performance by rating, for example, their communication skills, rapport with others, and decision making. There is evidence that possession of nonverbal and social skills does predict performance on many assessment center tasks (Riggio et al., 1997). Yet the question of whether it is worth the trouble to get these expensive and time-consuming performance-based assessments is one that parallels the work on measuring nonverbal skills and abilities.

The recent explosion of interest in emotional intelligence has fueled the development of measures, particularly those of Mayer, Salovey, and associates (Mayer et al., 1997, 2002), that assess components of nonverbal skill. These researchers are, in many ways, reinventing the decades-old measures of nonverbal decoding skill and encountering many of the same problems that plagued the nonverbal communication scholars (Ciarrochi, Chan, Caputi, & Roberts, 2001). Many emotional intelligence researchers, however, are simply opting for the easier to administer self-report measures. Despite their conceptual similarity, the two lines of research—skill in nonverbal communication and emotional intelligence—have rarely crossed. Perhaps, this will change with increasing recognition that both are focusing on the same phenomena.

◆ References

Ambady, N., Hallahan, M., & Rosenthal, R. (1995). On judging and being judged accurately in zero-acquaintance situations. *Journal of Personality and Social Psychology, 69*, 518–529.

Ambady, N., LaPlante, D., & Johnson, E. (2001). Thin-slice judgments as a measure of interpersonal sensitivity. In J. A. Hall & F. J. Bernieri (Eds.), *Interpersonal sensitivity: Theory and measurement* (pp. 89–101). Mahwah, NJ: Erlbaum.

Ambady, N., & Rosenthal, R. (1992). Thin slices of expressive behavior as predictors of interpersonal consequences: A meta-analysis. *Psychological Bulletin, 111,* 256–274.

Archer, D., & Costanzo, M. (1988). *The Interpersonal Perception Task.* Berkeley, CA: University of California Extension Media Center.

Archer, D., Costanzo, M., & Akert, R. (2001). The Interpersonal Perception Task (IPT): Alternative approaches to problems of theory and design. In J. A. Hall & F. J. Bernieri (Eds.), *Interpersonal sensitivity: Theory and measurement* (pp. 161–182). Mahwah, NJ: Erlbaum.

Argyle, M. (1999). Nonverbal vocalizations. In L. K. Guerrero, J. A. DeVito, & M. L. Hecht (Eds.). *The nonverbal communication reader: Classic and contemporary readings* (pp. 135–148). Prospect Heights, IL: Waveland Press.

Bar-On, R. (1997). *Bar-On Emotional Quotient Inventory: Technical manual.* Toronto, Canada: Multi-Health Systems.

Bernieri, F. J. (2001). Toward a taxonomy of interpersonal sensitivity. In J. A. Hall & F. J. Bernieri (Eds.), *Interpersonal sensitivity: Theory and measurement* (pp. 3–20). Mahwah, NJ: Erlbaum.

Bernieri, F. J., & Gillis, J. S. (2001). Judging rapport: Employing Brunswik's lens model to study interpersonal sensitivity. In J. A. Hall & F. J. Bernieri (Eds.), *Interpersonal sensitivity: Theory and measurement* (pp. 67–88). Mahwah, NJ: Erlbaum.

Bernieri, F. J, & Rosenthal, R. (1991). Coordinated movement in human interaction. In R. S. Feldman & B. Rime (Eds.), *Fundamentals of nonverbal behavior* (pp. 401–432). New York: Cambridge University Press.

Birdwhistell, R. L. (1970). *Kinesics and context: Essays on body motion communication.* Philadelphia: University of Pennsylvania Press.

Bonanno, G. A., Papa, A., Lalande, K., Wesphal, M., & Coifman, K. (2004). The importance of being flexible: The ability to both enhance and suppress emotional expression predicts long-term adjustment. *Psychological Science, 15,* 482–487.

Briggs, S. R., & Cheek, J. M. (1988). On the nature of self-monitoring: Problems with assessment, problems with validity. *Journal of Personality & Social Psychology, 54,* 663–678.

Briggs, S. R., Cheek, J. M., & Buss, A. H. (1980). An analysis of the self-monitoring scale. *Journal of Personality & Social Psychology, 38,* 679–686.

Brunswik, E. (1956). *Perception and the representative design of psychological experiments* (2nd ed.). Berkeley, CA: University of California Press.

Buck, R. (1976). A test of nonverbal receiving ability: Preliminary studies. *Human Communication Research, 2,* 162–171.

Buck, R. (1978). The slide-viewing technique for measuring nonverbal sending accuracy: A guide for replication. *Catalog of Selected Documents in Psychology, 8,* 62.

Buck, R. (2005). Measuring emotional experience, expression, and communication: The slide-viewing technique. In V. Manusov (Ed.), *The sourcebook of nonverbal measures: Going beyond words* (pp. 457–470). Mahwah, NJ: Erlbaum.

Buck, R., Miller, R. E., & Caul, W. F. (1974). Sex, personality and physiological variables in the communication of emotion via facial expression. *Journal of Personality and Social Psychology, 30,* 587–596.

Buck, R., Savin, V. J., Miller, R. E., & Caul, W. F. (1972). Nonverbal communication of affect in humans. *Journal of Personality and Social Psychology, 23,* 362–371.

Buller, D. B., & Burgoon, J. K. (1994). Deception: Strategic and nonstrategic communication. In J. A. Daly & J. M. Wiemann (Eds.), *Strategic interpersonal communication* (pp. 191–224). Hillsdale, NJ: Erlbaum.

Burgoon, J. K., & Bacue, A. E. (2003). Nonverbal communication skills. In J. O. Greene & B. R. Burleson (Eds.), *Handbook of communication and social interaction skills* (pp. 179–219). Mahwah, NJ: Erlbaum.

Caruso, D. R., Mayer, J. D., & Salovey, P. (2002). Emotional intelligence and emotional leadership. In R. E. Riggio, S. E. Murphy, & F. J. Pirozzolo (Eds.), *Multiple intelligences and leadership* (pp. 55–74). Mahwah, NJ: Erlbaum.

Ciarrochi, J., Chan, A., Caputi, P., & Roberts, R. (2001). Measuring emotional intelligence. In J. Ciarrochi, J. P. Forgas, & J. D. Mayer (Eds.). *Emotional intelligence in everyday life: A scientific inquiry* (pp. 25–45). Philadelphia: Psychology Press.

Costanzo, M. A., & Archer, D. (1989). Interpreting the expressive behavior of others: The Interpersonal Perception Task (IPT). *Journal of Nonverbal Behavior, 13,* 225–245.

Costanzo, M. A., & Archer, D. (1993). *The Interpersonal Perception Task-15 (IPT-15).* Berkeley, CA: University of California Extension Media Center.

Davis, M. H. (1983). Measuring individual differences in empathy: Evidence for a multidimensional approach. *Journal of Personality and Social Psychology, 44,* 113–126.

Davis, M. H. (1994). *Empathy: A social psychological approach.* Boulder, CO: Westview.

DePaulo, B. M., Blank, A. L., Swaim, G. W., & Hairfield, J. G. (1992). Expressiveness and expressive control. *Personality and Social Psychology Bulletin, 18,* 276–285.

DePaulo, B. M., & Friedman, H. S. (1998). Nonverbal communication. In D. T. Gilbert, S. T. Fiske, & G. Lindzey (Eds.), *The handbook of social psychology* (4th ed., pp. 3–40). New York: McGraw-Hill.

DePaulo, B. M., Lindsay, J. J., Malone, B. E., Muhlenbruck, L., Charlton, K., & Cooper, H. (2003). Cues to deception. *Psychological Bulletin, 129,* 74–118.

de Turck, M. A., Harszlak, J. J., Bodhorn, D. J., & Texter, L. A. (1990). The effects of training social perceivers to detect deception from behavioral cues. *Communication Quarterly, 38,* 189–199.

DiMatteo, M. R., Friedman, H. S., & Taranta, A. (1979). Sensitivity to bodily nonverbal communication as a factor in practitioner-patient rapport. *Journal of Nonverbal Behavior, 4,* 18–26.

Duke, M., & Nowicki, S., Jr. (2005). The Emory Dyssemia Index. In V. Manusov (Ed.), *The sourcebook for nonverbal measures: Going beyond words* (pp. 35–46). Mahwah, NJ: Erlbaum.

Eisenberg, N., Champion, C., & Ma, Y. (2004). Emotion-related regulation: An emerging construct. *Merrill-Palmer Quarterly, 50,* 236–259.

Ekman, P. (1985). *Telling lies: Clues to deceit in the marketplace, marriage, and politics.* New York: Norton.

Ekman, P., & Friesen, W. V. (1969). The repertoire of nonverbal behavior: Categories, origins, usage, and coding. *Semiotica, 1,* 49–98.

Ekman, P., & Friesen, W. V. (1974). Nonverbal behavior and psychopathology. In R. J. Friedman & M. Katz (Eds.), *The psychology of depression: Contemporary theory and research* (pp. 3–31). Washington, DC: Winston & Sons.

Ekman, P., Friesen, W. V., & Ellsworth, P. C. (1972). *Emotions in the human face: Guidelines for research and an integration of findings.* New York: Pergamon.

Ekman, P., O'Sullivan, M., & Frank, M. G. (1999). A few can catch a liar. *Psychological Science, 10,* 263–266.

Frank, M. G., & Ekman, P. (1997). The ability to detect deceit generalizes across different types of high-stake lies. *Journal of Personality and Social Psychology, 72,* 1429–1439.

Fridlund, A. J. (1994). *Human facial expression: An evolutionary view.* San Diego, CA: Academic Press.

Friedman, H. S. (1979). The concept of skill in nonverbal communication: Implications for understanding social interaction. In R. Rosenthal (Ed.), *Skill in nonverbal communication* (pp. 2–27). Cambridge, MA: Oelgeschlager, Gunn, & Hain.

Friedman, H. S. (1983). On shutting one's eyes to face validity. *Psychological Bulletin, 94,* 185–187.

Friedman, H. S., Prince, L. M., Riggio, R. E., & DiMatteo, M. R. (1980). Understanding and assessing nonverbal expressiveness:

The Affective Communication Test. *Journal of Personality and Social Psychology, 39,* 333–351.

Friedman, H. S., & Riggio, R. E. (1981). Effect of individual differences in nonverbal expressiveness on transmission of emotion. *Journal of Nonverbal Behavior, 6,* 96–104.

Friedman, H. S., & Riggio, R. E. (1999). Individual differences in ability to encode complex affects. *Personality and Individual Differences, 27,* 181–194.

Friedman, H. S., Riggio, R. E., & Casella, D. F. (1988). Nonverbal skill, personal charisma, and initial attraction. *Personality and Social Psychology Bulletin, 14,* 203–211.

Goleman, D. (1995). *Emotional intelligence: Why it can matter more than IQ.* New York: Bantam.

Goleman, D. (1998). *Working with emotional intelligence.* New York: Bantam.

Greene, J. O., & Burleson, B. R. (Eds.) (2003). *Handbook of communication and social interaction skills.* Mahwah, NJ: Erlbaum.

Gross, J. J. (1998). The emerging field of emotion regulation: An integrative review. *Review of General Psychology, 2,* 271–299.

Gross, J. J. (2001). Emotion regulation in adulthood: Timing is everything. *Current Directions in Psychological Science, 10,* 214–219.

Gross, J. J., & John, O. P. (1995). Facets of emotional expressivity: Three self-report factors and their correlates. *Personality and Individual Differences, 19,* 555–568.

Gross, J. J., & John, O. P. (2003). Individual differences in two emotion regulation processes: Implications for affect, relationships, and well-being. *Journal of Personality and Social Psychology, 85,* 348–362.

Hall, J. A. (2001). The *PONS* test and the psychometric approach to measuring interpersonal sensitivity. In J. A. Hall & F. J. Bernieri (Eds.), *Interpersonal sensitivity: Theory and measurement* (pp. 143–160). Mahwah, NJ: Erlbaum.

Hall, J. A., & Carter, J. D. (1999). Gender-stereotype accuracy as an individual difference. *Journal of Personality and Social Psychology, 77,* 350–359.

Hall, J. A., Carter, J. D., & Horgan, T. G. (2000). Gender differences in nonverbal communication of emotion. In A. H. Fischer (Ed.), *Gender and emotion: Social psychological perspectives* (pp. 97–117). New York: Cambridge University Press.

Harris, M. J., & Rosenthal, R. (2005). No more teachers' dirty looks: Effects of teacher nonverbal behavior on student outcomes. In R. E. Riggio & R. S. Feldman (Eds.), *Applications of nonverbal communication* (pp. 157–192). Mahwah, NJ: Erlbaum.

Hatfield, E., Cacioppo, J. T., & Rapson, R. (1994). *Emotional contagion.* Cambridge, England: Cambridge University Press.

Henley, N. (1977). *Body politics: Power, sex, and nonverbal communication.* Englewood Cliffs, NJ: Prentice-Hall.

Hodgins, H., & Zuckerman, M. (1990). The effect of nonverbal sensitivity on social interaction. *Journal of Nonverbal Behavior, 24,* 155–170.

Howard, A. (1997). A reassessment of assessment centers: Challenges for the 21st century. *Journal of Social Behavior and Personality, 12*(5), 13–52.

Iizuka, Y., Patterson, M. L., & Matchen, J. C. (2002). Accuracy and confidence on the Interpersonal Perception Task: A Japanese-American comparison. *Journal of Nonverbal Behavior, 26,* 159–174.

Kring, A. M., Smith, D. A., & Neale, J. M. (1994). Individual differences in dispositional expressiveness: Development and validation of the emotional expressivity scale. *Journal of Personality and Social Psychology, 66,* 934–949.

Losoya, S. H., & Eisenberg, N. (2001). Affective empathy. In J. A. Hall & F. J. Bernieri (Eds.), *Interpersonal sensitivity: Theory and measurement* (pp. 21–43). Mahwah, NJ: Erlbaum.

Malone, B. E., & DePaulo, B. M. (2001). Measuring sensitivity to deception. In J. A. Hall & F. J. Bernieri (Eds.), *Interpersonal sensitivity: Theory and measurement* (pp. 103–124). Mahwah, NJ: Erlbaum.

Mast, M. (2002). Dominance as expressed and inferred through speaking time: A meta-analysis. *Human Communication Research, 28,* 420–450.

Matsumoto, D. (2001). Culture and emotion. In D. Matsumoto (Ed.), *The handbook of culture and psychology* (pp. 171–194). New York: Oxford University Press.

Matsumoto, D., LeRoux, J., Wilson-Cohn, C., Raroque, J., Kooken, K., Ekman, P., et al. (2000). A new test to measure emotion recognition ability: Matsumoto and Ekman's Japanese and Caucasian Brief Affect Recognition Test (JACBART). *Journal of Nonverbal Behavior, 24,* 179–209.

Matsumoto, D., & Yoo, S. E. (2005). Culture and applied nonverbal communication. In R. E. Riggio & R. S. Feldman (Eds.), *Applications of nonverbal communication* (pp. 255–277). Mahwah, NJ: Erlbaum.

Mayer, J. D., & Salovey, P. (1997). What is emotional intelligence? In P. Salovey & J. D. Sluyter (Eds.). *Emotional development and emotional intelligence.* New York: Basic Books.

Mayer, J. D., Salovey, P., & Caruso, D. R. (1997). *Multifactor Emotional Intelligence Test (MEIS).* Needham, MA: Allyn & Bacon.

Mayer, J. D., Salovey, P., & Caruso, D. R. (2000). Models of emotional intelligence. In R. J. Sternberg (Ed.), *The handbook of intelligence* (pp. 396–420). New York: Cambridge University Press.

Mayer, J. D., Salovey, P., & Caruso, D. R. (2002). *Mayer-Salovey-Caruso Emotional Intelligence Test (MSCEIT) user's manual.* Toronto, Canada: MHS Publishers.

Mehrabian, A. (1969). Significance of posture and position in the communication of attitude and status relationships. *Psychological Bulletin, 71,* 359–372.

Nowicki, S., & Duke, M. P. (1994). Individual differences in the nonverbal communication of affect: The Diagnostic Analysis of Nonverbal Accuracy scale. *Journal of Nonverbal Behavior, 18,* 9–35.

Nowicki, S., & Duke, M. P. (2001). Nonverbal receptivity: The Diagnostic Analysis of Nonverbal Accuracy (DANVA). In J. A. Hall & F. J. Bernieri (Eds.), *Interpersonal sensitivity: Theory and measurement* (pp. 183–198). Mahwah, NJ: Erlbaum.

O'Sullivan, M. (2005). Emotional intelligence and deception detection: Why most people can't "read" others, but a few can. In R. E. Riggio & R. S. Feldman (Eds.), *Applications of nonverbal communication* (pp. 215–253). Mahwah, NJ: Erlbaum.

Patterson, M. L., Foster, J. L., & Bellmer, C. G. (2001). Another look at accuracy in social judgments. *Journal of Nonverbal Behavior, 25,* 207–219.

Perez, J. E., & Riggio, R. E. (2003). Nonverbal social skills and psychopathology. In P. Philippot, E. J. Coats, & R. S. Feldman (Eds.), *Nonverbal behavior in clinical settings* (pp. 17–44). New York: Oxford University Press.

Perez, J. E., Riggio, R. E., & Kopelowicz, A. (in press). Social skill imbalances as indicators of psychopathology: An exploratory investigation. *Personality and Individual Differences.*

Riggio, H. R., & Riggio, R. E. (2002). Emotional expressiveness, extraversion, and neuroticism: A meta-analysis. *Journal of Nonverbal Behavior, 26,* 195–218.

Riggio, R. E. (1986). Assessment of basic social skills. *Journal of Personality and Social Psychology, 51,* 649–660.

Riggio, R. E. (1989). *Manual for the Social Skills Inventory: Research edition.* Palo Alto, CA: Consulting Psychologists Press.

Riggio, R. E. (1992a). Social interaction skills and nonverbal behavior. In R. S. Feldman (Ed.), *Applications of nonverbal behavioral theories and research* (pp. 3–30). Hillsdale, NJ: Erlbaum.

Riggio, R. E. (1992b). Detecting lies and deception. *The Long Term View, 1,* 9–14.

Riggio, R. E. (2005). The Social Skills Inventory (SSI): Measuring nonverbal and social skills. In V. Manusov (Ed.), *The sourcebook of nonverbal measures: Going beyond words* (pp. 25–33). Mahwah, NJ: Erlbaum.

Riggio, R. E., Aguirre, M., Mayes, B. T., Belloli, C., & Kubiak, C. (1997). The use of assessment center methods for student outcome assessment. *Journal of Social Behavior and Personality, 12,* 273–288.

Riggio, R. E., & Carney, D. R. (2003). *Social Skills Inventory manual* (2nd ed.). Redwood City, CA: MindGarden.

Riggio, R. E., & Friedman, H. S. (1982). The interrelationships of self-monitoring factors, personality traits, and nonverbal social skills. *Journal of Nonverbal Behavior, 7,* 33–45.

Riggio, R. E., & Friedman, H. S. (1983). Individual differences and cues to deception. *Journal of Personality and Social Psychology, 45,* 899–915.

Riggio, R. E., & Friedman, H. S. (1986). Impression formation: The role of expressive behavior. *Journal of Personality and Social Psychology, 50,* 421–427.

Riggio, R. E., & Riggio, H. R. (2001). Self-report measurement of interpersonal sensitivity. In J. A. Hall & F. J. Bernieri (Eds.), *Interpersonal sensitivity: Theory and measurement* (pp. 127–142). Mahwah, NJ: Erlbaum.

Riggio, R. E., & Riggio, H. R. (2005). Self-report measures of emotional and nonverbal expressiveness. In V. Manusov (Ed.), *The sourcebook of nonverbal measures: Going beyond words* (pp. 105–111). Mahwah, NJ: Erlbaum.

Riggio, R. E., Riggio, H. R., Salinas, C., & Cole, E. J. (2003). The role of social and emotional communication skills in leader emergence and effectiveness. *Group Dynamics: Theory, Research, and Practice, 7,* 83–103.

Riggio, R. E., Watring, K., & Throckmorton, B. (1993). Social skills, social support, and psychosocial adjustment. *Personality and Individual Differences, 15,* 275–280.

Riggio, R. E., & Zimmerman, J. A. (1991). Social skills and interpersonal relationships: Influences on social support and support seeking. In W. H. Jones & D. Perlman (Eds.), *Advances in personal relationships* (Vol. 2, pp. 133–155). London: Jessica Kingsley Press.

Rosenthal, R. (Ed.). (1979). *Skill in nonverbal communication.* Cambridge, MA: Oelgeschlager, Gunn, & Hain.

Rosenthal, R., Hall, J. A., DiMatteo, M. R., Rogers, P. L., & Archer, D. (1979). *Sensitivity to nonverbal communications: The PONS test.* Baltimore, MD: Johns Hopkins University Press.

Rosenthal, R., & Jacobson, L. (1968). *Pygmalion in the classroom.* New York: Holt, Rinehart, and Winston.

Salovey, P., & Mayer, J. D. (1990). Emotional intelligence. *Imagination, Cognition, and Personality, 9,* 185–211.

Snyder, M. (1974). The self-monitoring of expressive behavior. *Journal of Personality and Social Psychology, 30,* 526–537.

Snyder, M. (1987). *Public appearances/private realities: The psychology of self-monitoring.* New York: W.H. Freeman.

Taylor, S. J. (2002). *Effects of a nonverbal skill training program on perceptions of personal charisma.* Unpublished doctoral dissertation, University of California at Riverside.

Thornton, G. C. (1992). *Assessment centers in human resource management.* Reading, MA: Addison-Wesley.

Tucker, J. S., & Riggio, R. E. (1988). The role of social skills in encoding posed and spontaneous facial expressions. *Journal of Nonverbal Behavior, 12,* 87–97.

Zaidel, S. F., & Mehrabian, A. (1969). The ability to communicate and infer positive and negative attitudes facially and vocally. *Journal of Experimental Research in Personality, 3,* 233–241.

Zuckerman, M., Koestner, R., & Alton, A. O. (1984). Learning to detect deception. *Journal of Personality and Social Psychology, 46,* 519–528.

Zuckerman, M., Koestner, R., & Colella, M. J. (1985). Learning to detect deception from three communication channels. *Journal of Nonverbal Behavior, 9,* 188–194.

Zuckerman, M., & Larrance, D. (1979). Individual differences in perceived encoding and decoding abilities. In R. Rosenthal (Ed.), *Skill in nonverbal communication* (pp. 171–203). Cambridge, MA: Oelgeschlager, Gunn, & Hain.

Zuckerman, M., Lipets, M. S., Koivumaki, J. A., & Rosenthal, R. (1975). Encoding and decoding nonverbal cues of emotion. *Journal of Personality and Social Psychology, 32,* 1068–1076.

6

NONVERBAL AND VERBAL COMMUNICATION

Hand Gestures and Facial Displays as Part of Language Use in Face-to-Face Dialogue[1]

◆ Janet Beavin Bavelas
   University of Victoria

◆ Nicole Chovil
   Independent Researcher and Education Consultant

Of the many different research perspectives on the fundamentals of nonverbal communication, one of the most taken for granted is the relationship between verbal communication and co-occurring non-verbal acts. Most researchers assume that conversational gestures (e.g., illustrators) and some facial actions (e.g., eyebrow emphasizers or a quizzical expression) contribute to the talk-in-progress. This chapter is the

Author's Note: The Social Sciences and Humanities Research Council of Canada has generously provided long-term support for the program of research from which this model developed. We owe a continuing debt to dis-cussions with members of the research team over the years and a particular debt to Jennifer Gerwing's survey of recent gesture research.

next step in a developing model on the contribution of nonverbal communication to face-to-face dialogue (proposed originally in Bavelas & Chovil, 2000). In addition to drawing on the evidence so far, we will suggest new directions for research in this relatively neglected area. Specifically, we will propose four theoretical propositions regarding the subset of nonverbal acts that function as part of language use in face-to-face dialogue and will discuss the logical and empirical evidence for each. We hope that the reader will agree that this area of research and theory is at an exciting point, with enough evidence to be promising but with many more questions and possibilities still open for investigation.

◆ Historical and Theoretical Context

Researchers who focus on face-to-face dialogue have long noted that some nonverbal behaviors can work closely with words, prosody, and each other in ordinary conversation. In our view, the beginning of a systematic theory was in 1955, with the highly influential, although mostly unpublished, Natural History of an Interview project (cf. Leeds-Hurwitz, 1987; McQuowan, 1971). We can then trace a line of proponents of an integrated approach in many disciplines, including Birdwhistell (1966), Scheflen (1968), Ekman and Friesen (1969), Kendon (1972, 1980), Blurton-Jones (1972), Pike (1972), Weiner, Devoe, Rubinow, and Geller (1972), Slama-Cazacu (1976), Duncan and Fiske (1977), Poyatos (1980), Scherer (1980), Linell (1982), McNeill (1985), Goodwin and Goodwin (1986), Sanders (1987), Leeds-Hurwitz (1989), Chovil (1989), Bavelas, Black, Chovil, and Mullett (1990, chap. 6), Fridlund (1991a), Streeck and Knapp (1992), Clark (1996, chap. 6), and Jones and LeBaron (2002). These authors have used a variety of terms for verbal-nonverbal

combinations of words, prosody, hand gestures, facial displays, or gaze, including *mixed syntax* (Slama-Cazacu, 1976), *comprehensive communicative act* (Linell, 1982), *multichannel process* (Leeds-Hurwitz, 1989; Sanders, 1987; Scherer, 1980), *composite signal* (Clark, 1996; Engle & Clark, 1995), *integrated message* (Bavelas & Chovil, 2000), and, most recently, *multimodal communication* (e.g., Engle, 2000), although the last term often includes computers or objects as well as human actions.

The broader context of the approach discussed in this chapter is our interest in the unique features of face-to-face dialogue as a primary mode of language use. Changes in conceptions of language itself have been a boon for conversational hand gestures and facial displays. Historically, when linguists and psycholinguists conceptualized language as an abstract entity or idealized it as written text or formal monologues, all nonverbal acts were either irrelevant or a completely separate communication channel. Recent interest in how interlocutors ordinarily *use* language has led to an emphasis on conversation and, eventually, to face-to-face dialogue. Indeed, many authors (e.g., Bavelas, 1990; Bavelas, Hutchinson, Kenwood, & Matheson, 1997; Clark, 1996, pp. 8–10; Fillmore, 1981; Goodwin, 1981; Levinson, 1983; Linell, 1982) have proposed that face-to-face dialogue, rather than written text or formal monologue, is the fundamental or basic site of language use, for at least three reasons: (1) face-to-face dialogue is arguably the first format for human language in evolutionary terms; (2) in typical development, it is the individual's first language; and (3) it is the most common format for language use in everyday life.

More specifically, we have proposed (e.g., Bavelas, 1990; Bavelas & Chovil, 2000; Bavelas, Coates, & Johnson, 2002; Bavelas, Hutchinson, Kenwood, & Matheson, 1997) that there are two features of dialogue that, in combination, do not occur in other forms of language use such as written text, public speaking, or e-mail. Face-to-face dialogue is, first of all, *dialogue* rather than monologue. It is a collaborative activity (Clark, 1996) with a high degree of reciprocity and mutual influence at a micro-social level (Bavelas, in press); that is, dialogue involves moment-by-moment or even simultaneous responses between the interlocutors. Second, once observed closely, face-to-face dialogue reveals the ubiquity and integral importance of *specific nonverbal acts* in the moment-by-moment interaction. Thus, in addition to rapid social reciprocity, the second key characteristic of face-to-face dialogue is the availability of elements other than words, such as hand gestures, facial displays, and some other nonverbal acts. We propose that these elements serve unique and essential roles in the dialogue.

In the rest of this chapter, we outline four theoretical propositions about the subset of nonverbal acts that are part of language use in face-to-face dialogue, with an emphasis on features that researchers can test both logically and empirically. The first, primary distinguishing characteristic is their *synchrony with spontaneous speech*. Second, these are *symbolic acts* with referents. Third, they are tightly *integrated with words*, although not necessarily redundant with them. Fourth, the participants in dialogue use them *to create and convey shared meanings*. We will review data for hand gestures and facial displays, data that imply possible programs of research for other acts, such as gaze (Bavelas, Coates, & Johnson, 2002). Because of space and the intended readership of this chapter, we will focus primarily on experimental or quantitative data and will not review the rich qualitative work that still leads the way. In our experience, both traditions combine to produce a more refined appreciation of how skillfully and precisely participants communicate in face-to-face dialogue.

Theoretical Propositions

♦ I. Synchrony With Spontaneous Speech in Face-to-Face Dialogue

As noted, our focus in this chapter is on a specific subset within the vast domain of nonverbal behaviors. We do not propose that all nonverbal behaviors function as part of language use. Instead, we propose sharp limits on the behaviors that might be part of integrated verbal and nonverbal messages; therefore, our model includes only certain behaviors when they occur in certain ways in certain settings. Somewhat similar physical behaviors might occur in other ways or in other settings, with no relationship to language use. And there are many, perhaps most, nonverbal behaviors that are unlikely to be related directly to language use. The nested criteria of *setting, timing,* and *meaning* are useful for making these distinctions, as elaborated in the following sections.

FACE-TO-FACE DIALOGUE

To be included in our model of language use, the setting in which the nonverbal acts occur must be spontaneous face-to-face dialogue. That is, both (or all) participants can see and hear each other and can interact freely as themselves.[2] This criterion puts many familiar research settings outside our focus of interest. For example, studies of individuals who are alone or of individuals who are looking at videos or photographs of other individuals do not yield data on face-to-face dialogue. When the speaker or the addressee is an experimenter or confederate, the dialogue is not reciprocally spontaneous; that is, one participant is following scripted guidelines rather than interacting freely.

Even within a dialogue, the nonverbal actions must be visible to the partner, which precludes dialogues through a visual barrier. Similarly, participants may produce muscle movements or physiological patterns that instruments can measure, but if these are not visible to the other participant, then they are not part of the overt face-to-face dialogue as we conceptualize it. All of the above settings and conditions can provide important background information, especially in experimental designs that contrast them to face-to-face dialogue (e.g., manipulating the visual availability of the receiver; cf. Chovil, 1997; Cohen & Harrison, 1973). Indeed, such experiments demonstrate that other settings are not the same as face-to-face dialogue and that we cannot assume generalizability.

SYNCHRONY WITH WORDS

Within the setting of face-to-face dialogue, a further essential criterion for our model is *timing*. The nonverbal acts we are focusing on are synchronized with the words that they accompany, which means that their typical duration will be seconds or even less. Conversational hand gestures, unlike emblems or hand signals in nonspeaking contexts, have a split-second relationship to words (e.g., McNeill, 1992, pp. 25–29). Similarly, although the face is capable of assuming precise stereotypic emotional configurations (e.g., Ekman, 1993), the face in dialogue can be highly mobile (Bavelas & Chovil, 1997), and many of its actions are synchronous with the words of the dialogue rather than the emotional state of a participant (Chovil, 1989, 1991/1992; Ekman, 1997).

The timing requirement also excludes many other nonverbal acts from our subset, including the following: involuntary or reflexive actions (e.g., blinking or breathing), static posture or appearance (e.g., arm or leg positions or cosmetic choices such as clothing or tattoos), and acts that have an obvious noncommunicative function (e.g., hand movements to reach for or manipulate objects or facial adaptors such as licking dry lips or squinting in bright light). None of the above acts is likely to be synchronous with precise words or phrases. It is readily observable, however, that speakers can co-opt almost any physical action conversationally (e.g., when they *demonstrate* blinking, reaching, or gazing; Clark & Gerrig, 1990). Timing as well as form and context make it clear when ordinary actions are being used conversationally, because only the stylized, communicative form would be synchronous with and supplement speech. In short, we are neither claiming nor excluding broad physical categories of behaviors but rather making functional distinctions based on identifiable parameters. Our focus is on what the behavior is *doing*, not on what kind of behavior it is.

CONVERSATIONAL MEANING

So far, we have described two aspects of synchrony between the verbal and nonverbal acts that are included in our model; the setting must be face-to-face dialogue, and the nonverbal acts must be tightly timed with speech. The third criterion is even more specific: The act must have meaning in its particular and immediate conversational context. Words and prosody are audible ways of creating meaning in conversation; we propose that certain nonverbal acts are *visible acts of meaning* (Bavelas & Chovil, 2000). Just like words, however, their meaning is not intrinsic to the isolated act but depends on the linguistic context (see Robinson, this volume). In contrast, emblematic hand gestures and facial expressions of emotion usually have stereotypic forms that are virtually independent of linguistic context. Similarly, the interpretation of many other nonverbal acts (such as those indicating intimacy or deception) does not necessarily depend on the micro-context in which they occur.

The context that determines the meaning of both audible and visible acts of meaning is multilayered and includes who the participants are, why they are talking, how they have been using the word or act so far, the particular topic in that phase of the conversation, the precise point in the utterance, and the simultaneous other elements of the integrated message of which it is a part at that moment. As an example of the importance of all of these layers of context for the meaning of words, the adjective *wide* has a couple dozen meanings in the *Random House Unabridged Dictionary* (1993). Like most words, it is polysemous, yet each meaning is ordinarily unambiguous when it occurs in a particular conversational context (i.e., from a *wide* turn to *wide* awake to nation*wide*).

Similarly, in the following gestural example, the speaker is describing a picture of a dress with an unusually wide hipline, which extends about a meter on either side of the waist (cf. Bavelas, Kenwood, Johnson, & Phillips, 2002, Figure 1). The underlining indicates where gestures occurred in relation to the words; the brackets contain an italicized description of each gesture; and S = speaker, A = addressee. (For readers who do not usually watch conversational actions frame by frame, the best way to understand a written example is to act it out oneself.)

Example 1.

S: "OK. Ah, <u>like a huge skirt that goes out like this</u>?" _____
            [both hands move from waist to full out]   *[holds width]*

A: "<u>Like one of the round ones</u>?" _____
  [hands curve out from waist] *[holds width]*

By moving her hands out and especially by holding them in place at the farthest extent, the speaker indicated, among other things, that the skirt was "wide." The addressee confirmed his understanding by replicating both movements.

In different conversational moments, her gesture for a wide skirt could have indicated the length of a fish that the speaker caught, the metaphorical amount of work the speaker has left to do, or the beginning of a tree-hugging gesture. Yet at the moment it occurred in its particular conversational context—even though there was no reference to "wide" in the words of either person—it was unambiguous. As Goodwin (2000) illustrated through a detailed micro-analysis of a hand gesture, simply "locating the lexical affiliate of a gesture does not constitute establishing its meaning" (p. 92) because the meaning of any word or gesture is usually inseparable from its linguistic and micro-social contexts.

Contextual specificity does not apply only to hand gestures. In the first systematic description of a conversational facial display, Ekman (1979) showed that the same physical eyebrow actions can have several different meanings (e.g., as a baton or a question mark), depending on conversational context. Chovil (1989) found that even stereotypic expressions can have varied meanings. The classic nose-wrinkle of disgust can also convey rejection of other kinds, which have nothing to do with smell (e.g., a disliked movie, an unpleasant chore), and an angry expression may not indicate concomitant anger. In the following example from Chovil's data, the speaker was humorously describing a past argument with her sister about whether she should cut her hair.

Example 2.

S: "I'm goin' like, 'I wanna cut my hair!'"_____

   [exaggerated, stylized anger display]   *[smiles]*

Exactly as she was describing her own part in the argument, she configured her eyes, brows, and mouth in a classic anger display. As soon as the relevant phrase was over, she smiled along with the addressee at her own humor. She was not angry when she made the display; indeed, she may not have been nearly as angry at the time of the argument as the current display indicated. She was exaggerating for effect, as confirmed by her immediate smile, which the addressee shared. We propose that, just as with words, the addressees seldom have difficulty selecting the correct meaning, largely because of the contextual redundancy that supports it.

◆ II. Symbolic Acts

In proposing that a hand gesture or facial display in dialogue is a *symbol*, we intend the simplest sense of the term: Symbols have referents; they are something that stands for something else (Quine, 1987, p. 763). Put in other terms, symbols are encoded acts, although the encoding is ordinarily analogic or iconic (see Bavelas & Chovil, 2000). The case for the proposition that some nonverbal acts are symbolic involves somewhat different issues for hand gestures and for facial displays, which will be treated separately in the following.

HAND GESTURES AS SYMBOLS

McNeill (1992) pointed out that "gestures are not just movements and can never be fully explained in purely kinesic terms. They are not just the arms waving in the air but symbols that exhibit meaning in their own right" (p. 105). Kendon (1985), Clark and Gerrig (1990), and Streeck and Knapp (1992) have also noted that hand gestures can depict, demonstrate, or reenact. There is a difference between a *hand action*, which has a practical function in the material world (e.g., turning on a light switch or holding a telephone) and a *hand gesture*, which has a communicative function in the social world (e.g., as part of telling someone to switch on the light or that you will call them later). Practical and material considerations shape the hand action, but social and communicative considerations shape the hand gesture. Because of these considerations, the hand action and gesture should look different in predictable ways (Gerwing & Bavelas, 2004). Very few studies have even recorded the difference between hand actions and hand gestures; an exception is LeBaron and Streeck's (2000) comparison of instrumental actions to later gestures for the same actions.

Several recent experiments have demonstrated a key part of our proposal, namely, if social and communicative factors shape hand gestures, then these factors should cause variation in gestures for the same referent. Ozyurek (2000, 2002) showed that speakers made a gesture depicting the same motion differently depending on their spatial relationship to their addressees. Other experiments have also demonstrated that the referent is not the sole determinant of the form of a gesture. Rather, linguistic principles unique to dialogue can influence the shape of gestures: When the participants shared common ground about an object, they made sketchier gestures to depict it than when the information was new to one of them (Gerwing & Bavelas, 2004). Similarly, within a dialogue, later gestures for familiar ("given") information were shorter than those for new information (Woods, 2005). These effects are identical to the effects of given-versus-new information on verbal communication, such as the length of verbal reference (e.g., Fowler, 1988). The results also accord with Grice's (1967/1989) maxims of manner and quantity: The sketchier or shorter gestures were sufficient for their purpose but no more than that.

FACIAL DISPLAYS AS SYMBOLIC

The distinction between symbol and referent is even more subtle and important for faces, because there is a strong tendency to equate a facial expression with an emotional expression. In this view, facial expressions of emotion are nonsymbolic, involuntary acts that reveal information about the individual's intrapsychic state. Ekman, the pioneer in the study of face and emotion, anticipated other functions of the face in his early work, however (e.g., Ekman, 1979). More recently, he also made several distinctions between facial expressions of emotion and facial actions that are conversational signals:

> Most importantly, the *conversational signals* [italics added] are part of the structure of the conversation, part of the flow of talk, and governed by the rules which govern the production of speech. While *facial expressions of emotion* [italics added] often occur during conversation, their location in the speech flow is related not to the structure of talk but to the semantics, revealing an emotional reaction to what is being said or not being said. (Ekman, 1997, p. 340)

Thus, Ekman's first criterion, synchrony with speech, is the same as ours. Kraut and Johnston (1979) also proposed a distinction between the facial expression of emotion and a socially oriented *facial display* (which is the term we use in this chapter).

Because of the vastly greater research interest in emotional expression, there is remarkably little scholarship on the use of the face for communication (for a more general discussion of emotional communication, however, see Fridlund & Russell, this volume). We know of three systematic descriptions: Ekman's (1979) above-mentioned description of eyebrow movements, Brunner's (1979) analysis of smiles as back-channels, and Chovil's systematic identification of conversational facial displays other than smiles (1989, 1991/1992). The latter study documented the wide variety of syntactic and semantic functions of participants' facial displays in spontaneous face-to-face dialogue. For example, speakers facially portrayed themselves as they might have appeared at another time, in another situation (see Example 2, earlier in this chapter); they also portrayed others' reactions (e.g., a disapproving relative), and they marked syntactic emphasis, questions, and other narrative features, usually with eyebrow movements.

One limitation of the research just discussed is that it has been almost entirely descriptive, documenting the nonemotional role of facial displays in face-to-face dialogue but not offering an alternative theoretical conception of them. We (Bavelas & Chovil, 1997) found a promising theory in Clark's (1996; Clark & Gerrig, 1990) concept of *demonstration* as a distinct method of signaling (adapted from Peirce, cited in Buchler, 1940). Clark and Gerrig (1990) proposed that many conversational actions, such as quoting what someone else said, are demonstrations rather than descriptions or indications (the other two methods of signaling). In addition, "people can demonstrate a cough, the rhythm of a part of a Chopin prelude, the sound of a car engine, ... or the appearance of a chimpanzee" (Clark & Gerrig, 1990, pp. 766–767). The speaker need not actually have a cough or be playing a Chopin prelude (and is certainly not a car engine or a chimpanzee), nor is he or she making such a claim, because a demonstration is not literal (it is "non-serious"; Goffman, 1974). The principle of demonstration means that speakers do not necessarily or even usually use their facial displays to portray the way they *feel* at that moment; rather, the speaker is *illustrating* some aspect of the conversational topic of the moment.

When demonstrating, the speaker does not simply reproduce the literal expression; a demonstration is *selective,* deleting irrelevant features and retaining or even exaggerating the relevant ones. For example, squinting one's eyes to indicate skepticism or disbelief may demonstrate looking more closely at something, but it is likely to be a highly stylized and different in form (e.g., quicker) than literally squinting to read fine print. In support of this, Gilbert, Fridlund, and Sabini (1987) showed that individuals who were demonstrating facial displays to various odors produced facial configurations that were clearer to observers than when they were actually smelling the odor and having the same reaction spontaneously. Arguably, these results illustrate the selective nature of demonstration. We proposed at the beginning of this section that if conversational hand gestures and facial displays are symbols, then social and communicative considerations would shape them. What we know about the principles of this selective process is encouraging but far too little; the determinants of the form of symbolic nonverbal acts are an important area for further research.

◆ III. Integrated (but Not Necessarily Redundant) With Words

One of our defining criteria for nonverbal acts that are part of language use in face-to-face dialogue was that they must be tightly synchronized with words in both timing and meaning. In this section, we propose that these two synchronies of timing and meaning work together to produce an *integrated but often complex whole.* Most of the available research relevant to this proposal has focused on gestures; at present, we have to rely on anecdotal observation for facial displays.

What may be the best evidence of the precise integration of audible and visible acts is easy to demonstrate: Speakers usually coordinate their hand gestures and facial displays to verbal syntax. McNeill (1985) found that "gestures synchronize with parallel linguistic units [and] almost never cross clause boundaries" (pp. 160–161). Ekman (1997) made the same general point about facial displays:

> Take for example, a person who says he had been afraid of what he would learn from a biopsy report, and was so relieved when it turned out to be negative. When the word "afraid" is said, the person stretches back his lips horizontally, referring facially to fear. (p. 340)

Ekman went on to point out that the above facial action, used to "refer to a fear not felt now," would not only be a transformed version of the emotional expression of fear but "would be likely to be made very quickly, much more quickly than the actual expression of emotion would be" (p. 340). Presumably, the display would be quicker in order to synchronize with the word "afraid." One important facility of the facial muscles is that they can track the speed of words or phrases. In Example 2, presented earlier in this chapter, the speaker's face changed rapidly from an angry expression to a smile exactly when her phrase ended.

We can illustrate the precise integration of all three elements (hand gestures, facial displays, and words) with a brief example from our data (Bavelas, 2000). The speaker was telling the addressee about a close call he once had, when he fell into a river and nearly drowned:

Example 3.

S: "So, <u>my-my-my head is in the water like this,</u>
    [head back, eyes shut, impassive face]
   and basically it's, <u>water's going over my head.</u>
   [head to vertical] [hands sweep beside head]
   <u>And it's str–I grew really, really calm.</u>"
   [puzzled   ] [serious face, looking at A]

During each underlined phrase, the speaker depicted some aspect of his dilemma gesturally or facially. In the first two lines, he demonstrated that "like this" meant a particular position of his head in the water and also his closed eyes and impassive facial display; then he returned his head to vertical and demonstrated that "water's going over my head" meant that the water (represented by his hands) was sweeping past the sides of his head. Altogether, this first sentence said and showed that he was on his back with the water flowing around, but not over, his face. At the same time, he illustrated his helplessness facially, with his eyes closed and an impassive expression, both also synchronous with the verbal description of his dilemma. Accomplishing these depictions required a high degree of coordination and integration. For example, in order to show how "water's going over my head," he had to return his head to vertical and lift his hands up to the sides of his head (the preparatory phase) before he started to say the phrase.

His impassive expression foreshadowed the latter part of his next sentence ("I grew really, really calm"), but first he interrupted his narration to insert a metacommunicative comment on his own reaction: He said a shortened version of "And it's strange," while making a very brief but clear facial display of puzzlement, as if still unable to understand what he was describing as his strange calmness in the situation. He then returned to the main narrative line by depicting, verbally, prosodically, and facially, the calmness he now found

puzzling. Each phrase of this example demonstrates precise coordination of words, hand (and head) gestures, and facial displays, all serving the immediate narrative purpose.

Coordination seems to be an important factor in creating the meaning of these speech-related nonverbal acts. Engle (2000; see also Engle, 1998; Engle & Clark, 1995) conducted an intensive analysis of multimodal signals (speech, gestures, diagrams, and object demonstrations), which yielded several lines of evidence for the temporal and linguistic integration of iconic and indexical conversational gestures with speech. For example, the gesture and the immediately accompanying speech segment were *co-expressive*, referring to the same underlying referent:

> For all but one of the 108 [communicative] nonverbal signals, a co-expressive speech segment could be found within [a] two intonation unit time window. . . . In stark contrast to communicative nonverbal signals, in 14 of [the] 17 non-communicative cases, no co-expressive speech was present. (Engle, 1998, pp. 323–324)

One implication of Engle's findings is that timing is a metacommunicative tool that speakers use to signal what is in the same integrated unit of meaning (Engle, 2000). Bavelas, Holt, and Allison (2000) analyzed over 1,700 gestures to learn how they were connected to co-occurring speech.

The data revealed that, whereas speakers sometimes used linguistic markers (e.g., a deictic expression or a dummy noun phrase), the most common link was simply timing (70% of the gestures). Unfortunately, we do not have comparable information for facial displays. There are to our knowledge no systematic studies of the precise temporal and linguistic relationship of facial displays to words, although advances in digital analysis make such frame-by-frame analysis possible, albeit still labor-intensive.

REDUNDANCY AND NONREDUNDANCY

Engle's (2000) data also confirmed that, although the gestures were virtually always consistent with the co-expressive speech, they were sometimes complementary rather than duplicating the speech. This observation contradicts the possibility that hand gestures are simply a redundant mode of expression. Examples 1 and 3 each illustrated that gestures can convey important information that is not in the speaker's words (e.g., the width of the dress and the way his head was in the water). Sometimes the simultaneous audible and visible elements of a message, taken separately, might appear to contradict each other. As Sanders (1987) pointed out, however, receivers integrate these apparent contradictions at the level of overall meaning (rather than at the level of components or physical source). For example, Bugental, Kaswan, and Love (1970; cited in Sanders, 1987) found

positively valued utterances paired with a negatively valued facial expression and vocal qualities were judged by respondents to be *sarcastic*. Negatively valued utterances paired with positively valued nonverbal displays were judged to involve *joking*. Thus, these inconsistent pairs of utterances and nonverbal displays

received *a single unitary interpretation distinct from the interpretation of either constituent,* not a preference for one rather than the other of two discrete messages. (Sanders, 1987, p. 142; italics added)

These interpretations are consistent with Engle's (1998) proposal that, following Grice's (1967/1989) "cooperative principle," both speaker and addressee assume that "all signals in a particular composite signal are intended to be treated from the start as contributing to a single, unified interpretation" (Engle, 1998, p. 321).

But what is the internal nature of a multimodal message that produces a single, unified interpretation? We propose that, primarily because of synchronous timing, multimodal elements can range from completely redundant to highly nonredundant and still remain unified. Our research group has examined the degree or rate of redundancy in hand gestures with different functions. Bavelas, Chovil, Lawrie, and Wade (1992), for example, examined the degree of redundancy of a gesture with its accompanying phonemic clause and found that, across several different descriptive tasks, gestures depicting features of the task topic were much more redundant with the words than were gestures that referred to the interlocutor or to the interaction itself. The latter (which we called *interactive gestures*) were usually completely nonredundant, although they depended on and contributed to the meaning of the clause.

An example from our data (Bavelas, Sutton, Gerwing, & Johnson, 2002) illustrates a nonredundant interactive gesture. At the beginning of their getting-acquainted conversation, one participant had answered the other's inquiry by saying that he was a Political Science major. A minute later, after they had been discussing another topic, the same speaker returned to his academic standing:

Example 4.

S: "This is my last term, and, ah, <u>Political Science.</u> I was a double major . . ."

[*flicks hand to A*]

Because his addressee already knew what his major was, naming it again was not new but given (i.e., shared) information. The speaker's words ("and, ah, Political Science") were cryptic and did not fit the syntax of his sentence; they also contained no reference to the addressee's prior knowledge. In our view, it was the hand flick at the addressee that made the socially necessary reference; we interpret this gesture to mean "as you already know," that is, as citing or acknowledging that the addressee obviously still remembered what the speaker's major was. The effective sentence would be, in words, "This is my last term and, as you know, I'm in Political Science. I was a double major . . ."

One limitation of our analysis in Bavelas et al. (1992) was that it did not distinguish among different experimental conditions and therefore included some conditions in which there was no addressee or in which the speaker and addressee were interacting through a partition. More recently, Bavelas, Gerwing, Sutton, and Prevost (2002, 2005) examined gestural redundancy as a function of the presence and visual availability of the addressee. When speaker and addressee were face to face, fewer than 20% of the speaker's gestures conveyed only information that was also in their words; over 80% also included some nonredundant information. In contrast, when the speakers were on the telephone or talking into a tape recorder to no one, their gestures were significantly more redundant; almost 60% of their gestures were entirely redundant with their words.

Likewise, Chovil (1989, 1991/1992; see also Bavelas & Chovil, 1997) reported redundancy data on 880 conversational facial displays. She found that 243 of the 405 *semantic* displays by speakers (e.g.,

portraying a past or present personal reaction) were redundant with speech; the other 162 semantic displays by speakers were nonredundant. The 315 *syntactic* facial displays by speakers (e.g., grammatical markers such as emphasis or question markers) were virtually always nonredundant with words, although not necessarily with prosody. Finally, the 160 facial displays by *listeners* were, by definition, nonredundant with speech, because the listener was the person who was not speaking at the moment. Thus, over 70% of all displays conveyed information that was not in the words. We speculate that the smiles by either speaker or listener, which were not analyzed in this study, would follow a similar pattern.

In sum, the third defining criterion of the nonverbal acts of interest in this chapter is that they form an integrated whole, with words and each other. Integration does not necessarily or even usually mean duplication, as there is at least some evidence that the various modalities can convey different (nonredundant) information from each other. When and how these diverse but unified elements operate is an important question for future research.

◆ IV. Communication in Dialogue

This final section examines evidence that the speakers and addressees use hand gestures and facial displays to communicate. To do so, it is first necessary to discuss methodology, because there are three different methods for examining these issues. The first two focus on speaker and addressee separately: An *encoding* design tests the conditions under which speakers do or do not produce hand gestures or facial displays; they should be more likely to do so in face-to-face dialogue than in other conditions. A *decoding* design seeks evidence that those who see such acts also understand their meaning. We have reviewed most of these studies in other places (Bavelas & Chovil, 2000; Bavelas, Gerwing, Sutton, et al., 2005; Chovil, 1997; see also Kendon, 1994; Gray & Ambady, this volume) and will only summarize the pattern here. The vast majority of studies show evidence for communication, in that (1) individuals tend to produce more gestures or facial displays when someone would see them and (2) observers can garner accurate information from these acts. Indeed, these studies have been so successful that we can now begin to see their limitations. Therefore, we will point out here what, in retrospect, appear as deficiencies in studies of isolated individuals (including some of our own experiments) and will suggest a third method, one that examines the speaker and addressee together, within their interaction.

ENCODING AND DECODING DESIGNS

The typical encoding design varies whether or not the speaker has a visually available recipient, for example, whether the speaker is alone or in the presence of another person. The main limitation of the existing encoding designs is that they seldom include a spontaneous face-to-face dialogue, which should be the baseline condition. For example, most studies of facial displays have instead used mere presence, eye contact, or social context instead of face-to-face dialogue (e.g., Bavelas, Black, Lemery, & Mullett, 1986; Fernandez-Dols & Ruis-Belda, 1995; Fridlund, 1991b; Jones, Collins, & Hong, 1991; Jones & Hong, 2001; Jones & Raag, 1989; Kraut &

Johnston, 1979; Schneider & Josephs, 1991). Only Chovil's (1989, 1991) experiment on addressees' facial displays involved a conversational dialogue.

In contrast, and for obvious reasons, encoding studies of conversational gestures have involved conversations, but virtually none of them have been spontaneous dialogues. In most of these gesture studies, the addressees were nonreactive confederates or the experimenter, or even an imagined other (e.g., Alibali, Heath, & Myers, 2001; Bavelas, Kenwood, et al., 2002; Beattie & Aboudan, 1994; Cohen, 1977; Cohen & Harrison, 1973; Emmorey & Casey, 2001; Krauss, Dushay, Chen, & Rauscher, 1995). Only three studies, to our knowledge, involved spontaneous dialogues between two participants (Bavelas et al., 1992; Bavelas, Gerwing, Sutton, et al., 2005; Rimé, 1982).

As shown in Bavelas and Chovil (2000), there are still far fewer decoding than encoding studies, and virtually all of them involve a similar design, one that tests whether outsiders to the interaction who later view the gesture or facial display can ascertain or at least agree on its meaning (e.g., Bavelas et al., 1986; Bavelas et al., 1990; Rosenfeld, Shea, & Greenbaum, 1979; Shea & Rosenfeld, 1976).[3] In one study, Graham and Argyle (1975) showed that the addressees were more accurate at drawing figures when the speaker who described them had been able to gesture, but there was little or no interaction involved between speakers and addressees.

Although these studies are encouraging for demonstrating some decoding of gestures or facial displays, the viewers were rarely the original addressees, a methodological choice that raises at least two problems. First, most decoder studies do not present the entire conversation, so that the decoding outsider has a fraction of the context that the addressee had. Our unpublished pilot studies with these designs showed that, in highly controlled presentations, decoders imagined contexts in order to make sense of a gesture, thereby escaping experimental control. Second, Schober and Clark's (1989) experiments on verbal dialogue showed that, even when outsiders had access to the entire conversation between speaker and addressee, they had a significantly poorer understanding because they were not part of the dialogue and could not participate in grounding, that is, in the interactive process of establishing mutual understanding (see also Roberts & Bavelas, 1996). The same effect may also apply to gestures or facial displays.

DIALOGUE DESIGNS

The above criticisms lead us to propose that the best studies of whether hand gestures or facial displays communicate are ones that focus on *the original speaker and addressee in dialogue.* There are two design alternatives: Because of the requirement of unscripted interaction between the participants, such studies often involve micro-analysis of events occurring spontaneously within the interaction rather than the effects of experimentally manipulation. As shown below, however, there are also true experiments, which use controlled tasks and systematic quantitative analysis; the independent variable applies to the dyad rather than to an individual. In any case, the best method is the one that goes where the phenomenon is happening.

Two early studies used nonexperimental designs. Camras (1977) created a situation in which two children would both want the same object. She showed that, when the child with the object made an aggressive facial display, the other child would stop trying to take it and would wait longer before trying again than when not met with an aggressive facial display. Brunner (1979) conducted a statistical analysis showing that listeners' smiles followed the

same pattern of relationships to speaker turn signals as did responses such as "mhm" or nodding. He concluded that these smiles also acted as back-channel responses.

More recently, we (Bavelas, Chovil, Coates, & Roe, 1995) used a similar statistical approach to examine the momentary effects of interactive gestures (which, as described above, are social gestures aimed at the addressee and are usually nonredundant with speech). The analysis required independently identifying (1) the perlocutionary meaning of each gesture in a large sample of interactive gestures and (2) the immediately following response of the addressee. In almost all cases, there was a significant relationship between the predictions based on the meaning of the gesture and the addressee's response to the gesture, even though the meaning did not appear in words.

Furuyama (2000) demonstrated that, when one person taught another how to make an origami figure without paper available, the teachers of course used gestures to demonstrate. The learners frequently joined in their teacher's gesture, acting in and on the same gesture space; for example, they pointed to or even touched the teacher's gesture as part of their dialogue about the figure. Furuyama called these "collaborative gestures." Clark and Krych (2004) analyzed one person teaching another how to build a Lego structure. The learner would often check with the teacher, for example, by pointing at a particular block, by picking it up and exhibiting it to the teacher, or by poising it over where it might go. These actions were not ones that actually placed the blocks; instead, they were arguably gestural demonstrations of intention or inquiry. The teachers seemed to use them as such, as evidenced by their responding immediately to them, even interrupting themselves to change what they were saying in response to what the learner was communicating with the gesture.

There is also an increasing number of true experiments involving two participants (i.e., neither experimenter nor confederate) in a spontaneous dialogue. For example, several studies described in an earlier section of this chapter showed that speakers in dialogue change the form of their gestures because of their addressee's location (Ozyurek, 2000, 2002) or current knowledge (Gerwing & Bavelas, 2004; Woods, 2005). Bavelas et al. (2002, 2005) found that speakers who were describing a picture of an unusual dress in face-to-face dialogue (compared with talking on the telephone or to a tape recorder) made significantly larger, life-sized gestures that were also less redundant with speech and more likely to be marked with a deictic expression.

Bangerter (2004) found that, when one person was identifying targets for another to choose, the speakers relied more on pointing than on words when their distance from the target object was short. At greater distances, pointing would be more ambiguous, and the speakers used words to describe the object. Finally, Bavelas, Gerwing, Allison, and Sutton (2005) asked two participants to design a floor plan across a table from each other, with no paper to draw on, which elicited a large proportion of nonredundant gestures. The experimental variable was the width of the table. When the table was narrow enough, they worked in the same space. When it was too wide, they had to work in different spaces, but they reached out significantly farther (toward each other), presumably so that the other person could see their gestures.

Thus, there are several examples each of experimental and nonexperimental studies that examine gestures between speakers and addressees in dialogue. It is worth noting that, in these more recent studies, the research question seems to have shifted from *whether* participants use gestures to communicate, using standard rate measures, to *how* they use gestures to communicate, using more subtle and varied measures.

◆ Conclusion

Some nonverbal acts are an intrinsic part of language use in face-to-face dialogue. In this chapter, we have focused on conversational hand gestures and facial displays because there is research support for their use in dialogue. The data so far suggest the outline of a model for how these acts function in dialogue: First, there are independent criteria for identifying this subset of nonverbal acts, all of which focus on their synchrony with speech. Second, these are analogically encoded symbolic acts, functionally distinguishable from the actions or objects they may represent. Third, they form integrated messages with the words they accompany, although they may frequently convey information that is not merely redundant with those words. Finally, there is a growing body of such evidence that the participants in a dialogue use gestures to communicate with each other; at present, there are only a few such studies for faces. New directions for research could include expanding and refining the evidence presented in any of these four areas; exploring other nonverbal acts, such as gaze, that might be added to gestures and facial displays; and beginning to reassemble the parts into the integrated messages that participants create, in order to understand how they function as a whole.

◆ Notes

1. The present chapter is an extension of the model proposed in Bavelas and Chovil (2000). It

includes a few sections adapted from that article, with the permission of the *Journal of Language and Social Psychology* and Sage Publications.

2. Clark (1996, chap. 1) has outlined in fuller detail the characteristics of face-to-face conversation as a fundamental setting for language use.

3. We are not including any method that isolates gestures from their verbal context (e.g., by using only the video without a sound track), because such procedures treat conversational gestures as if they were emblems.

◆ References

Alibali, M. W., Heath, D. C., & Myers, H. J. (2001). Effects of visibility between speaker and listener on gesture production: Some gestures are meant to be seen. *Journal of Memory and Language, 44,* 169–188.

Bangerter, A. (2004). Using pointing and describing to achieve joint focus of attention in dialogue. *Psychological Science, 15,* 415–419.

Bavelas, J. B. (1990). Nonverbal and social aspects of discourse in face-to-face interaction. *Text, 10,* 508.

Bavelas, J. B. (2000). Nonverbal aspects of fluency. In H. Riggenbach (Ed.), *Perspectives on fluency* (pp. 91–101). Ann Arbor: University of Michigan Press.

Bavelas, J. B. (in press). The micro-social dimension of face-to-face dialogue. In S. Duncan & E. Levy (Eds.), *Papers in honor of David McNeill.* Washington, DC: American Psychological Association.

Bavelas, J. B., Black, A., Chovil, N., & Mullett, J. (1990). *Equivocal communication.* Newbury Park, CA: Sage.

Bavelas, J. B., Black, A., Lemery, C. R., & Mullett, J. (1986). "I *show* you how you feel." Motor mimicry as a communicative act. *Journal of Personality and Social Psychology, 50,* 322–329.

Bavelas, J. B., & Chovil, N. (1997). Faces in dialogue. In J. A. Russell & J. M. Fernandez-Dols (Eds.), *The psychology of facial expression* (pp. 334–346). Cambridge: Cambridge University Press.

Bavelas, J. B., & Chovil, N. (2000). Visible acts of meaning. An integrated message model of language use in face-to-face dialogue. *Journal of Language and Social Psychology, 19,* 163–194.

Bavelas, J. B., Chovil, N., Coates, L., & Roe, L. (1995). Gestures specialized for dialogue. *Personality and Social Psychology Bulletin, 21,* 394–405.

Bavelas, J. B., Chovil, N., Lawrie, D. A., & Wade, A. (1992). Interactive gestures. *Discourse Processes, 15,* 469–489.

Bavelas, J. B., Coates, L., & Johnson, T. (2002). Listener responses as a collaborative process: The role of gaze. *Journal of Communication, 52,* 566–580.

Bavelas, J. B., Gerwing, J., Allison, M., & Sutton, C. (2005, June). *Evidence for grounding with non-redundant gestures: Co-constructing virtual spaces.* Paper presented at the second conference of the International Society for Gesture Studies, Lyon, France.

Bavelas, J. B., Gerwing, J., Sutton, C., & Prevost, D. (2002, June). *Gestures in face-to-face, telephone, and tape recorder conditions.* Paper presented at the first conference of the International Society for Gesture Studies, Austin, TX.

Bavelas, J. B., Gerwing, J., Sutton, C., & Prevost, D. (2005). *Gesturing on the telephone: Independent effects of dialogue and visibility.* Unpublished manuscript.

Bavelas, J. B., Holt, T., & Allison, M. (2000). *Links between gestures and words.* Unpublished research report.

Bavelas, J. B., Hutchinson, S., Kenwood, C., & Matheson, D. H. (1997). Using face-to-face dialogue as a standard for other communication systems. *Canadian Journal of Communication, 22,* 5–24.

Bavelas, J. B., Kenwood, C., Johnson, T., & Phillips, B. (2002c). An experimental study of when and how speakers use gestures to communicate. *Gesture, 2,* 1–17.

Bavelas, J. B., Sutton, C., Gerwing, J., & Johnson, T. (2002d). *Analysis of gestures in dialogue* [Training CD], Department of Psychology,

University of Victoria, Victoria, B.C.,
Canada.

Beattie, G., & Aboudan, R. (1994). Gestures,
pauses and speech: An experimental
investigation of the effects of changing
social context on their precise temporal
relationships. *Semiotica, 99,* 239–272.

Birdwhistell, R. L. (1966). Some relationships
between American kinesics and spoken
American language. In A. Smith (Ed.), *Communication and culture* (pp. 182–189).
New York: Holt, Rinehart & Winston.

Blurton-Jones, N. G. (1972). Criteria for use in
describing facial expressions of children. In
N. G. Blurton-Jones (Ed.), *Ethological studies of child behavior* (pp. 365–413).
Cambridge: Cambridge University Press.

Brunner, L. J. (1979). Smiles can be back
channels. *Journal of Personality and Social
Psychology, 37,* 728–734.

Buchler, J. (Ed.). (1940). *Philosophical writings of
Peirce.* London: Routledge and Kegan Paul.

Bugental, D. E., Kaswan, J. W., & Love, L. R.
(1970). Perception of contradictory meanings conveyed by verbal and nonverbal
channels. *Journal of Personality and Social
Psychology, 16,* 647–655.

Camras, L. A. (1977). Facial expressions used
by children in a conflict situation. *Child
Development, 48,* 1431–1435.

Chovil, N. (1989). *Communicative functions of
facial displays in conversation.* Unpublished
doctoral dissertation, Department of Psychology, University of Victoria, Victoria, British
Columbia, Canada.

Chovil, N. (1991). Social determinants of facial
displays. *Journal of Nonverbal Behavior,
15,* 141–154.

Chovil, N. (1991/1992). Discourse-oriented
facial displays in conversation. *Research
on Language and Social Interaction, 25,*
163–194.

Chovil, N. (1997). Facing others: A social communicative perspective on facial displays.
In J. A. Russell & J.-M. Fernandez-Dols
(Eds.), *The psychology of facial expression*
(pp. 321–333). Cambridge: Cambridge
University Press.

Clark, H. H. (1996). *Using language.*
Cambridge: Cambridge University Press.

Clark, H. H., & Gerrig, R. J. (1990). Quotations
as demonstrations. *Language, 66,* 764–805.

Clark, H. H., & Krych, M. A. (2004). Speaking
while monitoring addressees for understanding. *Journal of Memory and Language, 50,*
62–81.

Cohen, A. A. (1977). The communicative
functions of hand illustrators. *Journal of
Communication, 27,* 54–63.

Cohen, A. A., & Harrison, R. P. (1973).
Intentionality in the use of hand illustrators
in face-to-face communication situations.
*Journal of Personality and Social Psychology,
28,* 276–279.

Duncan, S., & Fiske, D. (1977). *Face-to-face
interaction: Research, methods, and theory.*
New York: Erlbaum.

Ekman, P. (1979). About brows: Emotional and
conversational signals. In J. Aschoof, M. von
Cranach, K. Foppa, W. Lepenies, & D. Ploog
(Eds.), *Human ethology* (pp. 169–202).
Cambridge, UK: Cambridge University Press.

Ekman, P. (1993). Facial expression and emotion. *American Psychologist, 48,* 384–392.

Ekman, P. (1997). Should we call it expression
or communication? *European Journal of
Social Sciences, 10,* 333–359.

Ekman, P., & Friesen, W. V. (1969). The repertoire of nonverbal behavior. Categories, origins, usage, and coding. *Semiotica, 1,* 49–98.

Emmorey, K., & Casey, S. (2001). Gesture,
thought and spatial language. *Gesture, 1,*
35–50.

Engle, R. A. (1998). Not channels but composite
signals: Speech, gesture, diagrams and object
demonstrations are integrated in multimodal
explanations. In M. A. Gernsbacher & S. J.
Derry (Eds.), *Proceedings of the Twentieth
Annual Conference of the Cognitive Science
Society* (pp. 321–326). Mahwah, NJ:
Erlbaum.

Engle, R. A. (2000). *Toward a theory of multimodal communication combining speech,
gestures, diagrams, and demonstrations
in instructional explanations.* Unpublished
doctoral dissertation, School of Education,
Stanford University.

Engle, R. A., & Clark, H. H. (1995, March).
Using composites of speech, gestures, diagrams and demonstrations in explanations

of mechanical devices. Paper presented at the American Association for Applied Linguistics Conference, Long Beach, CA.

Fernandez-Dols, J.-M., & Ruis-Belda, M.-A. (1995). Are smiles a sign of happiness? Gold medal winners at the Olympic Games. *Journal of Personality and Social Psychology, 69,* 1113–1119.

Fillmore, C. (1981). Pragmatics and the description of discourse. In P. Cole (Ed.), *Radical pragmatics* (pp. 143–166). New York: Academic Press.

Fowler, C. A. (1988). Differential shortening of repeated content words produced in various communicative contexts. *Language and Speech, 31,* 307–319.

Fridlund, A. J. (1991a). Evolution and facial action in reflex, social motive, and paralanguage. *Biological Psychology, 32,* 3–100.

Fridlund, A. J. (1991b). Sociality of solitary smiling: Potentiation by an implicit audience. *Journal of Personality and Social Psychology, 60,* 229–240.

Furuyama, N. (2000). Gestural interaction between the instructor and the learner in origami instruction. In D. McNeill (Ed.), *Language and gesture* (pp. 99–117). Cambridge: Cambridge University Press.

Gerwing, J., & Bavelas, J. (2004). Linguistic influences on gesture's form. *Gesture, 4,* 157–195.

Gilbert, A. N., Fridlund, A. J., & Sabini, J. (1987). Hedonic and social determinants of facial displays to odors. *Chemical Senses, 12,* 355–363.

Goffman, E. (1974). *Frame analysis.* New York: Harper & Row.

Goodwin, C. (1981). *Conversational organization. Interaction between speakers and hearers.* New York: Academic Press.

Goodwin, C. (2000). Gesture, aphasia, and interaction. In D. McNeill (Ed.), *Language and gesture* (pp. 99–117). Cambridge: Cambridge University Press.

Goodwin, M. H., & Goodwin, C. (1986). Gesture and coparticipation in the activity of searching for a word. *Semiotica, 62,* 51–75.

Graham, J. A., & Argyle, M. (1975). A cross-cultural study of the communication of extra-verbal meanings by gestures. *International Journal of Psychology, 10,* 57–67.

Grice, H. P. (1989). Logic and conversation. In *Studies in the way of words* (pp. 22–40). Cambridge, MA: Harvard University Press. (Original date of lectures 1967)

Jones, S., & Hong, H.-W. (2001). Onset of voluntary communication: Smiling looks to mother. *Infancy, 2,* 353–370.

Jones, S. E., & LeBaron, C. D. (2002). Research on the relationship between verbal and nonverbal communication: Emerging integrations. *Journal of Communication, 52,* 499–521.

Jones, S. S., Collins, K., & Hong, H.-W. (1991). An audience effect on smile production in 10-month-old infants. *Psychological Science, 2,* 45–49.

Jones, S. S., & Raag, T. (1989). Smile production in older infants: The importance of a social recipient for the facial signal. *Child Development, 60,* 811–818.

Kendon, A. (1972). Some relationships between body motion and speech. In A. W. Seigman & B. Pope (Eds.), *Studies in dyadic communication.* Elmsford, NY: Pergamon.

Kendon, A. (1980). Gesticulation and speech: Two aspects of the process of utterance. In M. R. Key (Ed.), *The relationship of verbal and nonverbal communication* (pp. 207–227). The Hague: Mouton.

Kendon, A. (1985). Uses of gesture. In D. Tannen & M. Saville-Troike (Eds.), *Perspectives on silence* (pp. 215–234). Norwood, NJ: Ablex.

Kendon, A. (1994). Do gestures communicate? A review. *Research on Language and Social Interaction, 27,* 175–200.

Krauss, R. M., Dushay, R. A., Chen, Y., & Rauscher, F. (1995). The communicative value of conversational hand gestures. *Journal of Experimental Social Psychology, 31,* 533–552.

Kraut, R. E., & Johnston, R. E. (1979). Social and emotional messages of smiling: An ethological approach. *Journal of Personality and Social Psychology, 37,* 1539–1553.

LeBaron, C., & Streeck, J. (2000). Gestures, knowledge, and the world. In D. McNeill (Ed.), *Language and gesture* (pp. 99–117). Cambridge: Cambridge University Press.

Leeds-Hurwitz, W. (1987). The social history of *The History of an Interview*: A multidisciplinary investigation of social communication. *Research on Language and Social Interaction, 20*, 1–51.

Leeds-Hurwitz, W. (1989). *Communication in everyday life: A social interpretation.* Parkside, WI: University of Wisconsin-Parkside Press.

Levinson, S. (1983). *Pragmatics.* Cambridge: Cambridge University Press.

Linell, P. (1982). *The written language bias in linguistics.* Linkoping, Sweden: University of Linkoping, Department of Communication.

McNeill, D. (1985). So you think gestures are nonverbal? *Psychological Bulletin, 92*, 350–371.

McNeill, D. (1992). *Hand and mind: What gestures reveal about thought.* Chicago: University of Chicago Press.

McQuowan, N. (Ed.). (1971). *The natural history of an interview. Microfilm collection of manuscripts on cultural anthropology.* Chicago: University of Chicago, Joseph Regenstein Library, Department of Photoduplicating.

Ozyurek, A. (2000). The influence of addressee location on spatial language and representational gestures of direction. In D. McNeill (Ed.), *Language and gesture* (pp. 99–117). Cambridge, UK: Cambridge University Press.

Ozyurek, A. (2002). Do speakers design their cospeech gestures for their addressees? The effects of addressee location on representational gestures. *Journal of Memory and Language, 46*, 665–875.

Pike, K. L. (1972). Towards a theory of the structure of human behavior. In R. M. Brend (Ed.), *Selected writings: To commemorate the 60th birthday of Kenneth Lee Pike* (pp. 106–116). The Hague: Mouton.

Poyatos, F. (1980). Interactive functions and limitations of verbal and nonverbal behaviors in natural conversation. *Semiotica, 30*, 211–244.

Quine, W. V. O. (1987). Symbols. In R. L. Gregory (Ed.), *The Oxford companion to the mind* (pp. 763–765). Oxford: Oxford University Press.

Random house unabridged dictionary (2nd ed.). (1993). New York: Random House.

Rimé, B. (1982). The elimination of visible behaviour from social interactions: Effects on verbal, nonverbal and interpersonal variables. *European Journal of Social Psychology, 12*, 113–129.

Roberts, G. L., & Bavelas, J. B. (1996). The communicative dictionary: A collaborative theory of meaning. In J. Stewart (Ed.), *Beyond the symbol model. Reflections on the nature of language* (pp. 139–164). Albany: SUNY Press.

Rosenfeld, N. M., Shea, M., & Greenbaum, P. (1979). Facial emblems of "right" and "wrong": Topographical analysis and derivation of a recognition test. *Semiotica, 26*, 15–34.

Sanders, R. E. (1987). The interconnection of utterances and nonverbal displays. *Research on Language and Social Interaction, 20*, 141–170.

Scheflen, A. (1968). Human communication: Behavioral programs and their integration in interaction. *Behavioral Science, 13*, 44–55.

Scherer, K. R. (1980). The functions of nonverbal signs in conversation. In R. N. St. Clair & H. Giles (Eds.), *The social and psychological contexts of language* (pp. 225–244). Hillsdale, NJ: Erlbaum.

Schneider, K., & Josephs, I. (1991). The expressive and communicative functions of preschool children's smiles in an achievement-situation. *Journal of Nonverbal Behavior, 15*, 185–198.

Schober, M. F., & Clark, H. H. (1989). Understanding by addressees and overhearers. *Cognitive Psychology, 21*, 211–232.

Shea, M., & Rosenfeld, H. M. (1976). Functional employment of nonverbal social reinforcers in dyadic learning. *Journal of Personality and Social Psychology, 34*, 228–239.

Slama-Cazacu, T. (1976). Nonverbal components in message sequence: "Mixed syntax." In W. C. McCormack & S. A. Wurm (Eds.), *Language and man: Anthropological issues* (pp. 217–227). The Hague: Mouton.

Streeck, J., & Knapp, M. L. (1992). The interaction of visual and verbal features in human communication. In F. Poyatos (Ed.), *Advances in nonverbal communication* (pp. 3–24). Amsterdam: Benjamins.

Weiner, M., Devoe, S., Rubinow, S., & Geller, J. (1972). Nonverbal behavior and nonverbal communication. *Psychological Review, 79,* 185–214.

Woods, J. (2005). *New vs. given information: Do gestures dance to the same tune as words?* Unpublished honours thesis, Department of Psychology, University of Victoria, Victoria, B.C., Canada.

PART II

FACTORS OF INFLUENCE

7

THE BIOLOGICAL FOUNDATIONS OF SOCIAL ORGANIZATION

The Dynamic Emergence of Social Structure Through Nonverbal Communication

◆ Ross Buck and Stacie Renfro Powers
University of Connecticut

The functioning of any system involves communication between system elements, and this chapter argues that social structure emerges during individual development via nonverbal communication

Authors' Note: The authors gratefully acknowledge the contributions of many students and colleagues to the research on which this chapter is based. Among those whose contributions have been particularly relevant to this chapter are R. Thomas Boone of St. Johns University; Benson Ginsburg of the University of Connecticut; David A. Kenny of the University of Connecticut; Makoto Nakamura of Utsunomiya University, Japan; Elliott Ross of the University of Oklahoma VA Medical Center; Edward Vieira of Simmons College; and Lesley Withers of Central Michigan University. Parts of this research were supported by NIMH RO1 MH48753; the Harry Frank Guggenheim Foundation; the EJLB Foundation—National Trust, Canada Council; the Russell Sage Foundation; and the University of Connecticut Research Foundation.

between elements—that is, between individuals. In this chapter, we present a view of social structure as an emergent, self-organizing dynamic system, and we seek to demonstrate the critical role of nonverbal communication in this emergence. We review evidence relevant to this thesis, arguing that even simple organisms show evidence of motivational-emotional systems underlying basic behavior and sociality. These systems exist not only within the individual organism but also "out there" in the communicative relationship associated with genetically structured *displays* in senders and *preattunements* in receivers. The result is a spontaneous communicative interplay from which, over time, social structure emerges. In human beings, this emergence proceeds so naturally and effortlessly that it is often taken for granted, but many of the deepest meanings conveyed by everyday nonverbal communication reflect these unseen, primordial biological imperatives.

This chapter considers how, through genetically structured displays and preattunements, spontaneous communicative interplay creates the basis for the social organization of species. The chapter moves from the biochemical bases of motivation and emotion that humans share with simpler species to the particular ways in which social and moral emotions emerge from this foundation. It examines the special role of language in human social organization and the interaction between spontaneous nonverbal communication and linguistically organized communication. Finally, it presents human interaction as a self-organizing dynamic system involving the direct communication of social and moral emotions, including pride and arrogance, guilt and shame, envy and jealousy, pity and scorn, and, potentially, moral emotions, such as triumph, humiliation, resentment, and contempt. These social and moral emotions are the foundation of human interaction, and

at the same time they reflect the primordial imperatives seen in simple creatures: arousal and quiescence, approach and avoidance, dominance and submission, cooperation and competition, courtship and sex.

◆ Selfishness, Altruism, and Communicative Genes

A fundamental issue in any discussion of communication and sociality is the question of cooperation and competition. Are living creatures responding to genetic influences that are fundamentally selfish? Is altruism a cultural ideal with no biological underpinning? Or is cooperation—and attachment and love—anchored in fundamental biological imperatives? The answers to these questions turn on the technical issue of the unit of selection in evolution, and communication theory has important contributions to make in this domain.

SELFISH GENES

The "selfish gene" theory of Richard Dawkins (1989) and others was based on the interpretation of natural selection as operating at the level of the gene (i.e., that individuals are motivated to maximize the number of genes contributed to subsequent generations; Hauser, 1996). A corollary of this gene selectionist account of evolution was that the gene is the ultimate unit of evolutionary selection: The gene is programmed only to make copies of itself. Dawkins (1982) argued that the unit of evolutionary selection must be self-replicating across the span of evolutionary time. He termed this unit an *active, germ-line replicator.* His candidate for replicator was the gene, which is maintained virtually intact from generation to generation across evolutionary timescales. Fitness in the evolutionary sense is based not on the survival of the individual but on the survival of the individual's genes, termed *inclusive fitness*.

One of the implications of this position is that genuine *altruism*—sacrificing one's own genetic fitness to preserve the genetic fitness of others—should not exist at the biological level. Instances of apparent altruism are explained as reflecting inclusive fitness, where helping others improves the survival of one's own genes through kin selection (helping genetic relatives) and reciprocity (helping with the probability of return). This position generated considerable debate, because it suggested that apparently prosocial and selfless acts are instances of selfish manipulation.

COMMUNICATIVE GENES

The *communicative gene hypothesis* accepts the gene-selectionist account but adds that communicative relationships of genes can be units of evolutionary selection (Buck & Ginsburg, 1991, 1997). Dawkins's argument assumed the gene was selected as an individual unit: "selection purely at the level of the individual gene" (Dawkins, 1989, pp. 84–85). This *genetic atomism*, however, does not take into account the fact that genes do not function alone: Whatever they do to enhance their own survival is in the context of interactive and communicative relationships with other genes.

Communication involves phenomena both at the level of the individual sender and receiver and at the level of the dyadic sender-receiver relationship, and the relative influence of these is potentially measurable. Extending Kenny's (1994) Social Relations Model, communication from A to B is a function of the general sending accuracy of A, the general receiving ability of B, and the unique ability of B to "read" A. Conversely, communication from B to A is composed of B's general sending accuracy, A's general receiving ability, and the unique ability of A to read B. The latter quantity reflects the unique relationship of A and B and is termed the "relationship effect."

$$\text{COMMa to b} = (\text{SENDINGa} + \text{RECEIVINGb} + \text{UNIQUEa to b})$$

$$\text{COMMb to a} = (\text{SENDINGb} + \text{RECEIVINGa} + \text{UNIQUEb to a})$$

The overall influence of individual and relationship factors on communication has been assessed in human beings by round-robin experimental designs in which A communicates not only with B but also with others—C and D—and B also communicates with C and D. This allows one to measure the abilities of A and B to send and receive not only vis-à-vis one another but also vis-à-vis C and D, so that one can estimate the average sending accuracy of A to B, C, and D; the average receiving ability of A from B, C, and D; and the same for B.

Knowing the overall communication accuracy of A and B, and the general sending accuracies and receiving abilities of A and B, the unique abilities of A and B to communicate with each other (plus error) can be assessed by solving the equation. For example, using a round-robin design in which young married couples communicated nonverbally vis-à-vis one another and also vis-à-vis groups of "other males" and "other females," Sabatelli, Buck, and Kenny (1986) found communication from wife to husband, and from husband to wife, to be composed of the following:

$$\text{COMMw to h} = (48\% \text{ SENDINGw} + 1\% \\ \text{RECEIVINGh} + 51\% \\ [\text{UNIQUEw to h} + \text{error}])$$

$$\text{COMMh to w} = (22\% \text{ SENDINGh} + 10\% \\ \text{RECEIVINGw} + 68\% \\ [\text{UNIQUEh to w} + \text{error}])$$

This analysis can be applied generally to any communication situation, including the communication of genes. Gene A has a communicative relationship with gene B and also with other genes, potentially all in the genome, just as an individual person A has a communicative relationship with person B and also with others. In theory, the sending and receiving of specific genes can be assessed and related to their communication with other genes, and unique communicative relationships between genes can be assessed.

The communicating genes in question may be in the same cell, in different cells, or in different individual organisms. For example, genes that produce pheromones function in the context of genes in other organisms that produce receptors for those pheromones. Sending genes persist across evolutionary time, dependent on receiving genes. So the *unique relationship of sending and receiving genes* can be an active, germ-line replicator in Dawkins's (1982) sense. This allows one to maintain a gene selectionist account of evolution, but by rejecting genetic atomism it also allows one to recognize genuine prosocial tendencies, including biologically based prosocial emotions and altruism, as based on the selection of communicative relationships between genes (Buck, 1999, 2002).

SPONTANEOUS, SYMBOLIC, AND PSEUDOSPONTANEOUS COMMUNICATION

Communication between genes is a fundamental example of *spontaneous communication*, which involves genetically based displays in a sender that can be "picked up" by genetically based preattunements in a receiver (Buck, 1984; Buck & VanLear, 2002). Spontaneous communication includes the nonverbal and nonintentional communication of motivational and emotional states in human beings: it is based on a biologically shared and genetically based signal system consisting of displays on the part of the sender and preattunements on the part of the receiver. The sender's displays are *signs*—readouts of the sender's internal motivational and emotional state—that function as social affordances (Gibson, 1966). Given attention, these are picked up by perceptual preattunements in the receiver, who gains an intuitive and affective knowledge of the sender. Spontaneous communication is direct, effortless, and nonpropositional.

In contrast, *symbolic communication* involves the intentional communication of propositions; it is based on a socially shared signal system that is learned rather than innate. Information is transmitted via symbols, including spoken language. These two streams of symbolic and spontaneous communication occur in every human conversation, although the relative importance of the two streams varies with the situation and the personal relationship. All else being equal, the spontaneous stream is relatively more important in intimate, affectively charged situations and relationships, but it has some role—often unconscious—in every communicative exchange.

Of course, the sender also attempts to *control* or manage the display via learned and culturally variable display rules, and the receiver responds to displays in others by learned and culturally variable decoding rules (Buck, 1984; Seyfarth & Cheney, 2003). *Pseudospontaneous communication* involves the intentional nonverbal display by the sender to manipulate the receiver: If the sender is successful, the receiver's affective "buttons are pushed" in a way that may be beneficial to the sender tactically or strategically and, possibly, detrimental to the receiver (Buck & VanLear, 2002). For example, charismatic leaders are often masters of pseudospontaneous communication. Through practice and refinement of their expressions of emotion, they are able to persuade their audiences by turning on preattunements for fear, anger, attraction, and so forth.

Communicative relationships based on spontaneous communication can persist across evolutionary timescales. An example is the dominant-submissive relationship in which one individual displays threat that may be responded to by another individual with actions such as counterthreat, submission, or withdrawal. Such communicative acts form the basis of the dominance hierarchy and territoriality across many species (Hauser, 1996; Wilson, 1975). There is evidence both in human beings and in other animals that confident dominance is associated with the neurochemical serotonin (5-hydroxytriptamine), and the relationship of serotonin and dominance may underlie the antidepressant effects of selective serotonin uptake inhibitors (SSRIs), such as Prozac © and Zoloft © (see Buck, 1999).

Another striking example of a display crossing evolutionary timescales involves the sexual pheromone in the yeast *Saccharomyces cerevisiae*, which is virtually identical to gonadotropin-releasing hormone (GnRH), a peptide neurochemical active in mammals and associated with erotic feelings in human beings (Panksepp, 1991). The similarity is so great that the yeast pheromone functions as the hormone in rodents, and rodent hormone functions as the pheromone in yeast. Loumaye, Thorner, and Catt (1982) stated, "It is intriguing that a pheromone responsible for mating and zygote formation in a unicellular organism is both structurally and functionally related to the peptide serving a key role in mammalian reproduction" (p. 1324). So, like the chemical organization of dominance, the sending and receiving genes associated with these molecules of sexual attraction have endured and maintained their essential functions across evolutionary timescales.

SUMMARY

Communication theory allows a useful approach to the conceptualization of the genetic bases of cooperation and competition. If communicative relationships between genes function as units of selection in evolution, it follows that genes not only compete selfishly with other genes but also depend directly on communicatively related genes for their own survival across evolutionary timescales: communicatively related genes co-evolve and survive as a collectivity. As a result, there are fundamental biological imperatives for tendencies toward both cooperation and competition, resulting in a relationship between these opposed predispositions that might be symbolized by the Yin and Yang (Buck, 2002). The next section presents evidence that nonverbal communication is critical to whether cooperation or competition actually occurs.

♦ Cooperation, Competition, and Deception

In *Expression of the Emotions in Man and Animals*, Charles Darwin (1872/1998) argued that expressive displays evolved to signal information about the sender's motivational-emotional state, and this account was largely accepted by early ethologists. This position was challenged by the *selfish-gene* account of evolution, however, which argued that selection should actually work against individuals whose displays are informative about their actual motivational-emotional state (Hauser, 1996). In the latter view, displays are actually designed like advertisements, to deceive and manipulate the receiver, concealing the actual state of the sender (Dawkins, 1989; Dawkins & Krebs, 1978). The receiver responds by "mind reading," attempting to see through the deception. The result is an evolutionary "arms race" in which senders evolve progressively more persuasive and manipulative "sales pitches," and receivers become increasingly sales resistant (Krebs & Dawkins, 1984). Zahavi (1977) moderated this view by suggesting that displays can be honest but if and only if they are costly to the sender: In the absence of costs, the display becomes unreliable because it is too easily imitated.

The question of honest versus manipulative communication can be approached from the viewpoint of economic game theory. Frank (1988, 2001, 2004) argued that cooperation can succeed only in the presence of markers that distinguish individuals who are willing to cooperate—that is, individuals who are "trustworthy"— from those who will not. Such markers must involve nonverbal behaviors that occur during the communication between players (Boone & Buck, 2003). For example, Frank, Gilovich, and Regan (1993) allowed partners to meet and interact before a one-shot Prisoner's Dilemma (PD) game but not discuss the game itself. Cooperation was enhanced overall, but more significantly, the participants could apparently predict the decision of partners to cooperate or compete, so that dyads tended to show either mutual cooperation or mutual defection, with relatively few cases of one partner taking advantage of the other. Apparently, the intent to cooperate *or* compete was somehow discernable in the partners' behavior during the face-to-face interaction.

Boone and Buck (2003) combined considerations about whether displays are honest or manipulative with evidence about superficially self-defeating cooperation in social dilemmas and suggested that a key marker of trustworthiness is spontaneous nonverbal expressivity. This argument was based on several considerations. First, as

noted, honest expressivity comes at a potential cost to the sender—those who show their feelings accurately put themselves at risk of exploitation—and costly signals are more reliable. Thus, the costly nature of the display is consistent with its representing an accurate readout of the sender's motivational-emotional state. Second, there is evidence that spontaneous emotional expressivity is in fact valued by others. Sabatelli and Rubin (1986) found that emotional expressivity is positively related to judgments of interpersonal attraction, independent of physical attractiveness. Third, studies demonstrating that personality judgments based on brief "thin slices" of nonverbal behavior have accurately predicted interpersonal outcomes (Ambady & Rosenthal, 1992) show that emotional expressivity has an immediate impact, which could allow fast and accurate evaluation of the trustworthiness of strangers.

For nonverbal expressiveness to function as an accurate "sincerity detector," spontaneous displays must differ from intentional pseudospontaneous behaviors. Indeed, spontaneous expressive behavior does differ from posed or intentionally enacted behavior, so that there is a signal basis for distinguishing between honest and manipulative displays. Cohn and Schmidt (2004) compared spontaneous smiles elicited by viewing a comedy film with deliberate smiles, using automatic feature tracking to extract and represent dynamic features of the behavior as well as its morphology. They found that spontaneous and deliberate smiles could be distinguished: There were differences in the timing of smile onsets, and there was a tight coupling between duration and amplitude in spontaneous smiles consistent with the contention that the spontaneous smile is automatic and involuntary. Also, there is initial empirical evidence that expressiveness predicts cooperation in the PD game. Rauh, Polonsky, and Buck (2004) found that cooperative behavior, as assessed by the participants' cooperation on the first move of a computer-simulated PD game, was positively related to friendly expressiveness.

In conclusion, genuine cooperation and altruism can be seen to have biological bases tied to nonverbal cues. If communicative relationships of genes are recognized to be active, germ-line replicators, it is consistent with a gene-selectionist account of evolution. Therefore, displays and pre-attunements are spontaneous sending and receiving mechanisms that co-evolve: Cooperation is fostered by communication that is friendly, open, direct, and genuinely expressive. It exists together with competition, antagonism, and manipulation, which are also biologically based and fostered by evasion, equivocation, and pretense.

◆ The Spontaneous Communication/Social Structure Relationship

We have shown that spontaneous communication is biologically based in both its sending and its receiving aspects and is a critical determinant of cooperation and competition. Indeed, we argue that spontaneous communication is the foundation of social organization. In some respects, this spontaneous communication/social structure relationship is easier to understand in simpler creatures, where behavior is under relatively close genetic control. Despite the relative simplicity of such creatures, their social structures are surprisingly complex and show basic characteristics found in all social structures: arousal-quiescence, approach-avoidance, dominance-submission, cooperation and competition, and some form of courting and sexuality.

PALEOSOCIALITY IN NONVERTEBRATE FORMS

"Paleosociality" refers to the social organization and behavior of relatively simple creatures. In these creatures, fundamental principles of social organization can be discerned. Given the intrinsic conservatism of evolution, these principles illuminate basic mechanisms underlying social organization by offering specific examples of how social organization arises as an emergent and self-organizing dynamic system. Moreover, it becomes clear that the mechanism of emergence through time is communication between elements—that is, between individual organisms. With nonvertebrates, and particularly with single-celled creatures, the system is uncomplicated enough so that the specific mechanisms of communication—the display molecules and receptor mechanisms—can be observed directly and their genetic origins established. To reveal this process, we consider two examples: quorum sensing in bacteria and the life cycle of the cellular slime mold. Our goal is to illustrate relatively simple examples of social organization as a self-organizing dynamic system emerging out of communicative interactions, which is based on general principles identical to those underlying the emergence of human social organization emerging out of communicative interactions.

Quorum Sensing in Bacteria. Quorum sensing is a remarkable example of bacterial communication leading to collective action through arousal and quiescence (Hentzer & Givskov, 2003; Waters & Bassler, 2005). "Quorum" refers to having a minimum number of individuals to perform a given action, as in a meeting that requires a certain number of participants. Quorum sensing in bacteria refers to the ability of individual bacteria to sense through the concentration of signaling molecules that their numbers in the area have reached a critical mass, and thereby to coordinate collective behavior. It is used by certain pathogenic bacteria to trick the immune systems of their hosts. The bacteria are quiescent—not activating a full immune system response—until their numbers are sufficient to overwhelm the victim. When a quorum is attained, the regulation of bacterial genes is changed so that toxic "virulence factors" are produced. For example, in cystic fibrosis, when the bacteria reach a certain concentration, they produce a "biofilm," a tough shell that protects them from attack from the immune system of the victim or from antibiotics. The bacteria can then reproduce, produce toxins, and damage tissues in relative safety (Riedel & Eberl, 2002).

The molecules that bacteria use to communicate have structures similar to those used by humans and many other creatures. The signals or displays used by bacteria typically involve amino acids or peptides functioning as pheromones (Gallio, Sturgill, Rather, & Kylsten, 2002). Peptides are critical signaling molecules in human beings, including the endorphins, oxytocin (OXY), vasopressin (VP), cholecystokinin, diazepam-binding inhibitor, GnRH, adrenocortico tropic hormone, and insulin. Many of these molecules exist virtually unchanged in simple creatures. Moreover, these molecules are also associated with subjectively experienced feelings and desires in human beings, including attachment, euphoria, pain, erotic feelings, panic, anxiety, and stress. Gallio and colleagues (2002) concluded that peptide-mediated signaling is a "widely conserved mechanism for signal release . . . not only the signal releasing mechanism seems conserved, but also the molecule that carries it out . . . (suggesting that) . . . these molecules share a common ancestry" (pp. 12212–12213).

Slime Molds. Whereas quorum sensing demonstrates that bacteria communicate,

the life cycle of the slime mold *Dictyostelium discoideum* illustrates the implications of cell communication for larger issues of overall social organization: the organization of multicelled organisms. Slime molds are abundant (a spoonful of rich garden soil contains millions), their principal food is rotting organic material, and they are responsible for the slimy material found on rotting wood. At one stage in their life cycle, *D. discoideum* are single-celled amoebae that live independently and display negative chemotaxis. That is, they produce pheromones that repel similar amoebae (Newell, 1981), a function analogous to territorial/threat displays in more complex species, that tend to spread individuals evenly over the available environment. When food in the environment becomes scarce, the negative chemotaxis ends, and a positive chemotaxis begins, attracting rather than repelling the amoebae. In *D. discoideum* the molecule on which the positive chemotaxis is based is cyclic adenosine monophosphate, a ubiquitous molecule involved in metabolism and in the functioning of many neurotransmitters in human beings. The result is an aggregation center where the single-celled amoebae come together and form a multicelled form termed a "grex," which may be made up of millions of individuals.

This journey culminates in the differentiation of the cells into a "fruiting body." Cells at the front end die and become a cellulose stalk anchored to a secure footing, and a mass of cells from the rear then literally climb over their fallen colleagues to the top of the stalk and form spores that become released into the environment. Given favorable conditions, the spores become individual amoebae and begin the life cycle anew (Waters & Bassler, 2005). In this process, the individual amoebae that form the stalk give up any possibility for passing on their genes, whereas the individuals that climb the stalk carry on the species. As noted, giving up the potential to pass on one's own genes while enhancing the genetic potential of other individuals is the biological definition of altruism (Wilson, 1975). Thus, *D. discoideum* in its life cycle demonstrates what might be termed *proto-threat behavior* in its negative chemotaxis, *proto-attachment behavior* in its positive chemotaxis, and *proto-altruistic* behavior in its stalk formation.

There are many other examples of paleosociality in simple creatures. In insect societies, for example, social organization is largely "hard wired"—that is, it is under close genetic control and has little to do with learning or flexibility. The genes accomplish social organization via spontaneous communication: genetically based displays and preattunements in different individual organisms interacting with one another over time.

SOCIALITY IN MAMMALS

In mammals, there is an additional consideration for understanding social organization: Unlike most reptiles, the mammal is helpless at birth. The brain and spinal cord do not come preprogrammed: They are programmed by the animal's experience over the course of development in the territorial and social environment. This experience requires communication mechanisms involving bonding, nurturance, and protection (i.e., *attachment*), to ensure that the young animal receives adequate parental attention until it is physically and socially mature enough to function on its own. An examination of voles can help demonstrate these communicative mechanisms.

Polygamous and Monogamous Voles. The vole is a particularly interesting case illustrating the biology of attachment. The vole is a mouse-size rodent, some species of which are monogamous, forming lasting female-male bonds, whereas other species

are polygamous. Prairie voles (*Microtus ochrogaster*) show monogamy as evidenced by selective and lasting partner preferences (pair bonds) that are activated by mating (Wang & Aragona, 2004). The bonds are lasting: If the bonded partner dies, a surviving prairie vole will live alone rather than take a new mate. Both male and female provide extensive care for their pups, with the male helping to build the nest and spending almost as much time as the female with the young. If separated from their parents, the pups become agitated and display ultrasonic distress calls and high stress evidenced by increases in cortisol. In contrast, closely related species—the meadow vole (*Microtus pennsylvanicus*) and montane vole (*Microtus montanus*)—are non-monogamous. The latter breed promiscuously and nest independently, and the males play no parenting role. Even the females abandon their pups soon after birth, and the pups do not appear to be distressed by abandonment (Carter, Lederhendler, & Kirkpatrick, 1997).

There is evidence that attachment in voles is related to the peptides OXY and VP. Brain areas associated with OXY are much larger in the prairie vole than in the montane vole (Insel, Young, & Wang, 1997), and the distribution of VP receptors in the male brain is different, with the prairie vole and other monogamous species having a relatively high density of VP receptors (termed V1aR) in the ventral forebrain, in an area of the brain also associated with dopamine-mediated reward (Lim et al., 2004; Young, Lim, Gingrich, & Insel, 2001). Moreover, OXY and VP are critical to the establishment of the pair bonds of prairie voles. In the natural setting, mating is associated with OXY release, which apparently functions to cement partner preferences in that the individuals prefer who they are with when OXY increase occurs (Carter, DeVries, & Getz, 1995). Thus, OXY is both *necessary and sufficient* for the development of pair bonds in the female prairie vole (Williams, Insel, Harbaugh, & Carter, 1994).

There is recent evidence that, rather incredibly, the ruggedly individualistic but philandering male meadow vole can be made to act like a sweet, sensitive, reliable male prairie vole by the alteration of a single gene. And, it is certainly a communicative gene. Lim et al. (2004) demonstrated that V1aR gene transfer into the ventral forebrain of male meadow voles substantially increased partner preference formation, indicating that "changes in the regional expression of a single gene can have a profound effect on the social behaviour of individuals within a species" (p. 756). The V1aR gene transfer increases VP receptors in the ventral forebrain, and the authors suggest that this has the effect of increasing social memory of the partner's olfactory signature and also associating that social memory with dopamine-mediated reward: "Monogamous social organization might be the result of the insertion of the V1aR system into the ancient pre-existing reward circuit" (p. 756).

Interestingly, dopamine-mediated reward is also associated with addiction, and it may be that the increased V1aRs induce the animal to become physically addicted to the partner (in this regard, Panksepp, 1991, noted a number of similarities between addiction and attachment). Recent studies have demonstrated such effects on cooperative and competitive behavior in the PD games considered previously. With human participants, Kosfeld, Heinrichs, Zak, Fischbacher, and Fehr (2005) found that OXY presented in an aerosol increased cooperative behavior in a PD game, and Wood, Rilling, Sanfey, Bhagwagar, and Rogers (2005) reported that the disruption of central serotonin function increases competitive tendencies. The implication is that these physiological manipulations involving

molecules relevant to attachment mechanisms can have significant effects on complex human behavior, and perhaps particularly on behavior involving communication. It is clear that these primordial affective motivational-emotional systems can influence complex choices in human beings involving cooperation and competition, and this is consistent with our view that such systems underlie basic behavior and sociality in humans.

Complex Mammalian Social Organization. More complex social mammals, such as wolves and nonhuman primates (monkeys and apes), demonstrate more complex social behavior accompanied by more complex communication patterns. With these creatures, bonding cannot be simply turned on and off chemically or genetically. Rather, bonding involves a long process of developmental experience in communicative relationships with other individuals. For example, Woolpy and Ginsburg (1967) raised unrelated wolves together from infancy with no adult tutors. Over the course of development the individuals generated a typical adult pack structure from their own communicative interactions. Often these communicative interchanges occur in the context of rough-and-tumble play, which may be accompanied by pleasure associated with endorphin mechanisms (Burgdorf & Panksepp, 2001).

Studies by Harry Harlow and colleagues demonstrated that rhesus monkeys show specific stages of socioemotional development based on experience in communicative relationships (Harlow, 1971). Interactions with the mother initiate the *maternal affectional system*, which establishes a basic sense of attachment and trust in other monkeys. This is followed by the *peer affectional system*, in which communicative displays—threats, submissive behaviors, courting behaviors—are "tried out" in the context of rough-and-tumble play relationships with peers. This sets the stage for the *heterosexual affectional system*, which is the basis for adult monkey communicative relationships and social organization. Harlow suggested that these are analogous to infancy, childhood, and adolescence in humans.

Harlow's work also demonstrated that early social deprivation can have devastating effects on an individual animal's abilities to participate in social behavior. Contact comfort—contact with a soft skinlike surface—was found to be sufficient to instill a basic sense of trust, but trusting individuals raised separately from peers showed significant deficits in courting and sexual behavior after puberty. Animals reared in wire cages were extremely fearful and aggressive as adults (Harlow, 1971). There is evidence that these social deficits are related to an inability to communicate. Specifically, Miller, Caul, and Mirsky (1967) demonstrated that monkeys isolated in infancy were unable as adults either to send or to receive accurately in Miller's cooperative conditioning paradigm measuring communication in monkeys (Miller, Banks, & Ogawa, 1962, 1963).

SUMMARY

Examples of social organization from simple bacteria to mammals including primates demonstrate common principles involving an unfolding of biological potential in the course of development. At all these levels, social organization emerges out of communicative interactions as a self-organizing dynamic system. In mammals, attachment systems involving bonding, nurturance, and protection of the young, are critical and demand communication systems through which attachment can function. We now turn to human social organization, where nonverbal communication

plays a similar role, but now in interaction with language, a new source of social organization missing in other animals.

◆ Language, Nonverbal Communication, and Human Social Organization

The human brain shares many features with the brains of other animals, particularly in the phylogenetically older subcortical and limbic regions, which are associated with motivational and emotional processing (Buck, 1999). In those regions, similar neurochemicals appear to function in ways analogous to those in other animals, and they do seem to have the ability in some cases to overwhelm more "rational" linguistic control mechanisms. Addiction provides many tragic examples. Indeed, it can be argued that these motivational-emotional systems set the agenda for human communication and underlie the human equivalents of the primordial characteristics found in all social structures—arousal-quiescence, approach-avoidance, dominance-submission, cooperation-competition, and courting-sexuality—all of which are communicated nonverbally.

Language introduces in human beings a source of behavioral control and social organization that is lacking in animals, creating a real discontinuity with other species (Buck, 1988). As complex propositions become expressible and recordable in language, questions of linguistic organization that are distinct from biological factors become important determinants of human social organization. On the other hand, language itself is based on biological mechanisms, associated particularly with the left hemisphere (LH) of the brain in almost all humans. For example, damage to the LH has long been associated with crippling language deficits collectively termed *aphasia*. Damage confined to Wernicke's area is associated with *receptive aphasia*, in which the patient can speak but cannot comprehend. Damage confined to Broca's area near the left motor cortex, associated with the control of the mouth, tongue, and larynx, is associated with *expressive aphasia*, in which the patient can comprehend but cannot speak. Damage to the right hemisphere (RH) in contrast is often associated with deficits in spontaneous communication. Patients damaged in the RH can express propositions normally, but often show deficits in both the sending and the receiving aspects of spontaneous communication. Specifically, the voice tends to be flat and lacking in affective prosody, the face is unexpressive, and there are often deficits in understanding emotion and other affective information in the voices and faces of others (Buck & Duffy, 1980; Ross, 1992).

Many nonverbal behaviors—gestures, illustrators, emblems, and so on—are linked closely with language (see Bavelas & Chovil, this volume), and there is evidence they are organized linguistically. For example, persons who use gestural forms of communication, such as sign language and finger spelling, typically lose their abilities after suffering LH damage. In a meta-analysis, Buck and VanLear (2002) showed that abilities at both sending and receiving via pantomime are generally lost with LH damage, suggesting that the LH is associated with intentional, symbolic, propositional communication and the RH with spontaneous, automatic, nonpropositional, affective communication. The implication is that the distinction between "spontaneous" and propositional or "symbolic" communication is more fundamental than that between verbal and nonverbal communication.

SUMMARY

In human beings, spontaneous and symbolic communication proceeds in simultaneous streams, spontaneous communication being entirely nonverbal and symbolic communication involving both verbal and nonverbal elements. We have argued that the spontaneous stream guides cooperative and competitive behavior, effortlessly and often unconsciously. The spontaneous stream is also involved in social comparison processes that can involve inequalities, where one partner is in a dominant position relative to the other. Such inequalities are the foundation of higher level social and moral emotions. The next sections consider how social and moral emotions emerge, naturally and effortlessly, from human interactions.

◆ Social and Moral Emotions in Human Social Organization

SOCIAL EMOTIONS

Social comparison processes occur constantly in animal social behavior, ranging from relatively straightforward considerations of who is bigger, smellier, louder, or more colorful to more complex issues involving establishing and maintaining enduring social relationships (de Waal & Tyack, 2003). In humans, linguistic competence adds enormously to the complexity of these considerations, but often social comparisons come down to whether the comparison person is better off or worse off than oneself. But this social comparison is not necessarily only rational: It is often fraught with strong emotion. Arguably, the emotional "fire" in social and moral emotions has its origin in that fundamental mammalian motivational-emotional system: attachment.

Fundamental Social Motives. The motivation arising from attachment has, arguably, two aspects: the *need to be loved* and the *need to meet or exceed expectations* (Buck, 1988). People are strongly motivated to be esteemed and loved and to do that which is expected and indeed to exceed expectations. Individuals can attain or fail to attain these two social goals themselves, and they can compare themselves with other persons who attain or fail to attain these goals. The relative strength of these two social motives should be related to the security of the attachment of the person to reference persons evaluating them. Persons who are insecurely attached are likely to need reassurance that they are loved, and that overwhelming need might overshadow needs to meet or exceed expectations. Secure individuals, in contrast, should be relatively assured of love, and they will instead be able to focus on meeting and exceeding expectations.

Fundamental Interpersonal Contingencies. The comparisons just described constitute *fundamental interpersonal contingencies,* which yield eight primary social emotions, including *pride-arrogance* when one is doing comparatively well, *guilt-shame* when one is not doing well, *envy-jealousy* when the other is doing well, and *pity-scorn* when the other is not doing well (Buck, 2004). More specifically, a person P who succeeds experiences what could be labeled in English pride or arrogance; if P fails, P experiences guilt or shame; if comparison person O succeeds, P tends to experience envy or jealousy; if O fails, P tends to experience pity or scorn. These comparisons involve relative dominance, which, as we have seen, is a fundamental characteristic of social structure and organization where one is in a position of relative strength and the other in a position of relative weakness. The difference between pride, shame, envy, and pity on the one hand and arrogance, shame,

jealousy, and scorn on the other relates to whether the responder is securely or insecurely attached in that particular comparison situation. A secure person may experience pride, guilt, envy, and pity in situations where an insecure person may experience arrogance, shame, jealousy, and scorn.

The Dynamics of Social Emotions. These fundamental interpersonal contingencies do not elicit social emotions in isolation from one another. Rather, because success and failure are relative, the social emotions are dynamically related one to the other. If P is successful and experiences pride-arrogance, P will tend to pity-scorn the less successful O. On the other hand, O will tend to be envious-jealous of P and will experience guilt-shame in comparison to P. The resulting dynamics of the social emotions are summarized in Figure 7.1a.

To test these predictions, American and Japanese students were asked to read a series of six simple scenarios, imagining they had gone home for a high school reunion and heard the scenario about an old acquaintance "O" (Buck, Nakamura, Vieira, & Polonsky, 2005). The scenarios involved positive or negative outcomes for O that were or were not deserved: for example, O won the lottery, was hit by lightning, invented a new computer chip, and was jailed for selling drugs to children. Participants were asked to rate how they would feel about O and how O would feel about them, using the list of the primary social emotions in English or Japanese as appropriate. The results relevant to the predictions about emotion dynamics are summarized in Table 7.1. Briefly, across both nations, in all cases save one, the average correlations were in the predicted direction and statistically significant. Thus, the predictions about the dynamics of social emotions in Figure 7.1a were strongly supported in both America and Japan.

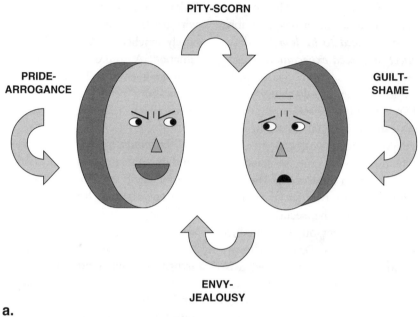

a.

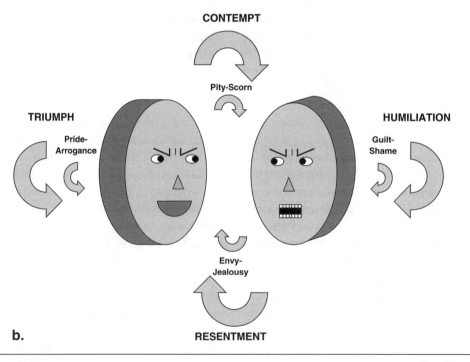

b.

Figure 7.1 (Continued)

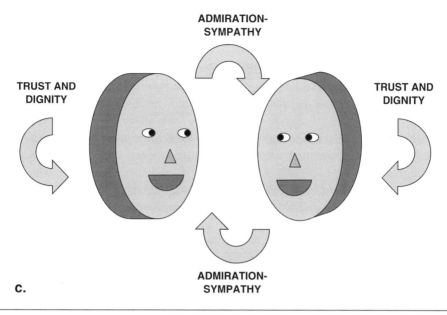

Figure 7.1 Hypothesized Dynamics of Social and Moral Emotions

NOTE: (A) Dynamics of eight primary social emotions. (B) Moral considerations can exacerbate conflict through the perception of unfairness. (C) Moral considerations can facilitate cooperation through the perception of fairness.

Table 7.1 Hypotheses About the Dynamics of Primary Social Emotions and Average Correlations From America and Japan		
	America	*Japan*
If one experiences the primary social emotion *pride*, it is		
Likely that one would simultaneously experience *arrogance*	.80***	.69***
Unlikely that one would experience *guilt-shame*	−.40***	−.33**
Likely that one would experience *pity-scorn* toward others	.25*	.13
Unlikely that one would experience *envy-jealousy* toward others	−.39***	−.41***
If one experiences the primary social emotion *pride*, the comparison other is		
Unlikely to simultaneously experience *pride-arrogance*	−.55***	−.46***
Likely to experience *guilt-shame*	.36***	.23**
Unlikely to experience *pity-scorn*	−.28**	−.31**
Likely to experience *envy-jealousy*	.68***	.77***

NOTE: Pride is given as an example. Data represent the average correlations computed across all relevant social emotions. English pronunciation of equivalent words in Japanese: *Hokori*, pride; *goumannsa*, arrogance; *zaiakukann*, guilt; *hazukashisa*, shame; *urayami*, envy; *sitto*, jealousy; *awaremi*, pity; *keibetsu*, scorn.

***$p < .001$. **$p < .01$. *$p < .05$.

This result supports the key proposition that social emotions emerge as dynamic systems from biologically based prosocial attachment, in interaction with fundamental interpersonal contingencies involving social comparison, over the course of individual development. Although the language used to label the social emotions is cultural, attachment and the eight unions of interpersonal contingencies are fundamentally similar in two nations with different values and languages. The implication is that this emergence is a pancultural phenomenon, common to all cultures and to all historical times.

The social emotions are "on," and the dynamic pattern of social emotions is present, in every human communicative exchange. The interchange depicted in Figure 7.1a is rather competitive, with the proud-arrogant individual clearly expressing dominance to the partner and the partner responding with a downcast, submissionlike display. Such feelings can be raised even in trivial encounters, as in passing on the street. Generalizing from Ambady and Rosenthal (1992), we can be exquisitely sensitive to thin slices suggesting even a hint of pride-arrogance: It can set off alarm bells that one is being put down, snubbed, and disrespected. Perhaps such signals—a smirk, a quick turning away of the eyes, a subtle raise of the chin—account for the ability of people in the Frank et al. (1993) study to calculate that their partner is likely to compete. Conversely, we quickly grasp weakness and submission in others—responding involuntarily with pity or scorn—and we can directly perceive honest and friendly trustworthiness.

MORAL EMOTIONS

When comparative success or failure is seen to be deserved or undeserved, it adds another level of consideration that elicits *moral emotions*. We propose that like social emotions, moral emotions involve issues of relative success or failure on the part of O: If we are winning and perceive that we deserve it, we respond with feelings of *triumph*; if we lose and deserve it, we experience *humiliation*. If O wins and deserves it, we experience *admiration* even as we may simultaneously experience envy-jealousy. But if we believe that O does not deserve success, our envy-jealousy is mixed with bitter *resentment*. If O loses and deserves it, we feel *contempt*, but if O's loss is not deserved, we feel *sympathy*. Morality is a double-edged sword, with the capacity to ameliorate potential conflict arising from inequities or greatly exacerbate such conflict.

Moral Indignation. When unfairness is perceived, moral considerations can greatly exacerbate the conflict shown in Figure 7.1a, evoking strikingly strong negative emotion: *moral indignation*, as illustrated in Figure 7.1b. P is triumphant and shows scorn toward O, who responds with humiliation and resentment: a powerful, poisonous combination fraught with potential conflict and aggression. Resentment can lead to increased conflict that can become deadly, with murderous assaults on O being perceived to be morally justified and even gratifying, eliciting *schadenfreude*: a delight in the discomfort and even agony of the other. Such perceptions can become socially shared, particularly through encouragement via media propaganda, and lead to long-term conflicts between peoples that can turn into war, ethnic cleansing, and genocide.

Civil Exchange. On the other hand, if P and O perceive that each is following the rules fairly, even though they may differ greatly in comparative success, the potential conflict shown in Figure 7.1 can be ameliorated. If P and O perceive that each is following the rules fairly, then each can view the other with *admiration* and *sympathy*. Moreover, they themselves feel a sense of *dignity* and *trust* in the relationship. Prosocial emotions can occur, such as *gratitude* and *appreciation*, when the other follows the rules and does the expected. These and other positive moral feelings constitute the emotional bases of *civil exchange* (see Figure 7.1c). Even bitter enemies may engage in civil interaction, albeit grudgingly, if they can mutually acknowledge that each is following the rules and acting with dignity. Seemingly trivial rituals of greeting, making brief eye contact, and saying "good day," function to remind interactants that each is following the rules and acting with dignity. It is possibly the nonverbal expression of civility that underlies the perception of mutual trustworthiness that enabled participants in Frank et al. (1993) to guess correctly that their partner would cooperate—that is, that their partner was trustworthy (Boone & Buck, 2003).

Moral emotions are based on the same elements as social emotions: an affective caring based biologically on attachment, interacting with fundamental interpersonal contingencies involving comparative success and failure. But, with moral emotions there is the additional element of fairness and justice, equity, or following the rules. Moral emotions emerge together with social emotions as dynamic systems, intuitively and effortlessly, during socioemotional development. They emerge, as Piaget (1971) suggested, from experiences in social interactions, particularly play. They have animal analogies in the pack structure that emerges spontaneously from the interactions of young wolves raised together by Woolpy and Ginsburg (1967) and in the need for peer interactions in young monkeys demonstrated in the work of Harlow (1971).

◆ Summary and Conclusions

Signs of basic sociality—arousal-quiescence, approach-avoidance, dominance-submission, cooperation-competition, courting-sexuality—are rooted in the deepest and most ancient regions and molecules of the brain. Their influence is almost unnoticed—they function largely below the radar of consciousness—but it is profound and pervasive. These signs constitute the mechanism by which social structure emerges and organizes itself, whether in bacteria and slime molds or in the rough-and-tumble play of children. The mechanism of the emergence is spontaneous nonverbal communication—unconscious, intuitive, and effortless—involving the direct perception of and preprogrammed responses to displays. Spontaneous communication links us one to another in a primordial biological dance.

We have seen that informal human communication involves social comparisons that evoke a dynamic system of social emotions including pride and arrogance, guilt and shame, envy and jealousy, and pity and scorn, and potentially also moral emotions, such as triumph, humiliation, resentment, and contempt. These potentially disruptive emotions are often finessed by common and virtually unconscious verbal and nonverbal rituals of politeness that establish the social lubricant of *civility*, evoking moral emotions of admiration, sympathy, trust, respect, and gratitude. They are leavened by other basic signals, including subtle signs of attraction that hint at courtship. These signs may be used to deceive and manipulate, but the very fact of deception implies their potential to reveal underlying truth.

Human social behavior retains a foundation in primordial sociality as evidenced by emergent systems of social and moral emotions that naturally, effortlessly, and largely unconsciously guide each and every human communicative exchange, mediated by nuances of nonverbal behavior that, although subtle, can engender deep and powerful emotions ranging from enraged humiliation and resentment to delight and triumph, tender nurturance and protectiveness, passionate desire, and compassionate love.

◆ References

Ambady, N., & Rosenthal, R. (1992). Thin slices of behavior as predictors of interpersonal consequences: A meta-analysis. *Psychological Bulletin, 2,* 256–274.

Boone, R. T., & Buck, R. (2003). Emotional expressivity and trustworthiness: The role of nonverbal behavior in the evolution of cooperation. *Journal of Nonverbal Behavior, 27,* 163–182.

Buck, R. (1984). *The communication of emotion.* New York: Guilford Press.

Buck, R. (1988). *Human motivation and emotion* (2nd ed.). New York: Wiley.

Buck, R. (1999). The biological affects: A typology. *Psychological Review, 106,* 301–336.

Buck, R. (2002). The genetics and biology of true love: Prosocial biological affects and the left hemisphere. *Psychological Review, 109,* 739–744.

Buck, R. (2004). The gratitude of exchange and the gratitude of caring: A developmental-interactionist perspective of moral emotion. In R. A. Emmons & M. McCullough (Eds.), *The psychology of gratitude* (pp. 100–122). New York: Oxford University Press.

Buck, R., & Duffy, R. (1980). Nonverbal communication of affect in brain damaged patients. *Cortex, 16,* 351–362.

Buck, R., & Ginsburg, B. (1991). Emotional communication and altruism: The communicative gene hypothesis. In M. Clark (Ed.), *Altruism: Review of personality and social psychology* (Vol. 11, pp. 149–175). Newbury Park, CA: Sage.

Buck, R., & Ginsburg, B. (1997). Communicative genes and the evolution of empathy. In W. Ickes (Ed.), *Empathic accuracy* (pp. 17–43). New York: Guilford Press.

Buck, R., Nakamura, M., Vieira, E. T., Jr., & Polonsky, M. (2005, November). *Dynamics of higher level social emotions: A cross-national comparison of America and Japan.* Paper presented at the annual conference of the National Communication Association, Boston.

Buck, R., & VanLear, C. A. (2002). Verbal and nonverbal communication: Distinguishing symbolic, spontaneous, and pseudo-spontaneous nonverbal behavior. *Journal of Communication, 52,* 522–541.

Burgdorf, J., & Panksepp, J. (2001). Tickling induces reward in adolescent rats. *Physiology & Behavior, 72,* 167–173.

Carter, C. S., DeVries, A. C., & Getz, L. L. (1995). Physiological substrates of mammalian monogamy: The prairie vole model. *Neuroscience & Biobehavioral Reviews, 19,* 303–314.

Carter, C. S., Lederhendler, I. I., & Kirkpatrick, B. (Eds.). (1997). The integrative neurobiology of affiliation. *Annals of the New York Academy of Sciences, 807,* 260–272.

Cohn, D. F., & Schmidt, K. L. (2004). The timing of facial motion in posed and spontaneous smiles. *International Journal of Wavelets, Multiresolution, and Information Processing, 2,* 1–12.

Darwin, C. (1998). *The expression of the emotions in man and animals* (3rd ed.). New York: Oxford University Press. (Original work published 1872)

Dawkins, R. (1982). *The extended phenotype: The gene as the unit of selection.* Oxford, UK: Oxford University Press.

Dawkins, R. (1989). *The selfish gene: New edition.* New York: Oxford University Press.

Dawkins, R., & Krebs, J. R. (1978). Animal signals: Information or manipulation? In J. R. Krebs & N. B. Davies (Eds.), *Behavioural ecology: An evolutionary approach* (pp. 282–309). Oxford, UK: Blackwell.

Frank, R. (1988). *Passions within reason: The strategic role of the emotions.* New York: Norton.

Frank, R. (2001). Cooperation through emotional commitment. In R. M. Hesse (Ed.), *Evolution and the capacity for commitment* (pp. 57–76). New York: Russell Sage Foundation.

Frank, R. H. (2004). In defense of sincerity detection. *Rationality and Society, 16,* 287–305.

Frank, R., Gilovich, T., & Regan, D. T. (1993). The evolution of one-shot cooperation: An experiment. *Ethology and Sociobiology, 14,* 247–256.

Gallio, M., Sturgill, G., Rather, P., & Kylsten, P. (2002). A conserved mechanism for extracellular signaling in eukaryotes and prokaryotes. *Proceedings of the National Academy of Sciences, 99,* 12208–12213.

Gibson, J. J. (1966). *The senses considered as perceptual systems.* Boston: Houghton Mifflin.

Harlow, H. F. (1971). *Learning to love.* San Francisco: Albion.

Hauser, M. D. (1996). *The evolution of communication.* Cambridge, MA: MIT Press.

Hentzer, M., & Givskov, M. (2003). Pharmacological inhibition of quorum sensing for the treatment of chronic bacterial infections. *Journal of Clinical Investigations, 112,* 1300–1307.

Insel, T. R., Young, L., & Wang, Z. (1997). Molecular aspects of monogamy. In C. S. Carter, I. I. Lederhendler, & B. Kirkpatrick (Eds.), *Annals of the New York Academy of Sciences: The integrative neurobiology of affiliation* (Vol. 807, pp. 302–316). New York: New York Academy of Sciences.

Kenny, D. A. (1994). *Interpersonal perception: A social relations analysis.* New York: Guilford.

Kosfeld, M., Heinrichs, M., Zak, P. J., Fischbacher, U., & Fehr, E. (2005). Oxytocin increases trust in humans. *Nature, 435,* 673–676.

Krebs, J. R., & Dawkins, R. (1984). Animal signals: Mind-reading and manipulation. In J. R. Krebs & N. B. Davies (Eds.), *Behavioural ecology: An evolutionary approach* (2nd ed., pp. 380–402). Sunderland, MA: Sinauer.

Lim, M. M., Wang, Z., Olazabal, D. E., Ren, X., Terwilliger, E. F., & Young, L. J. (2004). Enhanced partner preference in a promiscuous species by manipulating the expression of a single gene. *Nature, 429,* 754–757.

Loumaye, E., Thorner, J., & Catt, K. J. (1982). Yeast mating pheromone activates mammalian gonadotropins: Evolutionary conservation of a reproductive hormone? *Science, 218,* 1324–1325.

Miller, R. E., Banks, J., & Ogawa, N. (1962). Communication of affect in "cooperative conditioning" of rhesus monkeys. *Journal of Abnormal and Social Psychology, 64,* 343–348.

Miller, R. E., Banks, J., & Ogawa, N. (1963). Role of facial expression in "cooperative-avoidance conditioning" in monkeys. *Journal of Abnormal and Social Psychology, 67,* 24–30.

Miller, R. E., Caul, W. F., & Mirsky, I. A. (1967). Communication of affects between feral and socially isolated monkeys. *Journal of Personality and Social Psychology, 7,* 231–239.

Newell, P. C. (1981). Chemotaxis in the cellular slime moulds. In J. M. Lackie & P. C. Wilkinson (Eds.), *Biology of the chemotactic response* (pp. 89–114). Cambridge, UK: Cambridge University Press.

Panksepp, J. (1991). Brain opioids: A neurochemical substrate for narcotic and social dependence. In S. Cooper (Ed.), *Theory in psychopharmacology* (pp. 149–175). London: Academic Press.

Piaget, J. (1971). Piaget's theory. In P. Mussen (Ed.). *Handbook of child development* (Vol. 1, pp. 703–732). New York: Wiley.

Rauh, C., Polonsky, M., & Buck, R. (2004, July). *Cooperation on the first move: Emotional expressiveness and avatars in the Prisoners Dilemma Game.* Paper presented at the meeting of the International Society for Research on Emotions, New York.

Riedel, K., & Eberl, L. (2002). N-Acyl homoserinelactone-mediated cell-cell communication in bacterial biofilms. *Biomedical Progress 15,* 69–74.

Ross, E. D. (1992). Lateralization of affective prosody in the brain. *Neurology, 42* (Suppl. 3), 411.

Sabatelli, R. M., Buck, R., & Kenny, D. A. (1986). A social relations analysis of nonverbal communication accuracy in married couples. *Journal of Personality, 54,* 513–527.

Sabatelli, R. M., & Rubin, M. (1986). Nonverbal expressiveness and physical attractiveness as mediators of interpersonal perceptions.

Journal of Nonverbal Behavior, 10, 120–133.

Seyfarth, R. M., & Cheney, D. L. (2003). Signalers and receivers in animal communication. *Annual Review of Psychology, 54,* 145–173.

de Waal, F. B. M., & Tyack, P. L. (2003). *Animal social complexity: Intelligence, culture, and individualized societies.* Cambridge, MA: Harvard University Press.

Wang, Z., & Aragona, B. J. (2004). Neurochemical regulation of bonding in male prairie voles. *Physiology and Behavior, 83,* 319–328.

Waters, C. M., & Bassler, B. L. (2005). Quorum sensing: Cell-to-cell communication in bacteria. *Annual Review of Cell and Developmental Biology, 21,* 319–346.

Williams, J. R., Insel, T. R., Harbaugh, C. R., & Carter, C. S. (1994). Oxytocin administered centrally facilitates formation of a partner preference in prairie voles (*Microtus ochrogaster*). *Journal of Endocrinology, 6,* 247–250.

Wilson, E. O. (1975). *Sociobiology: The new synthesis.* Cambridge, MA: Belknap.

Wood, R. M., Rilling, J. K., Sanfey, A. G., Bhagwagar, Z., & Rogers, R. D. (2005). The effects of altering dietary L-tryptophan on the performance of an iterated Prisoner's Dilemma (PD) game in healthy volunteers. *Behavioural Pharmacology, 16,* S32.

Woolpy, J. H., & Ginsburg, B. E. (1967). Wolf socialization: A study of temperament in a wild social species. *American Zoologist, 7,* 357–363.

Young, L. J., Lim, M. M., Gingrich, B., & Insel, T. R. (2001). Cellular mechanisms of social attachment. *Hormones and Behavior, 40,* 133–138.

Zahavi, A. (1977). The costs of honesty (further remarks on the handicap principal). *Journal of Theoretical Biology, 67,* 603–605.

8

AN EVOLUTIONARY APPROACH TO UNDERSTANDING NONVERBAL COMMUNICATION

◆ Kory Floyd
Arizona State University

There are several excellent theories in nonverbal communication and new models to develop to meet emerging theoretic needs. This essay delineates how Darwin's (1859) *theory of evolution by means of natural selection* (TNS) can add to the theoretic sophistication in this area by explaining multiple aspects of nonverbal communication and behavior in human relationships. I have divided this chapter into three general sections, the first of which provides an introduction to evolution, in general, and TNS and evolutionary psychology, in particular. Such an introduction, although protracted, is essential to an appreciation of the evolutionary approach. The second section applies the principles of TNS and evolutionary psychology to the understanding of nonverbal communication and gives specific examples of how TNS can be used to study topics of importance to nonverbal communication researchers, including emotion and attraction. Finally, I discuss the efficacy of TNS as a guide for nonverbal communication scholars and offer brief suggestions for researchers wishing to incorporate the theory into their own work.

◆ *Evolution, Natural Selection, and Evolutionary Psychology*

Evolution itself is a remarkably simple concept: It refers to change over time in the characteristics of living organisms. Researchers generally address two types of evolution. The first is *ontogeny,* which references change in an individual person, animal, or plant over time (this term is synonymous with *development*). The physical growth and cognitive maturation observed when an infant grows into an adult is an example of ontogeny. The second is *phylogeny,* which relates to change in the characteristics of a group or species over time. For example, an observed change in the average length of the giraffe's neck or in the hue of the moth's wings over the course of many generations would be an example of phylogeny. It is this type of change, specifically, that most researchers refer to when using the word *evolution* (see, e.g., Buss, 1999).

It is simple enough, in many cases, to document that phylogenetic changes occur (albeit slowly, often over long spans of time). What eluded scientists for centuries, however, was an explanation for how the process of evolution works. Darwin (1859) offered such an explanation in his *theory of natural selection* (a theory that was simultaneously, and independently, proposed by Alfred Russel Wallace, 1858). The theory espouses four main principles: superfecundity, variation, heritability, and selection. The first principle, *superfecundity,* means that in any given generation, many more members of a species are born than can possibly survive and reproduce, creating what Darwin referred to as a "struggle for existence." The second principle, *variation,* indicates that all members of a species have different combinations of traits. Humans, for instance, vary one from another in any number of traits, including height, body shape, hair and eye color, bone density, sensory ability, and weight. According to the third principle, *heritability,* some of this variation is inherited, or passed down genetically from parents to their biological children.[1] For example, two parents with brown hair will tend to have brown-haired offspring, because hair color is heritable.[2]

The fourth (and, at the time it was proposed, the most innovative) principle in Darwin's theory is *selection.* Heritable characteristics that advantage an organism with respect to survival and procreation will be passed to future generations with a greater frequency than characteristics that do not provide these advantages. That is, genetic traits that prove advantageous to an organism (because they help meet an environmental challenge) are *selected for,* or retained from one generation to the next, whereas characteristics that do not prove advantageous are *selected against,* or not retained. For example, a long neck is advantageous to giraffes because it gives them access to food, which is necessary for survival. Giraffes with the longest necks, therefore, have access to more food than other giraffes, and thus, are more likely to survive to sexual maturity. Because they are more likely to survive to sexual maturity, they are more likely to procreate, and because neck length is heritable, succeeding generations of giraffes will have longer average necks than did previous generations. In the parlance of TNS, an environmental challenge (access to food) caused a heritable trait (neck length) to be advantageous in terms of survival and procreation.

This example illustrates the principle of *survival of the fittest* (a phrase coined by Herbert Spencer): Those organisms best adapted to the demands of their environment are the most likely to survive and reproduce themselves because the advantageous heritable characteristics are passed on to their progeny at a greater frequency than disadvantageous ones. The importance of the environment in this principle is clear, because traits that would prove adaptive in one environment may be maladaptive in another. (For example, the physical properties that make many water mammals fast swimmers make them slow movers on land, causing these properties to be adaptive for evading predators in the water but maladaptive for evading predators on land.)

Inherent in the theory of natural selection is the premise that all organisms, if they are to have evolutionary success, must attend to their needs for survival and procreation continually. Procreation, of course, is impossible barring survival to sexual maturity. Mere survival is not enough to succeed in the evolutionary process, however, because without procreation one's genetic materials are not contributed to future generations. Importantly, it need not be one's *own* procreation that contributes one's genetic materials to subsequent generations; such a task can be accomplished by anyone who also carries one's genes, such as a sibling, cousin, or niece. According to inclusive fitness theory, anything one does that furthers the reproductive success of these relatives also furthers one's own reproductive success, by a factor equal to the degree of genetic relatedness with that relative (which is higher for siblings than for nieces, and higher for nieces than for cousins; see Hamilton, 1964; Trivers, 1971).

Recognition of these premises has turned the attention of scholars in a number of disciplines toward the question of how particular characteristics of organisms contribute to survival and procreation. Specifically, researchers began in the mid-20th century to explore how psychological mechanisms might have evolved to meet environmental challenges in much the same way that physical mechanisms have. The possibility giving rise to this work was that human psychological experiences, such as sexual attraction, love, or jealousy, are evolved adaptations in the same way that physical features such as opposable thumbs are.

The discipline of evolutionary psychology brings two important principles to bear on Darwin's (1859) explanation of evolution. First, humans are no less subject to evolution than are any other living organisms. If a particular attribute advantages humans with respect to their survival and procreation abilities, evolutionary psychologists would expect that attribute to be "selected for" in humans just as it would in any other organism. The second principle is that psychological characteristics are no less subject to the process of evolution than physical characteristics are. If, for example, intelligence, empathy, emotional control, or a tendency toward jealousy are characteristics that improve a person's ability to survive and/or to procreate, then evolutionary psychologists would contend that these characteristics, to the extent that they are at all heritable, can be "selected for" just as physical stature, strength, or a long neck can be. Consequently, evolutionists examine the ways in which mental, emotional, or psychological attributes, and the behaviors that characterize them, might have been advantageous to our ancestors with respect to survival and procreation.

Following this brief overview, the primary purpose of this chapter is to delineate some of the ways in which TNS and the principles of evolutionary psychology can be used to model, predict, and explain nonverbal communication. Before engaging specific examples, however, it is necessary to consider some important principles about the application of TNS to human behavior. These concern the nature of evolutionary adaptations and are explained subsequently.

IMPORTANT PRINCIPLES OF THE EVOLUTIONARY APPROACH

Adaptations deal with proximal and ultimate levels of causation. The question of why a particular behavior occurs can be answered on at least two levels of abstraction.

A *proximal cause* is the condition or set of conditions that appears to facilitate the behavior in the specific time, place, and manner in which it occurred. In response to the question, "Why did you eat dinner tonight?" one might answer by identifying a proximal cause: "Because I felt hungry." By contrast, an *ultimate cause* is the condition or set of conditions that represents the original or higher-order cause of a behavior (and often dictates the connection between the behavior and its proximal causes). Thus, an ultimate answer to the question, "Why did you eat dinner tonight?" might be, "Because I must eat in order to survive, and so I have evolved the sensation of hunger as a way of motivating me to eat on a regular basis." This example illustrates how a given nonverbal behavior (e.g., eating) can be considered to be caused both by a proximal agent (hunger) and by an ultimate agent (human need for nutrients). Although both are valid causes, an evolutionary approach is concerned primarily with identifying ultimate causes that provide some clue as to the environmental challenges that adaptations evolved to meet. In many cases, however, there is an unmistakable link between ultimate and proximal causes.

Adaptations need not operate at a conscious level. When asked to account for their own behaviors, people commonly identify proximal causes with little or no regard for ultimate, higher-order causes. This is often because they are simply unaware of what the ultimate causes might be or how they might be operating through more proximal causes (Kenrick & Simpson, 1997). Evolutionary theories acknowledge that many ultimate causes operate outside of individuals' conscious awareness of them, and they contend that this is not problematic. For example, if people are asked to explain why they got married, they will likely say it is because they

fell in love with each other, couldn't imagine their lives without each other, and wanted to spend the rest of their lives together. Few are likely to say that they got married in order to pass their genetic materials on to future generations. The theory of natural selection posits that this is, indeed, the ultimate cause of pair bonding, irrespective of people's conscious awareness. That is, the evolutionary approach does not require individuals to be aware of the ultimate causes of their behaviors in order for those ultimate causes to be operative.

Adaptations need not be adaptive for modern living. When people think about their modern environments, it can be difficult to understand how particular adaptations are beneficial. Why, for instance, do humans have a preference for sweet, fatty, and salty foods? How could such a preference possibly be adaptive, when overindulgence in these types of foods can lead to obesity, high cholesterol, heart disease, and even death? Evolutionary theories do not try to explain human adaptations with reference to modern living. Rather, such theories focus on physical and psychological traits that would have been adaptive in the societies of our ancestors. Evolution usually operates slowly, and modern civilization is remarkably young when considered on an evolutionary timescale. Agriculture was invented only about 10,000 years ago, and civilization (let alone, modern civilization) is an even more recent phenomenon. Humankind has spent more than 99% of its history living in hunter-gatherer societies, and as Morris (2001) pointed out, it is not likely that natural selection has made any noticeable modifications in the human brain in the short period of time represented by modernity. As a result, some traits that were adaptive for our hunter-gatherer ancestors may be useless or even maladaptive in modern times.

Adaptations need not be adaptive for every person or in every instance. It can be difficult for an individual to see how particular traits might be adaptive if, for whatever reason, those traits do not produce the adaptive outcomes for that individual. The human sex drive can provide a useful example. The fact that sex is physically pleasurable for (most) humans can be considered to be adaptive in the sense that it motivates humans to engage in intercourse, which is necessary for reproduction of the species.[3] To be an adaptation, a trait must prove advantageous in solving an evolutionary challenge (in this case, the challenge of procreation). This does not mean, however, that the trait must produce its adaptive result for every person. The sex drive is adaptive because the challenge of reproduction is met more effectively *with it* than *without it*. Moreover, an adaptation need not produce its adaptive result in every instance. Of course, very few instances of sexual intercourse result in pregnancy, relative to the number of times humans engage in intercourse overall. Again, however, this does not mean that the sex drive is not adaptive (in fact, it would be quite maladaptive if every instance of intercourse *did* result in pregnancy). Adaptations need only provide advantages relative to their alternatives.

Adaptations operate at the individual level, not the group or species level. Humans belong to a number of important groups, including their families, social networks, and professional networks that, in various ways, help ensure their survival. In many cases, therefore, what is beneficial to the group is beneficial to the individual member, and vice versa. Often, however, individual and group priorities are in conflict. Consider, for example, a communal living situation in which each person's money and possessions are considered to be the collective property of all group members, and all group members are equally cared for. In such a situation, anything that benefits the group as a whole also benefits each member individually, because of the communal sharing of resources. Suppose, however, that a group member were to find a large sum of cash that the other group members did not know about. Would it benefit this member to contribute the money to the group? Yes, because an economic benefit to the group would benefit all members. It would benefit this individual *more* to keep the money and not to disclose its existence to the group, however, because this member would then be over-benefited in relation to his or her fellow members.[4] In a grave financial crisis, this member might even be able to survive, whereas others in the group—or the group as a whole—perished. Adaptations work in much the same way, to advantage the individual rather than any group to which he or she belongs. Therefore, when it comes to situations in which an individual's priorities conflict with a group's, evolved adaptations tend to privilege the success of the individual over that of the group.

Summary. These principles illustrate the application of TNS and related theories to various aspects of human behavior. Indeed, the breadth of behaviors evolutionary theories can explain is certainly one of their strengths (see Floyd & Haynes, 2005). Whereas many otherwise excellent theories used commonly in nonverbal communication research are limited to explaining specific behaviors or tendencies, such as expectancy violations (Burgoon & Hale, 1988), adaptation (Andersen, 1985), or arousal (Cappella & Greene, 1982), TNS and evolutionary psychology can be applied to multiple aspects of nonverbal behavior. In the second section of this chapter, I will discuss the application of evolutionary principles to the study of nonverbal communication, specifically, and discuss two examples in detail.

◆ Applications of TNS to the Understanding of Nonverbal Communication

TNS provides a rich explanatory basis for understanding human social behavior, including nonverbal communication. At the heart of any application of TNS to a characteristic or behavior is the question of how that characteristic or behavioral tendency ultimately serves the purposes of viability or fertility for the individual. Importantly, not all characteristics or behaviors that contribute to viability or fertility are necessarily evolutionary *adaptations* (which evolve specifically in reaction to environmental challenges to viability or fertility). They may nonetheless be evolutionarily *adaptive* through their contributions to these superordinate goals. (A complete discussion of the distinction between adaptations and evolutionary by-products is beyond the scope of this chapter; for a more in-depth discussion, see Tooby & Cosmides, 1990a, 1990b.)

In this section, I offer two examples of how TNS and principles of evolutionary psychology can be applied to topics of interest to nonverbal communication scholars. Because an application of the theory to all aspects of nonverbal communication is impossible for one chapter, I selected as examples two topics that receive a good deal of empirical attention from nonverbal researchers: emotion displays and attraction. For each, I offer examples of how TNS and evolutionary psychology can explain important aspects of the behavior, and then discuss empirical support relevant to such explanations.

EMOTION DISPLAYS

Emotion, and its related constructs and terms, is a topic that has drawn considerable interest from nonverbal communication scholars and students (e.g., Andersen & Guerrero, 1998; see also Fridlund & Russell, this volume). Evolutionary psychologists, too, have directed attention at explicating the evolutionary bases for both the experience and the expression of the emotions, and their applications have provided fertile ground for understanding how emotions, and the behaviors through which we communicate them, can be adaptive.

It is important to preface this discussion by distinguishing clearly between the *experience* of an emotion and the *expression* of it, the former being an internal affective state, and the latter encompassing specific behaviors through which such a state is represented. This distinction is important for two reasons. First, the experience and the expression of an emotion may be adaptive in different ways or to differing degrees. For instance, the experience of grief may serve to make maladaptive situations (e.g., the loss of one's livelihood) aversive, whereas the outward manifestation of grief may signal distress and elicit needed support and protection from others in one's social network. Second, the experience-expression distinction is important because emotional experiences and emotional expressions are, at least, partially independent of one another. That is, people can experience emotions without expressing them (e.g., concealing one's anger), and they can also express emotions without experiencing them (e.g., conveying affection that is not genuine) (see Guerrero, Andersen, & Trost, 1998; Ploog, 1986).

Much has been written on the evolutionary functions of emotional experiences (e.g., see Buss, 1994a, 1994b; Cannon, 1929; Frank, 1988; Nesse, 1990). Often of greater interest to nonverbal communication scholars, however, are the behaviors by which emotional experiences are conveyed to others. Seminal work on the evolutionary function of emotional expression was conducted by Darwin (1872), whose book, *The Expression of the Emotions in Man and Animals*, espoused three general principles regarding the evolution of emotion displays.

First, the *principle of serviceable associated habits* acknowledged that people perform certain physical actions to meet specific needs or desires (e.g., plugging one's nose in the presence of a foul odor to prevent the odor from entering the nasal passages). Whenever people experience states of mind similar to those associated with those needs or desires, they will perform the same actions, even though they may serve no functional purpose. For example, when presented with a particularly bad idea, one might plug one's nose to express contempt because one's state of mind is similar to that experienced in the presence of an offensive odor; thus, one plugs one's nose out of habit or association. Such a behavior is functional in the situation that initially provoked it (i.e., it protects one from the offensive odor), but in associated situations it is merely symbolic and serves to convey the message that "this idea stinks."

The second principle, the *principle of antithesis*, suggested that when one experiences a state of mind opposing one that is associated with a particular habit, one will perform an opposite action. For instance, when presented with a particularly pleasant idea, one might smile and take in a deep breath to convey contentment with the idea; because plugging one's nose is associated with an opposing state of mind (i.e., that summoned in the presence of a bad idea), the opposite state of mind elicits the opposite behavior.

Darwin's third principle is the *principle of actions due to the constitution of the nervous system*, which acknowledged that emotional expression is often the direct result of nervous system arousal. Being frightened, for instance, can induce sympathetic arousal that leads directly to certain components of the facial fear expression: dilated pupils, an open mouth, increased muscular tension, and a pronounced increase in perspiration. Darwin excluded from this third category explicitly those expressions that were due to the force of habit or its antithesis, distinguishing this principle from the former two.

These three principles are foundational to the evolutionary approach to emotional expression, which calls for the examination of (a) how emotion displays contribute to human viability and fertility and (b) how they are connected to their associated emotional experiences. As an example of the former point, the components of the fear expression mentioned above might all be said to serve particular functions with respect to survival. Pupil dilation allows for the increased intake of visual information that may be important in ascertaining the nature of the threat that provoked the fear response. An open mouth allows for increased oxygen intake, supplying the body with increased fuel for fighting, or fleeing from, the threat. Similarly, increased muscular tension also readies the body to fight or flee; additionally, it can serve to insulate the body from immediate injury. Increased perspiration is evoked to maintain thermoregulation in the face of changing blood flow to the muscles and skin tissues. Thus, from the vantage of evolutionary psychology, these common components of facial fear displays are elicited by the adaptive actions of the nervous system to invoke increased vigilance and increased energy for the purpose of dealing with the threat that initially evoked the fear.

This is just one example of how the logic behind TNS and evolutionary psychology could be used to link an emotion display to viability, fertility, or both. Of course, increases in vigilance and energy in the face of fear may seem to have a direct relationship with survival ability if the threat evoking the fear is physical (e.g., being chased by an animal, being stalked by a criminal), but their effect on survival may seem to be more dubious if the threat is psychological (e.g., facing impending exams or a visit to the dentist). This may well be the case. To the extent that dealing successfully even with psychological stressors can contribute to viability, however, even minutely or indirectly (e.g., conquering one's fear enough to do well in an exam, which helps secure a good grade, which contributes to the attainment of gainful employment and access to resources), the mechanisms that foster such abilities can be "selected for" through the process of natural selection. Because natural selection operates on an exceedingly slow time scale (e.g., producing changes over millennia), characteristics that confer even seemingly inconsequential advantages with respect to viability or fertility, and that are at least partially heritable, are likely to be selected for.

With respect to the link between emotion displays and their underlying emotional experiences, Darwin (1872) argued that displays of the primary emotions, at least, had evolved as a product of evolutionary pressures and were, therefore, as innate as the emotional experiences themselves (Ekman, 1973). Several forms of evidence can be examined as sources of support for Darwin's (1872) proposition. In this section, I identify three such forms of evidence. Two preliminary observations are warranted, the first of which is that Darwin's proposition referred to the primary or "chief" emotions, and contemporary scholars disagree on how many

primary emotions there are, and what they are (Cornelius, 1996; Ekman, 1972; Izard, 1977; Tomkins, 1962, 1963). Included on nearly every list of primary emotions, however, are fear, sadness, surprise, anger, and happiness or joy. Second, nonverbal communication scholars have debated the extent to which these forms of evidence provide logical support for Darwin's propositions (e.g., Ekman, 1992; Russell, 1994). Some, such as Fridlund (1994) and Fridlund and Russell (this volume), have offered alternative theoretic accounts. Although an analysis of these competing viewpoints is beyond the scope of this chapter, it is important to note that scholars have not always agreed about the merits of the Darwinian perspective or the extent to which the existing evidence supports it.

Cross-Cultural Consistency in Emotion Displays. As Ekman (1973) explained, Darwin's (1872) proposition that emotion displays are innate suggests that they are not the product of cultural socialization and should, therefore, show more consistency than variability from culture to culture.[5] An impressive body of research has accumulated that addresses this hypothesis with respect to *facial* emotion displays (arguably the most communicative of all nonverbal emotion displays; Knapp, 1978). Some early investigations conducted by researchers attempting to identify cultural variation in facial emotion displays, instead provided evidence of beyond-chance consistency in how people from different cultures interpret them. For example, Triandis and Lambert (1958) showed photos of an actress expressing different emotions to American college students, Greek college students, and Greek villagers from the Island of Corfu; their comparisons indicated that "Greek subjects, even when they come from very different populations, rate emotional expressions in the same way as American college students" (p. 323). Other investigations have also found substantial cultural consistency, in cultures ranging from American, Mexican, Japanese, Chinese, and Turkish (e.g., Cüceloglu, 1970; Dickey & Knower, 1941; Vinacke, 1949; Vinacke & Fong, 1955; Matsumoto, this volume).

Although these early studies provided preliminary evidence for cross-cultural consistency in facial displays of emotion, their contributions were constrained by a number of methodological limitations. Work by a range of scholars has remedied many of these shortcomings and demonstrated cross-cultural consistency in facial displays of emotion across both literate and preliterate cultures (e.g., Eibl-Eibesfeldt, 1972; Ekman, 1968; Ekman & Friesen, 1971; Ekman, Friesen, & Ellsworth, 1972; Ekman, Sorenson, & Friesen, 1969; Izard, 1971). Their collective finding is one of consistency across a range of cultures with respect to how emotions are conveyed (at least, facially). Although some studies have questioned the degree of cross-cultural consistency (e.g., Elfenbein & Ambady, 2002), and others have questioned its very existence (e.g., Fernández-Dols & Ruis-Belda, 1995), much of the evidence supports the hypothesis of cross-cultural consistency.

Consistency in Emotion Displays of Infants and Noninfants. If the means of conveying emotions are learned principally through socialization and enculturation, then it follows that newborn infants, being possessed neither of the cognitive capacity nor the experience to be functionally affected by enculturation messages, should display their emotions differently than children, adolescents, and adults, the latter groups having been subjected to the influences of socialization. Of course, differences between infants and noninfants are evident in terms of the ability to *control* emotion displays; infants

are relatively uninhibited in their expressions of emotions such as happiness, sadness, or fear, whereas older individuals have a greater capacity to control their emotion displays in the service of politeness or other social norms. If Darwin's (1872) proposition regarding the innateness of emotion displays is accurate, however, one should find consistency in the *forms* of emotion display from infancy onward through the life cycle. To address this question, Darwin began chronicling expressive behavior in his own child, and his observations were offered in his 1872 book and in a later essay titled *A Biographical Sketch of an Infant* (1877). His observations, although methodologically compromised, indicated the presence of at least seven distinctive facial emotion displays beginning as early as 45 days.

Systematic research on the ontology of emotion displays was relatively scarce in the century following Darwin's publications, but several more contemporary studies have addressed the enactment of facial emotion displays during infancy. Research on smiling, for instance, has indicated that externally elicited smiles begin to appear around the end of the first month (Sroufe, 1984), and that by the age of 12 weeks, infants have begun to smile selectively to newly mastered activities and familiar persons (Lewis, Sullivan, & Brooks-Gunn, 1985). Fox and Davidson (1988) also found that 10-month-olds produced more Duchenne smiles (accompanied by contraction of the lateral *orbicularis oculi*) with their mothers than with strangers and that only Duchenne smiles were associated with left frontal EEG activity (hypothesized to be an approach-related pattern). As Charlesworth and Kreutzer (1973) noted, there is little evidence of a one-to-one relationship between smiling and a specific class of external stimuli; rather, infant smiling can be elicited via a variety of auditory, visual, tactile, and kinesthetic stimuli. Most relevant to Darwin's proposition is the age at which facial emotion displays begin to be observed in infants; the earlier the displays, the less likely they are products of socialization or enculturation.

Several emotion displays, in addition to smiling, have been studied with infants, including displays of interest (Sullivan & Lewis, 1989), surprise (Camras, 1988), disgust (Rosenstein & Oster, 1988), fear (Schwartz, Izard, & Ansul, 1982), and anger (Stenberg, Campos, & Emde, 1983). Also instructive is research on congenitally blind children, whose condition eliminates their ability to imitate visually observed expressive behavior in others. Early work by Freedman (1965) indicated that congenitally blind infants smiled at expected times and (by 6 months of age) for expected durations, leading Freedman to conclude that smiling is an innate, rather than learned, behavior. Later work by Eibl-Eibesfeldt (1970) and Charlesworth (1970) further supported the parallels in expressions of blind and sighted infants, adding credence to Darwin's (1872) assertion regarding the evolution of emotion displays.

Physiological Correlates of Emotion Display. A third form of evidence buttressing Darwin's proposition derives from research showing that engaging in facial displays of emotion elicits physiological changes that mimic those associated with the experience of those emotions. As Levenson (1992) detailed, evidence from several laboratories has indicated distinctions between emotional experiences with respect to their effects on autonomic nervous system arousal. If Darwin's conjecture regarding the evolution of emotion displays is correct, one would also expect to find that emotion displays correspond to physiological profiles similar to those characterizing their associated emotions. This is the principle behind the *facial feedback*

hypothesis, which posits that merely engaging in a facial display of emotion will initiate physiological changes consistent with that emotion (e.g., smiling makes one feel happier).

In an experimental test of the facial feedback hypothesis, Ekman, Levenson, and Friesen (1983) instructed scientists and professional actors to enact facial displays of six emotions while their autonomic nervous system arousal was measured. Importantly, participants were told how to configure their faces physically in particular ways. Rather than being instructed to "display anger," for instance, participants were asked to pull their eyebrows down and together, press their lips together, raise their upper eyelids, etc. Each expression was held for 10 seconds. Facial displays of anger, fear, sadness, happiness, and surprise were accompanied by increases in heart rate, whereas displays of disgust elicited a small decrease in heart rate. Displays of anger, sadness, and happiness also elicited increases in skin temperature, whereas displays of fear, surprise, and disgust were accompanied by decreased skin temperature.

These physiological responses to *displaying* emotion closely resemble the correlates of *experiencing* emotion (see Levenson, 1992). Hess, Kappas, McHugo, Lanzetta, and Kleck (1992) also found that displaying anger and happiness increased participants' heart rates, whereas displaying peacefulness decreased it. Later experiments by Levenson, Carstensen, Friesen, and Ekman (1991) and Levenson, Ekman, and Friesen (1990) replicated the findings of Ekman et al. (1983). Ekman (1989) also replicated those results with a non-American culture, the Minangkabau of Sumatra, Indonesia (a fundamentalist Muslim, matrilineal society).

The findings that emotion displays are judged consistently across cultures, begin to appear early in life, and are associated with specific physiological reactions indicative of the underlying emotions do not unequivocally prove the validity of the evolutionary explanation, but these forms of evidence make it more difficult to argue that emotion displays are merely social or cultural constructions. A second active area of nonverbal communication research in which evolutionary principles can be applied is that of interpersonal attraction.

ATTRACTION

It is difficult to overstate the importance of attraction in human social interaction. Although a number of qualities may lead one person to be attracted to another as a friend or potential romantic partner (e.g., personality, similarity, propinquity), a great many markers of physical attractiveness are nonverbal, having to do with personal physical appearance (see Andersen, Guerrero, & Jones, this volume). Thus, for nonverbal communication researchers, these components of attractiveness are of clear relevance.

From an evolutionary perspective, physical attraction is important for one fundamental reason: It is often the instigating force behind the development of reproductive relationships. Without attraction to motivate initial interaction, many potentially significant relationships might simply be forgone. The evolutionary approach to understanding attractiveness therefore focuses on what aspects of physical appearance are judged to be attractive, and how attraction to these aspects of physical appearance is consequential with respect to reproductive success. This perspective proposes that humans (and many other species) are adaptively attuned to markers of physical attractiveness as signals of fertility and reproductive potential.

The causal links proffered by the evolutionary approach rest on at least two important assumptions. First, *people evaluate physical attractiveness with a high degree of consistency*. If beauty really were in the eye of the beholder (a notion that dates back at least to the third century, BC; Rubenstein, Langlois, & Roggman, 2002), then evaluating attractiveness as a signal of reproductive potential would not be a reliable strategy. The second assumption is that *the links between markers of attractiveness and reproductive potential are real, not socially or culturally contrived.* Just as the evolutionary perspective focuses attention on how facial displays of emotion might serve the evolutionary end of survival (as in the example of the fear expression detailed above), it also focuses on the ways in which markers of physical attractiveness are honest indicators of fitness, genetic quality, health, fertility, and reproductive value. As above, I will offer in this section several forms of evidence that support and are illustrative of the evolutionary perspective on attractiveness.

Intra- and Intercultural Consistency in Judgments of Attractiveness. The contention that "beauty is in the eye of the beholder" suggests both within-culture and, especially, between-culture variation in what people find physically attractive in others. Such variation does exist, particularly between cultures; however, research on human attraction has also identified a number of aspects of physical attraction that are remarkably consistent within and across cultures. In a series of studies, for example, Cunningham, Roberts, Wu, Barbee, and Druen (1995) asked people of different races to judge the attractiveness of Caucasian, Asian, Hispanic, and Black women and found a correlation of .93 between racial groups in their attractiveness ratings. In their second study, the researchers found that Taiwanese participants agreed strongly with the ratings of the other groups ($r = .91$) and that the degree of exposure to Western media did not moderate this effect. In their third study, Cunningham et al. found that Blacks and Caucasians agreed with each other strongly on attractiveness ratings ($r = .94$). Other studies have documented consensus in ratings of attractiveness between North Americans and South Africans, among Chinese, Indians, and the English, between Black and Caucasian Americans, and between Americans, Russians, and Ache Indians (see Cross & Cross, 1971; Jackson, 1992; Jones, 1996; Morse, Gruzen, & Reis, 1976; Thakerar & Iwawaki, 1979).

In a meta-analysis of the attractiveness literature, Langlois et al. (2000) examined 919 effect sizes from a sample of over 1,800 empirical studies focusing on the assessment of physical attractiveness. Their principal findings all supported the notions of intra- and intercultural consistency in how people rate others' attractiveness. Specifically, Langlois et al. found within-culture agreements of .90 for ratings of adults' attractiveness and .85 for ratings of children's attractiveness. Cross-ethnic agreement was .88 and cross-cultural agreement was .94. These findings contradict the "eye of the beholder" hypothesis and support the contention that many signals of physical attractiveness are judged consistently both within and between cultures.

Relationship of Attractiveness Markers to Reproductive Success. The evolutionary explanation assumes not only that people evaluate attractiveness with relative consistency but also that markers of attractiveness have real connections with reproductive success. In this section, I examine two physical characteristics that (1) are associated strongly and consistently with attractiveness and (2) have direct relationships with reproductive success. A first predictor of facial and bodily attractiveness is *symmetry*, or the extent to which two sides of a body mirror each other. During an individual's

development, genetic problems such as recessive genes and homozygosity, and environmental stressors such as parasites, pollutants, or extreme temperatures, cause the individual to exhibit *fluctuating asymmetry* (FA), or deviations from exact symmetry on bodily features that tend to be symmetrical (Møller & Pomiankowski, 1993). FA is assessed by taking precise measures of physical features such as the length of the ear, the breadth of the elbow, or the width of the feet on one side of the body and comparing them to the same measures taken from the opposite side. Larger discrepancies indicate higher FA. Only the most genetically fit individuals can maintain symmetry under conditions of developmental stress; low FA therefore serves as a marker of genetic quality (Møller, 1997).

A number of studies verify direct relationships between symmetry and perceptions of attractiveness. Grammer and Thornhill (1994), for example, measured the symmetry of adults' faces and found strong linear relationships between symmetry and perceptions of the attractiveness of those faces for both men and women. Similarly, Hume and Montgomerie (2001) examined the symmetry-attractiveness relationship by manipulating the amount of symmetry in facial photographs. They found the same direct relationship between symmetry and attractiveness ratings (see also Perrett et al., 1999).

Importantly, symmetry has also demonstrated direct effects on reproductive success. Thornhill and Gangestad (1994) found, for instance, that symmetry was linearly related to the number of sexual partners that male and female college students reporting having had. This effect held after controlling for the confounding effect of age (see also Gangestad & Thornhill, 1997). These results suggest that more symmetrical people have more sexual opportunities than less symmetrical people. Moreover,

Thornhill, Gangestad, and Comer (1995) found a direct relationship between the man's symmetry and his partner's likelihood of achieving orgasm. This is significant for reproductive success because female orgasm increases the proportion of her partner's sperm that is retained in her reproductive tract, boosting the chances of pregnancy (see Baxter & Bellis, 1993). Importantly, no other variables measured in the study (including the man's height, income, and sexual experience, and the couple's ratings of their mutual love) predicted the woman's likelihood of achieving orgasm.

A second example, relevant for women, is their *waist-to-hip ratio* (WHR), or the ratio of waist width to hip width. Across cultures, and even across time periods in Western cultures, a female WHR of approximately .70 has been seen as maximally attractive (i.e., when the waist is about 70% as wide as the hips; see Singh & Young, 1995). For example, Singh (1993) found that every single Miss America winner from 1923 to 1987 had a WHR between .69 and .72 and that the WHRs of *Playboy* centerfolds also ranged only from .68 to .71. Singh and Luis (1995) demonstrated that the preference for a .70 WHR was consistent across cultures.

As with symmetry, WHR also has direct effects on reproductive success, and research indicates that a WHR of .70 is the WHR of maximum female fertility. After puberty, estrogens lead to the accumulation of body fat in the gluteofemoral region (thighs and buttocks), whereas androgens (such as testosterone) promote fat accumulation in the abdominal region. WHR therefore serves as a reliable index of the distribution of fat between the upper and lower body and also of the relative proportions of intra-abdominal and extra-abdominal fat (Després, Prudhomme, Pouloit, Tremblay, & Bouchard, 1991).

This is significant for fertility, both because gluteofemoral fat is used nearly exclusively during pregnancy and lactation (Björntorp, 1987) and because a WHR of .70 or below corresponds to the absence of major obesity-related disorders, such as diabetes, carcinomas, or heart disease (Barbieri, 1990). Indeed, research indicates that higher WHRs are associated with women's difficulties in becoming pregnant (Kaye, Folsom, Prineas, Potter, & Gapstur, 1990). In a study of 500 women attending a fertility clinic, for instance, Zaadstra, Seidell, van Noord, te Velde, Habbema, Vrieswijk, and Karbaat (1993) reported that women who had a WHR under .80 were more than twice as likely to get pregnant following 12 rounds of artificial insemination as were women with ratios exceeding .80.

Symmetry and WHR are but two examples of physical characteristics that show both strong, reliable associations with attractiveness and direct relationships with reproductive success (others may include physical stature, skin clarity, and natural body odor). From the evolutionary perspective, therefore, one would contend that these characteristics are attractive to people *because* attraction to these characteristics is reproductively beneficial. I have argued elsewhere (Floyd & Haynes, 2005) that one of the great strengths of the evolutionary approach is its ability to explain multiple aspects of behavior and to do so at a level of explanation that often transcends the social, cultural, or political influences that are often the focus of social science research. Such a perspective allows researchers the breadth to investigate how human communicative behaviors are related to pervasive, engrained motivations that are often independent of the effects of gender, race, class, sexual orientation, or a host of other proximal influences. In this manner, human communicative behavior can be understood within a broad context that is relatively unbound by time, locale, or policy, and is often even unrestricted to humans. The evolutionary perspective allows one to understand how nonverbal communicative behaviors fit within a larger and broader picture than many other nonverbal theories point to.

◆ *Using TNS in Nonverbal Communication Research*

To conclude this chapter, I offer three recommendations for researchers wishing to capitalize on the advantages of evolutionary theories in their study of nonverbal behavior. The first is to *conceptualize research questions in terms of ultimate causality.* That is, researchers should consider the relationship that specific communicative behaviors might have either to survival or procreation (or both). The links for some behaviors might be fairly obvious; one can certainly identify how a behavior like flirting is related (eventually) to procreation, or how the fight-or-flight response to fear is related to survival. The links for other behaviors may be less apparent but are there nonetheless (e.g., the reproductive benefits of being attracted to symmetrical sexual partners). Researchers could apply evolutionary principles to the study of such diverse behaviors as immediacy, deception, touch avoidance, and cosmetic use to identify their implications for survival and procreation. Conceptualizing research questions in terms of ultimate causality requires researchers to consider the survival and procreative purposes that a given behavior might serve.

Equally important is that researchers *formulate hypothesis tests to rule out rival explanations.* This is a fundamental principle of the scientific design, but it is especially important for researchers studying communication from an evolutionary perspective because one can often deduce the same prediction using evolutionary and nonevolutionary theories. Although the explanations differ, the basic prediction

may be the same. For example, Floyd and Morman (2001) compared biological fathers and stepfathers in terms of the amount of affection they communicated to their sons. The hypothesis that fathers give more affection to biological sons than to stepsons can easily be derived on the basis of inclusive fitness theory. One might arrive at the same prediction, however, by reasoning that men feel closer to their biological sons than to stepsons because they have longer histories with biological sons.

To test an evolutionary hypothesis fairly, the researcher must design the test in such a way that one explanation can be ruled out. If it is a difference in closeness that causes fathers to be more affectionate with biological sons than stepsons, for instance, then the difference in affectionate communication should fail to manifest (or be diminished) if the level of closeness is covaried out. In fact, Floyd and Morman (2001) found that the mean difference in affectionate communication was maintained even when closeness and other relational characteristics were controlled for. Certainly, ruling out one rival hypothesis does not provide unequivocal evidence for another, but it strengthens one's claim. By crafting research designs carefully to rule out rival causes, researchers can test explanations derived from evolutionary theories while simultaneously ruling out explanations offered by other perspectives.

Finally, researchers must *consider context so as to avoid oversimplified hypotheses.* Although the evolutionary paradigm focuses on ultimate, rather than proximal, causes, the characteristics evolution selects for in individuals are often manifested only in particular contexts. Some may be more genetically prone than others to reciprocate nonverbal aggression, for instance, but this doesn't necessarily mean that such people have higher mean levels of aggressiveness than others, because an aggressive context is required to bring the tendency to fruition. Careful consideration of the environment and social context will help scholars avoid oversimplified hypotheses. Researchers must bear in mind that evolutionary adaptiveness matters, in terms of predicting behavior, but it is not the only thing that matters. Contextual influences, such as the history of a relationship or the constraints of a social context must also be considered in order to avoid the fallacy that evolutionary pressures are the only pressures that exert influence on interpersonal behavior.

◆ **Notes**

1. This is true, at least, for sexually reproducing species; see Bjorklund and Pellegrini (2002).

2. Not all characteristics are inherited; if a woman loses her hearing because of an injury, this will not make her more likely to have babies who are deaf.

3. Of course, advances in reproductive technology, such as in vitro fertilization, have eliminated intercourse as an absolute precursor to reproduction. Such technology was not available to our hunter-gatherer ancestors, for whom the adaptive nature of the human sex drive would have been selected.

4. Such a benefit does require that the others in the group be unaware of this member's good fortune. As Cosmides and Tooby (1989, 1992) have suggested, humans have evolved a type of *cheating detection mechanism* by which they notice, remember, and respond to perceived cheating on the part of others, so as to protect their self-interests.

5. For brevity's sake, I will use the term *emotion displays* in this section to refer to expressions of primary emotions, including fear, sadness, surprise, anger, and happiness.

◆ **References**

Andersen, P. A. (1985). Nonverbal immediacy in interpersonal communication. In A. W. Siegman & S. Feldstein (Eds.), *Multichannel*

integrations of nonverbal behavior (pp. 1–36). Hillsdale, NJ: Erlbaum.

Andersen, P. A., & Guerrero, L. K. (Eds.) (1998). *Handbook of communication and emotion: Research, theory, applications, and contexts.* San Diego, CA: Academic Press.

Barbieri, R. L. (1990). The role of adipose tissue and hyperinsulinemia in the development of hyperandrogenism in women. In R. E. Frisch (Ed.), *Adipose tissue and reproduction* (pp. 42–57). Basel, Switzerland: Karger.

Baxter, R. R., & Bellis, M. A. (1993). Human sperm competition: Ejaculate manipulation by females and a function for the female orgasm. *Animal Behavior, 46,* 887–909.

Bjorklund, D. F., & Pellegrini, A. D. (2002). *The origins of human nature: Evolutionary developmental psychology.* Washington, DC: American Psychological Association.

Björntorp, P. (1987). Fat cell distribution and metabolism. In R. J. Wurtman & J. J. Wurtman (Eds.), *Human obesity* (pp. 66–72). New York: New York Academy of Sciences.

Burgoon, J. K., & Hale, J. L. (1988). Nonverbal expectancy violations: Model elaboration and application to immediacy behaviors. *Communication Monographs, 55,* 58–79.

Buss, D. M. (1994a). *The evolution of desire: Strategies of human mating.* New York: Basic Books.

Buss, D. M. (1994b). The strategies of human mating. *American Scientist, 82,* 238–249.

Buss, D. M. (1999). *Evolutionary psychology: The new science of the mind.* Boston: Allyn & Bacon.

Camras, L. A. (1988, May). *Darwin revisited: An infant's first emotional facial expressions.* Paper presented at International Conference on Infant Studies, Washington, DC.

Cannon, W. (1929). *Bodily changes in pain, hunger, fear, and rage: Research into the function of emotional excitement.* New York: Harper & Row.

Cappella, J. N., & Greene, J. O. (1982). A discrepancy-arousal explanation of mutual influence in expressive behavior for adult and infant-adult interaction. *Communication Monographs, 49,* 89–114.

Charlesworth, W. R. (1970). *Surprise reactions in congenitally blind and sighted children.*

Bethesda, MD: National Institute of Mental Health Progress Report.

Charlesworth, W. R., & Kreutzer, M. A. (1973). Facial expressions of infants and children. In P. Ekman (Ed.), *Darwin and facial expression: A century of research in review* (pp. 91–168). New York: Academic Press.

Cornelius, R. R. (1996). *The science of emotion: Research and tradition in the psychology of emotion.* Upper Saddle River, NJ: Prentice Hall.

Cosmides, L. L., & Tooby, J. (1989). Evolutionary psychology and the generation of culture. Part II. Case study: A computational theory of social exchange. *Ethology and Sociobiology, 10,* 51–97.

Cosmides, L. L., & Tooby, J. (1992). Cognitive adaptations for social exchange. In J. Barkow, L. Cosmides, & J. Tooby (Eds.), *The adapted mind* (pp. 163–228). New York: Oxford University Press.

Cross, J. F., & Cross, J. (1971). Age, sex, race, and the perception of facial beauty. *Developmental Psychology, 5,* 433–439.

Cüceloglu, D. M. (1970). Perception of facial expressions in three cultures. *Ergonomics, 13,* 93–100.

Cunningham, M. R., Roberts, A. R., Wu, C-H., Barbee, A. P., & Druen, P. B. (1995). "Their ideas of beauty are, on the whole, the same as ours": Consistency and variability in the cross-cultural perception of female attractiveness. *Journal of Personality and Social Psychology, 68,* 261–279.

Darwin, C. (1859). *On the origin of species.* London: Murray.

Darwin, C. (1872). *The expression of the emotions in man and animals.* London: Murray.

Darwin, C. (1877). A biographical sketch of an infant. *Mind, 2,* 285–294.

Després, J. P., Prudhomme, D., Pouloit, M., Tremblay, A., & Bouchard, C. (1991). Estimation of deep abdominal adipose-tissue accumulation from simple anthropometric measurements in men. *American Journal of Clinical Nutrition, 54,* 471–477.

Dickey, E. C., & Knower, F. H. (1941). A note on some of the ethnological differences in recognition of simulated expressions of the emotions. *American Journal of Sociology, 47,* 190–193.

Eibl-Eibesfeldt, I. (1970). *Ethology: The biology of behavior.* New York: Holt.

Eibl-Eibesfeldt, I. (1972). Similarities and differences between cultures in expressive movements. In R. A. Hinde (Ed.), *Nonverbal communication* (pp. 297–314). Cambridge, UK: Cambridge University Press.

Ekman, P. (1968, September). *The recognition and display of facial behavior in literature and non-literate cultures.* Paper presented at symposium on the universality of emotions of the American Psychological Association, San Francisco, CA.

Ekman, P. (1972). Universal and cultural differences in facial expressions of emotion. In J. K. Cole (Ed.), *Nebraska symposium on motivation* (pp. 207–283). Lincoln, NE: University of Nebraska Press.

Ekman, P. (1973). Cross cultural studies of facial expression. In P. Ekman (Ed.), *Darwin and facial expression: A century of research in review* (pp. 169–222). New York: Academic Press.

Ekman, P. (1989). *A cross cultural study of emotional expression, language and physiology.* Symposium conducted at the annual meeting of the American Association for the Advancement of Science, San Francisco.

Ekman, P. (1992). Are there basic emotions? *Psychological Review, 99,* 550–553.

Ekman, P., & Friesen, W. V. (1971). Constants across cultures in the face and emotion. *Journal of Personality and Social Psychology, 17,* 124–129.

Ekman, P., Friesen, W. V., & Ellsworth, P. (1972). *Emotion in the human face.* New York: Pergamon.

Ekman, P., Levenson, R. W., & Friesen, W. V. (1983). Autonomic nervous system activity distinguishes among emotions. *Science, 221,* 1208–1210.

Ekman, P., Sorenson, E. R., & Friesen, W. V. (1969). Pan-cultural elements in facial displays of emotion. *Science, 164,* 86–88.

Elfenbein, H. A., & Ambady, N. (2002). On the universality and cultural specificity of emotion recognition: A meta-analysis. *Psychological Bulletin, 128,* 203–235.

Fernández-Dols, J. M., & Ruiz-Belda, M. A. (1995). Are smiles a sign of happiness? Gold medal winners at the Olympic Games. *Journal of Personality and Social Psychology, 69,* 1113–1119.

Floyd, K., & Haynes, M. T. (2005). Applications of the theory of natural selection to the study of family communication. *Journal of Family Communication, 5,* 79–101.

Floyd, K., & Morman, M. T. (2001). Human affection exchange: III. Discriminative parental solicitude in men's affectionate communication with their biological and nonbiological sons. *Communication Quarterly, 49,* 310–327.

Fox, N., & Davidson, R. (1988). Patterns of brain electrical activity during facial signs of emotion in 10 month old infants. *Developmental Psychology, 24,* 230–236.

Frank, R. (1988). *Passion within reason: The strategic role of the emotions.* New York: Norton.

Freedman, D. G. (1965). Hereditary control of early social behavior. In B. Foss (Ed.), *Determinants of infant behavior* (pp. 149–156). London: Methuen.

Fridlund, A. J. (1994). *Human facial expression: An evolutionary view.* San Diego, CA: Academic Press.

Gangestad, S. W., & Thornhill, R. (1997). Human sexual selection and developmental stability. In J. A. Simpson & D. T. Kenrick (Eds.), *Evolutionary social psychology* (pp. 169–195). Mahwah, NJ: Erlbaum.

Grammer, K., & Thornhill, R. (1994). Human (*Homo sapiens*) facial attractiveness and sexual selection: The role of symmetry and averageness. *Journal of Comparative Psychology, 108,* 233–242.

Guerrero, L. K., Andersen, P. A., & Trost, M. R. (1998). Communication and emotion: Basic concepts and approaches. In P. A. Andersen & L. K. Guerrero (Eds.), *The handbook of communication and emotion: Research, theory, applications, and contexts* (pp. 3–27). San Diego, CA: Academic Press.

Hamilton, W. D. (1964). The genetical evolution of social behavior. I & II. *Journal of Theoretical Biology, 7,* 1–52.

Hess, U., Kappas, A., McHugo, G. J., Lanzetta, J. T., & Kleck, R. E. (1992). The facilitative effect of facial expression on the self-generation of emotion. *International Journal of Psychophysiology, 12,* 251–265.

Hume, D. K., & Montgomerie, R. (2001). Facial attractiveness signals different aspects of "quality" in women and men. *Evolution and Human Behavior, 22,* 93–112.

Izard, C. E. (1971). *The face of emotion.* New York: Appleton.

Izard, C. E. (1977). *Human emotions.* New York: Plenum.

Jackson, L. A. (1992). *Physical appearance and gender: Sociobiological and sociocultural perspectives.* Albany: State University of New York Press.

Jones, D. (1996). *Physical attractiveness and the theory of sexual selection.* Ann Arbor: University of Michigan Press.

Kaye, S. A., Folsom, A. R., Prineas, R. J., Potter, J. D., & Gapstur, S. M. (1990). The association of body fat distribution with lifestyle and reproductive factors in a population study of postmenopausal women. *International Journal of Obesity, 14,* 583–591.

Kenrick, D. T., & Simpson, J. A. (1997). Why social psychology and evolutionary psychology need one another. In J. A. Simpson & D. T. Kenrick (Eds.), *Evolutionary social psychology* (pp. 1–20). Mahwah, NJ: Erlbaum.

Knapp, M. L. (1978). *Nonverbal communication in human interaction* (2nd ed.). New York: Holt.

Langlois, J. H., Kalakanis, L., Rubenstein, A. J., Larson, A., Hallam, M., & Smoot, M. (2000). Maxims or myths of beauty? A meta-analytic and theoretical review. *Psychological Bulletin, 126,* 390–423.

Levenson, R. W. (1992). Autonomic nervous system differences among emotions. *Psychological Science, 3,* 23–27.

Levenson, R. W., Carstensen, L. L., Friesen, W. V., & Ekman, P. (1991). Emotion, physiology, and expression in old age. *Psychology and Aging, 6,* 28–35.

Levenson, R. W., Ekman, P., & Friesen, W. V. (1990). Voluntary facial action generates emotion-specific autonomic nervous system activity. *Psychophysiology, 27,* 363–384.

Lewis, M., Sullivan, M., & Brooks-Gunn, J. (1985). Emotional behavior during the learning of a contingency in early infancy.

British Journal of Developmental Psychology, 3, 307–316.

Møller, A. P. (1997). Developmental stability and fitness: A review. *American Naturalist, 149,* 916–942.

Møller, A. P., & Pomiankowski, A. (1993). Fluctuating asymmetry and sexual selection. *Genetica, 89,* 267–279.

Morris, R. (2001). *The evolutionists: The struggle for Darwin's soul.* New York: W. H. Freeman.

Morse, S. T., Gruzen, J., & Reis, H. (1976). The "eye of the beholder": A neglected variable in the study of physical attractiveness. *Journal of Personality, 44,* 209–225.

Nesse, R. (1990). Evolutionary explanations of emotions. *Human Nature, 1,* 261–289.

Perrett, D. I., Burt, D. M., Penton-Voak, I. S., Lee, K. J., Rowland, D. A., & Edwards, R. (1999). Symmetry and human facial attractiveness. *Evolution and Human Behavior, 20,* 295–307.

Ploog, D. (1986). Biological foundations of the vocal expressions of emotions. In R. Plutchik & H. Kellerman (Eds.), *Emotion: Theory, research, and experience* (Vol. 3, pp. 173–197). New York: Academic Press.

Rosenstein, D., & Oster, H. (1988). Differential facial response to four basic tastes in newborns. *Child Development, 59,* 1555–1568.

Rubenstein, A. J., Langlois, J. H., & Roggman, L. A. (2002). What makes a face attractive and why: The role of averageness in defining facial beauty. In G. Rhodes & L. A. Zebrowitz (Eds.), *Facial attractiveness: Evolutionary, cognitive, and social perspectives* (pp. 1–33). Westport, CT: Ablex.

Russell, J. A. (1994). Is there universal recognition of emotion from facial expression? *Psychological Bulletin, 115,* 102–141.

Schwartz, G., Izard, C. E., & Ansul, S. (1982, May). *Heart rate and facial response to novelty in 7- and 13-month-old infants.* Paper presented at International Conference on Infant Studies, Austin, TX.

Singh, D. (1993). Adaptive significance of waist-to-hip ratio and female physical attractiveness. *Journal of Personality and Social Psychology, 65,* 293–307.

Singh, D., & Luis, S. (1995). Ethnic and gender consensus for the role of waist-to-hip ratio on judgment of women's attractiveness. *Human Nature, 6,* 51–65.

Singh, D., & Young, R. K. (1995). Body weight, waist-to-hip ratio, breasts, and hips: Role in judgments of female attractiveness and desirability for relationships. *Ethology and Sociobiology, 16,* 483–507.

Sroufe, L. A. (1984). The organization of emotional development. In K. R. Scherer & P. Ekman (Eds.), *Approaches to emotion* (pp. 109–128). Hillsdale, NJ: Erlbaum.

Stenberg, C., Campos, J., & Emde, R. (1983). The facial expression of anger in seven month old infants. *Child Development, 54,* 178–184.

Sullivan, M., & Lewis, M. (1989). Emotion and cognition in infancy: Facial expressions during contingency learning. *International Journal of Behavioral Development, 12,* 221–237.

Thakerar, J. N., & Iwawaki, S. (1979). Cross-cultural comparisons in interpersonal attraction of females toward males. *Journal of Social Psychology, 108,* 121–122.

Thornhill, R., & Gangestad, S. W. (1994). Human fluctuating asymmetry and sexual behavior. *Psychological Science, 5,* 297–302.

Thornhill, R., Gangestad, S. W., & Comer, R. (1995). Human female orgasm and mate fluctuating asymmetry. *Animal Behavior, 50,* 1601–1615.

Tomkins, S. S. (1962). *Affect, imagery, consciousness: Vol. 1. The positive affects.* New York: Springer.

Tomkins, S. S. (1963). *Affect, imagery, consciousness: Vol. 2. The negative affects.* New York: Springer.

Tooby, J., & Cosmides, L. (1990a). On the universality of human nature and the uniqueness of the individual: The role of genetics and adaptation. *Journal of Personality, 58,* 17–68.

Tooby, J., & Cosmides, L. (1990b). The past explains the present: Emotional adaptations and the structure of ancestral environments. *Ethology and Sociobiology, 11,* 375–424.

Triandis, H. C., & Lambert, W. W. (1958). A restatement and test of Schlosberg's theory of emotion with two kinds of subjects from Greece. *Journal of Abnormal and Social Psychology, 56*, 321–328.

Trivers, R. L. (1971). The evolution of reciprocal altruism. *Quarterly Review of Biology, 46*, 35–37.

Vinacke, W. E. (1949). The judgment of facial expressions by three national-race groups in Hawaii: I. Caucasian faces. *Journal of Personality, 17*, 407–429.

Vinacke, W. E., & Fong, R. W. (1955). The judgment of facial expressions by three national-race groups in Hawaii: II. Oriental faces. *Journal of Social Psychology, 41*, 185–195.

Wallace, A. R. (1858). On the tendency of varieties to depart indefinitely from the original type. *Journal of the Proceedings of the Linnean Society (Zoology), 3*, 53–62.

Zaadstra, B. M., Seidell, J. C., van Noord, P. A. H., te Velde, E. G., Habbema, J. D. F., Vrieswijk, B., et al. (1993). Fat and female fecundity: Prospective study of effect of body fat distribution on conception rates. *British Medical Journal, 306*, 484–487.

9

PERSONALITY AND NONVERBAL BEHAVIOR

A Complex Conundrum

◆ Robert Gifford
University of Victoria

A Boldly Sketched Portrait of Albrecht Dürer.

"Whoever examines this countenance cannot but perceive in it the traits of fortitude, deep penetration, determined perseverance, and inventive genius. At least every one will acknowledge the truth of these observations, when made."

SOURCE: J. C. Lavater (ca. 1844), *Essays on Physiognomy*, translated by Thomas Holcroft, 4th ed., London (publisher unknown), pp. 33–35, image and caption from Plate 1. (Retrieved August 9, 2005, from www.newcastle.edu.au/school/fine-art/publications/lavater; the Dürer image and the quotation from Lavater about Dürer were

Author's Note: Correspondence should be addressed to Robert Gifford, Department of Psychology, University of Victoria, Victoria, British Columbia, Canada, V8W 3P5; e-mail: rgifford@uvic.ca.

◆ 159

used, with permission, from the above Web site of Ross Woodrow.)

> It is possible to infer character from features, if it is granted that the body and the soul are changed together by the natural affections.
>
> Aristotle, *Prior Analytics*, 350 BCE

> Has he not a rogue's face? Speak brother, you understand physiognomy, a hanging look to me.
>
> William Congreve,
> *Love for Love*, 1695

From Aristotle's time, physiognomists have been certain they can discern personality solely from a person's facial features. The confidence expressed by famous physiognomists like the Swiss theologian Johann Caspar Lavater turned to respectable scientific optimism in the 1930s. But by the 1980s, researchers were generally pessimistic regarding the contention that personality is encoded clearly in nonverbal behavior or that personality could be decoded through nonverbal behavior. The pessimism was justifiable, given the mixed and unsatisfactory research results in the area. In this chapter, I argue that what appears to be a simple proposition—that nonverbal behavior and personality have simple or direct connections—actually is a very difficult problem with at least 10 types of complexity for researchers to manage. Nevertheless, some progress has been made in the last two decades, based mainly on adaptations of Brunswik's (1956) lens model. To show this development, and following discussion of relevant terms, I offer a larger description of these "10 complexities." I then review research assessing the connections between personality and nonverbal behavior, propose a paradigm

for future research that incorporates the complexities I detailed, and discuss an exemplar study that reflects this paradigm. I begin, however, with a brief history of scholarship connecting nonverbal cues to personality.

◆ A Short History

The idea that personal qualities are encoded in human physical features already was at least 100 years old when Aristotle wrote *Prior Analytics* about 2300 years ago. For centuries, physiognomy was assumed to be obvious and true. Until the time of Henry VIII, according to one Web site (www.answers.com/topic/physiognomy, retrieved August 9, 2005), its validity was assumed so widely that it was taught in many universities. Writers such as William Congreve apparently accepted physiognomy as fact in the 16th and 17th centuries, as the quotation above suggests. The 18th and 19th centuries were dominated by the works of Lavater, whose pronouncements about the psychological meaning of facial differences were extremely popular. His books went through about 150 editions (see www.newcastle.edu.au/school/fine-art/publications/lavater). Nineteenth-century writers such as Balzac, Hardy, and Dickens used physiognomic character descriptions frequently in their novels.

The premise of physiognomy, that personality is encoded in the face, has been discredited for decades, in part because static facial features represent only a small part of a person's nonverbal impression on others. This discrediting has not prevented contemporary pop psychology writers (e.g., Young, 1993) from making claims about what people can discern about one another. From Leonardo da Vinci's portrait of Mona Lisa, for example, Young divined that she was a liar, stubborn, a gifted abstract thinker with an IQ above average, greedy, an unreliable friend, and a sneak; that she would punish her enemies by any means; and that she needed at least 9 hours of sleep each night! Unlike a painting, however, human faces are dynamic, and they convey different dispositional impressions depending on the person's state. For example, when different emotions are *experienced* by an actor, different dispositions are *inferred* by observers (Montepare & Dobish, 2003). The first important scientific study relevant to the present chapter was summarized in Allport and Vernon's (1933) groundbreaking monograph. Allport and Vernon did not attempt to relate nonverbal behavior to personality dispositions. Rather, they sought to find unity (or something close to it) *among* the expressive movements of their subjects.

Their hypothesis appears to have been rooted in the Aristotelian proposition, quoted at the start of the chapter, that one's whole body and personality are a kind of unity in which every aspect is mirrored in every other aspect. This view was championed by German psychologists such as William Stern, who influenced Allport and Vernon profoundly. The purpose of the 1933 monograph was to demonstrate the existence of consistency among a person's expressive movements, which would, in the Aristotle-Stern sense, support the very construct and existence of personality. When Allport and Vernon were writing, personality was not a widely respected construct in psychology, and it was therefore in need of empirical support. Allport and Vernon's results showed promise, in that two clusters of expressive movements, one "general" and one "specific," were found, albeit with lower than desirable reliability. Their book was the basis for some optimism that personality and nonverbal behavior could be studied profitably.

Nevertheless, the Allport-Vernon book did not stimulate much new published research over the next three decades; only a few scattered studies may be found from the 1930s until the early 1960s. Perhaps the first modern study that would fit comfortably in this chapter was Ralph Exline's (1963) investigation of visual interaction in groups of men and groups of women who had been categorized in terms of their need for affiliation. He found that need for affiliation was related to mutual glances, but it worked differently for men and women. Exline's study has the further distinction of recognizing that nonverbal behavior should be examined *within interacting groups*, rather than assuming implicitly that people express themselves nonverbally without reference to others—that is, always in the same way (see the physiognomists).

In the four decades since the mid-1960s, a number of scientific studies (although perhaps fewer than one might expect) have been conducted on the relations between nonverbal behavior and personality, but progress has been slow and fitful. Twenty years after Exline's (1963) study, reviewers were forced to conclude that the expression of personality in nonverbal behavior "cannot be said to be strongly supported by the evidence" (Bull, 1983, p. 113) and that "in general, much of the research on personality correlates has shown . . . relatively weak relationships to nonverbal behavior" (Heslin & Patterson, 1982, p. 131).

Recognizing the complexity of nonverbal behavior, however, Patterson (1995, this volume) developed his parallel process model, which posits that nonverbal behavior is a balance of behavior and social cognitive judgment processes, often automatic or overlearned, but sometimes under control and in the service of a particular goal. Plausible as it is, the theory also is difficult to test empirically, as Patterson (this volume) attests. This chapter, then, while acknowledging the value of the parallel process model, focuses on the more modest, but more easily researched, social judgment aspect of communication. As will be seen, there are plenty of complexities even within this limited portion of the whole.

Thus, at the beginning of the 21st century, considerable research remains to be done before the complex connections among personality, nonverbal behavior, and inferences about personality made by observers of others' nonverbal behavior can be understood. This chapter summarizes recent work and offers a paradigm that might accelerate progress in the social judgment portion of the problem. The paradigm might be considered a subset of the ambitious framework proposed by Patterson (1995) for understanding nonverbal communication in general.

◆ Key Distinctions: Encoding, Decoding, Accuracy, and Agreement

Encoding is the outward, objective, visible manifestation of personal dispositions in nonverbal behavior. The fundamental hypothesis of researchers in this area is that valid encoding does occur. A crucial, and still largely unanswered, question remains, however. How much encoding occurs and for which dispositions? *Decoding* is the use by observers of nonverbal behavior to infer personal dispositions in others. The interesting question in this area concerns the accuracy of that decoding by different kinds of observers, for different dispositions, under different conditions. The wild card in this endeavor, however, is *accuracy*. How valid are our inferences of personality from nonverbal behavior?

Accuracy, in this sense, is itself problematic in two important ways. The first issue concerns the validity of personality measures.

Although this problem is beyond the scope of this chapter, suffice it to say there are problems with self-report measures as well as problems with ratings by significant others (see Funder, 2003; Kenny, 1994). The second main problem involving accuracy is this: How well do decoders detect the (true) level of a person's dispositions from the others' nonverbal behavior? In the typical study, decoding accuracy is measured as the discrepancy between the decoder's assessment of the disposition and the actor's self-rating (or the ratings of the actor's significant others). Given the uncertainty of self-ratings, and even those of significant others (Kenny, 1994), these assessments should not be granted the status of truth or treated as the criterion against which observers' ratings are measured. Nevertheless, they certainly have some face validity. They are, after all, the views of the actors by the actors or by those who know them well.

If the premise that even these assessments are fallible is accepted, it becomes unreasonable to tarnish any lack of agreement with these assessments on the part of other observers as a lack of achievement or error. The observer's assessment has its own inherent value as the view of another person after watching the actor's nonverbal behavior, with the advantage of some perspective, detachment, and often, objectivity. Thus, the two assessments of the disposition should be granted equal ontological status, and it is preferable to characterize any difference between the two assessments as a discrepancy rather than as observer error. In sum, neither the self's nor the observer's rating is valid necessarily, and the neutral term *agreement* should be used rather than *accuracy*.

The decoding of personality is itself fraught with problems. Assessments of a person's dispositions vary with the type of information given to the judge. For example, when judges in an interview study either saw a silent videotape of an interview with a manager (i.e., only the nonverbal behavior) or read a transcript of the same interview (thus, no nonverbal behavior), the correlations between their assessments of the managers' extraversion and conscientiousness were $r = .27$ and $r = .30$, respectively; that is, they shared about 9% of their variance (Motowidlo, Burnett, Maczynski, & Witkowski, 1996). Given that the overlap between the assessments was quite low, they cannot both be accurate. Which assessment was more accurate, that based on the manager's words, as written, or that based on the manager's wordless, nonverbal behavior?

TEN COMPLEXITIES

With these issues in mind, a summary of current knowledge may be essayed. All the following findings are subject to a blanket cautionary note, however, because most studies have not dealt with all the complexities of encoding and decoding research. Specifically, I argue that researchers must manage (at least) 10 complexities in their research designs and analyses (i.e., Type I or Type II errors in the relations between nonverbal behavior and personality that may occur if a researcher relies solely on a simple Pearson correlation or fails to take into account one or more of the accuracy or agreement issues). Some complexities are familiar and some less so; some are easier to manage than others.

The first complexity is perhaps the most obvious, but published studies that overlook it have appeared. *All the measures must have adequate internal consistency and interrater reliability.* Ordinarily, this should be at least .75, but .80 or better is very desirable. Adjustments for error and apologies for lower levels of reliability sometimes are made, but they are not convincing. Although interrater reliability is a prerequisite for decoding validity, even

that does not guarantee decoding validity (Kenny, 1991), as exemplified by (inaccurate) stereotyping. The second complexity concerns *the relevance of the disposition's domain to the context in which the nonverbal behavior occurs* (e.g., examining interpersonal traits in interpersonal contexts). A researcher should not expect conscientiousness, for example, to be encoded strongly in a casual conversation, but the same researcher could expect extraversion to be encoded strongly in a conversation.

The third complexity involves the *potential interference with encoding of situational factors.* One such factor is the mutual influence of interacting participants. Some writers have assumed that the presence of others will always affect the encoding for any individual (e.g., Kanki, 1985), but the effect of others can be tested with intraclass correlation analyses (e.g., Gifford, 1994). Sometimes the effect of others is found, empirically, to be minimal. The fourth complexity relates to another aspect of the situation, *the nature of the activity or interaction* during which encoding is investigated. For example, individuals may not merely enact a given behavior (e.g., smiling) more or less frequently depending on context (e.g., at a party vs. a funeral), but their encoding (the *correlation* with a given disposition, regardless of the *frequency* of the act) may differ with the situation. In a study that demonstrated this, dispositional public self-consciousness was encoded in hand movements differently when participants were lying than when they were telling the truth (Vrij, Akehurst, & Morris, 1997).

The fifth complexity is a matter of clear reporting more than a problem in itself. For example, in one study, neuroticism was correlated with touching the self more, fewer expressive gestures, and more gaze aversion (Campbell & Rushton, 1978). The first two encodings were based on a teacher's rating of the person's neuroticism, however, whereas the third encoding was based on a self-report measure of neuroticism. That is, the different assessments of neuroticism related to different nonverbal behaviors. Such results should be *reported as based on different measures of the disposition.* In a study that illustrated the problem of considering self-ratings and ratings by others to be equivalent, self-report measures of emotional expressiveness yielded different relations to a disposition (neuroticism again) than did rated behavioral assessments of emotional expressiveness (Riggio & Riggio, 2002).

A sixth complexity is that *relations between personality and nonverbal behavior can differ with different combinations of traits.* For example, individuals who are shy *and* sociable avert their gaze more and engage in more self-manipulation than others (Cheek & Buss, 1981), but this is not true of the other combinations (e.g., shy but *not* sociable persons). The value of the Cheek and Buss study lies in its demonstration that combinations of dispositions sometimes reveal more about encoding than individual dispositions do. A seventh complexity is that *dispositions can be encoded by a group of behaviors without any particular behavior doing so* (Aries, Gold, & Weigel, 1983). Sometimes a pattern or profile of nonverbal behaviors must be measured before significant encoding (in their case, dominance) can be detected. Eighth, in the same study, the encoding of dominance occurred only in same-sex groups, not in mixed-sex groups. Thus, *encoding may be different depending on the sex composition of an interacting group.*

The ninth form of complexity is also related to sex: *A given encoding relation may be true for one sex but not for the other.* For example, extraversion correlates strongly with the use of broad gestures among women but not among men (Lippa, 1998). The tenth complexity is that *personality is encoded by nonverbal behavior differently across cultures.* That is,

not only are there cultural differences in the amount or frequency of nonverbal behaviors (e.g., Hall, 1966; see Matsumoto, this volume), but nonverbal behavior may also differentially encode (correlate with) dispositions in different cultures (e.g., Andersen & Guerrero, 1998).

Summary. To learn whether nonverbal behavior truly encodes personality dispositions, researchers must navigate at least 10 design and analysis complexities: (1) True encoding can be obscured through the use of unreliable measures; (2) encoding should be studied in a context in which the disposition is salient; (3) others in the interaction might influence an individual's encoding; (4) encoding might occur differently when a person is engaged in different activities or purposes; (5) encoding may depend on who (e.g., self or significant others) assesses the disposition; (6) nonverbal behavior may encode combinations of dispositions without encoding that combination's constituent dispositions; (7) combinations of nonverbal behaviors may encode dispositions without the individual behaviors doing so; (8) encoding may depend on the gender composition of the group; (9) encoding sometimes differs for male and female individuals; and (10) cultural groups vary in their encoding patterns.

◆ Encoding and Decoding Personality

Keeping these complexities in mind, I turn now toward the research focused on encoding and decoding personality. An example of relatively straightforward *encoding* results comes from a study of interacting female dyads (Berry & Hansen, 2000). In Big Five personality terms, more agreeable women gestured more, used more open body postures, visually attended to their interaction partner more, used fewer visual dominance behaviors, and displayed fewer negative facial expressions than did less agreeable women. Women who were more open to experience visually attended to their interaction partners more than those who were less open to experience. More extraverted persons seem to use more animated, expressive, and animated gestures—that is, faster and more energetic gestures using the hands farther from the body (Lippa, 1998)—than more introverted persons. Children with more internal, rather than external, locus of control tendencies smile more and engage in fewer off-task activities (Carton & Carton, 1998). Individuals with avoidant attachment styles tend to choose larger interpersonal distances (Kaitz, Bar-Haim, Lehrer, & Grossman, 2004), as do those with greater trait anxiety (e.g., Patterson, 1973) and weaker affiliative tendencies (e.g., Mehrabian & Diamond, 1971).

Whether or not dispositions are encoded in nonverbal behavior, *decoders believe they are.* In an early study, personnel managers were quite confident that job application photographs revealed the applicants' character (Viteles & Smith, 1932). Observers' ratings may be reliable, which suggests accuracy, but they often do not correlate with any of the targets' physical features (e.g., Cleeton & Knight, 1924). Researchers still investigate alleged nonverbal "power codes" (Schwartz, Tesser, & Powell, 1982) and the "shared meaning" of postures (Kudoh & Matsumoto, 1985). "High-persuasive" nonverbal behavior patterns in actors (direct gaze, more gestures, fewer self-touches) are judged to be more assertive, forceful, powerful, and intelligent (Hart & Morry, 1997). Individuals who speak in a tight-lipped manner or who turn their heads while speaking may be judged as "uptight," those who speak with a hand over their mouths or smile with a closed

mouth as shy, and those who smile less as too serious (Ferrari & Swinkels, 1996).

Are these accurate assessments of a target person's personality or mere "decoding errors" (Bull, 1983)? Observers appear to decode *confidently* and with greater consensus (Gifford, 1994; Lippa & Dietz, 2000), but the evidence that they do so *accurately* is mixed or even discouraging, as shown, for example, by the Cleeton and Knight study. On the positive side, some research shows that *if* one is willing to define accuracy as observer agreement with target self-assessments, removing nonverbal behavior from a job interview (by conducting it by telephone, as opposed to in person) reduces accuracy (Blackman, 2002). Thus, nonverbal behavior certainly *can* contribute to accurate judgments.

A variant on the study of decoding is the study of decoding *ability*, sometimes called nonverbal sensitivity (e.g., Rosenthal, 1979; see Riggio, this volume). Decoding as a skill related to the judge's own experience and background is often applied to constructs other than personality (i.e., emotion; Mullins & Duke, 2004). More intelligent judges are also more accurate (Lippa & Dietz, 2000), at least for some dispositions: More intelligent university-student judges assessed dispositional extraversion and an omnibus (across dispositions) measure more accurately than less intelligent university-student judges. On the other side of the lens, which dispositions are easiest to decode from nonverbal behavior? Several studies (e.g., Ambady, Hallahan, & Rosenthal, 1995; Borkenau & Liebler, 1992; Gifford, 1994; Lippa & Dietz, 2000) report that sociability or extraversion is the most legible or accurately discernable disposition. This, however, may be a function of the second complexity mentioned previously. Most studies use conversations as the activity, and extraversion is particularly salient for conversations.

◆ *A Paradigm Proposal*

This section proposes a paradigm that may deal with the crucial accuracy problems in the most useful way. Its essential feature is that *encoding and decoding both are included in the same study*. Most prior studies have examined either encoding or decoding, which disallows the possibility of understanding the relations between the two processes, or they have compared self and observer ratings without investigating intervening variables such as nonverbal behavior. For example, one study showed that self and acquainted observer ratings were better correlated than self and unacquainted observer ratings, but the researchers did not investigate the behavioral cues on which the ratings were based (Funder & Colvin, 1988). Watson (1989) noticed this gap and called for studies of judgments that also include behavioral cues. Nevertheless, "cueless" studies are still reported (e.g., Ambady, Hallahan, & Rosenthal, 1995). For example, "sociable" actors were found to be more "legible" (i.e., easier to "read" or accurately decode) than less sociable actors, based on actor-observer agreement, but the pathways or mediating behaviors underlying this phenomenon were not examined. A few years later, these results were replicated, and many potential mediating cues were investigated. In this work, extraverts used more energetic gestures, kept their hands farther from their bodies, and changed their facial expression more than introverts (Lippa, 1998).

The proposed paradigm includes the following elements: reliably measured personality constructs that are investigated within the context to which they apply, using three independent groups of raters: (1) actors' self-rated personality or raters who know the actor well, (2) raters trained in a carefully developed nonverbal behavior scoring system, and (3) observer-raters who typically are unacquainted with the actors so that their ratings are not influenced by previous personal experience with the actor. More particularly or operationally, the paradigm's structure is an adaptation of Brunswik's (1956) lens model (Figure 9.1).

Encoding (or what Brunswik called *ecological validity*) is represented by the lines connecting personality to nonverbal behavior. Encoding, as defined here, occurs when reliable self-assessments correlate significantly with reliably scored nonverbal behaviors. Inferences from these cues (decoding, or what Brunswik called *cue utilization*) are represented by the lines connecting nonverbal behavior and impression formation on the part of the observers. Decoding, as defined here, occurs when reliable observer assessments are correlated with reliably scored nonverbal behaviors. The curved line linking the ratings of the actors' dispositions with the observers' ratings of those dispositions represents what Brunswik called *achievement*, or what is here called *agreement*. The large oval signifies the context in which the judgments are made.

Encoding and decoding are influenced by the context in which they occur. What transpires in a conversation may not flow the same way in a debate as during a romantic evening, a business discussion, a romantic interaction, or an interrogation, or in interactions within versus across cultures. One illustration of this comes from a study of deception (Vrij, Akehurst, & Morris, 1997). In this study, actors were interviewed twice, once when they told the truth and once when they lied. Actors with higher levels of public self-consciousness used their hands differently (less) when they lied than when they told the truth. Thus, the adapted lens model in Figure 9.1 requires its surrounding oval to signify the context in which the encoding

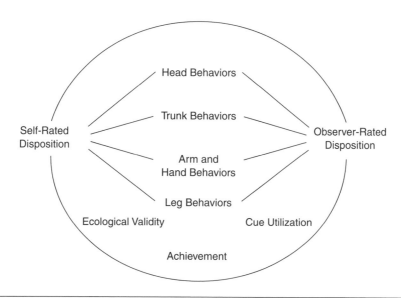

Figure 9.1   The Contextual Lens Model (updated)

SOURCE: Brunswik (1956).

and decoding occur. Few studies have done what seems most productive, however: (1) to investigate all three processes; (2) to assess the relative strengths of encoding, decoding, and agreement; and (3) to take the context into account to provide some understanding of how nonverbal behavior communicates (and miscommunicates) personality. Some other notable exceptions that focus on nonverbal behavior and dispositions include those by Borkenau and Liebler (1992) and Lippa (1998).

The paradigm is employed, in part, to understand the cue utilization policies of observers, individually or in aggregate. Some early studies focused on individual abilities, such as those of clinicians (e.g., Hoffman, 1960), and found that their judgments, as revealed through their use of cues, did not match well with their own impressions of how they use those cues. A more recent individual-level focus has been on the ability or sensitivity of individual observers (e.g., Rosenthal, 1979). When a researcher has more aggregate,

nomothetic goals ("How do *people* decode?"), the study combines the ratings of "everyone"—parents, supervisors, friends, partners, peers, or members of other cultures—as the observers of interest. Of course, if observers in general or from a particular group use nonverbal cues idiosyncratically, the interrater reliability of their target disposition ratings will be low, and it will be inappropriate to correlate their ratings with the nonverbal behavior scores (decoding correlations) or with the targets' self-ratings (agreement correlations). Thus, studies with any sort of nomothetic goals depend on the idea, and therefore must hypothesize, that a group of observers will reliably agree on actors' dispositions. If a specified group of observers do not agree, then conclusions about their cue-utilization policies cannot be stated, probably because members of that group do not use the same cues.

The earliest study that used this paradigm was one by Brunswik himself in 1945 (but not reported until later; Brunswik,

1956, pp. 26–29). The central cues he employed were, perhaps appropriately enough for a first and early study, physiognomic: actor's height of forehead, length of nose, and so on. A decidedly *verbal* study using the paradigm to study extraversion in relation to vocal behavior was published two decades later (Scherer, 1978). In one study that fulfilled most of the goals of the proposed paradigm, behavioral cues were examined as mediators of the encoding-decoding process (Borkenau & Liebler, 1992). The same judges served as raters of the physical cues and as decoders, however, which compromised the independence of the behavior scores and trait ratings.

Perhaps the first study that examined nonverbal behavioral mediators and used behavior scorers who were independent of both targets and observers was conducted by Gifford, Ng, and Wilkinson (1985). That study identified nonverbal cues exhibited by job applicants that mediated (and failed to mediate) agreement between job applicant and personnel officer assessments of the applicant's social skill and motivation to work. That study, however, did not employ personality dispositions as the psychological constructs. A subsequent study, with a coordinated set of independent targets, raters, and observers, that did investigate nonverbal behaviors and how they encode dispositions as well as which of these same nonverbal behaviors are employed by observers to infer targets' personality finally appeared just over a decade ago (Gifford, 1994).

Gifford (1994) will be described in some detail as an exemplar of the proposed paradigm. It examined the eight dispositions that comprise the interpersonal aspect of personality and form a circumplex (Wiggins, 1979). The primary axes of the circumplex (dominance and warmth) are interpreted by some theorists as two of the Big Five personality domains (McCrae & Costa, 1989; Peabody & Goldberg, 1989). Interpersonal dispositions were selected deliberately

because the actors in the study were engaged in a conversation; other dispositions (e.g., conscientiousness, openness to experience, and emotional stability, the other three dispositions in the Big Five) were not included because they would not have been examined in a context that should have made them particularly salient.

◆ *Interlude: Potential Outcomes of Encoding-Decoding Studies*

Before describing the exemplar study in detail, it may be useful to discuss the generic potential outcomes of studies that use this paradigm. The first assumption is that all the judgments (e.g., self-ratings, behavior scoring, and observer ratings) are reliable; if some are not, they cannot be used with any pretence of validity. In general, encoding, decoding, and agreement may be weak or strong for any disposition, and the pattern of results may be different for each disposition.

The first type of potential outcome occurs when, for a given disposition, encoding, decoding, and agreement all are weak. In this case, (1) personality is not reflected consistently in nonverbal behavior (at least not in the behaviors studied), (2) observers do not use this set of behavior cues to arrive at their inferences, and (3) observer inferences do not agree with the self or knowledgeable other assessments of actors. Second, if decoding is strong but encoding is weak, observers apparently are using invalid stereotypes. (One suspects, without the benefit of data, that this was the case with Lavater and his fellow physiognomists.) Agreement should be weak in such a case, because there are no true relations between personality and nonverbal behavior for observers to decode legitimately.

Third, if strong encoding but weak decoding is found, observers are unable to deduce correctly which nonverbal cues reflect the actors' personality. The potential for strong agreement is present, but it is unrealized. Fourth, if agreement is strong but both encoding and decoding are weak, observers must be using nonverbal behaviors for decoding that the researcher has not measured. Some nonverbal cue or other must have been providing valid information about the actor's personality, or agreement would not be possible. The researcher must explore the impression formation process, perhaps through interviews with observers, to learn which unstudied nonverbal cues the observers might have been using to succeed in matching the assessments of the actors.

Fifth, if weak encoding and high agreement are found, observers again must be using valid but unmeasured nonverbal cues, unless the unlikely case that the observers are clairvoyant holds true (Reichenbach, 1938). As Wiggins (1973) wryly notes, "Such a possibility is assigned rather low priority as a contemporary scientific explanation" (p. 159). This is a case in which researchers must rethink their choice of cues, seeking others that *do* encode the disposition. One way to accomplish this might be to interview the judges, asking them to reflect on their inferences.

Finally, if strong encoding, strong decoding, *and* strong agreement are found, the researcher may conclude that the whole process is working as researchers in this area dream it does, and they may be able to supply a satisfying account of this assessment process. A sober second thought, however, is that actors (or their intimates) and observers *could* be agreeing on an inaccurate view of the actors' personality, something akin to a folie à deux. A more likely interpretation is that the strong mediation of objective nonverbal behaviors, assessed reliably by independent observers, would be substantial evidence that the observers' decoding is valid, given that they have been demonstrated to rely on the

same objective (visible) aspects of reality as encoding. If so, the centuries-old conviction that dispositions truly are "legible" would receive convincing support.

◆ An Exemplar

The following study is presented partly for its results, which illustrate many specific encoding and decoding results with personality and nonverbal behavior. But it is also presented as a way of introducing many of the intricacies of conducting encoding-decoding research, including proposed solutions to problems that arise in the course of analyzing the data in such studies. Based on the available literature, the hypotheses of the exemplar study (Gifford, 1994) were that encoding would be weak to moderate but that observers would have a strong tendency to decode. Agreement, based on recent research that indicates dispositions are communicated to different degrees (Gifford et al., 1985; John, 1990), was expected to vary across dispositions. For dispositions with low agreement, self-observer encoding-decoding discrepancies were expected to be high. For dispositions with high agreement, self-observer discrepancies were expected to be low.

The target participants were 60 undergraduates drawn from a psychology department participant pool. Ten all-male and 10 all-female triads were formed into conversational groups, and one group at a time was filmed as it conversed. The participants were given a list of suggested topics, but they were encouraged to converse on any topic they chose. A week or so prior to the conversation, the participants were given Wiggins' (1979) Interpersonal Adjective Scales Inventory (IAS). The IAS covers two of the Big Five domains of personality, but it was chosen *to maximize the relevance of selected dispositions to the context.* From the top of the circumplex, these scales are ambitious-dominant, gregarious-extraverted, warm-agreeable, unassuming-ingenuous, lazy-submissive, aloof-introverted, cold-quarrelsome, and arrogant-calculating (see Gifford & O'Connor, 1987).

The videotapes were then scored using the Seated Kinesic Activity Notation System (SKANS IV; Gifford, 1986), in which 38 kinesic and facial behaviors are measured in one of three ways: frequency, duration, or time sampling. In a second sample of participants, 21 unacquainted peers of the targets were shown 5-minute selections from the middle of the conversations over several sessions with the audio track turned off. Each time the tape was played, each observer was asked to focus on only 1 of the 3 participants shown in the tape. The tape was then replayed and the observers watched another participant. Thus, all 21 observers viewed all 60 participants. After each tape was shown, each observer completed a 40-item short version of the IAS about one target. The observers' task was demanding, so they made their ratings over several sessions. They were paid $50 for their efforts and offered a prize of $50 for being the most accurate (defined as coming the closest to the self-ratings of the 60 target individuals—really, as noted, a measure of agreement).

Most measures (self-assessments, observer assessments, and SKANS IV measures) were adequately reliable. Some behaviors, however, occurred infrequently; they were difficult to score owing to camera placement; or interjudge agreement was low. Others were combined because they were highly correlated. Thus, the remaining analyses were based on 27 nonverbal behaviors. Pearson correlation coefficients between the actors' self-assessed dispositions and their nonverbal behaviors represent the left, or encoding, half of the lens diagram. Not every significant correlation

between a nonverbal behavior cue and a disposition, however, necessarily is a valid encoding link.

Three specific threats to the validity or generalizability of an encoding link may be identified. First, the correlation could be influenced by the actions of others in the conversation; a valid encoding link should be empirically attributable to an individual, uncontaminated by group influence, if it is to be considered a valid personality-nonverbal behavior link. Second, correlations may be due to chance; to be valid, an encoding link should have reasonable strength and be part of an ordered pattern of correlations around the interpersonal circle. If a behavior is truly relevant to interpersonal behavior, it should not merely correlate with one disposition on the circle. Its correlations should rise and fall around the interpersonal circle in an ordered manner (Gifford, 1991). Third, the possibility of sex differences raises the issue of generalizability of a given putative encoding link to both sexes. For example, a valid link between a disposition and a nonverbal behavior for women may not be valid for men, or vice versa. For example, using most of one's body when gesturing validly signals extraversion for women, but it does not work as a valid signal for men (Lippa, 1998).

Each of these threats was considered in preliminary analyses (for details, see Gifford, 1994). In all, because of significant group influence or failure to conclusively map onto the interpersonal circle, 19 of the 27 remaining nonverbal behaviors were rejected as not demonstrably valid encoders of interpersonal dispositions. The eight nonverbal behaviors identified as valid encoders of interpersonal circle traits are head orientation, nods, arm wrap, gestures, object manipulation, left leg lean, leg movement, and leg extension. Their significant links ($p < .05$) with the eight dispositions of the interpersonal circle are displayed in one

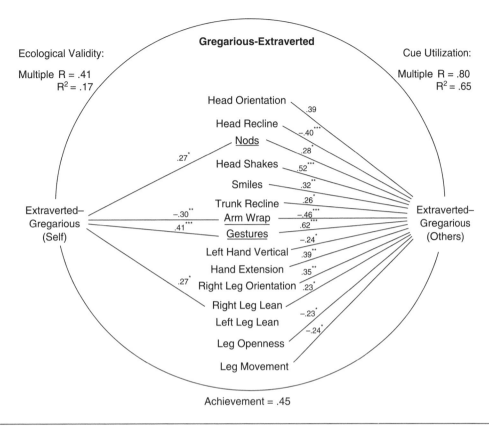

Figure 9.2   The Contextual Lens Model for Gregarious-Extraverted

typical disposition: gregarious-extraverted. See Figure 9.2 (also, see Gifford, 1994) for the other seven lens models.

Correlations between the nonverbal behaviors and the dispositions as inferred by the observers were computed. All 27 of the nonverbal behaviors were used for this purpose, rather than the subset of 8 behaviors used for the encoding half of the study. This was because the goal on the left half of the lens is to determine which nonverbal behaviors *actually* encode personality (to the best of our methods' abilities), whereas on the right side the goal is to determine which nonverbal behaviors are *believed* by observers to be cues to personality. This distinction follows from Brunswik's original labels for the two sides of the lens model: ecological *validity* (left half) and cue *utilization* (right half). Significant ($p < .05$)

cue utilization correlations are displayed on the right half of Figure 9.2; collectively, they describe the way in which typical observers decode.

THE STRENGTH OF ENCODING AND DECODING

Next, the magnitude of encoding and decoding was examined. Magnitude was computed as the multiple correlation and percentage of variance in each disposition accounted for by the nonverbal behaviors. Only nonverbal behaviors that had shown significant ($p < .05$) correlations with the dispositions were considered. Stepwise multiple regression analysis was used for this purpose. Magnitudes to be reported are conservative because, although all variables with significant Pearson correlations were given the opportunity to predict a given disposition, only those that made significant ($p < .05$) additional contributions to the equation were included. Figure 9.2 shows the values of multiple R and R^2 for the encoding and decoding for gregarious-extraverted.

One general tendency apparent from the results is that decoding is stronger than encoding. Beginning at the top of the interpersonal circle and proceeding clockwise, multiple correlations were (encoding followed by decoding) as follows: ambitious-dominant .54 versus .81, extraverted-gregarious .41 versus .80, warm-agreeable .30 versus .79, unassuming-ingenuous .41 versus .74, lazy-submissive .62 versus .81, aloof-introverted .54 versus .82, cold-quarrelsome .00 versus .79, and arrogant-calculating .25 versus .77. The median encoding magnitude is .41 and the median decoding magnitude is .80. Many more significant decoding links than encoding links are found.

GROUP VERSUS INDIVIDUAL DECODING

Despite these findings, however, decoding actually may not be much stronger than encoding. As noted, observer decoding ratings are based on 21 raters. Multiple raters almost necessarily increase the reliability of ratings. When ratings are more reliable, correlations involving them are stronger because less error is involved. Stronger correlations are more likely to be statistically significant and therefore to be included in the lens diagrams. Analyses that corrected for attenuation and estimated the reliability of single judges (see Gifford, 1994, for details) showed that one typical decoding link shrank from $r = -.58$ to $r = -.35$. The matched encoding link for this decoding link was $r = -.29$, not much less than $r = -.35$. Thus, observers as a *group* decode strongly, but researchers who wish to

generalize to typical *individual* observers would conclude that decoding is not particularly reliable, and this would attenuate the seemingly large magnitude of decoding.

Whether researchers examine group decoding or typical individual decoding value depends on the study's purpose. If it is to understand how observers (in general, nomothetically) decode, one would use the full observer sample; if it is to estimate the decoding skill of a single "typical" observer, the attenuation approach should be used; and if the goal is to understand how one particular observer decodes (e.g., a clinician under training), one could study decoding with an n of 1. The question for the researcher is, do I wish to learn how and how well observers in general decode, how and how well a typical single observer (e.g., a typical human resource officer in a large organization) decodes, or how and how well *this* observer (e.g., a person applying for a job as a human resource officer) decodes?

PARTICULAR ENCODING AND DECODING LINKS

For readers who are interested, considerable information about particular relations between interpersonal dispositions and nonverbal behaviors is available in Figures 3 to 10 of Gifford (1994). Here, only one lens model is presented, as an example, in the interest of saving space.

AGREEMENT AND NONVERBAL COMMUNICATION

Agreement is measured as the correlation between typical self-assessments and typical assessments by observers, and it is represented in Figures 9.1 and 9.2 by the curved line at the bottom. The use of correlations overcomes several of the classic Cronbach (1955) criticisms of accuracy research. Across the eight dispositions in the full study, agreement averaged .27 (*r*– to Z-transformed), which is significant (*p* < .02), if moderate in magnitude. Agreement ranged from .18 (NS) for both lazy-submissive and cold-quarrelsome to .45 (*p* < .001) for gregarious-extraverted and .41 (*p* < .001) for aloof-introverted.

The relations between encoding and decoding fall into two categories, each with two forms. First, *matched links* may be identified. One form of matched link occurs when a nonverbal behavior significantly encodes self-assessments and is also used to a significant degree by observers to decode or infer that self-assessment. Across the 8 dispositions, 14 matched links of this form were found. Matched links are underlined in Figure 9.2. Another form of matched link occurs when a link is significant on *neither* side of the lens: Observers are saying that a given behavior does not encode a given trait, and based on the self-assessments, it does not. In this study, 105 such matches occurred. Second, *mismatched links* may be identified. One form of mismatched link occurs when a nonverbal behavior does encode a self-assessed disposition, but observers do not use that cue. For example, more lazy-submissive persons manipulate objects (e.g., their clothing, pen, paper) more than others do, but observers do not use object manipulation as a cue to lazy-submissive. In this study, six mismatches of this kind occurred across the eight interpersonal dispositions. The other form of mismatched link occurs when observers use a particular nonverbal cue to form their impression but that cue does *not* encode that disposition. For example (see Figure 9.2), observers believe that more gregarious-extraverted persons orient their heads toward their companions more, but (based on self-assessments) this is not so.

In this study, 83 mismatches of this kind were observed across the eight dispositions. Decoders appear to use many more cues to infer self-assessed dispositions than were

necessary. As noted earlier, however, the greater number and magnitude of decoding links is due partly to psychometric considerations—that is, the superior reliability of decoding. Agreement is higher in general when there are more matched links. The existence of matched links, with their lines going from the disposition to a behavior and from the behavior to the observer's assessment, clearly suggests that agreement increases when information "flows" via such matched links. Conversely, agreement is lower when many mismatched links occur. The same trend was also demonstrated earlier in a personnel selection context by Gifford et al. (1985).

When information does *not* flow, either encoding has not occurred (no behaviors measured encode the disposition) or the observer has used cues other than those that the encoding analysis suggests are valid indicators of a disposition. The communication of self-assessed personality was quite good (i.e., agreement was relatively high) for some dispositions. Considering that observers saw only 5 minutes of a soundless conversation among individuals they had never met, their decoding of gregarious-extraverted, *r* = .45, and aloof-introverted, *r* = .41, for example, is quite an "achievement." This study demonstrates that (1) the encoding of interpersonal dispositions in nonverbal behavior is moderate (median multiple *R* = .41), (2) the decoding of the same dispositions is moderate by individual observers and strong by groups of observers (median multiple *R* = .80), and (3) agreement is low to moderate (mean *r* = .27), yet significant (*p* < .02). Each of these results will be discussed in turn. Apart from the specific magnitudes of these links, the combined findings show exactly *how* information appears to flow from the actor to the observer—that is, how personality and nonverbal behavior are connected, and how observers infer (and misinfer) personality by watching other people.

ENCODING

That encoding is at least moderate is an optimistic note in a literature that can be characterized as pessimistic (see Bull, 1983; Duncan & Fiske, 1985; Heslin & Patterson, 1982). These results are based on a conservative strategy that winnowed out apparently significant encoding links that manifested group influence or did not meet the criteria for behavior mapping (Gifford, 1991) and used a conservative variance-accounting strategy. Almost 40% of the variance in self-assessed lazy-submissiveness, for example, was accounted for. Even more encouraging, certain behaviors that have been linked to dominance or submissiveness in other encoding studies, such as postural relaxation (Mehrabian, 1981) and looking in relation to speaking (Exline, Ellyson, & Long, 1975), were not included in this study. When these behaviors are included in future studies, the evidence for encoding should be even stronger.

Dispositions that were not well encoded (e.g., cold-quarrelsome) may be encoded by behaviors that were not included in this study, may not be encoded in nonverbal behavior, or may not have been elicited often in the context of the conversations in this study. In a newly acquainted group of three students who have conversational freedom, any tendencies an individual may have toward cold-quarrelsome or arrogant-calculating have little reason or opportunity to be expressed. If so, any nonverbal behaviors that signal these dispositions will occur infrequently and not have much variance. This, in turn, means that correlations between disposition and behavior are unlikely to emerge. The context-based reason for poor encoding, however, may not always apply. For example, warm-agreeable is a disposition that one *would* expect to be expressed in this study's conversational context, but it was encoded poorly. Researchers, then, must consider other nonverbal behaviors as potential

encoders and vary the social context of their observations to encourage the expression of dispositions that may not show up in a pleasant exchange among previously unacquainted individuals before concluding that dispositions simply are not encoded in nonverbal behavior.

DECODING

Apparently, strong decoding was evident for all eight dispositions (the *smallest* multiple R was .74). Borkenau and Liebler (1992) also report stronger decoding than encoding. Because observers as a group produce very reliable ratings, they appear willing to make strong inferences about the targets' personalities based on nonverbal behavior. Typical individual observers may not decode any more strongly than the equivalent strength of encoding, however. Thus, personality theorists must be careful when interpreting observer decodings. Observer assessments are not necessarily any more or less valid than are self-ratings, particularly if neither self nor observer has any expert training. Observers may use "power codes" (Schwartz, Tesser, & Powell, 1982), and postures have shared meaning for observers (Kudoh & Matsumoto, 1985). This does not mean necessarily that dominance from the self's perspective is revealed by this same set of acts, however; it merely means that observers believe it is.

AGREEMENT

Agreement, as explained earlier, depends on the decoders' appropriate use of ecologically valid cues. For example, the observers believed that 14 nonverbal cues are good indicators of target cold-quarrelsomeness, but not one of the 14 cues encoded self-rated cold-quarrelsomeness, and agreement was only $r = .18$ (NS). In contrast, the observers believed that 14 nonverbal behaviors signal gregarious-extraverted, and 3 of those actually do; as a result, agreement was $r = .45$ ($p < .001$). Clearly, agreement varies across dispositions. The results indicate that, in general (around the interpersonal circle), self and observer both agree and disagree about self's dispositions. Self-other agreement depends heavily on the observer's use of appropriate nonverbal cues (i.e., those that do encode self's view of the disposition). "Disagreement" occurs when observers use inappropriate cues. If a way can be found to increase the reliability of self-assessment, perhaps through multiple self-assessments, error on the encoding side will shrink, and the magnitude and number of encoding links should rise, with a consequent increase in agreement.

VARIATIONS IN ENCODING ACROSS DISPOSITIONS

Interpersonal dispositions (in Big Five terms, agreeableness and extraversion, as opposed to the three others that are not particularly interpersonal in nature: conscientiousness, emotional stability, and openness to experience) are the focus in this study, because they are the dispositions one would expect to be salient in the conversational context we examined. This restriction of dispositions studied to contexts in which they may reasonably be expected to manifest themselves or to be salient is one of the precepts of this paradigm. In this study, the two major dimensions are treated as orthogonal axes of a circumplex; around the circumplex are eight gradations resulting from the high and low ends of the two dimensions, plus combinations of them. The resulting eight interpersonal constructs vary in the amount they are encoded in nonverbal behavior. What I call the "grexalin" axis (the line that bisects the interpersonal circle from

gregarious-extraverted to aloof-introverted) manifests the greatest agreement (the mean r for the two dispositions was .43). One implication is that grexalin is the most visible interpersonal axis. All the dispositions were strongly *perceived* (decoded) but without much agreement. Grexalin is perceived more *correctly* than the other axes. In attempting to explain this phenomenon, it is tempting to assert that grexalin is the most legible disposition because it is the most truly *interpersonal* disposition.

◆ Conclusion

IMPLICATIONS FOR EVERYDAY SOCIAL INTERACTION

One important implication of the findings is that when self and observer believe that different behaviors signify a given disposition (or that a given behavior signifies different dispositions), misinterpretation and conflict may result. If one person believes that the other is cold, he or she may well behave toward the other in accordance with this perception of coldness, that is, with generally negative responses. The other person consequently may be expected to be unpleasantly mystified by these actions and may then respond accordingly (i.e., not very positively). The first person may then react to the second person's negative reaction negatively, and so on. In this way, the innocent use of and consequent misinference from certain nonverbal behaviors could seriously damage the development of relations between persons who meet for the first time.

A PROCESS MODEL AS A FRAMEWORK

Brunswik's (1956) lens model serves as a useful way of conceptualizing social judgment, including the encoding and decoding of nonverbal behavior by actors and observers. Besides being clear intuitively, it offers an unambiguous path for empirical demonstrations of how encoding, decoding, and agreement operate through nonverbal behavior. A companion framework, which I have adapted from Craik's (1968) framework for understanding environmental perception and which offers a comprehensive overview of the different kinds of actors, media of presentation, form of judgments, types of criteria, types of observers, and types of analyses, is portrayed in Table 9.1. The process model is at once daunting, in that it suggests the huge number of possibilities in this research area in contrast to how little has been accomplished, and

heuristic, in that it can serve as a clear agenda for future researchers.

FINAL COMMENTS

Personality and nonverbal behavior are not linked in simple ways. This accounts for the undulations in optimism from the era of physiognomy and early (1930s) scientific efforts to the lacunae in research until the 1960s, followed by the slough of despond in the early 1980s and the slow rise of optimism since then. Progress will be difficult, given the 10 (or more) complexities, but if researchers are careful to at least describe how their studies deal with the complexities, understanding will grow. This will be a step

Table 9.1   A Process Model for the Encoding and Decoding of Nonverbal Behavior in Personality

Actor (A)	Mode of Presentation	Form of Judgment	Sample Criteria	Context	Observer (O)	Type of Analysis
Child	In Vivo	Self-report (A)	Big 5	Conversation	Peer	A-O Agreement
Student	Video	Rating (O)	Trait Anxiety	Personnel Selection	Partner	O-O Agreement
Partner	Audio	Scored Behavior	Self-Monitor	Deception	Employer	Encoding Correlation
Friend	Transcript	Specific	Attachment Style	Clinical	Employee	Decoding Correlation
Peer	Drawing	Pattern	Control Orientation	Attraction	Teacher	Mediators/ Moderators
Other Culture			Narcissism		Friend	Skill/ Sensitivity
Employee			Avoidant		Parent	Gender
Employer			Public Self-Consciousness		Stranger	Intelligence
Stranger			Secure			Personality
						Emotional State

toward a fuller understanding, which future researchers will achieve, of both social judgment and the delicate behavioral dance involved in nonverbal behavior (Patterson, this volume). Table 9.1 is an effort to create a process model of the problem, one that is adapted from Craik (1968), who used such a model for another area of research, environmental perception. Even this does not encompass the range of considerations that should be taken into account in any serious scientific study of personality and nonverbal behavior, but perhaps other observations made in this chapter will contribute to that goal.

◆ **References**

Allport, G., & Vernon, P. (1933). *Studies in expressive movement.* New York: Macmillan.

Ambady, N., Hallahan, M., & Rosenthal, R. (1995). On judging and being judged accurately in zero-acquaintance situations. *Journal of Personality and Social Psychology, 69,* 518–529.

Andersen, P. A., & Guerrero, L. K. (1998). The bright side of relational communication: Interpersonal warmth as a social emotion. In P. A. Andersen & L. K. Guerrero (Eds.), *Handbook of communication and emotion: Research, theory, applications, and contexts* (pp. 303–329). San Diego: Academic Press.

Aries, E. J., Gold, C., & Weigel, R. H. (1983). Dispositional and situational influences on dominance behavior in small groups. *Journal of Personality and Social Psychology, 44,* 779–786.

Berry, D. S., & Hansen, J. S. (2000). Personality, nonverbal behavior, and interaction quality in female dyads. *Personality and Social Psychology Bulletin, 26,* 278–292.

Blackman, M. C. (2002). The employment interview via the telephone: Are we sacrificing accurate personality judgments for cost efficiency? *Journal of Research in Personality, 36,* 208–233.

Borkenau, P., & Liebler, A. (1992). Trait inferences: Sources of validity at zero acquaintance. *Journal of Personality and Social Psychology, 62,* 645–657.

Brunswik, E. (1956). *Perception and the representative design of psychological experiments.* Berkeley, CA: University of California Press.

Bull, P. (1983). *Body movement and interpersonal communication.* New York: Wiley.

Campbell, A., & Rushton, J. P. (1978). Bodily communication and personality. *British Journal of Social and Clinical Psychology, 17,* 31–36.

Carton, J. S., & Carton, E. E. R. (1998). Nonverbal maternal warmth and children's locus of control of reinforcement. *Journal of Nonverbal Behavior, 22,* 77–86.

Cheek, J. M., & Buss, A. H. (1981). Shyness and sociability. *Journal of Personality and Social Psychology, 41,* 330–339.

Cleeton, G. U., & Knight, F. B. (1924). Validity of character judgments based on external criteria. *Journal of Applied Psychology, 8,* 215–231.

Craik, K. H. (1968). The comprehension of the everyday physical environment. *Journal of the American Institute of Planners, 34,* 29–37.

Cronbach, L. J. (1955). Processes affecting scores on "understanding of others" and "assumed similarity." *Psychological Bulletin, 52,* 177–193.

Duncan, S. F., Jr., & Fiske, D. W. (1985). *Interaction structure and strategy.* New York: Cambridge University Press.

Exline, R. V. (1963). Explorations in the process of person perception: Visual interaction in relation to competition, sex, and need for affiliation. *Journal of Personality, 31,* 1–20.

Exline, R. V., Ellyson, S. L., & Long, B. (1975). Visual behavior exhibited by males differing as to interpersonal control orientation in one- and two-way communication systems. In P. Pliner, L. Krames, & T. Alloway (Eds.), *Nonverbal communication of aggression* (Vol. 2, pp. 21–51). New York: Plenum.

Ferrari, J. R., & Swinkels, A. (1996). Classic cover-ups and misguided messages: Examining face-trait associations in stereotyped perceptions of nonverbal behavior. *Journal of Social Behavior and Personality, 11,* 27–42.

Funder, D. C. (2003). Toward a social psychology of person judgments: Implications for person perception *accuracy* and self-knowledge. In J. P. Forgas & K. D. Williams (Eds.), *Social judgments: Implicit and explicit processes* (pp. 115–133). New York: Cambridge University Press.

Funder, D. C., & Colvin, C. R. (1988). Friends and strangers: Acquaintanceship, agreement, and the accuracy of personality judgment. *Journal of Personality and Social Psychology, 55,* 149–158.

Gifford, R. (1986). SKANS IV: Seated Kinesic Activity Notation System (Version 4.1) [Computer software]. Victoria, BC, Canada: University of Victoria, Department of Psychology.

Gifford, R. (1991). Mapping nonverbal behavior on the interpersonal circle. *Journal of Personality and Social Psychology, 61,* 279–288.

Gifford, R. (1994). A lens-mapping framework for understanding the encoding and decoding of interpersonal dispositions in nonverbal behavior. *Journal of Personality and Social Psychology, 66,* 398–412.

Gifford, R., Ng, C. F., & Wilkinson, M. (1985). Nonverbal cues in the employment interview: Links between applicant qualities and interviewer judgments. *Journal of Applied Psychology, 70,* 729–736.

Gifford, R., & O'Connor, B. (1987). The interpersonal circumplex as a behavior map. *Journal of Personality and Social Psychology, 52,* 1019–1026.

Hall, E. T. (1966). *The hidden dimension.* New York: Doubleday.

Hart, A. J., & Morry, M. M. (1997). Trait inference based on racial and behavioral cues. *Basic and Applied Social Psychology, 19,* 33–48.

Heslin, R., & Patterson, M. L. (1982). *Nonverbal behavior and social psychology.* New York: Plenum.

Hoffman, P. J. (1960). The paramorphic representation of clinical judgment. *Psychological Bulletin, 57,* 116–131.

John, O. P. (1990, August). *Self-observer agreement: Differences between traits, differences between individuals.* Paper presented at the annual meetings of the American Psychological Association, Boston, MA.

Kaitz, M., Bar-Haim, Y., Lehrer, M., & Grossman, E. (2004). Adult attachment style and interpersonal distance. *Attachment and Human Development, 6,* 285–304.

Kanki, B. G. (1985). Participant differences and interactive strategies. In S. F. Duncan Jr. & D. W. Fiske (Eds.), *Interaction structure and strategy.* New York: Cambridge University Press.

Kenny, D. A. (1991). A general model of consensus and accuracy in interpersonal perception. *Psychological Review, 98,* 155–163.

Kenny, D. A. (1994). *Interpersonal perception: A social relations analysis.* New York: Guilford.

Kudoh, T., & Matsumoto, D. (1985). Cross-cultural examination of the semantic dimensions of body postures. *Journal of Personality and Social Psychology, 48,* 1440–1446.

Lippa, R. (1998). The nonverbal display and judgment of extraversion, masculinity, femininity, and gender diagnosticity: A lens model analysis. *Journal of Research in Personality, 32,* 80–107.

Lippa, R., & Dietz, J. K. (2000). The relation of gender, personality, and intelligence to judges' accuracy in judging strangers' personality from brief video segments. *Journal of Nonverbal Behavior, 24,* 25–43.

McCrae, R. R., & Costa, P. T., Jr. (1989). The structure of interpersonal traits: Wiggins's circumplex and the five-factor model. *Journal of Personality and Social Psychology, 56,* 586–595.

Mehrabian, A. (1981). *Silent messages.* Belmont, CA: Wadsworth.

Mehrabian, A., & Diamond, S. G. (1971). Seating arrangement and conversation. *Sociometry, 34,* 281–289.

Montepare, J. M., & Dobish, H. (2003). The contribution of emotion perceptions and their overgeneralizations to trait impressions. *Journal of Nonverbal Behavior, 27,* 237–254.

Motowidlo, S. J., Burnett, J. R., Maczynski, J., & Witkowski, S. (1996). Predicting managerial job performance from personality ratings based on a structured interview: An international replication. *Polish Psychological Bulletin, 27*, 139–151.

Mullins, D. T., & Duke, M. P. (2004). Effects of social anxiety on nonverbal accuracy and response time I: Facial expressions. *Journal of Nonverbal Behavior, 28*, 3–33.

Patterson, M. L. (1973). Stability of nonverbal immediacy behaviors. *Journal of Experimental Social Psychology, 9*, 97–109.

Patterson, M. L. (1995). A parallel process model of nonverbal communication. *Journal of Nonverbal Behavior, 19*, 3–29.

Peabody, D., & Goldberg, L. R. (1989). Some determinants of factor structures from personality-trait descriptors. *Journal of Personality and Social Psychology, 57*, 552–567.

Reichenbach, H. (1938). *Experience and prediction.* Chicago: University of Chicago Press.

Riggio, H. R., & Riggio, R. E. (2002). Emotional expressiveness, extraversion, and neuroticism: A meta-analysis. *Journal of Nonverbal Behavior, 26*(4), 195–218.

Rosenthal, R. (Ed.). (1979). *Skill in nonverbal communication: Individual differences.* Cambridge, MA: Oelgeschlager, Gunn & Hain.

Scherer, K. R. (1978). Personality inference from voice quality: The loud voice of extroversion. *European Journal of Social Psychology, 8*, 467–487.

Schwartz, B., Tesser, A., & Powell, E. (1982). Dominance cues in nonverbal behavior. *Social Psychology Quarterly, 45*(2), 114–120.

Viteles, M. S., & Smith, K. R. (1932). The prediction of vocational aptitude and success from photographs. *Journal of Experimental Psychology, 15*, 615–629.

Vrij, A., Akehurst, L., & Morris, P. (1997). Individual differences in hand movements during deception. *Journal of Nonverbal Behavior, 21*(2), 87–102.

Watson, D. (1989). Strangers' ratings of the five robust personality factors: Evidence of a surprising convergence with self-report. *Journal of Personality and Social Psychology, 57*, 120–128.

Wiggins, J. S. (1973). *Personality and prediction: Principles of personality assessment.* Reading, MA: Addison-Wesley.

Wiggins, J. S. (1979). A psychological taxonomy of trait-descriptive terms: The interpersonal domain. *Journal of Personality and Social Psychology, 37*, 395–412.

Young, L. (1993). *The naked face: The essential guide to reading faces.* New York: St. Martins Press.

10

FACTORING IN AGE

Nonverbal Communication Across the Life Span

◆ Robert S. Feldman
University of Massachusetts at Amherst

◆ James M. Tyler
Purdue University

Nonverbal behaviors comprise a fundamental component of human communication and represent the nature of communication in its earliest form. To use these behaviors in everyday social activities necessitates developing the ability to identify nonverbal expressions accurately and the capacity to respond nonverbally in an appropriate fashion (see Riggio, this volume). These skills not only serve a variety of communicative goals and functions but are also vitally important to the expression of emotions (see Fridlund & Russell, this volume; Matsumoto, this volume). Beginning as early as infancy and continuing into late adulthood, the ability to distinguish, interpret, and express nonverbal behaviors plays an essential role in the successful navigation of social interactions.

Typically, proficiency in nonverbal communication is described in terms of encoding and decoding activities, enhancing the course of a social interaction and the goals of the interactants. With respect to decoding, skillful nonverbal communication requires that people possess a "nonverbal sensitivity" to decode other people's expressions and behaviors accurately (DePaulo & Rosenthal, 1982). In comparable fashion, encoding nonverbal behaviors involves the expression of internal experiences in a manner that others can decode accurately, consequently enabling one to achieve one's desired goals (Burgoon, 1994). Importantly for this chapter, decoding and encoding ability improves generally from infancy through early adulthood, although both may begin to deteriorate at more advanced ages (Malatesta, 1981).

The primary goal of the present chapter is to examine the development and progression of nonverbal communication from infancy throughout late adulthood, focusing attention on two of the most commonly researched channels: facial expressions and body movements. The first section, Decoding Nonverbal Communication, involves the ability to decode facial expressions, first in infants and children and subsequently in younger and older adults, and focuses on the ability to decode body movements, again focusing on infants and children and then on adults. The second section, Encoding Nonverbal Communication, concerns the capacity to encode nonverbal communication, following the same outline as the previous section. In the final section, we describe potential directions for future research.

◆ Decoding Nonverbal Communication

DECODING FACIAL EXPRESSIONS: INFANTS AND CHILDREN

Facial expressions are characterized typically as a fundamental aspect of nonverbal communication, with the ability to decode such expressions playing an important role in the successful navigation of ongoing interactions (Burgoon, 1994).

Indeed, beginning with infancy and continuing throughout adulthood, the ability to differentiate, interpret, and understand facial expressions is a central component in developing and maintaining relationships. Evidence shows typically that the ability to identify facial expressions accurately improves with age, although even young infants distinguish among and appropriately respond to a variety of expressions (Walker-Andrews & Dickson, 1997).

It is difficult to assess how infants process facial displays, with most studies necessarily using visual preference or habituation to measure the distinctions that infants make between expressions. In broad terms, however, as early as the first few days of life, infants appear to possess some instinctive capacity for nonverbal communication (i.e., they imitate some facial expressions and gestures; Field, Woodson, Greenberg, & Cohen, 1982). Moreover, numerous features of infants' perceptual development indicate sensitivity to visual, acoustic, and motion information, connoting that infants are responsive to environmental stimuli (Bertenthal, Proffitt, Spetner, & Thomas, 1985). This early sensitivity may allow for the eventual recognition and discrimination of different facial expressions.

To determine infants' ability to distinguish facial expressions, researchers typically expose them to numerous stimuli, including a variety of posed faces. The results of such research indicate that within hours of birth, neonates look longer at and visually track stimuli that appear more face-like (Johnson, Dziurawiec, Ellis, & Morton, 1991). Infants also appear to differentiate between happy and surprised expressions and between happy and fearful expressions, but only if the happy expressions occur first (Young-Browne, Rosenfeld, & Horowitz, 1977). Moreover, infants discriminate between frowning and smiling, especially if posed by their mother, and they tend to look longer at joy expressions compared with neutral or angry ones (Barrera & Maurer, 1981). In short, this work suggests that infants may possess an early sensitivity to recognize and differentiate facial displays.

Because neonates can discern only blurry faces (i.e., they distinguish hairline, eyes, nose, and mouth), it is probable that they discriminate facial expressions primarily based on feature information (Ludemann, 1991). By 6 months, however, visual sharpness improves, and infants' sensitivity to contrasts enables them to make finer-grained affective distinctions between expressions (Gwiazda, Bauer, & Held, 1989). Thus, infants as young as 3 to 4 months old appear to discriminate between facial expressions, based initially on feature differences and later on affectively relevant information (Kestenbaum & Nelson, 1990). As infants approach 1 year of age, their gaze tends to focus increasingly on the facial area, and they start to process information conveyed by facial expressions in a more cognitively complex way (McClure, 2000). Specifically, infants move beyond simply distinguishing among expressions to assessing events and regulating behavior in accord with information derived from the facial expressions of adults. This ability—*social referencing*—is explored empirically by placing an infant in situations that involve conflicting outcomes and having their caretakers react with predetermined cues when the infant seeks her guidance (Saarni, Mumme, & Campos, 1998).

In a classic study of social referencing, Sorce, Emde, Campos, and Klinnert (1985) observed that the majority of 1-year-old infants crossed a visual cliff when their mothers posed happy expressions, whereas no infants crossed the cliff when their mothers posed fearful expressions. Similar examples of social referencing have been reported using various stimuli to trigger emotion, including toys, strangers, and animals (Feinman & Lewis, 1983). For instance, both 12- and 18-month-olds presented with a novel toy remained closer to their mother when she posed a fearful expression, moved to a middistance for neutral expressions, and wandered farthest when mothers portrayed happy expressions (Klinnert, 1984). Moreover, 12-month-olds played less with a toy if their mothers displayed negative expressions toward that toy (Hornik, Risenhoover, & Gunnar, 1987). By preschool, children match facial expressions of emotion to narrated stories (Borke, 1971) and label facial displays with basic emotions (i.e., happiness, sadness, anger, and fear) at better than chance accuracy (Denham & Couchoud, 1990; Philippot & Feldman, 1990).

In broad terms, positive emotions are recognized earlier and more accurately than negative ones (Camras & Allison, 1985). Specifically, 3- to 6-year-old-children can generally identify happiness more accurately than they can identify sadness and anger, and they identify sadness and anger better than fear, disgust, surprise, and shame (Harrigan, 1990). Moreover, when a facial expression conflicts with a situation (e.g., receiving a gift but displaying a sad face), preschoolers attend more to facial expressions than to circumstances to identify the emotion (Wiggers & Van Lieshout, 1985). For instance, 3- to 5-year-old children use facial cues to interpret whether people actually like a drink, particularly when the expressions are highly exaggerated (Eskritt & Lee, 2003). In other words, the degree to which nonverbal cues are salient influences preschool children's interpretation of facial expressions.

Although the speed that children process facial expressions improves with age overall, it varies with the specific emotion. For example, happiness is detected more quickly than anger, fear, and sadness (Boyatzis, Chazan, & Ting, 1993).

Moreover, even though young children identify negative facial expressions half as slow as adults, their accuracy improves with age. This finding is reflected most strongly in sadness expressions, with children's error rates decreasing from 17% at age 7 to 8% at age 10 (DeSonneville et al., 2002). Beyond the age of 10, comparison with adults makes it clear that children's processing speed and accuracy increases significantly. Indeed, by adolescence, most can organize facial expressions into six distinct categories (i.e., happiness, sadness, surprise, anger, fear, and disgust) and differentiate the intensity within each, thus allowing for a more detailed assessment of facial displays (Ley & Strauss, 1986). Even at very low levels of intensity, nearly 100% of older teens can recognize joy expressions, consistent with the "happy-face advantage," which shows higher overall accuracy rates for decoding happy faces (Hess, Blairy, & Kleck, 1997).

In short, the ability to decode facial expressions accurately improves with age, with preschool children showing better than chance accuracy at matching facial displays with emotions. Beyond the age of 10, children's accuracy is nearly comparable with adults'. Thus, as children get older, they are able to discriminate and understand increasingly complex facial displays across a wide range of social interactions.

DECODING FACIAL EXPRESSIONS: YOUNGER AND OLDER ADULTS

Although decoding capacity appears to improve from infancy through early adulthood, few studies have examined closely the interpretation and decoding of facial expressions in the context of adult developmental change over time. The evidence available suggests that older adults commit more decoding errors than younger and middle-aged adults when judging facial expressions, particularly when perceiving negative emotions (Levinson, Carstensen, Friesen, & Ekman, 1991). Older adults' accuracy does improve, however, when identifying expressions of people their own age (Malatesta, Izard, Culver, & Nicolich, 1987). In their research, Malatesta et al. found that, across three age groups (young to old), adults performed best when decoding facial expressions of adults their own age.

In more precise terms, older compared with younger adults rate sad, but not happy, facial expressions as significantly more intense, and are generally less accurate at identifying negative and neutral facial expressions in comparison with positive ones (McDowell, Harrison, & Demaree, 1994). In fact, older adults are less likely to attend to negative compared with neutral or positive expressions, thus decreasing the overall accuracy with which they decode negative displays (Mather & Carstensen, 2003). Moreover, compared with younger adults, older adults' arousal and amygdala activation diminishes when viewing negative facial expressions, suggesting that older adults' encoding of negative emotions may be somewhat constrained (Mather et al., 2004).

Other research has examined this potential age-related bias toward negative expressions more closely. For instance, in one study, participants viewed a pair of faces briefly presented on a computer screen, and then one face was subsequently replaced with a dot (Mather & Carstensen, 2003). Participants were instructed to respond as quickly as possible to indicate which side of the screen the dot was on. Younger adults' reaction times remained the same for both emotional (positive and negative) and neutral faces, whereas older adults responded significantly faster when the dot was located where a happy rather than neutral face had previously been. Conversely, older adults' reaction times were significantly slower when the dot was located where an angry or sad face had been in comparison with a neutral face. In brief, older adults showed a bias to attend to neutral rather than to negative facial expressions, and to positive rather than neutral ones, whereas younger adults did not exhibit these biases.

In addition, older adults decoded positive faces compared with negative ones more accurately and, in a recognition test, exhibited better recall for previously seen positive rather than negative faces (Mather & Carstensen, 2003). Moreover, similar results emerged using a forced choice memory test in which participants were shown pairs of faces matched for emotional expression and asked which face they had seen before. Specifically, senior adults were most accurate at discriminating between happy-new and happy-old faces, again also indicating that they recognize positive facial expressions better than negative ones; in contrast, type of emotional expression did not significantly affect younger adult's recognition.

In some respects, then, older adults tend not to fare as well as younger adults in decoding the facial expressions of others. This is not to say that older adults are unable to interpret facial displays successfully. Indeed, one study examining the facial expressions of physical therapists found that older adults decoded both positive and negative facial displays accurately (Ambady, Koo, Rosenthal, & Winograd, 2002). Specifically, older adults judged therapists accurately as warm, caring, concerned, and empathic when therapists displayed positive expressions and as indifferent, distant, and cold when they presented negative expressions. Whereas this study does not address age-related differences, it suggests that older adults certainly have the capacity to interpret and decode facial expressions accurately, although as other research documents, their skills are degraded in some respects compared with younger adults.

DECODING BODY MOVEMENTS: INFANTS AND CHILDREN

Although body movement has received considerably less research attention than has facial expression, the evidence available indicates that people decode body movements relatively less accurately than they decode facial expressions (Ambady & Rosenthal, 1992). Nonverbal communication has been investigated using various kinesic forms, including gait, geometric figures, and expressive movement performances. The research reveals that various body movements communicate important personal and social information.

A variety of evidence suggests that body movements communicate emotions reliably, whether they are posed, presented through dance, or elicited during scenes portraying interpersonal behavior (DeMeijer, 1989). In general, emotion-based body movement cues are characterized by variations in form, tempo, force, and direction (Montepare, Koff, Zaitchik, & Albert, 1999). For instance, movements characterized by extreme muscle exertion in the absence of an actual physical barrier may lead to inferences of fear or anger (Wallbott, 1980). Similarly, if an individual with no apparent physical reason unexpectedly steps backward, it may imply surprise or amazement. In short, body movements can be analyzed as communications that impart gross categories of emotions (e.g., like-dislike), with postural changes potentially reflecting corresponding changes in underlying interpersonal emotion structures (Ekman, 1965).

With respect to development, children are generally more skilled at decoding compared with encoding body movements, which may suggest that decoding ability develops first (Kumin & Lazar, 1974). Specifically, older children are more accurate than younger children at decoding emotional meaning in body movements and at using movement cues to judge emotional intensity (Michael & Willis, 1968). For example, 6-year-olds who viewed a film with a body movement only and a head movement only (masked faced) condition displayed better accuracy in the body compared with the head-only condition, whereas 4-year-olds were less accurate in both conditions (Pendleton & Snyder, 1982). Other studies indicate that even very young children—4- and 5-years-olds— when asked to choose a movement (from a video) that corresponds to a gestural message of a character depicted in a vignette, display a 60% decoding accuracy, suggesting that by age 4, children possess sufficient capacity to understand some gestural meanings (Boyatzis & Satyaprasad, 1994).

Other researchers suggest that sensitivity to body movement manifests as early as 4 to 6 months of age (Fox & McDaniel, 1982). Using Johansson's (1973) classic point light technique (i.e., points of lights on the main limbs and joints represent a moving person as small luminous dots moving against a black background), Fox and McDaniel presented targets to infants (2, 4, and 6 months) that consisted of biological body movement patterns and foils (i.e., moving dots that did not meet criteria for biological movement). Independent observers made target location judgments based on observing only the infants and not the stimuli. Results indicated that the judgment of observers associated with 2-month-old infants did not differ from chance. Those associated with the 4- and 6-month-olds, however, made judgments significantly better than chance, suggesting that sensitivity to body movement may appear by 4 months of age. The same experimenters also

using point light displays presented 4- and 6-month-old infants with a human running in place and a foil (the same form but converted 180°). Using the observer format as in the previous study, the data revealed that both infant groups were significantly above chance and that infants preferred the target rather than the foil. In short, evidence appears to indicate that sensitivity to body movement may manifest in infants between 4 and 6 months of age.

With respect to older children, in one study, 5-, 8-, 10-, and 12-year-olds made emotion attribution judgments, both in narrative form and by choosing one of four emotions that best matched a particular body movement (Van Meel, Verburgh, & deMeijer, 1993). In both cases (narrative/ forced choice), 5-year-olds' ability to identify emotion appropriately was significantly below older children. Although the study did not involve accuracy scores specifically, the results suggest that 5-year-olds failed to decode emotion meaning beyond chance level. Another study involving children aged 4, 5, and 8 years and adults, however, found that 5-year-olds did exceed chance identification of happiness, sadness, and fear, although not anger (Boone & Cunningham, 1998). Even 4-year-olds identified some emotional meaning in body movement by exceeding better than chance identification of sadness. Moreover, although 5-year-olds failed to identify anger beyond chance, they used cues that are associated with adult attributions of anger to make ratings of greater emotional intensity.

Relative to 4-year-olds, 5-year-olds appear to show increased skill in the ability to recognize emotional expression via body movement. The most significant growth in this ability appears to occur between the ages of 5 and 8, with 8-year-olds performing better than chance and showing little difference compared with adults in their capacity to recognize emotions in body movements.

Sadness was the earliest emotion to be recognized via body movement, in contrast to facial expression research, which suggests that happiness is the first recognized (Cunningham & Sterling, 1988).

Another classic study also suggests that attributions pertaining to social events may, in part, be grounded in body movement patterns (Heider & Simmel, 1944). When adults describe an animated film in which a large triangle, a small triangle, and a circle move at various speeds along different trajectories, they virtually never speak in purely geometric terms. Instead, they describe a series of interpersonal events that converge on a common theme. Specifically, they usually describe a scenario in which a woman (circle) is chased and trapped by a male bully (large triangle) until rescued by a second helpful male (small triangle). This description style suggests patterns of movement that when displayed by people, reveal states such as fear, aggression, and affiliation.

The tendency to attribute human characteristics to the figures depicted in such displays has been shown to appear at an early age (Kassin & Baron, 1986). For example, after viewing the film, adults and preschoolers produced open-ended anthropomorphic descriptions, although preschoolers did so less than adults (Berry & Springer, 1993). Specifically, 75% of adults described the film anthropomorphically (i.e., attribute human states and relations, e.g., fear and protectiveness, to the geometric figures), whereas only about half of the children did so. The open-ended verbalization task, however, may have underestimated younger children's abilities. A second experiment using a fixed-choice question format revealed clear distinctions between the responses of 3- and 4-year-olds and that of 5-year-olds and adults. Specifically, adults and 5-year-olds had higher canonical patterns of responses than 3- and 4-year-olds, and the attributions of 5-year-olds, but not 4-year-olds, were similar to adults.

DECODING BODY MOVEMENTS: YOUNGER AND OLDER ADULTS

Although variations in body movements convey important personal information concerning people's emotions, research investigating the differences in adults' ability to decode nonverbal expressions, particularly in older adults, is rather limited (Aronoff, Woike, & Hyman, 1992). Moreover, the studies that have examined these differences tend to focus primarily on decoding facial expressions. Consequently, with respect to age-related differences, relatively little is known concerning the extent to which body movements provide cues to decode nonverbal communication accurately.

The evidence available, however, suggests that certain features involving trunk movement, degree of openness, vertical direction, force, and speed serve as cues to the recognition of various emotions (Harrigan & Rosenthal, 1983). For example, trunk and head position and degree of body openness are associated with sadness, open arm movements are linked with warmth and empathy, and leaning forward and tilting one's head are tied to interpersonal positiveness (Matsumoto & Kudoh, 1987). Moreover, adults who were shown Heider and Simmel's (1944) film judge violence as associated with rapid movements, gentleness with slower movements, and hesitation with sudden reductions in speed (Berry, Misovich, Kean, & Baron, 1992). Another early study that used films of adults playing a ring-toss game also revealed that people tend to readily attribute psychological qualities to body movements (Wolff, 1943). Specifically, adults were characterized as weak, introverted, and pessimistic if they exhibited a stooped posture, shuffled their feet, or failed to bend their knees while walking. In contrast, adults were viewed as carefree and easygoing if they walked with a sauntering gait and as happy and optimistic if they briskly lifted their feet while walking.

Recent research using point light displays also supports the idea that adults frequently identify emotion via body movements and suggests further that older and younger adults use similar cues to decode such movements (Montepare & Zebrowitz-McArthur, 1988). For instance, angry gaits are associated with heavy footedness, sad gaits with less arm swing, and proud and angry gaits with greater stride length. More precisely, anger may be characterized by variations in velocity, force, abrupt tempo changes, and body angularity, sadness with contracted, soft, and smooth movements, and happiness with expanded, action-filled, loose, fast, and somewhat jerkier movements (DeMeijer, 1989). In contrast, neutral movements are related to minimal and contracted actions, in addition to loose, slow, soft, and smooth movements.

Evidence also suggests some differences in the ease of recognizing certain body movement-based emotions based on age and development. For example, younger adults are more adept at decoding anger compared with happiness or sadness on the basis of cues provided by a person's gait (Montepare, Goldstein, & Clausen, 1987). With respect to age differences, older adults make fewer accurate identifications than do younger adults, although both groups decode emotions from body movement at above chance levels (Malatesta et al., 1987). Specifically, older adults are less skilled than younger adults at decoding negative compared with positive emotion displays. This is particularly true for anger and sadness, which older adults frequently judge as neutral, although they are more accurate at identifying anger rather than sadness. In contrast, few age-related differences emerge with respect to the accurate decoding of happy and neutral emotions.

Another interesting line of research using expressive dance movements provides evidence that adults use body movements to decode particular emotions (Boone & Cunningham, 1998). Specifically, dancers enacted trunk and arm movements previously identified as emotion cues, and decoders rated each movement for 12 different emotions. In broad terms, adults used six cues—upward arm movement, muscle tension, forward leaning, directional changes in face and torso, tempo changes, and how long arms are kept close to the body—with better than 90% accuracy to distinguish among happiness, sadness, anger, and fear. Moreover, as the number of movement cues specifying an emotion increased, the frequency with which adults decoded the target emotion accurately increased.

Boone and Cunningham (1998) also found similarity between children and adults in their ability to decode body movements accurately. Specifically, adults and children identified anger by increased face and torso movement, happiness by increased upward arm movements, sadness by downward head movement and less muscle tension, and fear by rigid body posture with head positioned up. More interestingly, adults and 8-year-olds displayed better than chance accuracy on all four emotions, and minimal differences arose between adults' and 8-year-olds' ability to identify the different emotions accurately.

In summary, children's capacity to discriminate, identify, and understand the complex facial expressions of others show significant age-related improvement. Likewise, as children get older, they become increasingly more aware that people's body movements may reveal interpersonal events, relationships, and personal attributes. With respect to older adults, although they possess the capacity to decode facial expressions accurately, they commit more decoding errors than younger adults. Similarly, although older adults identify emotions via body movements at a better than chance rate, they do so less accurately than younger adults, especially when decoding negative emotions.

◆ Encoding Nonverbal Communication

ENCODING FACIAL EXPRESSIONS: INFANTS AND CHILDREN

An essential aspect underlying people's capacity to adapt to the social world involves knowing how to encode and control nonverbal emotion displays. From a developmental perspective, for instance, instructing children to follow rules or modulate their emotional behavior often represents more a request to control facial expressions rather than the direct control of emotions (Ceschi & Scherer, 2003). Examples of these *expression control behaviors* can be noted in young children, gradually increasing in frequency throughout adulthood (Saarni & von Salisch, 1993). Theorists have even argued that very young infants possess some basic signaling capacities in which facial expressions comprise a major component (Trevarthen, 1985).

Although encoding facial displays has been examined across a variety of contexts, systematic investigation of infants' facial expressions is still somewhat limited (Fox & Davidson, 1986). Evidence does suggest, however, that young infants exhibit a variety of distinct facial expressions in response to diverse stimuli (Campos, Campos, & Barrett, 1989). For example, the most common response to tickling is the

expression of joy, sour taste evokes expressions of sadness, and a jack-in-the-box, arm restraint, and masked stranger situations produce surprise and, in some cases, joyful expressions. Moreover, infants' facial movements display temporal patterns involving smiling, brow knitting, and pouting, and all but one of the facial muscle actions visible in adults can also be identified in infants (Oster, 1978).

Infants as early as 2 months of age can not only distinguish among and imitate happy, sad, and surprised facial expressions but also convey facial displays of interest, smiling, anger, and disgust (Izard & Malatesta, 1987). For instance, around 3 to 4 weeks of age, infants exhibit social smiling, coalescing into Duchenne smiles around the end of the first month, and becoming gradually stronger over the course of the next 5 months (Messinger & Fogel, 1998). In addition, after gazing at another's face, 1- to 3-month-old infants often smile spontaneously, although around the fourth month smiling becomes reserved increasingly for the infant's caregivers (Oster, 1978). Specifically, infants often respond as a function of their mothers' expressions of joy, sadness, and anger, and in part, they exhibit an age-related increase in the ability to match their mothers' facial expressions (Izard, Fantauzzo, Castle, & Haynes, 1995). For example, 2.5-month-old infants distinguish between and respond accurately to positive and negative conditions based, respectively, on their mother's expressions of interest and joy or sadness, anger, and withdrawal (Haviland & Lelwica, 1987). Notwithstanding this capacity to interpret and match their mothers' expressions, however, young infants are still prone to exhibit positive rather than negative expressions to their mothers' negative facial displays (Matias & Cohn, 1993).

Moreover, infants 2 to 8 months of age respond with facial expressions of frustration, predominantly anger, when expected rewards or consequences are changed (Alessandri, Sullivan, & Lewis, 1990). This response appears consistent with data that indicate infants' sad expressions often co-occur, in part, with anger, although displays of sadness alone do not represent a significant component of a frustration response (Camras, 1992). The clearest consensus suggests that by 5 months, infants experience expectancy violations as frustrating stimuli that are associated predominantly with facial expressions of anger (Sullivan & Lewis, 2003). Studies eliciting infants' negative responses suggest that anger is the most common reaction and sadness the least common (Camras & Sachs, 1991). With respect to expressions of fear, researchers agree generally that such displays do not emerge until around 7 months of age (Skarin, 1977).

Turning to older children, evidence suggests that preschoolers as early as 24 months of age use particular displays of emotion to elicit support from their caregiver (Buss & Kiel, 2004). In general, however, it is more difficult for them to produce facial expressions spontaneously on demand compared with imitating a model's expressions. When they are able to produce expressions, however, young children find happiness the easiest to enact and fear the most difficult to reflect spontaneously (Fridlund, Ekman, & Oster, 1987). Moreover, as children age they become progressively able to mimic specific actions embedded in facial expressions, and by 4 years of age, they are aware that distinct facial attributes are associated with specific emotions (Paliwal & Goss, 1981). Indeed, when asked how they would express or regulate emotion displays, young children rate the use of facial cues as the most common channel (Zeman & Garber, 1996). In addition, they associate situations that evoke negative affect with the increased use of facial displays to signal or mask emotions.

A number of studies have also examined children's ability to suppress their expressions to *hide* their actual feelings or reactions (e.g., Feldman, Tomasian, & Coats, 1999). One study in which 7- and 10-year-old children were instructed to suppress or express smiles and laughter freely indicated no age differences in facial expressions, except that 7-year-olds exhibited more facial activity than 10-year-olds (Ceschi & Scherer, 2003). Although in the suppression condition children did not laugh or show smiles less frequently; they did so for a significantly shorter length of time than in the expression condition. In another study, 6- and 13-year-old children consumed a bitter drink and tried to conceal their true response by feigning expressions of enjoyment. Adult judges detected the duplicitous expressions of younger children successfully, but they were unable to do so with older children. Thus, 13-year-olds were better able to suppress negative expressions on demand, while producing positive ones simultaneously (Feldman, Jenkins, & Popoola, 1979). Similarly, when faced with implicit demands to control facial expressions (e.g., an undesirable gift in a public situation), Cole (1986) found that 6-year-olds display more socially negative expressions than 10-year-olds, although a similar study reported that even 4-year-olds suppressed some negative expressions, albeit they seemed unaware they were doing so.

ENCODING FACIAL EXPRESSIONS: YOUNGER AND OLDER ADULTS

Although there is abundant evidence that associates facial expressions of adults with basic emotions, studies focusing specifically on age-related changes in facial expressions is rather limited and mixed (Carstensen, Gottman, & Levinson, 1995).

Some research suggests, however, that older adults are less successful than younger adults at posing facial expressions accurately (Malatesta, 1981). In contrast, other studies investigating spontaneous facial expressions or relived emotions show no age-related differences in the accuracy of facial displays and, in some cases, even indicate a more accurate expressivity in older adults (Levinson et al., 1991). For example, accuracy ratings for facial expressions generated when adults intentionally recalled an extreme emotional occurrence revealed no age-related effects (Malatesta et al., 1987). Levinson et al.'s (1991) study shows that older adults' relived emotions are experienced just as intensely, are just as likely to elicit facial expressions, and just as frequently elicit emotion-specific autonomic nervous system (ANS) activity as are younger adults' relived emotions. The capacity of older adults' facial expressions to recruit emotion-specific ANS activity, however, does show clear and significant age-related diminishment.

Notwithstanding the conflicting evidence regarding age-related differences in the capacity to encode facial expressions accurately, researchers agree that as people get older their expressiveness gradually declines, which may lead to increased difficulty in interpreting their facial expressions. Research supporting this perspective shows that older adults compared with younger adults have more closed and less expressive facial expressions, although some self-report studies indicate that older adults inhibit affective displays less often than do younger adults (Malatesta, 1981). Studies using more objective measures, however, indicate that older adults' facial expressions are more difficult to decode than younger adults and are perceived as sadder (Malatesta et al., 1987). In short, researchers agree that older adults' attempts to encode facial expressions may be complicated by facial changes associated with increased age,

which may increase the likelihood that older adults' expressions are misinterpreted at a higher rate than younger adults' expressions.

More precisely, as late adulthood unfolds, physiological characteristics of emotional experience, including somatic activity and skin conductance, tend to diminish (Levinson et al., 1991). In addition, other physical changes including surface musculature and wrinkling also make it more difficult to interpret older adults' facial expressions accurately (Malatesta et al., 1987). In short, although getting older does not necessarily result in decreased affectivity, understanding older adults' facial expressions may be obscured by wrinkles and other physiological changes. These changes create a situation in which it may be harder for other people to encode the older adults' facial displays successfully (Malatesta, 1981).

Not only may older adults' facial characteristics make it difficult to encode expressions, but stereotypic beliefs may also affect negatively their capacity to do so accurately. For example, Matheson (1997) found that judges' ratings of pain (facial displays) were more accurate when assessing older adults than younger adults. Although judges estimated more pain in older adults' expressions across all response types (i.e., genuine, posed, and baseline), older adults did not, however, report any more pain than younger adults. This suggests that judges may have been biased to note pain in older adult's facial expressions, undermining the impression that ratings of older adults' pain was more accurate. The stereotypic idea that increased pain is a "normal process of aging" may explain, in part, why higher pain ratings were ascribed to older adult's expressions, even though they did not necessarily report more pain. This finding adds to the idea that older adults' success at encoding facial expressions may be affected negatively by factors other than ability or developmental issues.

ENCODING BODY MOVEMENTS: INFANTS AND CHILDREN

As we turn to body movement, evidence reveals that infants' gestural movements can express affect, indicate requests, and draw attention to particular objects, which may represent a developmental step that suggests an increasing awareness that communication involves both active and reactive purposes (Goodwyn, Acredolo, & Brown, 2000). These results suggest that even infants' early gestural activity, consisting of physical explorations of the environment, may connote some degree of sensitivity to body movements. For example, infants look at, orient to, and focus on objects perceived to be within reach before reaching for the objects (Haslett & Samter, 1997). More specifically, 5-month-old infants reach for close objects, lean toward distant objects, and reduce reaching behavior as the distance from an object increases (Field, 1976). They develop awareness that reaching and leaning movements are related and that leaning is simply an extension of reach. Infants at 8 months recognize that leaning extends reaching distance. By 10 months, they grasp the limitations of leaning, and by 12 months, they start to understand that physical aids lengthen their reaching distances (McKenzie, Skouteris, Day, & Hartman, 1993).

Moreover, longitudinal and interview studies indicate that 14- to 16-month-old-infants employ a broad range of request and attribute gestures consistently when depicting various objects, desires, and states (Acredolo & Goodwyn, 1985). For example, gestures that involve offering and reaching for objects emerge routinely around the 1-year mark, although one study reported that object offering, but not

requests, appeared as early as 9 months, with significant increments occurring up to 15 months (Zinober & Martlew, 1985). By comparison, pointing and showing gestures start to increase between 12 and 14 months, with pointing used to identify referents clearly by 14 months (Masur, 1983). In short, it appears that around 1 year of age infants begin to use or elicit nonverbal gestural movements for communication purposes.

Interestingly, evidence also suggests that infants' emotion-related gestures tend to decrease after 11 months, congruent with evidence that infants begin to reduce negative affective expressions around 1 year of age (Blake, McConnell, Horton, & Benson, 1992). Moreover, it appears that specific body movements are associated with positive and negative affect, suggesting that early nonverbal communication may reveal particular emotions (Legerstee, Corter, & Kienapple, 1990). Specifically, infants' positive affect seems related to open-handed arm extensions, whereas negative affect is associated with closed hands and arms extended down to the sides. Overall, infants use a variety of gestures to express affective states, to indicate requests, and to attract attention (Goodwyn et al., 2000). They also employ showing or reference movements to direct adults' attention to objects; specifically they hold, offer, or point at objects to indicate interest or desire (Messinger & Fogel, 1998). These movements suggest an important developmental step indicating an infant's increasing awareness that the communication process entails both active and reactive aspects.

For toddlers and preschool children, the use of gestural movements to represent their knowledge of objects is difficult, even though they can, in part, substitute hand movements for objects (Boyatzis & Watson, 1993). In general, young children's pantomimic representation of actions progresses developmentally from, first, using body parts as substitutes for objects to, later, using empty-handed gestures in which they simply pretend to hold an object (O'Reilly, 1995). For example, after watching an adult model teeth-brushing behavior with an imaginary toothbrush, 3-year-old children typically used their finger to represent the toothbrush, suggesting that they still depend on substitute objects to facilitate their representations. In comparison, although 4-year-olds also relied on body parts more than on imaginary objects, they did so less than 3-year-olds, suggesting a reduced dependency on substitute objects. In contrast, 5-year-olds largely employed imaginary objects for all representations, reflecting apparent freedom from the perceptual cues of an actual substitute.

Several findings also suggest that young children encode emotion via body movements. For instance, children are able to encode body movements accurately using emotion cues that are depicted in narrative vignettes (Kumin & Lazar, 1974). In addition, children are sensitive to music cues that depict positive and negative emotions (Kastner & Crowder, 1990). Specifically, in one study, 4- and 5-year-olds were prompted to manipulate teddy bears to express an emotion conveyed by a specific music segment (Boone & Cunningham, 2001). Adult judges viewed the manipulations (no sound) to identify the emotion. Results indicated that children as young as 4 used body movements successfully to encode the specified emotion. Overall, children's encoding ability was strongest for sadness and happiness and less developed for anger and fear.

In broad terms, these results show that older children communicate emotions more effectively than do younger children. Specifically, 5-year-olds encoded happiness and sadness successfully, whereas 4-year-olds could only encode sadness, and neither group could encode anger or fear. In addition, both groups used less forceful movements to encode sadness, happiness, and anger, used less rotation and fewer and slower movements for sadness and fear, and used more upward movements for happiness and anger. Although cues used consistently to distinguish among these emotions are not yet fully developed by age 5, children, even at this early age, have begun to differentially use movement cues that are normally associated with how adults encode expressions of emotion.

ENCODING BODY MOVEMENTS: YOUNGER AND OLDER ADULTS

With respect to age-related changes, very little work has investigated directly adults' capacity to encode body movements successfully. One study, though, indicated minimal differences between older and younger female adults, except older adults used more body parts as imaginary objects and encoded fewer descriptive gestures than younger adults (Ska & Nespoulous, 1987). Notwithstanding the scarcity of direct evidence, a number of related research lines add indirectly to our understanding of encoding body movements. For example, one line of research that relates to the capacity to encode body movements involves people's gait patterns. Specifically, variations in people's gait may strongly influence how others perceive the person (i.e., their traits and emotional state) and thus, with or without intention, people's body movements may encode information about their internal state (Barclay, Cutting, & Kozlowski, 1978).

With respect to decoding body movements as a function of age, research indicates that older adults' gaits compared with children's, adolescents', and younger adults' gaits are perceived as reflecting less happiness, as physically weaker, as less dominant, and as less sexy (Montepare &

Zebrowitz-McArthur, 1988). These negatively valenced perceptions suggest that it may be difficult for older adults to use body movements to encode their genuine affective state accurately. In brief, increased hip swaying, knee bending, lifting of feet, more steps per second, larger arm swings, looser joints, and a bouncier pattern are used to decode gaits as youthful. Interestingly, younger adults who are perceived as having a youthful versus older gait are also judged as more powerful and happy.

Another interesting set of studies, although using only young adults, examined whether body movements represented in geometric patterns are encoded with the same affective meanings that are associated with facial movements (Aronoff et al., 1992). This work follows classic studies in which one ethnic group's gesture system, considered an angular one, was contrasted with the rounded gesture system of another, revealing the possibility of classifying and distinguishing among specific types of body movements (Efron, 1972). In particular, Aronoff et al. (1992) found that body movements communicated distinct affective meanings; for instance, roundedness was associated with warm characters and angular and diagonal forms with threatening characters. More precisely, "threatening" characters used diagonally oriented poses three times more often than "warm" characters, and warm characters used nearly four times as many round poses as did threatening characters. In addition, round-arm movements were associated primarily with warm characters and straight-arm movements principally with threatening characters.

Overall, evidence suggests that even infants convey a variety of facial expressions. And certainly as children get older, they mimic facial expressions and associate distinct facial characteristics with specific emotions accurately. Within adulthood, it appears that younger adults are more successful than older adults at posing facial expressions accurately. Older adults' attempts to encode facial expressions may be complicated by age-related facial changes, however, which increase the likelihood that their expressions will be misinterpreted. Similarly, older children are clearly more effective at communicating emotions through body movement than are younger children, and the cues that older children use to encode emotions, although not yet developed fully, are relatively similar to adults'. With respect to older adults' capacity to encode body movements, there is a clear need for more research. Indeed, the most that may be said presently is that it is simply difficult for many older adults to use body movements to encode their emotions accurately.

◆ Conclusions

Examining nonverbal behavior as it develops from infancy throughout late adulthood provides essential information to understand the emergent use and interpretation of such behaviors. The channels of communication that have received the most frequent study from a developmental perspective involve facial expressions and body movements, although the majority of research is centered on the former. Most of this work also centers on children and young adults rather than older adults. Notwithstanding these partial limitations, the available evidence recognizes broadly that infants and adults convey personal information involving their emotions, desires, and reactions through the distinct use of facial expressions and body movements. In short, how people express these nonverbal channels, and how they use these channels to interpret and understand others, has a significant influence on the quality of their social interactions.

FUTURE DIRECTIONS

Despite the number of strong conclusions that can be drawn from existing research, additional work is required. One empirical strategy that would provide further insight and knowledge concerning the development of nonverbal communication involves the use of longitudinal research. To our knowledge, no studies have employed such a design. Using such a method would, however, explicate a host of issues pertaining to the development and progression (i.e., age-related changes) of people's nonverbal behavior, ranging from cultural and biological aspects to more clinical and health-related issues.

Indeed, an important area that lacks significant investigation involves the broad differences among cultures in the development of people's nonverbal encoding and decoding abilities. Such cultural differences particularly include the development of nonverbal skills as a product of parental input and the learned cultural rules or norms concerning the appropriateness of showing certain expressions during certain situations (i.e., display rules; see Matsumoto, this volume). Although there is a scarcity of direct studies that examine these issues, some indirect ones suggest that parenting factors may contribute significantly to good adult decoding skills. Moreover, these studies also report a positive relation among family members' nonverbal abilities, again suggesting the potential affect of parental influences (Hodgins & Koestner, 1993). Research on the development of nonverbal communication would clearly benefit from more of this systematic exploration of cultural differences, especially those related to parenting styles and the cultural norms that parents invoke when interacting with their children.

Moreover, the population of older adults in the United States is increasing dramatically, and with that increase comes an urgent need to understand better how the nonverbal communication process changes over time. In particular, it is important to clarify how nonverbal processes unfold during the later stages of adulthood. Although research is increasing with respect to older adults, there is still an obvious need to examine the changes that the elderly may experience with respect to nonverbal communication and its subsequent affect on their interpersonal life.

◆ *References*

Acredolo, L. P., & Goodwyn, S. (1985). Symbolic gesturing in language development: A case study. *Human Development, 28,* 40–49.

Alessandri, S. M., Sullivan, M. W., & Lewis, M. (1990). Violation of expectancy and frustration in early infancy. *Developmental Psychology, 26,* 738–744.

Ambady, N., Koo, J., Rosenthal, R., & Winograd, C. H. (2002). Nonverbal communication predicts geriatric patients' health outcomes. *Psychology and Aging, 17,* 443–452.

Ambady, N., & Rosenthal, R. (1992). Thin slices of expressive behavior as predictors of interpersonal consequences: A meta-analysis. *Psychological Bulletin, 111,* 256–274.

Aronoff, J., Woike, B. A., & Hyman, L. M. (1992). Which are the stimuli in facial displays of anger and happiness? Configurational bases of emotion recognition. *Journal of Personality and Social Psychology, 62,* 1050–1066.

Barclay, C. D., Cutting, J. E., & Kozlowski, L. T. (1978). Temporal and spatial factors in gait perception that influence gender recognition. *Perception and Psychophysics, 23,* 145–152.

Barrera, M. E., & Maurer, D. (1981). Discrimination of strangers by the three-month-old. *Child Development, 52,* 558–563.

Berry, D. S., Misovich, S. J., Kean, K. J., & Baron, R. M. (1992). Effects of disruption of structure and motion on perceptions of social causality, *Personality and Social Psychology Bulletin, 18,* 237–244.

Berry, D. S., & Springer, K. (1993). Structure, motion, and preschoolers' perceptions of social causality. *Ecological Psychology, 5,* 273–283.

Bertenthal, B. I., Proffitt, D. R., Spetner, N. B., & Thomas, M. A. (1985). The development of infant sensitivity to biomechanical motions. *Child Development, 56,* 531–543.

Blake, J., McConnell, S., Horton, G., & Benson, N. (1992). The gestural repertoire and its evolution over the second year. *Early Development and Parenting, 1*(3), 127–136.

Boone, R. T., & Cunningham, J. G. (1998). Children's decoding of emotion in expressive body movement: Development of cue attunement. *Developmental Psychology, 34,* 1007–1016.

Boone, R. T., & Cunningham, J. G. (2001). Children's expression of emotional meaning in music through expressive body movement. *Journal of Nonverbal Behavior, 25,* 21–41.

Borke, H. (1971). Interpersonal perception of young children: Egocentrism or empathy? *Developmental Psychology, 5,* 263–269.

Boyatzis, C. J., Chazan, E., & Ting, C. Z. (1993). Preschool children's decoding of facial emotions. *Journal of Genetic Psychology, 154,* 375–382.

Boyatzis, C. J., & Satyaprasad, C. (1994). Children's facial and gestural decoding and encoding: Relations between skills and with popularity. *Journal of Nonverbal Behavior, 18,* 37–55.

Boyatzis, C. J., & Watson, M. W. (1993). Preschool children's symbolic representation of objects through gestures. *Child Development, 64,* 729–735.

Burgoon, J. K. (1994). Nonverbal signals. In M. L. Knapp & G. R. Miller (Eds.), *Handbook of interpersonal communication* (2nd ed., pp. 229–285). Thousand Oaks, CA: Sage.

Buss, K. A., & Kiel, E. J. (2004). Comparison of sadness, anger, and fear facial expressions when toddlers look at their mothers. *Child Development, 75,* 1761–1773.

Campos, J. J., Campos, R. G., & Barrett, K. C. (1989). Emergent themes in the study of emotional development and emotion regulation. *Developmental Psychology, 25,* 394–402.

Camras, L. A. (1992). Expressive development and basic emotions. *Cognition & Emotion, 6,* 269–283.

Camras, L. A., & Allison, K. (1985). Children's understanding of emotional facial expressions and verbal labels. *Journal of Nonverbal Behavior, 9,* 84–94.

Camras, L. A., & Sachs, V. B. (1991). Social referencing and caretaker expressive behavior in a day care setting. *Infant Behavior and Development, 14,* 27–36.

Carstensen, L. L., Gottman, J. M., & Levinson, R. W. (1995). Emotional behavior in long-term marriage. *Psychology and Aging, 10,* 140–149.

Ceschi, G., & Scherer, K. R. (2003). Children's ability to control the facial expression of laughter and smiling: Knowledge and behavior. *Cognition & Emotion, 17,* 385–411.

Cole, P. M. (1986). Children's spontaneous control of facial expression. *Child Development, 57,* 1309–1321.

Cunningham, J. G., & Sterling, R. S. (1988). Developmental change in the understanding of affective meaning in music. *Motivation and Emotion, 12,* 399–413.

DeMeijer, M. (1989). The contribution of general features of body movement to the attributions of emotions. *Journal of Nonverbal Behavior 13,* 247–268.

Denham, S. A., & Couchoud, E. A. (1990). Young preschoolers' ability to identify emotions in equivocal situations. *Child Study Journal, 20,* 153–169.

DePaulo, B. M., & Rosenthal, R. (1982). Measuring the development of nonverbal sensitivity. In C. E. Izard (Ed.), *Measuring emotions in infants and children.* New York: Cambridge University Press.

DeSonneville, L. M. J., Verschoor, C. A., Njiokiktjien, C., Op het Veld, V., Toorenaar, N., & Vranken, M. (2002). Facial identity and facial emotions: Speed, accuracy, and processing strategies in children and adults. *Journal of Clinical and Experimental Neuropsychology, 24,* 200–213.

Efron, D. (1972). *Gesture, race, and culture.* The Hague: Mouton.

Ekman, P. (1965). Differential communication of affect by head and body cues. *Journal of Personality and Social Psychology, 2,* 726–735.

Eskritt, M., & Lee, K. (2003). Do actions speak louder than words? Preschool children's use of the verbal-nonverbal consistency principle during inconsistent communications. *Journal of Nonverbal Behavior, 27,* 25–41.

Feinman, S., & Lewis, M. (1983). Social referencing at ten months: A second-order effect on infants' responses to strangers. *Child Development, 54,* 878–887.

Feldman, R. S., Jenkins, L., & Popoola, O. (1979). Detection of deception in adults and children via facial expressions. *Child Development, 50,* 350–355.

Feldman, R. S., Tomasian, J., & Coats, E. J. (1999). Adolescents' social competence and nonverbal deception abilities: Adolescents with higher social skills are better liars. *Journal of Nonverbal Behavior, 23,* 237–249.

Field, J. (1976). The adjustment of reaching behavior to object distance in early infancy. *Child Development, 47,* 304–308.

Field, T. M., Woodson, R., Greenberg, R., & Cohen, D. (1982). Discrimination and imitation of facial expressions by neonates. *Science, 218,* 179–181.

Fox, N. A., & Davidson, R. J. (1986). Psychophysiological measures of emotion: New directions in developmental research. In C. E. Izard & P. B. Read (Eds.), *Measuring emotions in infants and children* (Vol. 2, pp. 13–47). Boston: Cambridge University Press.

Fox, R., & McDaniel, C. (1982). The perception of biological motion by human infants. *Science, 218,* 486–487.

Fridlund, A. J., Ekman, P., & Oster, H. (1987). Facial expressions of emotion. In A. W. Siegman & S. Feldstein (Eds.), *Nonverbal behavior and communication* (2nd ed., pp. 143–223). Hillsdale, NJ: Lawrence Erlbaum.

Goodwyn, S. W., Acredolo, L. P., & Brown, C. A. (2000). Impact of symbolic gesturing on early language development. *Journal of Nonverbal Behavior, 24,* 81–103.

Gwiazda, J., Bauer, J., & Held, R. (1989). From visual acuity to hyperacuity: A 10-year update. *Canadian Journal of Psychology, 43,* 109–120.

Harrigan, J. A. (1990). The effects of task order on children's identification of facial expressions. *Motivation and Emotion, 8,* 157–169.

Harrigan, J. A., & Rosenthal, R. (1983). Physicians' head and body positions as determinants of perceived rapport. *Journal of Applied Social Psychology, 13,* 496–509.

Haslett, B. B., & Samter, W. (1997). *Children communicating: The first 5 years.* Hillsdale, NJ: Lawrence Erlbaum.

Haviland, J. M., & Lelwica, M. (1987). The induced affect response: 10-week-old infants' responses to three emotion expressions. *Developmental Psychology, 23,* 97–104.

Heider, F., & Simmel, M. (1944). An experimental study of apparent behavior. *American Journal of Psychology, 57,* 243–259.

Hess, U., Blairy, S., & Kleck, R. E. (1997). The intensity of emotional facial expressions and decoding accuracy. *Journal of Nonverbal Behavior, 21,* 241–257.

Hodgins, H. S., & Koestner, R. (1993). The origins of nonverbal sensitivity. *Personality and Social Psychology Bulletin, 19,* 466–473.

Hornik, R., Risenhoover, N., & Gunnar, M. (1987). The effects of maternal positive, neutral, and negative affective communications on infant responses to new toys. *Child Development, 58,* 937–944.

Izard, C. E., Fantauzzo, C. A., Castle, J. M., & Haynes, O. M. (1995). The ontogeny and significance of infants' facial expressions in the first 9 months of life. *Developmental Psychology, 31,* 997–1013.

Izard, C. E., & Malatesta, C. Z. (1987). Perspectives on emotional development I: Differential emotions theory of early emotional development. In J. D. Osofsky (Ed.), *Handbook of infant development* (pp. 494–554). New York: Wiley.

Johansson, G. (1973). Visual perception of biological motion and a model for its analysis. *Perception and Psychophysics, 14,* 201–211.

Johnson, M. H., Dziurawiec, S., Ellis, H., & Morton, J. (1991). Newborns' preferential tracking of face-like stimuli and its subsequent decline. *Cognition, 40,* 1–19.

Kassin, S. M., & Baron, R. M. (1986). On the basicity of social perception cues: Developmental evidence for adult processes? *Social Cognition, 4,* 180–200.

Kastner, M. P., & Crowder, R. G. (1990). Perception of the major/minor distinction: IV. Emotional connotations in young children. *Music Perception, 8,* 189–201.

Kestenbaum, R., & Nelson, C. A. (1990). The recognition and categorization of upright and inverted emotional expression by infants. *Infant Behavior and Development, 13,* 497–511.

Klinnert, M. D. (1984). The regulation of infant behavior by maternal facial expression. *Infant Behavior and Development, 7,* 447–465.

Kumin, L., & Lazar, M. (1974). Gestural communication in preschool children. *Perceptual and Motor Skills, 38,* 708–710.

Legerstee, M., Corter, C., & Kienapple, K. (1990). Hand, arm, and facial actions of young infants to a social and nonsocial stimulus. *Child Development, 61,* 774–784.

Levinson, R. W., Carstensen, L. L., Friesen, W. V., & Ekman, P. (1991). Emotion, physiology, and expression in old age. *Psychology and Aging, 6,* 28–35.

Ley, R. G., & Strauss, E. (1986). Hemispheric asymmetries in the perception of facial expression by normals. In R. Bruyer (Ed.), *The neuropsychology of face perception and facial expression* (pp. 269–290). Hillsdale, NJ: Erlbaum.

Ludemann, P. M. (1991). Generalized discrimination of positive facial expressions by seven- and ten-month-old infants. *Child Development, 62,* 55–67.

Malatesta, C. Z. (1981). Affective development over the lifespan: Involution or growth? *Merrill-Palmer Quarterly, 27,* 145–173.

Malatesta, C. Z., Izard, C. E., Culver, C., & Nicolich, M. (1987). Emotion communication skills in young, middle-aged, and older women. *Psychology and Aging, 2,* 193–203.

Masur, E. F. (1983). Gestural development, dual-directional signaling, and the transition to words. *Journal of Psycholinguistic Research, 12,* 93–109.

Mather, M., Canli, T., English, T., Whitfield, S., Wais, P., Ochsner, K., et al. (2004). Amygdala responses to emotionally valenced stimuli in older and younger adults. *Psychological Science, 15,* 259–263.

Mather, M., & Carstensen, L. L. (2003). Aging and attentional biases for emotional faces. *Psychological Science, 14,* 409–415.

Matheson, D. H. (1997). The painful truth: Interpretation of facial expressions of pain in older adults. *Journal of Nonverbal Behavior, 21,* 223–238.

Matias, R., & Cohn, J. F. (1993). Are max-specified infant facial expressions during face-to-face interaction consistent with differential emotions theory? *Developmental Psychology, 29,* 524–531.

Matsumoto, D., & Kudoh, T. (1987). Cultural similarities and differences in the semantic dimensions of body postures. *Journal of Nonverbal Behavior, 11,* 166–179.

McClure, E. B. (2000). A meta-analytic review of sex differences in facial expression processing and their development in infants, children, and adolescents. *Psychological Bulletin, 126,* 424–453.

McDowell, C., Harrison, D., & Demaree, H. (1994). Is right hemisphere decline in the perception of emotion a function of aging? *International Journal of Neuroscience, 79,* 1–11.

McKenzie, B. E., Skouteris, H., Day, R. H., & Hartman, B. (1993). Effective action by infants to contact objects by reaching and leaning. *Child Development, 64,* 415–429.

Messinger, D. S., & Fogel, A. (1998). Give and take: The development of conventional infant gestures. *Merrill-Palmer Quarterly, 44,* 566–590.

Michael, G., & Willis, F. N. J. (1968). The development of gestures as a function of social class, education, and sex. *Psychological Record, 18,* 515–519.

Montepare, J., Goldstein, S., Clausen, A. (1987). The identification of emotions from gait information. *Journal of Nonverbal Behavior, 11,* 33–42.

Montepare, J., Koff, E., Zaitchik, D., & Albert, M. (1999). The use of body movements and gestures as cues to emotions in younger and older adults. *Journal of Nonverbal Behavior, 23,* 133–152.

Montepare, J. M., & Zebrowitz-McArthur, L. (1988). Impressions of people created by age-related qualities of their gaits. *Journal of Personality and Social Psychology, 55,* 547–556.

O'Reilly, A. W. (1995). Using representations: Comprehension and production of actions with imagined objects. *Child Development, 66,* 999–1010.

Oster, H. (1978). Facial expression and affect development. In M. Lewis & L. Rosenblum (Eds.), *The development of affect* (pp. 43–76). New York: Plenum Press.

Paliwal, P., & Goss, A. E. (1981). Attributes of schematic faces in preschoolers' use of names of emotions. *Bulletin of the Psychonomic Society, 17,* 139–142.

Pendleton, K. L., & Snyder, S. S. (1982). Young children's perception of nonverbally expressed "preference": The effects of non-verbal cue, viewer age, and sex of actor. *Journal of Nonverbal Behavior, 6,* 220–237.

Philippot, P., & Feldman, R. S. (1990). Age and social competence in preschoolers' decoding of facial expression. *British Journal of Social Psychology, 29,* 43–54.

Saarni, C., Mumme, D. L., & Campos, J. J. (1998). Emotional development: Action, communication and understanding. In W. Damon (Ed.), *Handbook of child psychology* (5th ed., vol. 3), *Social, emotional, and personality development* (pp. 237–309). New York: Wiley.

Saarni, C., & von Salisch, M. (1993). The social-ization of emotional dissemblance. In M. Lewis & C. Saarni (Eds.), *Lying and deception in everyday life* (pp. 106–125). New York: Guilford.

Ska, B., & Nespoulous, J.-L. (1987). Panto-mimes and aging. *Journal of Clinical and Experimental Neuropsychology, 9,* 754–766.

Skarin, K. S. (1977). Cognitive and contextual determinants of stranger fear in six- and eleven-month-old infants. *Child Development, 48,* 537–544.

Sorce, J. F., Emde, R. N., Campos, J. J., & Klinnert, M. D. (1985). Maternal emo-tional signaling: Its effect on visual cliff behavior of 1-year-olds. *Developmental Psychology, 21,* 195–200.

Sullivan, M. W., & Lewis, M. (2003). Contextual determinants of anger and other negative expressions in young infants. *Developmental Psychology, 39,* 693–705.

Trevarthen, C. (1985). Facial expressions of emotion in mother-infant interaction. *Human Neurobiology, 4,* 21–32.

Van Meel, J., Verburgh, H., & de Meijer, M. (1993). Children's interpretations of dance expressions. *Empirical Studies of the Arts, 11,* 117–133.

Walker-Andrews, A. S., & Dickson, L. R. (1997). Infants' understanding of affect. In S. Hala (Ed.), *Development of social cognition* (pp. 161–186). Hove, UK: Psychology Press.

Wallbott, H. G. (1980). The measurement of human expression. In W. von Raffler-Engel (Ed.), *Aspects of nonverbal communication* (pp. 302–228). Lisse, The Netherlands: Swets & Zietlinger.

Wiggers, M., & Van Lieshout, C. F. (1985). Development of recognition of emotions: Children's reliance on situational and facial cues. *Developmental Psychology, 21,* 338–349.

Wolff, W. (1943). *The expression of personality.* New York: Harper.

Young-Browne, G., Rosenfeld, H. M., & Horowitz, F. D. (1977). Infant discrimination of facial expressions. *Child Development, 48,* 555–562.

Zeman, J., & Garber, J. (1996). Display rules for anger, sadness, and pain: It depends on who is watching. *Child Development, 67,* 957–973.

Zinober, B., & Martlew, M. (1985). Develop-mental changes in four types of gesture in relation to acts and vocalizations from 10 to 21 months. *British Journal of Develop-mental Psychology, 3,* 293–306.

11

WOMEN'S AND MEN'S NONVERBAL COMMUNICATION

Similarities, Differences, Stereotypes, and Origins

◆ Judith A. Hall
Northeastern University

Nonverbal cues are the "front lines" of contact between people. Information is conveyed via appearance, movement, and expression even before any words are spoken, and once the dialogue begins, a veritable torrent of cues is at the perceiver's disposal. People use nonverbal cues to draw first, and lasting, impressions about emotions, personality, character, and motives, as artists and novelists have always been aware. In turn, people know that their own nonverbal behavior is a primary vehicle by which they project their personas into the world. Thus, nonverbal behavior is a major medium of self-presentation (DePaulo, 1992; Keating, this volume). When presenting ourselves to the world, one of the major facets of identity to be presented is our gender.[1]

Presenting our gender—showing the world that we are male or female and that we know how to behave accordingly—is thus one contributing explanation for nonverbal gender differences. But other possible explanations have also been put forth. In this chapter, I review the nature of men's and women's nonverbal behavior and I work to provide explanations for differences in those behaviors. But, lest the reader expect too much, let me emphasize that description is much easier than explanation. Explaining effects as complex as those associated with gender is not done easily.

In the present chapter, I summarize stereotypes (i.e., everyday beliefs) about nonverbal gender differences, the actual differences as revealed by observational research, and some possible theoretical frameworks within which we might understand the differences. The nonverbal differences to be discussed include specific behaviors such as smiling and gazing and also accuracy in expression via nonverbal cues (both deliberate and spontaneous) and accuracy in receiving nonverbal cues (both noticing or recalling and interpreting cues). My overall goal is to summarize a large literature in a small space and in a way that is fair to different perspectives.

◆ **Stereotypes About Nonverbal Gender Differences**

Briton and Hall (1995a) asked over 400 college students for their opinions about 19 nonverbal behaviors and skills in relation to gender. Each student made a separate rating for men and for women on a 1–10 scale. For some behaviors, it was easy to predict the beliefs that would emerge, based on previous stereotype or self-rating studies: People would believe men to be louder, to have less variable voices, to smile less, to gaze less, to be less emotionally expressive, to use hand and arm gestures less, and to be less skilled in encoding (sending) and decoding (judging) nonverbal cues (Korzenny, Korzenny, & Sanchez de Rota, 1985; Kramer, 1977; Rosenkrantz, Vogel, Bee, Broverman, & Broverman, 1968; Zuckerman & Larrance, 1979).[2] Indeed, all the predictions based on

previous research were upheld, and many other differences emerged as well.

Table 11.1 shows the behaviors for which Briton and Hall (1995a) found significant differences in the ratings of men and women. The reader will probably find these results to be unsurprising because the beliefs are robust and probably widely shared. Only two behaviors did not show a significant perceived gender difference: "frowns at others" and "interacts facing directly." The stereotypes suggest that women are seen as more expressive, involved, warm, fluent, and skilled in their nonverbal communication than are men.

These beliefs also coincide with well-documented stereotypes that depict women as being more emotionally expressive and sensitive than men (e.g., Bem, 1974; Brody & Hall, 2000; Johnson & Shulman, 1988; LaFrance & Banaji, 1992; Spence & Helmreich, 1978), and they also coincide with the ways men and women describe themselves. Fischer and Manstead (2000) found that in all the 37 countries in which they gathered data, women rated themselves higher on the nonverbal expression of emotion than men rated themselves. In the United States, studies have shown predictable differences in men's and women's self-reports of emotional expressiveness (e.g., Gross & John, 1998), though sometimes the magnitude of the difference varies with the specific emotions being rated (Brody & Hall, 2000). Thus, stereotypic beliefs about the nonverbal behavior of men and women are well developed and widely shared.

◆ **What Are the Actual Nonverbal Differences Between Men and Women?**

In 1984, I published a meta-analysis of nonverbal gender differences that covered

Table 11.1   Beliefs About Female and Male Nonverbal Behavior

Women Rated Higher Than Men	*Men Rated Higher Than Women*
Smiles at others	Touches oneself
Has an expressive face	Has restless feet and legs
Gazes at others	Speaks with dysfluencies
Uses hand gestures	Speaks loudly
Interacts closely	Uses "um" and "ah"
Has an expressive voice	Interrupts others
Laughs	
Has encoding (expression) skill	
Pays attention to cues	
Recognizes faces	
Has decoding skill	

SOURCE: Summarized from Briton and Hall (1995a).

specific behaviors as well as communication skills. Effects for both the gender of the person whose nonverbal behavior is measured and the gender of the interaction partner were reviewed (though the latter had fewer results than the former), based on studies published in English up through 1983. This was the first quantitative treatment of this subject and it has stood the test of time rather well even though much research has been published since (its conclusions also concurred well with a qualitative review done by Vrugt & Kerkstra, 1984).

In the following sections, the main conclusions of the 1984 review (omitting those studies that included infants) are summarized and updated as space allows, under the two main headings of "nonverbal behaviors" and "nonverbal skills." The number of studies available for different behaviors and skills varies dramatically; because of space limitations, the present chapter focuses on the most well-substantiated results. Results that are not given a citation to a specific study are based

on the Hall (1984) review. Children are defined as 2 through 12 years, and adults are defined as college-age and older. Adolescents' behavior is mentioned when possible, but there is much less research on this age group. Because the present review is necessarily a simplification, the reader is referred to Hall and the other cited works for discussion of many additional methodological issues and qualifying points.

NONVERBAL BEHAVIORS

Smiling. The 1984 analysis found that when adolescents and adults were interacting with others, there was clear evidence based on 23 studies that women smiled more than men. Gender differences in smiling were negligible, however, when people were observed alone. Based on 20 studies among children, even when observed in a social situation, there was also little difference. There is also a well-documented gender difference in posed photographs. In one such study, Dodd, Russell, and Jenkins (1999) examined over 16,000 school yearbook photographs and found, as did Hall (1984), that the younger ages (kindergarten through Grade 3) showed little difference, but the gender difference was pronounced after that (including among college students and faculty or staff). The generality of the effect is evident in a study that found male and female physicians interacting with their patients to show a marked difference in smiling (Briton & Hall, 1995b).

LaFrance, Hecht, and Levy Paluck's (2003) recent meta-analysis included over 400 male-female comparisons. They concluded, consistent with Hall (1984), that women smiled more than men, that there was no gender difference in the absence of social interaction, that the difference was greatest in same-gender pairs, and that social tension was associated with a bigger difference. They also found numerous other moderators, including the following: The gender difference was especially large when people were aware of being observed, were under explicit instructions to get acquainted, were engaged in self-disclosure, and were adolescents. The latter result is especially interesting considering the overall lack of a gender difference for children. It seems that adolescence, a time of acute awareness of gender norms, is also the time when boys' and girls' smiling is most discrepant.

One potentially important moderator—the apparent sincerity of the smile—has been examined in only very limited fashion, but it is important because of the stereotype that women use smiles in an emotionally false way. Bugental, Love, and Gianetto (1971), in a much-cited study, found that the positivity of women's facial expressions was less concordant with the positivity of their spoken words than was the case for men. On the basis of this finding, the authors called women's smiles "perfidious." A larger, more recent, study not only did not find this but found the exact opposite (Halberstadt, Hayes, & Pike, 1988).

Another measure of apparent sincerity is the Duchenne smile (Ekman, Davidson, & Friesen, 1990), the term used to describe the combination of upturned mouth (zygomaticus muscle) and crinkles around the eyes (orbicularis oculi muscle). This configuration has been shown in a number of studies to reflect felt positive affect more than does the upturned mouth alone. Hecht and LaFrance (1998) measured Duchenne ("enjoyment") smiles and non-Duchenne ("social") smiles separately and found that women displayed more of both kinds than men. Thus, the idea that women's expressions are phony is not well supported by the available research.[3]

Hall and Halberstadt (1986) examined moderating factors for Hall's (1984) adult studies and found that when the circumstances of observation were rated as more anxiety provoking, the gender difference was larger. Whether women increased their smiling under such circumstances, or men reduced theirs, could not be ascertained. Finally, Hall (1984) also found evidence (as did Hinsz & Tomhave, 1991) that women *received* more smiles from others than men did.

Facial Expressiveness. Research on children's facial behavior is scanty and inconclusive, but five out of six published studies reviewed by Hall (1984) that measured objectively the extent or frequency of facial movements in adults found that women's faces were significantly more expressive than men's. It is not clear whether expressiveness means that more emotions are being shown or that there is simply more movement overall.

Gazing. Twenty-five studies of children and 61 studies of adults were located that measured overall gazing during conversation (frequency or duration). Females in both age groups engaged in higher levels of gazing than males did, with the difference being somewhat larger for adults. Subsequent research continues to find more gazing by women (e.g., McCormick & Jones, 1989, who observed couples in bars). Hall's review (1984) also found that women received more gaze than men did, making for a pattern also seen for smiling: The least gaze occurred when men interacted with men, and the most gaze occurred when women interacted with women.

A conspicuous moderator of women's elevated gaze tendencies was uncovered in a series of studies by Aiello (e.g., Aiello, 1977). As the physical distance between conversing interactants increased, men's gazing increased, as predicted by theories of intimacy compensation (Argyle & Dean, 1965). Women's gazing fell off abruptly, however, after a separation of about six feet, creating a reversal in the gender difference. It seems that women's heightened gazing is tied closely to the higher level of involvement produced by closer interactions.

The "visual dominance ratio" is a particular pattern of gazing during interaction, which refers specifically to the ratio of the percentage of gaze while speaking to the percentage of gaze while listening. A higher ratio indicates that the person is relatively more likely to gaze while speaking compared to listening. The visual dominance ratio is higher in more dominant or powerful persons (hence its name), as documented in numerous studies (reviewed by Dovidio & Ellyson, 1985). Dovidio, Ellyson, Keating, Heltman, and Brown (1988) measured the visual dominance ratio in cross-gender interactions in which neither person had a power or expertise advantage over the other. In these interactions, women displayed a lower visual dominance ratio than did men. Although it is not clear whether this is an effect of the actor's or the target's gender, it is nevertheless interesting because of its theoretical links to

the dominance or power construct (a topic to be taken up in a later section).

Head, Hand, and Arm Gestures. Hand gestures, as discussed here, are the fluid hand movements that accompany speech, rather than the discrete "emblematic" hand movements that can substitute for words (such as the A-okay sign or the slit-throat sign; Knapp & Hall, 2005). In terms of speech-dependent hand movements and other movements of the head and arms, Hall (1984) concluded, based on 15 studies, that women engage in more expressive movements during conversation than men do. This is in line with women's greater facial expressivity noted above.

Body Movements and Positions. The ways people sit, stand, and move their bodies have often been noted to distinguish men from women. Men were observed to be more restless (e.g., foot and leg movements, body shifts, fidgeting; 14 results), more expansive (e.g., wide knees, legs, or arms; six results), more relaxed (e.g., trunk lean, reclining, feet on table; six results), and less involved (e.g., nods, forward lean; 18 results) than were women (Hall, 1984). Finally, based on 11 results, Hall (1984) concluded that women engaged in more self-touching during interaction than men did, a result also found by McCormick and Jones (1989) for couples observed in bars. Interesting, for this behavior, Briton and Hall's (1995a) stereotype data were wrong.

Interpersonal Touch. Hall (1984) and Stier and Hall (1984) concluded that, in general, women were more likely to touch others than men were, based on 20 studies of children and 18 studies of adults. This result concurs with Willis and Rinck's (1983) study, in which college students kept logs of touches immediately after they occurred, and also with later studies of adults in public places (McCormick & Jones, 1989; Willis & Dodds, 1998). In an additional study that combined several age groups, Berkowitz (1971) observed touches in public in six areas of the world. The overall tendency of women to touch more than men was significant and evident in 23 of the 24 groups observed (four age groups across six areas of the world).

Interpersonal touch is, however, a complex topic both methodologically and theoretically, and several moderating variables are evident in its use. First, the preponderance of findings showing more female-initiated touch may be especially dependent on the high levels of touch typically shown *between* females. Stier and Hall (1984) and, later, Montemayor and Flannery (1989) noted that the most unambiguous differences were between female-female and male-male dyads. Because of the cultural norms and values prevailing in some countries, perhaps especially the United States, men may be particularly reluctant to touch other men in most public settings.

Apart from the gender composition of the dyad, several other moderators have been discussed. Sports settings show a disinhibition of male-male touch. The type of touch matters as well, with handshaking being much more notable between men than between women (Hall, 1984). Evidence also suggests that when touch in cross-gender dyads is observed, with the question being whether the man touches the woman more or vice versa, both the type of touch and the type of relationship matter. In younger, less committed couples, there is a stronger tendency for the male to touch the female (as in Henley, 1973), whereas in older and more established couples the balance of touching is likely to be shifted to the female (e.g., Hall & Veccia, 1990; Willis & Dodds, 1998). Several studies also suggest that men are more likely to touch women with their hand, but women are more likely to initiate nonhand touches with men (e.g., DiBiase & Gunnoe, 2004; Hall & Veccia, 1990). Notably, all this research has been on friendly or at least innocuous touches. For more aggressive touches, the gender differences are unknown, though one might surmise that they vary with the gender of the target and the specific kind of aggressive touch (Archer, 2002).

Interpersonal Distance and Facing Orientation. Hall (1984) summarized 28 studies of children and 59 studies of adults in which interpersonal distance was observed in relatively nonreactive ways (such as unobtrusive observation in public). In both age groups, males established larger interpersonal distances than females did, with the effects being more pronounced in adults than in children. Separate analyses of two other methodologies—staged (where participants are asked to set comfortable distances to others in the laboratory) and projective (where participants position humanoid figures on a board or in a picture)—show similar though weaker results; specifically, little gender difference among children and larger distances for men among adults. For the nonreactive studies, it was also possible to look at the gender of target effects. In five studies of children and 20 studies of adults, it was very evident that males were approached less closely than were females. As was the case for smiling and gazing, the separate actor gender and target gender effects combined such that distance was smallest in female-female dyads and largest in male-male dyads.

Regarding directness of orientation, five studies of children and 18 studies of adults indicated that females oriented their heads and bodies more directly toward a conversation partner than males did. Several studies that used naturalistic observation or confederates who invaded someone's space also found gender differences in preferred spatial orientation that varied with the identity of the other person (e.g., Fisher & Byrne, 1975). When the other was an acquaintance, women preferred side-by-side positions, and men preferred face-to-face positions, but these preferences were reversed when the other was a stranger.

Voice Qualities and Vocal Behaviors. The number of available studies assessing vocalics is typically smaller than for visible nonverbal behaviors, but Hall (1984) concluded that the following vocal gender differences were evident. Men's voices tend to be louder and lower pitched and to contain more speech disturbances (e.g., repetitions, omissions, stutters, sentence incompletions); men also tend to use fewer listener responses such as "uh-huh" and "I see" while listening to another speak (called back-channel responses) and more filled pauses (filled with sounds such as "uhh"). A later study (Viscovich et al., 2003) found that men's voices were less variable in pitch as well. Research has also found that men's voices were rated as different from women's on a number of global qualities—for example, less pleasant, more dominant, less enthusiastic, and less anxious. Studies based on listeners' global impressions may be biased by the listeners' stereotypes, thus reducing their value as evidence on actual gender differences.

Summary. This brief review paints a picture that most readers will find very familiar: Women are observed to be more direct, animated, and warm in interpersonal interaction than are men. Conversely, men behave in a less involved manner. These differences are closely associated with stereotypes of how men and women relate to others nonverbally. I turn now to accuracy in sending and receiving nonverbal cues.

ACCURACY IN NONVERBAL COMMUNICATION

Sending Nonverbal Cues. A person can be an accurate expressor in two ways: first, by being spontaneously expressive in a way that makes one's states (such as emotions) readily apparent to others and second, by being able to deliberately convey certain states so that others can judge them accurately. These two kinds of accuracy, which are called spontaneous and posed, are positively correlated (Cunningham, 1977; Zuckerman, Hall, DeFrank, & Rosenthal, 1976; see Riggio, this volume). Hall (1984) concluded, based on 49 studies, that females were more accurate on both definitions of accurate sending. Studies of adults showed somewhat larger effects than did studies of children. Furthermore, the difference between males and females was most pronounced for visible cues and, in fact, nearly nonexistent for vocally conveyed cues.

Noticing and Recalling Nonverbal Cues. Hall (1984) reviewed several studies that suggested that women noticed or were more influenced by nonverbal cues than men were. Recently, Horgan, Schmid Mast, Hall, and Carter (2004) and Schmid Mast and Hall (2006) documented in eight studies that women were more accurate than men in remembering the appearance (clothing, hair, and other physical characteristics) of others after having live interactions and after watching a videotape of people interacting. Also, women's appearance was easier to remember than was the appearance of men. Hall, Murphy, and Schimd Mast (in press) demonstrated in two studies that women were also more accurate than men at remembering dynamic nonverbal cues of others such as hand gestures, nodding, and shrugging, based on viewing live or recorded interactions.

Women's advantage in remembering appearance and visible movement is reminiscent of a related body of literature on accuracy of recognizing faces. Hall (1984) concluded, based on 28 studies of adults, that women recognized faces better than men, consistent with two previous reviews by other authors; also, several studies showed that females associated names with faces more accurately than men did. Shapiro and Penrod (1986) also did a meta-analysis of gender differences in face recognition, however, and concluded there was no difference.

Decoding Nonverbal Cues. Many studies have examined gender differences in accuracy of interpreting the meanings of nonverbal cues. The first meta-analysis of this topic was by Hall (1978), who located 75 studies of children through adults who were asked to identify the meanings of nonverbal cues in persons presented typically via photos, films, videos, or audiotape. Females' advantage was very evident and was relatively constant across a variety of cultures and age groups of perceivers, as well as across the gender of the people whose cues were judged. The greater accuracy for females tended to be more pronounced for visible than for vocal cues. Hall (1984) located an additional 50 studies for which the same conclusions held.

One particular test of decoding nonverbal cues—the Profile of Nonverbal Sensitivity (PONS test; Rosenthal, Hall, DiMatteo, Rogers, & Archer, 1979)—was given to 133 groups of many ages in 11 different countries. Only a small number of these groups were included in the two reviews described in the preceding paragraph so that the literature review would not be overweighted by one testing instrument. For the 133 PONS test samples, the average magnitude was exactly the same as in the preceding summaries (more on magnitude will be

said in a later section). Furthermore, the difference between men's and women's scores was just as strong in the non-U.S. groups as in the U.S. groups, and the difference was robust from third grade up into adulthood.

Later studies have continued to confirm that women's accuracy is higher than men's for judging the meanings of nonverbal cues in a variety of domains and contexts: for judging (a) personality traits (Ambady, Hallahan, & Rosenthal, 1995; Lippa & Dietz, 1998; Vogt & Colvin, 2003), (b) intelligence (Murphy, Hall, & Colvin, 2003), (c) facial expressions of emotion in six nations (Biehl et al., 1997), (d) vocal expressions of emotion in nine nations (Scherer, Banse, & Wallbott, 2001), (e) facial emotions judged by children and adolescents (meta-analysis by McClure, 2000), and (f) emotions conveyed by the eyes and brows alone (Baron-Cohen, Wheelwright, Hill, Raste, & Plumb, 2001). Women have also been shown to have more explicit knowledge of nonverbal cues, as demonstrated on a paper-and-pencil test of knowledge of nonverbal cue meanings and usages (Rosip & Hall, 2004).

Some domains, however, show markedly reduced or even nonexistent gender differences. A meta-analysis evidenced that women did not excel over men in judging deception (Zuckerman, DePaulo, & Rosenthal, 1981), and several studies have now suggested that women are no more accurate than men in judging status or dominance from nonverbal cues (e.g., Dovidio & Ellyson, 1982; Schmid Mast & Hall, 2004b). Both of these results are interesting, in part because deception and status (dominance) are arguably less female-stereotypical than are most of the other constructs measured in nonverbal sensitivity tasks (e.g., emotions, relationships, appearance). Perhaps future research will uncover not only areas of gender similarity in nonverbal skill, but even areas in which men's accuracy exceeds women's.

◆ How Accurate Are the Stereotypes?

Thus far, I have worked to document beliefs about, and actual differences in, men's and women's nonverbal behavior and skill. A comparison between the stereotypes and the actual gender differences indicates there can be no doubt that the stereotypes are overwhelmingly correct in substance. There are at least two ways to appraise the accuracy of people's beliefs in more precise quantitative terms. One way is to make a direct comparison (e.g., to gather people's beliefs about the rate of hand gesturing by men and women during conversation and then to compare this with the actual rate). In most research, however, people are asked to state their beliefs on an arbitrary rating scale that cannot be compared directly with measured behaviors. A second way is to correlate the beliefs with the actual differences, a method that does not require identical metrics for both beliefs and actual differences. This method, called *sensitivity correlation* (Judd & Park, 1993) or *profile correlation* (Vogt & Colvin, 2003), captures the covariation between believed and actual differences across behaviors.

To apply this method, the actual differences between males and females must be quantified on a common metric. In my meta-analysis (Hall, 1984), I used the point-biserial Pearson correlation between gender (coded male = 0, female = 1) and the behavior in question, although other indices of effect size are available, notably Cohen's *d*, defined as the difference between two means divided by their within-group standard deviation (Cohen, 1988).

I used the correlation metric because it has the broadest comparability across different domains of research (Lipsey & Wilson, 2001; Rosenthal, 1991).[4]

To assess accuracy of the gender difference beliefs, Briton and Hall (1995a) correlated the effect sizes for the belief data shown in Table 11.1, separately for male and female perceivers, with the effect sizes for the actual differences in Hall (1984). The resulting correlations were .74 for the averaged group of female perceivers and .68 for the averaged group of male perceivers, meaning that both men and women held very accurate beliefs about the patterning of the nonverbal gender differences. Hall and Carter (1999) also gathered stereotype data about nonverbal gender differences and were able to duplicate this group accuracy result almost exactly. In that study, accuracy was significantly higher for female than for male perceivers. Thus, women possessed more accurate knowledge than men about how the genders differ in their nonverbal behavior.

APPRAISING THE SIZE OF THE DIFFERENCES

How big are nonverbal gender differences? This is an important question that can be addressed in several different ways. One way is to ask whether the differences are big enough to be noticeable in everyday life. According to Cohen (1988), an effect size correlation (*r*) of about .25 is large enough to be visible to the naked eye, assuming repeated exposure. The average effect size of the nonverbal gender differences is in this range (.20 and above) for expression accuracy, smiling, facial expressiveness, decoding skill, recall of appearance, gazing (both gazing and being gazed at), interpersonal distance (both initiated and received), body restlessness, bodily expansiveness, bodily expressiveness (mainly hand gestures), self-touching, speech errors, and filled pauses. The fact that the observed differences are this large may help to explain why stereotypes about the differences are so accurate.

But there are other ways to ask the magnitude question. One is in terms of the variance explained by the gender differences. In other words, in an average study, how much of the variation in the observed behavior is accounted for by gender? The answer is "not much." Correlations in the range of .20 to .40 account for only small amounts of variance (4%–16%). This means that in absolute terms, very little of the variation in nonverbal behavior and skill is due to gender. Another way to express these differences is to examine the distributions for men and women. With effects in the range we find in this area of research, the male and female distributions will overlap a great deal. To be more exact, only about 30% of their joint distributions will not be overlapped (Cohen, 1988). This means that many men will exhibit behavior within the range of "women's behavior" and vice versa. For example, many men will smile more than the average woman.

Caution must be taken with the "magnitude" approach, however. Before we conclude that gender is only a trivial predictor of nonverbal behavior, we must ask a broader and more relativistic question: How do the nonverbal gender differences compare to other social psychological effects, other gender differences, and other correlates of the same nonverbal behaviors? Within these frames of reference, the nonverbal gender differences fare rather well. Richard, Bond, and Stokes-Zoota (2003) performed a summary of over 450 meta-analyses of social and personality phenomena (involving over 25,000 studies and 8 million participants). The overall effect was an average correlation of .21. Lipsey and Wilson (1993) did a nonoverlapping review of over 300 meta-analyses on the effects of interventions in education and psychology, finding an overall effect of $r = .24$. The nonverbal gender differences are comparable with these overall effects.

Richard et al.'s (2003) analysis of gender effects (for a long list of psychological variables) revealed an average correlation of .12, consistent with a similar quantitative summary of gender difference meta-analyses done by Hall (2006), suggesting that the nonverbal gender differences are larger on average than other gender differences reported in the social-personality literature. Finally, Hall (2006) compiled a list of other correlates (besides gender) for nonverbal sensitivity and smiling and found that gender correlated with nonverbal sensitivity as strongly (on average) as other variables did, and it correlated with smiling only slightly more weakly than other variables did. Thus, within a relative framework, gender differences in nonverbal communication are within the range typical of social-personality psychology in general, larger than other gender differences on average, and not very different from other correlates of the nonverbal behaviors.

WHERE DO THE DIFFERENCES COME FROM?

This most complex question has no simple answer, and before starting, several important observations must be made. First, because nonverbal behavior is often ambiguous in meaning (Knapp & Hall, 2005), and studies reporting gender differences hardly ever ascertain what the behaviors mean to the people observed, it is very difficult to know what interpretations to place on the gender differences in terms of intentions, motivations, correlated states, and so forth. Second, it is not possible to do controlled experiments that could lead to confident inferences about cause, given that we cannot assign people randomly to be either male or female. Third, because gender is a potent social variable whose impact on behavior begins at birth, it is likely not possible to pinpoint "the" cause of a gender difference. Indeed, considered in a wider historical perspective, social expectations, modeling, and force of habit may keep a gender difference alive even if the circumstances that were the original "cause" are no longer operative. Fourth, there is no reason to assume that one unified theory is required to explain the plethora of nonverbal gender differences that exist. Although a single grand explanation may succeed eventually in explaining all or most of the differences, it is also possible that there are many different causes that either coexist in producing a given gender difference or apply to different behaviors. Below, I offer a quick summary of several theoretical positions concerning possible causes for gender differences in nonverbal behavior.

Andersen (1998) proposed a biologically based explanation for women's advantage in decoding nonverbal cues. Women may, for example, have evolved to be more sensitive to nonverbal cues than men because of advantages in terms of survival of offspring. Some nonverbal differences (e.g., gazing) do appear in early infancy, which may support an inborn mechanism; on the other hand, social learning may occur even within the first year of life, and furthermore, some differences only appear years later (e.g., smiling). Perhaps because it is difficult to prove the biological case, or because sociocultural explanations are more compelling to social researchers, most writers have pursued an approach based on social factors.

Henley (1977, 1995) made the most ambitious theoretical proposition when she argued that nonverbal gender differences are rooted in gender differences in power, status, and dominance. Women, she argued, behave the way weak and low-status people behave, whereas men behave the way

strong and high-status people behave. Women's behaviors, therefore, are tied more to lower social status than to being female per se. Furthermore, the subtle and nonconscious nature of nonverbal communication provides an effective means not only to display power, status, and dominance but also to enforce and maintain domination over women. Henley's argument had a great deal of influence because it was consonant with the feminist psychology *zeitgeist* and it unified many findings under one parsimonious explanation (Vrugt, 1987). As a consequence, it has been presented—often as fact rather than hypothesis—in social psychology and psychology of women textbooks up to the present day. Furthermore, Henley's (1977, 1995) ideas were more provocative than systematic, in that she did not claim to put forth a fully developed theory that could account for all behaviors, all moderating factors, and all definitions of the power construct. And, of course, at the time of her seminal work there was much less empirical research available on which to base a comprehensive theory. From the perspective of some 30 years later, it is now possible to fill in a crucial empirical gap.

Henley's argument rested on three interlocking claims: that men have more power, dominance, and status than women; that men and women differ in their nonverbal communication; and that people high versus low in power, dominance, and status differ in their nonverbal communication in the same way that men and women differ. The first two of these claims are, broadly speaking, not in dispute. Interestingly, however, the third claim was assumed to be true without much empirical substantiation, and authors since Henley have not often questioned this assumption. Hall, Halberstadt, and O'Brien (1997) and Hall, Coats, and Smith LeBeau (2005) undertook an evaluation of this third claim by conducting meta-analyses of the relations of nonverbal behavior to power, dominance, and status (for simplicity, I will just say "power").

If Henley's (1977, 1995) power-based theory has viability, the gender differences should parallel the power differences.[5] Such parallelism is evident for the visual dominance ratio, bodily openness, loudness of voice, interruptions, and back-channel responses. Some nonverbal behaviors that are more prevalent in persons with higher power, however, are actually more characteristic of women (more facial expressiveness, smaller interpersonal distances, greater decoding skill, greater encoding skill),[6,7] and some nonverbal behaviors that are more characteristic of women do not show overall power effects (smiling, gazing, nodding, gesturing, and direct orientation). Thus, the parallelism required by the power-based theory is very inconsistent.

Though as an all-encompassing theory Henley's (1977, 1995) argument appears not to be viable, future research may still succeed in identifying circumstances and behaviors in which power underlies gender differences. Schmid Mast and Hall (2004b), for example, found that smiling was not related overall to either manipulated power or trait dominance in a laboratory study, but that smiling was in fact elevated in one circumstance: among women (not men) who wanted, and received, assignment to the lower power role. This suggests that future studies could profit from looking carefully at moderating factors.

If power is not the immediate cause of the gender differences, what is? One possibility is that power is the root cause of whatever is the more proximal cause. For example, although social norms that encourage women to be expressive, warm, approachable, interpersonally involved, sensitive, and the like may be the important direct influences in the lifetime of a given woman (with the complementary norms having direct influences on a man), one might still argue that it was the power differential that

produced those social norms in the first place. Thus, power would be a real but more distant cause. The difficulty of proving this "root cause" argument reduces its value, however.

Setting the power hypothesis aside for the moment, what explanations remain? As just noted, societal norms, roles, and expectations are clearly consistent with the observed gender differences. To review the literature on gender roles is clearly beyond the scope of this chapter, but it is clear that women in many cultures are expected to be competent in the social domain, indeed responsible for the positive outcomes of social interaction, and there are well-established gender norms on dimensions such as communion, relationship orientation, concern with feelings, social division of labor, and the experience and expression of affect (especially positive affect; Alexander & Wood, 2000; Clancy & Dollinger, 1993; Cross & Madson, 1997; Eagly, 1987; Jansz, 2000). Nonverbal cues and skills are relevant to such norms and expectations. The existence of norms and expectations creates a chicken-and-egg relation with observed differences, however: The one brings about and reinforces the other in a cycle.

In the most detailed theoretical statement to date, Hall, Carter, and Horgan (2000) offered a conceptual analysis of how various factors may impinge on women's smiling, expression skill, and interpersonal sensitivity. To illustrate with the case of smiling, we identified numerous potential factors that could serve to elevate women's smiling. At the heart of the analysis is the experience of positive affect and the facial feedback process whereby smiling itself produces positive affect (Strack, Martin, & Stepper, 1988). The fact that women are smiled at more than men could produce more smiling through the reciprocity process (Hinsz & Tomhave, 1991), which then produces positive affect through facial feedback, more smiling, and so forth. Women's superior awareness of social scripts and norms, and their attunement to others' needs, may also lead them into a heightened amount of prosocial smiling. People expect women to smile (be socially responsive, etc.), and people deliver social rewards to women accordingly, which again feeds into the affect-feedback-smiling cycle.

The differences between females and males, however, may not always be linked to immediate social purposes and messages. Nonverbal stylistic habits are undoubtedly learned, in part, through simple modeling processes of same-gender others. A child raised in isolation from same-gender models would likely display a very different profile of nonverbal behavior and skill than typically seen. Furthermore, the purpose of the gender-linked behaviors may be metacommunicative. For example, boys may smile less than girls in part because they do not want to be perceived as acting like girls. Clearly, social pressures bear down on both males and females (Jansz, 2000). Conformity to group standards can be a potent motivator all by itself, a point well supported by a number of the moderators uncovered in LaFrance et al.'s (2003) meta-analysis of smiling (i.e., the effect of being observed).

To summarize the state of theory regarding the origins of nonverbal gender differences, the weight of evidence points away from a power-based explanation and toward a sociocultural theory based on social norms, expectations, roles, and associated affective experiences. It is important to emphasize that the typical study that simply compares the nonverbal behavior of males and females is not conducive to unraveling the mystery of causation. Researchers need to distinguish better among subtly different nonverbal cues that have different interpersonal meanings. An example given earlier is smiling, for which there are variants that are more and less associated with concurrently felt positive emotion.

Researchers also need to understand better the meaning of behavior in context (see Bavelas & Chovil, this volume). For example, gazing may take on different meanings depending on other nonverbal behaviors, the task, the emotional tone of the interaction, and so forth. Furthermore, different processes may be operative for men versus women. For example, there may be situations in which men's smiling is tied to the urge to be influential, whereas women's smiling is tied to the belief that smiling makes them look more attractive. No meaningful conclusion could be drawn without knowing about these contingencies. Research on gender differences in nonverbal behavior and their explanations is still at a rather gross stage of description that lumps together many different variations with different possible meanings.

◆ Conclusion

Nonverbal gender differences and their associated stereotypes, because they connote much about emotion, motivation, and other personal characteristics, have implications for how men and women are viewed and treated. Self-fulfilling prophecies create a potent but usually invisible web of influence throughout our lives. Though the nonverbal gender differences are small in absolute terms, they are real and can have real consequences. Sometimes the differences may be noticed with gratitude or admiration, but sometimes they are a source of aggravation and frustration. Perhaps the ideal to strive for is an adaptable repertoire so that all individuals are able to adapt their nonverbal behavior to the needs of the situation and of the other people in it, as well as to their own emotional and strategic needs.

◆ Notes

Author's Note: This chapter is dedicated to Bob and Doris Gordon, who supplied the most pleasant possible setting in which to undertake its writing.

1. Rather than prejudge the origins of male-female differences by attributing some to "sex" and some to "gender," I prefer to use the terms interchangeably. To be consistent with the editors' preferences of using only one term, I use *gender* in the present chapter. Also, when I use the term *gender*, I refer to people who self-identify or are identified based on appearance as dichotomously male or female without consideration of possible complexities such as transgendered or transsexual identities, gender reassignment, or homosexual identity.

2. Kramer's (1977) respondents also believed that men's voices are lower pitched and that men lounge and lean back more than women do. Neither of these behaviors was included in the Briton and Hall (1995a) study, though both stereotypes were supported by Hall's (1984) review of actual nonverbal gender differences.

3. Of course, smiles have many meanings besides spontaneously revealing happy emotion. Smiles can be used as back-channel responses in conversation (i.e., cues that encourage the other person to continue speaking; Brunner, 1979), and smiles are used ubiquitously as social messages (greeting, apologizing, reassuring, acknowledging passersby, etc.). Therefore, even if women showed more non-Duchenne smiles than men, it would not necessarily mean that women's smiles are insincere, but rather could indicate more socially skilled behavior or other authentic interpersonal motives. The simple comparison of men's and women's Duchenne and non-Duchenne smiling is not meaningful without knowledge of current emotional states and motives.

4. For effects of $r = .20$ or smaller, the d statistic is simply $2r$ (Rosenthal, 1991). As r increases beyond this level, d increases at an accelerating rate. For example, the d corresponding to $r = .45$ is 1.00.

5. Of course, demonstrating such parallelism does not by itself validate the theory. At the least, one should find that controlling for power diminishes the gender differences. When this kind of analysis has been undertaken, however, no such reduction occurred (e.g., Hall & Friedman, 1999).

6. Snodgrass's research (e.g., Snodgrass, 1992) has often been cited as showing that low-power individuals are motivated to be better decoders of nonverbal cues in the dyadic context than high-power individuals. Later research (Hall, Rosip, Smith Le Beau, Horgan, & Carter, 2006; Snodgrass, Hecht, & Ploutz-Snyder, 1998), however, showed that this effect was actually due to the nature of expression and not to motivational factors related to decoding.

7. Fischer and Manstead (2000) used self-report of nonverbal emotional expressiveness to test the power hypothesis on a cross-cultural level, using questionnaires and archival data relating to women's status in 37 countries. There were few gender by status interactions, and those that did emerge showed that the gender difference in expressiveness was greater in more egalitarian countries, in contradiction to Henley's (1977) power-based theory.

◆ References

Aiello, J. R. (1977). Visual interaction at extended distances. *Personality and Social Psychology Bulletin, 3,* 83–86.

Alexander, M. G., & Wood, W. (2000). Women, men, and positive emotions: A social role interpretation. In A. H. Fischer (Ed.), *Gender and emotion: Social psychological perspectives* (pp. 189–210). Paris: Cambridge University Press.

Ambady, N., Hallahan, M., & Rosenthal, R. (1995). On judging and being judged accurately in zero-acquaintance situations. *Journal of Personality and Social Psychology, 69,* 518–529.

Andersen, P. A. (1998). Researching sex differences within sex similarities: The evolutionary consequences of reproductive differences. In D. J. Canary & K. Dindia (Eds.), *Sex differences and similarities in communication: Critical essays and empirical investigations of sex and gender in interaction* (pp. 83–100). Mahwah, NJ: Erlbaum.

Archer, J. (2002). Sex differences in physically aggressive acts between heterosexual partners: A meta-analytic review. *Aggression and Violent Behavior, 7*, 313–351.

Argyle, M., & Dean, J. (1965). Eye-contact, distance and affiliation. *Sociometry, 28*, 289–304.

Baron-Cohen, S., Wheelwright, S., Hill, J., Raste, Y., & Plumb, I. (2001). The "Reading the Mind in the Eyes" Test Revised Version: A study with normal adults, and adults with Asperger syndrome or high-functioning autism. *Journal of Child Psychology and Psychiatry, 42*, 241–251.

Bem, S. L. (1974). The measurement of psychological androgyny. *Journal of Consulting and Clinical Psychology, 42*, 155–162.

Berkowitz, W. R. (1971). A cross-national comparison of some social patterns of urban pedestrians. *Journal of Cross-Cultural Psychology, 2*, 129–144.

Biehl, M., Matsumoto, D., Ekman, P., Hearn, V., Heider, K., Kudoh, T., et al. (1997). Matsumoto's and Ekman's Japanese and Caucasian Facial Expressions of Emotion (JACFEE): Reliability data and cross-national differences. *Journal of Nonverbal Behavior, 21*, 3–21.

Briton, N. J., & Hall, J. A. (1995a). Beliefs about female and male nonverbal communication. *Sex Roles, 32*, 79–90.

Briton, N. J., & Hall, J. A. (1995b). Gender-based expectancies and observer judgments of smiling. *Journal of Nonverbal Behavior, 19*, 49–65.

Brody, L. R., & Hall, J. A. (2000). Gender, emotion, and expression. In M. Lewis & J. M. Haviland-Jones (Eds.), *Handbook of emotions* (2nd ed., pp. 338–349). New York: Guilford.

Brunner, L. J. (1979). Smiles can be back channels. *Journal of Personality and Social Psychology, 37*, 728–734.

Bugental, D. E., Love, L. R., & Gianetto, R. M. (1971). Perfidious feminine faces. *Journal of Personality and Social Psychology, 17*, 314–318.

Clancy, S. M., & Dollinger, S. J. (1993). Photographic depictions of the self: Gender and age differences in social connectedness. *Sex Roles, 29*, 477–495.

Cohen, J. (1988). *Statistical power analysis for the behavioral sciences* (2nd ed.). Mahwah, NJ: Erlbaum.

Cross, S. E., & Madson, L. (1997). Models of the self: Self-construals and gender. *Psychological Bulletin, 122*, 5–37.

Cunningham, M. R. (1977). Personality and the structure of the nonverbal communication of emotion. *Journal of Personality, 45*, 564–584.

DePaulo, B. M. (1992). Nonverbal behavior and self-presentation. *Psychological Bulletin, 111*, 203–243.

DiBiase, R., & Gunnoe, J. (2004). Gender and culture differences in touching behavior. *Journal of Social Psychology, 144*, 49–62.

Dodd, D. K., Russell, B. L., & Jenkins, C. (1999). Smiling in school yearbook photos: Gender differences from kindergarten to adulthood. *The Psychological Record, 49*, 543–554.

Dovidio, J. F., & Ellyson, S. L. (1982). Decoding visual dominance behavior: Attributions of power based on the relative percentages of looking while speaking and looking while listening. *Social Psychology Quarterly, 45*, 106–113.

Dovidio, J. F., & Ellyson, S. L. (1985). Patterns of visual dominance behavior in humans. In J. F. Dovidio & S. L. Ellyson (Eds.), *Power, dominance, and nonverbal behavior* (pp. 128–149). New York: Springer.

Dovidio, J. F., Ellyson, S. L., Keating, C. F., Heltman, K., & Brown, C. E. (1988). The relationship of social power to visual displays of dominance between men and women. *Journal of Personality and Social Psychology, 54*, 233–242.

Eagly, A. H. (1987). *Sex differences in social behavior: A social role interpretation.* Hillsdale, NJ: Erlbaum.

Ekman, P., Davidson, R. J., & Friesen, W. V. (1990). The Duchenne smile: Emotional expression and brain physiology: II. *Journal of Personality and Social Psychology, 58*, 342–353.

Fischer, A. H., & Manstead, A. S. R. (2000). The relation between gender and emotions in different cultures. In A. H. Fischer (Ed.), *Gender and emotion: Social psychological perspectives* (pp. 71–94). Paris: Cambridge University Press.

Fisher, J. D., & Byrne, D. (1975). Too close for comfort: Sex differences in response to invasions of personal space. *Journal of Personality and Social Psychology, 32,* 15–21.

Gross, J. J., & John, O. P. (1998). Mapping the domain of expressivity: Multimethod evidence for a hierarchical model. *Journal of Personality and Social Psychology, 74,* 170–191.

Halberstadt, A. G., Hayes, C. W., & Pike, K. M. (1988). Gender and gender role differences in smiling and communication consistency. *Sex Roles, 19,* 589–604.

Hall, J. A. (1978). Gender differences in decoding nonverbal cues. *Psychological Bulletin, 85,* 845–857.

Hall, J. A. (1984). *Nonverbal sex differences: Communication accuracy and expressive style.* Baltimore, MD: The Johns Hopkins University Press.

Hall, J. A. (2006). How big are nonverbal gender differences? The case of smiling and sensitivity to nonverbal cues. In K. Dindia & D. J. Canary (Eds.), *Sex differences and similarities in communication* (2nd ed., pp. 59–81). Mahwah, NJ: Erlbaum.

Hall, J. A., & Carter, J. D. (1999). Gender-stereotype accuracy as an individual difference. *Journal of Personality and Social Psychology, 77,* 350–359.

Hall, J. A., Carter, J. D., & Horgan, T. G. (2000). Gender differences in nonverbal communication of emotion. In A. H. Fischer (Ed.), *Gender and emotion: Social psychological perspectives* (pp. 97–117). Paris: Cambridge University Press.

Hall, J. A., Coats, E. J., & Smith LeBeau, L. (2005). Nonverbal behavior and the vertical dimension of social relations: A meta-analysis. *Psychological Bulletin, 131,* 898–924.

Hall, J. A., & Friedman, G. B. (1999). Status, gender, and nonverbal behavior: A study of structured interactions between employees of a company. *Personality and Social Psychology Bulletin, 25,* 1082–1091.

Hall, J. A., & Halberstadt, A. G. (1986). Smiling and gazing. In J. S. Hyde & M. C. Linn (Eds.), *The psychology of gender: Advances through meta-analysis* (pp. 136–158). Baltimore: The Johns Hopkins University Press.

Hall, J. A., Halberstadt, A. G., & O'Brien, C. E. (1997). "Subordination" and nonverbal sensitivity: A study and synthesis of findings based on trait measures. *Sex Roles, 37,* 295–317.

Hall, J. A., Murphy, N. A., & Schmid Mast, M. (in press). Recall of nonverbal cues: Exploring a new definition of interpersonal sensitivity. *Journal of Nonverbal Behavior.*

Hall, J. A., Rosip, J. C., Smith LeBeau, L., Horgan, T. G., & Carter, J. D. (2006). Attributing the sources of accuracy in unequal-power dyadic communication: Who is better and why? *Journal of Experimental Social Psychology, 42,* 18–27.

Hall, J. A., & Veccia, E. M. (1990). More "touching" observations: New insights on men, women, and interpersonal touch. *Journal of Personality and Social Psychology, 59,* 1155–1162.

Hecht, M. A., & LaFrance, M. (1998). License or obligation to smile: The effect of power and sex on amount and type of smiling. *Personality and Social Psychology Bulletin, 24,* 1332–1342.

Henley, N. M. (1973). Status and sex: Some touching observations. *Bulletin of the Psychonomic Society, 2,* 91–93.

Henley, N. M. (1977). *Body politics: Power, sex, and nonverbal communication.* Englewood Cliffs, NJ: Prentice Hall.

Henley, N. M. (1995). Body politics revisited: What do we know today? In P. J. Kalbfleisch & M. J. Cody (Eds.), *Gender, power, and communication in human relationships* (pp. 27–61). Hillsdale, NJ: Erlbaum.

Hinsz, V. B., & Tomhave, J. A. (1991). Smile and (half) the world smiles with you, frown and you frown alone. *Personality and Social Psychology Bulletin, 17,* 586–592.

Horgan, T. G., Schmid Mast, M., Hall, J. A., & Carter, J. D. (2004). Gender differences in memory for the appearance of others. *Personality and Social Psychology Bulletin, 30,* 185–196.

Jansz, J. (2000). Masculine identity and restrictive emotionality. In A. H. Fischer (Ed.), *Gender and emotion: Social psychological perspectives* (pp. 166–186). Paris: Cambridge University Press.

Johnson, J., & Shulman, G. (1988). More alike than meets the eye: Perceived gender differences in subjective experience and its display. *Sex Roles, 19,* 67–79.

Judd, C. M., & Park, B. (1993). Definition and assessment of accuracy in social stereotypes. *Psychological Review, 100,* 109–128.

Knapp, M. L., & Hall, J. A. (2005). *Nonverbal communication in human interaction* (6th ed.). Belmont, CA: Wadsworth.

Korzenny, B. A. G., Korzenny, F., & Sanchez de Rota, G. (1985). Women's communication in Mexican organizations. *Sex Roles, 12,* 867–876.

Kramer, C. (1977). Perceptions of male and female speech. *Language and Speech, 20,* 151–161.

LaFrance, M., & Banaji, M. (1992). Toward a reconsideration of the gender-emotion relationship. In M. S. Clark (Ed.), *Emotion and social behavior* (pp. 178–201). Newbury Park, CA: Sage.

LaFrance, M., Hecht, M. A., & Levy Paluck, E. (2003). The contingent smile: A meta-analysis of sex differences in smiling. *Psychological Bulletin, 129,* 305–334.

Lippa, R. A., & Dietz, J. K. (1998). The relation of gender, personality, and intelligence to judges' accuracy in judging strangers' personality from brief video segments. *Journal of Nonverbal Behavior, 24,* 25–43.

Lipsey, M. W., & Wilson, D. B. (1993). The efficacy of psychological, educational, and behavioral treatment: Confirmation from meta-analysis. *American Psychologist, 48,* 1181–1209.

Lipsey, M. W., & Wilson, D. B. (2001). *Practical meta-analysis.* Thousand Oaks, CA: Sage.

McClure, E. B. (2000). A meta-analytic review of sex differences in facial expression processing and their development in infants, children, and adolescents. *Psychological Bulletin, 126,* 424–453.

McCormick, N. B., & Jones, A. J. (1989). Gender differences in nonverbal flirtation. *Journal of Sex Education & Therapy, 15,* 271–282.

Montemayor, R., & Flannery, D. J. (1989). A naturalistic study of the involvement of children and adolescents with their mothers and friends: Developmental differences in expressive behavior. *Journal of Adolescent Research, 4,* 3–14.

Murphy, N. A., Hall, J. A., & Colvin, C. R. (2003). Accurate intelligence assessments in social interaction: Mediators and gender effects. *Journal of Personality, 71,* 465–493.

Noller, P., & Gallois, C. (1986). Sending emotional messages in marriage: Non-verbal behaviour, sex and communication clarity. *British Journal of Social Psychology, 25,* 287–297.

Richard, F. D., Bond, C. F., Jr., & Stokes-Zoota, J. J. (2003). One hundred years of social psychology quantitatively described. *Review of General Psychology, 7,* 331–363.

Rosenkrantz, P., Vogel, S., Bee, H., Broverman, I., & Broverman, D. M. (1968). Sex-role stereotypes and self-concepts in college students. *Journal of Consulting and Clinical Psychology, 32,* 287–295.

Rosenthal, R. (1991). *Meta-analytic procedures for social research* (rev. ed.). Newbury Park, CA: Sage.

Rosenthal, R., Hall, J. A., DiMatteo, M. R., Rogers, P. L., & Archer, D. (1979). *Sensitivity to nonverbal communication: The PONS test.* Baltimore: The Johns Hopkins University Press.

Rosip, J. C., & Hall, J. A. (2004). Knowledge of nonverbal cues, gender, and nonverbal decoding accuracy. *Journal of Nonverbal Behavior, 28,* 267–286.

Scherer, K. R., Banse, R., & Wallbott, H. G. (2001). Emotion inferences from vocal expression correlate across languages and cultures. *Journal of Cross-Cultural Psychology, 32,* 76–92.

Schmid Mast, M., & Hall, J. A. (2004a). Who is the boss and who is not? Accuracy of judging status. *Journal of Nonverbal Behavior, 28,* 145–165.

Schmid Mast, M., & Hall, J. A. (2004b). When is dominance related to smiling? Assigned dominance, dominance preference, trait dominance, and gender as moderators. *Sex Roles, 50,* 387–399.

Schmid Mast, M., & Hall, J. A. (2006). Women's advantage at remembering others' appearance: A systematic look at the why and when of a gender difference. *Personality and Social Psychology Bulletin, 32,* 353–364.

Shapiro, P. N., & Penrod, S. (1986). Meta-analysis of facial identification studies. *Psychological Bulletin, 100,* 139–156.

Snodgrass, S. E. (1992). Further effects of role versus gender on interpersonal sensitivity. *Journal of Personality and Social Psychology, 62,* 154–158.

Snodgrass, S. E., Hecht, M. A., & Ploutz-Snyder, R. (1998). Interpersonal sensitivity: Expressivity or perceptivity? *Journal of Personality and Social Psychology, 74,* 238–249.

Spence, J. T., & Helmreich, R. (1978). *Masculinity and femininity: Their psychological dimensions, correlates, and antecedents.* Austin, TX: University of Texas Press.

Stier, D. S., & Hall, J. A. (1984). Gender differences in touch: An empirical and theoretical review. *Journal of Personality and Social Psychology, 47,* 440–459.

Strack, F., Martin, L. L., & Stepper, S. (1988). Inhibiting and facilitating conditions of the human smile: A nonobtrusive test of the facial feedback hypothesis. *Journal of Personality and Social Psychology, 54,* 208–219.

Viscovich, N., Borod, J., Pihan, H., Peery, S., Brickman, A. M., Tabert, M., et al. (2003). Acoustical analysis of posed prosodic expressions: Effects of emotion and sex. *Perceptual and Motor Skills, 96,* 759–771.

Vogt, D. S., & Colvin, C. R. (2003). Interpersonal orientation and the accuracy of personality judgements. *Journal of Personality, 71,* 267–295.

Vrugt, A. (1987). The meaning of nonverbal sex differences. *Semiotica, 64,* 371–380.

Vrugt, A., & Kerkstra, A. (1984). Sex differences in nonverbal communication. *Semiotica, 50,* 1–41.

Willis, F. N., Jr., & Dodds, R. A. (1998). Age, relationship, and touch initiation. *Journal of Social Psychology, 138,* 115–123.

Willis, F. N., & Rinck, C. M. (1983). A personal log method for investigating interpersonal touch. *Journal of Psychology: Interdisciplinary and Applied, 113,* 119–122.

Zuckerman, M., DePaulo, B. M., & Rosenthal, R. (1981). Verbal and nonverbal communication of deception. In L. Berkowitz (Ed.), *Advances in experimental social psychology* (Vol. 14, pp. 1–59). New York: Academic Press.

Zuckerman, M., Hall, J. A., DeFrank, R. S., & Rosenthal, R. (1976). Encoding and decoding of spontaneous and posed facial expressions. *Journal of Personality and Social Psychology, 34,* 966–977.

Zuckerman, M., & Larrance, D. T. (1979). Individual differences in perceived encoding and decoding abilities. In R. Rosenthal (Ed.), *Skill in nonverbal communication: Individual differences* (pp. 171–193). Cambridge, MA: Oelgeschlager, Gunn & Hain.

12

CULTURE AND NONVERBAL BEHAVIOR

◆ David Matsumoto
San Francisco State University

◆ *Defining Culture*

Over the history of time, people have had to solve a host of distinct social problems in order to adapt and thus achieve reproductive success, including negotiating complex status hierarchies, forming successful work and social groups, attracting mates, fighting off potential rivals of food and sexual partners, giving birth and raising children, and battling nature (Buss, 1991, 2001). Universal biological imperatives are associated with a universal set of psychological problems that people need to solve in order to survive; thus, all individuals and groups of individuals must create ways to deal with these universal problems. The ways that each group develops then become their culture.

In my view, culture is the product of the interaction between universal biological needs and functions, universal social problems created to

Author's Note: I thank Marija Drezgic, Devon McCabe, and Joanna Schug for their aid in conducting the literature review; Seung Hee Yoo for her comments on a previous version of this chapter; and Sanae Nakagawa, Andres Olide, and Akiko Terao for their aid in the functioning of my laboratory.

◆ 219

address those needs, and the contexts in which people live. Culture is created as people adapt to their environments in order to survive, and it results from the process of individuals' attempts to adapt to their contexts in addressing the universal social problems and biological needs. Although many different definitions of culture exist (e.g., Berry, Poortinga, Segall, & Dasen, 1992; Jahoda, 1984; Kroeber & Kluckholn, 1963; Linton, 1936; Rohner, 1984; Triandis, 1972), I define culture as *a shared system of socially transmitted behavior that describes, defines, and guides people's ways of life, communicated from one generation to the next.*

Because people must deal with the same set of biological needs and functions and universal social problems, it is very possible and in many cases very likely that the ways in which they are addressed are the same. That is, universal biological needs and social problems can lead to similar solutions across cultures, especially over time in our evolutionary history. Thus, many aspects of our mental processes and behaviors can be considered universal. For example, all humans appear to have some degree of specific fears, such as to snakes, spiders, heights, and darkness, because these types of fears have led in our evolutionary history to greater probability of survival (Seligman & Hager, 1972). As well, people have a tendency to perceive their own ingroup as heterogeneous, fully recognizing the individual differences that exist in that group, whereas they perceive other groups as more homogeneous, assuming less diversity within the group (Linville & Jones, 1980; Triandis, McCusker, & Hui, 1990). People also seem to have a natural proclivity to fears of strangers and outgroup members, which may be a universal basis for ethnocentrism, prejudice, aggression, and even war (Buss, 2001; see also Dovidio & colleagues, this volume). Other universal processes, such as incest avoidance, facial expressions of

emotion, division of labor by sex, revenge and retaliation, mate selection and sexual jealousy, self-enhancement, and personality can be traced to the core aspect of a universal human nature based on biological imperatives and universal social problems of adaptation and living.

But many mental and behavioral processes are also culture-specific. Different cultures develop different ways of dealing with the biological imperatives and universal social problems based on their contexts. Language is an example of a very culture-specific behavior. Each culture has its own language, with its own vocabulary, syntax, grammar, phonology, and pragmatics (Barnlund & Araki, 1985; Barnlund & Yoshioka, 1990; Chen, 1995; Gudykunst & Mody, 2001; Kim et al., 1996; Minami & McCabe, 1995; Nomura & Barnlund, 1983). The need to have language may be a pancultural universal problem; and having a language may be a universal solution to this problem. But the specific way in which each culture solves this problem—that is, develops its own language—is different in every culture.

◆ The Role of Culture in the Nonverbal Communication Process

As with verbal communication, culture influences nonverbal behaviors in profound ways. By far the largest research literature on this topic is related to facial expressions of emotion, which I review later in this chapter. In this section, I highlight briefly the role of culture on other types of nonverbal behaviors before turning to the larger discussion of culture and emotional expressions.

Culture and Gestures. The study of culture and gestures has its roots in the study by

David Efron (Boas & Efron, 1936; Efron, 1941), who examined the gestures of Sicilian and Lithuanian Jewish immigrants in New York City. Efron found that there were distinct gestures among traditional Jews and Italians but that the traditional gestures disappeared as people were more assimilated into the larger American culture. This work was followed initially by that of Ekman and his colleagues (Ekman, 1976; Friesen, Ekman, & Wallbott, 1979), who documented cultural differences in emblematic gestures between Japanese, Americans, and New Guineans. Morris and his colleagues (Morris, Collett, Marsh, & O'Shaughnessy, 1980) have also well documented many cultural differences in gestures. The American A-OK sign, for example, is an obscene gesture in many cultures of Europe, having sexual implications. Placing both hands at the side of one's head and pointing upward with the forefingers signals one is angry in some cultures; in others, however, it means that one wants sex.

Culture and Gaze. Research on humans and nonhuman primates has shown that gaze is associated with dominance, power, or aggression (Fehr & Exline, 1987) and affiliation and nurturance (Argyle & Cook, 1976). Fehr and Exline suggested that the affiliative aspects of gazing begin in infancy, as infants attend to adults as their source of care and protection. Cultures create rules concerning gazing and visual attention, however, because both aggression and affiliation are behavioral tendencies that are important for group stability and maintenance. Cross-cultural research has documented differences in these rules. Arabs, for example, have been found to gaze much longer and more directly at their partners than do Americans (Hall, 1963; Watson & Graves, 1966). Watson (1970), who classified 30 countries as either a "contact" culture (those that facilitated physical touch or contact during interaction) or a "noncontact" culture, found that contact cultures engaged in more gazing and had more direct orientations when interacting with others, less interpersonal distance, and more touching. Within the United States, there are also differences in gaze and visual behavior between different ethnic groups (Exline, Jones, & Maciorowski, 1977; LaFrance & Mayo, 1976).

Culture and Interpersonal Space. Hall (1966, 1973) specified four different levels of interpersonal space use depending on social relationship type: intimate, personal, social, and public. Whereas people of all cultures seem to make these distinctions, they differ in the spaces they attribute to them. Arab males, for example, tend to sit closer to each other than American males, with more direct, confrontational types of body orientations (Watson & Graves, 1966). They also were found to use greater eye contact and to speak in louder voices. Arabs, at least in the past, learned to interact with others at distances close enough to feel the other person's breath (Hall, 1963). Furthermore, Latin Americans tend to interact more closely than do students of European backgrounds (Forston & Larson, 1968), and Indonesians tend to sit closer than Australians (Noesjirwan, 1977, 1978). Italians interact more closely than either Germans or Americans (Shuter, 1977), and Colombians were found to interact at closer distances than did Costa Ricans (Shuter, 1976).

Culture and Other Nonverbal Behaviors. Other studies have documented cultural differences in other nonverbal behaviors as well, such as in the semantic meanings attributed to body postures (Kudoh & Matsumoto, 1985; Matsumoto & Kudoh, 1987) and vocal characteristics and hand and arm movements (Vrij & Winkel, 1991, 1992). Collectively, the evidence provides more than ample support for the contention that culture plays a large role in molding our nonverbal behaviors, which comprise an important part of the communication process. The largest research literature in the area of culture and nonverbal behavior, however, concerns facial expressions of emotion. In the next section, I review the most relevant research in this area of study, illustrating the universal and culture-specific aspects of both the encoding and decoding of facial expressions of emotion.

◆ Culture and Facial Expressions of Emotion

THE UNIVERSALITY OF FACIAL EXPRESSIONS

Questions concerning the universality of facial expression find their roots in Charles Darwin's work. Darwin's thesis, summarized in *The Expression of Emotion in Man and Animals*, suggested that emotions and their expressions had evolved across species, were evolutionarily adaptive, biologically innate, and universal across all human and even nonhuman primates. According to Darwin (1872/1998), humans, regardless of race or culture, possess the ability to express emotions in exactly the same ways, primarily through their faces. Between the time of Darwin's original writing and the 1960s, however, only seven studies attempted to test the universality of facial expression. These studies were flawed methodologically in a number of ways, so that unequivocal data speaking to the issue of the possible universality of emotional expression did not emerge at that time (Ekman, Friesen, & Ellsworth, 1972).

It was not until the mid-1960s when psychologist Sylvan Tomkins, a pioneer in modern studies of human emotion, joined forces independently with Paul Ekman and Carroll Izard to conduct the first of what have become known today as the "universality studies." These researchers obtained

judgments of faces thought to express emotions panculturally and demonstrated that all cultures agreed on the emotions portrayed in the expressions, providing the first evidence for their universality (Ekman, 1972, 1973; Ekman & Friesen, 1971; Ekman, Sorenson, & Friesen, 1969; Izard, 1971). Collectively, these findings demonstrated the existence of six universal expressions—anger, disgust, fear, happiness, sadness, and surprise—as judges from around the world agreed on what emotion was portrayed in the faces.

Yet the judgment studies were not the only evidence that came to bear on the question of emotion universality. Some of the most important findings related to universality were from Ekman's (1972) cross-cultural study of expressions that occurred spontaneously in reaction to emotion-eliciting films. In that study, American and Japanese participants viewed a neutral and highly stressful film (comprised of four separate clips), while their facial behaviors were recorded throughout the entire experiment. Ekman coded the last 3 minutes of facial behavior videotaped during the neutral films and the entire 3 minutes of the last stress film clip. The coding identified facial muscle configurations associated with the six emotions mentioned previously; all corresponded to the facial expressions portrayed in the stimuli used in their judgment studies (Ekman, 1972; Ekman et al., 1969, 1972). Research following Ekman's original study described above and using American, Japanese, German, Canadian, and French participants has continued to mount convincing evidence for the universality of facial expressions of emotion (see Table 12.1).

Considerable evidence documenting and converging in their support of the universality of facial expressions of emotion has come from studies with different bases than those following Ekman (1972). For

Table 12.1   Studies Examining Spontaneous Facial Expressions of Emotion

Citation	Participants	Eliciting Stimuli	Measurement System	Emotions[a]
Rosenberg & Ekman, 1994	American university students	Videos selected for their ability to elicit primarily disgust and secondarily fear	FACS	Disgust, sadness, fear, happiness, contempt, and anger
Ruch, 1995	German university students	Slides of jokes and cartoons	FACS	Happiness
Ruch, 1993	German university students	Slides of jokes and cartoons	FACS	Happiness
Frank, Ekman, & Friesen, 1993, Study 1	American university students	Films designed to elicit various emotions	FACS	Happiness
Gosselin, Kirouac, & Dore,1995, Study 1	Actors from the Conservatory of Dramatic Arts in Quebec	Actors were asked to interpret 2 of 24 scenarios designed to elicit happiness, fear, anger, surprise, sadness, and disgust	FACS	Happiness, fear, anger, surprise, sadness, and disgust
Ekman, Matsumoto, & Friesen, 1997	Depressed inpatients	Intake and discharge interviews	FACS and EMFACS	Happiness, contempt, anger, disgust, fear, and sadness
Berenbaum & Oltmanns, 1992	German schizophrenic and psychosomatic patients, and healthy controls	Engaging in a political conversation with a partner they had never met before	EMFACS	Contempt, disgust, anger, sadness, fear, surprise, and happiness
Ellgring, 1986	German depressed patients	Interviews	FACS	Happiness
Heller & Haynal, 1994	French depressed patients	Interviews with the patient's psychiatrists	FACS and EMFACS	Contempt
Keltner, Moffitt, & Stouthamer-Loeber, 1995	American adolescents with behavior problems	Administration of the WISC-R	EMFACS	Anger, fear, and sadness

(Continued)

Table 12.1 (Continued)

Citation	Participants	Eliciting Stimuli	Measurement System	Emotions[a]
Chesney et al., 1990	American salaried employees in managerial positions at an aerospace firm	Structured interview designed to assess Type A behavior	FACS	Disgust, fear, sadness, happiness, anger, contempt, and surprise
Camras, Oster, Campos, Miyake, & Bradshaw, 1992	American and Japanese infants	Arm restraint that produces distress	FACS	Anger, sadness, fear, and happiness

NOTE: FACS, Facial action coding system; EMFACS, emotion facial action coding system; JACFEE, Japanese and Caucasian facial expressions of emotions; WISC-R, Weschler Intelligence Scale for Children—Revised.

a. Corresponding to facial muscle configurations coded in the face that match those in JACFEE.

instance, studies have shown that the universal facial expressions of emotion occur in congenitally blind individuals (Charlesworth & Kreutzer, 1973). Research on nonhuman primates has also demonstrated that the expressions that are universal to humans also occur in animals, and that animals have many different yet stable signals of emotion (Chevalier-Skolnikoff, 1973; Geen, 1992; Hauser, 1993; Snowdon, 2003). Likewise, the emotions portrayed in the universal facial expressions correspond to emotion taxonomies in different languages around the world (Romney, Boyd, Moore, Batchelder, & Brazill, 1996; Romney, Moore, & Rusch, 1997; Shaver, Murdaya, & Fraley, 2001; Shaver, Wu, & Schwartz, 1992).

There is also cross-cultural similarity in the physiological responses to emotion when these facial expressions are used as markers, in both the autonomic nervous system and brain activity (Davidson, 2003; Ekman, Levenson, & Friesen, 1983; Levenson, Ekman, & Friesen, 1990; Levenson, Ekman, Heider, & Friesen, 1992; Tsai & Levenson,

1997). This similarity exists in people of as widely divergent cultures as the United States and the Minangkabau of West Sumatra, Indonesia. In addition, there is universality in the antecedents that bring about emotion (Scherer, 1997a, 1997b).

CULTURAL DIFFERENCES IN EXPRESSING EMOTION: CULTURAL DISPLAY RULES

Despite the existence of universal facial expressions of emotion, people around the world do express emotions differently. The first evidence for cultural differences in expression was Friesen's (1972) study, in which the spontaneous expressions of Americans and Japanese were examined as they viewed highly stressful films in two conditions, first alone and then a second time in the presence of an older, male experimenter. In the first condition, the American and Japanese participants were similar in their expressions of disgust, sadness, fear, and anger; in the second condition, however, cultural differences emerged. Whereas the Americans continued to express their negative emotions, the Japanese were more likely to smile.

Other researchers have also examined cultural differences in emotional expression (Argyle, Henderson, Bond, Iizuka, & Contarello, 1986; Edelmann et al., 1987; Gudykunst & Nishida, 1984; Gudykunst & Ting-Toomey, 1988; Noesjirwan, 1978; Waxer, 1985). A recent study from my laboratory extended Ekman and Friesen's (Ekman, 1972; Friesen, 1972) original findings. In this study (Matsumoto & Kupperbusch, 2001), European American females were classified as either individualistic or collectivistic based on their responses to an individual difference measure (Matsumoto, Weissman, Preston, Brown, & Kupperbusch, 1997) and were then videotaped unobtrusively as they watched films designed to elicit positive and negative emotion, first alone and then in the presence of an experimenter. They self-rated their emotional responses to both films in both conditions, and samples of their emotional expressions were judged by a separate group of decoders.

Both individualists and collectivists experienced the films as intended, and there was no difference in their expressions when they were alone. With the experimenter, however, the collectivists attenuated their negative expressions and more often masked them with smiles. This finding is the same that Ekman and Friesen (Ekman, 1972; Friesen, 1972) reported previously, and the remarkable thing about this study is that the entire sample was of European American females who were classified based solely on their responses to a questionnaire assessing individualism and collectivism. The collectivists also attenuated their expressions of positive emotion when in the presence of the experimenter (Ekman and Friesen's studies did not test positive emotions); thus, the effects of culture on expression were not limited to negative emotions.

Ekman and Friesen (1969) coined the term *cultural display rules* to account for cultural differences in facial expressions of emotion. These are rules learned early in childhood that help individuals manage and modify their emotional expressions depending on social circumstances. Ekman and Friesen used the concept to explain the American–Japanese cultural differences in expression they observed, suggesting that in the first condition of their experiment there was no reason for display rules to modify expressions because the participants were alone and their display rules were inoperative; in the second condition display rules dictated that the Japanese mask their negative emotions in the presence of the experimenter (Ekman, 1972; Friesen, 1972).

After the original inception and documentation of display rules, published cross-cultural research was dormant until Matsumoto's (1990) study examining display rules in Americans and Japanese. Participants saw faces portraying seven emotions and rated the appropriateness of each in eight social situations involving people of varying intimacy and status. Americans rated negative emotions more appropriately than did the Japanese in ingroups, whereas the Japanese rated negative emotions more appropriately than Americans in outgroups; the Japanese also rated negative emotions more appropriately than Americans toward lower status individuals. Matsumoto (1993) used the same methodology to document differences in display rules among four ethnic groups within the United States.

When the concept of display rules was proposed originally as a mechanism of expression management, Ekman and Friesen (1969, 1975) noted six ways in which expressions may be managed when emotion is aroused. Of course, individuals can express emotions as they feel them with no modification. But individuals can also amplify (exaggerate) or deamplify (minimize) their expressions; for instance, feelings of sadness may be intensified (amplification) at funerals or minimized (deamplification) at weddings. People can mask or conceal their emotions by expressing something other than what they feel, as when nurses or physicians hide their emotions when speaking with patients with terminal illness, or when employees in service industries (e.g., flight attendants) interact with customers. Individuals may also learn to neutralize their expressions, expressing nothing, such as when playing poker (poker face) and to qualify their feelings by expressing emotions in combination, such as when feelings of sadness are mixed with a smile, with the smile commenting on the sadness, saying "I'll be OK." All these behavioral responses have been found to occur when spontaneous expressive behaviors have been studied (Cole, 1986; Ekman & Rosenberg, 1998).

Recently, my colleagues and I created the Display Rule Assessment Inventory (DRAI), in which participants choose a behavioral response when they experience different emotions in different social situations (Matsumoto, Takeuchi, Andayani, Kouznetsova, & Krupp, 1998; Matsumoto, Choi, Hirayama, Domae, & Yamaguchi, 2005). The emotions were those that previous research has shown to be universally expressed and recognized: anger, contempt, disgust, fear, happiness, sadness, and surprise; these were selected because universality served as a basis by which to examine display rules initially and by which comparisons across cultures would be meaningful. To build internal consistency, a synonym for each emotion label was also included in the initial DRAI—hostility, defiance, aversion, worry, joy, gloom, and shock, respectively— resulting in a total of 14 emotions terms. Participants are asked to consider what they

would do if they felt each emotion in four social situations: with family members, close friends, colleagues, and strangers. These categories were chosen because they represent a broad range of social categories within which people interact, and because previous research has demonstrated considerable variability in cultural values and attitudes across these social situations (Brewer & Kramer, 1985; Tajfel, 1982).

In our first study using the DRAI (Matsumoto, Takeuchi, Andayani, Kouznetsova, & Krupp, 1998), participants from the United States, Japan, South Korea, and Russia completed the DRAI along with an individual-level measure of individualism-collectivism. Our results showed that Russians exerted the highest control over their expressions, followed by South Koreans and Japanese; Americans had the lowest scores. Significant sex differences were also found, with females exerting more control on anger, contempt, disgust, and across all emotions when with family members, and males exerting more control on fear and surprise.

Our most recent study involving the DRAI (Matsumoto, Yoo, Hirayama, & Petrova, 2005) provided evidence for its internal and temporal reliability and for its content, convergent (with measures of emotion regulation), discriminant (correlations with personality controlling for emotion regulation), external, and concurrent predictive validity (with personality). The findings also indicated that expression regulation occurs in the various ways discussed earlier, and not on a simple expression-suppression dimension. Additionally, there were consistent and predictable cultural differences among American, Russian, and Japanese participants. For instance, Americans and Russians both expressed anger and contempt more than Japanese. Americans expressed fear and disgust more than Russians, and Americans expressed happiness more than did Russians and

Japanese. The Japanese participants de-amplified more than both the Americans and the Russians. Americans amplified more than Russians on sadness and disgust, whereas Japanese amplified surprise and fear more than Russians. Japanese qualified sadness more than Russians, but the Russians qualified their happiness more than both Japanese and Americans.

CULTURAL INFLUENCES ON JUDGMENTS OF EMOTION

As discussed earlier, studies examining judgments of facial expressions were instrumental in the original universality studies and have been replicated by many authors, and Elfenbein and Ambady's (2002) meta-analysis of judgment studies of emotion (not limited to facial expressions) demonstrated convincingly that people around the world recognize emotions at levels well above chance accuracy. Research of the last decade and a half has demonstrated that people of different cultures are similar in other aspects of emotion judgment as well. For example, there is pancultural similarity in judgments of relative intensity among faces; that is, when comparing expressions, people of different countries agree on which is more strongly expressed (Ekman et al., 1987; Matsumoto & Ekman, 1989). There is also evidence of pancultural agreement in the association between perceived expression intensity and inferences about subjective experiences (Matsumoto, Kasri, & Kooken, 1999). People of different cultures have also been found to agree on the secondary emotions portrayed in an expression (Biehl et al., 1997; Ekman et al., 1987; Matsumoto & Ekman, 1989), suggesting pancultural agreement in the multiple meanings derived from universal faces. This agreement may exist because of overlap in the semantics of the emotion categories, antecedents and elicitors of emotion, or in the facial configurations themselves.

There are many cultural differences in emotion judgments as well. Although people of all cultures recognize the universal faces at levels well beyond chance, they differ on the absolute level of recognition (Biehl et al., 1997; Elfenbein & Ambady, 2002; Matsumoto, 1989, 1992; Matsumoto et al., 2002). In an attempt to explain why cultures differ in emotion recognition rates, Matsumoto (1989) compiled recognition accuracy data from 15 cultures reported in four studies, and correlated them with Hofstede's (1980) four cultural dimensions. Individualism was positively correlated with recognition rates of negative emotions. An independent meta-analysis by Schimmack (1996) also indicated that individualism predicted emotion recognition levels. These findings may be related to the fact that individualism is also correlated positively with emotional expression (Matsumoto & Koopmann, 2004). Individualistic cultures may foster the free and open expression of emotion, thereby promoting the more accurate judgment of emotion as well. Just as cultures have display rules that govern the management of emotional expression, they may have "cultural decoding rules" that help manage the judgments of emotions in others.

There are cultural differences in judgments of the intensity of expressions as well. Ekman et al.'s (1987) study of 10 countries was the first to document such differences, with Asians rating emotions at lower intensity than non-Asians. Although this finding has been replicated a number of times (Biehl et al., 1997; Matsumoto, 1990, 1993), more recent research indicated that the cultural differences differ depending on whether observers rate the external display or the presumed internal experience. Matsumoto et al. (1999) tested this idea by comparing American and Japanese judgments on both types of ratings and found that Americans rated external display more intensely than the Japanese, but that the Japanese rated internal experience more intensely than Americans. Within-country analyses indicated no significant differences between the two ratings for the Japanese; the Americans, however, rated external displays more intensely than they rated subjective experience.

These findings were extended by Matsumoto and colleagues (2002) by having American and Japanese observers rate expressions expressed at 0%, 50%, 100%, and 125% intensities. The data for the 100% and 125% expressions replicated the previous findings: Americans rated external display significantly higher than internal experience, whereas there were no differences for the Japanese. Also, there were no differences between external and internal ratings for either Americans or Japanese on 0% expressions, which were expected. On 50% expressions, however, the findings were intriguing. Whereas there was no difference between external and internal ratings for the Americans, the Japanese rated internal experience higher than external display. We interpreted these findings as suggesting that for weaker expressions, Japanese may assume that a display rule is operating, and may thus infer more emotion being felt than is actually displayed. When Americans see a weak expression, however, there need not be any such assumption; thus, they interpret the same amount of emotion felt as expressed. For strong expressions, Japanese may assume that the context was such that the expression was justified; thus, they infer a level of emotion felt that is commensurate with what is shown. When Americans see a strong expression, however, they know that there is a display rule to exaggerate one's feelings; thus, they compensate for this display rule by inferring less emotion felt.

One limitation of all the studies cited in this section was that, although the findings were interpreted as occurring as a function of cultural display rules, none actually measured display rules and linked them to the judgments. A recent study from our laboratory, however, has closed this loop. In this study, American and Japanese participants completed the DRAI and viewed a series of facial expressions of emotion portrayed at high and low intensities (Matsumoto, Choi, et al., 2005). They made three judgments for each face: a categorical judgment of which emotion was portrayed, and intensity ratings of the strength of the external display and the presumed subjective experience of the expressor. American and Japanese judges thought that the expressors of high intensity expressions displayed the emotions more strongly than they felt them. When judging the low intensity expressions, Americans and Japanese also rated the expressor's internal experience higher than they did the external display, but the effect was significantly larger for the Japanese. All these differences were mediated by display rules as assessed by the DRAI, suggesting that one's own rules for expression management influences one's judgments of expression management in others.

A POSSIBLE INGROUP ADVANTAGE IN RECOGNIZING EMOTIONS?

One type of cultural difference in judgment that has recently received attention concerns the possibility of an ingroup advantage in emotion recognition (Elfenbein & Ambady, 2002). This is defined as the tendency for *members of a cultural group to be more accurate in recognizing the emotions of members of their own cultural group than of other, relatively more disparate groups.* Although previous research testing this hypothesis (Boucher & Carlson, 1980; Kilbride & Yarczower, 1983; Markham & Wang, 1996) provided mixed results, Elfenbein and her colleagues have recently reported a number of studies in support of it (Elfenbein & Ambady, 2002, 2003a, 2003b; Elfenbein, Mandal, Ambady, & Harizuka, 2002).

Elsewhere, I have suggested that studies must meet two methodological requirements to test the ingroup hypothesis adequately (Matsumoto, 2002). First, studies should employ balanced designs in which all judge cultures view expressions portrayed by members of all the other cultures in the study. Second, because balanced studies include stimuli expressed by people of multiple cultures, it is necessary to ensure that the stimuli are equivalent across the cultural groups in terms of their physical signaling properties related to emotion. Given both of these concerns, Matsumoto (2002) concluded that Elfenbein and Ambady's (2002) original meta-analysis could not support the ingroup hypothesis because they did not review the studies as to whether or not they met these two requirements.

When balanced studies are examined as to whether or not they employed stimuli that were equivalent in their physical signaling properties or not, the data are clear: All the studies reported by Elfenbein and colleagues to date supporting the ingroup hypothesis have used stimuli that were not equivalent across the cultural groups (Elfenbein & Ambady, 2003a, 2003b; Elfenbein et al., 2002; Elfenbein, Mandal, Ambady, Harizuka, & Kumar, 2004). Furthermore, a close examination of the balanced studies they reviewed in Table 4 of their original meta-analysis (Elfenbein & Ambady, 2002) shows that only five studies provide evidence that the physical signaling properties of the expressions used as stimuli were equivalent across the expressor ethnicities (Albas, McCluskey, & Albas, 1976; Kilbride & Yarczower, 1983; McCluskey, Albas, Niemi, Cuevas, & Ferrer, 1975; McCluskey & Albas, 1981; Mehta, Ward, & Strongman, 1992).

Four of these were associated with non-significant interaction *F*s that test the ingroup effect. Two involved studies of facial expressions (Kilbride & Yarczower, 1983; Mehta et al., 1992), and both these involved facial action coding system (FACS) coding of the facial muscles in the expressions. The FACS codes were equivalent but not exactly the same across the expressor ethnicities as they are in the Japanese and Caucasian facial expressions of emotion (JACFEE), thus allowing for minor cultural differences in the expressions to exist (perhaps, corresponding to Elfenbein and Ambady's, 2002, 2003a; Elfenbein et al., 2002, "emotion dialects").

When balanced studies employ expressions that are equivalent in their physical signaling properties (the JACFEE), there is no support for the ingroup hypothesis (Matsumoto, 2002; Matsumoto & Choi, 2004). This is the case whether the expressions being judged are full-face, high intensity expressions, or low intensity expressions where signal clarity is weaker (Matsumoto & Choi, 2004). Future studies will need to isolate differences in expressions across encoder cultures while holding constant nonmorphological features of the face that may contribute to emotion signaling. There are many aspects of the face that may contribute to emotion signaling, including facial physiognomy, cosmetics, and hairstyle, in addition to the actual expressions themselves (Ekman, 1979; Matsumoto & Choi, 2004). Research is yet to test the possible contributory roles of these aspects of the face to emotion signaling, which is a possible rich source of information in the future.

◆ **Conclusion**

In considering cultural influences on nonverbal behavior, it is first important to recognize the universal bases of those behaviors, and to realize that culture's influence on nonverbal behaviors occurs above and beyond the universal bases of those behaviors that we are all born with. With regard to emotion communication, we all start with the same base of universal, pancultural expressions. We learn rules about how to modify and manage these expressions based on social circumstance (cultural display rules), and we learn rules about how to manage our judgments of them (cultural decoding rules). Whereas we all recognize universal emotions at levels well beyond chance, there are cultural influences on the *absolute* levels of recognition accuracy and on judgments of external intensity and internal subjective experience.

Most of our knowledge concerning culture and nonverbal behaviors comes from studies of facial expressions of emotion. The few cross-cultural studies on other nonverbal behaviors that do exist suggest considerable cultural differences in these. Yet there may be universal aspects to these other nonverbal behaviors that research has just not yet uncovered. Examples include the raising of one or both arms in achievement or clapping as a sign of approval. Future research will not only continue to unravel the influence of culture on facial expressions but will also need to delve into these other possibilities for other nonverbal behaviors.

◆ References

Albas, D. C., McCluskey, K. W., & Albas, C. A. (1976). Perception of the emotional content of speech: A comparison of two Canadian groups. *Journal of Cross-Cultural Psychology, 7,* 481–490.

Argyle, M., & Cook, M. (1976). *Gaze and mutual gaze.* New York: Cambridge University Press.

Argyle, M., Henderson, M., Bond, M., Iizuka, Y., & Contarello, A. (1986). Cross-cultural variations in relationship rules. *International Journal of Psychology, 21,* 287–315.

Barnlund, D., & Araki, S. (1985). Intercultural encounters: The management of compliments by Japanese and Americans. *Journal of Cross-Cultural Psychology, 16,* 9–26.

Barnlund, D., & Yoshioka, M. (1990). Apologies: Japanese and American styles. *International Journal of Intercultural Relations, 14,* 193–206.

Berenbaum, H., & Oltmanns, T. (1992). Emotional experience and expression in schizophrenia and depression. *Journal of Abnormal Psychology, 101,* 37–44.

Berry, J. W., Poortinga, Y. H., Segall, M. H., & Dasen, P. R. (1992). *Cross-cultural psychology: Research and applications.* New York: Cambridge University Press.

Biehl, M., Matsumoto, D., Ekman, P., Hearn, V., Heider, K., Kudoh, T., et al. (1997). Matsumoto and Ekman's Japanese and Caucasian facial expressions of emotion (JACFEE): Reliability data and cross-national differences. *Journal of Nonverbal Behavior, 21,* 3–21.

Boas, F., & Efron, D. F. (1936). A comparative investigation of gestural behavior patterns in "racial" groups living under different as well as similar environmental conditions. *Psychological Bulletin, 33,* 760.

Boucher, J. D., & Carlson, G. E. (1980). Recognition of facial expression in three cultures. *Journal of Cross-Cultural Psychology, 11,* 263–280.

Brewer, M. B., & Kramer, R. M. (1985). The psychology of intergroup attitudes and behavior. *Annual Review of Psychology, 36,* 219–243.

Buss, D. M. (1991). Evolutionary personality psychology. *Annual Review of Psychology, 42,* 459–491.

Buss, D. M. (2001). Human nature and culture: An evolutionary psychological perspective. *Journal of Personality, 69,* 955–978.

Camras, L. A., Oster, H., Campos, J., Miyake, K., & Bradshaw, D. (1992). Japanese and American infants' responses to arm restraint. *Developmental Psychology, 28,* 578–583.

Charlesworth, W. R., & Kreutzer, M. A. (1973). Facial expressions of infants and children. In P. Ekman (Ed.), *Darwin and facial expression* (pp. 91–168). New York: Academic Press.

Chen, G. M. (1995). Differences in self-disclosure patterns among Americans versus Chinese: A comparative study. *Journal of Cross-Cultural Psychology, 26,* 84–91.

Chesney, M. A., Ekman, P., Friesen, W. V., Black, G. W., et al. (1990). Type a behavior pattern: Facial behavior and speech components. *Psychosomatic Medicine, 52,* 307–319.

Chevalier-Skolnikoff, S. (1973). Facial expression of emotion in nonhuman primates. In P. Ekman (Ed.), *Darwin and facial expression* (pp. 11–89). New York: Academic Press.

Cole, P. M. (1986). Children's spontaneous control of facial expression. *Child Development, 57,* 1309–1321.

Darwin, C. (1998). *The expression of emotion in man and animals.* New York: Oxford University Press. (Original work published 1872)

Davidson, R. J. (2003). Parsing the subcomponents of emotion and disorders of emotion: Perspectives from affective neuroscience. In R. J. Davidson, K. R. Scherer, & H. H. Goldsmith (Eds.), *Handbook of affective sciences* (pp. 8–24). New York: Oxford University Press.

Edelmann, R. J., Asendorpf, J., Contarello, A., Georgas, J., Villanueva, C., & Zammuner, V. (1987). Self-reported verbal and nonverbal strategies for coping with embarrassment in five European cultures. *Social Science Information, 26,* 869–883.

Efron, D. (1941). *Gesture and environment.* Oxford, England: King's Crown Press.

Ekman, P. (1972). Universal and cultural differences in facial expression of emotion. In J. R. Cole (Ed.), *Nebraska symposium on motivation, 1971* (pp. 207–283). Lincoln: Nebraska University Press.

Ekman, P. (1973). *Darwin and facial expression; A century of research in review.* New York: Academic Press.

Ekman, P. (1976). Movements with precise meanings. *Journal of Communication, 26*(3), 14–26.

Ekman, P. (1979). Facial signs: Facts, fantasies, and possibilities. In T. Sebeok (Ed.),

Sight, sound, and sense (pp. 124–156). Bloomington: Indiana University Press.

Ekman, P., & Friesen, W. (1969). The repertoire of nonverbal behavior: Categories, origins, usage, and coding. *Semiotica, 1,* 49–98.

Ekman, P., & Friesen, W. (1971). Constants across culture in the face and emotion. *Journal of Personality and Social Psychology, 17,* 124–129.

Ekman, P., & Friesen, W. V. (1975). *Unmasking the face; a guide to recognizing emotions from facial clues.* Englewood Cliffs, NJ: Prentice Hall.

Ekman, P., Friesen, W. V., & Ellsworth, P. (1972). *Emotion in the human face: Guidelines for research and an integration of findings.* New York: Pergamon Press.

Ekman, P., Friesen, W. V., O'Sullivan, M., Chan, A., Diacoyanni-Tarlatzis, I., Heider, K., et al. (1987). Universals and cultural differences in the judgments of facial expressions of emotion. *Journal of Personality and Social Psychology, 53,* 712–717.

Ekman, P., Levenson, R. W., & Friesen, W. V. (1983). Autonomic nervous system activity distinguishes among emotions. *Science, 221,* 1208–1210.

Ekman, P., Matsumoto, D., & Friesen, W. (1997). Facial expression in affective disorders. In P. Ekman & E. L. Rosenberg (Eds.), *What the face reveals: Basic and applied studies of spontaneous expression using the facial action coding system (FACs)* (pp. 331–341). New York: Oxford University Press.

Ekman, P., & Rosenberg, E. L. (Eds.). (1998). *What the face reveals: Basic and applied studies of spontaneous expression using the facial action coding system (FACs).* New York: Oxford University Press.

Ekman, P., Sorenson, E. R., & Friesen, W. V. (1969). Pancultural elements in facial displays of emotion. *Science, 164,* 86–88.

Elfenbein, H. A., & Ambady, N. (2002). On the universality and cultural specificity of emotion recognition: A meta-analysis. *Psychological Bulletin, 128,* 205–235.

Elfenbein, H. A., & Ambady, N. (2003a). Cultural similarity's consequences: A distance perspective on cross-cultural differences in emotion recognition. *Journal of Cross-Cultural Psychology, 34,* 92–110.

Elfenbein, H. A., & Ambady, N. (2003b). When familiarity breeds accuracy: Cultural exposure and facial emotion recognition. *Journal of Personality and Social Psychology, 85,* 276–290.

Elfenbein, H. A., Mandal, M. K., Ambady, N., & Harizuka, S. (2002). Cross-cultural patterns in emotion recognition: Highlighting design and analytic techniques. *Emotion, 2,* 75–84.

Elfenbein, H. A., Mandal, M. K., Ambady, N., Harizuka, S., & Kumar, S. (2004). Hemifacial differences in the in-group advantage in emotion recognition. *Cognition and Emotion, 18,* 613–629.

Ellgring, H. (1986). Nonverbal expression of psychological states in psychiatric patients. *European Archives of Psychiatry and Neurological Sciences, 236,* 31–34.

Exline, R. V., Jones, P., & Maciorowski, K. (1977, August). *Race, affiliative-conflict theory and mutual visual attention during conversation.* Paper presented at the American Psychological Association Annual Convention, San Francisco.

Fehr, B. J., & Exline, R. V. (1987). Social visual interactions: A conceptual and literature review. In A. W. Siegman & S. Feldstein (Eds.), *Nonverbal behavior and communication* (Vol. 2, pp. 225–326). Hillsdale, NJ: Erlbaum.

Forston, R. F., & Larson, C. U. (1968). The dynamics of space: An experimental study in proxemic behavior among Latin Americans and North Americans. *Journal of Communication, 18,* 109–116.

Frank, M. G., Ekman, P., & Friesen, W. V. (1993). Behavioral markers and recognizability of the smile of enjoyment. *Journal of Personality and Social Psychology, 64,* 83–93.

Friesen, W. V. (1972). *Cultural differences in facial expressions in a social situation: An experimental test of the concept of display rules.* Unpublished doctoral dissertation, University of California, San Francisco.

Friesen, W. V., Ekman, P., & Wallbott, H. (1979). Measuring hand movements. *Journal of Nonverbal Behavior, 4,* 97–112.

Geen, T. (1992). Facial expressions in socially isolated nonhuman primates: Open and closed programs for expressive behavior. *Journal of Research in Personality, 26,* 273–280.

Gosselin, P., Kirouac, G., & Dore, F. (1995). Components and recognition of facial expression in the communication of emotion by actors. *Journal of Personality and Social Psychology, 68,* 83–96.

Gudykunst, W. B., & Mody, B. (Eds.). (2001). *Handbook of international and intercultural communication.* Newbury Park, CA: Sage.

Gudykunst, W. B., & Nishida, T. (1984). Individual and cultural influences on uncertainty reduction. *Communication Monographs, 51,* 23–36.

Gudykunst, W. B., & Ting-Toomey, S. (1988). Culture and affective communication. *American Behavioral Scientist, 31,* 384–400.

Hall, E. T. (1963). A system for the notation of proxemic behaviors. *American Anthropologist, 65,* 1003–1026.

Hall, E. T. (1966). *The hidden dimension.* New York: Doubleday.

Hall, E. T. (1973). *The silent language.* New York: Anchor.

Hauser, M. (1993). Right hemisphere dominance for the production of facial expression in monkeys. *Science, 261,* 475–477.

Heller, M., & Haynal, V. (1994). Depression and suicide faces. *Cahiers Psychiatriques Genevois, 16,* 107–117.

Hofstede, G. H. (1980). *Culture's consequences: International differences in work-related values.* Beverly Hills: Sage.

Izard, C. E. (1971). *The face of emotion.* East Norwalk, CT: Appleton-Century-Crofts.

Jahoda, G. (1984). Do we need a concept of culture? *Journal of Cross-Cultural Psychology, 15,* 139–151.

Keltner, D., Moffitt, T., & Stouthamer-Loeber, M. (1995). Facial expressions of emotion and psychopathology in adolescent boys. *Journal of Abnormal Psychology, 104,* 644–652.

Kilbride, J. E., & Yarczower, M. (1983). Ethnic bias in the recognition of facial expressions. *Journal of Nonverbal Behavior, 8,* 27–41.

Kim, M. S., Hunter, J. E., Miyahara, A., Horvath, A. M., Bresnahan, M., & Yoon, H. J. (1996). Individual vs. culture-level dimensions of individualism and collectivism: Effects on preferred conversation styles. *Communication Monographs, 63,* 29–49.

Kroeber, A. L., & Kluckholn, C. (1963). *Culture: A critical review of concepts and definitions.* Cambridge, MA: Harvard University.

Kudoh, T., & Matsumoto, D. (1985). Cross-cultural examination of the semantic dimensions of body postures. *Journal of Personality and Social Psychology, 48,* 1440–1446.

LaFrance, M., & Mayo, C. (1976). Racial differences in gaze behavior during conversations: Two systematic observational studies. *Journal of Personality and Social Psychology, 33,* 547–552.

Levenson, R. W., Ekman, P., & Friesen, W. V. (1990). Voluntary facial action generates emotion-specific autonomic nervous system activity. *Psychophysiology, 27,* 363–384.

Levenson, R. W., Ekman, P., Heider, K., & Friesen, W. V. (1992). Emotion and autonomic nervous system activity in the Minangkabau of West Sumatra. *Journal of Personality and Social Psychology, 62,* 972–988.

Linton, R. (1936). *The study of man: An introduction.* New York: Appleton.

Linville, P. W., & Jones, E. E. (1980). Polarized appraisals of out-group members. *Journal of Personality and Social Psychology, 38,* 689–703.

Markham, R., & Wang, L. (1996). Recognition of emotion by Chinese and Australian children. *Journal of Cross-Cultural Psychology, 27,* 616–643.

Matsumoto, D. (1989). Cultural influences on the perception of emotion. *Journal of Cross-Cultural Psychology, 20,* 92–105.

Matsumoto, D. (1990). Cultural similarities and differences in display rules. *Motivation and Emotion, 14,* 195–214.

Matsumoto, D. (1992). American-Japanese cultural differences in the recognition of universal facial expressions. *Journal of Cross-Cultural Psychology, 23,* 72–84.

Matsumoto, D. (1993). Ethnic differences in affect intensity, emotion judgments, display rule attitudes, and self-reported emotional expression in an American sample. *Motivation and Emotion, 17,* 107–123.

Matsumoto, D. (2002). Methodological requirements to test a possible ingroup advantage in judging emotions across cultures: Comments on Elfenbein and Ambady and evidence. *Psychological Bulletin, 128,* 236–242.

Matsumoto, D., & Choi, J. W. (2004). *Exploring decoder sources of the ingroup advantage effect in recognizing facial expressions of emotions.* Unpublished manuscript.

Matsumoto, D., Choi, J. W., Hirayama, S., Domae, A., & Yamaguchi, S. (2005). *Culture, display rules, emotion regulation, and emotion judgments.* Manuscript submitted for publication.

Matsumoto, D., Consolacion, T., Yamada, H., Suzuki, R., Franklin, B., Paul, S., et al. (2002). American-Japanese cultural differences in judgments of emotional expressions of different intensities. *Cognition and Emotion, 16,* 721–747.

Matsumoto, D., & Ekman, P. (1989). American-Japanese cultural differences in intensity ratings of facial expressions of emotion. *Motivation and Emotion, 13,* 143–157.

Matsumoto, D., Kasri, F., & Kooken, K. (1999). American-Japanese cultural differences in judgments of expression intensity and subjective experience. *Cognition and Emotion, 13,* 201–218.

Matsumoto, D., & Koopmann, B. (2004). *Ecology, culture, personality, and emotional expression.* Unpublished manuscript.

Matsumoto, D., & Kudoh, T. (1987). Cultural similarities and differences in the semantic dimensions of body postures. *Journal of Nonverbal Behavior, 11,* 166–179.

Matsumoto, D., & Kupperbusch, C. (2001). Idiocentric and allocentric differences in emotional expression and experience. *Asian Journal of Social Psychology, 4,* 113–131.

Matsumoto, D., Takeuchi, S., Andayani, S., Kouznetsova, N., & Krupp, D. (1998). The contribution of individualism-collectivism to cross-national differences in display rules. *Asian Journal of Social Psychology, 1,* 147–165.

Matsumoto, D., Weissman, M., Preston, K., Brown, B., & Kupperbusch, C. (1997).

Context-specific measurement of individualism-collectivism on the individual level: The IC interpersonal assessment inventory (ICIAI). *Journal of Cross-Cultural Psychology, 28*, 743–767.

Matsumoto, D., Yoo, S. H., Hirayama, S., & Petrova, G. (2005). Validation of an individual-level measure of display rules: The display rule assessment inventory (DRAI). *Emotion, 5*, 23–40.

McCluskey, K., Albas, D., Niemi, R., Cuevas, C., & Ferrer, C. (1975). Cultural differences in the perception of the emotional content of speech: A study of the development of sensitivity in Canadian and Mexican children. *Developmental Psychology, 11*, 551–555.

McCluskey, K. W., & Albas, D. C. (1981). Perception of the emotional content of speech by Canadian and Mexican children, adolescents and adults. *International Journal of Psychology, 16*, 119–132.

Mehta, S. D., Ward, C., & Strongman, K. (1992). Cross-cultural recognition of posed facial expressions of emotion. *New Zealand Journal of Psychology, 21*, 74–77.

Minami, M., & McCabe, A. (1995). Rice balls and bear hunts: Japanese and North American family narrative patterns. *Journal of Child Language, 22*, 423–445.

Morris, D., Collett, P., Marsh, P., & O'Shaughnessy, M. (1980). *Gestures: Their origins and distribution.* New York: Scarborough.

Noesjirwan, J. (1977). Contrasting cultural patterns on interpersonal closeness in doctors: Waiting rooms in Sydney and Jakarta. *Journal of Cross-Cultural Psychology, 8*, 357–368.

Noesjirwan, J. (1978). A rule-based analysis of cultural differences in social behavior: Indonesia and Australia. *International Journal of Psychology, 13*, 305–316.

Nomura, N., & Barnlund, D. (1983). Patterns of interpersonal criticism in Japan and the United States. *International Journal of Intercultural Relations, 7*, 1–18.

Rohner, R. P. (1984). Toward a conception of culture for cross-cultural psychology. *Journal of Cross-Cultural Psychology, 15*, 111–138.

Romney, A. K., Boyd, J. P., Moore, C. C., Batchelder, W. H., & Brazill, T. J. (1996). Culture as shared cognitive representations. *Proceedings of the National Academy of Sciences of the United States of America, 93*, 4699–4705.

Romney, A. K., Moore, C. C., & Rusch, C. D. (1997). Cultural universals: Measuring the semantic structure of emotion terms in English and Japanese. *Proceedings of the National Academy of Sciences of the United States of America, 94*, 5489–5494.

Rosenberg, E. L., & Ekman, P. (1994). Coherence between expressive and experiential systems in emotion. *Cognition and Emotion, 8*, 201–229.

Ruch, W. (1993). Extraversion, alcohol, and enjoyment. *Personality and Individual Differences, 16*, 89–102.

Ruch, W. (1995). Will the real relationship between facial expression and affective experience stand up: The case of exhilaration. *Cognition and Emotion, 9*, 33–58.

Scherer, K. R. (1997a). Profiles of emotion-antecedent appraisal: Testing theoretical predictions across cultures. *Cognition and Emotion, 11*, 113–150.

Scherer, K. R. (1997b). The role of culture in emotion-antecedent appraisal. *Journal of Personality and Social Psychology, 73*, 902–922.

Schimmack, U. (1996). Cultural influences on the recognition of emotion by facial expressions: Individualist or Caucasian cultures? *Journal of Cross-Cultural Psychology, 27*, 37–50.

Seligman, M. E., & Hager, J. (1972). *Biological boundaries of learning.* New York: Appleton-Century-Crofts.

Shaver, P., Murdaya, U., & Fraley, R. C. (2001). The structure of the Indonesian emotion lexicon. *Asian Journal of Social Psychology, 4*, 201–224.

Shaver, P. R., Wu, S., & Schwartz, J. C. (1992). Cross-cultural similarities and differences in emotion and its representation. In M. S. Clark (Ed.), *Emotion: Review of personality and social psychology* (Vol. 13, pp. 175–212). Thousand Oaks, CA: Sage.

Shuter, R. (1976). Proxemics and tactility in Latin America. *Journal of Communication, 26*, 46–52.

Shuter, R. (1977). A field study of nonverbal communication in Germany, Italy, and the United States. *Communication Monographs, 44*, 298–305.

Snowdon, C. T. (2003). Expression of emotion in nonhuman animals. In R. J. Davidson, K. Scherer, & H. H. Goldsmith (Eds.), *Handbook of affective sciences* (pp. 457–480). New York: Oxford University Press.

Tajfel, H. (1982). Social psychology of intergroup relations. *Annual Review of Psychology, 33*, 1–39.

Triandis, H. C. (1972). *The analysis of subjective culture.* New York: Wiley.

Triandis, H. C., McCusker, C., & Hui, C. H. (1990). Multimethod probes of individualism and collectivism. *Journal of Personality and Social Psychology, 59*, 1006–1020.

Tsai, J. L., & Levenson, R. W. (1997). Cultural influences of emotional responding: Chinese American and European American dating couples during interpersonal conflict. *Journal of Cross-Cultural Psychology, 28*, 600–625.

Vrij, A., & Winkel, F. W. (1991). Cultural patterns in Dutch and Surinam nonverbal behavior: An analysis of simulated police/citizen encounters. *Journal of Nonverbal Behavior, 15*, 169–184.

Vrij, A., & Winkel, F. W. (1992). Cross-cultural police-citizen interactions: The influence of race, beliefs, and nonverbal communication on impression formation. *Journal of Applied Social Psychology, 22*, 1546–1559.

Watson, O. M. (1970). *Proxemic behavior: A cross-cultural study.* The Hague, The Netherlands: Mouton.

Watson, O. M., & Graves, T. D. (1966). Quantitative research in proxemic behavior. *American Anthropologist, 68*, 971–985.

Waxer, P. H. (1985). Video ethology: Television as a data base for cross-cultural studies in nonverbal displays. *Journal of Nonverbal Behavior, 9*, 111–120.

13

CASTING NONVERBAL BEHAVIOR IN THE MEDIA

Representations and Responses

◆ Valerie Manusov
University of Washington

◆ Adam Jaworski
Cardiff University

N onverbal behavior is often regarded as a set of actions that occur between interactants in face-to-face settings. Indeed, many of the nonverbal cues that we enact are done for and with other people in our everyday interactions. We also learn a great deal about how to behave nonverbally and what certain cues may mean through those interactions, particularly in our encounters with family (Halberstadt, 1986). Simultaneously, however, we are presented with a nonverbal code in our exposure to an array of *mediated* sources. By providing normative behaviors, interpretations for cues in context, and potential sanctions for not adhering to the code, media present and encourage a particular set of communication practices and ideologies.

This chapter focuses on the portrayal of nonverbal behavior in what have been defined as "traditional" media: television, film, and the press (for a review of online communication, see Walther, this volume). We argue that non-verbal cues as they occur within mediated coverage[1]—*and the talk about those cues within the coverage*—affect and reflect many deeply held beliefs about the nature, importance, and meaning of nonverbal behavior. To make this argument, we try to answer four questions: (1) How are nonverbal codes learned? (2) What is the content of those codes? (3) What codes exist in media talk about nonverbal cues? and (4) What consequences do such codes have for media users? Our goal in answering these questions is to reveal the processes—and the implications—of the media as an influencing factor for our understanding and use of nonverbal cues. We begin with how nonverbal cues may be learned.

◆ Learning the Nonverbal Code: Socialization

Socialization can be defined as a process of acquiring the cultural (including verbal and nonverbal) knowledge and skills needed to become competent members of particular communities. Communicative competencies are included within the larger socialization process (Hymes, 1972) and involve "socialization through language and socialization to use language" (Ochs & Schieffelin, 1986, p. 2) and learned nonverbal communication (see Feldman & Tyler, this volume). Saville-Troike (2003), in examining the socialization processes involved in nonverbal communication, discusses how, apart from universal nonverbal patterns, such as some of the facial expressions of emotion identified by Darwin (1872) (see also Ekman, 1972), children in different societies are exposed to—or taught explicitly—appropriate age-, gender-, class-, and other-related nonverbal behavior. These learned behavioral patterns

include when not to talk (i.e., to use silence; Jaworski, 1997), how to gesture (Morris, Collett, Marsh, & O'Shaughnessy, 1980), and rules for the use of time (Levine, 1997). Media play a large part in teaching the non-verbal code, at least within some societies.

AFFECTIVE SOCIALIZATION

An important part of being socialized into a particular communication community, and one that is particularly important for understanding nonverbal behavior and media exposure, involves learning the ways in which emotions ought to be expressed and experienced. Nonverbal cues are connected commonly with emotional expression (Ekman, 1972; but see Fridlund & Russell, this volume), and research has found that media perform a number of roles in the development and understanding of affect. These roles include the normative occurrence of nonverbal expressions of emotion (i.e., how often such emotions occur in everyday life) and the type of emotion presented as most common in interaction. Research has also examined media exposure and the development of particular affective skills. In addition, researchers have investigated the connection between nonverbal images in media and peoples' affective reactions to those presentations. This section reviews some arguments regarding the connection between media and affective understanding and response.

One of the most common areas of research connecting nonverbal media displays and affective socialization revolves around *what children may learn about emotional expression from media exposure*, particularly from television. Coats and Feldman (1995) (see also Coats, Feldman, & Philippot, 1999) argue that television is a primary means through which children (and others) learn how to encode and decode emotions and to discover when specific emotional expressions are appropriate (see also Saarni, 1985). More specifically, Wilson and Smith (1998) noted that many "young children encounter certain emotions and affective situations on television long before they experience those same phenomena in real life" (p. 533). Some children's shows even focus on teaching viewers to recognize and label feelings (Wilson & Smith, 1998).

Researchers have speculated on the reason for television's primacy in teaching young viewers about affect. For instance, Collins (1983) argues that young children are particularly affected by television portrayals of nonverbal expressions because, in part, their cognitive development may not yet allow them to focus as fully on verbal content; thus, nonverbal elements are more likely to capture their attention. Researchers suggest, however, some problems with such learning. For Houle and Feldman (1991), "Television presents salient, engaging, even prestigious models of emotionality and emotional expression . . . [But] it appears that the models television presents . . . are different from [the] models presented in children's social environments" (p. 329). Specifically, (1) televised emotional expressions appear, in general, much more often than they do in everyday interactions and (2) certain emotions (e.g., happiness, sadness, and anger) occur more commonly than others and in different proportions than they are likely to do in nonmediated contexts (Houle & Feldman, 1991). Furthermore, several studies have documented that families on television are more likely to deal with simple, rather than complex, emotions (e.g., Larson, 1993), which may be one explanation for why certain simple skills, but not complex skills, are facilitated by increased television viewing.

As would be expected, the *amount* of exposure appears to play a role in affective socialization. But the specific findings regarding affective learning and television viewing are less easy to predict. For example, Coats and Feldman (1995) assessed some of the potential outcomes of exposure to television on the use of nonverbal emotional expressions and found that children who were frequent TV watchers were *better* encoders of those emotions expressed commonly on television shows than were infrequent watchers; they were also better at encoding spontaneous (but poorer at encoding posed) emotional displays. The authors interpreted the findings about overall encoding skill cautiously, suggesting that children who watch TV frequently are less able to regulate their emotional expressions than are children less often exposed to television. An additional study found that frequent viewers could better decode others' facial expressions, but they "had a less differentiated, more simplistic view of the consequences of nonverbal self-presentation" (Feldman, Coats, & Spielman, 1996, p. 1718).

Other researchers have focused on what is being learned from media: the affective content and responses to affect. Weiss and Wilson (cited in Wilson & Smith, 1998), for instance, found that subplots in a television show that were humorous led children to have less negative evaluations of the story's main plot (i.e., an earthquake). Specifically, children who saw shows with a humorous subplot rated the main character's mood more positively and, perhaps more important, judged the occurrence of earthquakes in real-life as less severe than did those who did not have the positively affective subplot. Media images have also been found to induce feelings of horror: Wilson and Smith (1998) argued that children tend to be frightened by horrific images, with younger children more likely to be scared by visually frightening characters and older children frightened by seeing a televised victim's terror reactions.

COGNITIVE SOCIALIZATION

The work just reviewed suggests that media, particularly television, may play a role in emphasizing the expression of certain emotions over others, increasing skill for the spontaneous expression and interpretation of those emotions but possibly lessening other affective abilities. Socialization relevant to nonverbal communication is not only about affect, however. Semioticians and critical discourse analysts have long emphasized the role the media play in developing group consciousness: constructing, reinforcing, and legitimizing popular ideologies—or commonsense and normative attitudes and beliefs—about social reality (see Barthes, 1977; Fairclough, 1995).

Some of these ideas are, inevitably, about affect. As Wilson and Smith (1998) argue, for example, "Children's beliefs about emotional events in the real world can be influenced by television" (p. 540). Furthermore, the type and frequency of emotional expressions on television are not consistent with what occurs in everyday interactions, often leading frequent viewers to have an unrealistic image of "normal" social expression and self-presentation (Coats & Feldman, 1995; Zillmann, 1991). In particular, the typical straightforward connection between what a character is feeling and his or her expression of that feeling may lead to a simplified view of the strategic nature of nonverbal behavior, one that does not take dissemblance into account (Feldman et al., 1996; Houle & Feldman, 1991).

Additionally, however, the media provide cognitive structures about physical appearance. Specifically, scholars argue that media provide repeated images of ideal physical appearance that help to create relatively stable appearance schemata (Hargreaves & Tiggemann, 2002). Like affect schemata, appearance schemata have been found to be distortions from "actual" appearances. Most notably, "current societal standards for beauty inordinately emphasize the desirability of thinness" (Hargreaves & Tiggemann, 2002, p. 288), and the media—particularly fashion magazines—are a primary source of those standards. Thus, a likely schema resulting from media exposure is that thinness is desirable. Such exposure does not mean that people's schemata reflect the belief that most bodies are thin, however. Instead, one study showed that viewing appearance-related advertisements led people to believe that people's actual body size was, on average, *larger* than it is (Myers & Biocca, 1999).

Such beauty schemata are more common for females than for males, reflecting part of what Goffman (1976) labeled *gender stereotypes* and showing the importance of media in cognitive socialization about gender (which is often linked to physical appearance schemata). Using print advertising as a source of data, Goffman showed that pose, facial expression, and other forms of "body language" worked to depict women as shy, dreamy, gentle, helpless, and likely to be manipulated. Males' behaviors, what Browne (1998) calls "executive behaviors" (i.e., active and aggressive), engendered images of power, control, and dominance. For both female and male images, however, Goffman (1976) contended that the advertisements worked to create beliefs about sex differences that were unrealistic. More recent analyses of advertisements reflect that such images—represented in nonverbal cues—persist in adult-targeted advertisements (Klassen, Jasper, & Schwartz, 1993) as well as advertisements oriented to children (Browne, 1998; Kolbe, 1990; for a broader discussion of sex or gender and nonverbal communication, see Hall, this volume).

Gender schemata related to appearance are instituted in other ways. In his assessment of television commercials in India, for example, Roy (2005) followed other scholars in asserting that females are often presented as the province and property of men by the nonverbal cues directed toward them in photographic images. In his study, Roy addressed specifically where males in two commercials looked. His analysis confirmed that in addition to other choices regarding camera angle, dress, and music, males gazed at females in the commercial, but females did not gaze at males, and the gaze direction suggested that the females were there to be looked at and, in some cases, owned. Roy argued as well that the females in the commercials acted in a way that was complicit nonverbally with the gendered ideology (i.e., accepting the gaze).

Additionally, researchers have examined what children learn from media *about being consumers.* For example, Derscheid, Kwon, and Fang (1996) focused their argument on the processes of consumer socialization (i.e., how children learn about shopping, products, and stores). They argued that young children cannot read labels on products but can and do recognize nonlinguistic symbols (McNeal, 1987). This recognition may increase as media exposure increases. Furthermore, Derscheid et al. (1996) found that more exposure to TV or books by preschoolers was related to a greater ability to recognize nonlinguistic product symbols. More important, perhaps, this recognition often leads to product preference, and such preference has been linked with developing identities. Specifically, products and their affective symbols may become part of how children choose to identify themselves to others (Seiter, 1993). As Derscheid et al. (1996) assert, "TV, videos, and books allow children to imitate different personalities and act out fantasies while they construct their identity from media role models"

(p. 1173). Although learning about products and their linkage to self-identity may occur in the process of shopping with family and friends (Derscheid et al., 1996), it also is brought about through exposure to media (Seiter, 1993).

SUMMARY

The research on socialization relevant to nonverbal cues has focused primarily on two areas: (1) patterns of use in emotional expressions and development and (2) effects of schemata regarding ideal physical types and other aspects of identity. In both kinds of socialization, certain patterns and types of nonverbal cues are portrayed as more common or appropriate than others, and individuals' view of the self may be created and judged in relation to those patterns and types. In addition, media representations of emotional expressions, body size, and gender cues are often inconsistent with actual, everyday behavior, creating a code that exists in the media but not within the larger communicative system in which the code is embedded.

◆ The Content of Media Representations: What Is the Code?

To discern more fully the prevalence and nature of media portrayals of nonverbal behavior, a range of studies have investigated the content of nonverbal cues in the media. Many of these projects have used content analysis (or other quantitative approaches) to discern the message value of nonverbal cues within a particular media source; others provide a qualitative (often semiotic or critical discourse) analysis to identify the content of media coverage. The current section reviews some of this work, including scholarship whose aim is to critique the code's content.

UNCOVERING THE CODE

Considerable research has focused on media sources to discover the content of certain types of coverage, the relative frequency of such coverage, and possible links between the coverage and other important variables. Most commonly, researchers have investigated the coverage of particular *ideologies* and their potential associations with viewers' reactions. Content analyses have revealed, for instance, that television emphasizes physical attractiveness for women (Furnham & Mak, 1999), although recent trends suggest that attractiveness is emphasized increasingly for males as well (Bordo, 1999; Coupland, 2005).

The focus on appearance appears to reflect other ideologies. Coupland (2003) argues that advertisements, epitomized in skin-care and other beauty-product marketing, display an ageist ideology, representing getting older solely in physical terms and as fundamentally negative. In an analysis of the texts in British magazine skin-care advertisements, Coupland (2003) found that discourses are "scientized" and "marketized" and employed to provide desirable solutions to alleviate "premature ageing," particularly for women. She also argues that the ethos of body management and modification for the sake of maintaining a youthful appearance is sanctioned by the normalization of plastic surgery procedures, to which cosmetics have become an "inexpensive" precursor or temporary replacement (Coupland, 2005).

Other research has focused on the representation of different physical types in the media, presenting an ideology regarding a preference for thinness. For example, White, Brown, and Ginsburg (1999) content analyzed prime-time shows and afternoon soap operas and discerned that female characters tend to reflect only a few body types, whereas males are portrayed with more variation (although televised body types are, overall, thinner than in the actual population). Also, characters with larger bodies tended to be cast in fewer "romantic" contexts and are outfitted less revealingly than thinner characters. Larger bodied characters also tend to be older than their thinner counterparts (White et al., 1999).

CRITIQUING THE CODE

Although research has not investigated all aspects of the cultural code presented nonverbally in media sources, it has revealed an overall tendency to present idealized images (young, attractive, thin consumers). In response to this apparent code, a number of sociologic and discourse analytic scholars have critiqued the presentation of these ideologies (e.g., Bancroft, 1998; Jaworski, 2003; Shaw, 1998), with a particular concern with those ideologies surrounding the body. Their studies share a common premise that in late-modern, capitalist societies, personal identities have become more fluid and changeable than they used to be in traditional, premodern societies. In the contemporary world, scholars argue that identity has taken the form of a highly reflexive "project of self" linked to lifestyle choices and stances, consumption of goods and services, and mass media mediation of personal experience (i.e., a persistent but contingent and ongoing, often aspirational "program" that provides a focus for our daily activities, narratives, and encounters with others; c.f. Bauman, 1998; Coupland, Nussbaum, & Grossman, 1993; Giddens, 1991).

More central to nonverbal cues, Featherstone (1991) and Shilling (1993) provide evidence that the body has become a project site, fueled by media images of the "ideal" body, leading some to strive for "perfection" and leaving the others frustratingly "inadequate." Moreover, the theme of the ideal and "deviant" bodies is the dominant one in the literature dealing with media representations of the body and the viewers' or readers' reactions to these images. For example, a clear pattern emerged in Jaworski's (2003) discourse analytic study of the interviews with "ordinary" members of the public in the BBC four-part series *Naked*, broadcast in the United Kingdom in November and December 1998. Specifically, Jaworski observed that the four, roughly identified, age groups of the interviewees—middle aged, young adults, teenagers, and elderly—positioned talk about their bodies in terms of an ideal of youthful looks, good health, and sexual attractiveness and fulfillment. In contrast, the groups associated the deviant body image with prepuberty, old age, illness, and loss of sexual drive or partners.

The findings of this work are consistent with Urla and Terry's scholarship (1995) distinguishing between *normal* and *deviant* bodies (where *normal* does not equate with *natural*). Urla and Terry argued, like Jaworski (2003), that the power constraints imposed on body representations have led to the widespread acceptance of a binary split between acceptable and unacceptable body images: "normal versus deviant" or "healthy versus pathological." This is problematic because "deviance" is not so much linked to a particular set of body traits as to their perceived connotations imposed by a hegemonic social order and value system. In the case of the *Naked* documentary, the problem is exemplified in the comment by *The Sunday Times* TV critic, Edwards (1998), who sums up the program's impact as follows:

[Whereas] some people might tune in to Naked because of the promise of nudity, what keeps you watching is the stories, not the pictures, most dramatically that of Louise, a 15-year-old girl, deaf since birth, who says she would rather have a nose job than her hearing. Needless to say, there is nothing wrong with her nose at all. (Edwards, 1998, p. 29)

The concept of deviant bodies can be related to Goffman's presentation of *stigma* as "an undesired differentness from what we had anticipated" (Goffman, 1997, p. 74). The fear of the deviant body implies and can only be made meaningful in relation to the ideal, desirable, and normal body. Of course, neither is the ideal or idealized image of the body a given, nor is it the same and unchanging for all people and at all times. Just as individuals' identities, self-perceptions, other representations, and so on are flexible, changeable, and multiplex, so are the representations of the ideal body. At any given time in a specific community (social, gender, professional, or any other group), however, there are certain well-recognized and accepted principles on which the idea of an ideal body is based. This is, for example, evident from the different representations of the "ideal" body in the history of (Western) art, whether the representation is Leonardo da Vinci's drawing of the classically perfect *Vitruvian Man* (ca. 1490), Jacques-Louis David's painting, *Napoleon in His Study* (1812), depicting the Emperor as fusing the monarchichal body politic with revolutionary symbolism, or the practices of "normalizing" whiteness through the colonial photography of the 19th century representing the imperfect body of the racial "other" (Mirzoeff, 1995).

The discursive or visual representations of such ideal bodies are constituted by and are constitutive of the power relations operating within the community. With regard to the issue of social preoccupation with the "ideal versus deviant" bodies, Douglas (1966) argues that because the body can be used as a symbol of any bounded system, such as society, negotiating the margins of bodily acceptability can be indicative of negotiating the margins of society, and the shifting of these margins may have consequences for the centers of power. This preoccupation can explain our fear of, and at the same time fascination with, "freaks," "monsters," "cyborgs," "aliens," and so on (Eubanks, 1996). Yet our fascination with such pathologized and stigmatized bodies also has more of a personal dimension. Shildrick (2002) argues that "monsters" (i.e., the excluded bodies that fail to conform to any corporeal norm) may sometimes turn up in our own self-perceptions.

Instead of remaining at the outer regions of our embodied selves, "monsters" may at times reflect aspects of our own subjectivities, creating uncertainties and anxieties of our self-perception and self-identification (Stafford, 1991). For example, as far as our humanity is defined in contrast to nonhuman creatures (e.g., monsters), we often project a "monstrous" image onto our own bodies through negative self-perception (the extreme case being *dysmorphophobia*) or, in an instance of carnivalesque play with identities, by putting on a mask of a Halloween monster. As Shaw (1998) observes, however, the women she interviewed on the role of media images of the body, their self-perception, and identity

> are not deluded "cultural dopes." . . . Rather, they are an active, interpreting, knowledgeable and diverse audience, who attribute meaning to cultural images of female "beauty," and negotiate their relationship with their own bodies within the constraints of the "fashion beauty complex." (p. 22)

Although most of the discourses in *Naked* (Jaworski, 2003) seem to conform to the dominant ideologies of the body that conceptualize the normative body as young, attractive, sexualized, and so on, a number of participants in the program appear to

subvert and challenge these ideologies. This reflexivity of the interviewees is consistent with other forms of reflexivity associated with the late-modern era (Beck, 1992, 1994; Giddens, 1990, 1991), allowing individuals to tackle their anxieties and uncertainties concerning the changing beliefs and value systems and their own shifting identities as seen and experienced through their bodies (Lupton & Tulloch, 1998).

SUMMARY

In this section, we discussed scholarship that has investigated and critiqued the content of media portrayals of at least some nonverbal cues (i.e., those focusing primarily on appearance cues or the body). This work reflects several ideologies common to media representations, helping to reveal the larger cultural code reflected in these representations, which may be, at once, both utilitarian and problematic for the overall culture. In some cases, these implied ideologies are derived from the nonverbal images. In other cases, they are apparent in how media talk about the nonverbal cues. The latter, an analysis of *metacommunication*, is at the core of studying ideological stances in media texts (as well as in face-to-face interaction), because it is at this level that we can gain insight into how social groups value and orient to language and communication (varieties, processes, effects) through the study of folk beliefs about communication, people's attitudes, and awareness about their verbal and nonverbal conduct. We turn now more directly to the metacommunicative role of the media.

◆ Metapragmatic Discourse

In the previous section, we discussed several studies dealing with media discourses to assess what media sources (e.g., talk show guests) presume about various nonverbal cues (e.g., Greenberg, Sherry, Busselle, Hnilo, & Smith, 1997; Shaw, 1998). Additional work has concerned itself with the media's own portrayals of specific nonverbal acts (e.g., Featherstone, 1991). These discourses or "stories" form part of what we term here *verbal and visual metadiscourses* of nonverbal behavior (i.e., talk or visual presentation that comments on the meaning of the nonverbal cues). In our own work, which we review in this section, we argue that metadiscursive representations may enter the public consciousness and come to constitute structured understandings, perhaps even "common-sense" understandings of how communication works, what it is usually like, what certain ways of speaking and nonverbal behavior connote and imply, and what they *ought* to be like. That is, metadiscourse works at an ideological level and influences people's actions and priorities in a wide range of ways, some clearly visible and others much less so.

JAWORSKI AND GALASIŃSKI

Through metadiscourse commentary (remarking on communicative performance, style, rhetorical function, or silence; Jaworski, 1997), people can influence and negotiate how an utterance is or should have been heard or try to modify the values attributed to it (e.g., "What I meant to say was . . ."). At the metalevel of communication, we can mark our personal or group identities, display expertise, claim incompetence, and do many other sorts of "personal identification work" or "social relationship work" (Jaworski, Coupland, & Galasiński, 2004). Therefore, as an important site of "ideological work," metadiscursive studies have been especially fruitful in unraveling the underlying code (or codes) held by the media. In a qualitative discourse analytic study, for example, Jaworski and Galasiński (2002) examined U.K. press reports of President Clinton's testimony to the grand jury in the Clinton-Lewinsky affair as seen in the video released on September 21, 1998. This study focuses on the papers' choices of the descriptors and interpretations of Clinton's nonverbal behavior in the video, particularly in the ways they combined written text and still pictures from the video in reporting how Clinton "looked" and "behaved" during the testimony.

The relative indeterminacy and immediacy of nonverbal behavior (e.g., facial expressions, gestures, body posture) allow the media as well as the social actors in noninstitutional, face-to-face contexts to use metapragmatic manipulation of nonverbal behavior (i.e., strategic [re-] interpretation) or glossing of a particular nonverbal expression. Jaworski and Galasiński's analysis revealed that the metapragmatic nature of the reports was not so much aimed at the "accurate" reporting of what happened regarding Clinton's facial expressions, gestures, tone of voice, and certain physiological reactions (e.g., perspiration). Rather, they aimed at constructing a particular version of reality, a version that is ideologically compatible with the dominant ideologies subscribed to by the newspapers.

Overall, the comparison of the eight newspapers' accounts of Clinton's nonverbal behavior demonstrates a rather clear split between broadsheet and tabloid newspapers. The former tended to be positive (*The Guardian, Financial Times, The Independent, The Daily Telegraph*) or at least nonjudgmental (*The Western Mail*). Of the broadsheets, only *The Daily Telegraph* in its editorial was strongly critical of Clinton, which is not very surprising given the newspaper's conservative bias. The tabloids, on the other hand, tended to be mildly critical (*The Daily Mail*), at a minimum, or, more commonly, sensationally negative and disparaging (*The Sun, The Mirror*). With regard to the last three papers, despite its conservatism, *The Daily Mail*'s position was relatively uncritical of the Democratic President. The other two tabloids, despite their opposing political leanings (*The Sun* to the right and *The Mirror* to the left), seemed to adopt a unanimous stance with regard to the coverage of this story by overriding their political differences with the overarching ethos of sensationalism and focusing on human interest stories in tabloid publishing (Allan, 1999).

MANUSOV AND COLLEAGUES

As critical discourse analysts, Jaworski and Galasiński's (2002) work involves assessing the performative value of metadiscursive commentary. Manusov and her colleagues (Manusov & Bixler, 2003; Manusov & Milstein, 2005), on the other hand, focused on metadiscourse as a way to learn about how the media talk about nonverbal cues and, in doing so, reflect a way of thinking about the nature and meaning of nonverbal cues. To explore media reflections regarding the way nonverbal cues may work and what they may mean, Manusov and her colleagues accessed media texts that commented on the 1993 handshake between Yitzhak Rabin and Yasser Arafat. The handshake event, while not representative of everyday interaction, is recognized as a highly significant and public nonverbal cue. It has also been talked about in media sources for the past 13 years.

Manusov and Bixler (2003) set out to look at U.S. metadiscourse specifically to uncover the media's implied portrayal of the nature of nonverbal behavior (i.e., whether it was a set of natural signs, strategic symbols, etc.) in its coverage of the event. Across 218 texts, derived from an array of print, radio, and television discussions of the handshake, the authors argued that three potentially competing views on nonverbal behavior emerged. These portrayed nonverbal cues

(1) as *informative* (i.e., reflecting emotions, statements of the relationship between the two men and their cultures, and indicators of personal characteristics), (2) as *performative* (i.e., as strategic, symbolic, and performed for a larger audience), and (3) as *transformative* (having the potential to alter the nature of interaction and future events). (p. 2; italics ours)

The same behaviors (the handshake and surrounding nonverbal cues, such as facial expressions and other arm movements) were legitimately given a range of interpretations, reflecting very different conceptions of how nonverbal cues work in communication. These findings comment on the "relative indeterminacy of nonverbal behavior" as argued by Jaworski and Galasiński (2002), and they are consistent with Patterson (1983) and Manusov (1990) in showing that the same behaviors allow for diverse interpretations, even of their very origin.

Manusov and Milstein (2005) found a similar variability in frames for the handshake and its accompanying cues in their analysis of Israeli and Palestinian press coverage of the same event. Somewhat similar to Manusov and Bixler (2003), Manusov and Milstein (2005) found two primary frames for presenting the meaning of nonverbal cues in this press, which they labeled representations (a combination of nonverbal cues' informative and performative natures) and transformations. *Representations* involved the conceptualization of nonverbal cues as a "stand-in" for a larger process, issue, or state, often something intangible or abstract and based in the larger event or context in which the behaviors occurred. The more specific meanings for the nonverbal cues framed as representations were peace-hope-optimism, violence, betrayal, anguish, authority-legitimacy, agreement-promise, and dislike. Finally, *transformative* meanings focused on the potential of nonverbal cues to bring about a new state or process or to serve as a time marker from which events could be measured. The more specific transformations included gaining legitimacy, increasing status, working as a curse, and moving backward.

SUMMARY

Together, the work on metadiscourse provides an indirect, or even ironic, means for understanding the role of the media in nonverbal communication by focusing on the "talk" about the nonverbal cues. Thus, unlike much of the work described earlier, our work focusing on metadiscourse allows the larger nonverbal code to be understood by investigating the way it is discussed or presented in the media, with an assumption that such presentations may work to promote particular beliefs and ideologies rather than others. We turn now toward other implications of the media code for nonverbal cues.

◆ The Consequences of the Code

Many of the studies mentioned in the previous sections concern not only *what* is covered in media portrayals of nonverbal cues. They are also concerned deeply with the *consequences or outcomes* of the portrayals, especially if viewed over time and over contexts. For instance, immediate affective responses have been investigated as resulting from particular kinds of advertising strategies. Specifically, Chaudhuri and Buck (1995) argued that there is an important link between an advertisement model's facial expression and the likelihood that an audience will share the emotion vicariously (for a more general discussion of emotional contagion, see Tickle-Degnen, this volume). Furthermore, the authors argued that, "The consumer comes to associate the brand with the emotion generated (happiness, or relief from fear and anxiety) and sees the brand as a status instrument that obtains rewards and stays punishment" (Chaudhuri & Buck, 1995, p. 425). In their study, advertising strategies designed to enhance mood were associated positively with actual affective response. Attempts to portray status were linked positively with audience arousal.

SELF-IMAGE

The work locating a link between media portrayals of ideal attractiveness and the development of attractiveness schemata have also found important connections to the effects or consequences of such schemata. Many of these consequences revolve around one's own image and esteem. In particular, activating appearance schemata prior to watching appearance-related commercials has led female viewers to feel more anger, less confidence, and greater overall body dissatisfaction (Hargreaves & Tiggemann, 2002). Body dissatisfaction is often associated with such outcomes as lowered self-esteem (Henderson-King & Henderson-King, 1997; Richards, Casper, & Larson, 1990) and eating disorders (Harrison, 1997; Twamley & Davis, 1999). Activation of appearance schemata may also lead to discrimination against larger body types (White et al., 1999).

The way people talk about the body, as revealed by Shaw (1998) and Jaworski

(2003), is equally ideologized, informed by scientific, medical, and especially commercial (Coupland, 2003) discourses of the body. As Foucault (1978, 1979) has argued, body representations, both lay and scientific, are guided by similar truth-seeking principles leading to modes of regulation, containment, incitement, and resistance. As such, these representations turn bodies from purely "natural" to socially "constructed" entities (Lupton, 2000; Synnott, 1993), constrained by relations of power (Foucault's systems of knowledge or knowledge production) and by social and material inequality (see Urla & Terry, 1995, p. 3).

PERSUASION

Whereas esteem (especially low esteem) is unlikely to be the persuasive intent of mediated nonverbal cues, the larger ideologies mentioned in this chapter may well be. Indeed, research has shown that nonverbal cues in the media appear to have additional, widespread consequences, and most of these implications center around the persuasive impact of nonverbal cues. One notable body of research has looked at the effects of politicians' nonverbal behaviors (as well as the behaviors of people talking about or to politicians) on outcomes such as voting. Much of this research focuses on nonverbal cues during televised debates.

Gregory and Gallaher (2002) suggest that in addition to appearing presidential, candidates fare better when they also *sound* presidential. In their analysis of the fundamental frequency of candidates' voices during 19 televised debates from the 1960 to 2000 presidential elections, they found that certain frequencies were linked with the perceived dominance and "commanding presence" of some candidates. The metric the authors determined from this frequency also predicted accurately the popular vote outcomes across all eight elections they analyzed, confirming the authors' contention about the importance of vocal cues in determining status and the effect of status on election outcomes.

But looks or sound work differently, as would be expected, depending on the media form used. Across two studies, Patterson, Churchill, Burger, and Powell (1992) focused on this issue, which they labeled *presentation modality,* and found a range of interesting results. Using tapes of the 1984 debates between presidential candidates Ronald Reagan and Walter Mondale, Patterson et al. found evidence for a visual modality effect. Specifically, in their second study, the authors noted that viewers who only *saw* the debates (i.e., had visual information but no audio) judged Mondale much lower than they judged Reagan on expressiveness and physical attractiveness. This "benefit" for Reagan had not occurred in the audiovisual and audio presentations when the audiences had the opportunity to hear— or could be distracted by listening to—what the debaters said. Thus, certain nonverbal cues (e.g., the tendency to blink more, exchange gaze, or use fewer head movements) appeared to work against Mondale, but only when those cues were the sole focus of the participants' evaluations.

In addition to televised debates, research on nonverbal cues in other election coverage has also found that such cues may play an important role in image creation and, ultimately, in audiences' voting behavior. Rosenberg, Bohan, McCafferty, and Harris (1986), who argue for the importance of candidate perception in election outcome, also found specifically that a candidate's appearance (as judged from a photograph) affects judgments of the candidate. Specifically, certain candidates were seen as "more congressional" or as having more integrity and competence than were others.

Those rated more favorably were more likely to win a mock election by both university students and a sample from the general population. Although not stated by the researchers, the candidates in the favorable conditions tended to be smiling and had good posture, which, arguably, is what affected the election outcome.

An *affective* consequence of televised nonverbal behaviors was found in a study of political leaders' facial displays. In their analysis of the emotional responses viewers had to videotaped excerpts of the candidates in the 1984 U.S. presidential election, Sullivan and Masters (1988) found that for most of the candidates, neutral and happy or reassuring facial displays evoked (self-reported) positive emotions in audience members. These reactions were more intense in displays that came closest to the election, particularly for Ronald Reagan (the pattern was reversed for Reagan's primary Democratic rival, Walter Mondale). Importantly, the authors found that emotional responses predicted attitudes toward the candidates, such that audience members viewed more favorably those candidates (such as Gary Hart) whose facial expressions evoked the most positive self-reported emotional responses (Sullivan & Masters, 1988).

Newscasters' nonverbal behaviors when discussing a candidate also appear to play a role in audiences' judgments about political candidates. An initial analysis of 227 segments of the 1976 U.S. presidential election coverage documented that newscasters may use more positive facial expressions when talking about one candidate or another (Friedman, Mertz, & DiMatteo, 1980). Later research (e.g., Mullen et al., 1986) found evidence that such facial "bias" may affect viewers' attitudes toward the candidates: The only U.S. station (ABC) whose broadcaster showed facial favoritism toward a candidate in 1984 (Peter Jennings used more positive facial cues when talking

about Ronald Reagan than when discussing Walter Mondale) also had an audience that was significantly more likely to vote for Reagan than the audiences of CBS or NBC. In the study, the authors provide a case for the role of facial expressions, rather than audience selectivity, as the likely causal variable in voting behavior.

Such bias may occur when talking to, in addition to talking about, politicians. In three studies of Israeli television interviewers, Babad (1999) asked U.S. participants (who did not understand the language in the interviews) to judge the interviewers' nonverbal behaviors. Despite Israeli law that demands broadcasters act neutrally to candidates of all parties, Babad's first study reflected that all six interviewers studied used different nonverbal behaviors with different interviewees, although some of the interviewers were more consistent than were others. In the second study, analysis of one interviewer's behaviors when talking to two candidates for prime minister in 1996 (Shimon Peres and Benjamen Netanyahu) showed that the interviewer's nonverbal cues were judged as much more favorable when talking to one candidate than to the other. The third study included a more detailed analysis of the first set of data. In it, Babad found that the positive impressions emitted by the interviewers were based on more smiling and nodding, a relaxed face, and more round hand movements. Negative impressions were tied to "beating" hand movements, nonverbal regulation of the interview, forward lean, head thrusting, blinking, and appearing sarcastic. Overall, more "aggressive" interviewers were those likely to use nonverbal cues more differentially across interviewees (Babad, 1999).

But it is not just interviewers who may act or react differently and affect audience's views. Other research has looked at the nonverbal reactions of other parties in and watching an interaction. Seiter (2001), for example, noted that "cues communicated by one person may influence other people's perceptions of a third party's veracity" (p. 335). Specifically, and following (in some of the experimental conditions) the split-screen format of televised political debates when an opponent's nonverbal reactions are shown, Seiter asked students to watch a videotaped debate that allowed him to assess the role of opponents' nonverbal cues of apparent disbelief for what the speaker was saying. He found that both the speaker's *and his opponent's* veracity were harmed by the nonverbal expressions, even when the expressions of disbelief were only moderate. Seiter cites previous research that shows an opponent's negative nonverbal cues are more likely to influence audiences' judgment of the opponent in a negative way (i.e., lowering perceptions of competence and character) than of the speaker.

Additionally, research has examined the persuasive impact of "overheard audiences," sounds of approval or disapproval made by a real or apparent studio of listeners. Axsom, Yates, and Chaiken (1987) found that auditory reactions by an audience (in their case, enthusiastic or unenthusiastic responses) had an effect on listeners' persuasion, but only if the listeners were not highly involved in the issue. For those with low involvement, audience response affected their postmessage opinions in the direction of the audience's affect. "Seen" audience reactions also appear to have an important effect on viewers' attitudes but in an interesting and complex way. Wiegman's (1987) analysis of an interview with the Liberal leader in the Dutch Parliament found that the audience's attractiveness played a central role in the effects of their reactions. For audiences judged as attractive, research participants (members of the Dutch Socialist and Liberal parties) were particularly influenced by their positive reactions, tending to be more favorable toward the politician. For unattractive

audiences, negative nonverbal reaction played a greater role than did positive reactions, encouraging participants to take a less favorable view of the politician. From this, Wiegman concluded that "the audience is a mediating factor between the source and the receiver" (p. 38).

Davis (1999) also found an important connection between actual audience reaction shots on television and viewers' postmessage opinions on issues that were modified, in her study, by issue position. Nabi and Hendricks (2003) also revealed that positive audience reactions could affect persuasion, but only if they were consistent with the talk show host's nonverbal cues. Given that "reaction shots are one of the most commonly used editing devices used to capture and manipulate non-verbal cues in film and television" (Davis, 1999, p. 477), such effects, even when moderated by prior opinion and others' behaviors, are vital to assess.

SUMMARY

Overall, research focusing on the implications of the mediated nonverbal code has addressed image and, more commonly, persuasion. This work has found that certain presentations of nonverbal cues, viewed over time, are likely to affect, often negatively, people's own identities. More forcefully, research has looked at the persuasive effects of visual and aural cues on voting, character judgments, affective responses, and issue position, among other outcomes. These results suggest that the media may work effectively as a factor underlying the use and interpretation of nonverbal cues.

◆ Conclusion

Whereas nonverbal cues are studied often as they occur between—and are affected by—people in interaction, the media are also, for many, an important factor of influence. We argue in this chapter that they work to shape their audience to have certain expectations, which are often at odds with what everyday life would lead audiences to expect. Those expectations involve, among other things, the frequency and type of emotional expressions, standards of appearance, and gender roles. The affective and cognitive responses that audiences have to, and take away from, media are part of a larger communicative code, which includes judgments of others, expected behaviors, and interpretations of actions, that the media work to affect and reflect. The code, as revealed in media talk and visual and aural content, also appears to bring about certain kinds of behaviors, such as particular consumption and voting patterns. Looking at the media as a "factor of influence" creating and re-creating a larger code for its users necessitates a larger critique of the code. In this chapter, we reviewed some of the published critiques that others have done. We offer here one additional comment.

As Ron Scollon (1998) has argued, all mediated communication is, at some level, produced as face-to-face, interpersonal communication. In this sense, nonverbal cues displayed in the media, although more self-conscious, scripted, rehearsed, and aided by image consultants and makeup artists, are inevitably subject to the same rules of production and interpretation as nonverbal behavior in other, unmediated contexts. What is important, however, is the immense influence the media have on their audiences through the propagation of certain modes of behavior and types of body image while suppressing and devaluing others. Some of these processes are not new. After all, looking at ancient Greek statues or 17th-century European portraits, we tend to see mostly idealized images of men and women. As the media wield a huge amount of power in steering our lives in

terms of how we act, how we look (or aspire to look), or who we find desirable, powerful, or trustworthy, we need to continue to examine critically the portrayals and the (meta)commentaries of nonverbal displays in the media.

◆ Note

1. In this chapter, we discuss research primarily on media use in developed (First World) nations.

◆ References

Allan, S. (1999). *News culture.* Buckingham: Open University Press.

Axsom, D., Yates, S., & Chaiken, S. (1987). Audience response as a heuristic cue in persuasion. *Journal of Personality and Social Psychology, 53,* 30–40.

Babad, E. (1999). Preferential treatment in television interviewing: Evidence from nonverbal behavior. *Political Communication, 16,* 337–358.

Bancroft, A. (1998). The model of a man: Masculinity and body image in men's lifestyle magazines. In J. Richardson & A. Shaw (Eds.), *The body in qualitative research* (pp. 26–38). Aldershot, UK: Ashgate.

Barthes, R. (1977). *Image–music–text.* London: Fontana.

Bauman, Z. (1998). *Globalization: The human consequences.* Cambridge, UK: Polity Press.

Beck, U. (1992). *Risk society: Towards a new modernity.* London: Sage.

Beck, U. (1994). The reinvention of politics: Towards a theory of reflexive modernization. In U. Beck, A. Giddens, & S. Lash (Eds.), *Reflexive modernization: Politics, tradition and aesthetics in the modern social order* (pp. 1–55). Cambridge, UK: Polity Press.

Bordo, S. (1999). *The male body.* New York: Farrar, Straus and Giroux.

Browne, B. A. (1998). Gender stereotypes in advertising on children's television in the 1990s: A cross-national analysis. *Journal of Advertising, 27,* 83–97.

Chaudhuri, A., & Buck, R. (1995). Affect, reason, and persuasion: Advertising strategies that predict affective and analytic cognitive responses. *Human Communication Research, 21,* 422–441.

Coats, E. J., & Feldman, R. S. (1995). The role of television in the socialization of nonverbal behavioral skills. *Basic and Applied Social Psychology, 17,* 327–341.

Coats, E. J., Feldman, R. S., & Philippot, P. (1999). The influence of television on children's nonverbal behavior. In P. Philippot, R. S. Feldman, & E. J. Coates (Eds.), *The social context of nonverbal behavior* (pp. 156–181). Cambridge, UK: Cambridge University Press.

Collins, W. A. (1983). Interpretation and inference in children's television. In J. Bryant & D. R. Anderson (Eds.), *Children's understanding of television.* New York: Academic Press.

Coupland, J. (2003). Ageist ideology and discourses of control in skincare product marketing. In J. Coupland & R. Gwyn (Eds.), *Discourse, the body and identity* (pp. 127–150). Basingstoke, UK: Palgrave Macmillan.

Coupland, J. (2005). *Let surgery wait: Consumerised discourses on the "problem" of ageing.* Unpublished manuscript.

Coupland, N., Nussbaum, J. F., & Grossman, A. (1993). Introduction: Discourse, self-hood, and the lifespan. In N. Coupland & J. F. Nussbaum (Eds.), *Discourse and lifespan identity* (pp. x–xxviii). Newbury Park, CA: Sage.

Darwin, C. (1872). *The expression of emotions in men and animals.* London: John Murray.

Davis, S. (1999). The effects of audience reaction shots on attitudes towards controversial issues. *Journal of Broadcasting & Electronic Media, 43,* 476–491.

Derscheid, L. E., Kwon, Y.-H., & Fang, S-R. (1996). Preschoolers' socialization as consumers of clothing and recognition of symbolism. *Perceptual and Motor Skills, 82,* 1171–1181.

Douglas, M. (1966). *Purity and danger.* Baltimore, MD: Penguin.

Edwards, M. (1998, November 22). I just can't bare it. *The Sunday Times, Culture,* 29.

Ekman, P. (1972). Universals and cultural differences in facial expressions of emotions. In J. K. Cole (Ed.), *Nebraska symposium on motivation* (pp. 207–283). Lincoln: University of Nebraska Press.

Eubanks, V. (1996). Zones of dither: Writing the postmodern body. *Body & Society, 2,* 73–88.

Fairclough, N. L. (1995). *Media discourse.* London: Edward Arnold.

Featherstone, M. (1991). The body in consumer culture. In M. Featherstone, M. Hepworth, & B. S. Turner (Eds.), *The body: Social processes and cultural theory* (pp. 170–196). London: Sage.

Feldman, R. S., Coats, E. J., & Spielman, D. A. (1996). Television exposure and children's decoding of nonverbal behavior. *Journal of Applied Social Psychology, 26,* 1718–1733.

Foucault, M. (1978). *The history of sexuality: An introduction* (R. Huxley., Trans.). London: Penguin.

Foucault, M. (1979). *Discipline and punish: The birth of the prison* (A. M. Sheridan Smith, Trans.). New York: Vintage Books.

Friedman, H. S., Mertz, T. J., & DiMatteo, M. R. (1980). Perceived bias in the facial expressions of television news broadcasters. *Journal of Communication, 30,* 103–111.

Furnham, A., & Mak, T. (1999). Sex-role stereotyping in television commercials: A review and comparison of fourteen studies done on five continents over 25 years. *Sex Roles, 41,* 413–437.

Giddens, A. (1990). *The consequences of modernity.* Cambridge, UK: Polity Press.

Giddens, A. (1991). *Modernity and self-identity: Self and society in the late modern age.* Cambridge, UK: Polity Press.

Goffman, E. (1976). *Gender advertisements.* Cambridge, MA: Harvard University Press.

Goffman, E. (1997). The stigmatized self. In C. Lemert & A. Branman (Eds.), *The Goffman reader* (pp. 73–79). Oxford, UK: Blackwell. (Originally published as *Stigma: Notes on the management of spoiled identity.* Boston: Simon & Schuster, 1963)

Greenberg, B. S., Sherry, J. L., Busselle, R. W., Hnilo, L. R., & Smith, S. L. (1997). Daytime television talk shows: Guests, content, and interactions. *Journal of Broadcasting & Electronic Media, 41,* 412–426.

Gregory, S. W., Jr., & Gallagher, T. J. (2002). Spectral analysis of candidates' nonverbal vocal communication: Predicting U.S. presidential election outcomes. *Social Psychology Quarterly, 65,* 298–308.

Halberstadt, A. (1986). Family socialization of emotional expression and nonverbal communication of styles and skills. *Journal of Personality and Social Psychology, 51,* 827–836.

Hargreaves, D., & Tiggemann, M. (2002). The effect of television commercials on mood and body dissatisfaction: The role of the appearance–schema activation. *Journal of Social and Clinical Psychology, 21,* 287–308.

Harrison, K. (1997). Does interpersonal attraction to thin media personalities promote eating disorders? *Journal of Broadcasting & Electronic Media, 41,* 478–500.

Henderson-King, E., & Henderson-King, D. (1997). Media effects on women's body esteem: Social and individual difference factors. *Journal of Applied Social Psychology, 27,* 167–173.

Houle, R., & Feldman, R. S. (1991). Emotional displays in children's television programming. *Journal of Nonverbal Behavior, 15,* 261–271.

Hymes, D. (1972). On communicative competence. In J. Pride & J. Holmes (Eds.), *Sociolinguistics* (pp. 269–293). Harmondsworth, UK: Penguin.

Jaworski, A. (1997). "White and white": Metacommunicative and metaphorical silences. In A. Jaworski (Ed.), *Silence: Interdisciplinary perspectives* (pp. 381–401). Berlin, Germany: Mouton de Gruyter.

Jaworski, A. (2003). Talking bodies: Representations of norm and deviance in the BBC *Naked* programme. In J. Coupland & R. Gwyn (Eds.), *Discourse, the body and identity* (pp. 151–176). Basingstoke, UK: Palgrave Macmillan.

Jaworski, A., Coupland, N., & Galasiński, D. (Eds.). (2004). *Metalanguage: Social and ideological perspectives.* Berlin, Germany: Mouton de Gruyter.

Jaworski, A., & Galasiński, D. (2002). The verbal construction of non-verbal behaviour: British press reports of President Clinton's grand jury testimony video. *Discourse & Society, 13,* 629–649.

Klassen, M. L., Jasper, C. M., & Schwartz, A. M. (1993). Men and women: Images of their relationships in magazine advertisements. *Journal of Advertising Research, 22,* 30–39.

Kolbe, R. H. (1990). Gender roles in children's advertising: A longitudinal content analysis. In J. H. Leigh & C. R. Martin (Eds.), *Current issues and research in advertising* (pp. 197–206). Ann Arbor: University of Michigan, Graduate School of Business Administration.

Larson, M. S. (1993). Family communication on prime-time television. *Journal of Broadcasting and Electronic Media, 37,* 349–357.

Levine, R. (1997). *A geography of time.* New York: Basic Books.

Lupton, D. (2000). The social construction of medicine and the body. In G. L. Albert, R. Fitzpatrick, & S. C. Scrimshaw (Eds.), *Handbook of social studies in health and medicine* (pp. 50–63). London: Sage.

Lupton, D., & Tulloch, J. (1998). The adolescent "unfinished body," reflexivity and HIV/AIDS risk. *Discourse & Society, 4,* 19–34.

Manusov, V. (1990). An application of attribution principles to nonverbal messages in romantic dyads. *Communication Monographs, 57,* 104–118.

Manusov, V., & Bixler, N. R. (2003, November). *The polysemous nature of nonverbal behavior: Variety in media framing of the Rabin-Arafat handshake.* Paper presented to the National Communication Association, Miami.

Manusov, V., & Milstein, T. (2005). Interpreting nonverbal behavior: Representation and transformation frames in Israeli and Palestinian coverage of the 1993 Rabin-Arafat handshake. *Western Journal of Communication, 69,* 183–201.

McNeal, J. U. (1987). *Children are consumers: Insights and implications*. Lexington, MA: Lexington Books.

Mirzoeff, N. (1995). *Bodyscape: Art, Modernity and the Ideal Figure*. London: Routledge.

Morris, D., Collett, P., Marsh, P., & O'Shaughnessy, M. (1980). *Gestures: Their origins and distribution*. New York: Scarborough.

Mullen, B., Futrell, D., Stairs, D., Tice, D. M., Baumeister, R. F., Dawson, K. E., et al. (1986). Newscasters' facial expressions and voting behavior of viewers: Can a smile elect a president? *Journal of Personality and Social Psychology, 51*, 291–295.

Myers, P. N., & Biocca, F. A. (1999).The effect of television advertising and programming on body image distortions in young women. In L. K. Guerrero, J. A. Devito, & M. L. Hecht (Eds.), *The nonverbal communication reader: Classic and contemporary readings* (2nd ed., pp. 92–100). Prospect Heights, IL: Waveland Press.

Nabi, R. L., & Hendricks, A. (2003). The persuasive effect of host and audience reaction shots in television talk shows. *Journal of Communication, 53*, 527–543.

Ochs, E., & Schieffelin, B. (1986). *Language socialization across cultures*. New York: Cambridge University Press.

Patterson, M. L. (1983). *Nonverbal behavior: A functional perspective*. New York: Springer.

Patterson, M. L., Churchill, M. E., Burger, G. K., & Powell, J. L. (1992). Verbal and nonverbal modality effects on impressions of political candidates: Analysis from the 1984 presidential debates. *Communication Monographs, 59*, 231–242.

Richards, M. H., Casper, R. C., & Larson, R. W. (1990). Weight and eating disorders among pre- and young adolescent boys and girls. *Journal of Adolescent Health Care, 11*, 85–89.

Rosenberg, S. W., Bohan, L., McCafferty, P., & Harris, K. (1986). The image and the vote: The effect of candidate presentation on voter preference. *American Journal of Political Science, 30*, 108–127.

Roy, A. (2005). The "male gaze" in Indian television commercials: A rhetorical analysis. In T. Carilli & J. Campbell (Eds.), *Women and the media: National and global perspectives* (pp. 3–18). Lanham, MD: University Press of America.

Saarni, C. (1985). Indirect processes in affect socialization. In M. Lewis & C. Saarni (Eds.), *The socialization of emotions* (pp. 187–212). New York: Plenum.

Saville-Troike, M. (2003). *The ethnography of communication: An introduction* (3rd ed.). Oxford: Blackwell.

Scollon, R. (1998). *Mediated discourse as social interaction*. London: Longman.

Seiter, E. (1993). *Sold separately: Children and parents in consumer culture*. New Brunswick, NJ: Rutgers University Press.

Seiter, J. S. (2001). Silent derogation and perceptions of deceptiveness: Does communicating nonverbal disbelief during an opponent's speech affect perceptions of a debater's veracity? *Communication Research Reports, 18*, 334–344.

Shaw, A. (1998). Images of the female body: Women's identities and the media. In J. Richardson & A. Shaw (Eds.), *The body in qualitative research* (pp. 7–25). Aldershot, UK: Ashgate.

Shildrick, M. (2002). *Embodying the monster: Encounters with the vulnerable self*. London: Sage.

Shilling, C. (1993). *The body and social theory*. London: Sage.

Stafford, B. M. (1991). *Body criticism: Imaging the unseen in enlightenment art and medicine*. Cambridge, MA: MIT Press.

Sullivan, D. G., & Masters, R. D. (1988). "Happy warriors": Leaders' facial displays, viewers' emotions, and political support. *American Journal of Political Science, 32*, 345–368.

Synnott, A. (1993). *The body social: Symbolism, self and society*. London: Routledge.

Twamley, E. W., & Davis, M. C. (1999). The sociocultural model of eating disturbance in young women: The effects of personal attributes and family environment. *Journal of Social and Clinical Psychology, 18,* 467–489.

Urla, J., & Terry, J. (1995). Introduction: Mapping embodied deviance. In J. Terry & J. Urla (Eds.), *Deviant bodies: Critical perspectives on difference in scenic and popular culture* (pp. 1–18). Bloomington: Indiana University Press.

White, S. E., Brown, N. J., & Ginsburg, S. L. (1999). Diversity of body types in network television programming: A content analysis. *Communication Research Reports, 16,* 386–392.

Wiegman, O. (1987). Attitude change in a realistic experiment: The effect of party membership and audience reaction during an interview with a Dutch politician. *Journal of Applied Social Psychology, 17,* 37–49.

Wilson, B. J., & Smith, S. L. (1998). Children's responses to emotional portrayals on television. In P. A. Andersen & L. K. Guerrero (Eds.), *Handbook of communication and emotion: Theory, application, and contexts* (pp. 533–569). San Diego, CA: Academic Press.

Zillmann, D. (1991). Television viewing and physiological arousal. In J. Bryant & D. Zillmann (Eds), *Responding to the screens: Reception and reaction processes* (pp. 103–133). Hillsdale, NJ: Erlbaum.

PART III

FUNCTIONS

14

NONVERBAL BEHAVIOR IN INTIMATE INTERACTIONS AND INTIMATE RELATIONSHIPS

◆ Peter A. Andersen
San Diego State University

◆ Laura K. Guerrero
Arizona State University

◆ Susanne M. Jones
University of Minnesota, Twin Cities

Intimacy is a complex concept about which researchers legitimately create various conceptualizations and reach different conclusions (Acitelli & Duck, 1987; Prager, 1995). For this reason, intimacy has been conceptualized variously as a relationship type, as an emotion, as interpersonal warmth or closeness, as a subjective experience, as a communication trait, as an interpersonal process, as a motive, as a behavior, as sexual interaction, and as an interpersonal goal (Andersen & Guerrero, 1998; McAdams, 1988; Prager, 1995; Reis & Shaver, 1988). Whereas all these conceptualizations have value, consistent with Prager (2000), we are concerned primarily in this chapter with intimacy as a

Relational Context

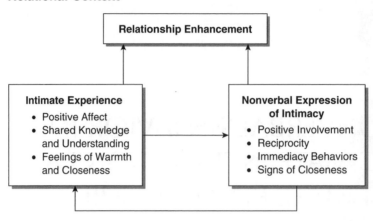

Figure 14.1 An Interaction-Centered Model of Intimacy Processes Related to Nonverbal Behavior Relational Context

type of interaction, a focus that has two primary foundations: (1) that intimate interactions are necessary to develop and maintain intimate relationships and (2) that emotions and behaviors associated with the experience of intimacy are displayed within the context of intimate interaction.

Although intimacy can be conceptualized as an experience consisting of felt emotions and perceptions of understanding, or as a relationship that is characterized by affection and trust, ultimately intimacy is located in interaction (Prager, 2000). Intimate interaction is the vehicle through which people exchange intimate actions, thoughts, and feelings. Relationships are creations of interaction, with partners labeling relationships as intimate (or nonintimate) based on the communication patterns that have occurred between them. Thus, we argue that intimacy is experienced *and* expressed in interaction. Although verbal factors are an important component of intimate interaction, we shall demonstrate in this chapter that nonverbal behaviors play a critical role in creating and sustaining intimate interactions and relationships. More pointedly,

we argue that nonverbal communication is the sine qua non of intimacy. Although intimacy can be created by talk, we contend that nonverbal communication is intimacy's primary vehicle.

As a framework for exploring the role that nonverbal behavior plays in the intimacy process, we present an interaction-centered model of intimacy processes related to nonverbal behavior (see Figure 14.1).

This model modifies and extends Prager's (1995, 2000; Prager & Roberts, 2004) conceptualization of intimacy. Positive nonverbal involvement cues occupy a central position in the model. Although individuals typically manifest positive involvement when they experience intimate thoughts and feelings, it is the expression of intimacy (through positive involvement cues) that sustains and enhances those intimate thoughts and feelings. Ultimately, both the experience and expression of intimacy lead to relationship enhancement; relational partners who engage in intimate interaction frequently and routinely are more likely to be satisfied and committed as well as to manage conflict effectively (Prager, 2000). Variables associated with relational context, such as the type and stage of a relationship, frame the experience and expression of intimacy and provide guidelines for what constitutes appropriate levels of intimacy within interactions.

With our interaction-centered model serving as a guide, this chapter is organized around three issues. First, we distinguish between the experience and expression of intimacy. Second, we examine nonverbal cues of positive involvement and argue that these cues are the basic building blocks of intimate interaction. Third, we examine positive involvement behaviors in the context of intimate relationships, showing that these behaviors are associated with relationship maintenance and enhancement.

THE EXPERIENCE VERSUS THE EXPRESSION OF INTIMACY

Scholars have distinguished between the experience and expression of intimacy, sometimes referring to these components as latent versus manifest intimacy, respectively (e.g., Sternberg, 1986). The experience of intimacy is located in internal processes related to perceptions and felt emotions. At the perceptual level, Prager and Roberts (2004) argued that intimacy is experienced through shared knowledge. This knowledge, which is gained through intimate interaction, is stored in cognitive schemas. The extent to which these schemas are accurate and reflect shared meaning defines the quality of intimate relationships. The perception of understanding is also important. Prager (2000) noted that perceiving oneself to be "liked, accepted, understood, cared for, or loved" is an essential part of the intimacy experience (p. 231; see also, Reis & Shaver, 1988).

At the emotional level, people experience intimacy as an affective state characterized by subjective feelings of warmth and affection (Andersen & Guerrero, 1998; Prager,

1995). In his triangular theory of love, Sternberg (1986) conceptualized intimacy as the experience of warm, affectionate feelings that occur during interaction with close friends and others we hold dear. Similarly, Clarke, Allen, and Dickson (1985) defined warmth as a positive emotion that characterizes close, intimate relationships, and Andersen and Guerrero (1998) argued that warmth is a "pleasant, contented, intimate feeling that occurs during positive interactions" with others (p. 306). As these conceptualizations suggest, intimate feelings are sustained, enhanced, and created through intimate interaction with others. This illustrates the complexity of intimacy. Intimacy is experienced typically during interaction in close relationships in the presence of positive verbal and nonverbal behavior that reflects and creates feelings of warmth. The experience of interpersonal warmth can lead people to engage in more positive behavior, just as positive behavior can trigger feelings of warmth and intimacy.

NONVERBAL INVOLVEMENT CUES

The expression of intimacy involves verbal and nonverbal behavior (Prager, 2000). Verbal expressions of intimacy include self-disclosure, verbal responsiveness, and intimate words (Andersen, 1998). Self-revealing statements that express vulnerable emotions are especially conducive to intimacy (Prager & Roberts, 2004). Statements expressing agreement and validation also foster intimacy (Andersen & Guerrero, 1998). Nonverbal expressions of intimacy include a wide range of behaviors that reflect both positive affect and involvement, such as gaze, smiling, forward lean, and affirming head nods. According to Prager (2000), positive involvement behaviors contribute "substantially to people's intimate experiences" (p. 233) and are a defining feature of interactions in close, satisfying relationships.

Most nonverbal behavior is spontaneous and exerts a powerful effect because of its perceived authenticity (Andersen, 1999; Prager, 2000). We contend that nonverbal behavior plays a special role in the creation and maintenance of intimacy for two additional reasons. First, in contrast to verbal communication, nonverbal communication is multimodal; people can say only one word at a time, yet they can engage in numerous positive involvement cues simultaneously. Indeed, scholars have contended that intimacy is communicated through multichanneled composites of nonverbal cues (Andersen, 1999; Patterson, 1983), and nonverbal involvement behaviors are perceived typically as a gestalt, with people processing a package of behaviors rather than focusing on a single cue (Andersen, 1985, 1998). Second, people tend to express emotions such as warmth and affection via nonverbal rather than verbal cues (Burgoon, Buller, & Woodall, 1996; Planalp, DeFrancisco, & Rutherford, 1996). Although different models of intimacy offer diverse predictions for how this process works (see Patterson, this volume), increases in nonverbal involvement behavior (such as eye contact, touch, and smiling) often lead to emotional reactions and changes in arousal that can trigger affective states related to intimacy (Andersen, 1985, 1998; Cappella & Greene, 1982).

As depicted in Figure 14.1, the experience and expression of intimacy are interdependent processes. When people feel positive affect and perceive shared knowledge and understanding, they are likely to express those internal experiences through communication. In initial interactions, variables such as social and physical attraction (which involve positive affect) and perceived similarity (which is likely related to shared knowledge and understanding) may

help predict how intimate an interaction is (e.g., Byrne, 1997). In developed relationships, intimate interaction is positively associated with a number of relational quality indicators, such as satisfaction and trust (Prager, 1995).

Importantly, however, if intimate feelings and perceptions are not manifest in communication, they remain internal processes and have little direct effect on relationships. Intimate interaction helps sustain and enhance intimate feelings and perceptions that enhance relationships. In some cases, intimate interaction even creates the experience of intimacy. For example, an individual may feel neutral toward an acquaintance until the pair is thrown together in a situation that leads them to disclose personal information and act warmly toward one another. Relational context also influences how intimacy is experienced and expressed. In beginning relationships, trust, shared knowledge, and understanding are still developing, so intimate thoughts and feelings may be hidden or expressed more cautiously (e.g., Altman & Taylor, 1973; Aune, Aune, & Buller, 1994). Prager (2000; Prager & Roberts, 2004), as well as other scholars (e.g., Hatfield, 1984) have noted that intimacy expression is inhibited when people feel vulnerable, as is often the case during initial interactions. In fact, Prager (2000) argued that the expression of thoughts and emotions that make one vulnerable is a critical component of both intimate interactions and intimate relationships.

POSITIVE INVOLVEMENT BEHAVIOR IN INTIMATE RELATIONSHIPS

The search for a catalog of behaviors that foster and express intimacy has led down various paths to lists of behaviors

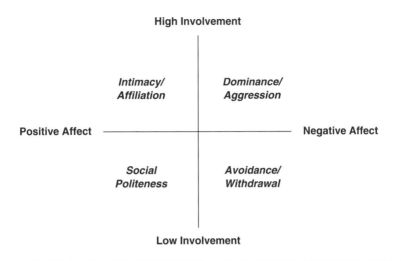

Figure 14.2   Involvement and Affect as Dimensions Underlying Relational Messages

labeled representing involvement, positive affect, or immediacy, but ultimately these lists are similar. Prager's (2000) term *positive involvement behavior* represents the intersection of these lines of research. Consistent with Prager's theorizing, we believe that nonverbal behaviors related to intimacy have two fundamental characteristics: They reflect involvement and positive affect. Figure 14.2 shows how the dimensions of involvement (or intensity) and affect combine to produce various relational messages. To understand the behaviors that communicate intimacy we turn to a discussion of work on involvement and immediacy. Although various scholars use these two terms somewhat differently, each approach leads to the same conclusion: Behaviors that reflect engagement and positive affect contribute to intimate interaction. Moreover, regardless of the approach taken, behaviors identified as constituting intimate interaction are strikingly similar, indicating that they are part of the same construct.

Nonverbal involvement is the degree to which a person is an engaged, active participant in a social interaction (Coker & Burgoon, 1987). Scholars have argued that

involvement is a behavioral reflection of the intimacy level of an interaction. For example, Patterson (1988) described intimacy as the degree of union or openness with another person, which is manifested by a high degree of spontaneous nonverbal involvement. Earlier, Patterson (1983) noted, "the construct of nonverbal involvement overlaps with proxemics, intimacy, and immediacy, but it is more comprehensive than each of those constructs" (p. 5). According to Patterson, involvement is communicated via nonverbal behaviors such as decreased distance, more gaze and touch, direct body orientation, forward lean, facial and vocal expressiveness, and postural openness.

Burgoon and Newton (1991) defined involvement via five dimensions: immediacy (e.g., touch), expressiveness (e.g., facial animation), altercentrism (e.g., attention to the partner), smooth interaction management (e.g., coordinated turn-taking), and composure (e.g., few vocal pauses). Importantly, altercentrism reflects caring and shared understanding, which Prager (2000) identified as essential to the intimacy experience. Shared knowledge may also be related to smooth interaction management because partners would be more familiar with one another's communication style. Burgoon and Newton (1991) added a sixth dimension, affect, as relevant but not essential to nonverbal involvement. According to this perspective, the simultaneous manifestation of involvement behaviors and positive affect cues (such as smiling and vocal warmth) helps create or sustain intimacy. In contrast, when involvement behaviors are paired with negative affect cues (e.g., scowling and a loud, angry voice), dominance or aggression is communicated.

Dillard, Solomon, and Palmer (1999) argued that involvement is conceptualized by the level of intensity or engagement present within an interaction. Involvement cues are present in interactions characterized as either affiliative-intimate or dominant-aggressive, depending on the type of affect present in the interaction (see also, Cappella, 1983; Guerrero, 2004; Prager, 1995; see Figure 14.2). Thus, nonverbal involvement and displays of positive affect combine to produce intimate interactions. Studies demonstrate that both participants and observers perceive people to be more intimate when they use involvement behaviors such as eye contact and forward leans, coupled with positive affect cues such as smiling (e.g., Burgoon, Buller, Hale, & deTurck, 1984; Burgoon & Le Poire, 1999; Burgoon & Newton, 1991).

Researchers have also identified a host of behaviors associated with positive affect and interpersonal warmth (see Andersen & Guerrero, 1998, for a review). Interpersonal warmth is part of a cluster of social emotions related to intimacy and affection that includes love, liking, and joy. These emotions are expressed via positive involvement (Guerrero & Andersen, 2000; Guerrero & Floyd, 2006). Love is communicated nonverbally by physical closeness, positive touch, smiling, mutual gaze, spending time together, warm vocal tones, and giving gifts

(Marston, Hecht, & Robers, 1987; Shaver, Schwartz, Kirson, & O'Connor, 1987). Liking is communicated through eye contact, smiling, facial and gestural animation, and head nodding (Floyd & Ray, 2003; Palmer & Simmons, 1995). Finally, joy is associated with being physically energetic, smiling, laughing, approaching others, and sounding enthusiastic (Shaver et al., 1987). When these emotions are exchanged, an intimate interaction is created that helps produce and sustain an intimate relationship.

Instead of using the term *positive involvement,* some scholars use the term *immediacy* to describe a set of behaviors that communicates *both* involvement and positive affect (Andersen, 1985). Mehrabian (1967, 1969b) coined the term *immediacy* to describe approach behaviors that reflect the intensity level of interaction. Later, Mehrabian (1981) argued that immediacy behaviors also signal attentiveness, heighten sensory stimulation, and communicate liking, with individuals moving toward people and things they like, and away from people and things they dislike. On the basis of these characteristics, Mehrabian's conceptualization of immediacy seems to capture intensity (or involvement) and liking (or warm feelings). Andersen (1985) added that immediacy behaviors increase physical and psychological closeness, signal availability for interaction, are physiologically arousing, and communicate positive affect.

Mehrabian's (1967, 1969b) work focused on five immediacy behaviors: interpersonal distance, touch, gaze, body orientation, and lean. Andersen (1985) expanded the domain of immediacy behaviors to include a wide variety of kinesic, vocalic, and chronemic cues (e.g., smiling, warm vocal tone, and time spent together). As noted earlier, some scholars view immediacy as one of several dimensions under the broader construct of involvement

(Burgoon & Newton, 1991; Dillard et al., 1999). For these scholars, immediacy is limited to involvement behaviors reflecting physical and psychological closeness between two people during interaction, with Mehrabian's (1969b) original list of immediacy behaviors—distance, touch, gaze, body orientation, and lean—providing the best exemplars. Regardless of the approach taken, however, scholars studying involvement and immediacy appear to agree that behaviors representing the intersection of involvement and positive affect are the building blocks of intimate interaction. Like Prager (1995), we refer to these behaviors as positive involvement cues.

Specific Behaviors Reflecting Positive Involvement

Next, we identify specific nonverbal behaviors that have been categorized as positive involvement cues. This discussion is organized by examining various subcodes of nonverbal communication, such as proxemics and haptics. Our review focuses on dynamic nonverbal behaviors rather than nonverbal cues that are typically static, such as appearance and the environment. Although cues related to appearance and the environment undoubtedly shape perceptions and intimate experiences, we believe static cues have less potential for influencing the ongoing process of intimate interaction than do dynamic cues such as touch and gesturing, which frequently change throughout the course of interaction (Guerrero & Floyd, 2006). This perspective is consistent with work by scholars studying involvement and immediacy; although these scholars have not differentiated between dynamic and static nonverbal cues, the behaviors they have identified as constituting involvement and immediacy have tended to fall under the subcodes of proxemics, haptics, kinesics, vocalics, and to a lesser extent,

chronemics. When discussing the behaviors associated with each of these subcodes, we also comment on relational context variables (such as type and stage of relationship) that influence the display and interpretation of various positive involvement cues.

Proxemics. At least four types of proxemic behavior are related to the experience or communication of intimacy: interpersonal distance, lean, body orientation, and the physical plane (Andersen, 1999). Interpersonal distance refers to the physical space between two people. Hall's (1966) classic work on conversational distances suggests that in North American culture, the distance ranging from 0 to 18 inches is the "intimate" zone, reserved generally for intimate interaction with close relational partners. Mehrabian (1969a) contended that close interpersonal distances are related to liking under most circumstances, and early empirical research showed that close distances are related to positive interpersonal attitudes (Mehrabian & Ksionsky, 1970), liking, and friendship (Priest & Sawyer, 1967).

Mehrabian (1969a) also suggested, however, that close distances can lead to *less* liking and intimacy under certain circumstances. Burgoon and her colleagues (e.g., Burgoon & Hale, 1988; Burgoon, Manusov, Mineo, & Hale, 1985) have shown that close distance only produces increased liking and positive perceptions if a person is perceived to be rewarding (e.g., attractive, high status). When someone judged as nonrewarding gets close, people tend to evaluate that person more negatively. Research shows that relationships also matter. Morton (1977), for example, verified that people are less comfortable standing or sitting close to a stranger than a friend. Guerrero (1997) revealed that people tend to sit closer to romantic partners than to friends.

Together, these studies suggest that interpersonal distance reflects the intimacy level of relationships and that relational context helps determine how people interpret and respond to positive involvement behavior.

Lean, body orientation, and the physical plane decrease the vertical and horizontal distance between people. Forward leans communicate immediacy, involvement, and affection and tend to lead to perceptions of greater intimacy (e.g., Burgoon, 1991; Palmer, Cappella, Patterson, & Churchill, 1990; Ray & Floyd, 2000). People comfortable with intimacy expression are more likely to lean forward than are those fearful of intimacy (Guerrero, 1996). Face-to-face body orientation is related to intimacy (Andersen, 1999). In one study, couples who expressed support for each other during disagreements (with support potentially being a reflection of intimacy) were more likely to use direct body orientation and close distancing (Newton & Burgoon, 1990). Studies suggest that women friends are especially likely to use direct body orientation to express intimacy (e.g., Guerrero, 1997). Communicating on the same physical plane also reduces height differentials, leading to more intimate interaction (Andersen, 1999).

Haptics. Touch is vital to human development; loving physical contact, for example, enables children to reach full social and intellectual potential and helps them become comfortable with intimacy (Guerrero, 2000; Montagu, 1978). Some scholars have even suggested that intimacy is impossible in the absence of touch (e.g., Morris, 1971). Research has confirmed that across many contexts, including friendships, romances, family relationships, and therapeutic and medical treatments, touch is associated with intimacy. Indeed, Prager (1995, 2000) considers touch to be a fundamental component of intimate interaction. As she put it, "Touch further intensifies the experience of intimacy" with welcome touch on

vulnerable body parts such as the face or torso "always . . . experienced as intimate" (Prager, 2000, p. 233).

Despite the consistency with which touch is perceived as intimate, touch may function to express intimacy differentially depending on the stage of a relationship. In field studies conducted at airports, zoos, and theaters, for example, more touch was associated with feelings of greater intimacy during relationship escalation (Guerrero & Andersen, 1991; Heslin & Boss, 1980; McDaniel & Andersen, 1998). In these studies, touch was observed unobtrusively and correlated positively to participants' or observers' ratings of intimacy in developing relationships. In long-term relationships, touch tends to level off or decline. Likewise, in a study of dating and married couples, Emmers and Dindia (1995) found a nonlinear relationship between touch and relational intimacy in self-reported private touch, with touch peaking and then leveling off or decreasing slightly at the highest reported levels of intimacy. These studies suggest that touch is more than a reflection of intimate experience. Instead, touch may be an essential part of developing and escalating intimate relationships. Once the experience of intimacy is stable in longer-term relationships, touch may become less necessary.

Touch also appears to be important in communicating intimacy across a variety of relationship types. Monsour (1992) argued that physical contact is essential to perceptions of intimate interaction for friends. Similarly, Marston, Hecht, Manke, McDaniel, and Reeder (1998) found that tactile behavior (e.g., embracing, hugging, or kissing) is the primary way people communicate intimacy in romantic relationships. The criss-cross hug may be perceived as especially intimate across various types of relationships (Floyd, 1999).

Studies comparing other types of nonsexual touch suggest that face touching is seen as particularly intimate, presumably because the face is a sensitive and vulnerable part of the body (Burgoon, 1991; Lee & Guerrero, 2001), which comports with Prager's (1995, 2000) argument that intimacy requires one to become vulnerable. In Burgoon et al.'s (1984) study, observers who viewed videotaped tactile interactions rated touch conditions as more intimate than nontouch conditions. Because touch is considered an intimate behavior, however, interactants must be sure that touch is welcome (Andersen, 1998; Prager, 2000). Studies show that some people are highly touch avoidant and do not like intimate touch, will not volunteer for touch experiments, stand and sit out of reach of other interactants, and dislike a situation if they are touched (see Andersen, 2005). Touch-avoidant people will adjust to greater levels of touch, however, depending on relational stage and their partner's tactile preferences. In short, the relationship trumps the trait when the two conflict (Guerrero & Andersen, 1991, 1994), illustrating the importance of relational context.

Of course, touch is inappropriate in some relationships. Interpretations of excessively intimate behaviors, such as touch, can lead to employees' reports of sexual harassment. Lee and Guerrero (2001) found that among ambiguous touches, a gentle facial touch or an arm around a coworker's waist were rated as the most intimate and, therefore, inappropriate for coworkers. In another study, soft touches were viewed as less harmful and harassing than were hard touches (Black & Gold, 2003). Whether touch is perceived as sexually harassing is not just a function of the area touched and the type of touch, but also of the physical attractiveness of the transgressor (Black & Gold, 2003; Cartar, Hickes, & Slane, 1996). Generally, the more attractive the transgressor, the more acceptable the tactile behavior is rated.

Kinesics. Kinesics encompass nonverbal behaviors that include facial expressions, eye behavior, body movements, and gestures (Burgoon et al., 1996). Intimate kinesic expressions include smiling, facial pleasantness, increased eye contact, and gestures that connote immediacy, affection, closeness, and warmth (Kleinke, 1986). The face is considered the primary and most trusted source of emotional information (Ekman & Friesen, 1975; Knapp & Hall, 2006; Planalp et al., 1996). Therefore, the face carries important messages of positive affect that help create intimate interaction. Burgoon and Newton (1991) found that both facial and gestural animation predict relational intimacy. Additionally, when couples are intimate, they also tend to synchronize their gestures, body movements, and facial expressions (Tickle-Degnen & Rosenthal, 1990; see also Tickle-Degnen, this volume).

Eye behavior typically is crucial to the experience of intimacy. The primary oculesic behaviors are gaze (i.e., a person looks at another person) and eye contact (i.e., simultaneous gaze). The latter is particularly important for initiating social interactions because it serves as an invitation to communicate and is vital to attributions of intimacy (Andersen, 1985). Argyle (1972) and Breed (1972) found mutually causal relationships between eye contact and intimacy. Eye contact is essential for communicating positive involvement and fostering the experience of intimacy in face-to-face contexts (Andersen & Andersen, 1984; Mehrabian, 1981). Experiments by Burgoon, Coker, and Coker (1986) showed that less eye contact had a negative effect on perceived intimacy compared with normal or greater levels of eye contact.

Vocalics. Most of the research focusing on vocal cues has not addressed their potential for communicating intimacy. Rather, research has focused on the related constructs of affect, liking, closeness, immediacy, and affection. Next to the face, the vocal channel is the key medium for transmitting emotional information (Knapp & Hall, 2006). Given that subtle vocal cues are hard to control, the voice is a reliable indicator of emotion. Planalp et al. (1996) found that people relied most frequently on vocal cues, especially loudness, speed of talking, and amount of talking when interpreting emotional expressions from others.

People tend to match vocal cues to signal liking and closeness (Tickle-Degnen & Rosenthal, 1990). Likewise, vocal pleasantness is an important facet of positive involvement that helps people initiate and maintain intimate relationships (Guerrero, 2004). Positive affect is conveyed via vocal warmth, vocal pleasantness, and relaxed laughter (Burgoon & Newton, 1991; Guerrero, 1997). As Knapp and Hall (2006) pointed out, the presence of a smile is also evident in the voice. Affection, a construct closely related to intimacy, is also communicated via pitch (number of vocal vibrations per second) as well as variance in pitch. Floyd and Ray (2003) found that men and women were rated as showing more affection when their voices varied in pitch. Men were perceived as more affectionate, however, when their average pitch level was low, whereas women were perceived as more affectionate when their average pitch level was high.

Chronemics. Spending time with a relational partner often sends compelling, intimate messages. Studies reveal that a potent predictor of relational satisfaction, interpersonal understanding, and intimacy, is the amount of time people spend together. Egland, Stelzner, Andersen, and Spitzberg (1997) reported that among 20 nonverbal behaviors, spending time together was the most powerful predictor of both relational satisfaction and perceived interpersonal understanding, accounting for 30% and 25% of the variance in satisfaction and understanding,

respectively. Hatfield and Rapson (1987) suggested that intimacy is comprised of several elements, including behavioral intimacy, operationalized primarily as spending time in close proximity to one's partner. Factor analytic studies have found that spending time with someone is a central component of nonverbal intimacy or immediacy (Andersen & Andersen, 2005). In a study of the subjective nature of intimacy, Marston et al. (1998) demonstrated that an important component of intimacy was time together, including private moments.

As discussed above regarding kinesics, interactional matching or synchrony between two interactants is vital to the creation of intimacy. Theories of interpersonal adaptation (e.g., Burgoon, Stern, & Dillman, 1995), communication accommodation theory (Giles & Street, 1994), rapport (Tickle-Degnen & Rosenthal, 1990), and interpersonal sensitivity (Hall & Bernieri, 2001) suggest that timing and synchronicity are essential to establishing intimacy. More specifically, studies indicate that interactional timing is crucial for developing intimacy in both adult-adult and infant-adult interaction (Cappella, 1981, this volume; Stern, 1980). Children tend to be more secure and comfortable with intimacy when they have parents who respond to their needs consistently and appropriately, using moderate levels of stimulation and highly synchronized nonverbal behavior (Ainsworth, Blehar, Waters, & Wall, 1978; Isabella & Belsky, 1991). In addition, many researchers report that careful timing and sequencing of intimacy behaviors such as eye contact and proximity are essential to perceptions of interpersonal intimacy (see Andersen, 1998, for a review). Initiating intimacy too quickly, too slowly, or in the wrong sequence can be perceived as excessive intimacy, sexual harassment, or interpersonal desperation (Wertin & Andersen, 1996). Similarly, dissynchronous behaviors such as arriving late for a meeting or social engagement communicate less friendliness and sociability (Baxter & Ward, 1975).

Interpreting Positive Involvement Cues as a Reflection of Intimacy

Intensifications of positive involvement behavior usually have a direct, positive relationship with experienced intimacy. This is the position of the direct effects model (Andersen, 1985, 1999) and a related perspective, the social meaning model (Burgoon et al., 1986), both of which have been widely supported. The direct effects model posits that although immediacy (or positive involvement behavior) is moderated by situational, relational, cultural, and personality factors, in most circumstances greater nonverbal immediacy inherently produces positive person perceptions and greater relational intimacy (Andersen, 1998, 1999). The social meaning model is based on the principle that there are consensually recognized meanings for nonverbal communication within social communities or the broader society (Burgoon & Newton, 1991; Burgoon et al., 1985). Research on the social meaning model has confirmed that people interpret positive involvement cues as a reflection of intimacy (Burgoon & Le Poire, 1999; Burgoon & Newton, 1991).

Positive involvement behavior is, however, most likely to lead to intimate interactions and intimate relationships when two conditions are met. The first of these conditions—that the behavior is welcome— was alluded to earlier in this chapter. Behaviors such as touch and close proxemic distancing, in particular, can be interpreted as threatening or aggressive if uninvited and unwanted, even if positive affect cues are present. The experience of intimacy, in terms of how much positive affect one feels

and how much shared understanding one perceives initially, is likely to exert a strong influence on how people react to positive involvement behavior. The second condition revolves around the concept of reciprocity. If one person engages in positive involvement behavior and the other person responds by compensating (e.g., backing away) rather than reciprocating (e.g., smiling and increasing eye contact), intimate interaction has *not* occurred. It is our position that intimate interaction requires participation by both partners rather than the simple display of positive involvement behavior by one partner.

Our position regarding reciprocity is supported by scholarship on intimacy as well as theories of nonverbal communication. In Prager's (2000) model of intimacy, partners are viewed as highly interdependent. Prager described the interdependent processes underlying intimate interaction this way: "The experiences (feelings and perceptions) that Partner A's behavior elicits in Partner B prompt Partner B to behave intimately. The intimate behaviors performed by Partner B then shape the experiences of Partner A and so on" (p. 230). As this scenario illustrates, the creation of intimate interaction requires individuals to express their intimate feelings to each other, as well as to respond positively to one another's expressions of intimacy. Theories focusing on patterns of nonverbal communication come to similar conclusions. For example, according to Andersen's (1985, 1998) cognitive valence theory, positive reactions to immediacy behavior lead to reciprocity and increased intimacy. Similarly, in Cappella and Greene's (1982) discrepancy arousal theory, individuals who feel positive emotion in response to a partner's increase in expressive, warm behavior are theorized to reciprocate by engaging in similarly expressive and warm behavior that creates intimate interaction. Research stemming from an expectancy violations theory has also demonstrated that interactions are rated as more intimate when positive involvement cues are reciprocated (see Burgoon et al., 1995, for a review).

Scholarship demonstrating an emotional contagion effect (Hatfield, Cacioppo, & Rapson, 1994) also suggests that reciprocity contributes to intimacy. Emotional contagion occurs when one person catches the emotions of the other, creating a likely reciprocity effect. If an individual does not express her or his intimate feelings, however, there is no opportunity for contagion to occur. Catching one another's emotions may also foster shared understanding, which is an important construct in Prager and Roberts' (2004) model of intimacy.

◆ Intimate Interactions as Relationship Enhancing

Partners who display and reciprocate positive involvement also enhance their relationships. Prager (2000) took the position that "intimate relationships are built on frequently occurring intimate interactions" (p. 236), with intimate interaction fostering satisfaction, trust, and understanding. Such a view is consistent with the perspective of communication scholars who have argued that relationships emerge across ongoing interactions. Wilmot (1995) contended that relationships represent a collection of all the interactions that two people have engaged in over time. Cappella (1988) argued, "Interactions reflect the kind of relationship that exists between the partners" (p. 325). This position is consistent with the idea that relationships are characterized as intimate because partners have a history of using positive involvement behaviors when interacting with one another.

Scholars have demonstrated that intimacy is the vital characteristic differentiating close

relationships from casual relationships (Hays, 1988; Monsour, 1992; Prager, 2000). Because positive involvement behaviors reflect intimacy (Prager, 2000), these behaviors help people maintain and enhance close relationships. Nonverbal involvement cues, however, vary across relationship type. In one study, people used more head nods, vocal fluency, vocal interest, and shorter response latencies when interacting with same-sex friends than with cross-sex friends or romantic partners (Guerrero, 1997), yet people maintained larger distances with same-sex friends. Women friends were most likely to use direct body orientation, and romantic partners used the most eye contact, touch, and closest proximity (Guerrero, 1997), suggesting different positive involvement cues emerge in intimate interactions depending on the type of relationship.

Positive involvement cues are also related to emotional support and comforting, both of which are associated with intimacy and relationship maintenance (Burleson & Samter, 1994). Jones and Guerrero (2001) found that both verbal person-centeredness (i.e., verbal comments validating the distressed person) and nonverbal immediacy exerted strong effects on comforting quality. Participants also reported feeling better (Jones, 2004) and liking the helper more (Jones & Burleson, 2003) when he or she was nonverbally immediate rather than nonimmediate. Comforting is most likely to occur in the context of an intimate relationship, suggesting a bidirectional relationship between intimacy and comforting (Burleson & Goldsmith, 1998).

Extensive evidence also links positive involvement behavior, including the expression of positive emotion, to relational satisfaction and the experience of intimacy (Guerrero & Floyd, 2006). As Kelly, Fincham, and Beach (2003) concluded, "it is often not the verbal content that stands out" when distinguishing between happy and unhappy couples. Instead, "what is remarkable is the pleasurable emotions couples appear to be experiencing—the smiles, laughs, affection, and warmth that couples show" (p. 729). During ordinary interaction and conflict episodes, satisfied couples express more positive affect than do dissatisfied couples (e.g., Broderick & O'Leary, 1986; Gottman, Markman, & Notarius, 1977). Satisfied couples in intimate relationships also reciprocate nonverbal displays of involvement, activity, and positive affect more than dissatisfied couples (Manusov, 1995). Although these studies measured satisfaction rather than intimacy, the results are consistent with Prager's (2000) theorizing about the connection between intimate interaction and relationship enhancement. Couples who create intimate interaction through the mutual display of positive involvement are likely to reinforce intimate feelings and perceptions while also enhancing their relationships.

Expressing positive involvement may also counterbalance negativity within romantic relationships. Fincham, Bradbury, Arias, Byrne, and Karney (1997) found that among couples displaying negative behavior, those who exhibited more positive behavior rated themselves as happier. Prager (2000) also noted that effective conflict management is essential for sustaining intimacy within relationships. Of course, it is often difficult to engage in positive involvement behavior in the midst of the negative emotion that tends to characterize many conflict interactions. Often, people respond to conflict by withdrawing or becoming demanding and competitive (Heavey, Christensen, & Malamuth, 1995). When people withdraw from conflict, they are likely to engage in behaviors that indicate a lack of involvement, such as using less gaze, a more closed posture, and more head down positions (Feeney, Noller, Sheehan, & Peterson, 1999). When individuals become demanding or competitive, they are likely to

engage in hostile or aggressive behaviors that reflect the intersection of involvement and negative affect (see Figure 14.2).

In a study on nonverbal correlates of conflict, Newton and Burgoon (1990) found that people who used antisocial verbal statements also tended to use nonverbal behaviors such as a loud or sharp vocal tone, head shaking, fast speaking rate, and animated gestures—all of which suggest involvement but not positive affect. By contrast, Newton and Burgoon showed that people who made supportive statements during conflict interactions were more likely to display positive involvement behaviors such as direct body orientation, kinesic animation, vocal warmth, and vocal interest. Given the considerable body of research showing that people tend to reciprocate negative nonverbal behavior during conflict interaction (for a review see Guerrero & Floyd, 2006), being able to break this negative cycle by using positive involvement cues may not only help couples deal with conflict more effectively, but also help them sustain intimate feelings and perceptions that enhance their relationships.

The experience of intimacy is also related to reading emotions accurately, particularly positive ones. Decoding positive emotions accurately is linked to satisfaction (Gottman & Porterfield, 1981) as well as to perceptions of shared understanding, which are part of the intimacy experience (Prager, 2000). Gaelick, Bodenhausen, and Wyer (1985) reported that people reciprocated emotions they *thought* their spouses were experiencing. People had more difficulty decoding affectionate emotions than hostile emotions, however, leading to more negative communication cycles. Similarly, Manusov, Floyd, and Kerssen-Griep (1997) found that partners in intimate dyads were more likely to notice negative nonverbal cues than positive cues, and positive perception of nonverbal behavior was linked to relational satisfaction. Partners in happy relationships attribute negative affect expression to external causes and positive affect expression to the relationship (Koerner & Fitzpatrick, 2002). Decoding nonthreatening emotional displays accurately is associated with relational closeness and experienced intimacy for couples, whereas accurately decoding relationship-threatening emotion is associated with less intimacy (Simpson, Orina, & Ickes, 2003).

◆ Summary and Conclusion

Intimate interactions play a pivotal role in the development and maintenance of relationships. Nonverbal cues of positive involvement are a critical component that helps define interaction as intimate. Behaviors such as gaze, smiling, touch, and close distancing are all related to perceptions of intimacy and liking, especially when they are welcome and reciprocated. These behaviors also differentiate close relationships from casual relationships, and satisfied couples from dissatisfied couples. Along with self-disclosure and verbal responsiveness, nonverbal behaviors that signal positive involvement are key ingredients in the recipe for intimate interaction.

Taking an interaction-based approach to the study of intimacy provides scholars with many challenges and exciting directions for new research. First, scholars need to continue examining interactions between people to determine which specific positive involvement behaviors are associated most strongly with intimacy across various types of relationships. Second, scholars should investigate the extent to which variables such as attraction and perceived similarity influence both intimacy experience and intimacy expression in initial interaction. Third, to get a more complete picture of intimacy in developed relationships, researchers will need to examine how intimacy experience and expression influence one another as well as relational characteristics such as trust, love, satisfaction, and commitment. The perceptions and behaviors of both relational partners need to be explored and patterns of reciprocity should be investigated. Researchers studying relational maintenance may also want to look at how intimate interaction helps sustain and enhance close relationships.

Intimacy is a complex construct that emerges from dynamic interaction patterns. To appreciate this complexity fully, scholars must understand the specific nonverbal and verbal behaviors that work in tandem with perceptions, emotions, and relationship characteristics in creating and sustaining intimate interaction.

◆ References

Acitelli, L. K., & Duck, S. W. (1987). Intimacy as the proverbial elephant. In D. Perlman & S. W. Duck (Eds.), *Intimate relationships: Development, dynamics, and deterioration* (pp. 297–308). Newbury Park, CA: Sage.

Ainsworth, M. D. S., Blehar, M. C., Waters, E., & Wall, S. (1978). *Patterns of attachment: A psychological study of the strange situation.* Hillsdale, NJ: Erlbaum.

Altman, I., & Taylor, D. A. (1973). *Social penetration: The development of interpersonal relationships.* New York: Holt, Rinehart & Winston.

Andersen, P. A. (1985). Nonverbal immediacy in interpersonal communication. In A. W. Siegman & S. Feldstein (Eds.), *Multichannel integrations of nonverbal behavior* (pp. 1–36). Hillsdale, NJ: Erlbaum.

Andersen, P. A. (1998). The cognitive valence theory of intimate communication. In M. T. Palmer & G. A. Barnett (Eds.), *Progress in communication sciences, Volume XIV:*

Mutual influence in interpersonal communication: Theory and research in cognition, affect, and behavior (pp. 39–72). Stamford, CT: Ablex.

Andersen, P. A. (1999). *Nonverbal communication: Forms and functions*. Mountain View, CA: Mayfield.

Andersen, P. A. (2005). The touch avoidance measure. In V. Manusov (Ed.), *The sourcebook of nonverbal measures: Going beyond words*. (pp. 57–66). Mahwah, NJ: Erlbaum.

Andersen, P. A., & Andersen, J. F. (1984). The exchange of nonverbal immediacy: A critical review of dyadic models. *Journal of Nonverbal Behavior, 8,* 327–349.

Andersen, P. A., & Andersen, J. F. (2005). Measurement of perceived nonverbal immediacy. In V. Manusov (Ed.), *The sourcebook of nonverbal measures: Going beyond words*. (pp. 113–126). Mahwah, NJ: Erlbaum.

Andersen, P. A., & Guerrero, L. K. (1998). The bright side of relational communication: Interpersonal warmth as a social emotion. In P.A. Andersen & L. K. Guerrero (Eds.), *Handbook of communication and emotion: Research, theory, applications and contexts* (pp. 303–324). San Diego, CA: Academic Press.

Argyle, M. (1972). *The psychology of interpersonal behavior* (2nd ed.). London: Penguin.

Aune, K. S., Aune, R. K., & Buller, D. B. (1994). The experience, expression, and perceived appropriateness of emotion across levels of relationship development. *Journal of Social Psychology, 134,* 141–150.

Baxter, L., & Ward, J. (1975). Newsline. *Psychology Today, 8,* 28.

Black, K. A., & Gold, D. J. (2003). Men's and women's reactions to hypothetical sexual advances: The role of initiator socioeconomic status and level of coercion. *Sex Roles, 49,* 173–178.

Breed, G. (1972). The effect of intimacy: Reciprocity or retreat? *British Journal of Social and Clinical Psychology, 2,* 135–142.

Broderick, J. E., & O'Leary, K. D. (1986). Contributions of affect, attitude and behavior to marital satisfaction. *Journal of Consulting and Clinical Psychology, 54,* 514–517.

Burgoon, J. K. (1991). Relational message interpretations of touch, conversational distance, and posture. *Journal of Nonverbal Behavior, 15,* 233–259.

Burgoon, J. K., Buller, D. B., Hale, J. L., & deTurck, M. A. (1984). Relational messages associated with nonverbal behaviors. *Human Communication Research, 10,* 351–378.

Burgoon, J. K., Buller, D. B., & Woodall, W. G. (1996). *Nonverbal communication: The unspoken dialogue* (2nd ed.). New York: McGraw-Hill.

Burgoon, J. K., Coker, D. A., & Coker, R. A. (1986). Communicative effects of gaze behavior: A test of two contrasting explanations. *Human Communication Research, 12,* 495–524.

Burgoon, J. K., & Hale, J. L. (1988). Nonverbal expectancy violations: Model elaboration and application to immediacy behaviors. *Communication Monographs, 55,* 58–79.

Burgoon, J. K., & Le Poire, B. A. (1999). Nonverbal cues and interpersonal judgments: Participant and observer perceptions of intimacy, dominance, composure, and formality. *Communication Monographs, 66,* 105–124.

Burgoon, J. K., Manusov, V., Mineo, P., & Hale, J. L. (1985). Effects of eye gaze on hiring, credibility, attraction, and relational message interpretation. *Journal of Nonverbal Behavior, 9,* 133–146.

Burgoon, J. K., & Newton, D. A. (1991). Applying a social meaning model to relational message interpretations of conversational involvement: Comparing observer and participant perspectives. *Southern Communication Journal, 56,* 96–113.

Burgoon, J. K., Stern, L. A., & Dillman, L. (1995). *Interpersonal adaptation: Dyadic interaction patterns.* New York: Cambridge University Press.

Burleson, B. R., & Goldsmith, D. J. (1998). How the comforting process works: Alleviating emotional distress through conversationally induced reappraisals. In P. A. Andersen & L. K. Guerrero (Eds.), *Handbook of communication and emotion: Research, theory, applications and contexts* (pp. 245–280). San Diego, CA: Academic Press.

Burleson, B. R., & Samter, W. (1994). A social skills approach to relationship maintenance: How individual differences in communication skills affect the achievement of relationship functions. In D. J. Canary & L. Stafford (Eds.), *Communication and relational maintenance* (pp. 61–90). San Diego, CA: Academic Press.

Byrne, D. (1997). An overview (and underview) of research and theory within the attraction paradigm. *Journal of Social and Personal Relationships, 14,* 417–431.

Cappella, J. N. (1981). Mutual influence in expressive behavior: Adult-adult and infant-adult dyadic interaction. *Psychological Bulletin, 89,* 101–132.

Cappella, J. N. (1983). Conversational involvement: Approaching and avoiding others. In J. M. Wiemann & R. P. Harrison (Eds.), *Nonverbal interaction* (pp. 113–148). Beverly Hills, CA: Sage.

Cappella, J. N. (1988). Personal relationships, social relationships and patterns of interaction. In S. Duck (Ed.), *Handbook of personal relationships: Theory, research and interventions* (pp. 325–342). Chichester, UK: Wiley.

Cappella, J. N., & Greene, J. O. (1982). A discrepancy-arousal explanation of mutual influence in expressive behavior for adult and infant-adult interaction. *Communication Monographs, 49,* 89–114.

Cartar, L., Hicks, M., & Slane, S. (1996). Women's reactions to hypothetical male touch as a function of initiator attractiveness and level of coercion. *Sex Roles, 35,* 737–750.

Clarke, D. D., Allen, C. M. B., & Dickson, S. (1985). The characteristic affective tone of seven classes of interpersonal relationships. *Journal of Social and Personal Relationships, 2,* 117–130.

Coker, D. A., & Burgoon, J. K. (1987). The nature of conversational involvement and

nonverbal encoding patterns. *Human Communication Research, 13,* 463–494.

Dillard, J. P., Solomon, D. H., & Palmer, M. T. (1999). Structuring the concept of relational communication. *Communication Monographs, 66,* 49–65.

Egland, K. I., Stelzner, M. A., Andersen, P. A., & Spitzberg, B. S. (1997). Perceived understanding, nonverbal communication, and relational satisfaction. In J. E. Aitken & L. J. Shedletsky (Eds.), *Intrapersonal communication processes* (pp. 386–396). Annandale, VA: Speech Communication Association.

Ekman, P., & Friesen, W. V. (1975). *Unmasking the face: A guide to recognizing emotions from facial clues.* Englewood Cliffs, NJ: Prentice Hall.

Emmers, T. M., & Dindia, K. (1995). The effect of relational stage and intimacy on touch: An extension of Guerrero and Andersen. *Personal Relationships, 2,* 225–236.

Feeney, J. A., Noller, P., Sheehan, G., & Peterson, C. (1999). Conflict issues and conflict strategies as contexts for nonverbal behavior in close relationships. In P. Philippot, R. S. Feldman, & E. J. Coats (Eds.), *The social context of nonverbal behavior* (pp. 348–371). Paris: Cambridge University Press.

Fincham, F. D., Bradbury, T. N., Arias, I., Byrne, C. A., & Karney, B. R. (1997). Marital violence, marital distress, and attributions. *Journal of Family Violence, 11,* 367–372.

Floyd, K. (1999). All touches are not created equal: Effects of form and duration on observers' perceptions of an embrace. *Journal of Nonverbal Behavior, 23,* 283–299.

Floyd, K., & Ray, G. B. (2003). Human affection exchange: VI. Vocalic predictors of perceived affection in initial interactions. *Western Journal of Communication, 67,* 56–73.

Gaelick, L., Bodenhausen, G. V., & Wyer, R. S., Jr. (1985). Emotional communication in close relationships. *Journal of Personality and Social Psychology, 49,* 1246–1265.

Giles, H., & Street, R. L. (1994). Communication characteristics and behavior.

In M. L. Knapp & G. R. Miller (Eds.) *Handbook of interpersonal communication* (2nd ed., pp. 103–161). Thousand Oaks, CA: Sage.

Gottman, J. M., Markman, H. J., & Notarius, C. I. (1977). The topography of marital conflict: A sequenced analysis of verbal and nonverbal behaviors. *Journal of Marriage and the Family, 39,* 461–477.

Gottman, J. M., & Porterfield, A. L. (1981). Communicative competence in the nonverbal behavior of married couples. *Journal of Marriage and the Family, 43,* 817–824.

Guerrero, L. K. (1996). Attachment-style differences in intimacy and involvement: A test of the four-category model. *Communication Monographs, 63,* 269–292.

Guerrero, L. K. (1997). Nonverbal involvement across interactions with same-sex friends, opposite-sex friends, and romantic partners: Consistency or change? *Journal of Social and Personal Relationships, 14,* 31–58.

Guerrero, L. K. (2000). Intimacy. In D. Levinson, J. Ponzetti, & P. Jorgensen (Eds.), *Encyclopedia of human emotions.* (pp. 403–409) New York: Macmillan Reference.

Guerrero, L. K. (2004). Observer ratings of nonverbal involvement and immediacy. In V. Manusov (Ed.), *The sourcebook of nonverbal measures: Going beyond words* (pp. 221–235). Mahwah, NJ: Erlbaum.

Guerrero, L. K., & Andersen, P. A. (1991). The waxing and waning of relational intimacy: Touch as a function of relational stage, gender and touch avoidance. *Journal of Social and Personal Relationships, 8,* 147–165.

Guerrero, L. K., & Andersen, P. A. (1994). Patterns of matching and initiation: Touch behavior and avoidance across romantic relationship stages. *Journal of Nonverbal Behavior, 18,* 137–153.

Guerrero, L. K., & Andersen, P. A. (2000). Emotion in close relationships. In C. Hendrick & S. S. Hendrick (Eds.), *Close relationships: A sourcebook* (pp. 171–186). Thousand Oaks, CA: Sage.

Guerrero, L. K., & Floyd, K. (2006). *Nonverbal communication in close relationships.* Mahwah, NJ: Erlbaum.

Hall, E. T. (1966). *The hidden dimension.* Garden City, NY: Doubleday.

Hall, J. A., & Bernieri, F. J. (2001). *Interpersonal sensitivity theory and measurement.* Mahwah, NJ: Erlbaum.

Hatfield, E. (1984). The dangers of intimacy. In V. J. Derlega (Ed.), *Communication, intimacy, and close relationships* (pp. 191–217). New Haven, CT: Yale University Press.

Hatfield, E., Cacioppo, J. T., & Rapson, R. L. (1994). *Emotional contagion.* New York: Cambridge University Press.

Hatfield, E., & Rapson, R. L. (1987). Gender difference in love and intimacy: The fantasy vs. the reality. *Journal of Social Work and Human Sexuality, 5,* 12–26.

Hays, R. B. (1988). Friendship. In S. W. Duck (Ed.), *Handbook of personal relationships* (pp. 391–408). New York: Wiley.

Heavey, C. L., Christensen, A., & Malamuth, N. M. (1995). The longitudinal impact of demand and withdrawal during marital conflict. *Journal of Consulting and Clinical Psychology, 63,* 797–801.

Heslin, R., & Boss, D. (1980). Nonverbal intimacy in arrival and departure at an airport. *Personality and Social Psychology Bulletin, 6,* 248–252.

Isabella, R. A., & Belsky, J. (1991). Interactional synchrony and the origins of infant-mother attachment: A replication study. *Child Development, 62,* 373–384.

Jones, S. M. (2004). Putting the person into person-centered and immediate emotional support: Emotional change and perceived helper competence as outcomes of comforting in helping situations. *Communication Research, 32,* 338–360.

Jones, S. M., & Burleson, B. R. (2003). Effects of helper and recipient sex on the experience and outcomes of comforting messages: An experimental investigation. *Sex Roles, 48*(1/2), 1–19.

Jones, S. M., & Guerrero, L. K. (2001). Nonverbal immediacy and verbal person centeredness in the emotional support process. *Human Communication Research, 27,* 567–596.

Kelly, A. B., Fincham, F. D., & Beach, S. R. H. (2003). Communication skills in couples:

A review and discussion of emerging perspectives. In J. O. Greene & B. R. Burleson (Eds.), *Handbook of communication and social skills* (pp. 723–751). Mahwah, NJ: Erlbaum.

Kleinke, C. L. (1986). Gaze and eye contact: A research review. *Psychological Bulletin, 100,* 78–100.

Knapp, M. L., & Hall, J. A. (2006). *Nonverbal communication in human interaction* (6th ed.). Belmont, CA: Wadsworth-Thomson.

Koerner, A. F., & Fitzpatrick, M. A. (2002). Nonverbal communication and marital adjustment and satisfaction: The role of decoding relationship relevant and relationship irrelevant affect. *Communication Monographs, 69,* 33–51.

Lee, J. W., & Guerrero, L. K. (2001). Types of touch in cross-sex relationships between co-workers: Perceptions of relational and emotional messages, inappropriateness, and sexual harassment. *Journal of Applied Communication, 29,* 197–220.

Manusov, V. (1995). Reacting to changes in nonverbal behaviors: Relational satisfaction and adaptation patterns in romantic dyads. *Human Communication Research, 21,* 456–477.

Manusov, V., Floyd, K., & Kerssen-Griep, J. (1997). Yours, mine, and ours: Mutual attributions for nonverbal behaviors in couples' interactions. *Communication Research, 24,* 234–260.

Marston, P. J., Hecht, M. L., Manke, M. L., McDaniel, S., & Reeder, H. (1998). The subjective experience of intimacy, passion, and commitment in heterosexual loving relationships. *Personal Relationships, 5,* 15–30.

Marston, P. J., Hecht, M. L., & Robers, T. (1987). True love ways: The subjective experience and communication of romantic love. *Journal of Social and Personal Relationships, 4,* 387–407.

McAdams, D. P. (1988). Personal needs and personal relationships. In S. Duck (Ed.), *Handbook of personal relationships* (pp. 7–22). New York: Wiley.

McDaniel, E., & Andersen, P.A. (1998). International patterns of tactile communication: A field study. *Journal of Nonverbal Behavior, 21,* 59–75.

Mehrabian, A. (1967). Orientation behaviors and nonverbal attitude in communicators. *Journal of Communication, 17,* 324–332.

Mehrabian, A. (1969a). Significance of posture and position in the communication of attitude and status relationships. *Psychological Bulletin, 71,* 359–372.

Mehrabian, A. (1969b). Some referents and measures of nonverbal behavior. *Behavior Research Methods and Instrumentation, 1,* 203–207.

Mehrabian A. (1981). *Silent messages: Implicit communication of emotions and attitudes* (2nd ed.). Belmont, CA: Wadsworth.

Mehrabian, A., & Ksionsky, S. (1972). Categories of social behavior. *Comparative Group Studies, 3,* 425–436.

Monsour, M. (1992). Meanings of intimacy in cross- and same-sex friendships. *Journal of Social and Personal Relationships, 9,* 277–295.

Montagu, A. (1978). *Touching: The human significance of the skin* (2nd ed.). New York: Harper and Row.

Morris, D. (1971). *Intimate behavior.* New York: Random House.

Morton, T. L. (1977). *The effects of acquaintance and distance on intimacy and reciprocity.* Unpublished doctoral dissertation, University of Utah, Salt Lake City.

Newton, D. A., & Burgoon, J. K. (1990). Nonverbal conflict behaviors: Functions, strategies, and tactics. In D. D. Cahn (Ed.), *Intimates in conflict: A communication perspective* (pp. 77–104). Hillsdale, NJ: Erlbaum.

Palmer, M. T., Cappella, N. J., Patterson, M. L., & Churchill, M. (1990, June). *Mapping conversation behaviors onto relational inferences I: A cross-sectional analysis.* Paper presented at the meeting of the International Communication Association, Dublin, Ireland.

Palmer, M. T., & Simmons, K. B. (1995). Communicating intentions through nonverbal behaviors: Conscious and unconscious encoding of liking. *Human Communication Research, 22,* 128–160.

Patterson, M. L. (1983). *Nonverbal behavior: A functional perspective.* New York: Springer.

Patterson, M. L. (1988). Functions of nonverbal behavior in close relationships. In S. Duck (Ed.), *Handbook of personal relationships* (pp. 41–56). New York: Wiley.

Planalp, S., DeFrancisco, V. I., & Rutherford, D. (1996). Varieties of cues to emotion in naturally occurring situations. *Cognition and Emotion, 10,* 137–153.

Prager, K. J. (1995). *The psychology of intimacy.* New York: Guilford.

Prager, K. J. (2000). Intimacy in personal relationships. In C. Hendrick & S. S. Hendrick (Eds.), *Close relationships: A sourcebook* (pp. 229–242). Thousand Oaks, CA: Sage.

Prager, K. J., & Roberts, L. J. (2004). Deep intimate connection: Self and intimacy in couple relationships. In D. J. Mashek & A. P. Aron (Eds.), *Handbook of closeness and intimacy* (pp. 43–60). Mahwah, NJ: Erlbaum.

Priest, R. F., & Sawyer, J. (1967). Proximity and peership: Bases of balance in interpersonal attraction. *American Journal of Sociology, 72,* 633–649.

Ray, G. B., & Floyd, K. (2000, May). *Nonverbal expressions of liking and disliking in initial interaction: Encoding and decoding perspectives.* Paper presented at the meeting of the Eastern States Communication Association, Pittsburgh, PA.

Reis, H. T., & Shaver, P. (1988). Intimacy as an interpersonal process. In S. Duck (Ed.), *Handbook of personal relationships* (pp. 367–389). New York: Wiley.

Shaver, P. R., Schwartz, J., Kirson, D., & O'Connor, C. (1987). Emotion knowledge: Further explorations of a prototype approach. *Journal of Personality and Social Psychology, 52,* 1061–1086.

Simpson, J. A., Orina, M., & Ickes, W. (2003). When accuracy hurts and when it helps: A test of the empathic accuracy model in marital interactions. *Journal of Personality and Social Psychology, 85,* 881–893.

Stern, D. (1980). *The first relationship: Mother and infant.* Cambridge, MA: Harvard University Press.

Sternberg, R. J. (1986). A triangular theory of love. *Psychological Review, 93,* 119–135.

Tickle-Degnen, L., & Rosenthal, R. (1990). The nature of rapport and nonverbal correlates. *Psychology Inquiry, 1,* 285–293.

Wertin, L., & Andersen, P. A. (1996, February). *Cognitive schema and the perceptions of sexual harassment: A test of cognitive valence theory.* Paper presented at the annual meeting of the Western States Communication Association, Pasadena, CA.

Wilmot, W. W. (1995). *Relational communication.* New York: McGraw-Hill.

15

NONVERBAL EXPRESSIONS OF DOMINANCE AND POWER IN HUMAN RELATIONSHIPS

◆ Judee K. Burgoon
University of Arizona

◆ Norah E. Dunbar
California State University, Long Beach

Fundamental to all social species is the negotiation and expression of dominance and power relationships. Whether it is establishing a pecking order or a marching order, proclaiming privileges or prohibitions, exercising leadership or intimidation, humans, like other mammals, have evolved intricate means of signaling in any social encounter who are "one up" or "one down," who can "have" or "have not," who "goes before" or "goes after." Such signaling is a necessity for creating

Authors' Note: Preparation of this manuscript was supported by funding from the U.S. Air Force Office of Scientific Research under the U.S. Department of Defense University Research Initiative (Grant No. F49620-01-1-0394). The views, opinions, and/or findings in this report are those of the authors and should not be construed as an official Department of Defense position, policy, or decision.

◆ 279

and maintaining social order. And, as with so many other aspects of social behavior, much of this work is done nonverbally. It is the nonverbal signals of dominance-submission and power-powerlessness that constitute the focus of this chapter.

The social significance of nonverbal expressions of dominance and power is underscored by the panoply of scientific research and commentary it has attracted. Ellyson and Dovidio (1985) note such diverse tributaries as Charles Darwin's *The Expression of Emotion in Man and Animals* (1872/1965), Sigmund Freud's psychoanalytic treatises, works by personality and social psychologists in the early 1900s, and anthropological works by Ray Birdwhistell (1970) and Edward Hall (1959, 1966). A confluence of research on such interrelated constructs as status, authority, rank, control, influence, expertise, leadership, domineeringness, assertiveness, and aggressiveness has galvanized interest further in this fundamental social dimension. Though these various constructs are not synonymous, they all fall under what Edinger and Patterson (1983) referred to as the *social control* aspects of interaction and what Hall, Coats, and Smith LeBeau (2005) labeled the *vertical dimension* of human relationships.

In this chapter, we conceptualize dominance and power as incorporating not only reflexive, fixed action patterns that are under the control of external stimuli but also deliberate, adaptive, and changeable ones that are under the control of actors themselves (consistent with some ethologists and behavioral ecologists, e.g., Bernstein, 1980; Fridlund, 1991a, 1991b; Liska, 1992). Greater emphasis on the strategic aspects of dominance squares with our writings on interpersonal dominance as social, interactional, situational, intentional, and dynamic (Burgoon & Dunbar, 2000; Burgoon, Johnson, &

Koch, 1998). This chapter is meant to further that discussion.

◆ Conceptualizing Power, Dominance, and Status

Decades of scholarly debate on what constitutes power have produced a consensual view of *power* as the capacity to produce intended effects, and in particular, the ability to influence the behavior of another person (Berger, 1994; Burgoon et al., 1998; Dunbar, 2004; French & Raven, 1959). Power takes many forms, and its multidimensional nature is reflected in the classification of power into three domains: power bases, power processes, and power outcomes (Olson & Cromwell, 1975). *Power bases* refer to resources such as rewards or knowledge that form the foundation for control over others (French & Raven, 1959). Several of the nonverbal display patterns to be discussed in this chapter are linked to these bases of power. *Power processes,* on the other hand, are the specific strategies (often nonverbal) used to exert power in interactions. *Power outcomes* are the compliance, conformity, cooperation, or obedience that one secures; that is, they are the actual influence that is achieved over others' beliefs and actions (Wheeless, Barraclough, & Stewart, 1983).

The conceptualization of *dominance* has varied according to disciplinary perspective. For personality psychologists, dominance is considered an enduring individual trait that designates one's characteristic temperament and behavioral predispositions (e.g., Cattell, Eber, & Tatsuoka, 1970; Ridgeway, 1987). Social skills are part of this equation, as the ability to be forceful, to take initiative, and to be expressive yet relaxed and poised are all facets of dominance displays that correspond with characterizations of a skillful communication style (Burgoon & Dunbar, 2000). For biologists and sociobiologists, dominance designates a pattern of imbalance in interactions within a dyadic relationship (Hinde, 1978) or an organism's position in a social hierarchy (Sebeok, 1972), which accords it preferential access to resources (Omark, 1980). For sociologists, power and dominance are intertwined with *status*, which designates one's position in a socially agreed-upon hierarchy, something that is prevalent in all types of societies (Lips, 1991). A person's social position is often based on possession of commodities valued by the society (e.g., money, occupation, good looks) or position within a prestige hierarchy of relations in a social unit.

Communication and social psychology scholars largely view dominance as a social rather than organismic variable but *one that is defined at the interpersonal level* (i.e., in relation to another actor). Dominance constitutes one of two superordinate topoi of relational communication (Burgoon & Hale, 1984). Whereas power may remain latent, dominance is manifest and behavioral, referencing those communicative acts by which one actor's assertion of influence and control is met with acquiescence from another (Burgoon & Dunbar, 2000; Rogers-Millar & Millar, 1979). Moreover, even though dominance-submission is conceptualized as a universal dimension along which all social relationships can be arrayed, dominance displays may be instigated by a combination of individual temperament and situational features that encourage dominant behavior (Aries, Gold, & Weigel, 1983; Burgoon & Dunbar, 2000) and that are responsive to changing goals, interlocutors, situations, and time, among other factors. Thus, within the same episode, individuals may adjust their dominance-submission displays to changing circumstances.

Overall, power, dominance, and status are best conceptualized as interrelated though not synonymous. High status often gives the appearance of power and may facilitate dominance because one is endowed with legitimate authority, and legitimate authority confers on the individual the potential for greater influence (Rollins & Bahr, 1976). But high status does not guarantee the exercise of power or the display of dominant behavior, and dominance displays in the absence of legitimate power may fail to achieve influence (Ridgeway, Diekema, & Johnson, 1995). In this chapter, we focus on "power" and "dominance" and use them as shorthand for the dimensions of *dominance-submission* and *power-powerlessness*. We ask the reader to interpret dominance and power, not as discrete categories, but as continua that span the extremes of each dimensional pole and all points in between.

◆ Operationalizing Power and Dominance

Power and dominance can be understood more concretely through their typical operationalizations. Power is often operationalized as *potential* influence and measured as a perceptual variable, despite claims that perceptions do not necessarily constitute "real" power differences (e.g., Olson & Cromwell, 1975). Measures range from self-reports and overlapping circles that represent various levels of equality in a relationship, to role-plays, projective tests, and story writing (e.g., Berger, 1994; Dunbar & Burgoon, 2005a; Neff & Harter, 2002). Such measures often make little or no mention of nonverbal behavior.

By contrast, dominance is operationalized commonly in ways that incorporate nonverbal behavior, whether through self-reports of an individual's own dominance, partner or observer perceptions of another person's dominance, or trained coders' ratings of particular markers of dominance (Dunbar & Burgoon, 2005b). Measurements can be made at the microlevel, in which case they entail objective physical behaviors, or at the macrolevel, in which case they entail holistic interpretations of whether an actor appears dominant or submissive (see Dunbar & Burgoon, 2005b, for samples of both types in separate studies and Burgoon & Le Poire, 1999, or Moscowitz, 1988, 1990, for examples of both measurement approaches in the same study). Dominant microbehaviors that have been measured include talk time, loudness, gaze, eyebrow raise, posture, arm and leg positions, physical assertiveness, smiling, threat gestures, proximity, and touch (e.g., Aries et al., 1983; Schwartz, Tesser, & Powell, 1982).

In contrast to examinations of particular behaviors made by an individual, relationally based measurement examines dominance at the dyadic level. A relational perspective distinguishes between *domineeringness*—individual attempts to control the interaction—and dominance. The former is assessed as an individual-level characteristic; the latter is defined according to pairs of adjacent conversational turns by which interlocutors position themselves as "one up" or "one down" vis-à-vis the other. Specifically, dominance is said to occur when one individual's assertive actions elicit complementary acquiescence by another. Hence, dominance or submission is defined according to "interacts" (pairs of acts) rather than individual acts (Rogers-Millar & Millar, 1979; for an incorporation of nonverbal cues and the application in group settings, see Siegel, Friedlander, & Heatherington, 1992). Overall, however, the operationalizations of power and dominance reflect their definitional differences. Power is often measured through an individual's perceptions based on his or her relationship to another, whereas dominance is measured by the behavioral manifestations of that power, whether recorded by third parties or the interactants themselves.

♦ Theoretical Perspectives

There is an array of theories and models that provide the foundation for principles of nonverbal dominance, power, and status. Organismic approaches view dominance and power as inhering in characteristics or behavioral patterns of individuals, and status as associated with classes of individuals. More social models envision dominance and power as transacted between actors at dyadic or group levels. Uniting these respective perspectives on social conduct is an interest in socially acquired behavioral routines. Several of these models are discussed in the following sections.

PERSONALITY AND EVOLUTIONARY PSYCHOLOGY

The history of personality assessment is rife with constructs that are linked explicitly or implicitly to dominance and power: *n*Dominance, *n*Power, authoritarianism, locus of control, and Machiavellianism, among others. Because personality is expected to be fairly stable, nonverbal indicators associated with personality traits should form stable behavioral profiles by which individuals could be typed. In support of this view, Gifford (1994) used a Brunswikian lens model to analyze 27 behaviors and concluded that eight were valid indicators that accounted for 30% of the variance in ambitious-dominant personality and 39% of the variance in lazy-submissive personality. Other research, discussed in detail below, points to a fairly stable behavioral profile associated with expressivity, which some (e.g., Gallaher, 1992) have viewed as a personality style that would be associated closely with dominance or extraversion.

Ethology and evolutionary psychology perspectives, on the other hand, focus on physiological, anatomical, and behavioral features that are adaptive in responding to survival-related problems (see Floyd, this volume). Within the ethological perspective is a bifurcation between viewing dominance-submission as (1) inborn attributes possessed by individual organisms that confer on them greater or lesser survival success than other species mates or (2) emergent properties of social interaction that entail the ability to manipulate others and form alliances. Those who subscribe to the former viewpoint see in many intraspecific and interspecific displays vestiges of inborn tendencies to exert power and domination, to elicit deference and acquiescence, or to appease and submit to a stronger conspecific (see Andrew, 1972; Keltner, 1995; Smith, 1974; Thorpe, 1972). Displays such as fight-flight, or more abbreviated intention signals of approach-avoidance, are thought to be universal and innate, the result of natural selection leading to *ritualized* displays. Behaviors such as sprawling, relaxed postures and sweeping gestures that signal lack of fear among humans find parallels in the expansive posture or tail-in-the-air gait of other warm-blooded creatures.

Yet many behaviors that appear to be homologs across species do not necessarily share a genetic origin. Some signals may actually be *conventionalized*, the result of learning at critical periods in an animal's development (Fridlund, 1991a). Contemporary ethological work is shifting away from viewing dominance strictly as an innate pattern based on aggressiveness, toward one in which

dominance is also socially negotiated; away from partitioning variance into separate individual and social components, toward understanding the interaction between organisms and their social environment (Burgoon & Dunbar, 2000). Representative of this view is the behavioral ecology perspective, a term coined by Fridlund (1991a, 1991b), that acknowledges the fundamentally social and communicative nature of these dominance displays, their inborn origins notwithstanding. Display forms and intensity are seen as responsive to the relationship between sender and receiver and no longer viewed as primitive reflexes but rather as inclinations, because unequivocally announcing one's intentions would risk heightened resistance and therefore be detrimental to survival.

Appeasement displays are linked closely to the submissive end of the dominance-submission continuum. Keltner, Young, and Buswell (1997) conjecture that emotional states such as modesty, shyness, embarrassment, and shame have all evolved from appeasement systems in other species and serve appeasement-related functions in humans. Appeasement signals are intended to placate or pacify others when social relationships are disrupted and conflicts arise. Violations of social rules or breeches of expected social distance may prompt appeasement gestures in the form of submissiveness, affiliative displays, or inhibitions of other actions. Acceptance of an appeasement gesture may take the form of reduced aggressiveness and increased social approach.

SOCIAL EXCHANGE MODELS

Social exchange models move dominance, power, and status from the personality or biological into a social arena and share the assumption that individuals will act to maximize their interpersonal rewards and minimize their interpersonal costs (Rusbult & Arriaga, 1997; Thibaut & Kelley, 1959). Social exchange theories view power as a characteristic *of a relationship,* not an individual. Power is achieved dyadically when a person is valued as an exchange partner and there are few alternatives; people depend more on partners who hold high exchange value (Emerson, 1962). This power-dependence relationship may be expressed nonverbally through influence strategies related to making oneself appear more attractive as a partner or signaling one's interest or disinterest in an exchange relationship (Burgoon, Dunbar, & Segrin, 2002).

One social exchange theory that focuses on nonverbal cues specifically is *dyadic power theory* (DPT) (Dunbar, 2004; Rollins & Bahr, 1976). It proposes that perceptions of legitimate authority and access to resources increase individuals' perceptions of power compared with interaction partners. Perceptions of power, in turn, influence the use of dominant communication to control the interaction, which results in greater influence over decisions. In DPT, the relationship between power and dominance is theorized to be curvilinear, because power is sometimes latent rather than overt (Komter, 1989). For example, *powerless* individuals may remain silent if they fear retaliation or termination of the relationship from their more powerful partner (Cloven & Roloff, 1993; Leung, 1988). On the other hand, extremely powerful individuals may maintain control without ever having to initiate any control attempts (Bugental & Shennum, 2002; Christensen & Heavey, 1990; Dunbar, 2004). In a test of DPT, Dunbar and Burgoon (2005a) found that the most powerful individuals (i.e., with the most influence) were the most facially and gesturally expressive, the least controlled in their body

actions, and perceived by their partners as nondominant.

GENDER POLITICS

Another social model of power is what has become known as the "gender politics hypothesis" (Henley, 1977, 1995; LaFrance & Henley, 1993; also see Hall, this volume). In this model, nonverbal behaviors are a primary means by which those in positions of power (usually men) exercise social control and interpersonal dominance. Henley argued that many behaviors that may seem unimportant are actually reflections of societal biases founded in power differences. For example, she claimed that women are more likely to exhibit circumspect demeanor, tense posture, gaze aversion or vigilant watching, more smiling, touch avoidance, and greater emotional expressivity. Henley drew a parallel between the behaviors associated with status and the behaviors associated with sex: "The same behaviors exhibited by superior to subordinate are those exhibited by men to women; and women exhibit to men the behaviors typical of subordinate to superior" (Henley, 1977, p. 180). Undergirding the gender politics hypothesis are three key premises: (1) that nonverbal differences between men and women are substantial; (2) that observed nonverbal patterns reflect social disparities; that is, nonverbal patterns are systematically correlated with degree of power or dominance; and (3) those who occupy the subordinate role (usually women) are more socially perceptive and vigilant by virtue of their position of greater weakness and vulnerability.

Research has documented large sex or gender differences in nonverbal behavior. For example, several reviews by Hall (1998, this volume; Hall et al., 2005) and others (e.g., Andersen, 1998; Burgoon & Dillman,

1995; LaFrance, Hecht, & Levy Paluck, 2003; Riggio, this volume) have found that, compared with men, women generally smile, gaze, nod, and gesture more; use more direct body orientation; receive but do not give more touch; are less relaxed posturally but also exhibit less shifting of body and feet; have more speech errors, and give more back-channel responses. Women are also more skilled decoders and encoders of nonverbal and emotional communication and exhibit nonverbal behaviors indicative of docility and openness to others.

Nevertheless, many of the empirical findings do not comport with the gender politics hypothesis. For example, the meta-analysis by Hall et al. (2005) found only four behaviors that were associated with higher actual verticality (their term for dominance, status, and power): closer physical distances to others, using more open body postures, interrupting more, and speaking more loudly (see also, Hall, Rosip, Smith LeBeau, Horgan, & Carter, 2006; Snodgrass, Hecht, & Ploutz-Snyder, 1998). The great heterogeneity in results and lack of parallelism between nonverbal gender differences and power, dominance, or status have led many scholars to conclude that research results on the gender politics hypothesis are equivocal, that there are more commonalities than differences between the sexes in dominance displays, that purported sex differences are often based on stereotypes, and that observed differences may not be attributable to women holding more subservient roles (Burgoon & Dillman, 1995; Dindia & Canary, 2006; Hall et al., 2005).

EXPECTANCY THEORIES

Other models of power draw upon expectations. For example, expectation states theory, which focuses on influence and task performance in groups, revolves around expectations that establish a "power and prestige order" (Berger, Conner, & Fisek, 1974; Ridgeway & Berger, 1986; Ridgeway & Walker, 1995). According to this theory, group members develop expectations about others' likely contributions to the task based on status characteristics, and these performance expectations confer an "expectation advantage or disadvantage," depending on whether the individual is expected to contribute favorably or unfavorably to successful task completion.

Status characteristics within this model involve any quality of actors around which evaluations of and beliefs about them come to be organized (e.g., age, sex, race, ethnicity, education, occupation, physical attractiveness, and intelligence; Berger, Rosenholtz, & Zelditch, 1980). Furthermore, expectation states theory differentiates between specific and diffuse status characteristics. *Specific* status characteristics are socially valued skills, expertise, or social accomplishments that imply a specific and bounded range of competencies, such as computer or mathematical skills. *Diffuse* status characteristics, such as gender or race, not only are associated culturally with some specific skills but also carry general expectations for competence that are diffuse and unbounded in range (Ridgeway & Walker, 1995). Many of these characteristics are signaled nonverbally through demeanor and appearance, making this theory especially relevant to nonverbal dominance. Those who possess status-valued external characteristics "are more likely (1) to have chances to perform, (2) to initiate problem-solving performances, (3) have their performances positively evaluated, and (4) are less likely to be influenced when there are disagreements" (Berger, Ridgeway, Fisek, & Norman, 1998, p. 381) than those lacking such characteristics or those who possess negatively valued ones.

Related to performance expectations are *reward expectations:* expectations about whether the status characteristics are more or less likely to create benefits for individual perceivers or the group. Three classes of reward structures that have been identified are categorical, ability, and outcome (Ridgeway & Berger, 1986). *Categorical structures* are related to diffuse social status characteristics such as age, gender, or physical strength. These expectations are like the physical attractiveness stereotypes discussed earlier in their ability to engender attraction and confer credibility. *Ability structures* are associated with the specific task to be performed. Speaking with an authoritative voice or using dramatic gestures may imply greater confidence and expertise (i.e., greater ability). *Outcome structures* are associated with actual accomplishments during the group task. Those with high expectation advantages not only are more likely to take the initiative (talking first, establishing seating arrangements, etc.) and to be more participative but also are likely to be accorded more deferential treatment by others. In this manner, they will have more of their recommendations acknowledged and accepted.

Another expectancy-based theory is expectancy violations theory (EVT), which addresses the effects of noticeable deviations from both societal and individual expectations for nonverbal communication (Burgoon, 1978, 1995; Burgoon & Burgoon, 2001). EVT is relevant to nonverbal dominance and power in several respects. Nonverbal behaviors are the locus of the expectations (or their violations). Interpretations of nonverbal behavior may include dominance connotations, and effects may include perceived power and actual influence. Additionally, effects may be moderated by characteristics of the actor that include his or her status, dominance, and power.

In EVT, *expectancies* are enduring patterns of anticipated behavior for a particular

individual that are appropriate, desired, or preferred. Deviant or unexpected behaviors, by virtue of their novelty, can heighten attention to the violation and the communicator committing the violation. *Reward valence* refers to whether interactions with the communicator are viewed as desirable or not. Someone who is physically attractive, has high status, controls valued resources, or gives positive feedback, for instance, should be more positively regarded than someone who is physically repulsive, has lower status, controls nothing of value, or gives negative feedback. Tests of EVT have demonstrated that for highly rewarding communicators, *violations* of expectancies can engender more positive interpretations of ambiguous or polysemic nonverbal behaviors, such that positive violations produce more favorable outcomes than expectancy confirmations. The same act committed by low-reward communicators can backfire, eliciting uncharitable evaluations that make it a negative violation. For low-reward communicators, expectancy *confirmation* is therefore best (Burgoon, 1991; Burgoon, Newton, Walther, & Baesler, 1989; Le Poire & Burgoon, 1994). Nonverbal indicators of status, power, and dominance may be understood in many contexts from an EVT frame to the extent that they impinge on reward valence, constitute expectancy violations, or are the result of violations.

SUMMARY

Scholars have identified many theoretical explanations for differences in status, dominance, or power. Whereas some theorists place the emphasis on personality or individual characteristics, many scholars consider perceptions of power and the resultant dominance displays to be interpersonal or relational in nature. They are often influenced by context in that interactants' past experiential history or larger societal norms can influence the dynamic interplay of dominance-submission. This view allows us to examine the particular ways in which power-powerlessness or dominance-submission are typically manifest in interaction. The next section introduces three general principles for the nonverbal expression of dominance and power.

◆ Nonverbal Strategies for Signaling Dominance-Submission and Power-Powerlessness

Based on an extensive survey of the empirical nonverbal literature, Burgoon and colleagues (Burgoon, Buller, & Woodall, 1996; Burgoon & Hoobler, 2002) have proposed a number of principles (rules or abstractions) underlying the nonverbal expression of dominance and power. We group these principles into three general categories: (1) physical potency, (2) resource control, and (3) interaction control.

PHYSICAL POTENCY

Physical potency represents most closely the stereotypic views of what it means to signify dominance or submission, power or powerlessness. The components that are included within the general conception of potency are (1) threat, (2) size or strength, and (3) expressivity.

Threat. Perhaps the most obvious signals of dominance and submission recognized in the ethological literature (e.g., Keltner, 1995; Smith, 1974; Thorpe, 1972) are threat and fright displays, the former to intimidate and the latter to show timidity.

These displays map onto the most primitive fight-flight and approach-avoidance response patterns (Keltner, Gruenfeld, & Anderson, 2003). Threats may signal not only readiness to strike but also the ability to fight if provoked (Maynard Smith, 1982). Less indicative of impending physical aggression, but still intimidating, are threat stares and penetrating gazes (Ellsworth, Carlsmith, & Henson, 1972; Exline, Ellyson, & Long, 1975; Le Poire & Burgoon, 1994). Although Hall et al. (2005) found that actual gaze was not associated with their dimension of verticality, it is possible that distinguishing among glares, stares, and timing of breaks in eye contact might produce differences. Hinde (1978, 1985) proposed that threat displays show conflicting intentions to attack and to escape. Such ambivalence and the likely development of finely graded rather than crude signals of threat may account for mixed empirical findings.

Another symbolic form of threat comes from silence, which can convert its target from personhood to nonperson (or object) status, with concomitant loss of belongingness and protection accorded members of the same social unit. As explained by Bruneau (1973), the "silent treatment" can force

> subordinates into awkward positions whereby they exhibit behaviors detrimental to their own cause—because their frustration is aggravated by silent response to their efforts. Silence as absence of response to or lack of recognition of subordinates may very well be the main source of protection of power in socio-political orders where physical restraint has lost repute. (p. 39)

Other signals intended to show subordination, supplication, and appeasement include stooped and contractive postures, crouching, drawing the head into the shoulders, a hesitant gait, a slow and tentative approach, retreating body orientations, and exposing vulnerable body regions such as the jugular vein or palm (Mehrabian, 1981). Targets of impending attack may rely on these fright signals to show submission symbolically. Those low in power and in subservient roles may also exhibit far less expressivity due to a host of inhibitory and avoidant tendencies associated with the position of vulnerability (Keltner et al., 2003).

Size and Strength. All species appear to respond to speed, agility, and energy expenditure as indicators of potency. By contrast, lethargy and torpidity are associated typically with weakness and ineffectualness. Thus, any nonverbal action that entails a high degree of intensity and dynamic action is likely to connote power and to secure avoidance, flight, or submission from less dominant others. In the human repertoire, height, weight, bulk, and muscularity may signal sufficient physical strength and endurance to render the displayer victorious in a physical conflict. Other nonverbal behaviors that connote size or strength are rapid gait, erect postures, firm stances, animated gesturing, loud and deep-pitched voices, rapid speaking tempo, clear articulation, and clothing or hair styles that create a bulky appearance (Apple, Streeter & Krauss, 1979; Burgoon, Birk, & Pfau, 1990; Hall et al., 2006; Mehrabian, 1981; Schwartz et al., 1982). Size and strength can be signaled also by "strength in numbers," such as a celebrity's entourage, a gang member's comrades, or an army battalion's compatriots.

Implicit signals of strength or weakness are facial and vocal maturity or babyishness. Nonverbal appearance features that connote maturity or immaturity, and actions that emphasize or deemphasize these features, may capitalize on innate responses to visible physical attributes of potential harm or harmlessness that can be deciphered from a safe distance. Mature faces are broader ones with square jaws, larger noses, more prominent eyebrows, thinner lips, and smaller ratios of eye size to face size, whereas baby-faced features included more rounded and softer features, smaller noses, less pronounced brows and eyebrows, larger lips, and larger eye sizes relative to total face size (Keating, 1985, this volume; Rhodes & Zebrowitz, 2002; Zebrowitz, Fellous, Mignault, & Andreoletti, 2003). Baby-faced and smiling faces are seen as submissive, weak, and helpless; mature and unsmiling or frowning faces with furrowed brows are seen as dominant, threatening or aggressive. Similarly, high-pitched, thin voices are babyish; deep-pitched, louder, and more resonant ones are considered mature (Montepare & Zebrowitz-McArthur, 1987).

Expressivity. In addition to threat and size, dominance has been associated with more energetic and animated behavior such as variable facial expressions, inflected speech, high-pitched voice, head shaking and nodding, frequent and broad gestures, wide smiles, peppy, not sluggish or lethargic movement, erect posture, quick movement, upright torso, vertical sitting posture, more expansive and emphatic postures and vocalizations, loud voice, vigorous behaviors, heavy step, legs wide apart, elbows akimbo, hands away from body, emphatic and centrifugal gestures and movements, and more coordinated nonverbal behavior (e.g., smooth voice, fluid and graceful walk, rhythmic speech, flowing voice and speech) (Gallaher, 1992). These behaviors connote a high degree of actual or potential energy expenditure.

Gifford (1994) found several behaviors associated with *perceptions* of individuals as more dominant-ambitious (direct head orientation, lack of forward head tilt, more head shaking, direct trunk orientation, less arm wrap, more gestures, more self-manipulations, right leg orientation, more right leg lean, and more leg extension). Additionally, gregarious-extraverted individuals, who also might be regarded as dominant, displayed more nods, less arm wrap, more gestures, and more left leg lean; those individuals *perceived* as gregarious-extraverted displayed most of the same behaviors as associated with dominance plus more nods, smiles, forward lean, and hand extension and less left-hand verticality, leg openness, and leg movement. In general, then, behaviors that connote a high degree of actual or potential energy expenditure are associated with dominance and power.

RESOURCE CONTROL

In addition to the displays of potency just described, nonverbal cues signaling dominance and power do so because they constitute displays of "resource holding potential" (Fridlund, 1991a). Animals signify privileged access to such valued resources as food, protective shelter, or fecund females. In humans, these may be signified through (1) command of space, (2) precedence, (3) prerogative, and (4) possession of other valued commodities. We discuss each of these briefly.

Command of Space. Powerful people have access to more space, larger territories, and more private territories (Remland, 1981), which also afford their occupants or owners greater insulation from intrusion by others and more space in which to display other visible indications of their status and power. They may display more territorial markers (i.e., tangible objects that signify a

space is "taken"), have easy access to others, and may have others' access regulated by gatekeepers—people such as receptionists who can prevent intrusions. In addition to access to space, dominance may also be expressed by taking up more physical space (i.e., a combination of enlarging one's size and occupying more space). Dominant individuals often sit in more open body positions (as opposed to defensive positions), adopt stances with arms akimbo, and use more expansive gestures. Submissive people take up less space by contracting their postures, sitting with closed arm and leg positions, and using diminutive, if any, gestures (Burgoon, Buller, Hale, & deTurck, 1984).

Precedence. Precedence refers to "who gets to go first" and likely extends from an evolutionary basis (Burgoon & Hoobler, 2002). Just as alpha males in the animal kingdom are the first to feast on prey, so dominant humans are the first to appropriate the spoils of war. High-ranking personages also have the first right of refusal on acquiring socially valued goods and services. The principle of precedence is reinforced through rituals that symbolically signify one's social position, such as entering a space first, walking ahead of others of lower rank, going to the head of the line, leading a parade, or being given a first turn.

Prerogative. People may mark their power through having the "right" to behave in certain ways. Consistent with EVT (Burgoon, 1978; Burgoon & Burgoon, 2001; Burgoon & Ebesu Hubbard, 2005) and the gender politics hypothesis, dominant, powerful, and high-ranking personages are free to deviate from norms and expectations, and may actually accrue more power by doing so, compared with those in subordinate positions, who must conform to social norms or risk adverse consequences. Dominant individuals have the prerogative to initiate touch as well as to determine the frequency, intensity, and intimacy of touch (Burgoon, 1991; Burgoon et al., 1989; Burgoon & Hale, 1988), and people high in verticality commonly interact at closer interaction distances than those low in verticality (Hall et al., 2006).

Possession of Valued Commodities. Beyond the survival-related resources of food, shelter, and safety are the goods and services that every society designates as status symbols. Those who can afford luxuries and other status symbols, or who can appropriate such valued intangibles as another's time, should accrue both rank and influence. Thus, symbolic actions that mark one's position explicitly or implicitly in a status hierarchy may be socially ritualized extensions of an evolutionary-based principle of resource control. Together with the other means just mentioned, the possession of valued items works to reflect people's power, dominance, and status.

INTERACTION CONTROL

Like the prerogative to control resources, powerful people are able to control interactions with others (e.g., by summoning others to their home turf, calling for and adjourning meetings, and changing the direction of a conversation). They can dictate that interactions take place in their territory, which may elicit deferential and submissive behavior from visitors, especially if the territory is personalized with plaques, framed degrees, elegant furnishings, and other symbolic markers of status (Edney, 1976). Those who interact on their "home court" gain greater confidence typically from the familiarity of their surroundings. This territorial advantage is so universally recognized that international diplomacy and other serious negotiations are slated to take place on neutral ground to prevent any one party from having a territorial advantage. Among the principles that enable interaction control are (1) centrality, (2) elevation, (3) initiation, (4) nonreciprocation, and (5) task performance cues.

Centrality. Centrality of position in a social setting arguably affords the central figure not only insulation from threats on the perimeter of the group but also maximal capacity to monitor and influence the actions of those in immediate proximity. Within social interactions, leaders sit or stand in more central positions in a group, such as the head of a table or wherever visual access to the most people is maximized (Sommer, 1971). Centrality may also be marked by gaze patterns. Submissive or low-status individuals look at superiors more when they are listening (as a sign of attention and respect) than when they are speaking, whereas powerful people show relatively more gaze at others when speaking than when listening. This produces what is called a *visual dominance ratio* (Exline et al., 1975). Central positioning can also confer status on those whose offices, workspaces, parking spaces, and the like are centrally located. For example, offices that are located closer to the "center of power" are typically inhabited by higher-status organizational members, with the center of power defined by the office inhabited by the highest-ranking member of all. Interestingly, however, this principle is overridden by the principle of privileged access. Where the central territory has been "contaminated" (Lyman & Scott, 1967), as in deteriorating inner cities and graffiti-ridden neighborhoods, powerful and dominant individuals seek and secure more protected spaces. Thus, centrality can be associated with the most *and* least powerful in a society.

Elevation. Like physical mass and size that convey control of the horizontal sphere, height may convey control of vertical space. Elevated perches give predators an advantage over their prey; raised thrones, daises, theater "box seats," pedestals, penthouses, top-floor offices, and prison guard posts give people greater surveillance and control over others. The power bias toward height "is deeply embedded in the visual grammar of western civilization. For a speaker, it has functional advantages. The elevation . . . gives him or her a much larger field of vision. Elevation gathers and keeps attention" (King, cited in Jaworski, 1993, p. 14). Behaviors that increase height differentials, such as standing over another person or "looking down at someone," likewise function as dominant behaviors. It follows, then, that tall people would be seen as more powerful than short people (Frieze, Olson, & Good, 1990). Social rituals, such as bowing to the higher status individual in Japan (Nixon & West, 1995), have evolved to accord elevation symbolically to individuals of higher rank.

Initiation. A corollary to the principle of precedence discussed earlier is initiation. Deciding where people will sit or stand, changing interactional distances, initiating touch, starting or stopping conversation, and setting interaction rhythms are all interaction-based extensions of the "going first" principle. For example, dominant individuals may initiate handshakes, dictate conversational distancing, and set the pattern for seated or standing interaction. Sheer proximity to, and surveillance of, more individuals enables a powerful person to dictate who talks to whom and when. By being accorded the privilege of speaking first, they then can nominate the next

speaker through eye contact, gesturing, or direct verbal address. They also may control the conversational floor by initiating and switching topics, picking up conversational turns more rapidly, interrupting others, and talking longer (Hall et al., 2005; Wiemann, 1985), which results in them talking more, influencing others more, and being perceived as leaders (Leffler, Gillespie, & Conaty, 1982).

Nonreciprocation. Another form of conversational control is *nonreciprocation* of others' nonverbal behavior patterns. Whereas people on an equal plane may signal their equality through matching and mirroring of another's kinesic, proxemic, and vocalic patterns, dominant individuals may meet another's smile with a blank expression or counter an expressive voice with a bored one. Dominant individuals may also become the *zeitgeber,* the one who sets the interactional pace and to whom others orient as they attempt to establish interactional synchrony (Burgoon, Stern, & Dillman, 1995). All these patterns work to reflect the lack of power symmetry.

Task Performance Cues. A final principle of conversational control is a culmination of many of the foregoing principles applied to a task context. Task performance cues are nonverbal indicators of status and task-related ability from which group members infer one's potential to contribute effectively to a group's task performance (Berger et al., 1980; Ridgeway & Walker, 1995). High-status apparel, possession of artifacts that are culturally defined status symbols (e.g., an expensive briefcase or pen), and actions indicative of centrality, privileged access, precedence, and prerogative, connote likely expertise, experience, and leadership. These set up expectations for the person to contribute favorably to a group's task and set into motion a self-fulfilling prophecy whereby such individuals are accorded more and longer speaking turns, are allowed to initiate or change topics, and thus exert more influence on the group, which then reinforces their prestige and position of power. In this manner, the "strong" may become stronger and the "weak," weaker.

◆ **Conclusions**

The expression of dominance-submission and power-powerlessness is a form of communication that has a universal vocabulary. The theories, lines of research, and principles for nonverbal display of dominance and power that we have reviewed here point to a strong grounding in ethological and related behavioral ecology perspectives. Even those forms of expression that have clear social derivations and constitute symbolic rather than sign behavior often have more primitive biological analogs. Thus, the study of nonverbal expressions of dominance, power, and status offer insights more generally into societal hierarchies and social functioning.

Notwithstanding the evidence of universality and possible innate foundations for many power and dominance displays, we share with Hall et al. (2006) a conviction that such displays are also responsive to culture, context, relationships, social motives, and the psychological makeup of actors. This responsivity to a panoply of antecedent factors helps explain what might otherwise seem to be a dismal record of nonverbal expressions of status, power, and dominance in predicting the vertical dimension of human relationships. The need for flexibility and adaptability for all species argues for behavioral repertoires that are rich in alternative forms of expression and that can be adjusted or substituted as circumstances demand. We, therefore,

should not expect simple and unidimensional behavioral profiles of status, dominance-submission, or power-powerlessness. Moreover, because human actors are not bundles of instincts but rather active agents who choose among alternative strategies to accomplish their goals, variability in forms of dominance and power expressions is to be expected.

The nonexhaustive review we have presented here illustrates the various ways in which nonverbal behaviors can be enacted to accomplish these ends. These include principles for displaying physical potency, signifying resource holding potential, and accomplishing interaction control. We hope this review promotes insights into what behavioral patterns carry dominance-submission and power-powerlessness connotations as well as what theoretical explanations can be advanced for understanding their meanings and impact. It provides a template for future research into the critical role played by nonverbal behavior in negotiating this elemental facet of social life.

◆ **References**

Anderson, J. R. (1998). *Cognitive psychology and its implications.* New York: Freeman.

Andrew, R. J. (1972). The information potentially available in mammal displays. In R. A. Hinde (Ed.), *Non-verbal communication* (pp. 179–204). Cambridge, UK: Cambridge University Press.

Apple, W., Streeter, L. A., & Krauss, R. M. (1979). Effects of pitch and speech rate on personal attributions. *Journal of Personality and Social Psychology, 37,* 715–727.

Aries, E. J., Gold, C., & Weigel, R. H. (1983). Dispositional and situational influences on dominance behavior in small groups. *Journal of Personality and Social Psychology, 44,* 779–786.

Berger, C. R. (1994). Power, dominance, and social interaction. In M. L. Knapp & G. R. Miller (Eds.), *Handbook of interpersonal communication* (2nd ed., pp. 450–507). Thousand Oaks, CA: Sage.

Berger, J., Conner, T. L., & Fisek, M. H. (1974). *Expectation states theory: A theoretical research program.* Cambridge, MA: Winthrop.

Berger, J., Ridgeway, C. L., Fisek, M. H., & Norman, R. Z. (1998). The legitimation and delegitimation of power and prestige orders. *American Sociological Review, 63,* 379–405.

Berger, J., Rosenholtz, S. J., & Zelditch, M., Jr. (1980). States organizing processes. *Annual Review of Sociology, 6,* 479–508.

Bernstein, I. S. (1980). Dominance: A theoretical perspective for ethologists. In D. R. Omark, F. F. Strayer, & D. G. Freedman (Eds.), *Dominance relations* (pp. 71–84). New York: Garland.

Birdwhistell, R. (1970). *Kinesics and context: Essays on body motion communication.* Philadelphia: University of Pennsylvania Press.

Bruneau, T. J. (1973). Communicative silences: Forms and functions. *Journal of Communication, 23,* 17–46.

Bugental, D. B., & Shennum, W. (2002). Gender, power, and violence in the family. *Child Maltreatment, 7,* 56–64.

Burgoon, J. K. (1978). A communication model of personal space violations: Explication and an initial test. *Human Communication Research, 4,* 129–142.

Burgoon, J. K. (1991). Relational message interpretations of touch, conversational distance, and posture. *Journal of Nonverbal Behavior, 15,* 233–258.

Burgoon, J. K. (1995). Cross-cultural and intercultural applications of expectancy violations theory. In R. L. Wiseman (Ed.), *Intercultural communication theory* (International and intercultural communication annual, Vol. 19, pp. 194–214). Thousand Oaks, CA: Sage.

Burgoon, J. K., Birk, T., & Pfau, M. (1990). Nonverbal behaviors, persuasion, and credibility. *Human Communication Research, 17,* 140–169.

Burgoon, J. K., Buller, D. B., Hale, J. L., & deTurck, M. (1984). Relational messages associated with nonverbal behaviors. *Human Communication Research, 10,* 351–378.

Burgoon, J. K., Buller, D. B., & Woodall, G. W. (1996). *Nonverbal communication: The unspoken dialogue.* New York: McGraw-Hill.

Burgoon, J. K., & Burgoon, M. (2001). Expectancy theories. In P. Robinson & H. Giles (Eds.), *Handbook of language and social psychology* (2nd ed., pp. 79–101). Sussex, UK: Wiley.

Burgoon, J. K., & Dillman, L. (1995). Gender, immediacy and nonverbal communication. In P. J. Kalbfleisch & M. J. Cody (Eds.), *Gender, power, and communication in human relationships* (pp. 63–81). Hillsdale, NJ: Erlbaum.

Burgoon, J. K., & Dunbar, N. (2000). An interactionist perspective on dominance-submission: Interpersonal dominance as a dynamically, situationally contingent social skill. *Communication Monographs, 67,* 96–121.

Burgoon, J. K., Dunbar, N. E., & Segrin, C. (2002). Nonverbal influence. In M. Pfau & J. P. Dillard (Eds.), *The persuasion handbook: Theory and practice* (pp. 445–473). Thousand Oaks, CA: Sage.

Burgoon, J. K., & Ebesu Hubbard, E. (2005). Expectancy violations theory and interaction adaptation theory. In W. Gudykunst (Ed.), *Theorizing about intercultural communication* (pp. 149–171). Thousand Oaks, CA: Sage.

Burgoon, J. K., & Hale, J. L. (1984). The fundamental topoi of relational communication. *Communication Monographs, 51,* 193–214.

Burgoon, J. K., & Hale, J. L. (1988). Nonverbal expectancy violations: Model elaboration and application to immediacy behaviors. *Communication Monographs, 55,* 58–79.

Burgoon, J. K., & Hoobler, G. (2002). Nonverbal signals. In M. L. Knapp & J. Daly (Ed.), *Handbook of interpersonal communication* (pp. 240–299). Thousand Oaks, CA: Sage.

Burgoon, J. K., Johnson, M. L., & Koch, P. T. (1998). The nature and measurement of interpersonal dominance. *Communication Monographs, 65,* 309–335.

Burgoon, J. K., & Le Poire, B. A. (1999). Nonverbal cues and interpersonal judgments: Participant and observer perceptions of intimacy, dominance, composure, and formality. *Communication Monographs, 66,* 105–124.

Burgoon, J. K., Newton, D. A., Walther, J. B., & Baesler, E. J. (1989). Nonverbal expectancy violations and conversational involvement. *Journal of Nonverbal Behavior, 13,* 97–120.

Burgoon, J. K., Stern, L., & Dillman, L. (1995). *Interpersonal adaptation: Interaction adaptation theory.* New York: Cambridge University Press.

Cattell, R. B., Eber, H. W., & Tatsuoka, M. M. (1970). *Handbook for the sixteen personality factor questionnaire (16PF).* Champaign, IL: Institute for Personality and Ability Testing.

Christensen, A., & Heavey, C. L. (1990). Gender and social structure in the demand/withdraw pattern of marital conflict. *Journal of Personality and Social Psychology, 59,* 73–81.

Cloven, D. H., & Roloff, M. E. (1993). The chilling effect of aggressive potential on the expression of complaints in intimate relationships. *Communication Monographs, 60,* 199–219.

Darwin, C. (1965). *The expression of the emotions in man and animals.* Chicago: University of Chicago Press. (Original work published 1872)

Dindia, K., & Canary, D. J. (Eds.). (2006). *Sex differences and similarities in communication* (2nd ed.). Mahwah, NJ: Erlbaum.

Dunbar, N. E. (2004). Dyadic power theory: Constructing a communication-based theory of relational power. *Journal of Family Communication, 4,* 235–248.

Dunbar, N. E., & Burgoon, J. K. (2005a). Perceptions of power and interactional dominance in interpersonal relationships. *Journal of Social and Personal Relationships, 22,* 231–257.

Dunbar, N. E., & Burgoon, J. K. (2005b). The measurement of nonverbal dominance. In V. Manusov (Ed.), *Beyond words: A sourcebook of methods for measuring nonverbal cues* (pp. 361–374). Mahwah, NJ: Erlbaum.

Edinger, J. A., & Patterson, M. L. (1983). Nonverbal involvement and social control. *Psychological Bulletin, 93,* 30–56.

Edney, J. J. (1976). Human territories: Comment on functional properties. *Environment and Behavior, 8,* 31–47.

Ellsworth, P. C., Carlsmith, J. M., & Henson, A. (1972). The stare as a stimulus to flight in human subjects: A series of field experiments. *Journal of Personality and Social Psychology, 33,* 117–122.

Ellyson, S. L., & Dovidio, J. F. (1985). Power, dominance, and nonverbal behavior: Basic concepts and issues. In S. L. Ellyson & J. F. Dovidio (Eds.), *Power, dominance, and nonverbal behavior* (pp. 1–28). New York: Springer.

Emerson, R. M. (1962). Power-dependence relations. *American Sociological Review, 27,* 31–41.

Exline, R. V., Ellyson, S. L., & Long, B. (1975). Visual behavior as an aspect of power role relationships. In P. Pliner, L. Krames, & T. Alloway (Eds.), *Nonverbal communication of aggression* (pp. 21–52). New York: Plenum.

French, J. R. P., & Raven, B. (1959). The bases of social power. In D. Cartwright (Ed.), *Studies in social power* (pp. 150–167). Ann Arbor, MI: Institute for Social Research.

Frieze, I. H., Olson, J. E., & Good, D. C. (1990). Perceived and actual discrimination in the salaries of male and female managers. *Journal of Applied Social Psychology, 20,* 46–67.

Fridlund, A. J. (1991a). Evolution and facial action in reflex, social motive, and paralanguage. *Biological Psychology, 32,* 3–100.

Fridlund, A. J. (1991b). Sociality of solitary smiling: Potentiation by an implicit audience. *Journal of Personality and Social Psychology, 60,* 229–240.

Gallaher, P. (1992). Individual differences in nonverbal behavior: Dimensions of style. *Journal of Personality and Social Psychology, 63,* 133–145.

Gifford, R. (1994). A lens-mapping framework for understanding the encoding and decoding of interpersonal dispositions in nonverbal behavior. *Journal of Personality and Social Psychology, 66*, 398–412.

Hall, E. T. (1959). *The silent language.* Garden City, NY: Anchor/Doubleday.

Hall, E. T. (1966). *The hidden dimension* (2nd ed.). Garden City, NY: Anchor/Doubleday.

Hall, J. A. (1998). How big are nonverbal sex differences? The case of smiling and non-verbal sensitivity. In D. Canary & K. Dindia (Eds.), *Sex differences and similarities in communication* (pp. 59–81). Mahwah, NJ: Lawrence Earlbaum Associates.

Hall, J. A., Coats, E., & Smith LeBeau, L. (2005). Nonverbal behavior and the vertical dimension of social relations: A meta-analysis. *Psychological Bulletin, 131*, 898–924.

Hall, J. A., Rosip, J. C., Smith LeBeau, L., Horgan, T. G., & Carter, J. D. (2006). Attributing the sources of accuracy in unequal-power dyadic communication: Who is better and why? *Journal of Experimental Social Psychology, 42*, 18–27.

Henley, N. M. (1977). *Body politics: Power, sex, and nonverbal, communication.* Englewood Cliffs, NJ: Prentice Hall.

Henley, N. M. (1995). Gender politics revisited: What do we know today? In P. J. Kalbfleisch & M. J. Cody (Eds.), *Gender, power, and communication in human relationships* (pp. 27–61). Hillsdale, NJ: Erlbaum.

Hinde, R. A. (1974). *Biological bases of human social behavior.* New York: McGraw-Hill.

Hinde, R. A. (1978). Dominance and role—two concepts with dual meanings. *Journal of Social and Biological Structures, 1*, 27–38.

Hinde, R.A. (1985). Expression and negotiation. In G. Zivin (Ed.), *The development of expressive behavior* (pp. 103–116). Orlando, FL: Academic Press.

Jaworski, A. (1993). *The power of silence: Social and pragmatic perspectives.* Newbury Park, CA: Sage.

Keating, C. F. (1985). Human dominance signals: The primate in us. In S. L. Ellyson & J. F. Dovidio (Eds.), *Power, dominance, and nonverbal behavior* (pp. 89–108). New York: Springer.

Keltner, D. (1995). The signs of appeasement: Evidence for the distinct displays of embarrassment, amusement, and shame. *Journal of Personality and Social Psychology, 68*, 441–454.

Keltner, D., Gruenfeld, D. H., & Anderson, C. (2003). Power, approach, and inhibition. *Psychological Review, 110*, 265–284.

Keltner, D., Young, R. C., & Buswell, B. N. (1997). Appeasement in human emotion, social practice, and personality. *Aggressive Behavior, 23*, 359–374.

Komter, A. (1989). Hidden power in marriage. *Gender & Society, 3*, 187–216.

LaFrance, M., Hecht, M. A., & Levy Paluck, E. (2003). The contingent smile: A meta-analysis of sex differences in smiling. *Psychological Bulletin, 129*, 305–334.

LaFrance, M., & Henley, N. M. (1993). On "oppressing hypotheses" or differences in nonverbal sensitivity revisited. In L. Radtke & H. Stam (Eds.), *Power/gender: Social relations in theory and practice* (pp. 287–311). London: Sage.

Leffler, A., Gillespie, D. L., & Conaty, J. C. (1982). The effect of status differentiation on nonverbal behavior. *Social Psychology Quarterly, 45*, 153–161.

Le Poire, B. A., & Burgoon, J. K. (1994). Two contrasting explanations of involvement violations: Expectancy violations theory versus discrepancy arousal theory. *Human Communication Research, 20*, 560–591.

Leung, K. (1988). Some determinants of conflict avoidance. *Journal of Cross-Cultural Psychology, 19*, 125–136.

Lips, H. M. (1991). *Women, men and power.* Mountain View, CA: Mayfield.

Liska, J. (1992). Dominance-seeking language strategies: Please eat the floor, dogbreath, or I'll rip your lungs out, okay? In S. A. Deetz (Ed.), *Communication yearbook 15* (pp. 427–456). New Brunswick, NJ: International Communication Association.

Lyman, S. M., & Scott, M. B. (1967). Territoriality: A neglected sociological dimension. *Social Problems, 15*, 236–249.

Maynard Smith, J. (1982). *Evolution and the theory of games.* Cambridge, UK: Cambridge University Press.

Mehrabian, A. (1981). *Silent messages: Implicit communication of emotions and attitudes* (2nd ed.). Belmont, CA: Wadsworth.

Montepare, J. M., & Zebrowitz-McArthur, L. (1987). Perceptions of adults and children with childlike voices in two cultures. *Journal of Experimental Social Psychology, 23,* 331–349.

Moskowitz, D. S. (1988). Cross-situational generality in the laboratory: Dominance and friendliness. *Journal of Personality and Social Psychology, 54,* 829–839.

Moskowitz, D. S. (1990). Convergence of self-reports and independent observers: Dominance and friendliness. *Journal of Personality and Social Psychology, 58,* 1096–1106.

Neff, K. D., & Harter, S. (2002). The role of power and authenticity in relationship styles emphasizing autonomy, connectedness, or mutuality among couples. *Journal of Social and Personal Relationships, 19,* 835–857.

Nixon, J. C., & West, J. F. (1995). Intercultural preparation for managers going to Japan. *Mid-American Journal of Business, 10,* 57–64.

Olson, D. H., & Cromwell, R. E. (1975). Power in families. In R. E. Cromwell & D. H. Olson (Eds.), *Power in families* (pp. 3–11). Beverly Hills, CA: Sage.

Omark, D. R. (1980). The group: A factor or an epiphenomenon in evolution. In D. R. Omark, F. F. Strayer, & D. G. Freedman (Eds.), *Dominance relations* (pp. 21–64). New York: Garland.

Remland, M. (1981). Developing leadership skills in nonverbal communication: A situational perspective. *Journal of Business Communication, 18,* 18–31.

Rhodes, G., & Zebrowitz, L. A. (Eds.). (2002). *Facial attractiveness: Evolutionary, cognitive, and social perspectives.* Westport, CT: Ablex.

Ridgeway, C. L. (1987). Nonverbal behavior, dominance, and the basis of status in task groups. *American Sociological Review, 52,* 683–694.

Ridgeway, C. L., & Berger, J. (1986). Expectations, legitimation, and dominance behavior in task groups. *American Sociological Review, 62,* 218–35.

Ridgeway, C. L., Diekema, D., & Johnson, C. (1995). Legitimacy, compliance, and gender in peer groups. *Social Psychology Quarterly, 58,* 298–311.

Ridgeway, C. L., & Walker, H. A. (1995). Status structures. In K. S. Cook, G. A. Fine, & J. S. House (Eds.), *Sociological perspectives on social psychology* (pp. 281–310). Boston: Allyn & Bacon.

Rogers-Millar, E. L., & Millar, F. E. (1979). Domineeringness and dominance: A transactional view. *Human Communication Research, 5,* 238–246.

Rollins, B. C., & Bahr, S. J. (1976). A theory of power relationships in marriage. *Journal of Marriage and the Family, 38,* 619–627.

Rusbult, C. E., & Arriaga, X. B. (1997). Interdependence theory. In S. Duck (Ed.), *Handbook of personal relationships* (2nd ed., pp. 221–250). Chichester, UK: Wiley.

Schwartz, B., Tesser, A., & Powell, E. (1982). Dominance cues in nonverbal behavior. *Social Psychology Quarterly, 45,* 114–120.

Sebeok, T. (1972). *Perspectives in zoosemiotics.* The Hague, The Netherlands: Mouton.

Siegel, S. M., Friedlander, M. L., & Heatherington, L. (1992). Nonverbal relational control in family communication. *Journal of Nonverbal Behavior, 16,* 117–139.

Smith, W. J. (1974). Displays and messages in intraspecific communication. In S. Weitz (Ed.), *Nonverbal communication: Readings with commentary* (pp. 331–340). New York: Oxford University Press.

Snodgrass, S. E., Hecht, M. A., & Ploutz-Snyder, R. (1998). Interpersonal sensitivity: Expressivity or perceptivity? *Journal of Personality and Social Psychology, 74,* 238–249.

Sommer, R. (1971). Spatial parameters in naturalistic research. In A. H. Esser (Ed.), *Behavior and environment: The use of space in animals* (pp. 281–290). New York: Plenum.

Thibaut, J. W., & Kelley, H. H. (1959). *The social psychology of groups.* New York: Wiley.

Thorpe, W. H. (1972). The comparison of vocal communication in animals and man.

In R. A. Hinde (Ed.), *Non-verbal communication* (pp. 27–48). Cambridge, UK: Cambridge University Press.

Wheeless, L. R., Barraclough, R., & Stewart, R. (1983). Compliance-gaining and power in persuasion. *Communication yearbook, 7* (pp. 105–145). Newbury Park, CA: Sage.

Wiemann, J. M. (1985). Interpersonal control and regulation in conversation. In R. L. Street Jr., & J. N. Cappella (Eds.), *Sequence and pattern in communicative behaviour* (pp. 85–102). London: Edward Arnold.

Zebrowitz, L. A., Fellous, J-M., Mignault, A., & Andreoletti, C. (2003). Trait impressions as overgeneralized responses to adaptively significant facial qualities: Evidence from connectionist modeling. *Personality and Social Psychology Review, 7*, 194–215.

16

THE FUNCTIONS
OF FACIAL EXPRESSIONS

What's in a Face?

◆ Alan J. Fridlund
University of California, Santa Barbara

◆ James A. Russell
Boston College

H umans are quintessentially social beings, and our faces occupy a central role in our social interactions. How and why they do so is the focus of this chapter. This chapter is not intended to be comprehensive, an inevitable choice given the explosion of research on facial expressions that has occurred in the past 20 years. Instead, we focus on one central contention: that the traditional focus on *emotion* as the way to explain our facial expressions is erroneous. We argue instead that facial cues are better seen as "social tools" that modify the trajectory of our social interactions. We begin with a brief look at how faces have been interpreted historically. Next, we examine more current views of the *face* and *facial expression*. In doing so, we touch upon the face's anatomy and physiology, the properties of the face that can convey information, and the ways that others are affected by our faces. We end by discussing facial paralanguage and suggest that the traditional division between facial paralanguage and "facial expressions of emotion" is illusory and counterproductive.

◆ Older Views of Facial Expression

History shows the variety of possible interpretations of faces. "Face reading," or *physiognomy,* goes back to antiquity (see Fridlund, 1994, for a more detailed review of this history). It existed in ancient Egypt and Arabia and was a profession in China before Confucius. Pythagoras probably originated the scientific study of physiognomy, which Hippocrates and Galen applied to their medical diagnoses. Aristotle constructed a system of physiognomy which likened people's personalities to the animals whose faces they resembled. For example, people with prominent upper lips were said to be stupid like apes and donkeys, and those with "hawk" noses were magnanimous. Two thousand years later, the Renaissance figure, Giambattista Della Porta, joined Aristotle's physiognomy with Hippocrates' system of temperament, arguing that a person's face indicated whether he was sanguine, choleric, phlegmatic, or melancholic. But physiognomy reached its zenith with the 18th-century Swiss pastor and poet, Johann Caspar Lavater, who believed he could recognize the God in man by divining his subjects' traits from the shapes and lines in their faces.

Much of physiognomy concerned static features of the face, but changes in the face were also thought to convey changes in the person. Aristotle had read faces as indicating the "passions," which Descartes understood as turbulence in the bodily humors. The 17th-century French painter Charles LeBrun, who ruled the arts in France for two generations, argued that the face "reads out" the Cartesian passions, much like the face of the clock reads out the time. The French neurologist Guillaume Duchenne, who invented the biopsy and discovered Duchenne muscular dystrophy, pioneered the scientific study of facial movement, based on the assumption that the ability to express emotions was God-given. But the chief expositor of this theological view of the facial muscles was the celebrated Scottish surgeon, anatomist, and artist Charles Bell (discoverer of Bell's palsy), who published his celebrated *Essays on the Anatomy of Expression in Painting* in 1806.

Bell's theological view was the implicit target for Charles Darwin, whose *Expression of the Emotions in Man and Animals* (1872) aimed systematically to replace creationist accounts of human behavior by providing an onslaught of natural-history ones. As Fridlund (1992a) discussed, Darwin (1872) countered Bell (1806) by arguing that human facial expressions were not there *for* expression at all: They were either vestigial reflexes or accidents of nervous system wiring. If faces were vestiges or accidents, then the argument of divine design was undermined. Thus, for Darwin, we don't bare our teeth when we're angry *in order to* show anger; we just do it because evolutionary ancestors tended to bite when they were aggressive, and we simply inherited this outdated habit.

In the 20th century, accounts of facial expression bifurcated (Russell & Fernandez-Dols, 1997). Almost no one continued Darwin's (1872) nonadaptationist account. Those who focused on humans continued to see facial expressions as readouts of the passions, modernized with an evolutionary patina to say that facial expressions *evolved* to express the passions. Those who studied nonhuman animals saw faces as signal movements, which, like other animal signals, evolved to convey likely actions and thereby alter the course of ongoing social interaction. Later in this chapter, we contrast these as the Facial Expression Program (FEP) and the Behavioral Ecology View (BEV). We will show that the latter view both restores continuity between our conceptions of human facial expressions and nonhuman displays and provides a more productive way to understand how we use our faces in everyday social commerce. For now, however, we turn toward the face itself.

◆ *Components of Facial Expression*

Our faces are exquisitely complex, in both appearance and movement, and people use *both* to make inferences about us. In describing appearance and movement we are, technically, speaking of the face's *static* and *dynamic* features.

STATIC FEATURES OF THE FACE

Our faces influence our social interactions even before they move, because of how much we draw from the face's *static features*. Although some reviews omit their discussion, these features form the background against which our facial expressions arise, and their inclusion is critical. These features are as follows.

First, we use static facial features to infer the owner's sex, age, and race. Beyond that, group identifications are often inferred from cultural ornamentation that can include grooming, face painting, tattooing, nose or lip piercing, or hair coloration. Second, we use the face's static features to make inferences about the owner's personality, much along the lines of ancient physiognomy (although we are likely to be incorrect in our judgments; see Gifford,

this volume). Craniofacial anomalies or deformities like harelips, scarring, eye folds or skin discoloration (e.g., blotching or vitiligo), and overbites can lead to aversion reactions and, like all stigma, result in social marginalization (Heatherton, Kleck, Hebl, & Hull, 2000). Mental disorder was once thought to be deducible strictly from physiognomy, and history is replete with racist stereotypes about personality and criminality based on facial features (see Gilman, 1985, 1996).

Although such inferences as these (whether valid or not) play a role in guiding the social interactions we have with their owners, it is less clear whether some static facial features were *designed* to be signals. To use Goffman's (1959) terms, are they *given* (produced with the aim of communication) or *given off* (where any communication is incidental)? The best answer is *maybe,* for *some.* Facial angularity, for instance, is an approximate indicator of circulating testosterone (as is a plethora of other signs like height, hairiness, and muscularity), and females tend to prefer angular faces when they are ovulating more than when they are menstruating (Penton-Voak et al., 1999). Youthful ("neotenous") features among females of reproductive age (e.g., wide eyes, full lips) are an approximate indicator of greater fecundity (Johnson & Franklin, 1993) and more reproductive years ahead, and males judge youthful females to be more beautiful (Cunningham, Roberts, Barbee, Druen, & Wu, 1994; Perrett, May, & Yoshikawa, 1994). In several accounts, angularity in males and big eyes in females were shaped by sexual selection. On the other hand, both features may simply be incidental offshoots of other traits; so for example, females may have preferred mating with stronger males, with angularity "tagging along," as a *correlated variation*, to use Darwin's (1872) term.

Because evolutionary accounts of behavior amount to historical reconstructions, which account applies is difficult to determine. The argument hinges on whether the sign in question is exaggerated beyond what would be expected of an offshoot, often to the point that it becomes a physiological liability or handicap. For example, a male widow bird drags along a tail of feathers four to five times the length of the female's tail. His tail adds weight, is metabolically costly to grow, and hinders flight. It *does* attract females, and that seems to be its only virtue (Andersson, 1982). Thus, it is reasonable to conclude that the male's tail evolved to do so and that it is not simply an offshoot of the hormonal requirements of maleness.

No comparable clear-cut argument for any human static facial feature has been made. Perhaps the best candidate is the eyebrows, which enhance the visibility of our brow movements and—although some have conjectured that they are sweat catchers (see Porter, 1993)—they have no other convincing *raison d'etre*. Although static features of the face provide information, much more research has focused on the dynamic features of the face, specifically its coloration and muscular movements.

DYNAMIC FEATURES OF THE FACE

Facial Coloration Changes. Faces change color when the blood vessels constrict or dilate, thereby regulating how much blood flows through the facial muscles and skin. In facial *flushing,* all or part of the face reddens, often over a period of hours. Facial flushing may occur after changes in ambient temperature, eating spicy foods, or with fever. It can also occur in a variety of disorders, such as rosacea, and after taking certain vasoactive substances, like alcohol or niacin. Flushing is also common during menopause. It appears to be thermoregulatory, because running

blood through the dense, superficial vasculature of the face (and, often, the hands and the chest) exhausts heat. Prolonged flushing is accompanied by burning and sweating, and this combination is not only painful but embarrassing (Gerlach, Wilhelm, Gruber, & Roth, 2001).

Vasodilation can also occur rapidly, as in intense exercise. In *blushing,* the entire face (and usually, the ears and upper neck) reddens within 2 seconds of the event that evoked it. Blushes last on average about 20 seconds, although they may endure up to 15 min (Shields, Mallory, & Simon, 1990). People blush commonly in various kinds of social interactions. The interactions are usually intense ones, such as when we (1) lash out and yell ("reddening with anger"), (2) grieve, and (3) are made the subject of undue social attention, whether being praised ("flushed with pride"), found guilty of a transgression, or caught off guard and made to go off role (e.g., embarrassment and other "self-presentational predicaments"; see Schlenker, 1980). As one might predict, blushing is more likely among people with low self-esteem or those who are especially sensitive about others' judgments of them (Leary, Britt, Cutlip, & Templeton, 1992).

Based on the fact that most blushing is social, Leary et al. (1992) suggested that blushes are, at least in part, intrinsically communicative. In their account, our blushes notify others that we care about what they think of us, a strategy that may appease those who would judge us harshly. Social blushes can occur in solitude, as well, when we *imagine* the appropriate social circumstances, and then place ourselves before an imaginary audience (see Fridlund, Sabini, et al., 1990; Fridlund, Kenworthy, & Jaffey, 1992; for the influence of imaginary audiences of facial expressions).

Whether blushes evolved as a signal hinges on whether the coloration changes are

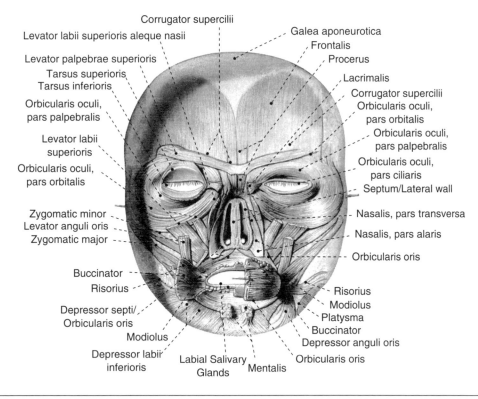

Corrugator supercilii
Levator labii superioris aleque nasii
Levator palpebrae superioris
Tarsus superioris
Tarsus inferioris
Orbicularis oculi,
pars palpebralis
Levator labii
superioris
Orbicularis oculi,
pars orbitalis
Zygomatic minor
Levator anguli oris
Zygomatic major
Buccinator
Risorius
Depressor septi/
Orbicularis oris
Modiolus
Depressor labii
inferioris
Labial Salivary
Glands
Mentalis

Galea aponeurotica
Frontalis
Procerus
Lacrimalis
Corrugator supercilii
Orbicularis oculi,
pars orbitalis
Orbicularis oculi,
pars palpebralis
Orbicularis oculi,
pars ciliaris
Septum/Lateral wall
Nasalis, pars transversa
Nasalis, pars alaris
Orbicularis oris
Risorius
Modiolus
Platysma
Buccinator
Depressor anguli oris
Orbicularis oris

Figure 16.1   The Superficial (Mimetic) Muscles of the Face Seen From the Inside Out

SOURCE: Reprinted from Pernkopf (1938), with permission from Elsevier.

beyond what would be expected as incidental offshoots of other vascular reactions. Specifically, the circumstances that might make us blush socially are often those in which "the heat is on," and when we would blush as a natural part of thermoregulation. That others might read blush as a sign of that reaction would be incidental. The jury is still out on the issue, but some evidence of an intrinsic display component was found by Drummond and Mirco (2004), who measured the cheek temperatures of participants who were asked either to sing (an embarrassing task) or read aloud (a less-embarrassing task). During the singing, cheek temperatures were symmetrical if the experimenter watched the participant sing head-on. But if the experimenter watched the participant off to one side, the participant's cheek temperature was higher on that side.

Muscular Changes. Our facial coloration changes proceed over periods of seconds or minutes, but it is the muscular changes in our face that allow it to accomplish split-second signaling and social engagement. Our exquisitely complex facial movements are caused by fewer than 30 muscles (Figure 16.1) precisely controlled by more nerves than any other muscles save those of the fingers.

The face collects together the organs for tasting, smelling, eating (including suckling), seeing, and speaking. All these involve orifices—the mouth, nose, and eyes—that require control and protection. These are the primary function of our facial muscles.

At least some of the information a face provides to an observer stems from these simple functions: shouting or whispering, looking toward or away or down, sniffing or tasting, orienting or listening—information given off. The facial muscles also display messages—information given. But the same question arises for the facial muscles as it did for static features and vascular changes: Were the muscles themselves shaped by natural selection, at least in part, for these *display* purposes?

Here, ironically, the case is harder to make. Any proof that muscles were shaped for signaling would require demonstrating that they possess shapes or actions that do not accord with their physiological functions, or perhaps even handicap their physiological functions (like the piloerection of feathers on the peacock's tail). Muscles used in producing speech, for example, were likely just co-opted (technically, preadapted or *exapted;* Gould & Vrba, 1982) because mammalian suckling had already required fine control and flexibility. There is also little evidence on this issue. Of course, humans use facial muscles to create displays, and the role of natural selection in this *use* is a separate question.

Measuring Facial Muscular Changes. Whatever their use, studying the facial muscles requires measuring them precisely, and this task is difficult. Most of the facial muscles originate in bone and insert into skin. Because they distend skin, we are seldom able to measure the contractions of our facial muscles exactly; we measure instead the *displacement* of facial features as an indication of their contractions. Perhaps the most common method of doing so is direct observation. In its simplest form, raters watch people and tally the numbers of smiles, frowns, grimaces, pouts, and so on, in a given period. In this case, many raters are typically needed to achieve adequate

reliability, and validity remains questionable. Terms such as "smile" and "frown" are vague, and we have no guarantee that they cover the range of facial behavior exhaustively or parse nature at its joints. The Maximally Discriminative Facial Movement Coding System developed by Izard (1979) uses theoretically defined categories of facial features.

A major advance in facial measurement was an anatomically based system devised by the anatomist Hjortsjö (1970). His system was later revised by Ekman and Friesen (1978) as their Facial Action Coding System (FACS). Specific facial actions are given "action unit" codes; for example, brow knitting is an "Action Unit 4" (AU 4) and cheek-corner retraction is AU 12. A second major technique for facial measurement is facial electromyography (EMG), in which tiny electrodes are affixed to the skin over major facial muscles. The electrical signals produced by the contracting muscles are then digitized and recorded. The facial EMG technique can render precise estimates of even weak muscle contractions, but its limitations include lack of selectivity (frequently, there is crosstalk from neighboring muscles), reactivity (participants are usually quite aware of the electrodes), and imperfect relationship to visual appearance (co-contracting antagonistic muscles can be electrically quite active but result in little change in facial appearance) (see Fridlund & Cacioppo, 1986).

SUMMARY

As we have seen, people make a wide range of inferences about others from both the appearance and the movements of faces. By far, most research on facial expression has focused on the face's muscular movements, under the presupposition that they "express emotion." We now turn to the use of facial musculature in expression and evaluate this presupposition.

♦ The Facial Expression Program

Scientists since the end of the 18th century have adopted the ancient and by then common-sense assumption that what faces express are emotions. Indeed, by the 1980s, the psychology of facial expression was dominated by a network of assumptions, theories, and methods that Russell and Fernandez-Dols (1997) termed the Facial Expression Program (FEP). Table 16.1 summarizes the FEP.

What we offer is but a prototype, and so no one theorist would support all 12 of the following claims. The FEP guided research on facial expression, indeed on emotion, for several decades. Some of the basic assumptions have been severely questioned by the data; for evidence against the 12th claim, for example, see Russell and Fehr (1987) and Carroll and Russell (1996). More recently, questions have arisen about *all* of the assumptions (for reviews see Fridlund, 1994; Russell, 1994; Russell & Fernandez-Dols, 1997). Here we consider two central issues: universality and the relationship of facial expressions to emotions.

ARE FACIAL EXPRESSIONS OF EMOTION UNIVERSAL?

There are many arguments regarding the universality of facial expression. Demonstration of *Strong Universality* as presupposed in the FEP would require three sets of findings: (1) the same patterns of facial movement occur in all normal humans, with the specific patterns now offered illustrated in Figure 16.2; (2) observers in different societies attribute

the same specific basic emotions to those universal facial patterns; and (3) those same facial patterns are, indeed, manifestations of those very same emotions in all humans. The principal method used in support of this premise was to show people of various cultures photographs of posed facial expressions (see Figure 16.2) and then ask each participant to match the photos with emotionally laden scenarios or emotion-words. Peoples from many parts of the world were tested, including, most famously, relatively isolated, non-Western and illiterate peoples from Papua New Guinea.[1]

Russell (1994) reviewed the 34 cross-cultural studies that used the standard method just described. The overall findings from the matching-to-word design are depicted in Figure 16.3. The leftmost set of bars comes from Western literate societies (mostly college students). The second set of bars comes from non-Western societies, although the participants were also largely college students. The rightmost set is comprised of the findings from the isolated, non-Western, illiterate cultures. All groups showed matching of still faces to words at greater-than-chance rates (Elfenbein & Ambady, 2003; Russell, 1994), but as the participants' level of westernization decreased, so did their matching rates. In the case of the studies involving non-Western, isolated, illiterate participants, even the lower rates are likely to be inflated by a concatenation of technical shortcomings within the studies themselves—namely, that they used a within-subjects design (known to inflate matching relative to a between-subjects design), using a forced-choice response format (another known source of inflation), with experimenters who were not blind to the stimuli or the hypotheses, and with questionable experimental control (Sorenson, 1975).

The studies show *something*, to be sure, but rejecting the null hypothesis of random matching does not confirm Strong

Table 16.1 Stipulations of the Facial Expression Program

1. There is a small number (7 ± 2) of basic emotions.

2. Each basic emotion is genetically determined, universal, and discrete, and includes a unique conscious experience, physiology, instrumental action, and—most important—a characteristic facial expression.

3. The production (encoding) and recognition (decoding) of these distinct facial expressions constitute a signaling system, similar across species, which is an evolutionary adaptation to some of life's major problems. The 7 (± 2) facial expressions are thus easily recognized by all human beings regardless of their culture.

4. Any state lacking its own facial expression is not a basic emotion, and so discovering which facial expressions signal the same emotion universally provides a list of candidate basic emotions. The seven candidates found so far are happiness, surprise, fear, anger, contempt, disgust, and sadness.

5. All emotions other than the basic ones are subcategories or mixtures (patterns, blends, combinations) of the basic emotions.

6. Voluntary facial movements can simulate spontaneous expressions. Voluntary expressions are deceptive in nature, and culturally conditioned according to "display rules" dictating when an expression can be displayed freely or inhibited, exaggerated, or masked with a different expression. The true emotion "leaks" through the camouflage and can be detected through facial measurement.

7. Emotional state is revealed by facial measurement. Thus, verbal reports can be bypassed, permitting access to the emotions of newborns and of others unable or unwilling to speak truthfully.

8. The distinct subjective feelings associated with each emotion are due, at least in part, to proprioceptive feedback from facial movements. This "facial feedback hypothesis" has been offered as one means by which an individual "knows" which emotion he or she is feeling.

9. Deliberately manipulating the face into the appropriate configuration creates the neurological pattern of the corresponding emotion. For instance, wrinkling the nose creates the neurological pattern of disgust. Facial manipulation can then be used in the laboratory to reveal the physiological signature of each emotion.

10. The ability to recognize the emotion in a facial expression is innate rather than culturally determined, and may be seen as early as just after birth.

11. The mental categories by means of which recognition occurs (in the self as facial feedback or in others through facial signaling) are genetically rather than culturally determined, and the emotion-words we use thus designate innate and universal categories. Other languages may use other names, but the categories named are the same.

12. The meaning ("signal value") of a facial expression is fixed by nature and invariant across changes in the context in which it occurs.

Universality stated above. Many interpretations are possible. For example, one parsimonious alternative account, which Russell (1995) labeled *Minimal Universality*, as stated above (1) Certain patterns of facial movement occur in all human beings;

Figure 16.2   Four of the Facial Expressions of Emotion ("Happy," "Sad," "Angry," and "Fear" Faces, Respectively) That Are Claimed Within the Facial Expression Program to Be Innate, Universally Produced and Understood, and Tied Intimately to Emotional State

SOURCE: Photographs by Alan Fridlund (model: Jason Fridlund)

(2) facial movements are coordinated with psychological states, which might include actions, preparations for actions, physical states, emotional states, cognitive states, and other psychological conditions (which they are would require other evidence); (3) most people everywhere can infer something of another's psychological state from facial movement, just as they can from almost anything else that other person does; and (4) people in Western cultures have a set of beliefs in which specific types of facial actions are expressions of specific types of emotions (e.g., the smile is a familiar symbol for happiness). These four premises predict that, when asked, people everywhere can form nonrandom associations between faces and emotions. People in Western cultures will be particularly adept at associating faces with emotions. At this time, we argue that anything beyond Minimal Universality has yet to be proved.[2]

IS THE RELATIONSHIP BETWEEN FACIAL EXPRESSIONS AND EMOTION PRIVILEGED?

Untested in the famous cross-cultural studies was the assumption of a *privileged*

relationship between facial expressions and emotion. At least in Western societies, people interpret many stimuli—not just faces—in terms of emotion: angry storms, weeping willows, joyous birdsong, and the melancholic baying of wolves. Conversely, humans interpret faces in many ways, not just as emotions. For example, people interpret faces in terms of action tendencies (e.g., Frijda & Tcherkassof, 1997) and social messages (e.g., Yik & Russell, 1999).

The assumption of a *privileged* relation is that faces and emotions are linked in some more fundamental and specific way: Specific "basic" emotions *cause* specific facial expressions. Specific facial expressions were shaped by evolution to express *precisely* those specific, basic emotions. What are these "basic emotions" that are held to cause specific facial expressions and to be expressed by them? How would one determine them? Ortony and Turner (1990) exposed a host of conceptual problems with the supposition of "basic emotions," but pragmatically, one could imagine sidestepping the complexities. Only three simple steps would be required: (1) develop inclusion and exclusion criteria for stipulating whether people are having a particular emotion. In other words, what specific signs and

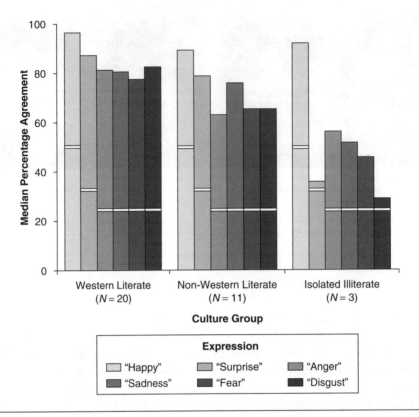

Figure 16.3   Overall Face-Matching Rates in Cross-Cultural Studies

SOURCE: From Russell (1994).

symptoms must be present to say that the emotion is present, and what specific signs and symptoms must be present to say that it is absent? This criterion cannot include the face, else one would simply be proving a tautology; (2) measure what these people do with their faces; and (3) investigate whether there is a relationship between Steps 1 and 2.

We argue that Step 3 has not been accomplished, because the prerequisite Step 1 has not been accomplished. For some, "emotion" means subjective emotional *experience*; for others, it means emotional *behavior* or changes in peripheral *physiology*; for still others, it means certain kinds of *cognition*. For many theorists, "emotion" is a complex of all these components, and not all need be

present at once. The absence of agreed upon inclusion and exclusion criteria for "emotion" means that the hypothesis of a privileged relation of emotion to facial expression remains fuzzy. It will remain untestable so long as "emotion" is operationally undefinable.

Setting aside the fuzzy edges of the concept of emotion, one runs into difficulty even with the prototypical cases created in the laboratory. Empirical examination of specific emotions as highly coherent packages has produced surprisingly weak results. Research has repeatedly uncovered weak associations among components of an emotion (Lang, 1968; Lazarus, Speisman, & Mordkoff, 1963; Mandler, Mandler, Kremen, & Sholiton, 1961).

In the most sophisticated set of laboratory studies on this topic, Reisenzein (2000) examined the intercorrelations among four components of surprise: & cognitive appraisal, self-reported experience of surprise, reaction time, and facial expression. Correlations were modest, with the exception of one relation that is close to a tautology: a correlation between self-reported feeling of surprise and self-reported appraisal of the stimulus as unexpected.

The assumption that emotions cause facial expressions has fared poorly as well. Little evidence is available on production of faces, and what exists largely goes against the hypothesis that emotions are the immediate cause. Fernandez-Dols and Ruiz-Belda (1997) reviewed available evidence on the question, "What is the actual behavior of a happy person, an angry person, and so on?" (p. 256); their review led them to conclude that the "conventional answer, known to artists, actors, and everyone else throughout the ages, is wrong" (p. 256). In support of this contention, Camras (1992) examined one child for over a year and failed to find the predicted expressions in the predicted emotional circumstances.

More notably, Fernandez-Dols and Ruiz-Belda (1995) studied people in a clearly ecstatic state (having just won a gold medal at the Olympic games) and noted that they failed to smile except in specific social circumstances. Reisenzein (in press) extended his research program on surprise and found that the predicted "facial expression of surprise" occurred rarely in surprised persons, although, tellingly, those same persons reported (mistakenly) that their faces had shown the predicted pattern. In Parkinson's (2005) thoughtful and thorough review of the literature most relevant to the relation of emotion to faces, he argued that overall, the research shows only moderate correlations between facial expressions and emotion.

Such correlations are compatible with many theories about facial expression, including those that assume no privileged relation.

Altogether, two major planks of the FEP—Strong Universality and a privileged link between facial expressions and emotion—have been shown to be quite controvertible. As a result, beginning in the 1980s, theorists began to search for accounts of our facial expressions that better suited the evidence.

◆ *The Behavioral Ecology View*

Modern evolutionary theory has inspired new accounts of facial and vocal expression (e.g., Owren & Bachorowski, 2001; Owren & Rendall, 2001). Here we focus on Fridlund's (1991a, 1992b, 1994, 1997, 2003) BEV. BEV is a pragmatic, functionalist view of facial displays centered on how we use our faces in everyday life. BEV assumes facial displays are simply signals that influence others' actions. No assumption is made that the recipient's response is mediated by a conscious reading of the sender's display or a classification of that display into categories like "emotion."

Evolutionary theory provides strong basic premises for the BEV of facial displays (see Floyd, this volume). In the first place, the generation of facial displays co-evolves with others' vigilance for them. The display must benefit the displayer, but the recipient is also indispensable: Signals that do not end up influencing the behavior of recipients, either because they are not received or because they are moot, would not be selected. Furthermore, recipients of displays should attend only to cues that provide predictions about the future *behavior* of the displayer. Therefore, facial displays and vigilance for them must co-evolve and could do so only if displays provided *mutually beneficial* signals of contingent future action. These signals would allow interactants to proceed with reciprocation or counteraction that promoted mutual survival (Alcock, 1984; Hinde, 1985; Smith, 1977, 1986). This does not imply that recipients can use *only* formalized cues; everyday behavior in a given context also allows prediction of the others' next moves (Argyle, 1972; Kendon, 1981).

Second, for the human face to broadcast its owner's ongoing internal state, just as the face of a clock reads out the time, would be foolhardy in its altruism, because it ignores the potential conflict of interest between signaler and recipient. Signals do not evolve to provide information detrimental to the signaler. Signalers must not be honest automatically, but only when it is beneficial to do so. Automatic readouts of emotion would thus be extinguished early in phylogeny in the service of deception, economy, and privacy.

Third, individuals who survived conflict by signaling their intentions would include not only those who produced more schematized facial behavior (technically, "ritualized" if the evolution is genetic and "conventionalized" if it is cultural) but also those with a heightened sensitivity to faces (see Nelson & de Haan, 1997). This "ecology" of signaling and vigilance, countersignaling and countervigilance, is analogous to the balance of resources and consumers, and predator and prey, which characterize all natural ecosystems.

Fourth, the costs and benefits of signaling, and of emitting a particular kind of signal, would vary with the momentary social context and the animal's intentions within it. This sociality of animal signals is well documented in a number of animals and a variety of social settings (Fridlund, 1994; Marler & Evans, 1997). Human signals,

like the signals of other animals, should be no less dependent on motive and context. Because displays exert their influence in the particular context of their issuance, they may be interpretable only within that context. The evidence supports this: For example, a face interpreted as "afraid" in one context may be interpreted as "angry" in another (Carroll & Russell, 1996).

EMOTIONS OR MOTIVES?

From these premises, the BEV offers an alternative to the FEP. In Table 16.2, we provide contrasting interpretations of commonly studied facial displays. Just as Yik and Russell (1999) showed that people in three different societies interpret faces in terms of social motive with about as much agreement as they do in terms of emotion, in each case in the table, an emotion is contrasted with a social motive or intention. The table must be interpreted with two strong caveats, however. First, the prototypical facial displays used in FEP research are highly selected, posed, melodramatic faces of unknown ecological validity (indeed, their ecological validity is dubious; see Russell & Carroll, 1999). The more appropriate faces to examine are those that actually occur in the ecology. Second, as we discussed above, for BEV— but not for FEP—the meaning of a facial display depends on its context. As such, the interpretations offered for the BEV in Table 16.2 are but samples, and they would change along with the context in which the faces occurred.

A common criticism of the BEV is that it supplants one ineffable, internal psychological construct, *emotion,* with another, *social motive,* or that "emotion" can be defined easily so as to subsume social motive. Doing so would make "emotion" even slipperier than it already is. A better approach is to

Table 16.2 Emotions and Behavioral Ecology Interpretations of Common Human Facial
Displays

Facial Expression Program ("facial expressions of emotion")	*Behavioral Ecology View (signification of intent and verbal equivalent)*
"Felt" ("Duchenne") smile (readout of happiness)	Readiness to affiliate or play ("Good to see you," "Let's play [keep playing]," or "Let's be friends")
"False" smile (feigned happiness)	Readiness to appease ("Whatever you say" or "I give in")
"Sad" face (readout of sadness)	Recruitment of succor ("Take care of me," "Hold me" or "Look what you [he/she] did to me")
"Anger" face (readout of anger)	Readiness to attack ("Back off or I'll attack")
"Leaked" anger (inhibited anger)	Conflict about attacking ("I want to attack and I don't want to attack" or "I'm so close to attacking you")
"Fear" face (readout of fear)	Readiness to submit or escape ("Don't hurt me!" or "Take what you want!")
"Contentment" face (readout of contentment)	Readiness to continue current interaction ("Everything [you're doing] is just fine")
"Contempt" face (readout of contempt	Declaration of superiority ("I can't even bother with you" or "You're not worth the trouble")
"Poker" face (suppressed emotion)	Declaration of neutrality ("I'm taking no position [on what you're doing/saying]")

sharpen and narrow concepts through empirical confrontation of competing hypotheses. Motives as used in BEV are not about feelings or, indeed, any necessarily conscious state. Rather, motive is *the projected plan of action and its goal*. BEV therefore offers a different program of research, with different questions, premises, and hypotheses than those comprising the FEP. Although Fridlund (1994) has been critical of the concept of emotion, within the BEV "emotion" is, at best, secondary in understanding of faces. We argue that the concept of *emotion* is not needed to understand how our facial expressions evolved or operate in modern life. Our expressions participate in and guide our

interaction trajectories, just like our words, our tone of voice, and our gestures. All these are like switches on a railway, diverting the interactional train this way and that as it barrels down the track. Emotion is the accompanying plume of steam. We offer two additional lines of research that add fuel to this perspective.

SOCIALITY OF FACES

If facial displays are intrinsically social, as we contend, then it would seem that when alone we wouldn't produce them. As Ekman, Davidson, and Friesen (1990) argued, "Facial expressions do occur when people are alone . . . and contradict the theoretical proposals of those who view expressions solely as social signals" (p. 351). We know of no evidence that the kind of prototypical facial expressions of emotion seen in Figure 16.2 occur when the displayer is alone, and Reisenzein's (in press) data that people believe they show faces when in fact they do not suggest that evidence ought to replace assumption here. But being social versus being alone does not conform to the all-or-none law. Even when an interactant has been removed physically from the room, he or she may still be present psychologically. Actually, the physical presence of others is one of the *least* important ways of assessing the sociality of facial displays.

There are several ways in which people can be structurally alone, with their facial behavior implicitly social (see Fridlund, 1994, for a complete exposition). First, *when we are alone we often treat ourselves as interactants.* We reward or punish ourselves, hit, touch, and stroke ourselves, and likely move our faces in the course of these acts. Most important, we speak to ourselves (without undermining the social and communicative nature of language), and the facial expressions involved may be a part (see paralanguage section below). Second, *we often act as if others are present when they are not.* In their absence, we curse them and utter words of love to them. In many of these acts we deploy facial displays. These faces, too, are social and communicative, although they are emitted when we are alone.

Third, *we often imagine that others are present when they are not.* In our imagination we engage in interactions with others who are not there; that is, we "simulate" interaction with them. We imagine talking to them, arguing with them, making love with them, and we often deploy facial displays. That "implicit audiences" mediate

solitary faces has been documented in several experiments of affective imagery, which showed that, controlling for self-reported emotion, subjects showed more facial behavior in high- than in low-sociality imagery. In other words, people display to the people "in their heads" (Fridlund, Sabini, et al., 1990; Fridlund, Kenworthy, & Jaffey, 1992).

Fridlund (1991b) attempted to circumvent the imprecision of imagery manipulations by manipulating implicit audiences directly. Subjects watched an amusing videotape in one of four viewing conditions: (1) alone; (2) alone, but with the belief that a friend nearby was performing an irrelevant task; (3) alone, but with the belief that a friend nearby was viewing the same videotape in another room; and (4) when a friend was physically present. Viewers' smiles were measured using facial EMG over the *zygomatic major* muscles responsible for smiling. Smiling among solitary viewers who believed a friend was viewing nearby equaled that shown in the actual presence of the friend, but it was greater than that shown by subjects who simply viewed alone. Reported happiness did not differ among the viewing conditions, and within conditions it correlated negligibly with smiling.

Similar findings emerged from another study involving gradations in sociality. Chovil (1991b) visually coded the types of gestures made in different social contexts. Her subjects (all females) heard stories about close calls in one of four conditions: (1) alone, from an audiotape recording; (2) alone, over the telephone; (3) from another subject across a partition; and (d) talking to another subject face to face. When these conditions were ordered according to their "psychological presence," as determined by separate raters, Chovil's subject's exhibited facial displays—largely wincing and grimacing—that increased monotonically with sociality, a finding that mapped nearly identically onto that provided by Fridlund (1991b).

These kinds of audience effects have been found in many studies, although not all found facial behavior to be independent of reported emotion; the relationship of the two has become a focus of debate (Kappas, 1997, and the special 1997 issue of *Journal of Nonverbal Behavior*). Some studies have found independence (Devereux & Ginsburg, 2001; Jakobs, Manstead, & Fischer, 1999a), whereas others have not (Hess, Banse, & Kappas, 1995; Jakobs, Manstead, & Fischer, 1999b). In these sociality studies, face-to-face interaction resulted in maximal facial behavior. This should not always be the case, however, because in many contexts we do *not* issue communications to others. Friends sharing a humorous experience face to face should exhibit greater facial behavior than if they are separated by a partition; friends asked to play poker should exhibit less. Likewise, facial behavior that is socially censored (e.g., crying in front of strangers or casual friends) may produce less facial behavior with increasing sociality (see Jakobs, Manstead, & Fischer, 2001). Indeed, the social role we play toward others has proven critical in understanding the displays we make toward them, whether they are present or not (see Wagner & Smith, 1991).

Fourth, *we often rehearse, forecast, or prepare for interaction and deploy displays appropriately*, consciously or not, even though no interactant is immediately present. Some displays function to deter interaction, like scowls, or the tongue-showing display seen in both gorillas and humans (Dolgin & Sabini, 1982; Smith, Chase, & Lieblich, 1974). On the other hand, "readiness to interact" displays (cf., Smith, 1977) are omnipresent. We deploy a smile seconds before greeting a neighbor at the front door. Indeed, Kraut and Johnston (1979) found that bowlers were unlikely to smile when they had just made a spare or strike, but were likely to do so when they turned around to meet the gaze of those in their bowling party. In analogous studies involving infants and their play toys, smiling was almost entirely dependent on visual contact with the caregiver (Jones, Collins, & Hong, 1991; Jones & Raag, 1989).

Fifth, *we often treat nonhumans, and animate and inanimate objects, as interactants*. That we often treat nonhuman animals as humans is self-evident to any pet owner. We also treat inanimate objects as though they were social interactants. Devotees of indoor gardening talk, gesture, and make faces to their houseplants. Children do the same to their stuffed animals, dolls, or toy soldiers (see exposition by Fridlund & Duchaine, 1996). Thus, even those "solitary" facial displays that are offered as decisive evidence against BEV actually support it, and they reveal the extent to which we are social, even when we are alone.

FACIAL PARALANGUAGE AND GESTURE

For FEP theorists, facial expressions of emotion are a thing apart from language. Indeed, Ekman and Friesen's (1978) FACS specifies that certain Action Units cannot be scored if they occur during speech. This omission is not trivial, because most facial displays occur amid speech. Indeed, we have seen various indications that facial displays are tied to speech more closely than is commonly understood. Fridlund and Gilbert (1985) argued that the face's chief display role was to accompany and supplement speech. Such a close association between facial movements and speech might be expected, given that the entire orofacial apparatus (lips, cheeks, tongue, pharynx) changes in the course of making speech sounds.

TYPOLOGIES OF FACIAL PARALANGUAGE

An early typology of facial paralanguage was the inductive scheme suggested by Ekman and Friesen (1969). Their typology distinguished four main types: (1) *emblems,* which are arbitrary symbols that substitute for speech (a nod in place of "yes") and can be used, for example, to circumvent speech taboos; (2) *[self-] manipulators (adaptors),* which include biting or wiping our lips, or running our tongues in the crevices between our teeth and cheeks, clamping and then widening our eyelids, working our jaws, or bruxing our teeth; (3) *illustrators,* which, as Darwin (1872, p. 366) put it, "give vividness and energy to our spoken words," and serve to accent our speech or substitute for finger-pointing, as when we tilt our heads to indicate a location or object; and (4) *regulators,* which, within a stream of conversation, prevent either awkward speech gaps or colliding utterances; these include facial and head movements to help us hold or yield the floor, indicate that we have gotten the point, show that we wish to squeeze in a word or two, or enable us to regulate the other speakers' content and pacing. Precise, quantitative evidence would be required to determine how often each of Ekman and Friesen's categories occurs and whether their scheme is exhaustive.

These questions prompted Chovil (1991a) to videotape 12 dyads of different sex compositions while they were having three short conversations. She then coded the participants' facial movements from the videotape records. Chovil developed a typology of facial paralanguage inductively based on whether a facial movement (1) was issued by speakers or listeners and (2) conveyed syntactic, semantic, or nonlinguistic information. Across the 12 dyads and 3 conversations, Chovil and her judges scored 1,184 facial movements. From this data set, Chovil achieved a parsimonious hierarchical scheme that accounted for 99% of these movements. Overall, the frequencies of facial movements in her typology did not change with either the conversation topic or the sex composition of the dyad.

Chovil identified five primary types of facial displays, along with several illustrative subtypes. (In parentheses, we give the percentage of the 1,184 instances so classified.): First are *syntactic displays* (27%), which are connected with either speech intonation or syntactical features and are redundant with what we are saying. They consist largely of eyebrow raising and lowering, with tightening or widening of the eyes. These syntactic displays included "emphasizers," which place stress on words ("He's really bad"), and "question markers," which indicate that the utterance should be taken as a question. Second are *speaker illustrators* (21%) that depict or represent what we are saying. Like Ekman and Friesen's (1969) "illustrators," they include "personal reactions," which depict our sentiments about what we are saying (e.g., our making a "yuck" face when we say, "Rap music is vile"), and "facial shrugs" ("You've got me"). Third are *speaker comments* (14%) that convey information that is *non*redundant with what we are saying. These comments include personal reactions, which add our sentiments to our otherwise neutral utterances, thinking or remembering displays, which signify that we are thinking or reminiscing, facial shrugs, which are similar to speaker illustrators but with nonequivalent words, and interactive displays, which recruit or enhance another's attention or reaction. Fourth are *listener comments* (14%), made when we have yielded the floor, that have connotations typically distinct from what the other is saying. The most common listener comments are backchannel displays, personal reactions to the speaker's utterances, motor mimicry displays that echo the speaker's sentiments, and understanding displays, which signify our comprehension of the substance of the speaker's utterance, as if to say, "I know what you mean." Fifth (25%) *nonlinguistic adaptors,* occurring with no clear relation to ongoing speech, that include biting the lips or wiping them with the tongue.

Chovil's (1991a) findings are reminiscent of findings on facial expressions, in that her facial paralanguage categories do not specify precise facial muscular patterns (except for the brow movements of syntactic displays), because she found no facial movements that were peculiar to *any* specific paralinguistic category. Rather, specific movements were categorizable only in the context of the ongoing conversation. In addition, most facial movements (with the exception of the "personal reaction displays") had nothing obvious to do with emotion.

Chovil's (1991a) data demonstrate the overwhelming predominance of the paralinguistic role of the face. Given this predominance, we argued that facial expressions of emotion have received too much attention relative to paralinguistic functions of faces. Furthermore, the distinction between faces that accompany speech and those that do not is superficial, and several explanations can be offered for it. One possibility is that "facial expressions" are a type of interjection into speech. Like the verbal interjections we insert in our ongoing speech, the facial expressions of emotion that are bracketed off by FEP theorists may actually be nonverbal interjections, once necessarily linked to vocalization but now separable from it, making them appear autonomous and wholly apart from the stream of our facial paralanguage.

◆ *Concluding Comment*

Faces differ in their static configurations, and the face changes dynamically in coloration and movement as we look,

look away, stare, listen, taste, sniff, attend or ignore, speak or shout, and so on. Little we do fails to change the face, and observers make use of this information "given off." During conversation, the face supplements and complements the verbal message. The research we have reviewed in this chapter suggests that the boundary between facial paralanguage and facial expressions of emotion may be illusory: The face and the spoken word each modifies the other, and together, they form a package that modifies the trajectory of ongoing social interaction. We can indicate disbelief, for example, by rolling our eyes, "scrunching up" one side of our face, or saying "Yeah, right" as innuendo, and each form of communication has a similar effect. In everyday social commerce, face, voice, and gesture are all co-conspirators. They are *all* paralanguage, all signals that serve the same social end, and none of them has a privileged relationship to emotion (see Bavelas & Chovil, 2000; this volume, for their Integrated Message Model from this understanding).

New neurological findings support this suggestion by pointing to common neurological underpinnings and, possibly, evolutionary origins of vocal, facial, and gestural expressions (see Rizzolatti & Arbib, 1998; Rizzolatti & Craighero, 2004). These findings begin with the discovery in monkeys of the so-called mirror neurons in the frontal lobe. These mirror neurons do not fire when the animal possessing them sees an object but rather when he sees a certain action performed *toward* the object—whether he is executing the action or watching someone else do it. Mirror neurons were found for actions that included grasping between index finger and thumb, placement on a plate, or tearing.

Of course, the discovery of mirror neurons is in one sense trivial. Because we imitate, we must have neurons *for* imitation. But the location of these neurons is surprising. The area containing them is the monkey homolog to our Broca's area, which is intimately involved with generating the orofacial motor sequences associated with speech. Just as surprising is the finding from neuroimaging studies that, in humans, this so-called "speech area" is also active when we move our arms and hands (or imagine moving them), and in deaf people it is Broca's area that becomes activated when the individual uses sign instead of spoken language. The data suggest that, during our evolution, we developed both "brachio-manual" and "oro-facial" communication systems in which we, by virtue of our "mirror systems," could enact what we saw others do (Rizzolatti & Arbib, 1998). In this general model, gestural, facial, and vocal displays may have all co-evolved, from the same sets of circuits, and they may have constituted the background against which speech arose. These signs, readily mirrorable, could have formed the "toolset" for social signaling.

◆ Notes

1. Having participants match posed faces to emotion terms or scenarios says nothing about how people deal with the fleeting, ever-changing faces of everyday life, or what information they naturally draw from them. Moreover—and this is an essential point—the logic of this design means that the results address the second premise. The first and third remain untested.

2. We argue that the assumption that universal faces and our reading of them must be part of our biological heritage is unwarranted (and would remain so even, counterfactually, had the studies supported Strong Universality). Natural selection can spawn both uniformity *and* diversity. Both evolutionary and sociocultural accounts are compatible with *either* cross-cultural commonality or diversity (see Fridlund, 1994).

◆ References

Alcock, J. (1984). *Animal behavior: An evolutionary approach* (3rd ed.). Sunderland, MA: Sinauer.

Andersson, M. (1982). Female choice selects for extreme tail length in a widowbird. *Nature, 99*, 818–820.

Argyle, M. (1972). Non-verbal communication in human social interaction. In R. A. Hinde (Ed.), *Nonverbal communication* (pp. 243–269). New York: Cambridge University Press.

Bavelas, J. B., & Chovil, N. (2000). Visible acts of meaning. An integrated message model of language in face-to-face dialogue. *Journal of Language and Social Psychology, 19*, 163–194.

Bell, C. (1806). *Essays on the anatomy of expression in painting.* London: Longman.

Camras, L. (1992). Expressive development and basic emotions. *Cognition & Emotion, 6*, 269–283.

Carroll, J. M., & Russell, J. A. (1996). Do facial expressions signal specific emotions? Judging emotion from the face in context. *Journal of Personality and Social Psychology, 70*, 205–218.

Chovil, N. (1991a). Discourse-oriented facial displays in conversation. *Research on Language and Social Interaction, 25*, 163–194.

Chovil, N. (1991b). Social determinants of facial displays. *Journal of Nonverbal Behavior, 15*, 141–154.

Cunningham, M. R., Roberts, A. R., Barbee, A. P., Druen, P. B., & Wu, C. (1995). "Their ideas of beauty are, on the whole, the same as ours": Consistency and variability in the cross-cultural perception of female physical attractiveness. *Journal of Personality and Social Psychology, 68*, 261–279.

Darwin, C. R. (1872). *Expression of the emotions in man and animals.* London: Albemarle.

Devereux, P. G., & Ginsburg, G. P. (2001). Sociality effects on the production of laughter. *Journal of General Psychology* [*Special Issue Humor and Laughter*], *128*, 227–240.

Dolgin, K. M., & Sabini, J. (1982). Experimental manipulation of a human non-verbal display: The tongue show affects an observer's willingness to interact. *Animal Behaviour, 30,* 935–936.

Drummond, P. D., & Mirco, N. (2004). Staring at one side of the face increases blood flow on that side of the face. *Psychophysiology, 41,* 281–287.

Ekman, P., Davidson, R. J., & Friesen, W. V. (1990). The Duchenne smile: Emotional expression and brain physiology II. *Journal of Personality and Social Psychology, 58,* 342–353.

Ekman, P., & Friesen, W. V. (1969). The repertoire of nonverbal behavior: Categories, origins, usage, and coding. *Semiotica, 1,* 49–98.

Ekman, P., & Friesen, W. V. (1978). *Facial action coding system: A technique for the measurement of facial movement.* Palo Alto, CA: Consulting Psychologists Press.

Elfenbein, H. A., & Ambady, N. (2003). When familiarity breeds accuracy: Cultural exposure and facial emotion recognition. *Journal of Personality and Social Psychology, 85,* 276–290.

Fernandez-Dols, J.-M., & Ruiz-Belda, M.-A. (1995). Are smiles a sign of happiness? Gold medal winners at the Olympic Games. *Journal of Personality and Social Psychology, 69,* 1113–1119.

Fernandez-Dols, J.-M., & Ruiz-Belda, M.-A. (1997). Spontaneous facial behavior during intense emotional episodes: Artistic truth and optical truth. In J. A. Russell & J.-M. Fernandez-Dols (Eds.), *The psychology of facial expression* (pp. 255–274). New York: Cambridge University Press.

Fridlund, A. J. (1991a). Evolution and facial action in reflex, social motive, and paralanguage. *Biological Psychology, 32,* 3–100.

Fridlund, A. J. (1991b). Sociality of solitary smiling: Potentiation by an implicit audience. *Journal of Personality and Social Psychology, 60,* 229–240.

Fridlund, A. J. (1992a). Darwin's anti-Darwinism and the *Expression of the emotions in man and animals.* In K. T. Strongman (Ed.), *International review of emotion* (Vol. 2, pp. 117–137). New York: Wiley.

Fridlund, A. J. (1992b). The behavioral ecology and sociality of human faces. In M. S. Clark (Ed.), *Review of personality and social psychology* (Vol. 13, pp. 90–121). Newbury Park, CA: Sage.

Fridlund, A. J. (1994). *Human facial expression: An evolutionary view.* San Diego, CA: Academic Press.

Fridlund, A. J. (1997). The new ethology of human facial expressions. In J. A. Russell & J.-M. Fernandez-Dols (Eds.), *The psychology of facial expression* (pp. 103–129). New York: Cambridge University Press.

Fridlund, A. J. (2003). The behavioral ecology view of smiling and other facial expressions. In M. Abel (Ed.), *An empirical reflection on the smile* (pp. 45–82). New York: Mellen Press.

Fridlund, A. J., & Cacioppo, J. T. (1986). Publication guidelines for human electromyographic research. *Psychophysiology, 23,* 567–589.

Fridlund, A. J., & Duchaine, B. (1996). "Facial expressions of emotion" and the delusion of the hermetic self. In R. Harré & W. G. Parrott, *The emotions* (pp. 259–284). Cambridge, UK: Cambridge University Press.

Fridlund, A. J., & Gilbert, A. N. (1985). Emotions and facial expressions (Letter to the Editor). *Science, 230,* 607–608.

Fridlund, A. J., Kenworthy, K. G., & Jaffey, A. K. (1992). Audience effects in affective imagery: Replication and extension to affective imagery. *Journal of Nonverbal Behavior, 16,* 191–212.

Fridlund, A. J., Sabini, J. P., Hedlund, L. E., Schaut, J. A., Shenker, J. I., & Knauer, M. J. (1990). Social determinants of facial expressions during affective imagery: Displaying to the people in your head. *Journal of Nonverbal Behavior, 14,* 113–137.

Frijda, N. H., & Tcherkassof, A. (1997). Facial expressions as modes of action readiness. In J. A. Russell & J.-M. Fernández-Dols (Eds.), *The psychology of facial expression* (pp. 78–102). New York: Cambridge University Press.

Gerlach, A. L., Wilhelm, F. H., Gruber, K., & Roth, W. T. (2001). Blushing and physiological arousability in social phobia. *Journal of Abnormal Psychology, 110,* 247–258.

Gilman, S. L. (1985). *Difference and pathology: Stereotypes of sexuality, race and madness.* Ithaca, NY: Cornell University Press.

Gilman, S. L. (1996). *Seeing the insane.* Lincoln: University of Nebraska Press.

Goffman, E. (1959). *The presentation of self in everyday life.* Garden City, NY: Doubleday.

Gould, S. J., & Vrba, E. S. (1982). Exaptation: A missing term in the science of form. *Paleobiology, 8,* 14–15.

Heatherton, T. F., Kleck, R. E., Hebl, M. R., & Hull, J. G. (Eds.). (2000). *The social psychology of stigma.* New York: Guilford.

Hess, U., Banse, R., & Kappas, A. (1995). The intensity of facial expression is determined by underlying affective state and social situation. *Journal of Personality and Social Psychology, 69,* 280–288.

Hinde, R. A. (1985). Expression and negotiation. In G. Zivin (Ed.), *The development of expressive behavior* (pp. 103–116). Orlando, FL: Academic Press.

Hjortsjö, C. B. (1970). *Man's face and mimic language.* Lund: Student-litteratur.

Izard, C. E. (1979). *The Maximally Discriminative Facial Movement Coding System (MAX).* Unpublished manuscript. (Available from Instructional Resource Center, University of Delaware, Newark, DE)

Jakobs, E., Manstead, A. S. R., & Fischer, A. H. (1999a). Social motives and emotional feelings as determinants of facial displays: The case of smiling. *Personality and Social Psychology Bulletin, 25,* 424–435.

Jakobs, E., Manstead, A. S. R., & Fischer, A. H. (1999b). Social motives, emotional feelings, and smiling. *Cognition & Emotion, 13,* 321–345.

Jakobs, E., Manstead, A. S. R., & Fischer, A. H. (2001). Social context effects on facial activity in a negative emotional setting. *Emotion, 1,* 51–69.

Johnson, V. S., & Franklin, M. (1993). Is beauty in the eye of the beholder? *Ethology and Sociobiology, 14,* 183–199.

Jones, S. S., Collins, K., & Hong, H.-W. (1991). An audience effect on smile production in 10-month-old infants. *Psychological Science, 2,* 45–49.

Jones, S. S., & Raag, T. (1989). Smile production in older infants: The importance of a social recipient for the facial signal. *Child Development, 60,* 811–818.

Kappas, A. (1997). The fascination with faces: Are they windows to our soul? *Journal of Nonverbal Behavior, 21,* 157–161.

Kendon, A. (1981). Introduction: Current issues in the study of "nonverbal communication." In A. Kendon (Ed.), *Nonverbal communication, interaction, and gesture* (pp. 1–53). Paris: Mouton.

Kraut, R. E., & Johnston, R. E. (1979). Social and emotional messages of smiling: An ethological approach. *Journal of Personality and Social Psychology, 37,* 1539–1553.

Lang, P. J. (1968). Fear reduction and fear behavior: Problems in treating a construct. In J. M. Shlien (Ed.), *Research in Psychotherapy, 1,* 90–102.

Lazarus, R. S., Speisman, J. C., & Mordkoff, A. M. (1963). The relationship between autonomic indicators of psychological stress: Heart rate and skin conductance. *Psychosomatic Medicine, 25,* 19–30.

Leary, M. R., Britt, T. W., Cutlip, W. D., & Templeton, J. L. (1992). Social blushing. *Psychological Bulletin, 112,* 446–460.

Mandler, G., Mandler, J. M., Kremen, I., & Sholiton, R. D. (1961). The response to threat: Relations among verbal and physiological indices. *Psychological Monographs, 75*(9, Whole No. 513), 22.

Marler, P., & Evans, C. (1997). Animal sounds and human faces: Do they have anything in common? In J. A. Russell & J.-M. Fernandez-Dols (Eds.), *The psychology of facial expression* (pp. 133–157). New York: Cambridge University Press.

Nelson, C. A., & de Haan, M. (1997). A neurobehavioral approach to the recognition of facial expressions in infancy. In J. A. Russell & J.-M. Fernandez-Dols (Eds.), *The psychology of facial expression* (pp. 176–204). New York: Cambridge University Press.

Ortony, A., & Turner, T. J. (1990). What's so basic about basic emotions? *Psychological Review, 97,* 315–331.

Owren, M. J., & Bacharowski, J.-A. (2001). The evolution of emotional experience: A "selfish-gene" account of smiling and laughter in early hominids and humans. In T. J. Mayne & G. A. Bonanno (Eds.), *Emotions: Current issues and future directions. Emotions and social behavior* (pp. 152–191). New York: Guilford Press.

Owren, M. J., & Rendall, D. (2001). Sound on the rebound: Bringing form and function back to the forefront in understanding nonhuman primate vocal signaling. *Evolutionary Anthropology, 10,* 58–71.

Parkinson, B. (2005). Do facial movements express emotions or communicate motives? *Personality and Social Psychology Review, 9,* 278–311.

Penton-Voak, I. S., Perrett, D. I., Castles, D. L., Kobayashi, T., Burt, D. M., Murray, L. K., et al. (1999). Menstrual cycle alters face preferences. *Nature, 399,* 741–742.

Pernkopf, E. (1938). *Atlas of topographical and applied human anatomy.* Philadelphia: Saunders.

Perrett, D. I., May, K. A., & Yoshikawa, S. (1994). Facial shape and judgments of female attractiveness. *Nature, 368,* 239–242.

Porter, A. M. W. (1993). Sweat and thermoregulation in hominids. *Journal of Human Evolution, 25,* 417–423.

Reisenzein, R. (2000). Exploring the strength of association between the components of emotion syndromes: The case of surprise. *Cognition & Emotion. 14,* 1–38.

Reisenzein, R. (in press). Evidence for strong dissociation between emotion and facial displays: The case of surprise. *Journal of Personality and Social Psychology.*

Rizzolatti, G., & Arbib, M. A. (1998). Language within our grasp. *Trends in Neurosciences, 21,* 188–194.

Rizzolatti, G., & Craighero, L. (2004). The mirror-neuron system. *Annual Review of Neuroscience, 27,* 169–192.

Russell, J. A. (1994). Is there universal recognition of emotion from facial expression? *Psychological Bulletin, 115,* 102–141.

Russell, J. A. (1995). Facial expressions of emotion: What lies beyond minimal universality? *Psychological Bulletin, 118,* 379–391.

Russell, J. A, & Carroll, J. M. (1999). The phoenix of bipolarity: Reply to Watson and Tellegen (1999). *Psychological Bulletin, 125,* 611–617.

Russell, J. A., & Fehr, B. (1987). Relativity in the perception of emotion in facial expressions. *Journal of Experimental Psychology: General, 116,* 223–237.

Russell, J. A., & Fernandez-Dols (Eds.). (1997). *The psychology of facial expression* (pp. 295–320). New York: Cambridge University Press.

Schlenker, B. R. (1980). *Impression management: The self-concept, social identity, and interpersonal relations.* Monterey, CA: Brooks/Cole.

Shields, S. A., Mallory, M. E., & Simon, A. (1990). The experience and symptoms of blushing as a function of age and reported frequency of blushing. *Journal of Nonverbal Behavior. 14,* 171–187.

Smith, W. J. (1977). *The behavior of communicating.* Cambridge, MA: Harvard University Press.

Smith, W. J. (1986). An "informational" perspective on manipulation. In R. W. Mitchell & N. S. Thompson (Eds.), *Perspectives on human and nonhuman deceit* (pp. 71–87). Albany: State University of New York Press.

Smith, W. J., Chase, J., & Lieblich, A. K. (1974). Tongue showing: A facial display of humans and other primate species. *Semiotica, 11,* 201–246.

Sorenson, E. R. (1975). Culture and the expression of emotion. In. T. R. Williams (Ed.), *Psychological anthropology* (pp. 364–372). The Hague: Mouton.

Wagner, H. L., & Smith, J. (1991). Facial expression in the presence of friends and strangers. *Journal of Nonverbal Behavior, 15,* 201–214.

Yik, M. S. M., & Russell, J. A. (1999). Interpretation of faces: A cross-cultural study of a prediction from Fridlund's theory. *Cognition & Emotion, 13,* 93–104.

17

WHY AND HOW THE SILENT SELF SPEAKS VOLUMES

Functional Approaches to Nonverbal Impression Management

◆ Caroline F. Keating
Colgate University

My mother said it wasn't important to *be* confident, but it *was* important to *look* confident. Martha Stewart's mother must have told Martha the same thing. On the day the celebrity CEO appeared in court to receive a 10-month sentence for lying to federal prosecutors about a stock sale, those who watched the defendant stride into the courtroom could only imagine what Martha was feeling and thinking. To manage, perhaps, the audience's imaginings, Martha crafted an impression of herself using nonverbal signals: Her posture was erect, her walk was energetic, and she projected just enough anger to seem powerful but not out of control. Her crinkly, narrow blue eyes and firm, well-defined chin conveyed determination and toughness. But the long blond bangs that tumbled across her forehead made her look girlishly innocent, and her voice cracked with emotion. In essence, Martha presented herself as the entrepreneurial Joan of Arc, marching toward an uncertain future, affected but undaunted by her downturn in fortune.

Martha's calibrated self-presentation throughout the ordeal seems to have been effective: Her release from prison coincided with a 6% spike in the value of the Martha Stewart Company. On paper, she was estimated to be much wealthier after leaving prison than when she entered. Martha returned to a million dollar a year position in her company and set to star in two new television shows (Kaufman, 2005). Yet it is doubtful that in her heart, Martha Stewart was as sanguine about her personal fate and corporate future as she appeared to be on the day of her sentence.

What Martha Stewart's courtroom drama illustrates is that faces and bodies do not speak solely from the heart. The corpus may be moved or silenced by purpose, effort, and habit. Its signal is checked and balanced by processes that warp spontaneous expression to influence audiences strategically. In these ways, nonverbal communication is tuned to motives and orchestrated to accomplish goals. Thus, displays of anger can be used to cloak signs of guilt (Ekman, 1992), smiles can serve as a disguise for psychological pain (Bonanno et al., 2002), and "blank" looks may be enacted to convey irony or sarcasm (Attardo, Eisterhold, Hay, & Poggi, 2003). This brand of *nonverbal impression management* reflects how individuals "spin" nonlanguage cues in ways intended to project images that produce desired social outcomes.

My main objective in this chapter is to integrate functional approaches to nonverbal communication with theoretical perspectives on impression management and self-presentation. To accomplish this task, the introductory section identifies essential aspects of the relationship between nonverbal communication and impression management. The second section applies specific types of functional approaches to impression management and identifies

their distinctive and shared features. The final section exposes some of impression management's important unfinished business.

◆ Impression Management and Nonverbal Communication

Broadly defined, *impression management* is "the goal-directed activity of controlling information in order to influence the impressions formed by an audience" (Schlenker, 2003, p. 492). Audience impressions of people (e.g., self, family members, job and political candidates), groups (e.g., organizations, nations), objects (e.g., products, gifts), events (e.g., performances, disasters), and ideas (e.g., policies, theories) may all be managed (Schlenker, 2003). This chapter pinpoints the first category of manageable entities—people—in which individuals serve as units of analysis.

The control of information about the self is sometimes referred to as impression management and sometimes as *self-presentation* (Goffman, 1959; Schlenker & Pontari, 2000). Many researchers use these constructs interchangeably (e.g., Jones & Pittman, 1982; Leary, 1995; Vohs, Baumeister, & Ciarocco, 2005), and they are considered together here. I emphasize, however, their application to social outcomes rather than to intrapersonal consequences such as self-concept or self-regulation. In social contexts, the actor's impression management goal is not simply to wield momentary influence over others in the sense of "selling" something or getting compliance. Instead, the goal is to gain advantage by projecting an image or identity to interactants and to the *observers* of interactions (Burgoon, Buller, & Woodall, 1996; Patterson, 2001). Such nonverbal forms of self-presentation have surprising power. For instance, whereas blatant, verbal self-promotion can create a backlash against women who use it (Rudman, 1998), nonverbal tactics such as firm handshakes can be an effective way for women to self-promote in a sexist environment (Chaplin, Phillips, Brown, Clanton, & Stein, 2000).

Functional explanations for impression management combine how individuals control the presentation of self-relevant information with how others respond to it (Schlenker, 2003; Schlenker & Pontari, 2000). As DePaulo (1992) pointed out, nonverbal cues are more accessible to audiences than to communicators, because those signaling cannot see the messages they send. Signalers are stuck relying largely on audience reactions to gauge the impressions they leave. In the end, impression management may depend as much on the audience as on the actor because it requires the dynamic interplay between the two (Goffman, 1959; Schlenker, 2003). Thus, the way to successful self-presentation is both to "Know Thy Self" and "Know Thy Audience."

The importance of actor and audience dynamics has encouraged some researchers to analyze nonverbal interaction using dyads or groups as units of analysis (e.g., Bernieri, Gillis, & Davis, 1996). Approaches like these fuse the moment-by-moment interdependence of one person's action with another's reaction. However, most analyses of impression management processes have been extracted from the vantage point of the individual actor or encoder (Burgoon et al., 1996). To fortify these types of approaches, Patterson (2001; see also Patterson, this volume) hinged actor-audience dynamics together by analyzing the actors' dual tasks as encoders of messages and decoders of audience reactions.

In her overview of nonverbal behavior and self-presentation, DePaulo (1992) articulated the special relationship nonverbal behavior has with impression formation. She noted that the impressions nonverbal cues generate are typically "off the record" in that they are resistant to precise identification and assessment (p. 206). Nonverbal cues are like journalists' anonymous sources: Their messages are crucial but hard to name. A literary example comes from columnist Maureen Dowd (2004), who attributed the Bush Administration's decision to invade Iraq to "body language" that amplified verbal exchanges between the President and his advisors. In this case, the President's nonverbal actions made his words "speak louder" by rendering images of a man whose mind was already made up. Nonverbal impression management can also distract audiences from verbal messages. Adaval and Wyers (2004) found that when memory for impressions and nonverbal actions was sharp, recall for verbal messages was dull. In this instance, actions appeared to speak louder than words, perhaps even drowning them out.

Muscling nonverbal cues into sculpted impressions is not always easy. It is particularly difficult to manage impressions that require suppressing or neutralizing spontaneous nonverbal responses (Ekman, 1992). Individuals pressured to appear invulnerable can often control verbal self-reports better than they can monitor nonverbal behavior. Gay child care workers, for example, may express little anxiety verbally when faced with stereotype threats, whereas kinesic cues belie their verbal expression of confidence by conveying tension (Bosson, Haymovitz, & Pinel, 2004). Moreover, the successful neutralization of nonverbal expression is no guarantee that a desirable image will be projected. For instance, overcontrolling nonverbal output can make others suspicious of highly motivated liars (DePaulo, Lindsay, Malone, & Muhlenbruck, 2003; see also Vrij, this volume). Lack of expressivity tends to convey disinterest, aloofness, and coldness (Burgoon et al., 1996; Mehrabian, 1972). When it comes to the nonverbal engine that powers self-presentation, there seems to be no "neutral" gear, only "forward" and "reverse." Cues such as mutual gaze while smiling, nodding, and forward lean generally draw approach, whereas mouth and brow frowns, gaze avoidance or aggressive stares, tense body postures, and interpersonal space violations usually propel avoidance (Burgoon et al., 1996; Mehrabian, 1972).

Managing images to regulate approach and avoidance could be considered a cross-species phenomenon. As any horse rancher knows, stallions never limp in the presence of their mares: Revealing signs of lameness telegraphs vulnerability to mates and competitors and would be a stallion's reproductive undoing. Primate-care workers in laboratories and zoos are often amazed to discover animals that, overnight, seem to fall fatally ill and die. Sick or injured individuals apparently protect themselves from becoming the target of conspecifics' rejection and aggression by cloaking signs of weakness up to the bitter end. The best-known human examples of this kind of impression management may come from the White House. The ability of American presidents to disguise physical and psychological illness and project false images of health and fortitude has kept many in office despite the odds (Gilbert, 1998). From a functional perspective, honesty about one's physical condition may not always be the best policy when the social goal is to maintain power. Indeed, the difficulty in detecting pain from gestures has stymied veterinarians and physicians alike for years (e.g., Hyden & Peolsson, 2002; Leary, Tchividjian, & Kraxberger, 1994).

Individuals are proficient at "spinning" images, even in experimental settings where the image "spun" has been arbitrarily assigned to them (Albright, Forest, & Reiseter, 2001). How can perceivers be so readily beguiled by others' nonverbal performances? At times, perceivers may "want" to be fooled and accept impressions at face value. For example, socially anxious people are especially poor lie detectors (DePaulo & Tang, 1994) and seem to avoid gazing at emotion-laden faces presumably because they fear negative social appraisals (Mansell, Clark, Ehlers, & Chen, 1999). Women often resist probing the veracity of ingratiating comments (DePaulo, Stone, & Lassiter, 1985). Thus, accepting as well as projecting contrived images may have a lot to do with the fear of looking too closely into the proverbial social mirror (Tice & Baumeister, 2001).

There are, nevertheless, nonverbal checks and balances on human gullibility in response to others' managed impressions. One unlikely defense against skewed nonverbal presentations is the snap judgment. Nonverbal behavior is often decoded early and quickly during interactions (DePaulo, 1992), and researchers have found, for example, that deception is best detected rapidly (Vrij, Evans, Akehurst, & Mann, 2004) before a person's "acting" takes effect. Audiences also have defenses against bad acting: Self-presentations that do not seem genuine are not effective. So when women read a script meant to project powerful leadership, they were not nearly as effective as when they performed the identical script in a mindful way, not straying from the content but adding personal, feminine touches to the tone (Kawakami, White, & Langer, 2000). Overlearned, scripted behavior can lead to stilted performances that are not compelling, especially if the image one attempts to project does not come naturally (Schlenker & Pontari, 2000).

Nevertheless, some individuals have better self-presentational skills than others.

Researchers have attributed these differences to variations in temperament, appearance, or environment or to combinations of traits, skills, and experiences (e.g., Anderson, John, Keltner & Kring, 2001; DePaulo et al., 2003; Gangestad & Snyder, 2000). Examples come from studies of leadership. Undergraduates identified by their same-sex peers as socially dominant seem to be especially good at disguising the truth (Keating & Heltman, 1994). Presenting an image of intellectual competence is just as good as the real thing (i.e., possessing intelligence) when leaders are judged for intelligence (Rubin, Bartels, & Bommer, 2002). Furthermore, charismatic nonverbal performances are contagious and enhance leadership effectiveness and liking (Cherulnick, Donely, Wiewel, & Miller, 2001). Yet deciphering exactly what these powerfully appealing nonverbal impression management skills are and teaching them has proven to be difficult (Riggio, Riggio, Salinas, & Cole, 2003).

NONVERBAL IMPRESSION MANAGEMENT: TECHNIQUES OF THE TRADE

Static Physical Appearance Cues. The sizes, shapes, qualities, and spatial relationships of static morphological cues influence how individuals are perceived (see Rhodes & Zebrowitz, 2002). Moreover, static signals can alter the interpretation of dynamic nonverbal cues: Thus, the same behavior may get a different "read" when displayed by individuals with different facial structures, body types, or genders (Keating, 2002). After all, morphological cues "arrive" first and set expectations about traits and abilities (Zebrowitz, 1997). So potent are these cues that they are difficult for perceivers to ignore even when given explicit instructions

to do so (Hassin & Trope, 2000). At the same time, perceivers are unaware that morphological cues often guide their assessment and treatment of others (Keating, Randall, & Kendrick, 1999; Keating, Randall, Kendrick, & Gutshall, 2003; Todorov, Mandisodza, Goren, & Hall, 2005).

People direct remarkable amounts of time, effort, and resources toward modifying outward appearances. Across cultures and millennia, face and body parts have been dressed, painted, pierced, shaved, plucked, injected, molded, stretched, cut, and sewn to manage images of self and identity (Guerrero & DeVito, 1999; Zebrowitz, 1997). These (pre)occupations often reflect cultural values. In parts of the West, fascination with individual physical appearance has led to the popularity of television series such as ABC's *Extreme Makeover*, which on a typical night musters an audience of over 8 million U.S. viewers, who watch as plastic surgeons, cosmetic artists, and physical trainers transform appearances (C. Whipple, personal communication, July 26, 2005; see Manusov & Jaworski, this volume).

Clothing is part of this nonverbal arsenal of impression management techniques. Women and men select clothing styles strategically to make their bodies appear to fit cultural ideals (e.g., Frith & Gleeson, 2004; see also Guerrero & DeVito, 1999). These physical ideals, and their accompanying fashions, change with the times in what could arguably be an adaptive pattern (Pettijohn & Jungeberg, 2004). Even the color of clothing can spark impressions in a big way. For example, the aggressiveness of national athletic teams has been linked to the color of their uniforms. Football and hockey teams wearing black uniforms receive disproportionately high numbers of penalties, in part because they are perceived as more aggressive; cued by their own clothing, team members may actually behave that way (Frank & Gilovich, 1988).

On or off the athletic field, height conveys status and power (Montepare, 1995). The taller of U.S. Presidential contenders win elections a disproportionate amount of the time (Cialdini, 2001). Moreover, adult height is correlated with salary (Collins & Zebrowitz, 1995). In China, job advertisements sometimes contain minimum height requirements, and individuals go to surprising lengths, literally, to achieve greater height. Chinese physicians have nearly perfected surgical techniques that succeed in permanently increasing adult height by as much as 5 or 6 inches. In this procedure, the legs are broken below the knee and extenders are attached to the leg bones. The patients spend months in hospital, during which time an apparatus gradually stretches the broken bones apart just enough for them to regrow in between (Gifford, 2004). Apparently, size does matter in China and elsewhere.

Physical appearance cues can also be manipulated through weight loss or gain and molded through exercise routines designed to shift distributions of fat and muscle in the body. Drugs are sometimes used to enhance these effects: In particular, the use of anabolic steroid develops muscle more quickly than weight training alone (Wroblewska, 1997). These types of practices can be carried to extremes: *Machismo nervosa* describes a psychological disorder characterized by excessive weight training, abnormal eating habits, and distorted body image (Connan, 1998). For many, morphing body parts to transform physical images is worth considerable effort and risk.

Dynamic Behavioral Cues. Nonverbal messages activated by body movements include facial expressions, gestures, postures, gaze, touch, and paralanguage. Behavioral signals may be intensified, attenuated, masked, neutralized, ritualized, or allowed spontaneous expression in the service of self-presentation (Burgoon et al., 1996). Despite their dependence on motion, expressive behavioral cues are often indexed as if they were static entities. Only a few researchers have probed for information transmitted purely by motion (e.g., Berry, 1990; Grammer, Honda, Juette, & Schmitt, 1999).

The meaning of movements can be altered by the context of speech. Some actions regulate or complement speech (Duncan, 1972; see Bavelas & Chovil, this volume), cue speakers' or learners' memory for speech-related cognitions (e.g., Krauss, 1998; Singer & Goldin-Meadows, 2005), or serve as signs and have specific meanings in particular cultures (e.g., Birdwhistell, 1970). Paralinguistic or vocalic cues consist of dynamic information about the voice (e.g., variation in pitch, tone, timbre, loudness, and tempo) and nonlanguage characteristics of speech that find their way into conversations (e.g., pauses, silences, sighs, laughs, throat clearing) (Burgoon et al., 1996). Speakers routinely alter their voice qualities and speech characteristics to "play" to different audiences (DePaulo, 1992), and these alterations impact the impressions they leave behind. Judgments about speakers' politeness, for example, are affected by voice tone as well as language content (LaPlante & Ambady, 2003). They also happen quickly: Impressions that form in the earliest moments of interaction are largely based on nonverbal information and possess the tenacity of other types of primacy effects (e.g., Kenny, Horner, Kashy, & Chu, 1992). Perceivers tend to attribute durable character traits from initial exposures to strangers' nonverbal behavior (Gifford, 1994; Manusov & Rodriguez, 1989).

First impressions are not only both durable and influential, but tiny samples of behavior are sometimes all it takes to create them. Perceivers may draw conclusions about others based on exceedingly "thin slices" of behavior (i.e., in a matter of 5 or 10 seconds; Ambady, Bernieri, & Richeson, 2000). Once impressions are fixed, perceivers are generally motivated to go about confirming what they already believe (e.g., Dougherty, Turban, & Callender, 1994). For instance, job applicants' initial handshakes predict who is likely to be offered the job by the end of the interview process (Ambady et al., 2000). Whether or not these brief, initial impressions are linked to real dispositional qualities (for more on this issue, see Albright et al., 2001), interpretations of subsequent movements, gazes, vocalizations, and smiles are often guided by them.

The manipulation of the *relative* timing of body movements and expression can also leave lasting impressions. Depending on the situation, mimicry, complementarity, or synchrony of action can enhance impressions. Actors and perceivers who mimic one another's behavior generally report greater rapport and greater mutual liking (Hess, Philippot, & Blairy, 1999; see also Lakin, this volume; Tickle-Degnen, this volume). Interactants' motives can, however, shift this formula. For example, individuals seeking to dominate others are more favorably impressed by actors who behave in a complementary, appeasing manner than in a matching, assertive one (Tiedens & Fragale, 2003). Human courtship behavior—the successful kind, anyhow—usually has a synchrony to it, too (Grammer, Kruck, & Magnujsson, 1998). Characteristics of motion, such as the speed of offset and onset of behaviors, rather than the specific behaviors themselves, predict female interest in males (Grammer et al., 1999).

Summary. Nonverbal communication provides powerful platforms for impression management: Both static (morphological) and dynamic (behavioral) nonverbal cues can be managed to shape impressions. The next section of this chapter presents different functional approaches to understanding why and how these platforms operate. The basic premises, promises, and shortcomings of each approach are described and illustrated. Implications of their common attributes are considered in the final section of this chapter.

◆ Functional Approaches to Nonverbal Impression Management

The intellectual centerpiece of functional approaches is that behavioral systems are goal directed or organized by purpose. Classic designs of what it means to engage in functional analyses are found in the writings of Darwin (1872/1991) and Brunswik (1955). These theorists fashioned natural selection and adaptation as ultimate explanations for trait development and behavior. Many current functional approaches to nonverbal impression management can be traced to the thinking of these theorists (e.g., Cunningham, Druen, & Barbee, 1997; Keating, 2002). Other kinds of functional analyses project more immediate or proximate intentions and outcomes as opposed to distal, biological adaptations (e.g., Patterson, 2001; Saarni & Weber, 1999). These models identify relatively short-term communication goals and specify the processes by which they are achieved.

The theoretical approaches featured in this section are meant to represent a variety of functional perspectives on nonverbal impression management; they do not comprise an exhaustive accounting of viewpoints. Contemporary, empirically based theoretical perspectives are included that (1) are concerned directly with strategic impression management or the outcomes of self-presentation, (2) identify goal-directed functions, (3) focus on nonverbal means of crafting impressions, and (4) specify a role for audiences. Approaches meeting these

Table 17.1   Selected Functional Approaches to Nonverbal Impression Management

Main Theme	Function	Nonverbal Cues	Research Examples
Evolutionary	Biological fitness	Neoteny, senescence, expressive, grooming	Cunningham, Barbee, and Philhower (2002)
		Status cues	Keating (2002) and Mueller and Mazur (1996)
		Sexual dimorphism	Perrett et al. (1998)
		Fluctuating asymmetry	Gangestad, Simpson, DiGeronimo, and Biek (1992)
Ecological	Adaptive social responding	Physiognomic maturity/immaturity	Zebrowitz (1997) and Montepare and Zebrowitz (1998)
		Gestures and body movements	Bernieri, Gillis, and Davis (1996) and Gifford (1994)
Emotional	Regulation of others' emotions	Emotional displays	Saarni and Weber (1999) and Clark, Pataki, and Carver (1996)
	Self-regulation norms		Saarni and Weber (1999)
			Ekman (1971)
Social-cognitive	Social goal attainment	Encoding and decoding	Patterson (1999, 2001)
		Courtship behaviors	Grammer, Kruck, and Magnujsson (1998)
		Thin slices	Ambady, Bernieri, and Richeson (2000)
		Deception	DePaulo, Lindsay, Malone, and Muhlenbruck (2003)

criteria were distinguishable by one of four overlapping, theoretical emphases: evolutionary, ecological, emotional, or social-cognitive. Table 17.1 outlines distinguishing features and cites research related to each.

EVOLUTIONARY PERSPECTIVES ON IMPRESSION MANAGEMENT

Evolutionary perspectives are perhaps best at projecting *why* individuals manage nonverbal cues to produce particular images and *what messages* are likely to be advantageous (or disadvantageous) to impression formation (for a more general discussion of evolutionary perspectives on nonverbal communication, see Floyd, this volume). The intellectual inspiration for evolutionary approaches can be traced to Darwin (1872/1991), who applied notions of random variation and selective retention of genetically based traits to communication in animals and humans. Darwinian logic requires that genetic substrates (however direct or indirect) underlie appearances and communication abilities. Gene-based appearances and behaviors that confer reproductive benefits to individuals and to their kin are selected for and retained in offspring.

Courtship displays in birds, piloerection in felines, play bows in canines, appeasement grimaces in primates, and neoteny in humans are all examples of cues rooted in phyletic histories. They illustrate that the essential function or "why" of signaling systems is the enhancement of *biological fitness*. Behavioral and appearance cues that signal sex and sexual interest, developmental maturity, status, health, and reproductive potential are imbued with information essential to fitness. For example, symmetrical faces and bodies look attractive presumably because symmetry reflects pathogen resistance, health, good genes, and, ultimately, reproductive potential (e.g., Gangestad, Thornhill, & Yeo, 1994), and there are image management techniques for those who do not measure up to the ideal. For instance, some believe that the disguise of body asymmetry may be accomplished through the careful design and placement of tattoos and piercings (Singh & Bronstad, 1997).

Cunningham's multiple fitness model (Cunningham, Barbee, & Philhower, 2002; Cunningham et al., 1997) provides a relatively comprehensive approach to impression management from an evolutionary point of view. For Cunningham and his colleagues, "each face and body provides an opportunity for natural and sexual selection to increase or decrease the success of the individual conveying that appearance" (Cunningham et al., 2002, p. 109). Success is achievable physically (e.g., by developing traits that enhance health or strength) and socially (e.g., by developing traits that enhance dominance or devotion). According to the model, individuals display multiple fitness messages that function in complementary ways to influence heterosexual attractiveness and bonding. Consistent with the idea of a multiple-message advantage, Keating and Doyle (2002) found that the physiognomies of desirable dates and mates contained mixed signals of dominance and warmth rather than strong forms of either message.

The multiple fitness model specifies five types of features that skew perceptions of faces and bodies. These include (1) the appearance of neonate features such as large eyes, small nose, and smooth skin, which signal dependence, cuteness, and vulnerability; (2) sex-linked sexual maturity features, which enhance sexual attractiveness; (3) expressive features such as large smiles, high eyebrows, and relaxed vocal tones, which invite social interchange; (4) grooming features including hairstyle, cosmetics, clothing; and (5) senescence features such as male pattern baldness, gray hair, and slow gait, which signal nurturance and appeasement (Cunningham et al., 1997, 2002). These features may be augmented, altered, or contrived to achieve desirable impressions.

Blond hair, for example, is a neonate feature that can be mimicked by adults. The offspring of European parents often signaled their ontogenetic status by remaining blond until after puberty (Cunningham et al., 1997, 2002; Guthrie, 1976). Adults who dye their hair blond can mimic, to some extent, the youthful impressions blond locks convey. So when Cunningham and his colleagues portrayed 21 women as blonds and as brunettes, trait attributions differed. As blonds, the women were perceived as more attractive, feminine, emotional, and pleasure seeking. As brunettes, they were rated as more intelligent (Cunningham et al., 1997). Though consistent with evolutionary thinking, it is impossible to tell from such data whether ultimate (evolutionary) or proximate (learned through association) mechanisms direct this perceptual bias. Much evolutionary theorizing is vulnerable to this kind of uncertainty, because deriving testable predictions and reasonable measures of fitness is difficult. In other words, the question to be posed in this instance is not whether blonds have more fun, but whether they have more offspring and kin who themselves are reproductively successful.

ECOLOGICAL PERSPECTIVES ON IMPRESSION MANAGEMENT

Although displays ultimately enhance reproductive potential far downstream, proximate goals, say for social approval or financial reward, may be served in their more immediate wake. From an ecological perspective, the benefits of impression management involve *adaptive social functioning* in which the fit between signal and social context or "ecology" is imperative. The theoretical perspectives categorized as following an ecological tradition reflect the thinking of early functionalists like Brunswik (1955), who applied his ideas to perception and social perception (e.g., to face cues, nations). Brunswik argued that perceptual systems were adapted to their environments by expectancies developed through experience in a particular environment or ecology. Perception operated probabilistically, meaning that cue perception was biased toward interpretations that had worked in the past (e.g., Segall, Campbell, & Herskovitz, 1966). Because probabilistic judgments were mostly correct in specific ecologies, these perceptual habits or attunements were thought to be adaptive (McArthur & Baron, 1983). Like a Vegas gambler at the blackjack table, Brunswik (1955) reckoned that perceivers need only beat the odds some percentage of the time to come away with a winning perceptual formula. This implies that a certain degree of error is acceptable in social perception. That is, there may be some "slippage" in the matchup between cue

validity and cue utilization. It could be said that Brunswikian approaches are more generous than evolutionary ones in the degree to which they anticipate and tolerate error in the (social) perceptual system.

The application of Brunswik's paradigm to nonverbal self-presentation reveals that the cues encoded by a communicator may or may not match those used (decoded) by observers to derive impressions of the communicator. Gifford (1994) noted this slippage when he adapted a Brunswikian lens model to nonverbal impression formation. He found that communicators who scored high on the measurements of warmth and agreeableness nodded their heads often during interactions. When observers judged the communicators' traits, however, they relied on more than just the valid cue of nods; observers used a host of postural cues unassociated with the dispositions of communicators. Similarly, object manipulation predicted communicators' scores on measurements of dominance and submissiveness, yet observers neglected to use this cue in their assessments of them. One explanation for the discrepancy may relate to perceiver's motivation. When the dispositions judged are highly relevant to perceivers, they tend to increase their use of valid cues (Gangestad, Simpson, DiGeronimo, & Biek, 1992).

Ecological approaches relevant to impression management include research on social perception derived from static physical appearances as well as behavior. The Brunswikian idea of affordances has been championed by Zebrowitz and her colleagues (e.g., Montepare & Zebrowitz, 1998; Zebrowitz, 1997). For example, facial structures may convey affordances defined as opportunities for certain types of interactions. Sensitivity toward these signals is adaptive but can result in overinterpretation, a kind of perceptual error we may be biologically prepared to make (Zebrowitz, 1997). Affordances proffered by "age-related physical qualities" (Montepare & Zebrowitz, 1998, p. 95) such as infantile facial cues, for example, overgeneralize when displayed by adults and influence cognitions about social traits. Hence, baby-faced adults are perceived as having characteristics associated with babies: dependent, weak, approachable, and warm (Montepare & Zebrowitz, 1998; Zebrowitz, 1997). By creating initial impressions, facial structure thus sets the stage for impression management strategies (e.g., Keating, 2002; Zebrowitz, 1997).

EMOTIONAL PERSPECTIVES ON IMPRESSION MANAGEMENT

Humans seem hot-wired to read and write emotion-related nonverbal communication. Emotions can project from brain to body quickly with little input from higher, cortical areas of the brain (LeDoux, 1996). Emotion *decoding* can be fast, too. Brain responses to facial displays of fear, anger, happiness, sadness, disgust, and surprise register distinct patterns of processing activity that appear rapid and automatic (Batty & Taylor, 2003). But the fact that the presence of others modifies the quality and intensity of an individual's expression (e.g., Ekman, 1971; Fridlund, 1994) indicates that humans come biologically prepared not simply to express and detect affective states but also to control their display (LeDoux, 1996). These "audience effects" are complex: Audiences and co-actors sometimes attenuate expression, sometimes amplify it, and at other times alter the type of emotion conveyed (e.g., Manstead, Fischer, & Jakobs, 1999).

When drafted into the service of impression management, emotional cues become powerful allies. In fact, both the regulation of one's own and others' emotions, accomplished largely through nonverbal means, is a key component of emotional intelligence (see Bar-On & Parker, 2000). Expressions may forecast intentions and the nature of subsequent interactions (Fridlund, 1994; Fridlund & Russell, this volume). They can be contagious and used to "infect" others' internal states and cognitions (Hatfield, Cacioppo, & Rapson, 1994). Knowing which emotions to project, to what degree, when, and with whom constitutes a form of impression management aimed at strategic emotional self-presentation. Such self-presentation may also enhance emotion regulation and coping (Holodynski, 2004; Saarni & Weber, 1999). The "bad management" of emotional displays can have dramatic— actually historic—consequences: Democratic candidate Howard Dean arguably wrecked his 2004 bid for the U.S. presidency in under 5 seconds by letting loose over the airwaves a volatile, hot-blooded, untamed scream that was captured and immortalized in the national media as the "Dean Scream" (Stolberg, 2004).

Saarni (1989; Saarni & Weber, 1999) emphasizes the self-presentational functions of managed emotional displays and identifies the proximate, social goals they serve. In her view, emotional displays are calibrated to cast desired self-images and to cope with stressful situations. Saarni distinguishes emotional display management, or what others derive about a person's emotional experience, from emotion regulation, or a person's internal experience of emotion. Display management involves the strategic or habitual dissembling of expressive behavior (Saarni & Weber, 1999). The expression of internal emotion states may be attenuated, exaggerated, replaced by feigned emotion, or suppressed and neutralized.

Whereas Ekman (1971) attributed behavioral modifications like these to cultural "display rules" or norms for public expressivity, Saarni (1989), a functionalist at heart, attaches the dissembling of emotional expressivity to an individuals' social goal striving. According to Saarni, children learn to dissemble to avoid negative consequences, to craft displays so as to avoid hurting another's feelings, and to adopt social conventions for dissembling. Whether these or other lessons are part of a cross-cultural curriculum of emotional self-presentation remains to be studied (e.g., Manstead et al., 1999). But it is clear that control over emotional expression is a skill that individuals are prepared to learn and use strategically to accomplish social goals throughout their lives (Keating & Heltman, 1994; see Feldman & Tyler, this volume).

Emotional displays aimed at attaining social goals sometimes score as congruent, and at other times as incongruent, with privately held feelings. In one experiment (Pataki & Clark, 2004), men expressed happiness publicly, but not privately, just before meeting with a socially undesirable woman. Prior to meeting a socially *desirable* woman, men tended to report more happiness privately than they expressed publicly. Apparently the men's social goalposts moved from "confident politeness" in the first instance to "don't appear too accommodating" in the second. These findings help show that emotional displays may reflect social motives and goals, acting skill, emotional intelligence, and more (e.g., Clark, Pataki, & Carver, 1996; Fernandez-Dols, 1999; Fridlund, 1994; Manstead et al., 1999).

SOCIAL-COGNITIVE PERSPECTIVES ON IMPRESSION MANAGEMENT

Functional social-cognitive approaches identify particular proximate social goals as energizing presentations of the self. Some impose single primary goals, such as interpersonal power or social attractiveness (Tedeschi & Norman, 1985). Baumeister (1993) projected three main goals: (1) social belonging and acceptance, (2) the construction of self-identity with desirable qualities, and (3) the establishment and protection of self-esteem or positive self-images. But attempts to delineate particular social goals and images, and to prescribe the social conditions most favorable to impression management, led to specifications that clashed (see DePaulo, 1992; Schlenker, 2003; Schlenker & Pontari, 2000). For instance, emotional displays and scripted behaviors were considered "management-free" episodes by some and viewed as exemplary impression management opportunities by others. There were controversies as to whether managed self-presentations ever exposed the authentic self and whether awareness was needed to produce them.

Conceptual clashes like these could be rectified, argued Schlenker (2003), by unleashing impression management from ties to singular social goals frozen in time. Schlenker and his colleagues (e.g., Schlenker & Pontari, 2000) made the case for broadening the conceptualization of impression management. In essence, they argued that impression management comprises a dynamic process serving a hierarchy of goals and that it glides continually between the cognitive fore and aft of interactions depending on the resources individuals direct toward it. Resource allocation depends on many things, including the relative importance of the goals served, the effort needed to perform goal-relevant behavior, competition from additional tasks at hand, features of the audience such as their expertise or attractiveness, and the skills and personality characteristics of the actor.

These ideas help explain how signals from our body and face sometimes undermine us just when we need them the most: when managing impressions to look credible. Situations in which communicators have a large personal stake in being believed may be made tense by that fact alone (DePaulo et al., 2003; Ekman, 1992). Add to this factor certain characteristics of the communicator (e.g., low confidence) plus features of the audience (e.g., suspiciousness) and competition for attentional resources (e.g., impressing cohorts), and the derived formula predicts either an unsuccessful bid for a date or a collapsed courtroom testimony, each undermined by nonverbal tension leakage and untrustworthy appearances.

This way of thinking about impression management highlights important issues for nonverbal communication processes. First, neither goals nor the situations that trigger them need be conscious to produce nonverbal impression management strategies (e.g., Cheng & Chartrand, 2003; see Lakin, this volume). Second, resource availability and allocation may influence the success of presentations (e.g., Vohs et al., 2005).

These two key elements of impression management are contained in the parallel process model of nonverbal communication presented by Patterson (2001; see also Patterson, this volume). According to Patterson, processes at or below the level of consciousness can launch the dynamics of sending and receiving nonverbal messages. Patterson's parallel process model could be helpful in determining how cognitive and affective mediators or filters operate differently for individuals high and low in traits such as social anxiety or self-monitoring. Parts of the model could also be used to predict when and how cognitive resources would be redirected, for example, under different status conditions (e.g., Snodgrass, 1992) or for different age groups or in different cultures. To date, components of the parallel processing model have heuristic value, but specific hypotheses are yet to be formulated and tested.

Summary of Approaches. The variety of approaches presented in this section reveal three tasks of nonverbal impression management: the enhancement of biological fitness, the production of adaptive social responses, and the pursuit of social goals. The ultimate and proximate functions they comprise are interwoven into the fabric of human life history and fashion two important qualities of nonverbal impression management.

The first quality is that nonverbal impression management may be performed without awareness. This is despite the fact that its operation is described typically as "strategic," thereby implying conscious processes and control (Burgoon et al., 1996; DePaulo, 1992). Implicitly or explicitly, functional approaches accept that nonverbal impression management may result from either conscious or nonconscious (automatic) processes. Second, functional approaches treat the integrity of the nonverbal signal as relatively arbitrary: imposters, self-deceivers, honest signalers, and the misread attract equal attention on the impression management runway. These two qualities have important implications for understanding impression management and are the focus of this chapter's final section.

◆ The Unfinished Business of Nonverbal Impression Management

Connie, a young graduate student who showed up at class each day wearing jeans and a tee shirt, charged her professor with sexual harassment. But as the professor saw it, Connie was the one behaving in sexually provocative ways. The professor claimed that Connie flirted with him regularly by smiling and gazing at him with open legs as she sat around the conference table in the graduate seminar classroom. Connie was stunned by this accusation; she did not feel sexually attracted to her professor. What kind of impression management was this? Or was it? And whose was it? Maybe Connie's nonverbal behavior expressed an attraction toward her professor that she was unaware of and Connie was simply self-deceptive. Alternatively, the professor was perhaps motivated to misread Connie's body cues and perceive messages that were not really there. But either way, could the professor defend himself by claiming that he was victimized by Connie's nonconscious goal of seduction played out on a nonverbal stage? Is Connie responsible? Is her professor responsible?

This example highlights the fact that nonconscious goal activation and its intersection with deceptive and self-deceptive cognitive processes have potentially important practical consequences for the performers and audiences of nonverbal impression management. At the same time, they present conceptual and measurement challenges for researchers studying impression management. These conceptual and measurement issues are intertwined. Given that nonverbal impression management can be driven by nonconscious goals and stimulated by nonconscious processes (e.g., Cheng & Chartrand, 2003), nonverbal behavior may be the best—or only—way to track their operation. These measurements will have especially complex iterations in "live" impression management situations where nonconscious processes simultaneously energize actors, audiences, and their relationships. Teasing nonverbal communicative processes apart as well as pasting them together will be necessary to elucidate how nonverbal impression management is orchestrated between actors and audiences.

Previous conceptualizations of impression management characterized it as a Machiavellian enterprise of strategy and manipulation in which the "mini-Mach"

within us sought to control our social world (see Leary, 1995; Schlenker & Pontari, 2003, for discussions). Contemporary evolutionary and ecological perspectives give impression management, especially its nonverbal forms, a place in the larger scheme of adaptive social behavior. New knowledge about connections between emotion and cognition offers fresh insights into nonverbal emotional self-presentation, self-regulation, and social context. Contemporary social-cognitive approaches put conscious and nonconscious processes within the boundaries of nonverbal impression management frameworks and highlight the importance of nonverbal measurement techniques.

At the same time, these new insights have a troubling side. Freed from the imposition of conscious control, where is the "management" in nonverbal impression management? How is successful nonverbal impression management different from just getting lucky in the context of impression formation? Is impression management simply the mirror image of person perception, a contest for best performance of expressive scripts, or a relatively honest form of deception? The usefulness of the impression management concept may lie in a renewed emphasis on its most unique aspect: the interdependence of actor-audience psychologies (Goffman, 1959; Patterson, 2001). Those who invest in future research on nonverbal impression management must give due diligence by distinguishing its functions and effects from those of other social influence processes, testing them in an orderly way, and revealing their superior predictive validity.

◆ References

Adaval, R., & Wyers, R. S. (2004). Communicating about a social interaction: Effects on member for protagonists' statement and nonverbal behaviors. *Journal of Experimental Social Psychology, 40,* 450–465.

Albright, L., Forest, C., & Reiseter, K. (2001). Acting, behaving, and the selfless basis of metaperception. *Journal of Personality and Social Psychology, 81,* 910–921.

Ambady, N., Bernieri, F. J., & Richeson, J. A. (2000). Toward a histology of social behavior: Judgmental accuracy from thin slices of the behavioral stream. In M. P. Zanna (Ed.), *Advances in experimental social psychology* (Vol. 32, pp. 201–271). San Diego, CA: Academic Press.

Anderson, C., John, O. P., Keltner, D, & Kring, A. M. (2001). Who attains social status? Effects of personality and physical attractiveness in social groups. *Journal of Personality and Social Psychology, 81,* 116–132.

Attardo, S., Eisterhold, J., Hay, J, & Poggi, I. (2003). Multimodal markers of irony and sarcasm. *International Journal of Humor Research, 16,* 243–260.

Bar-On, R., & Parker, J. D. A. (2000). *Handbook of emotional intelligence.* San Francisco: Jossey-Bass.

Batty, M., & Taylor, M. J. (2003). Early processing of the six basic facial emotional expressions. *Cognitive Brain Research, 17,* 613–620.

Baumeister, R. (1993). Self-presentation: Motivational, cognitive, and interpersonal patterns. In G. van Heck, P. Bonaiuto, I. J. Deary, & W. Nowack (Eds.), *Personality psychology in Europe* (Vol. 4, pp. 257–280). Tilburg, The Netherlands: Tilburg University Press.

Bernieri, F. J., Gillis, J. S., & Davis, J. M. (1996). Dyad rapport and the accuracy of its judgment across situations: A lens model analysis. *Journal of Personality and Social Psychology, 71,* 110–129.

Berry, D. S. (1990). What can a moving face tell us? *Journal of Personality and Social Psychology, 58,* 1004–1014.

Birdwhistell, R. (1970). *Kinesics and context: Essays on body motion communication.* Philadelphia: University of Pennsylvania Press.

Bonanno, G. A., Keltner, D., Noll, J. G., Putnam, F. W., Trickett, P. K., LeJeune, J., et al. (2002). When the face reveals what words do not: facial expressions of emotion, smiling, and the willingness to disclose childhood sexual abuse. *Journal of Personality and Social Psychology, 83,* 94–110.

Bosson, J. K., Haymovitz, E. L., & Pinel, E. C. (2004). When saying and doing diverge: The effects of stereotype threat on self-reported versus nonverbal anxiety. *Journal of Experimental Social Psychology, 40,* 247–255.

Brunswik, E. (1955). Representative design and probabilistic theory in a functional theory. *Psychological Review, 62,* 193–217.

Burgoon, J. K., Buller, D. B., & Woodall, W. G. (1996). *Nonverbal communication* (2nd ed.). New York: McGraw-Hill.

Chaplin, W. F., Phillips, J. B., Brown, J. D., Clanton, N.R., & Stein, J. L. (2000). Handshaking, gender, personality, and first impressions. *Journal of Personality and Social Psychology, 79,* 110–117.

Cheng, C. M., & Chartrand, T. L. (2003). Self-monitoring without awareness: Using mimicry as a nonconscious affiliation strategy. *Journal of Personality and Social Psychology, 85,* 1170–1179.

Cherulnick, P. D., Donely, K. A.,Wiewel, T. S. R., & Miller, S. R. (2001). Charisma is contagious: The effect of leaders' charisma on observers' affect. *Journal of Applied Social Psychology, 31,* 2149–2159.

Cialdini, R. B. (2001). *Influence: Science and practice* (4th ed.). Boston: Allyn & Bacon.

Clark, M. S., Pataki, S. P., & Carver, V. H. (1996). Some thoughts and findings on self-presentation of emotions in relationships. In G. J. O. Fletcher & J. Fitness (Eds.), *Knowledge structures in close relationship: A social psychological approach* (pp. 247–274). Hillsdale NJ: Erlbaum.

Collins, M. A., & Zebrowitz, L. A. (1995). The contributions of appearance to occupational outcomes in civilian and military settings. *Journal of Applied Social Psychology, 25,* 129–163.

Connan, F. (1998). Machismo nervosa: An ominous variant of bulimia nervosa. *European Eating Disorders Review, 6,* 154–159.

Cunningham, M. R., Barbee, A. P., & Philhower, C. L. (2002). Dimensions of facial physical attractiveness: The intersection of biology and culture. In G. Rhodes & L. A. Zebrowitz (Eds.), *Facial attractiveness: Evolutionary, cognitive, and social perspectives* (pp. 193–238). Westport, CT: Ablex.

Cunningham, M. R., Druen, P. B., & Barbee, A. P. (1997). Angels, mentors, and friends: Trade-offs among evolutionary, social, and individual variables in physical appearance. In J. A. Simpson & D. T. Kendrick (Eds.), *Evolutionary social psychology* (pp. 109–140). Mahwah, NJ: Erlbaum.

Darwin, C. (1991). *The expression of the emotions in man and animals.* London: John Murray. (Original work published 1872)

DePaulo, B. M. (1992). Nonverbal behavior and self-presentation. *Psychological Bulletin, 111,* 203–243.

DePaulo, B. M., Lindsay, J. J., Malone, B. E., & Muhlenbruck, L. (2003). Cues to deception. *Psychological Bulletin, 129,* 74–118.

DePaulo, B. M., Stone, J. I., & Lassiter, G. D. (1985). Telling ingratiating lies: Effects of target sex and target attractiveness on verbal and nonverbal deceptive success. *Journal of Personality and Social Psychology, 48,* 1191–1203.

DePaulo, B. M., & Tang, J. (1994). Social anxiety and social judgment: The example of detecting deception. *Journal of Research in Personality, 28,* 142–153.

Dougherty, T. W., Turban, D. B., & Callender, J. C. (1994). Confirming first impression in the employment interview: A field study of interviewer behavior. *Journal of Applied Psychology, 79,* 659–665.

Dowd, M. (2004, April 22). The body politic. *New York Times.* Retrieved April 22, 2004, from http://www.nytimes.com

Duncan, S. D., Jr. (1972). Some signals and rules for taking speaking turns in conversations. *Journal of Personality and Social Psychology, 23,* 283–292.

Ekman, P. (1971). Universal and cultural differences in facial expressions of emotion. In J. K. Coles (Ed.), *Nebraska symposium on motivation* (pp. 207–283). Lincoln: University of Nebraska Press.

Ekman, P. (1992). *Telling lies.* New York: Norton. (Original work published 1985)

Fernandez-Dols, J. (1999). Facial expression and emotion: A situationist view. In P. Philippot, R. S. Feldman, & E. J. Coats (Eds.), *The social context of nonverbal behavior* (pp. 242–261). Cambridge, UK: Cambridge University Press.

Frank, M. G., & Gilovich, T. (1988). The dark side of self- and social perception: Black uniforms and aggression in professional sports. *Journal of Personality and Social Psychology, 54,* 74–85.

Fridlund, A. J. (1994). *Human facial expression: An evolutionary view.* San Diego, CA: Academic Press.

Frith, H., & Gleeson, K. (2004). Clothing and embodiment: Men managing body image and appearance. *Psychology of Men and Masculinity, 5,* 40–48.

Gangestad, S. W., Simpson, J. A., DiGeronimo, K., & Biek, M. (1992). Differential accuracy in person perception across traits: Examination of a functional hypothesis. *Journal of Personality and Social Psychology, 62,* 688–698.

Gangestad, S. W., & Snyder, M. (2000). Self-monitoring: Appraisal and reappraisal. *Psychological Bulletin, 126,* 530–555.

Gangestad, S. W., Thornhill, R., & Yeo, R. A. (1994). Facial attractiveness, developmental stability, and fluctuating asymmetry. *Ethology and Sociobiology, 15,* 73–85.

Gifford, R. (1994). A lens-mapping framework for understanding the encoding and decoding of interpersonal dispositions in nonverbal behavior. *Journal of Personality and Social Psychology, 66,* 398–412.

Gifford, R. (2004, December 5). *Weekend edition* [Radio broadcast]. Washington, DC: National Public Radio.

Gilbert, R. E. (1998). *The mortal presidency: Illness and anguish in the White House.* New York: Fordham University Press.

Goffman, E. (1959). *The presentation of self in everyday life.* Garden City, NY: Doubleday.

Grammer, K., Honda, M., Juette, A., & Schmitt, A. (1999). Fuzziness of nonverbal courtship communication unblurred by motion energy detection. *Journal of Personality and Social Psychology, 77,* 487–508.

Grammer, K., Kruck, K. B., & Magnujsson, M. S. (1998). The courtship dance: Patterns of nonverbal synchronization in opposite-sex encounters. *Journal of Nonverbal Behavior, 22,* 3–29.

Guerrero, L. K., & DeVito, J. A. (Eds.). (1999). *Nonverbal communication reader: Appearance and adornment cues.* Prospect Heights, IL: Waveland Press.

Guthrie, R. D. (1976). *Body hotspots.* New York: Van Nostrand Reinhold.

Hassin, R., & Trope, Y. (2000). Facing faces: Studies on the cognitive aspects of physiognomy. *Journal of Personality and Social Psychology, 78,* 837–852.

Hatfield, E., Cacioppo, J. T., & Rapson, R. (1994). *Emotional contagion.* Cambridge, UK: Cambridge University Press.

Hess, U., Philippot, P., & Blairy, S. (1999). Mimicry: Facts and fiction. In P. Philippot, R. S. Feldman, & E. J. Coats (Eds.), *The social context of nonverbal behavior* (pp. 213–241). Cambridge, UK: Cambridge University Press.

Holodynski, M. (2004). The miniaturization of expression in the development of emotional self-regulation. *Developmental Psychology, 40,* 16–28.

Hyden, L., & Peolsson, M. (2002). Pain gestures: The orchestration of speech and body gestures. *Health, 6,* 325–345.

Jones, E. E., & Pittman, T. S. (1982). Toward a general theory of strategic self-presentation. In J. Suls (Ed.), *Psychological perspectives on the self* (Vol. 1, pp. 231–263). Hillsdale, NJ: Erlbaum.

Kaufman, W. (2005, March 3). *All things considered* [Radio broadcast]. Washington, DC: National Public Radio.

Kawakami, C., White, J. B., & Langer, E. J. (2000). Mindful and masculine: Freeing women leaders from the constraints of gender roles. *Journal of Social Issues, 56,* 49–63.

Keating, C. F. (2002). Charismatic faces: Social status cues put face appeal in context. In G. Rhodes & L. A. Zebrowitz (Eds.), *Facial attractiveness: Evolutionary, cognitive, and social perspectives* (pp. 153–192). Westport, CT: Ablex.

Keating, C. F., & Doyle, J. (2002). The faces of desirable mates and dates contain mixed social status cues. *Journal of Experimental Social Psychology, 38,* 414–424.

Keating, C. F., & Heltman, K. R. (1994). Dominance and deception in children and adults: Are leaders the best misleaders? *Personality and Social Psychology Bulletin, 20,* 312–321.

Keating, C. F., Randall, D. W., & Kendrick, T. (1999). Presidential physiognomies: Altered images, altered perceptions. *Political Psychology, 20,* 593–610.

Keating, C. F., Randall, D., Kendrick, T., & Gutshall, K. A. (2003). Do babyfaced adults receive more help? The (cross-cultural) case of the lost resume. *Journal of Nonverbal Behavior, 27,* 89–109.

Kenny, R. D., Horner, C., Kashy, D. A., & Chu, L. (1992). Consensus at zero acquaintance: Replication, behavioral cues, and stability. *Journal of Personality and Social Psychology, 62,* 88–97.

Krauss, R. M. (1998). Why do we gesture when we speak? *Current Directions in Psychological Science, 7,* 54–60.

LaPlante, D., & Ambady, N. (2003). On how things are said: Voice tone, voice intensity, verbal content, and perceptions of politeness. *Journal of Language and Social Psychology, 22,* 434–441.

Leary, M. R. (1995). *Self-presentation: Impression management and interpersonal behavior.* Madison, WI: Brown & Benchmark.

Leary, M. R., Tchividjian, L. R., & Kraxberger, B. E. (1994). Self-presentation can be hazardous to your health: Impression management and health risk. *Health Psychology, 13,* 461–470.

LeDoux, J. (1996). *The emotional brain.* New York: Simon & Schuster.

Mansell, W., Clark, D. M., Ehlers, A., & Chen, Y. (1999). Social anxiety and attention away from emotional faces. *Cognition and Emotion, 13,* 673–690.

Manstead, A. S. R., Fischer, A. H., & Jakobs, E. B. (1999). The social and emotional functions of facial displays. In P. Philippot, R. S. Feldman, & E. J. Coats (Eds.), *The social context of nonverbal behavior* (pp. 287–316). Cambridge, UK: Cambridge University Press.

Manusov, V., & Rodriguez, J. S. (1989). Intentionality behind nonverbal messages:

A perceiver's perspective. *Journal of Nonverbal Behavior, 13,* 15–24.

McArthur, L. Z., & Baron, R. M. (1983). Toward an ecological theory of social perception. *Psychological Review, 90,* 215–238.

Mehrabian, A. (1972). *Nonverbal communication.* Chicago: Aldine-Atherton.

Montepare, J. M. (1995). The impact of variations in height on young children's impressions of men and women. *Journal of Nonverbal Behavior 19,* 31–47.

Montepare, J. M., & Zebrowitz, L. A. (1998). Person perception comes of age: The salience and significance of age in social judgments. *Advances in Experimental Social Psychology, 30,* 93–161.

Mueller, U., & Mazur, A. C. (1996). Facial dominance in *Homo sapiens* as honest signaling of male quality. *Behavioral Ecology, 8,* 569–579.

Pataki, S. P., & Clark, M. S. (2004). Self-presentations of happiness: Sincere, polite, or cautious? *Personality and Social Psychology Bulletin, 30,* 905–914.

Patterson, M. L. (1999). The evolution of a parallel process model of nonverbal communication. In P. Philippot, R. S. Feldman, & E. J. Coats (Eds.), *The social context of nonverbal behavior* (pp. 317–347). Cambridge, UK: Cambridge University Press.

Patterson, M. L. (2001). Toward a comprehensive model of non-verbal communication. In W. P. Robinson & H. Giles (Eds.), *The new handbook of language and social psychology* (pp. 159–176). New York: Wiley.

Perrett, D. I., Lee, K. J., Penton-Voak, I., Rowland, D., Yoshikawa, S., Burt, D. M., et al. (1998). Effects of sexual dimorphism on facial attractiveness. *Nature, 394,* 884–887.

Pettijohn, T. E., III, & Jungeberg, B. J. (2004). Playmate curves: Changes in facial and body feature preferences across social and economic conditions. *Personality and Social Psychology Bulletin, 30,* 1186–1197.

Rhodes, G., & Zebrowitz, L. A. (2002). (Eds.). *Facial attractiveness: Evolutionary, cognitive, and social perspectives.* Westport, CT: Ablex.

Riggio, R., Riggio, H. R., Salinas, C., & Cole, E. J. (2003). The role of social and emotional communication skills in leaders emergence and effectiveness. *Group Dynamics: Theory, Research, and Practice, 7,* 83–103.

Rubin, R. S., Bartels, L. K., & Bommer. W. H. (2002). Are leaders smarter or do they just seem that way? Exploring perceived intellectual competence and leadership emergence. *Social Behavior and Personality, 30,* 105–118.

Rudman, L. A. (1998). Self-promotion as a risk factor for women: The costs and benefits of counterstereotypical impression management. *Journal of Personality and Social Psychology, 74,* 629–645.

Saarni, C. (1989). Children's understanding of strategic control of emotional expression in social transactions. In C. Saarni & P. Harris (Eds.), *Children's understanding of emotion* (pp. 181–208). New York: Cambridge University Press.

Saarni, C., & Weber, H. (1999). Emotional displays and dissemblance in childhood: implications for self-presentation. In P. Philippot, R. S. Feldman, & E. J. Coats (Eds.), *The social context of nonverbal behavior* (pp. 317–347). Cambridge, UK: Cambridge University Press.

Schlenker, B. R. (2003). Self-presentation. In M. R. Leary & J. P. Tangney (Eds.), *Handbook of self and identity* (pp. 462–518). New York: Guilford Press.

Schlenker, B. R., & Pontari, B. A. (2000). The strategic control of information: Impression management and self-presentational in daily life. In A. Tesser, R. Felson, & J. Suils (Eds.), *Perspective on self and identity* (pp. 199–232). Washington, DC: American Psychological Association.

Segall, M. H., Campbell, D. T., & Herskovitz, M. J. (1966). *The influence of culture on visual perception.* Indianapolis, IN: Bobbs Merrill.

Singer, M. A., & Goldin-Meadows, S. (2005). Children learn when their teacher's gestures and speech differ. *Psychological Science, 16,* 85–89.

Singh, D., & Bronstad, P. M. (1997). Sex differences in the anatomical locations of human body scarification and tattooing as a function of pathogen prevalence. *Evolution and Human Behavior, 18,* 403–416.

Snodgrass, S. E. (1992). Further effects of role versus gender on interpersonal sensitivity. *Journal of Personality and Social Psychology, 62,* 154–158.

Stolberg, S. G. (2004, January 25). Whoop, oops and the state of the political slip. *New York Times Week in Review,* sec. 4, pp. 1, 3.

Tedeschi, J. T., & Norman, N. (1985). Social power, self-presentation, and the self. In B. R. Schlenker (Ed.), *The self in social life* (pp. 293–321). New York: McGraw-Hill.

Tice, D. M., & Baumeister, R. F. (2001). The primacy of the interpersonal self. In C. Sedikedes & M. Brewer (Eds.), *Individual self, relational self, collective self* (pp. 71–88). Philadelphia: Psychology Press.

Tiedens, L. Z., & Fragale, A. R. (2003). Power moves: Complementarity in dominant and submissive nonverbal behavior. *Journal of Personality and Social Psychology, 84,* 558–568.

Todorov, A., Mandisodza, A. N., Goren, A., & Hall, C. C. (2005). Inferences of competence from faces predict election outcomes. *Science, 308,* 1623–1626.

Vohs, K. D., Baumeister, R. F., & Ciarocco, N. J. (2005). Self-regulation and self-presentation: Regulatory resource depletion impairs impression management and effortful self-presentation depletes regulatory resources. *Journal of Personality and Social Psychology, 88,* 632–657.

Vrij, A., Evans, H., Akehurst, L., & Mann, M. (2004). Rapid judgements in assessing verbal and nonverbal cues: Their potential for deception researches and lie detection. *Applied Cognitive Psychology, 18,* 283–296.

Wroblewska, A. M. (1997). Androgen-anabolic steroids and body dysmorphia in young men. *Journal of Psychosomatic Research, 42,* 225–234.

Zebrowitz, L. A. (1997). *Reading faces: Window to the soul?* Boulder, CO: Westview Press.

18

NONVERBAL COMMUNICATION AND DECEPTION

◆ Aldert Vrij
University of Portsmouth, United Kingdom

A re there behavioral differences between liars and truth tellers? Most people think there are. Can we spot whether people are lying by looking at their behavior? Many police officers (and parents) think they can (Boon & McLeod, 2001; Elaad, 2003). These beliefs reflect the assumption that communicative behavior, particularly non-verbal cues, function as signals of deception or truth telling. Despite our assumptions about our abilities, however, most people are poor at detecting deception (Bond & DePaulo, 2005; Vrij, 2000a; see also Riggio, this volume). This inability may be due to the expectations that people have about what cues reveal deception. Unlike the clarity of Pinocchio's growing nose, however, researchers have found no single cue that is related to deception uniquely and reliably; and deception theories, such as those included in this chapter, do not predict that such cues exist. To help make sense of the general inability to detect deception, this chapter discusses the discrepancy between attempts at deception detection and cues to deception. Several reasons why people fail to spot deceit will also be discussed, including ways in which they can improve. I start this chapter with discussing the importance of nonverbal communication in deception more generally.

◆ Importance of Nonverbal Communication in Deception

People can rely on what people say or how they act when attempting to determine their truthfulness. To assess what cues are relied on under what circumstances, Park, Levine, McCornack, Morrison, and Ferrara (2002) asked college students to recall an instance in their life in which they had detected that another person had lied to them. They then reported how they had discovered the lie. The results suggested that people's main method of detecting lies was by comparing someone's speech content with other sources of information (third parties and physical evidence) to prove that the statement was incorrect. When people hear different statements from the same person about a particular topic, they focus primarily on speech content, checking for consistency between the different statements (Granhag & Vrij, 2005). In situations where there is no information to check and only one statement is made, however, people pay primary attention to nonverbal communication to detect lies (Vrij & Mann, 2005).

There are several reasons for this focus. First, nonverbal communication might actually be more revealing than speech (DePaulo, 1992; Vrij, 2000a). Specifically, there may be automatic links between strongly felt emotions and certain behaviors (Ekman, 1985/2001), but there are no such links between emotions and speech content. Also, because we exchange information predominantly, certainly consciously, via words, we are more practiced in using words than in using other behaviors. The predominance of words in the exchange of information also makes people more aware of what they are saying than of how they are behaving. Being aware of one's own speech and other behavior underlies attempts to control those behaviors. Finally, although people can refrain from

speech, they cannot be silent nonverbally. When a question takes one by surprise, one can afford a little rest to think of an appropriate answer. Nonverbally, however, there is no possibility of taking such a rest. That person will display behavior throughout the entire conversation, even when remaining silent, and the receiver can observe and interpret this behavior (DePaulo & Kirkendol, 1989).

A second reason why people often attend to nonverbal communication is that observers may not know which verbal cues to pay attention to. Speech content can reveal a lie if only observers know what to pay attention to (Vrij, 2005). Third, unlike verbal-only lie detection for which written transcripts of the statements are required (Vrij, 2005), nonverbal lie detection can take place without any tools or equipment. It is therefore the only lie detection method that can be employed spontaneously and the only method that could be used in situations where immediate observations are required. Nonverbal lie detection can only be successful, however, if the behavior shown by liars differs from that shown by truth tellers. The next two sections address this issue. In the first of these sections, I discuss three theories addressing how and why nonverbal behavior could be linked to deception. This is followed by an overview of research examining nonverbal cues to deceit, discussed in light of these theories.

◆ Deception Theories

ZUCKERMAN, DEPAULO, AND ROSENTHAL'S MULTIFACTOR MODEL

All three deception theories discussed in this chapter have one important feature in common: The mere fact that people lie will not necessarily affect their nonverbal behavior. Sometimes, however, liars may show different behaviors than do truth tellers. According to Zuckerman, DePaulo, and Rosenthal (1981), three factors could influence cues to deception: (1) emotional reactions, (2) content complexity, and (3) attempted behavioral control. Each of these factors may influence a liar's nonverbal behavior and emphasize a different aspect of deception.

Telling a lie is associated most commonly with three different emotions: fear, guilt, or delight (Ekman, 1985/2001). Liars might feel guilty because they are lying, might be afraid of getting caught, or might be excited about having the opportunity to fool someone. The strength of these emotions depends on the personality of the liar and on the circumstances under which the lie takes place (Ekman, 1985/2001; Vrij, 2000a). Importantly, the experience of guilt, fear, and excitement may influence a liar's behavior. For example, guilt might result in gaze aversion if the liar does not dare to look the target straight in the eye while telling a lie. Fear and excitement might result in signs of stress, such as an increase in movements, an increase in speech hesitations (mm's and errrr's) and speech errors (stutters, repetition of words, omission of words), or a higher pitched voice. The stronger the emotion, the more likely it is that some of these behaviors will reveal deceit (Ekman, 1985/2001).

Lying may be a cognitively demanding task. To avoid getting caught, liars need to provide plausible answers while avoiding contradicting themselves. They must tell a lie that is consistent with everything the observer knows or might find out. Liars also need to remember what they have said, so that they can say the same things again when asked to repeat their story. They may also feel an urge to control their demeanor so that they will appear honest (as emphasized in the attempted control process below), and they may observe the target person's reactions

carefully to assess whether they are getting away with their lie.

The extent to which lying is demanding often depends on the type of lie. Telling an outright lie might be more cognitively challenging than concealing information, and telling an elaborate lie might well be more demanding than providing short yes or no answers. Lying may be more demanding when the lie is not well prepared or rehearsed. People engaged in cognitively complex tasks make more speech hesitations (e.g., stutters) and speech errors, speak slower, pause more, and wait longer before giving an answer (Goldman-Eisler, 1968). Cognitive complexity also leads to fewer hand and arm movements (Ekman & Friesen, 1972) and to more gaze aversion, because looking the conversation partner in the eye can be distracting (Doherty-Sneddon, Bruce, Bonner, Longbotham, & Doyle, 2002).

Liars may realize that observers look at their behavioral reactions to judge whether they are lying and may, therefore, attempt to control their behavior to appear credible. To be successful, typically, liars must suppress their nervousness while masking evidence of having to think hard. They should also be able to show "honest-looking" behaviors and avoid "dishonest-looking" behaviors (Hocking & Leathers, 1980). These "requirements" mean that liars may need to act, but they must also avoid behavior appearing planned, rehearsed, and lacking in spontaneity. According to this theoretical perspective, liars' motivation and efforts to control their behavior will increase when the stakes (negative consequences of getting caught or positive consequences of succeeding) increase (Ekman, 1985/2001).

DEPAULO'S SELF-PRESENTATIONAL PERSPECTIVE

Zuckerman et al.'s (1981) perspective predicts that the more liars experience one or more of the three factors (emotion, content complexity, behavioral control), the more likely it is that cues to deception will occur. These factors are present only to a limited extent in the majority of lies that people tell (DePaulo, Kashy, Kirkendol, Wyer, & Epstein, 1996). In her self-presentational perspective, DePaulo (1992; DePaulo et al., 2003) argues that emotions, content complexity, and behavioral control might also influence *truth tellers'* behavior. Thus, liars may be afraid of not being believed in high-stakes situations, but so will truth tellers, because they too could face negative consequences if they fail to convince others. Given the similarities between liars and truth tellers, this perspective thus predicts that clear, diagnostic nonverbal cues to deception are unlikely to exist.

According to DePaulo et al. (2003), liars and truth tellers will succeed in their social interaction goals only if they appear sincere. The difference between lying and truth telling is that the liar's claim to honesty is illegitimate, and this lack of legitimacy has two implications. First, deceptive self-presentations might be less embraced as truthful self-presentations less convincingly (e.g., because liars have moral scruples, lack emotional investment in their false claims, or lack the knowledge and experience to back up their deceptive statements convincingly). Second, liars typically experience a greater sense of awareness and deliberateness in their performances than truth tellers, because they may take their credibility less for granted than truth tellers. Trying to appear convincing deliberately, however, might be counterproductive.

BULLER AND BURGOON'S INTERPERSONAL DECEPTION THEORY

A third perspective on deception, Buller and Burgoon's (1996) interpersonal deception theory (IDT), postulates that during face-to-face encounters, liars must accomplish numerous communication tasks simultaneously. They must produce a credible verbal message while projecting credible nonverbal behavior simultaneously. They must also manage their emotions, attend to their conversation partner while keeping the dialogue running smoothly, send desired relational messages to their conversation partner and respond appropriately to what is said, and be discreet about any intentions to deceive their partner. IDT embraces Zuckerman et al.'s (1981) factors (emotion, content complexity, and attempted behavior control) as underlying reasons for cues to deceit (Burgoon, Buller, White, Afifi, & Buslig, 1999). In addition, it emphasizes that when deception occurs in interactive contexts, it is not a unidirectional activity. Rather, both liar and receiver mutually influence each other (Burgoon, Buller, Floyd, & Grandpre, 1996).

According to IDT, receivers' behavior may influence senders' behavioral displays both directly, via synchrony, and indirectly, because it may trigger behavioral adjustments (Burgoon et al., 1999). Regarding the direct effects, when people communicate with each other, matching and synchrony may take place (Burgoon et al., 1999; Chartrand & Bargh, 1999; see Tickle-Degnen, this volume). People may mirror each other's posture, or they may converge in how quickly and how loudly they speak. They may also reciprocate each other's gazing, nodding, accents, and smiling behavior (DePaulo & Friedman, 1998). This "chameleon effect" (Chartrand & Bargh, 1999) emerges even when strangers interact with each other, and it happens typically within a few minutes (Chartrand & Bargh, 1999). Furthermore, the indirect effects are related to feedback from the receiver: When liars are exposed to negative feedback from the receiver, expressed through either verbal comments or through nonverbal behavior, liars might realize that their performance is lacking credulity. Consequently, liars might respond by making behavioral adjustments to diminish suspicions.

SUMMARY

The three perspectives discussed here make clear that the relationship between lying and deceptive behavior is complex. Zuckerman et al.'s (1981) assumptions that liars might show signs of emotions and cognitive load seem straightforward, yet liars often do not experience emotions and high cognitive load (DePaulo et al., 1996). DePaulo et al.'s (2003) self-presentation perspective stresses that such experiences are not the exclusive domain of liars. Truth tellers may experience them as well, and, as a result, may also display nonverbal cues associated with emotion or cognitive load. The attempted behavioral control prediction is not straightforward given that the behaviors shown by deceptive senders, as a result of this deliberate control, will depend on both their perceptions of what constitutes a credible nonverbal display and their acting skills in performing this display. Finally, IDT's interactive approach implies that deceptive behavior might be influenced directly by the behavior of the receiver (a result of the chameleon effect) or indirectly influenced by the suspicions raised by the receiver (Burgoon et al., 1999). The complex relationship between nonverbal communication and deception thus makes it unlikely that clear, diagnostic, nonverbal cues to deception exist. Deception research, summarized in the next section, has supported this view.

◆ Liars and Nonverbal Cues

NO CUE AKIN PINOCCHIO'S GROWING NOSE

DePaulo et al.'s (2003) meta-analysis of cues to deception is the most comprehensive

review to date assessing the consistency and strength of certain nonverbal cues indicating deception. Their meta-analysis includes 116 studies, although not all these projects focus on nonverbal cues to deception, and involves 102 different nonverbal cues. Most of the studies were experimental studies where university students lied or told the truth for the sake of the experiment. Sometimes efforts were made to motivate the participants, for example, by promising them a financial reward if they were convincing.

Significant findings emerged for 23 cues, and these are listed in Table 18.1. Nine of those cues, listed in the bottom half of Table 18.1, were investigated in only a few studies and will not be discussed further. The cues are ranked in terms of their effect sizes. Cohen (1977) suggested that effect sizes of .20, .50, and .80 should be interpreted as small, medium, and large effects, respectively. The effect sizes in the meta-analysis were typically small. No one cue was related significantly to deception across studies. The highest effect sizes were found in the cues that were not often investigated (bottom half of Table 18.1), but if the concentration is only on the cues that were investigated more often, then the largest effect size was found for verbal and vocal immediacy, $d = -.55$. The second highest cue, pupil dilation, obtained a d-score of .39. Most other cues obtained effect sizes of around .20 (see DePaulo et al., 2003, for all effect sizes, information about the individual studies, definitions of the nonverbal cues, and the impact of several moderating factors on these cues).

SUPPORT FOR THE THEORETICAL PERSPECTIVES

The results of the meta-analysis provide general support for the theoretical perspectives discussed previously. Several cues

Table 18.1   Nonverbal Cues to Deception

Cues	d
Nonverbal cues to deception	
Verbal and vocal immediacy	−.55
Pupil dilation	.39
Talking time	−.35
Discrepant/ambivalent	.34
Verbal and vocal uncertainty	.30
Nervous, tense	.27
Vocal tension	.26
Chin raise	.25
Words and phrase repetitions	.21
Verbal and vocal involvement	−.21
Pitch, frequency	.21
Lip pressing	.16
Illustrators	−.14
Facial pleasantness	−.12
Cues based on a small number of studies	
Changes in foot movements	1.05
Pupillary changes	.90
Genuine smile	−.70
Indifferent, unconcerned	.59
Interrupted words and repeated words	.38
Specific hand and arm movements	−.36
Seems planned, not spontaneous	.35
Intensity of facial expression	−.32
Direct orientation	−.20

SOURCE: Derived from DePaulo et al. (2003).

(pupil dilation, nervousness, vocal tension, and pitch) indicate that liars may be tenser than are truth tellers. The findings that liars talk less, make more word and phrase repetitions, and make fewer illustrators (movements tied to speech directly and serving to illustrate what is being said verbally; Ekman & Friesen, 1969) suggest that lying is somewhat more cognitively demanding than truth telling. The remaining cues reveal that liars appear less spontaneous, more ambivalent, less involved, and more uncertain, and this fits well with the predictions that liars endorse their statements less convincingly than do truth tellers (DePaulo et al., 2003) and that liars often fail to control their behavior in a convincing manner (DePaulo et al., 2003; Zuckerman et al., 1981).

In the overwhelming majority of deception studies, however, no interaction takes place between sender and receiver, making them inappropriate for Buller and Burgoon's (1996) IDT. Studies in which an interactional interview style has been employed have provided mixed results regarding whether liars avoid displaying suspicious behaviors (Levine & McCornack, 1996). It might be that liars aim to suppress all behaviors that they believe are suspicious, but they often do not succeed (Buller, Stiff, & Burgoon, 1996; Vrij, 2000a).

◆ Reasons for Few Nonverbal Cues to Deception

The complex relationship between nonverbal behavior and deception, outlined above, already predicted that research would reveal only a few, and usually weak, relationships between nonverbal cues and deception. There are more explanations for the limited success that people have when they attempt to detect deception. This section highlights two such reasons.

SOME CUES ARE OVERLOOKED

One explanation for not finding consistent and reliable cues to deception is that some nonverbal cues are overlooked by researchers, sometimes because the scoring systems used to measure them are not detailed enough. Ekman (1985/2001) has identified a number of different smiles, including a distinction between felt and false smiles. Felt smiles include smiles in which the person actually experiences a positive emotion, whereas false smiles are deliberately contrived to convince another person that a positive emotion is felt, when in fact it is not. Felt smiles are accompanied by the action of two muscles: the zygomatic major that pulls the lip corners upward toward the cheekbone and the orbicularis oculi that raises the cheek and gathers skin inward from around the eye socket. The latter change produces bagged skin below the eyes and crow's-feet creases beyond the eye corners. In false smiles, the action of the orbicularis oculi muscle causing the effects around the eye is often missing (Frank, Ekman, & Friesen, 1993). Ekman and colleagues found that truth tellers displayed more felt smiles than did liars, whereas liars displayed more false smiles than did truth tellers. When the distinction between felt and false smiles was not made, truth tellers

smiled as frequently as liars (Ekman, Friesen, & O'Sullivan, 1988). Other differences between felt and false smiles include that false smiles are more asymmetrical, appear too early or too late, and often last longer (Ekman, Davidson, & Friesen, 1990; see Ekman, 1985/2001, for more examples about how facial expressions could be related to deceit).

Similar patterns may occur with different behaviors. Nonverbal communication researchers have identified numerous types of hand movements (Bavelas, Chovil, Coates, & Roe, 1995; Ekman & Friesen, 1969, 1972; McNeill, 1985, 1992). For example, based on the work of Efron (1941), Ekman and Friesen (1969) made a distinction between five movement categories: emblems, illustrators, affect displays, regulators, and adaptors. In their later writings (Ekman & Friesen, 1972; Friesen, Ekman, & Wallbott, 1979), they restricted themselves to only three of these categories, emblems, illustrators, and adaptors, because "these three classes include all hand movement except for those times when the hand moves simply to establish a new position or rest" (Friesen et al., 1979, p. 99). This three-class categorization is often used in deception research, and all three categories appear in DePaulo et al.'s (2003) meta-analysis.

Ekman and Friesen (1972) make further distinctions into eight types of illustrators, but these subdivisions are not used by deception researchers typically. In one experiment, however, Caso, Maricchiolo, Bonaiuto, Vrij, and Mann (2006) did differentiate between different types of illustrators. Truth tellers described objects they had in their possession, whereas liars had to imagine that they had these objects in their possession. Liars made fewer deictic movements (pointing gestures) than did truth tellers, perhaps due to the lack of real objects they could point at, but liars made more metaphoric gestures, which are typically made when people describe abstract ideas (McNeill, 1992). Illustrators as a whole entity (i.e., all the different types combined) were not linked to deception. Like smiles, it was only when specific types of distinctions were made among subclasses of behavior that deception cues were detected.

INDIVIDUAL AND SITUATIONAL DIFFERENCES

Another reason for limited number of nonverbal indicators of deceit may be that a meta-analysis cannot capture signs of deceit at an individual level. That is, different individuals may give their lies away in different ways (DePaulo et al., 2003); such idiosyncratic cues do not become apparent when the focus is across studies. Similarly, cues to deception could be dependent on the situational context for the lie. A meta-analysis that accumulates findings across contexts would not apprehend those trends either.

Furthermore, more cues to deception are likely to occur when the stakes are high rather than low. In high-stakes situations, liars might feel stronger emotions, might experience more cognitive demand, and might be more motivated to manage their behavior to appear credible. In their meta-analysis, DePaulo et al. (2003) compared higher-stakes studies (e.g., studies where financial incentives were promised if the participant appeared credible) with lower-stakes studies. Some cues to deception, such as an increase in blinking, a decrease in leg and foot movements, and an increased speech rate, appeared only in higher-stakes situations. The differences between liars and truth tellers were still small, however, perhaps because a high-stakes situation will also affect truth tellers or, alternatively, because the stakes were still not high enough in these laboratory-based, higher-stakes studies.

What happens in situations where the stakes are really high, for example, when guilty suspects lie in police interviews, when smugglers go through customs at airports, or when adulterous husbands are challenged by their wives? To examine how liars respond in high-stakes situations, one of the few options is to analyze such real-life high-stakes situations. It is difficult, however, to capture such lies on tape and to establish the *ground truth* in such situations, that is, to know for certain that someone was actually lying or telling the truth (Vrij & Mann, 2003), making such studies difficult to undertake.

Mann, Vrij, and Bull (2002) published the most comprehensive study to date about people's behavior in real-life high-stakes situations. They examined the behavioral responses of 16 suspects while they lied and told the truth during their police interviews. The police interviews were videotaped, and the tapes were made available for detailed scoring of the suspects' behavioral responses. The suspects were interviewed in connection with serious crimes such as murder, rape, and arson and were facing long custodial sentences if found guilty. Regarding the ground truth, clips of video footage were selected where other sources (reliable witness statements and forensic evidence) provided conclusive evidence that the suspect lied or told the truth.

Results revealed that compared with when they told the truth, the suspects exhibited more pauses, fewer eye blinks, and fewer hand and arm movements (by male suspects) when they lied. Indicators of being tense (such as fidgeting and gaze aversion) did not emerge. These indicators are the behavioral patterns that police officers expect typically in lying suspects. Mann et al.'s results suggest that the suspects' cues to deception were more likely the result of increased cognitive demand than of nervousness. The strongest evidence for this was the reduction in eye blinks during deception. Research has shown that nervousness results in an increase in eye blinking (Harrigan & O'Connell, 1996), whereas increased cognitive load results in a decrease in eye blinking (Wallbott & Scherer, 1991).

The apparent predominance of cognitive load processes compared with emotional processes in those suspects is perhaps not surprising. Many of the suspects included in Mann et al.'s (2002) study have had regular contact with the police and were probably familiar with the police interview situation, thereby decreasing their nervousness. Suspects in police interviews are typically of below average intelligence, however (Gudjonsson, 2003). There is evidence that less intelligent people will have particular difficulty in inventing plausible and convincing stories (Ekman & Frank, 1993). Alternatively, it might well be that the suspects were more tense when they lied but that this was momentarily suppressed when they had to think hard. There is evidence that cognitive demand results in an automatic and momentary suppression of arousal (Jennings, 1992; Leal, 2005).

The absence of clear diagnostic nonverbal cues to deceit makes detecting deceit a difficult task. People's ability to detect deceit and reasons why they sometimes fail to catch liars will be discussed in the next two sections.

◆ Accuracy in Detecting Deceit

LAYPERSONS' LIE DETECTION IN STRANGERS

In a typical lie detection study, observers (normally undergraduate students) are shown video clips of strangers who are either lying or telling the truth. They are asked to indicate after each clip whether the person was lying or telling the truth. There is no opportunity for the lie detectors to check the veracity of the statement via physical evidence, third parties, and so on, so the only source of information is the verbal and nonverbal behavior displayed in the videos. In such a study, simply guessing whether the person lied or spoke the truth would result in an accuracy rate (percentage of correct classifications) of 50%.

Vrij (2000a) reviewed 37 of such studies. In most studies, the accuracy rates varied between 45% and 60%, with an average accuracy rate of 56.6%, only just above the level of chance. When accuracy at detecting lies was computed separately from accuracy at detecting truth, results showed that observers were reasonably good at detecting truths (correctly judging that someone was telling the truth: 67% accuracy rate) but particularly poor at detecting lies (correctly judging that someone was lying: 44% accuracy rate). This rate is below the level of chance, and people would be more accurate at detecting lies if they simply guessed.

The superior accuracy rate for truthful messages is likely caused at least in part by the *truth bias:* Judges are more likely to consider that messages are truthful than deceptive and, as a result, truthful messages are identified with more accuracy than are deceptive messages. There are at least four explanations for the truth bias (Gilbert, 1991; Vrij & Mann, 2003). First, in daily life people are more often confronted with truthful than with deceptive statements, so they are more inclined to assume that the behavior they observe is honest (what has been labeled the *availability heuristic;* O'Sullivan, Ekman, & Friesen, 1988). Second, social conversation rules discourage people from displaying suspicion. It is often necessary, however, to challenge what the person is saying and ask for more information to detect deceit (Vrij, 2000a, 2004b). Third, people may be unsure as to whether deception is actually occurring. Given this uncertainty, the safest and most polite strategy may be to believe what is expressed overtly (DePaulo, Jordan, Irvine, & Laser, 1982). Fourth, based on a Spinozan model of knowledge representation, Gilbert (1991) argues that everything is taken to be true initially, and that disbelief requires extra effort. In other words, the truth bias is the default setting when interacting with strangers.

Lie detection is not only difficult when adults are involved. When adults are asked to detect truths and lies in children with whom they are not familiar, particularly in situations where they can only rely on the child's verbal and nonverbal behavior, they do not perform much better than when they are asked to detect lies in adults. Parents, however, seem to be better than other adults at detecting lies told by their own children (see Vrij, 2002, for a review of child deception literature). Deception is also harder to spot across cultures (e.g., when natives and immigrants in a country interact) than within the same culture (see Bond & Rao, 2004, for a review of cross-cultural lie detection).

LAYPERSONS' LIE DETECTION IN FRIENDS, PARTNERS, OR CHILDREN

Boon and McLeod (2001) reported that people believe that they are fairly successful in detecting lies in their partners. They also believe that they themselves are more successful in deceiving their partners than their partners are at deceiving them. In several experiments, however, observers were shown videotaped truthful or deceptive statements of people they know, and were asked to judge the veracity of each statement (Anderson, Ansfield, & DePaulo, 1999; Vrij, 2000a). As in most studies, there was no physical evidence or third-party information to rely on.

The results of these studies did not support the idea that it is easier to detect lies in friends or lovers than in strangers. As relationships become more intimate, partners develop a strong tendency to judge the other, a tendency that has been called the *relational truth-bias heuristic* (Stiff, Kim, & Ramesh, 1992). As the relationship between two people intensifies, they often become more confident that they can detect each other's lies. High levels of confidence tend to result in the belief that the other person would probably not dare to lie, which subsequently reduces the need of trying to discover whether that person is lying (Levine & McCornack, 1992).

Anderson et al. (1999) provided additional explanations as to why people may fail to detect deceit in their close friends or romantic partners. They suggested that when close relationship partners attempt to detect deceit in each other, they bring to mind a great deal of information about each other. This information could be overwhelming, and the lie detector might deal with this load by processing the information heuristically instead of searching carefully for genuine cues to deceit. Also, in close relationship interactions, the lie detector must engage simultaneously in social behavior (e.g., the need to appear supportive in those interactions) and social cognition (e.g., decoding possible cues to deception) (Patterson, 1995). This might be too much for the lie detector and, as a result, valuable cues may remain unnoticed. Finally, it could be that as relationships develop, the partners become more skilled at crafting communications designed uniquely to fool each other.

PROFESSIONAL LIE CATCHERS

Granhag and Vrij (2005) reviewed 10 studies in which professional lie catchers, such as police officers, participated as judges. In these studies, the professionals saw clips of people they did not know, and no physical or third-party evidence was available to them. Granhag and Vrij found an accuracy rate (lies and truths combined) of 55%. This accuracy rate is similar to the accuracy rate found with students. Results revealed, however, that professionals are equally good at detecting truths (55%) and lies (55%), suggesting that the truth bias, typically found in students, does not seem to occur with professional lie catchers.

In another study, Mann, Vrij, and Bull (2004) showed 99 police officers videotapes consisting of a total of 54 truths and lies told by suspects during their police interviews. These clips were derived from the Mann et al. (2002) study described previously. Again, no physical or third-party evidence was available to the observers. In this study, however, the officers were capable of detecting, on average, 63% of the truths and 66% of the lies. These accuracy rates were higher than those found in most previous lie detection studies. One explanation for this greater accuracy is that the stakes for the suspects in this study were considerably higher than the stakes for the liars and truth tellers in most lie detection studies, and as noted, high-stake lies may be easier to detect than low-stake lies (see, Vrij, 2000b, for a review).

◆ Reasons Why Lies Remain Undetected

Despite some evidence that certain kinds of lies may be easier to detect, most lies are not detected easily. There are numerous reasons why lies often remain undetected (Vrij, 2004a, 2004b). Those related to nonverbal communication are discussed here. As already argued, the most basic reason for the failure to detect lies is that there is no single verbal, nonverbal, or physiological cue uniquely related to deception. The other reasons are a little more complicated and merit more discussion.

THE USE OF HEURISTICS

Rather than scrutinizing another's reactions actively for cues to deceit, observers may instead rely on rule of thumb decision rules or cognitive heuristics (Levine, Park, & McCornack, 1999). Such heuristics easily lead to systematic errors and biases. Two heuristics that are thought to influence veracity judgments, the availability heuristic and the relational truth-bias heuristic, were discussed earlier. Another heuristic sis the *probing heuristic* (Levine & McCornack, 2001), and it refers to judges' tendency to believe a source more after the source has been probed. Receivers often have a strong belief in the efficacy of probing as a lie detection strategy. In cases where probing does not result in clear signs of deceit, and it often will not (Levine & McCornack), the source is more likely to be believed. The *representativeness heuristic* (Stiff et al., 1989) refers to the tendency to evaluate a particular reaction (e.g., nervous behavior) as an example of a broader category (e.g., deception). The *expectancy-violation heuristic* (Vrij, 2004b) relates to observers' tendency to judge reactions that are odd or infrequent, such as keeping the eyes closed or staring while speaking, as deceptive (Bond et al., 1992). In addition, the *facial appearance heuristic* (Vrij, 2004b) refers to observers' tendency to judge people with attractive faces or with a baby-faced appearance as more honest (Aune, Levine, Ching, & Yoshimoto, 1993; Bull & Rumsey, 1988).

Furthermore, O'Sullivan (2003) demonstrated that the fundamental attribution error (FAE) can undermine lie detection. The FAE is the tendency, when forming impressions of others, to overestimate dispositional causes of that person and to underestimate situational causes. When observers believe that someone is generally a trustworthy person, they will have the tendency to judge that person as truthful in any given situation. Similarly, when observers believe that someone is an untrustworthy person, they will be inclined to judge that person as dishonest in any given situation.

LOOKING AT THE WRONG CUES

Studies investigating how people think liars behave have been carried out worldwide, albeit overwhelmingly with Caucasian participants. These studies suggest that people predominantly expect liars to react nervously, with "liars look away" being the most often mentioned belief (see Bond & Rao, 2004; Strömwall, Granhag, & Hartwig, 2004; Vrij, Akehurst, & Knight, in press; Vrij, 2004b, for reviews). The belief that liars increase their movements is also widespread (Strömwall et al., 2004). Gaze, however, does not appear to be reliably related to deception (DePaulo et al., 2003; Vrij, 2000a). In addition, liars tend to *decrease* rather than increase their movements (DePaulo et al., 2003; Vrij, 2000a; see Table 18.1).

There are several reasons why these incorrect beliefs exist. First, because media often promote the idea that liars look away and fidget, many people may have been exposed to and absorbed this information. Even police manuals often suggest that liars fidget and look away, which may explain why police officers also endorse these beliefs overwhelmingly (Vrij, 2004b). Second, people believe mistakenly that they show nervous behaviors themselves when they lie (Vrij, Edward, & Bull, 2001a), and, during lie detection, observers may look for cues they mistakenly believe they themselves show while lying. Third, once incorrect

beliefs are established, people tend to seek information that confirms rather than disconfirms these beliefs (*confirmation bias*) and therefore have a biased evaluation of new information. Consequently, they will discount information that contradicts their beliefs (*belief perseverance*). These processes result in people thinking that their beliefs are more grounded in reality than they are. In turn, this makes it unlikely that they will change their beliefs (Granhag & Vrij, 2005; Strömwall et al., 2004).

Fourth, it is often difficult for people to test the accuracy of their beliefs because of a lack of reliable feedback (i.e., we seldom learn whether our lie detection strategy is accurate). Interestingly, research suggests that prisoners have the most accurate beliefs about deception (Hartwig, Granhag, Strömwall, & Andersson, 2004; Vrij & Semin, 1996). They may well live in a world that involves a lot of deception. Success in such a culture may depend in part on being able to tell when one is the target of deception.

PEOPLE DO NOT TAKE INDIVIDUAL AND SITUATIONAL DIFFERENCES INTO ACCOUNT

There are large individual differences in people's behavior. People may fail to catch liars because they do not take such individual differences into account when they attempt to detect deceit. People whose normative behavior looks suspicious are in a particularly disadvantageous position. Some individuals' nonverbal behavior gives the impression that they are telling the truth (*honest demeanor bias*), whereas others' natural behavior leaves the impression that they are lying (*dishonest demeanor bias*) (Frank & Ekman, 2004; Riggio, Tucker, & Throckmorton, 1988).

Such demeanor biases are related to personality traits. Expressive people, for example, exude credibility, regardless of the truth of their assertions, because their spontaneity tends to disarm suspicion (Riggio, 1986). People with a strong sense of public self-consciousness tend to make a less credible impression on others. When these individuals lie, they are concerned about being scrutinized by others, which changes their behavior in such a way that it appears dishonest. Introverts and socially anxious people also tend to make a suspicious impression. The social clumsiness of many introverts and the impression of tension, nervousness, or fear of socially anxious individuals are often interpreted by observers as indicators of deceit. Interestingly, introverts' demeanor seems not to reflect their actions accurately. Specifically, research has found that introverted people lie infrequently (Kashy & DePaulo, 1996).

Errors in interpreting someone's behavior arise easily in cross-ethnic or cross-cultural interactions because of differences in behavior that may be displayed by different groups. For example, African Americans display more gaze aversion generally than do Euro-Americans (LaFrance & Mayo, 1976). Such differences are, in part, based on the fact that gaze patterns are influenced by culture, and that looking into the eyes of a conversation partner is regarded as polite in some Western cultures but is considered to be rude in several other cultures (Vrij & Winkel, 1991). In support of this argument, several experimental studies revealed that behaviors displayed typically by members of some ethnic groups living in the Netherlands make a suspicious impression on Caucasian Dutch police officers, a phenomenon labeled *cross-cultural nonverbal communication errors* (see Vrij, 2000a, for an overview of these studies). That is, nonverbal behavioral patterns normative for certain ethnic groups may be interpreted by members of other ethnicities as revealing attempts to hide the truth.

Not only do different people behave differently in the same situation (interpersonal differences); the same person also behaves differently across situations (intrapersonal differences). For example, people show different behaviors when with friends in a restaurant than while interviewed for a job application. Establishing how people behave in the former setting can therefore not be used to establish whether they are lying in the latter setting. Yet police manuals advise police detectives to establish a suspect's baseline behavior on the initial small talk part of the interrogation, and to compare this with the behavior shown during the accusational part of the interrogation (Inbau, Reid, Buckley, & Jayne, 2001).

◆ Discussion

This chapter makes clear that the relationship between deception and nonverbal communication is complex, and distinguishing accurately between lies and truths is often challenging. Having difficulty with detecting deceit, however, does not harm people in many daily life situations. On the contrary, being ignorant about the truth often serves us well. What would we think of ourselves if we come to know the truth about every flattering comment we receive? And how would we respond if other people could detect every lie we tell, including our white lies? Telling lies is very much part of everyday life (DePaulo et al., 1996; Goffman, 1959; Vrij, in press) and something that is expected in the smooth working of social relations. Sometimes, however, it is important to be able to detect lies. For example, it would benefit police investigations if police detectives were able to tell when suspects are lying and when they are telling the truth during police interviews. There are opportunities for improving lie detection ability by paying attention to people's behavior. To conclude this chapter, I will discuss these ideas.

PAY ATTENTION TO DIAGNOSTIC CUES

Observers *can* become more accurate when they are trained to attend to more diagnostic cues (Frank & Feeley, 2003). Determining the greatest number of diagnostic cues may, however, be difficult. One means for doing so is to examine the strategies that good lie detectors use. For example, Frank and Ekman (1997) found that accurate lie detectors appear to be good at spotting facial micro-expressions of emotion. Other studies have revealed that good lie detectors report paying attention to vocal cues while attempting to detect deceit (Anderson, DePaulo, Ansfield, Tickle, & Green, 1999; Feeley & Young, 2000). This finding matches well with DePaulo et al.'s (2003) meta-analysis, which showed that many of the cues distinguishing liars from truth tellers are vocal cues. Other studies have shown that people become better lie detectors when they cannot see the person's face (DePaulo, Stone, & Lassiter, 1985). Lie detectors are inclined to look at someone's eye movements when they are available to them, even though eye movements are quite easy to control and not related to deception in most cases.

IMPLICIT LIE DETECTION

There is evidence that people are better lie detectors when they are asked indirectly whether or not someone is lying (DePaulo & Morris, 2004). In some studies, after watching a truthful or deceptive story, participants were asked to detect deception both in a direct way (i.e., Is the person lying?) and in an indirect way (i.e., Does the speaker sincerely like the person he or she just described?). These studies found greater accuracy when using the indirect measures (see Vrij, 2001, for a review). This

might be the result of conversation rules, which regulate politeness. It is impolite or undesirable typically to accuse someone of being a liar (e.g., "I do not believe you"), but it might be possible to challenge the words of a speaker more subtly (e.g., "Do you really like that person so much?").

Alternatively, people might look at different cues when detecting lies than when applying an indirect method. In Vrij, Edward, and Bull's (2001b) lie detection experiment, half of the sample of police officers was asked to indicate whether or not certain people were lying. The other half was asked to indicate whether or not these people had to think hard while making their statements. Police officers could only distinguish between truths and lies by using the latter, implicit, method. Moreover, only in the implicit method did they pay attention to the cues that actually discriminated between the truth tellers and liars, such as a decrease in hand movements. In the explicit method they paid attention to stereotypical, but unreliable, cues to deceit such as an increase in foot and leg movements.

COMPARABLE TRUTH

Because of individual differences in nonverbal behavior, the response of one individual in a specific situation cannot be used as a comparison to judge the veracity of the response of another person in the same situation. Intraindividual comparisons (comparing the responses of the same person in different situations) are, in that respect, better, as they control for individual differences in responses. For this technique to be effective, however, it is essential that appropriate comparisons are made (Vrij & Mann, 2003) and that the known truthful response to be used as a comparison (baseline) is truly comparable with the response under investigation. Thus, if the response under investigation is a high-stakes situation, then the baseline situation should also be a high-stakes situation. Moreover, there is evidence that some behaviors are topic related. While analyzing the behavior shown by Saddam Hussein in an interview with Peter Arnett during the First Gulf War (the interview was broadcasted on CNN), Davis and Hadiks (1995) found that the topic Hussein discussed was related to the illustrators he made. Only when discussing Israel and Zionism did Hussein make specific movements with his left forearm. Likely, Israel has a special meaning to an Arab leader, and issues such as personal involvement should be taken into account as well.

Vrij and Mann (2001) employed the comparable truth technique in an actual police interview. During a videotaped real-life police interview, a man suspected and later convicted of murder was asked to describe his activities on a particular day. The murder suspect described his activities during the morning (went to work), afternoon (visited a market), and evening (visited a neighbor). Detailed analyses of the videotape revealed a sudden change in behavior as soon as he started to describe his activities during the afternoon and evening. One reason for this change may have been that he was lying and evidence supported this view. Police investigations could confirm his story with regard to his morning activities but revealed that his statements about the afternoon and evening were fabricated. In reality, he met the victim in the afternoon and killed her later on that day. In this case, my colleague and I were able to make a good comparison. The comparable truth method would benefit, however, from instant, accurate, and detailed coding of all sorts of behaviors shown by a target person. Progress is being made in developing technical equipment that can observe nonintrusively and code

instantly the nonverbal behavior displayed by target persons (see Vrij, 2004b).

INTERVIEWING TO DETECT DECEPTION

Mann et al.'s (2002) examination of real-life police interviews, discussed earlier, suggested that when suspects lie, they experience high cognitive demand. Police interviewers could use this knowledge by employing interview techniques that increase the cognitive demand in suspects. This should have a greater effect on liars than on truth tellers, thus facilitating discrimination between them. There are several ways in which cognitive demand could be increased. For example, suspects could be asked to elaborate on or repeat what they have just said. Using this technique, lies could well fail if the liar did not plan the lie in sufficient detail.

Moreover, liars tend to speak of events in a more fixed chronological order (this happened first, and then this, and then that, etc.) than truth tellers. It has been suggested that it is difficult for liars to fabricate a story in a nonchronological order (Vrij, 2005). Lie detectors could exploit this difficulty by asking interviewees to tell their stories in a nonchronological order, for example, in reverse order. Police officers could also use the evidence they have against a suspect strategically. Inbau et al. (2001), for example, advise the police to present such evidence at the beginning of the interview (e.g., "Our CCTV footage shows that you were in Commercial Road on Saturday evening at 8 p.m."). The task the lying suspect then faces is to fabricate an alibi that is consistent with this factual evidence. Alternatively, the police do not reveal the evidence initially but first let the suspect talk about his whereabouts. In an experiment where the timing of presenting the evidence was manipulated (it was presented either before or after the interviewee was given the opportunity to discuss his or her activities) lies were more readily detected by observers when the evidence was presented at a later stage (Hartwig, Granhag, Strömwall, & Vrij, 2005).

People have considerable difficulty in accurately distinguishing between truths and lies, among other factors, because they often fail to take individual and situational differences into account; attend to the wrong, nondiagnostic, cues, and use heuristics that lead to systematic errors and biases. It is argued in this chapter, however, that people could become better lie detectors if they used alternative lie detection strategies.

◆ References

Anderson, D. E., Ansfield, M. E., & DePaulo, B. M. (1999). Love's best habit: Deception in the context of relationships. In P. Philippot, R. S. Feldman, & E. J. Coats (Eds.), *The social context of nonverbal behavior* (pp. 372–409). Cambridge, UK: Cambridge University Press.

Anderson, D. E., DePaulo, B. M., Ansfield, M. E., Tickle, J. J., & Green, E. (1999). Beliefs about cues to deception: Mindless stereotypes or untapped wisdom? *Journal of Nonverbal Behavior, 23,* 67–89.

Aune, R. K., Levine, T., Ching, P., & Yoshimoto, J. (1993). The influence of perceived source reward value and attributions of deception. *Communication Research Reports, 10,* 15–27.

Bavelas, J. B., Chovil, N., Coates, L., & Roe, L. (1995). Gestures specialized for dialogue. *Personality and Social Psychology Bulletin, 21,* 394–405.

Bond, C. F., & DePaulo, B. M. (2005). *Accuracy of deception judgments.* Unpublished manuscript.

Bond, C. F., Omar, A., Pitre, U., Lashley, B. R., Skaggs, L. M., & Kirk, C. T. (1992). Fishy-looking liars: Deception judgment from expectancy violation. *Journal of Personality and Social Psychology, 63,* 969–977.

Bond, C. F., & Rao, S. R. (2004). Lies travel: Mendacity in a mobile world. In P. A. Granhag & L. A. Strömwall (Eds.), *Deception detection in forensic contexts* (pp. 127–147). Cambridge, UK: Cambridge University Press.

Boon, S. D., & McLeod, B. A. (2001). Deception in romantic relationships: Subjective estimates of success at deceiving and attitudes toward deception. *Journal of Social and Personal Relationships, 18,* 463–476.

Bull, R., & Rumsey, N. (1988). *The social psychology of facial appearance.* New York: Springer-Verlag.

Buller, D. B., & Burgoon, J. K. (1996). Interpersonal deception theory. *Communication Theory, 6,* 203–242.

Buller, D. B., Stiff, J. B., & Burgoon, J. K. (1996). Behavioral adaptation in deceptive transactions. *Human Communication Research, 22,* 589–603.

Burgoon, J. K., Buller, D. B., Floyd, K., & Grandpre, J. (1996). Deceptive realities: Sender, receiver, and observer perspectives in deceptive conversations. *Communication Research, 23,* 724–748.

Burgoon, J. K., Buller, D. B., White, C. H., Afifi, W., & Buslig, A. L. S. (1999). The role of conversation involvement in deceptive interpersonal interactions. *Personality and Social Psychology Bulletin, 25,* 669–685.

Caso, L., Maricchiolo, F., Bonaiuto, M., Vrij, A., & Mann, S. (2006). The impact of deception and suspicion on different hand movements. *Journal of Nonverbal Behavior, 30,* 1–19.

Chartrand, T. L., & Bargh, J. A. (1999). The chameleon effect: The perception-behavior link and social interaction. *Journal of Personality and Social Psychology, 76,* 893–910.

Cohen, J. (1977). *Statistical power analysis for the behavioral sciences.* New York: Academic Press.

Davis, M., & Hadiks, D. (1995). Demeanor and credibility. *Semiotica, 106,* 5–54.

DePaulo, B. M. (1992). Nonverbal behavior and self-presentation. *Psychological Bulletin, 111,* 203–243.

DePaulo, B. M., & Friedman, H. S. (1998). Nonverbal communication. In D. T. Gilbert, S. T. Fiske, & G. Lindzey (Eds.), *The handbook of social psychology* (pp. 3–40). Boston, MA: McGraw-Hill.

DePaulo, B. M., Jordan, A., Irvine, A., & Laser, P. S. (1982). Age changes in the detection of deception. *Child Development, 53,* 701–709.

DePaulo, B. M., Kashy, D. A., Kirkendol, S. E., Wyer, M. M., & Epstein, J. A. (1996). Lying in everyday life. *Journal of Personality and Social Psychology, 70,* 979–995.

DePaulo, B. M., & Kirkendol, S. E. (1989). The motivational impairment effect in the communication of deception. In J. C. Yuille (Ed.), *Credibility assessment* (pp. 51–70). Dordrecht, The Netherlands: Kluwer.

DePaulo, B. M., Lindsay, J. L., Malone, B. E., Muhlenbruck, L., Charlton, K., & Cooper, H. (2003). Cues to deception. *Psychological Bulletin, 129,* 74–118.

DePaulo, B. M., & Morris, W. L. (2004). Discerning lies from truths: Behavioral cues to deception and the indirect pathway of intuition. In P. A. Granhag & L. A. Strömwall (Eds.), *Deception detection in forensic contexts* (pp. 15–40). Cambridge, UK: Cambridge University Press.

DePaulo, B. M., Stone, J. L., & Lassiter, G. D. (1985). Deceiving and detecting deceit. In B. R. Schlenker (Ed.), *The self and social life* (pp. 323–370). New York: McGraw-Hill.

Doherty-Sneddon, G., Bruce, V., Bonner, L., Longbotham, S., & Doyle, C. (2002). Development of gaze aversion as disengagement of visual information. *Developmental Psychology, 38,* 438–445.

Efron, D. (1941). *Gesture and environment.* New York: King's Crown.

Ekman, P. (2001). *Telling lies.* New York: W. W. Norton. (Original work published 1985)

Ekman, P., Davidson, R. J., & Friesen, W. V. (1990). The Duchenne smile: Emotional expression and brain physiology II. *Journal of Personality and Social Psychology, 58,* 342–353.

Ekman, P., & Frank, M. G. (1993). Lies that fail. In M. Lewis & C. Saarni (Eds.), *Lying and deception in everyday life* (pp. 184–201). New York: Guildford Press.

Ekman, P., & Friesen, W. V. (1969). The repertoire of nonverbal behavior. *Semiotica, 1,* 49–98.

Ekman, P., & Friesen, W. V. (1972). Hand movements. *Journal of Communication, 22,* 353–374.

Ekman, P., Friesen, W. V., & O'Sullivan, M. (1988). Smiles when lying. *Journal of Personality and Social Psychology, 54,* 414–420.

Elaad, E. (2003). Effects of feedback on the overestimated capacity to detect lies and the underestimated ability to tell lies. *Applied Cognitive Psychology, 17,* 349–363.

Feeley, T. H., & Young, M. J. (2000). The effects of cognitive capacity on beliefs about deceptive communication. *Communication Quarterly, 48,* 101–119.

Frank, M. G., & Ekman, P. (1997). The ability to detect deceit generalizes across different types of high-stake lies. *Journal of Personality and Social Psychology, 72,* 1429–1439.

Frank, M. G., & Ekman, P. (2004). Appearing truthful generalizes across different deception situations. *Journal of Personality and Social Psychology, 86,* 486–495.

Frank, M. G., & Ekman, P., & Friesen, W. V. (1993). Behavioral markers and recognizability of the smile of enjoyment. *Journal of Personality and Social Psychology, 64,* 83–93.

Frank, M. G., & Feeley, T. H. (2003). To catch a liar: Challenges for research in lie detection. *Journal of Applied Communication Research, 31,* 58–75.

Friesen, W. V., Ekman, P., & Wallbott, H. (1979). Measuring hand movements. *Journal of Nonverbal Behavior, 4,* 97–112.

Gilbert, D. T. (1991). How mental systems believe. *American Psychologist, 46,* 107–119.

Goffman, E. (1959). *The presentation of self in everyday life.* New York: Doubleday.

Goldman-Eisler, F. (1968). *Psycholinguistics: Experiments in spontaneous speech.* New York: Doubleday.

Granhag, P. A., & Vrij, A. (2005). Deception detection. In N. Brewer & K. Williams (Eds.), *Psychology and law: An empirical perspective* (pp. 43–92). New York: Guilford Press.

Gudjonsson, G. H. (2003). *The psychology of interrogations and confessions: A handbook.* Chichester, UK: Wiley.

Harrigan, J. A., & O'Connell, D. M. (1996). Facial movements during anxiety states. *Personality and Individual Differences, 21,* 205–212.

Hartwig, M., Granhag, P. A., Strömwall, L. A., Andersson, L. O. (2004). Suspicious minds: Criminals' ability to detect deception. *Psychology, Crime, and Law, 10,* 83–95.

Hartwig, M., Granhag, P. A., Strömwall, L. A., & Vrij, A. (2005). The strategic use of disclosing evidence. *Law and Human Behavior, 29,* 469–484.

Hocking, J. E., & Leathers, D. G. (1980). Nonverbal indicators of deception: A new theoretical perspective. *Communication Monographs, 47,* 119–131.

Inbau, F. E., Reid, J. E., Buckley, J. P., & Jayne, B. C. (2001). *Criminal interrogation and confessions* (4th ed.). Gaithersburg, MD: Aspen.

Jennings, J. R. (1992). Is it important that the mind is in a body? Inhibition and the heart. *Psychophysiology, 29,* 369–383.

Kashy, D. A., & DePaulo, B. M. (1996). Who lies? *Journal of Personality and Social Psychology, 70,* 1037–1051.

LaFrance, M., & Mayo, C. (1976). Racial differences in gaze behavior during conversations: Two systematic observational studies. *Journal of Personality and Social Psychology, 33,* 547–552.

Leal, S. (2005). *Central and peripheral physiology of attention and cognitive demand: Understanding how brain and body work together.* Unpublished doctoral dissertation, University of Portsmouth, England.

Levine, T. R., & McCornack, S. A. (1992). Linking love and lies: A formal test of the McCornack and Parks model of deception detection. *Journal of Social and Personal Relationships, 9,* 143–154.

Levine, T. R., & McCornack, S. A. (1996). A critical analysis of the behavioral adaptation explanation of the probing effect. *Human Communication Research, 22,* 575–588.

Levine, T. R., & McCornack, S. A. (2001). Behavioral adaptation, confidence, and

heuristic-based explanations of the probing effect. *Human Communication Research, 27,* 471–502.

Levine, T. R., Park, H. S., & McCornack, S. A. (1999). Accuracy in detecting truths and lies: Documenting the "veracity effect." *Communication Monographs, 66,* 125–144.

Mann, S., Vrij, A., & Bull, R. (2002). Suspects, lies and videotape: An analysis of authentic high-stakes liars. *Law and Human Behaviour, 26,* 365–376.

Mann, S., Vrij, A., & Bull, R. (2004). Detecting true lies: Police officers' ability to detect deceit. *Journal of Applied Psychology, 89,* 137–149.

McNeill, D. (1985). So you think gestures are nonverbal? *Psychological Review, 92,* 350–371.

McNeill, D. (1992). *Hand and mind.* Chicago: University of Chicago Press.

O'Sullivan, M. (2003). The fundamental attribution error in detecting deception: The boy-who-cried-wolf-effect. *Personality and Social Psychology Bulletin, 29,* 1316–1327.

O'Sullivan, M., Ekman, P., & Friesen, W. V. (1988). The effect of comparisons on detecting deceit. *Journal of Nonverbal Behavior, 12,* 203–216.

Park, H. S., Levine, T. R., McCornack, S. A., Morrison, K., & Ferrara, M. (2002). How people really detect lies. *Communication Monographs, 69,* 144–157.

Patterson, M. L. (1995). Invited article: A parallel process model of nonverbal communication. *Journal of Nonverbal Behavior, 19,* 3–29.

Riggio, R. E. (1986). Assessment of basic social skills. *Journal of Personality and Social Psychology, 51,* 649–660.

Riggio, R.E., Tucker, J., & Throckmorton, B. (1988). Social skills and deception ability. *Personality and Social Psychology Bulletin, 13,* 568–577.

Stiff, J. B., Kim, H. J., & Ramesh, C. N. (1992). Truth biases and aroused suspicion in relational deception. *Communication Research, 19,* 326–345.

Stiff, J. B., Miller, G. R., Sleight, C., Mongeau, P., Garlick, R., & Rogan, R. (1989). Explanations for visual cue primacy in judgments of honesty and deceit. *Journal of Personality and Social Psychology, 56,* 555–564.

Strömwall. L. A., Granhag, P. A., & Hartwig, M. (2004). Practitioners' beliefs about deception. In P. A. Granhag & L. A. Strömwall (Eds.), *Deception detection in forensic contexts* (pp. 229–250). Cambridge, UK: Cambridge University Press.

Vrij, A. (2000a). *Detecting lies and deceit: The psychology of lying and its implications for professional practice.* Chichester: Wiley.

Vrij, A. (2000b). Telling and detecting lies as a function of raising the stakes. In C. M. Breur, M. M. Kommer, J. F. Nijboer, & J. M. Reintjes (Eds.), *New trends in criminal investigation and evidence II* (pp. 699–709). Antwerpen, Belgium: Intersentia.

Vrij, A. (2001). Implicit lie detection. *The Psychologist, 14,* 58–60.

Vrij, A. (2002). Deception in children: A literature review and implications for children's testimony. In H. Westcott, G. Davies, & R. Bull (Eds.), *Children's testimony* (pp. 175–194). Chichester: Wiley.

Vrij, A. (2004a). Guidelines to catch a liar. In P. A. Granhag & L. A. Strömwall (Eds.), *Deception detection in forensic contexts* (pp. 287–314). Cambridge, UK: Cambridge University Press.

Vrij, A. (2004b). Invited article: Why professionals fail to catch liars and how they can improve. *Legal and Criminological Psychology, 9,* 159–181.

Vrij, A. (2005). Criteria-based content analysis: A qualitative review of the first 37 studies. *Psychology, Public Policy, and Law, 11,* 3–41.

Vrij, A. (in press). Deception: A social lubricant and a selfish act. In K. Fiedler (Ed.), *Frontiers of social psychology: Social communication.* New York: Psychology Press.

Vrij, A., Akehurst, L., & Knight, S. (in press). Police officers', social workers', teachers' and general public's beliefs about deception in children, adolescents and adults. *Legal and Criminological Psychology.*

Vrij, A., Edward, K., & Bull, R. (2001a). People's insight into their own behaviour and speech content while lying. *British Journal of Psychology, 92,* 373–389.

Vrij, A., Edward, K., & Bull, R. (2001b). Police officers' ability to detect deceit: The benefit of indirect deception detection measures. *Legal and Criminological Psychology, 6,* 185–197.

Vrij, A., & Mann, S. (2001). Telling and detecting lies in a high-stake situation: The case of a convicted murderer. *Applied Cognitive Psychology, 15,* 187–203.

Vrij, A., & Mann, S. (2003). Telling and detecting true lies: Investigating and detecting the lies of murderers and thieves during police interviews. In M. Verhallen, G. Verkaeke, P. J. van Koppen, & J. Goethals (Eds.), *Much ado about crime: Chapters on psychology and law* (pp. 185–208). Brussels, Belgium: Uitgeverij Politeia.

Vrij, A., & Mann, S. (2005). Police use of nonverbal behavior as indicators of deception. In R. E. Riggio & R. S. Feldman (Eds.), *Applications of nonverbal communication* (pp. 63–94). Mahwah, NJ: Erlbaum.

Vrij, A., & Semin, G. R. (1996). Lie experts' beliefs about nonverbal indicators of deception. *Journal of Nonverbal Behavior, 20,* 65–80.

Vrij, A., & Winkel, F. W. (1991). Cultural patterns in Dutch and Surinam nonverbal behaviour: An analysis of simulated police/citizen encounters. *Journal of Nonverbal Behavior, 15,* 169–184.

Wallbott, H. G., & Scherer, K. R. (1991). Stress specifics: Differential effects of coping style, gender, and type of stressor on automatic arousal, facial expression, and subjective feeling. *Journal of Personality and Social Psychology, 61,* 147–156.

Zuckerman, M., DePaulo, B. M., & Rosenthal, R. (1981). Verbal and nonverbal communication of deception. In L. Berkowitz (Ed.), *Advances in experimental social psychology* (Vol. 14, pp. 1–57). New York: Academic Press.

19

THE INTERACTION MANAGEMENT FUNCTION OF NONVERBAL CUES

Theory and Research About Mutual Behavioral Influence in Face-to-Face Settings

◆ Joseph N. Cappella
University of Pennsylvania

◆ Darren M. Schreiber
University of California, San Diego

There are two important senses in which conversations are regulated. The more typical connotation of the word *regulate* implies that a person seeks intentionally to alter the content, tenor, or events of a conversation toward some preordained end. Regulation of this type exhibits control in the sense that actions are undertaken to achieve what one perceives to be an important need or purpose. Such conversational behaviors are sometimes called "deliberate." The second sense assumes that regulation of interaction is more "automatic" (i.e., weighed less cognitively; for more on this topic, see Lakin, this volume).

The research that will be reviewed in this chapter will show that this automatic sense of management involves control over the more microscopic events during interaction. People are, in general, quite unaware that such influences exist and, under most circumstances, do not employ such responses intentionally (Berger & Roloff, 1980; Langer, 1978). More generally, this chapter updates recent reviews of the patterns of behavioral coordination that characterize social interaction and focuses on the explanations behind these patterns. We will show that recent research has added to the fact base about coordination in ways that strengthen and extend previous research while, at the same time, offering some new empirical puzzles that need resolving. We will explore some possible answers beyond those available in the current theoretical literature.

◆ Coordination in Interaction

Interaction is not simply the generation of social symbols or signals; neither is it reducible solely to the reception or interpretation of such symbols or signals. In this chapter, interaction is conceptualized as *the regularized patterns of messages from one person that influence the messages sent in turn by the other over and above what they would otherwise be* (Cappella, 1985). This definition emphasizes the *pattern* of exchange between two persons and *not* the behavior of one or the other person, even though that behavior occurred in the context of an interaction with another. These regularized patterns are labeled *coordination*.

◆ Research on Coordination

Numerous reviews of the literature on coordination in adult dyads and adult-infant dyads have appeared. These include reviews by Cappella (1981, 1991, 1993, 1994) and by Burgoon (1978, 1993, 1994) and her colleagues (Burgoon, Stern, & Dillman, 1995), among others (Bernieri & Rosenthal, 1991; Hatfield, Cacioppo, & Rapson, 1994; Hess, Philippott, & Blairy, 1999; Patterson, 1976, 1982, 1999). These reviews have focused on vocal and kinesic behaviors primarily, but

some linguistic behaviors have been included as well (see especially Burgoon et al., 1995; Cappella, 1994). This section will not repeat the content of these prior detailed reviews but instead will report selectively on key studies that advance the research base on coordination.

Recent research in three broad arenas pertinent to mutual coordination of behavior will be presented in this section: studies of (1) mutual coordination, (2) the relationship between behavioral coordination and outcome for the relationship or social group, and (3) the first two types but focused on infants and children. In contrast to previous reviews, this one will not focus on behavioral coordination exclusively but will expand to include emotional contagion in the sense of yoked emotional response (i.e., self-reported affect) among interactants. This expansion recognizes that behavioral coordination in emotions may also produce emotional synchrony, which in turn can be consequential in relational connection and performance.

MUTUAL COORDINATION

A substantial body of research indicates that social interactions exhibit mutual coordination for behaviors as diverse as accents, speech rate, vocal intensity, postural and gestural behaviors, movement, gaze, facial affect, self-disclosure, excuses, and other behaviors (Cappella, 1981, 1985, 1998). The variety of behaviors implicated is testimony to the centrality of this process, and the mechanisms behind it, in human behavior. Recent research in this area has developed in two directions: one increasingly microscopic and physiological and the other more macroscopic and less behavioral. Both developments are welcome.

The first moves from the study of nonverbal behaviors, such as eye gaze, that are often "multifunctional." These behaviors often have several interpretations depending on the context. The physiological responses are less susceptible—but certainly not immune—to interpretive variation. The less behavioral, more macroscopic behaviors, move the research on coordination into a different research domain (e.g., the role of emotional and other types of contagion in groups, organizations, and other social units). The implication of these two developments is to direct that theories be capable of explaining both the automatic responses characteristic of physiological coordination and the more subjective, deliberate processes of emotional yoking between partners, perhaps with expressive imitation mediating the subjective yoking of emotional experience. The following details examples of research with these characteristics.

The first of these concerns *microcoordination*. Electromyography (EMG) is the study of facial muscle activity in response to various stimuli. Visual stimuli can elicit facial muscle activity depending on the affective valence of the stimuli to the subject. For example, studies suggest that stimuli related to positive affect increase activity in the cheek muscle region—smiling—and stimuli related to negative affect increase activity in the brow muscle region—frowning (Hietanen, Surakka, & Linnankoski, 1998). Some studies have investigated facial electromyographic responses during actual interaction. Lundqvist (1995), for example, explored whether people exposed to facial expressions responded with specific facial muscle reaction patterns that correspond to specific emotional experiences. Participants were shown pictures of faces expressing sadness, anger, fear, surprise, disgust, happiness, as well as neutral facial expressions. At the same time, facial electromyographs from the M. zygomaticus major, the

M. levator labii, the frontal M. lateralis, and the M. corrugator supercilii muscle regions were obtained as were emotional experiences. The results revealed that people both mimicked and experienced an emotion similar to that expressed by the stimulus person.

The focus on coordination in emotions has extended to vocal emotion. Neuman and Strack (2000) had people listen to philosophical essays read in a slightly happy or slightly sad tone of voice. Listeners reported a more positive mood with the happier reading and a more negative mood with the sadder reading. In a second study, they also repeated the essay in a tone that independent raters found to be happier or sadder depending on hearing the slightly happy or sad initial rendition—a kind of vocal coordination of emotion. Additionally, Hietanen et al. (1998) obtained facial EMG responses to vocal affect expressions as participants listened to single words uttered by two actors stimulating different emotions. Three categories of expressions were selected: emotional neutrality, anger, and contentment. The EMG activity over two facial muscle regions was measured: corrugator supercilii (the muscle that knits the brows together) and orbicularis oculi (the muscle that produces bagging below the eyes and wrinkles in the corners of the eyes). Hearing the expression of anger increased EMG activity in the participants' brow region more than did hearing the expression of contentment. In contrast, the expression of contentment activated the periocular muscle region more than did anger. The results support the view that negative and positive affects are "contagious" from hearing human vocal affect expressions.

The linkage between emotional expression and felt emotion within the person is an important set of facts that theories must explain. In interpersonal contexts, if person A mimics person B and if both A and B experience emotion consistent with their facial displays, then we might reasonably expect coordination between A and B in their subjective experiences of emotional or mood. This *coordination in subjective emotion and mood* is examined next. Specifically, Totterdell, Kellett, Teuchmann, and Briner (1998) explored "mood linkage" in the context of work groups. They investigated whether people's moods are influenced by the collective mood of their work teammates over time.

In their first study, a time-series analysis showed a significant association between the nurses' moods and the collective mood of their teammates independent of shared hassles. In their second study, a team of accountants rated their own moods and the moods of their teammates three times a day for 4 weeks using pocket computers. The accountants' moods and their judgments of their teammates' moods were significantly associated with the collective mood of their teammates. The findings suggest that people's moods can become linked to the mood of their coworkers, offering a compelling line of evidence for affective or, in this case, mood synchrony during adult interaction.

Similar effects have been reported for teacher burnout (i.e., emotional exhaustion and depersonalization; Bakker & Schaufeli, 2001), in sales contexts (Verbeke, 1997), and in clinical environments (Hsee, Hatfield, Carlson, & Chemtob, 1992). Thompson, Nadler, and Kim (1999), for example, argued that the ability of negotiators at the bargaining table is enhanced to the extent that they are successful in perceiving emotions of participants, reacting appropriately to them, and being "in tune" with those emotions. Pugh (1998) found that in a service context sales people were more effective when they were emotionally congruent with their customers. Furthermore, Ingram (1997) studied the coordination of

depression between spouses where one was primarily the caretaker and one the caregiver. Depression scores for the care receiver tended to determine those of the caretaker at a later point in time, suggesting coordination but with the caregiver dominant. The opposite influences were not found with regard to depression or a variety of other emotional states. Specifically, Goodman and Shippy (2002) studied elderly spouses where one was experiencing serious vision problems. After controlling for other factors, depression by one spouse predicted the partner's depression.

Individual differences in sensitivity to emotions from others and the ability to transmit emotions to others may affect the existence and strength of observed contagion. Verbeke (1997) explored whether these individual differences are assets or liabilities over the long term for salespersons. Doherty (1997) explored the individual differences in susceptibility to emotional coordination by crafting an Emotional Contagion Scale, a 15-item measure of individual differences in susceptibility to catching others' emotions. Participants were videotaped while watching videotapes of emotionally expressive stimulus persons relating their happiest and saddest memories. Doherty found that susceptibility to emotional contagion was positively related to reactivity, emotionality, sensitivity to others, social functioning, and self-esteem. Doherty, Orimoto, Singelis, Hatfield, and Hebb (1995) showed further that women in a variety of occupations illustrated higher total emotional contagion scores than did men.

Findings on mood transfer observed in more applied settings have also been obtained in more controlled environments (Gump & Kulik, 1997). In one study (Neuman & Strack, 2000), participants were tested on their listening comprehension in response to a neutral text that was read to them in a happy or sad tone of voice. Listeners reported being in an emotional state that was like that of the read materials and when required to repeat portions of the text read to them, employed a vocal tone similar to the one they had heard. Similar findings by Hess and Blairy (2001) suggest that aspects of facial mimicry of emotion may account for the subjective emotional reactions that viewers of the videotaped faces reported. Direct evidence of mediation from facial stimuli to facial mimicry by viewers to reports of emotional state by viewers was not obtained. These reactions to facial displays are likely to occur quickly (presentations less than half a second) and exhibit a dose-response relationship with more intense displays eliciting more intense emotional reactions (Wild, Erb, & Bartels, 2001).

Summary. Overall, four conclusions can be drawn from the recent literature: (1) relatively automatic responses to emotional stimuli are manifest in facial and vocal reactions; (2) these automatic reactions are sometimes accompanied by subjective feelings of emotion; (3) mood and emotional contagion in subjective experience—emotional yoking—is common in applied and more controlled settings; and (4) the question of which mechanisms might account for emotional yoking is an open question, although the possibility of expressive mimicry is suggested.

MUTUAL COORDINATION IN INFANT-MOTHER INTERACTION

Studies reviewed by Cappella (1997, 1998) and Field (1987) show that infants weeks and, in a few cases, even hours old adapt to their adult partners in vocal, gaze, facial, and movement behaviors. Such evidence underscores the centrality of mutual coordination in human social interaction

(but see Ullstadius, 1998, who offered contrary evidence for the imitation of tongue protrusions and mouth openings in 18 newborn infants). Other studies support the claim of mutual coordination between infants and adults. Stack and Arnold (1998), for example, focused on maternal touch and its ability to influence infants' gaze and affect during interactions. The results from this study indicated that (1) infants were sensitive to subtle changes in maternal tactile-gestural behavior, (2) maternal touch and hand gestures can attract infants' attention to their faces even when still and expressionless, and (3) there were associations between infant expressiveness and gaze at mothers' faces and hands during these periods.

Symons and Moran (1994) extended the idea of maternal influence to *mutual* influence—that is, observing infants' smiling behavior as being both responsive to and dependent on maternal smiling behavior. Twenty-five mothers were observed engaged in face-to-face interactions with their 8-, 12-, 16-, and 20-week-old infants, the ages at which face-to-face interaction is most common. Maternal dependency and infant responsiveness were not found to have occurred at significant levels, but maternal responsiveness and infant dependency were, and at all ages. Although mothers were responsive to their infants, mothers smiled a lot independently of their infants' smiling behavior; hence, infant behavior is sufficient but not necessary to elicit smiles from the mother. Infants responded to their mothers' smiles with smiles of their own. The proportion of mother smiles followed by infant smiles did not exceed the levels expected by chance. Mother smiling behavior seems necessary, but not sufficient, to elicit smiles from the infants.

In an important, and related, line of study, empathic responsiveness and affective reactivity to infant stimuli were studied in mothers at high and low risk for physical child abuse (Milner, Halsey, & Fultz, 1995). Compared with baseline, high-risk mothers reported no change in empathy across infant conditions such as baseline, smiling, quiet, and crying. Low-risk mothers did report an increase in empathy. Following the presentation of a crying infant, high-risk mothers reported more distress and hostility. These data agree with other studies showing that child abusers are less empathic and more hostile in response to a crying child.

Although these conclusions are compelling, one of the problems with many of the studies of infant-adult interaction is that the samples are usually small and unrepresentative of the population at large. The National Institute of Child Health and Human Development (NICHD), however, has undertaken a large-scale study of more than 1,100 infants and their mothers at 10 different sites around the country. One of the first reports from this study (NICHD Early Child Care Research Team, 1997) focused on the relationship between child care and quality of later attachment between the mother and her infant. Although the quality, amount, and type of child care outside the home (6–15 months) were unrelated to attachment quality at 15 months, maternal responsiveness to the infant did interact with child care arrangements. When mothers were low in responsiveness and their children also experienced poor quality child care outside the home, the infants tended to be less securely attached at 15 months.

Parents can also be trained to be more responsive to their infants. Wendland-Carro, Piccinini, and Millar (1999) exposed parents of newborns (2–3 days old) to a video on the importance of parental interaction or a video on basic caregiving. One month later, those exposed to the interaction video exhibited more behavioral co-occurrences between infant and mother involving vocal, touch, and gaze behaviors. A meta-analysis tracked the value of interventions in improving parental sensitivity in interacting with their infants across available studies (Bakermans-Kranenburg, van Ijzendoorn, & Juffer, 2003). Interventions that altered parental sensitivity also had favorable consequences on subsequent attachment, adding evidence to the claim that responsive interactions are important for the development of attachment.

The absence of responsive interaction in the early weeks and months of an infant's life can be deleterious to the infant's development in the absence of other buffering social and psychological conditions. Despite this understanding, many parents may not be responsive to their child. There are many reasons for lower responsiveness by parents, including depression. Field (1998) argues that early maternal depression is associated with two different interactional styles: withdrawn or intrusive. Both can affect the infant's physiology and biochemistry through inadequate stimulation or its opposite, overstimulation. Field argues that others in the infant's life who are not themselves depressed may buffer the negative consequences of interaction with a depressed mother.

In addition to the more one-sided responsiveness, synchrony in the expressed behaviors between infants and their caregivers has become a staple of researchers and is slowly achieving the stature of a diagnostic tool in assessing developmental progression and responsive parenting. Some recent studies have used synchrony between infant and mother (and sometimes father) to assess the risk status of triplets in comparison to twins and singletons (Feldman & Eidelman, 2004), the development of symbolic competence at 2 years from synchrony at 3 and 9 months

(Feldman & Greenbaum, 1997), the development of self-control at 2 years (Feldman, Greenbaum, & Yirmiya, 1999), and the development of emotional differentiation with mothers and with fathers (Feldman, 2003). Not only does infant-adult coordination occur early in the infant's development, but the presence of these behaviors is also predictive of subsequent attachment and, very possibly, other cognitive and behavioral advances. The fact that parents can be primed to be responsive and sensitive to their infants' behaviors is evidence that intervention can benefit infants and their parents by enhancing the bonding process as well as other desirable social and cognitive competencies.

Summary. Despite the occasional contrary study, research on coordination between infants and adults (1) has been consistent with earlier research; (2) has been consistent across studies in meta-analytical summaries; (3) has been manifest in more representative populations; and (4) has begun to be treated as an indicator of normal behavioral, emotional, and cognitive development. These conclusions imply that coordination in adult social interaction has its roots in infant-adult social interaction.

MUTUAL COORDINATION AND RELATIONAL AND INDIVIDUAL CONDITIONS

Coordination between partners in expressed emotion (and other behaviors) and in subjectively experienced emotion does not imply necessarily desirable or undesirable outcomes for the persons or their relationship. Earlier research on this issue (e.g., Cappella, 1991, 1998) has shown mostly, but not exclusively, beneficial outcomes for infants and mostly favorable outcomes in adult relationships. Positive social

evaluations have been associated, for example, with coordination in speech latency (Welkowitz & Kuc, 1973), speech rate and duration (Street, 1982), and pronunciation (Giles & Smith, 1979). Generalized responsiveness is associated with attraction (Davis & Martin, 1978) and the provision of pleasurable stimulation (Davis & Perkowitz, 1979). Movement synchrony and mimicry are associated with rapport (Bernieri, 1988; Hess et al., 1999; see Tickle-Degnen, this volume). Our own research has produced modest positive correlations between measures of dynamic coordination and interpersonal attraction (see Cappella, 1996, 1998; Cappella & Flagg, 1992; Cappella, Palmer, & Donzella, 1991).

In the context of marital relationships, Gottman's (1979) widely cited findings are still the exemplar. Although all his couples tended to show reciprocity in hostile affect in discussions about common problems in their marriages, the less well-adjusted couples showed greater hostile affect than did the better-adjusted couples. Pike and Sillars (1985) also found greater reciprocity in negative vocal affect for dissatisfied as opposed to satisfied married couples. Using face-directed gaze rather than negative affect, Noller's (1984) satisfied couples exhibited greater correlation between partners than did the dissatisfied couples (see also Manusov, 1995). Overall, partners in satisfying, established relationships appear to differ in the type of mutual influence that their interaction shows relative to those in less satisfied relationships.

Some of the recent studies in emotional contagion and relational outcomes have focused more on the similarity of reported emotion than on expressed emotion (e.g., Totterdell, 2000; Totterdell, Wall, Holman, Diamond, & Epitropaki, 2004). Anderson, Keltner, and John (2003) completed a controlled version of the contagion hypothesis. Their study evaluated the development of emotional similarity over time. They defined emotional similarity as the coordination of thoughts and behaviors leading to greater understanding and cohesion among partners. Studies 1 and 2 in Anderson et al. were longitudinal, investigating dating partners and college roommates at two points in time separated by 6 months. The third was experimental. Study 1 showed an increase in reported emotional similarity—both positive and negative—over time, whereas personality similarity remained relatively stable in the same time period. Over the same time period, positive emotional convergence was associated with relational satisfaction, but negative emotional similarity was not. Relational breakup from Time 1 to Time 2 was also predicted by emotional similarity at Time 1: Couples with greater emotional similarity at Time 1 stayed together, whereas those without emotional similarity tended to part.

Although emotional contagion is common among coworkers, dating couples, college roommates, and spouses, and its suppression can disrupt communication and relationship formation and elevate blood pressure (Butler et al., 2003), it is less clear whether emotional contagion and synchrony in behavior are as consequential to the success of a relationship. Gottman and Levenson (1999) compared four classes of predictors in accounting for deterioration in marital interaction over a 4-year period. Two classes of predictors were physiological, one cognitive, and one interactional. The *ratio* of positive to negative expressions was the best predictor of deterioration of interaction, which, in turn, was an excellent predictor of future marital dissolution and dissatisfaction.

Despite the association between some type of coordination and some form of rapport or attachment for adult and infant-adult dyads, a strong claim of a causal relationship between the two cannot be made from the available empirical results without inducing some skepticism. The "causality problem" is both theoretical and empirical. On empirical grounds, even if there is both covariation and temporal order, as is the case in Gottman's research and in many of the infant-adult studies, these criteria do not eliminate the possibility of spurious correlation or mutual attraction prior to the interaction affecting the initial levels of coordination. Whereas the data for infants are more convincing, those for adults are less convincing. On theoretical grounds, the mechanisms through which rapport might grow from behavioral coordination between partners are not well described by prevailing explanations. In the remainder of this section, we will focus on empirical considerations.

Although this issue was not their primary motivation, Chartrand and Bargh (1999) have taken on the causal question directly in a series of studies. In their first study, the authors established a mimicry effect between confederate and respondent using two uncommon behaviors: face rub and foot shake. When confederates used one of the unusual behaviors, then so did the respondent. In effect, there was imitation of the behavior over and above baseline. These imitations were independent of whether the confederate was smiling or not. In their second study, confederates imitated the "posture, movement, and mannerisms" (p. 902) of the respondent while maintaining a neutral facial expression and avoiding gaze. Results indicated that when the confederates imitated the behavior of the participants, the participants rated the interactions as smoother and reported liking the confederate more. Careful checking of the confederates' other nonverbal behaviors indicated no differences in rated eye contact, smiling, friendliness, or liking of the participant by the confederates across the mimicry/no mimicry conditions. The authors employed a careful debriefing procedure to determine whether the participants were aware of imitation by the confederate. They were not.

The results of this study establish a clear causal relationship between imitation and positive relational consequences. What differentiates this study from several others that seem to test the same hypothesis is the careful control over confederate behavior and attention to initial levels of liking or cues to liking and attraction (such as smiling or other nonverbal cues). Other studies have used confederates to enact behaviors that are themselves clear indicators of positive feeling, such as eye gaze and smiling. These behaviors can create positive regard right away. Instead of studying the impact of coordination on subsequent positive feeling, a design allowing initially positive nonverbal behavior confounds initial positive regard with coordination. In the Chartrand and Bargh (1999) study, however, the imitated behaviors are hardly noticed by participants, and initial behaviors by the confederate are not inherently positive. Yet they create positive social perceptions automatically. The authors argue strongly for an automatic perception-behavior linkage based on these and other data.

This recent work in social psychology on imitation of behaviors has produced a surge of other studies operating under the label *mimicry*. These studies have reinvigorated the study of contagion and coordination processes but have done so, at least initially, in ignorance of a long history of research on similar, if not exactly the same, processes. New findings supporting and extending Chartrand and Bargh's initial work have cascaded into the literature. Van Baaren, Holland, Kawakami, and van Knippenberg (2004), for example, found in three separate studies that people who were mimicked by others were more helpful and generous toward third parties not involved in the mimicry. Their results suggest that being mimicked enhanced a prosocial attitude in general. Several personality and situation factors enhance or retard the likelihood of mimicry, including self-monitoring (Cheng & Chartrand, 2003), context dependence (Van Baaren, Horgan, Chartrand, & Dijkmans, 2004), self-construal orientation (Van Baaren, Maddux, Chartrand, de Bouter, & van Knippenberg, 2003), affiliation goals (Lakin & Chartrand, 2003), and attachment patterns (Sonnby-Borgstrom & Jonsson, 2004).

Summary. The research on the association between coordination and relational outcomes finds that at both the micro- and macrolevels, coordination affects relational outcomes. Studies at the microlevel show clearly that mimicry of unobtrusive behaviors is causally linked to rapport, and those at the macrolevel show that emotional yoking between partners is a necessary condition for bonding.

◆ Implications for Theory

The review of previous and newer empirical findings produces four broad conclusions that should guide our tour into the theoretical realms. The first of these is *automaticity*. Many behaviors produce coordination between partners automatically, operating well below conscious awareness (see Lakin, this volume). The consistent observation of automatic coordination of behaviors suggests strongly that theory must be based on mechanisms that allow for automatic, nonconscious behavioral and emotional coordination. Second, the evidence establishing a *causal linkage between behavioral coordination and some form of positive relational outcome, particularly rapport,* is difficult to treat with skepticism any longer. The absence of a good explanation for this relationship leaves the empirical causal findings without a strong explanatory basis, however, and therefore undermines their believability.

Third, research in various domains has begun to produce findings showing that persons in work groups, in relationships, in social groups, living together, and so on develop (and report) similar emotional responses over the course of time. This suggests an *emotional yoking in social groups*. The impact for successful relationships and performance of emotional similarity and dissimilarity is only beginning to be understood. Theories must begin to explain the mechanisms through which yoked emotion develops (other than through spurious external events that must be controlled), especially given the failure of several studies to show that expressed emotion mediates the relationship between partners' reports of yoked emotion. Theory must account for the link between synchrony in expressed emotion and emotional contagion. Finally, the strong and consistent findings of synchrony in infant-adult interactions and the possibility that synchrony (or its absence) might be a diagnostic tool for normal developmental progression of infants argue that *coordination is a deep-seated and abiding process in human social and behavioral life*. Explaining how and why these processes came to be is an important goal for theory, particularly evolutionary theories, which aim to explain how processes came to be in the first place (Cappella, 1991; Buck & Renfrow Powers, this volume).

◆ Theories About Coordination

In this section, we take up theoretical approaches to explaining the existing data on coordination in social interaction. Space

limitations will not allow a comprehensive review, but we will discuss extant theories in terms of their ability to account for the recent findings reported above (see Patterson, this volume). Specifically, what can theories tell us about automatic responding, the linking between synchrony and outcome, emotional yoking, and how coordination came to be so central a process in human social interaction?

EVALUATING THEORIES OF COORDINATION

A number of competing accounts have been put forward to meet the basic requirements of explaining coordination. These include drive explanations (Argyle & Dean, 1965; Firestone, 1977), arousal-mediated explanations (Andersen, 1985; Burgoon, 1978; Burgoon & Jones, 1976; Burgoon & Hale, 1988; Cappella & Greene, 1982; Patterson, 1976, 1982), cognitive explanations (Giles & Powesland, 1975; Giles, Mulac, Bradac, & Johnson, 1987; Street & Giles, 1982), and various combinations of these (Andersen, Guerrero, Buller, & Jorgensen, 1998; Burgoon et al., 1995). With the upsurge of research emphasizing the automatic nature of certain aspects of coordination in the adult (Chartrand & Bargh, 1999) and in the infant-adult arenas (De Wolff & van Ijzendoorn, 1997), however, and the clear causal evidence for a coordination-rapport link, theories must be capable of accounting for these developments, not as an afterthought but as a central feature.

Despite their elegance, careful attention to the research literature, and attempts to be comprehensive, none of these theories has risen to the top of the empirical heap in contrastive tests. In three such tests, the findings are mostly mixed, with one or the other theory taking precedence in some results but no one theory clearly accounting for all findings. O'Connor and Gifford (1988) tested their social cognitive approach against arousal labeling and discrepancy arousal theories, reporting that the social cognitive model fared best in accounting for behavioral responses but the self-report results were less clearly supported. Other contrastive tests have produced a mixture of findings favoring no one explanation indicative of the complexity of realistic social interactions or the difficulty of producing true critical tests (Andersen et al., 1998; Le Poire & Burgoon, 1996).

One possible explanation for the inability of one of the several extant theories to account successfully for the results is not only the complexity of the testing environments and the requirements of careful, controlled manipulation by confederates but also the breadth of the theories themselves. Each of the theories makes a concerted effort to encompass the full range of behaviors, explain the conditions promoting compensation and reciprocity, and take into account mitigating and aggravating conditions. For example, discrepancy-arousal theory (Cappella & Greene, 1982) particularly tries to offer an account of infant-adult as well as adult-adult patterns of coordination. This very strength, however, might produce generalities in the theories that make them less able to predict particular outcomes in particular social contexts. A different strategy is to craft theories of much narrower scope that seek to provide very specific predictions of specific empirical phenomena. We turn now to such a case, which provides explanations for results about behavioral mimicry.

EXPLAINING MIMICRY

The intriguing findings reported by Chartrand and Bargh (1999) beg for an explanation. In particular, two components of their findings need explaining: mimicry and rapport. What explains people's mimicry of each other's (inconsequential) behaviors? Furthermore, what explains why mimicry should be associated with positive social regard for the partner? Other issues arise as we interrogate this process. Do people always imitate? The answer of course is "no," but what are the conditions promoting mimicry and its absence? Can mimicry create hostility rather than rapport?

Bargh and his colleagues have offered some answers (Bargh, 2003; Bargh & Chartrand, 1999; Bargh & Ferguson, 2000; Ferguson & Bargh, 2004), even carrying their views into the evolutionary domain (Lakin, Jefferis, Cheng, & Chartrand, 2003). Their essential claim is that a much larger proportion of human activity is driven by automatic processes than people and psychology have been willing to admit. Although there has been a very rich tradition of environmental primes stimulating cognitions and evaluations automatically (Bargh & Ferguson, 2000), it is only recently that automatic primes for behavior have been investigated and found operational.

Bargh and his colleagues posit a perception-behavior linkage that shows itself in media effects on behavior (Berkowitz, 1984, 1997), in behavior consistent with the activation of stereotypes (Dijksterhuis & van Knippenberg, 1998), and, of course, in social interaction (Chartrand & Bargh, 1999). The mechanisms through which perception leads to behavior and the limiting conditions are as yet not completely explored or understood. "Mirror neurons" are a viable candidate for perception-behavior activation and interpersonal facial feedback (IFF) a potential mechanism for establishing rapport through imitation.

INTERPERSONAL FACIAL FEEDBACK

The interpersonal facial feedback hypothesis (IFFH; Cappella, 1993) offers a speculation that accounts for the development of relational outcomes from behavioral coordination. None of the causal theories currently in the literature accounts specifically for the association between coordination patterns and relational outcomes, either in adults or in children. Neither do the mimicry-rapport explanations make a good case for the mechanism through which mimicry might breed rapport. The IFFH may help with this set of issues.

The IFFH is a series of simple claims. First, facial displays, especially emotional ones, tend to be imitated by both infants and adults. Imitation can be overt (i.e., observable by others) or covert (i.e., observable only via micromomentary displays or through changes in muscle potential [EMG]). Second, the act of producing a facial display of emotion alters the underlying experience of emotion, intensifying it toward the more positive or more negative valence. The mechanism for this intensification effect may be through the phenomenon of facial efferance (Adelman & Zajonc, 1989). Third, if person A expresses a valenced emotion, and B imitates with a similar display, the subjective experiences of emotion between A and B are yoked through facial feedback, so that subjective emotional similarity accompanies expressive similarity. If the IFFH is correct, it explains several results from the coordination-mimicry literature, including (1) the link between coordination and relational outcomes, at least for facial displays; (2) how attachment between infants and their parents might come about; and (3) how the recent observations of subjective emotional contagion (e.g., coworkers having yoked emotional responses) might be produced.

The IFFH has, to our knowledge, never been tested directly. A study by Kleinke and Walton (1982), however, comes closest. They used techniques of reinforcement to alter the frequency of smiles emitted by subjects. Those who emitted more smiles gave the interview and the interviewer higher ratings than those who emitted fewer smiles even though they were not able to ascertain that they were being reinforced to smile. Although suggestive, this study did not check the quality and number of reinforcements, and so the results could be due to differences in reinforcement frequency or quality rather than differences in smiling.

Although we have not carried out a serious test of the IFFH, a secondary analysis of some previous data is suggestive. To assess whether one's own smiling affects one's attraction to a conversational partner, as the IFFH would suggest, we began with the predictors that accounted for variance in attraction due to experimental condition (attitude similarity, relational history, and their interaction) and to effects from the partner's behavior (in this case the interaction of the partner's gaze) (Cappella & Palmer, 1990, p. 175). We added one's own smiling at the partner to this regression predicting one's attraction (in both linear and quadratic forms). The results (Cappella, 1993) suggest that the effects of experimental condition and partner's behavior are roughly the same as reported previously by Cappella and Palmer (1990) without any additional predictors, but that there is a positive linear effect and a negative, albeit small and marginal, quadratic effect of one's own smiling on one's own attraction to the partner. In effect, one's own smiling adds significant and positive variation to the prediction of attraction to the partner.

With the IFFH and its more speculative counterparts pertinent to vocal and physical imitation (see Cappella, 1993), certain puzzles in the interactional literature are explained. The IFFH assumes that behavioral adaptation is temporally prior to one's own affective response. By invoking the IFFH, physiological and, as we will see below, neurological pathways are implicated as the causal linkages from behavioral activation in the muscles of the face and voice to the subjective affective response (Zajonc, Murphy, & Englehart, 1989). In effect, a clear, if controversial, causal mechanism is posited to account for the association between behavioral coordination and interpersonal affect.

NEUROLOGICAL BASES FOR INTERPERSONAL FACIAL FEEDBACK, INTERPERSONAL VOCAL FEEDBACK, AND MIMICRY

One line of research that supports Bargh's (2003) explanation of mimicry as well as the IFFH is found in recent work in neuroscience, specifically the isolation of a mirror neuron reflex. In the mid-1990s, neuroscientist Vitorio Gallese was observing neural activity in the cortex of a macaque monkey during object manipulation. After returning to his laboratory with an ice-cream cone, Gallese noticed that each time he licked the ice-cream cone, the neurons in the monkey's premotor cortex fired. This was intriguing, given that the monkey was not making any motor movements.

Further study revealed a set of 92 neurons in the premotor cortex that were active both when the monkey performed an action and when the experimenter performed the same action (Gallese, Fadiga, Fogassi, & Rizzolatti, 1996; Rizzolatti, Fadiga, Gallese, & Fogassi, 1996). Although canonical neurons in the premotor cortex would activate only when the monkey performed a motor hand action, these neurons were described as mirror neurons because of their apparent ability to represent the

action of another. Additional research soon identified clusters of mirror neurons in a number of different locations in the brain (Rizzolatti & Craighero, 2004). Support for the theory that these neurons were providing mental representations of the action increased when it was discovered that neurons representing the final part of a motor sequence continued to fire even when the final portion of the sequence was hidden from the monkey's view (Umilta et al., 2001).

Mirror neurons have been posited as the foundation on which imitation (Buccino et al., 2004), empathy (Carr, Iacoboni, Dubeau, Mazziotta, & Lenzi, 2003), and even our capacity to understand another's state of mind rests (Gallese & Goldman, 1998; Schulkin, 2000; Williams, Whiten, Suddendorf, & Perrett, 2001). Evidence from a variety of sources including neurological impairment, direct neuron recordings, evolutionary biology, and neuroimaging have been marshaled in support of these arguments, at least in part because mirror neurons enable a plausible story to be told about how we have come to the capacity to communicate emotionally.

There is also mounting evidence suggesting that mirror neurons allow humans to use the same neural mechanisms both to express emotions and perceive the expression of emotion in others. Furthermore, these neural substrates appear connected to the emotion (changes in body and brain states triggered by the content of perceptions) as well as feelings (those changes in brain state that reach sufficient intensity to be perceived by conscious awareness) (Damasio, 1999, 2003). The insula, for instance, appears to become activated not only when we experience a disgusting smell but also when we perceive someone else's experience of disgust or imitate a disgusted expression. The region appears to facilitate our recognition of our physical, emotional, and mental states and the physical, emotional, and mental states of others. And it may well be that the insula is one part of the network involved in the experience of disgust after adopting a disgusted facial expression.

Mirror neurons offer a plausible, causal mechanism for explaining the "perception-behavior" linkage that is central to the new research on automatic mimicry and older research on automatic responding in infants and adults as well. Coupled with the IFF hypothesis, the two mechanisms provide a plausible, if speculative, account of automatic behavioral responding, imitation (both gestural and facial), the occurrence of rapport, and emotional yoking. Empirical testing for these regulative processes awaits.

◆ Conclusions

In this chapter, we have tried to bring previous reviews of the literature on nonverbal coordination up to date by highlighting key studies and trends in the literature. In addition, we have tried to offer some speculations for theory development that would help to resolve some puzzles and paradoxes in the existing literature. In closing, however, three empirical conclusions should be brought out, lest they be lost in the details that the review entails. First, *yoked emotional response among social actors characterizes work groups, dating and longer term relationships, roommates, and even professional sports teams.* The mechanism of the production of this yoking of emotion is less well established and its consequences—for good or ill— have not yet been fully explored. Second, *coordination shows itself through mimicry of unnoticed behaviors.* Mimicry, in turn, produces a sense of rapport with the person mimicking that may even generalize to others in the social environment. Importantly, the evidence is strong with causal direction clear and possible confounders minimized. Third, *coordination in the form of synchrony between infants and their parents has become sufficiently well established as to be a sign of normal (and, in its absence, abnormal) social development.* These findings are evidence of the maturation of a field of study.

At the theoretical level, the active formulation of general explanations of coordination that has marked the past 40 years of its study has not produced conceptual or theoretical consensus on which of several similar competitors is the most effective. We speculate that the move toward broad theories that encompass the range of behaviors and circumstances characteristic of coordination may be part of the problem along with the difficulty of providing unequivocal contrastive tests. One alterative is explanations that are more limited in scope. We explored "automatic perception-behavior" account of mimicry, arguing that it offers clear predictions and links well with other theories of automatic responding. Whereas the perception-behavior link works well, it is also clear that the behavior-rapport link is less obvious a consequence of mimicry. As a suggestive resolution, we presented IFFH to account for the behavior-rapport link and some evidence from the neurosciences on mirror neurons to strengthen the association between perception and behaviors enacted through imitation (or coordination).

◆ References

Adelman, P. K., & Zajonc, R. B. (1989). Facial efference and the experience of emotion. *Annual Review of Psychology, 40,* 249–280.

Andersen, P. A. (1985). Nonverbal immediacy in interpersonal communication. In

A. W. Siegman & S. Feldstein (Eds.), *Multichannel integrations of nonverbal behavior* (pp. 1–36). Hillsdale, NJ: Erlbaum.

Andersen, P. A., Guerrero, L. K., Buller, D. B., & Jorgensen, P. F. (1998). An empirical comparison of three theories of nonverbal immediacy exchange. *Human Communication Research, 24,* 501–535.

Anderson, C., Keltner, D., & John, O. P. (2003). Emotional convergence between people over time. *Journal of Personality and Social Psychology, 84,* 1054–1068.

Argyle, M., & Dean, J. (1965). Eye contact, distance, and affiliation. *Sociometry, 28,* 289–304.

Bakermans-Kranenburg, M. J., van Ijzendoorn, M. H., & Juffer, F. (2003). Less is more: Meta-analyses of sensitivity and attachment interventions in early childhood. *Psychological Bulletin, 129,* 195–215.

Bakker, A. B., & Schaufeli, W. B. (2001). Burnout contagion processes among teachers. *Journal of Applied Social Psychology, 30,* 2289–2308.

Bargh, J. A. (2003). Why we thought we could prime social behavior. *Psychological Inquiry, 14,* 216–218.

Bargh, J. A., & Chartrand, T. L. (1999). The unbearable automaticity of being. *American Psychologist, 54,* 462–479.

Bargh, J. A., & Ferguson, M. J. (2000). Beyond behaviorism: On the automaticity of higher mental processes. *Psychological Bulletin, 126,* 925–945.

Berkowitz, L. (1984). Some effects of thoughts on anti- and prosocial influences of media events: A cognitive neo-association analysis. *Psychological Bulletin, 95,* 410–427.

Berkowitz, L. (1997). Some thoughts extending Bargh's argument. In R. S. Wyer (Ed.), *Advances in social cognition* (Vol. 10, pp. 83–94). Mahwah, NJ: Erlbaum.

Berger, C. R., & Roloff, M. E. (1980). Social cognition, self awareness, and interpersonal communication. In B. Dervin & M. J. Voight (Eds.), *Progress in communication sciences* (Vol. 2, pp. 1–50). Norwood, NJ: Ablex.

Bernieri, F. J. (1988). Coordinated movement and rapport in teacher-student interactions. *Journal of Nonverbal Behavior, 12,* 120–138.

Bernieri, F., & Rosenthal, R. (1991). Interpersonal coordination: Behavior matching and interactional synchrony. In R. S. Feldman & B. Rime (Eds.), *The fundamentals of nonverbal behavior* (pp. 401–432). New York: Cambridge University Press.

Buccino, G., Vogt, S., Ritzl, A., Fink, G. R., Zilles, K., Freund, H. J., et al. (2004). Neural circuits underlying imitation learning of hand actions: An event-related fMRI study. *Neuron, 42,* 323–334.

Burgoon, J. K. (1978). A communication model of interpersonal space violations: Explication and initial test. *Human Communication Research, 4,* 129–142.

Burgoon, J. K. (1993). Interpersonal expectations, expectancy violations, and emotional communication. *Journal of Language and Social Psychology, 12,* 30–48.

Burgoon J. K. (1994). Nonverbal signals. In M. L. Knapp & G. R. Miller (Eds.), *Handbook of interpersonal communication* (2nd ed., pp. 229–271). Thousand Oaks, CA: Sage.

Burgoon, J. K., & Hale, J. L. (1988). Nonverbal expectancies violations: Model elaboration and application to immediacy behaviors. *Communication Monographs, 55,* 58–79.

Burgoon, J. K., & Jones, S. B. (1976). Toward a theory of personal space expectations and their violations. *Human Communication Research, 2,* 131–146.

Burgoon, J. K., Stern, L. A., & Dillman, L. (1995). *Interpersonal adaptation: Dyadic interaction patterns.* New York: Cambridge University Press.

Butler, E. A., Egloff, B., Wilhelm, F. H., Smith, N. C., Erickson, E. A., & Gross, J. J. (2003). The social consequences of expressive suppression. *Emotion, 3,* 48–67.

Cappella, J. N. (1981). Mutual influence in expressive behavior: Adult and infant-adult dyadic interaction. *Psychological Bulletin, 89,* 101–132.

Cappella, J. N. (1985). The management of conversations. In M. L. Knapp & G. R. Miller (Eds.), *The handbook of interpersonal communication* (pp. 393–438). Beverly Hills, CA: Sage.

Cappella, J. N. (1991). The biological origins of automated patterns of human interaction. *Communication Theory, 1,* 4–35.

Cappella, J. N. (1993). The facial feedback hypothesis in human interaction: Review and speculations. *Journal of Language and Social Psychology, 12,* 13–29.

Cappella, J. N. (1994). The management of conversational interaction in adults and infants. In M. L. Knapp & G. R. Miller (Eds.), *Handbook of interpersonal communication* (2nd ed., pp. 380–419). Thousand Oaks, CA: Sage.

Cappella, J. N. (1996). Dynamic coordination of vocal and kinesic behavior. In J. Watt & C. A. VanLear (Eds.), *Dynamic patterns in communication processes* (pp. 353–386). Thousand Oaks, CA: Sage.

Cappella, J. N. (1997). The development of theory about automated patterns of face-to-face human interaction. In G. Philipsen & T. Albrecht (Eds.), *Theories in human communication* (pp. 57–84). Albany, NY: SUNY Press.

Cappella, J. N. (1998). The dynamics of nonverbal coordination and attachment: Problems of causal direction and causal mechanism. In M. T. Palmer (Ed.), *Progress in communication sciences: Vol. 14. Mutual influence in interpersonal communication: Cognitive, behavioral, and affective components* (pp. 19–37). Greenwich, CT: Ablex.

Cappella, J. N., & Flagg, M. E. (1992, July). *Interactional adaptation, expressiveness and attraction: Kinesic and vocal responsiveness patterns in initial liking.* Paper presented at the 6th International Conference on Personal Relationships, University of Maine, Orono.

Cappella, J. N., & Greene, J. O. (1982). A discrepancy-arousal explanation of mutual influence in expressive behaviors for adult-adult and infant-adult interactions. *Communication Monographs, 49,* 89–114.

Cappella, J. N., & Palmer, M. T. (1990). Attitude similarity, relational history, and attraction: The mediating effects of kinesic and vocal behaviors. *Communication Monographs, 57,* 161–183.

Cappella, J. N., Palmer, M. T., & Donzella, B. (1991, May). *Individual consistency in temporal adaptations in nonverbal behavior in dyadic conversations: High and low expressive groups.* Paper presented at the International Communication Association conference, Chicago.

Carr, L., Iacoboni, M., Dubeau, M. C., Mazziotta, J. C., & Lenzi, G. L. (2003). Neural mechanisms of empathy in humans: A relay from neural systems for imitation to limbic areas. *Proceedings of the National Academy of Sciences, 100,* 5497–5502.

Chartrand, T. L., & Bargh, J. A. (1999). The chameleon effect: The perception-behavior link and social interaction. *Journal of Personality and Social Psychology, 76,* 893–910.

Cheng, C. M., & Chartrand, T. L. (2003). Self-monitoring without awareness: Using mimicry as a non-conscious affiliation strategy. *Journal of Personality and Social Psychology, 85,* 1170–1179.

Damasio, A. R. (1999). *The feeling of what happens: Body and emotion in the making of consciousness.* New York: Harcourt Brace.

Damasio, A. R. (2003). *Looking for Spinoza: Joy, sorrow, and the feeling brain.* New York: Harcourt.

Davis, D., & Martin, H. J. (1978). When pleasure begets pleasure: Recipient responsiveness as a determinant of physical pleasuring between heterosexual dating couples and strangers. *Journal of Personality and Social Psychology, 36,* 767–777.

Davis, D., & Perkowitz, W. T. (1979). Consequences of responsiveness in dyadic interaction: Effects of probability of response and proportion of content-related responses on interpersonal attraction. *Journal of Personality and Social Psychology, 37,* 534–550.

De Wolff, M. S., & van Ijzendoorn, M. H. (1997). Sensitivity and attachment: A meta-analysis on parental antecedents of infant attachment. *Child Development, 68,* 571–591.

Dijksterhuis, A., & van Knippenberg, A. (1998). The relation between perception and behavior, or how to win a game of Trivial Pursuit. *Journal of Personality and Social Psychology, 74,* 865–877.

Doherty, R. W. (1997). The Emotional Contagion Scale: A measure of individual differences. *Journal of Nonverbal Behavior, 21*, 131–153.

Doherty, R. W., Orimoto, L., Singelis, T. M., Hatfield, E., & Hebb, J. (1995). Emotional contagion: Gender and occupational differences. *Psychology of Women Quarterly, 19*, 355–371.

Feldman, R. (2003). Infant-mother and infant-father synchrony: The coregulation of positive arousal. *Infant Mental Health Journal, 24*, 1–23.

Feldman, R., & Eidelman, A. I. (2004). Parent-infant synchrony and the social-emotional development of triplets. *Developmental Psychology, 40*, 1133–1147.

Feldman, R., & Greenbaum, C. W. (1997). Affect regulation and synchrony in mother-infant play as precursors to the development of symbolic competence. *Infant Mental Health Journal, 18*, 4–23.

Feldman, R., Greenbaum, C. W., & Yirmiya, N. (1999). Mother-infant affect synchrony as an antecedent of the emergence of self-control. *Developmental Psychology, 35*, 223–231.

Ferguson, M. J., & Bargh, J.A. (2004). How social perception can automatically influence behavior. *Trends in Cognitive Sciences, 8*, 33–39.

Field, T. (1987). Affective and interactive disturbances in infants. In J. D. Osofsky (Ed.), *Handbook of infant development* (2nd ed., pp. 972–1007). New York: Wiley.

Field, T. (1998). Maternal depression effects on infants and early interventions. *Preventive Medicine: An International Journal Devoted to Practice & Theory, 27*, 200–203.

Firestone, I. (1977). Reconciling verbal and nonverbal models of dyadic communication. *Environmental Psychology and Nonverbal Behavior, 2*, 30–44.

Gallese, V., Fadiga, L., Fogassi, L., & Rizzolatti, G. (1996). Action recognition in the premotor cortex. *Brain, 119*, 593–609.

Gallese, V., & Goldman, A. (1998). Mirror neurons and the simulation theory of mind reading. *Trends in Cognitive Science, 2*, 493–501.

Giles, H., & Powesland, P. F. (1975). *Speech style and social evaluation.* London: Academic Press.

Giles, H., Mulac, A., Bradac, J. J., & Johnson, P. (1987). Speech accommodation theory: The first decade and beyond. In M. L. McLaughlin (Ed.), *Communication yearbook 10* (pp. 13–48). Newbury Park, CA: Sage.

Giles, H., & Smith, P. M. (1979). Accommodation theory: Optimal levels of convergence. In H. Giles & R. St. Clair (Eds.), *Language and social psychology* (pp. 45–65). Baltimore, MD: University Park Press.

Goodman, C. R., & Shippy, R. A. (2002). Is it contagious? Affect similarity among spouses. *Aging & Mental Health, 6*, 266–274.

Gottman, J. M. (1979). *Marital interaction.* New York: Academic Press.

Gottman, J. M., & Levenson, R. W. (1999). What predicts change in marital interaction over time? A study of alternative models. *Family Process, 38*, 143–158.

Gump, B. B., & Kulik, J. A. (1997). Stress, affiliation, and emotional contagion. *Journal of Personality and Social Psychology, 72*, 305–319.

Hatfield, E., Cacioppo, J., & Rapson, R. L. (1994). *Emotional contagion.* Paris: Cambridge University Press.

Hess, U., & Blairy, S. (2001). Facial mimicry and emotional contagion to dynamic emotional facial expressions and their influence on decoding accuracy. *International Journal of Psychophysiology, 40*, 129–141.

Hess, U., Philippot, P., & Blairy, S. (1999). Mimicry: Facts and fiction. In P. Philippot, R. S. Feldman, & E. J. Coats (Eds.), *The social context of nonverbal behavior* (pp. 213–241). New York: Cambridge University Press.

Hietanen, J. K., Surakka, V., & Linnankoski, I. (1998). Facial electromyographic responses to vocal affect expressions. *Psychophysiology, 35*, 530–536.

Hsee, C. K., Hatfield, E., Carlson, J. G., & Chemtob, C. (1992). Assessments of the emotional state of others—Conscious judgments versus emotional contagion. *Journal of Social and Clinical Psychology, 11*, 119–128.

Ingram, L. A. (1997). Congruence and contagion of affect in elderly caregiver-care recipient spousal pairs. *Dissertation Abstracts International, 58* (3-B), 1595B.

Kleinke, C. L., & Walton, J. H. (1982). Influence of reinforced smiling on affective responses in an interview. *Journal of Personality and Social Psychology, 42,* 557–565.

Lakin, J. L., & Chartrand, T. L. (2003). Using non-conscious behavioral mimicry to create affiliation and rapport. *Psychological Science, 14,* 334–339.

Lakin, J. L., Jefferis, V. E., Cheng, C. M., & Chartrand, T. L. (2003). The chameleon effect as social glue: Evidence for the evolutionary significance of nonconscious mimicry. *Journal of Nonverbal Behavior, 27,* 145–162.

Langer, E. J. (1978). Rethinking the role of thought in social interaction. In J. H. Harvey, W. J. Ickes, & R. F. Kidd (Eds.), *New directions in attribution research* (Vol. 2, pp. 35–58). Hillsdale, NJ: Erlbaum.

Le Poire, B. A., & Burgoon, J. K. (1996). Usefulness of differentiating arousal responses within communication theories: Orienting response or defensive arousal within nonverbal theories of expectancy violation. *Communication Monographs, 63,* 208–230.

Lundqvist, L.O. (1995). Facial EMG reactions to facial expressions: A case of facial emotional contagion. *Scandinavian Journal of Psychology, 36,* 130–141.

Manusov, V. (1995). Reacting to changes in nonverbal behaviors: Relational satisfaction and adaptation patterns in romantic dyads. *Human Communication Research, 21,* 456–477.

Milner, J. S., Halsey, L. B., & Fultz, J. (1995). Empathic responsiveness and affective reactivity to infant stimuli in high- and low-risk for child abuse mothers. *Child Abuse and Neglect, 19,* 767–780.

Neumann, R., & Strack, F. (2000). "Mood contagion": The automatic transfer of mood between persons. *Journal of Personality and Social Psychology, 79,* 211–223.

NICHD Early Child Care Research Team. (1997). The effects of infant child care on infant-mother attachment security: Results of the NICHD study of early child care. *Child Development, 68,* 860–879.

Noller, P. (1984). *Nonverbal communication and marital interaction.* Oxford: Pergamon Press.

O'Connor, B. P., & Gifford, R. (1988). A test among models of nonverbal immediacy reactions: Arousal-labeling, discrepancy-arousal, and social cognition. *Journal of Nonverbal Behavior, 12,* 6–30.

Patterson, M. L. (1976). An arousal model of interpersonal intimacy. *Psychological Review, 83,* 235–245.

Patterson, M. L. (1982). A sequential functional model of nonverbal exchange. *Psychological Review, 89,* 231–249.

Patterson, M. L. (1999). The evolution of a parallel process model of nonverbal communication. In P. Philippot, R. S. Feldman, & E. J. Coats (Eds.), *The social context of nonverbal behavior* (pp. 317–347). New York: Cambridge University Press.

Pike, G. R., & Sillars, A. L. (1985). Reciprocity and marital communication. *Journal of Personal and Social Relationships, 2,* 303–324.

Pugh, S. D. (1998). Service with a smile: The contagious effects of employee affect on customer attitudes. *Dissertation Abstracts International, 58* (11-B), 6267B.

Rizzolatti, G., & Craighero, L. (2004). The mirror-neuron system. *Annual Review of Neuroscience, 27,* 169–192.

Rizzolatti, G., Fadiga, L., Gallese, V., & Fogassi, L. (1996). Premotor cortex and the recognition of motor actions. *Cognitive Brain Research, 3,* 131–141.

Schulkin, J. (2000). Theory of mind and mirroring neurons. *Trends in Cognitive Science, 4,* 252–254.

Sonnby-Borgstrom, M., & Jonsson, P. (2004). Dismissing-avoidant pattern of attachment and mimicry reactions at different levels of information processing. *Scandinavian Journal of Psychology, 45,* 103–13.

Stack, D. M., & Arnold, S. L. (1998). Changes in mothers' touch and hand gestures influence infant behavior during face-to-face interchanges. *Infant Behavior and Development, 21,* 451–468.

Street, R. L. (1982). Evaluation of noncontent speech accommodation. *Language and Communication, 2,* 13–31.

Street, R. L., & Giles, H. (1982). Speech accommodation theory: A social cognitive approach to language and speech behavior. In M. Roloff & C. R. Berger (Eds.), *Social cognition and communication* (pp. 193–226). Beverly Hills, CA: Sage.

Symons, D., & Moran, G. (1994). Responsiveness and dependency are different aspects of social contingencies: An example from mother and infant smiles. *Infant Behavior and Development, 17,* 209–214.

Thompson, L. L., Nadler, J., & Kim, P. H. (1999). Some like it hot: The case for the emotional negotiator. In L. L. Thompson & J. M. Levine (Eds.), *Shared cognition in organizations: The management of knowledge* (pp. 139–161). Mahwah, NJ: Erlbaum.

Totterdell, P. (2000). Catching moods and hitting runs: Mood linkage and subjective performance in professional sport teams. *Journal of Applied Psychology, 85,* 848–859.

Totterdell, P., Kellett, S., Teuchmann, K., & Briner, R. B. (1998). Evidence of mood linkage in work groups. *Journal of Personality and Social Psychology, 74,* 1504–1515.

Totterdell, P., Wall, T., Holman, D., Diamond, H., & Epitropaki, O. (2004). Affect networks: A structural analysis of the relationship between work ties and job-related affect. *Journal of Applied Psychology, 89,* 854–867.

Ullstadius, E. (1998). Neonatal imitation in a mother-infant setting. *Early Development and Parenting, 7,* 1–8.

Umilta, M. A., Kohler, E., Gallese, V., Fogassi, L., Fadiga, L., Keysers, C., et al. (2001). I know what you are doing: A neurophysiological study. *Neuron, 31,* 155–165.

Van Baaren, R. B., Holland, R. W., Kawakami, K., & Van Knippenberg, A. (2004). Mimicry and prosocial behavior. *Psychological Science, 15,* 71–74.

Van Baaren, R. B., Horgan, T. G., Chartrand, T. L., & Dijkmans, M. (2004). The forest, the trees, and the chameleon: Context dependence and mimicry. *Journal of Personality & Social Psychology, 86,* 453–459.

Van Baaren, R. B., Maddux, W. W., Chartrand, T. L., de Bouter, C., & van Knippenberg, A. (2003). It takes two to mimic: Behavioral consequences of self-construals. *Journal of Personality and Social Psychology, 84,* 1093–1102.

Verbeke, W. (1997). Individual differences in emotional contagion of salespersons: Its effect on performance and burnout. *Psychology & Marketing, 14,* 617–636.

Welkowitz, J., & Kuc, M. (1973). Interrelationships among warmth, genuineness, empathy, and temporal speech patterns in interpersonal interaction. *Journal of Consulting and Clinical Psychology, 41,* 472–473.

Wendland-Carro, J., Piccinini, C. A., & Millar, W. S. (1999). The role of an early intervention on enhancing the quality of mother-infant interaction. *Child Development, 70,* 713–721.

Wild, B., Erb, M., & Bartels, M. (2001). Are emotions contagious? Evoked emotions while viewing emotionally expressive faces: Quality, quantity, time course and gender differences. *Psychiatry Research, 102,* 109–124.

Williams, J. H., Whiten, A., Suddendorf, T., & Perrett, D. I. (2001). Imitation, mirror neurons and autism. *Neuroscience Biobehavior Review, 25,* 287–295.

Zajonc, R. B., Murphy, S. T., & Englehart, M. (1989). Feeling and facial efference: Implications of the vascular theory of emotion. *Psychological Review, 96,* 395–416.

20

NONVERBAL BEHAVIOR AND ITS FUNCTIONS IN THE ECOSYSTEM OF RAPPORT

◆ Linda Tickle-Degnen

Boston University

The term *rapport* is used to indicate a meaningful human experience of close and harmonious connection that involves common understanding *(Compact Oxford English Dictionary, 2005)*, and being *in rapport* with someone requires mutual responsiveness to intention, attitude, and affect (Park & Burgess, 1924). Rapport is self-affirming, satisfying, and enjoyable for the individual—a desired internal state of optimal experience (Csikszentmihalyi, 1990)—and it involves the experiential bonding of individuals into relationship with one another. This bonding sustains mutual involvement in single interactions of short duration as well as across repeated interactions over extended periods of time.

Author's Note: This chapter was supported in part by Grant No. NS048059 from the National Institute of Neurological Disorders and Stroke of the National Institutes of Health (NIH). Its contents are solely the responsibility of the author and do not necessarily represent the official views of NIH.

Rapport creates a powerful medium for social influence (Freud, 1914/1924; LaFrance, 1990) and for the accomplishment of tasks that are challenging and require mutual commitment to accomplish (Tickle-Degnen & Gavett, 2003). Individuals in rapport are likely to cooperate with one another to accomplish tasks and objectives that could not be accomplished alone as effectively, as efficiently, or at all. Cooperation facilitates many of the tasks of everyday living, including those most basic to species survival—eating, protection against harm, or procreation—as well as those involved in the actualization of human potential. The child in rapport with the parent is fed and nourished, workers in rapport achieve the project deadline, and the student and teacher in rapport pass knowledge on to the next generation.

Importantly for this chapter, rapport is created, sustained, and marked by action. More specifically, it involves the coupling of internal experience and purposeful, often nonverbal, action into a perception-action system that has adaptive value for the individual, the dyad, and the human species (Dijksterhuis & Bargh, 2001; Fridlund, 1997; Patterson, 1999). The perception-action system of rapport is not separate from its context but is rather emergent within it (Gibson, 1986; McArthur & Baron, 1983; Zebrowitz & Collins, 1997), and the immediate contextual elements for one individual are the features of the other individual, including static nonverbal features such as facial structure and signs of gender as well as dynamic features from verbal and nonverbal behavior.

Perceivers respond rapidly to informative physical features in the face, body, and voice of potential cooperative partners as they negotiate the natural social environment. Whether this response is due to an attunement of attention that is learned (Gibson, 1986), an automatic expression of perceived qualities (Dijksterhuis & Bargh, 2001), or a strategic process (Brunswik, 1955) is beyond the scope of this chapter (but see Lakin, this volume), although arguably both automaticity and cognitive mediation are involved (Patterson, 1999, 2003; Strack & Deutsch, 2004). Once in rapport, however, individuals form a physical and social ecosystem—an interdependence of two entities' perceptions and actions—that operates in relation to the larger physical and social environment in which it is embedded. People develop, maintain, and indicate their rapport through a stream of interlinked signals and responses that are shaped by their personal physical and psychological properties, the parameters of the task in which they are engaged, and the physical and social environment of their actions.

Research studies on rapport, with a few exceptions (Bernieri, Gillis, Davis, & Grahe, 1996; Puccinelli, Tickle-Degnen, & Rosenthal, 2003, 2004), have not addressed nonverbal behavior as emergent from context explicitly and as part of an ecosystem of rapport, that is, from an ecological perspective. As a result, accumulating evidence has little theoretical coherence and appears to be complex and conflicting. The purpose of this chapter is to explore the role of nonverbal behavior within the ecosystem of rapport and to demonstrate that *a systematic investigation of context* resolves apparently conflicting results and promotes the theoretical coherence needed to move this area of research forward. To do so, the chapter describes the functions of nonverbal behavior and presents a three-component model of rapport that is consistent with an ecological perspective.

The chapter also reviews recent research findings on nonverbal behavior and rapport and describes how a model of optimal experience developed by Csikszentmihalyi and his colleague (Csikszentmihalyi, 1990;

Csikszentmihalyi & Csikszentmihalyi, 1988) can be applied flexibly to the systematic investigation of rapport and nonverbal behavior in context. Specifically, this model places optimal experiences such as rapport within the broader theoretical perspective of how dyads regulate themselves to achieve smooth, harmonious, and enjoyable interaction as constrained by the tasks that they are doing. The model provides a framework for showing how nonverbal behavior varies in relation to the degree that task parameters support or undermine the achievement of rapport. The chapter concludes with implications for future research.

◆ The Functions of Nonverbal Behavior in the Ecosystem of Rapport

As part of the dyadic ecosystem, nonverbal behavior is functional (Patterson, 1994). Nonverbal behavior provides information about each interacting participant's initial intentions, attitudes, and feelings and, as such, serves an expressive function in the development and maintenance of rapport. Furthermore, each participant's nonverbal behavior functions to create *affordances* (Gibson, 1986) or opportunities for action by the other participant. To the perceiver, an actor's behavior affords differing degrees of interpersonal contact, enjoyment, information exchange, mutual task engagement, and so on. The nonverbal reactions of the perceiver, now actor, function to signal the degree of "pick up" of the other participant's intentions, attitudes, and feelings as well as the acceptance or agreement with them. These functions operate within a continuous signal-perception-action-signal loop of interpersonal interaction, and they often occur spontaneously, within seconds and in parallel across both participants within a

dyad (Ambady, Bernieri, & Richeson, 2000; Patterson, 1999). This ecosystem as a whole serves the function of regulating dyadic connection and rapport to accomplish interpersonal tasks and meet personal, dyadic, and group needs.

In contrast to a view that specific patterns of nonverbal behavior map one-to-one with discrete emotions (Ekman & Keltner, 1997; Izard, 1994) or that nonverbal behavior expresses an actor's social intentions, not emotions (Fridlund, 1997), the position taken here is that a nonverbal action or event is best understood as *expressive of many psychological states, traits, and action tendencies at once.* The stream of perception and behavior is such that participants' intentions, attitudes, and feelings are not parsed out into entities that are expressed in mutually exclusive behavioral markers. Rather internal states, perceptions, and behaviors are convergent aspects of a meaningful event that is understood within context (Heft, 2003; James, 1890). That is, from an ecological perspective, nonverbal behavior is constrained, or shaped, in relation to (a) the capacities and tendencies of the interacting individuals to experience, perceive, and express rapport-relevant intentions, attitudes, and feelings; (b) parameters of the interactive task; and (c) features of the physical and societal environment.

More specifically, individuals vary in their sensitivity to experiencing rapport, their expressiveness of internal states, and their ability to pick up information relevant to others' states. For one individual, a vertical wrinkle between the brows may be an expression of anger, an emotion relevant to rapport, and, in another, it may be an indication of far-sightedness, a condition less relevant to rapport. Also, interactive tasks vary in difficulty, required actions and object manipulations, bodily positioning to accomplish the task, and amounts of verbal and nonverbal communication. Furrowing the brow during an easy task can indicate confusion and be associated with feelings not conducive to rapport, such as incompetence, but during a challenging task can indicate careful, effortful decision making and be associated with feelings congruent with rapport (Tamir, Robinson, Clore, Martin, & Whitaker, 2004). Finally, physical and social environments vary in features such as type and position of furniture, size of interactive space, the presence and number of potential observers to the interaction, and the cultural setting and social roles of the participants. A couple's frowning at each other in public, when social pressures would tend to suppress negative affect, may indicate stronger negativity than the same degree of frowning in the privacy of home, where intimacy is expected to generate more open expression of frustration.

◆ A Three-Component Model of Rapport

For nonverbal behavior to serve the functions relative to rapport (i.e., as information about internal states, as affordances, and as information about the congruence of internal states between interactive partners), the perceiver must be able to glean information relevant to rapport from variable and context-dependent combinations and physical forms of behavior (such as a brow furrow and eye contact). A problem for research and theory in this area is how these variable combinations can indicate similar experiences (i.e., being in or out of rapport) across varying contexts. One solution proposed by Tickle-Degnen and Rosenthal (1987, 1990) is that the experience and behavioral manifestations of rapport can be described

generally as consisting of the components of mutual attentiveness, positivity, and interpersonal coordination.

Mutual attentiveness refers to participants' focus on one another or on the same object or environmental feature. Behavioral attention demonstrates and affords interpersonal interest and engagement. *Positivity* refers to an affectively positive rather than negative experience of one another. Behavioral positivity demonstrates and affords respect and beneficence toward another person. *Interpersonal coordination* refers to an immediate and spontaneous behavioral and experiential mutual responsiveness, a being "in sync" rather than "out of sync" with one another, and the affordance of well-regulated and effective interaction. Although this three-component model did not involve the concept of affordance explicitly, the components relate implicitly to an affordance function, as do many social psychological constructs (McArthur & Baron, 1983; Zebrowitz & Collins, 1997).

The concepts of attentiveness, positivity, and coordination are socially meaningful because they require a context-dependent assessment of behavior. To come back to the example of brow furrowing, a brow furrow is not separable from context in naturalistic and daily life interaction, just as the meaning of the word "furrowing" is not separable from the utterance and context in which it is spoken (Fridlund, 1997). In some contexts, the furrow may indicate high levels of attentiveness, positivity, and coordination, yet in other contexts it may signify low levels. Rosenthal (1982) captured this contention in his advocacy to augment the standard molecular coding of physical behavior with a *molar* judging of the social meaning of behavior. The molar approach, now identified with the "thin slice" method, has been validated extensively in the prediction of important social phenomena and outcomes (Ambady et al.,

2000) and in the explanation of how individuals form their judgments of rapport (Grahe & Bernieri, 2002). It is the approach taken in the three-component model of rapport (Tickle-Degnen & Rosenthal, 1987, 1990).

◆ **Research on Nonverbal Behavior and Rapport**

The three-component model is partially represented in the recent research on nonverbal behavior and rapport. The bulk of recent and relevant research is on interpersonal coordination, followed by nonverbal expressivity, a construct that encompasses but is not limited to positivity. Little research has systematically examined the component of mutual attentiveness. The review that follows describes first the findings for expressivity, and second, the findings for coordination, because nonverbal expressivity appears to be the raw behavioral material for the development of interpersonal coordination. Both sets of findings demonstrate the need for a more systematic investigation of context and of more complex patterns among the different behavioral components of rapport.

NONVERBAL EXPRESSIVITY

From their review of the literature on emotional expressivity, Boone and Buck (2003) conclude that to be openly self-expressive is a claim to one's own trustworthiness and one's ability to trust. By displaying feelings openly, vividly, and dynamically, people invite others to know their feelings, intentions, and attitudes. Such openness allows the perceiver to determine the potential for an interaction with the actor that is responsive to the perceiver's own needs and inner states. Expressivity tends to elicit liking, rapport, and other positive social outcomes (Riggio & Riggio, 2002). In an experimental manipulation of the suppression of emotional behavior (Butler et al., 2003), female dyads watched an upsetting film and, then, after receiving the experimental manipulation, discussed it. Women who had been instructed to suppress their emotional behavior were less expressive, both positively and negatively, less responsive, and more distracted than were those women who had not received any specific instructions. The uninstructed partners of the "suppressing" women reportedly felt less rapport and willingness to form friendships with those women. Dyads in which both members were uninstructed, and, therefore, more expressive, had better rapport outcomes.

Expressivity and Positivity. That expression of both positive and negative feelings is conducive to rapport is counter to the proposal that positivity alone, not general expressivity, is a basic component of rapport (Tickle-Degnen & Rosenthal, 1987, 1990). Some research studies, however, have implied the importance of positivity by finding that negative expressivity is a negative correlate of rapport. In a study of women who interviewed one another about their daily lives and aspirations, dyads experienced lower rapport when the more expressive partner of the dyad was also the partner with the more negatively emotional personality (Tickle-Degnen & Puccinelli, 1999). Rapport was higher when the less negatively emotional partner was the more expressive partner of the dyad. Other findings suggest that dyads containing partners who are sensitive to detecting negative emotionality in others tend to have compromised experiences of rapport (Elfenbein & Ambady, 2002; Puccinelli & Tickle-Degnen, 2004).

Context factors may explain the inconsistency in research results about negative expressivity. In Tickle-Degnen and Puccinelli's (1999) study, the task of discussing one's daily life and aspirations with a relatively new acquaintance implicitly required a pleasant self-presentation (DePaulo, 1992). In this context, rapport was higher when expressivity was more positive than negative. Expressed negativity by one partner may have been off-putting given the context demands. In contrast, in Butler et al.'s (2003) study, the task of watching an upsetting film with another person would have implicitly required a social acknowledgment of the shared negative experience. Suppression of negative expressivity may have been off-putting in this context. Perhaps, this suppression was a message of dissimilarity or nonacceptance of not only the suppressing woman's inner state but also the partner's inner state. Furthermore, suppression would afford the partner little responsive action, such as commiseration. In the context of this study, unsuppressed negative expressivity would be "positive" because it would imply mutual acceptance and understanding of one another's experience.

If such an interpretation is correct, the implication is that expressivity can have meaning that is positive, neutral, or negative, depending on the context. Specifically, it is expressivity that has positive meaning-in-context that is the correlate or facilitator of rapport. Lending support to this contextual explanation, Bernieri et al. (1996) found that nonverbal expressivity had a lower correlation with experienced rapport in an adversarial context, in which expressivity may have had a less positive, more negative quality, than in a cooperative one, in which expressivity may have had a more positive, less negative quality.

Nonlinear and Dynamic Patterns of Nonverbal Expressivity. Boone and Buck (2003) note that expressivity of an unusually intense or chaotic nature among newly acquainted individuals would be perceived as untrustworthy and not conducive to cooperation. From this perspective, a moderate level of positivity and negativity of expression would be more favorable to rapport than either very low levels (unexpressive) or very high levels (unusually intense). Related to this nonlinear perspective is Gottman's (1994) finding that when happily married couples openly express negative emotion in a manner that is modulated by positive interpersonal strategies, such as humor, they return to a nonnegative state. Unhappy couples, on the other hand, descend into unalleviated and intense negativity. Positive and negative expressivity events may cycle relative to one another, and the dynamic pattern of these cycles may drive the rapport experience.

Tickle-Degnen and Gavett (2003) observed nonlinear and dynamic patterning of nonverbal behavior in six speech therapists and their new child clients over eight weekly clinic sessions. There appeared to be a higher degree of fluctuating, up-down changes in levels of nonverbal positivity and attentiveness within dyads from session to session during the first four sessions compared with the last four sessions, which showed a stable leveling of behavior. The therapists' self-reported experience of rapport, competence, and success, as well as their supervisors' analysis of the sessions, suggested that the greater degree of behavioral fluctuation in the earlier set of sessions was due to conditions that challenged effective communication and collaboration. The greater degree of behavioral stability in the later set appeared to be due to less challenging conditions. More concretely, the therapists and children were learning about each other and how to communicate and work together effectively in their earlier sessions, and they were more informed and skilled in their interactive patterns in later sessions.

Furthermore, across the entire set of sessions, therapists who felt the highest level of rapport demonstrated intermediate levels of attentiveness and positivity. Therapists who felt the lowest level of rapport demonstrated low or high—not intermediate—attentiveness and positivity. These findings support a view of nonlinearity in the association between nonverbal behavior and rapport that is consistent with Boone and Buck's (2003) view that a moderate level of expressivity is more conducive to feelings of trustworthiness and motives to cooperate than extremely low or high levels of expressivity.

INTERPERSONAL COORDINATION

The research on nonverbal expressivity points toward rapport as emerging from *multicomponent, nonlinear, and dynamic behavior in context.* The research on interpersonal coordination leads to a similar conclusion. The concept of interpersonal coordination is particularly useful for understanding rapport because the concept of interpersonal coordination incorporates the dynamic and bidirectional, person-to-person interdependence of behavior. Each partner is part of the context for the other partner, and each partner's expressivity is the "raw action" material that affords the responsive action necessary to link partners into a coordinative unit. Coordination emerges from the context of interpersonal action. For example, individuals who move more are more likely to show a behavioral responsiveness to one another beyond that expected by chance alone (Grammer, Kruck, & Magnusson, 1998). It is this above-chance responsiveness that defines interpersonal coordination.

The terms *coordination, responsiveness,* and *accommodation* are used interchangeably to refer to a whole class of coordinative

patterns that are not mutually exclusive of one another. Three frequently measured coordinative patterns are *matching, interactional synchrony,* and *mimicry* (Burgoon, Stern, & Dillman, 1995). *Matching* refers to behavioral similarity, often measured as a couple's shared positioning of arms and legs. In my work, I have operationalized matching as the similarity in the degree of observed attentiveness and positivity of partners (Tickle-Degnen & Gavett, 2003). *Interactional synchrony* refers to similarity in the rhythm of behavior and to a measurable enmeshment or interdependence of the timing of movements. *Mimicry* is a matching of the behavior of one participant, such as foot shaking, by another participant close in time to the original behavior.

Of the three hypothesized components of rapport (Tickle-Degnen & Rosenthal, 1987, 1990), interpersonal coordination has the most evidence supporting its validity. Parent-infant studies suggest that there are innate pressures for individuals to accommodate to one another behaviorally (Crown, Feldstein, Jasnow, Beebe, & Jaffe, 2001; Papoušek & Papoušek, 1997). When an interaction is going well or supported by the context, coordinated patterning tends to increase over the course of an encounter (Bernieri, Reznick, & Rosenthal, 1988; Cappella, 1996, this volume; Warner, 1992). Such patterning, however, does not always occur. Kritzer and Valenti (1990) showed that synchrony did not increase among untrained therapists and their clients, but it did so with trained therapists. Bernieri et al. (1988) found synchrony to increase in mothers with their own infants but not among mothers with infants with whom they were interacting for the first time.

It is possible that individuals who coordinate behaviorally recognize consciously that their actions are easy, predictable, efficient, and coordinated and, consequently, infer that these qualities are due to an experiential understanding of one another (Bem, 1972). But recent research demonstrates that consciousness is not required. Studies in which mimicry is manipulated experimentally suggest that another's mimicry of one's own behavior induces liking of and rapport with the mimicker unconsciously (Chartrand & Bargh, 1999; Lakin, Jefferis, Cheng, & Chartrand, 2003; see Lakin, this volume) and promotes prosocial behavior toward mimickers as well as those not involved in mimicking (van Baaren, Holland, Kawakami, & van Knippenberg, 2004).

Interpersonal Coordination and Attentiveness. Despite the persuasive evidence that interpersonal coordination is a behavioral correlate and antecedent of rapport across various contexts, it is possible that coordination is an automatic and spontaneous correlate of any type of interpersonal experience that involves engagement and mutual attention (Bernieri et al., 1996; Burgoon et al, 1995; Dijksterhuis & Bargh, 2001; Hatfield, Cacioppo, & Rapson, 1994). An example that coordination is not a sufficient component of rapport is demonstrated in the findings of a study of people interacting via typing in an Internet-style chat room (Niederhoffer & Pennebaker, 2002). Accommodation to one another's linguistic styles occurred regardless of rapport levels (Giles & Coupland, 1991). Engagement in the form of attentive interest appeared to be a better indicator of rapport than the coordinative process of accommodation.

Other studies suggest that attentiveness and synchrony are additive or interactive with respect to rapport. Kendon (1970) found that observers who were present and attentive to, but not involved in, a conversation between two people tended to synchronize their movement to the speaker. The two people who were engaged with each other showed more pronounced

degrees of synchrony than those who were less involved. Renfro and Rauh (2005) found that manipulated disruption of interpersonal coordination during video-mediated discussions had a more negative effect on communication satisfaction and emotion when individuals were more rather than less interested and involved in the topic of their discussion.

Interpersonal Coordination and Positivity. Another example that coordination is not a sufficient component of rapport is demonstrated in the mixed findings of research on postural matching, one type of coordinative structure. In naturalistic interactions of people in established relationships, matching is a positive correlate of rapport experience (LaFrance, 1979; LaFrance & Broadbent, 1976). Alternatively, in interactions of strangers involved in experimental tasks that had unusual or ambiguous purposes, matching has been found to be indicative of communication anxiety or nervousness rather than rapport (Bernieri, 1988; LaFrance & Ickes, 1981). The matching in these latter contexts was relatively static and unchanging, appearing rigid and strained (Bernieri, 1988). LaFrance and Ickes (1981) have suggested such matching in anxiety-provoking contexts may reflect an intention or effort to connect rather than an actual expression of rapport. Even though coordinative behavior in these contexts reflects feelings that are negative, such patterns also reflect a prosocial, and therefore, positive intention; that is, the intention or desire to be in rapport. Such an intention, in the long run, actually may promote rapport but, perhaps, not in short-lived, experimental encounters.

Nonlinear and Dynamic Patterns of Interpersonal Coordination. Some research has demonstrated that interpersonal coordination varies along a looseness-to-tightness dimension, and that this dimension is important for understanding its role in rapport (Bernieri & Rosenthal, 1991; Burgoon et al., 1995; Cappella, 1996; Gottman, 1994; Warner, Malloy, Schneider, Knoth, & Wilder, 1987; Watzlawick, Beavin, & Jackson, 1967). In general, a moderate degree of coordination between individuals indicates effective communication, bonding, and positive interpersonal outcomes (Bernieri et al., 1988; Jaffe, Beebe, Feldstein, Crown, & Jasnow, 2001; Kritzer & Valenti, 1990; Warner, 1992). Based on this research, Tickle-Degnen and Gavett (2003) divided speech therapy dyads into three categories—those having interpersonal coordination that was loose, tight, or intermediate—based on the absolute difference score between the therapist's and child's rated levels of attentiveness or positivity, across three slices in time within a session. The higher the difference score, the "looser" the pattern of coordination. Consistent with previous research findings, therapists experienced higher rapport when there was an intermediate degree of matched attentiveness or matched positivity, and experienced lower rapport when the match was loose or tight.

The results from some studies suggest that very tightly coordinated action, as reflected in a relatively high degree of symmetry, regularity, periodicity, or predictability in the interaction pattern, appears to be indicative of a challenging, uncomfortable social situation or an effort to overcome a problematic interaction. Cappella (1996), for example, found that strangers were more likely to accommodate to one another in their speech turn-taking than were well-acquainted individuals, suggesting that "hyperpoliteness" operates in initial encounters. In another study, therapist-client dyads with ultimately unsuccessful, compared with successful, outcomes were characterized by tighter coordination,

with the therapist accommodating more to the client than vice versa (Lichtenberg et al., 1998).

These findings suggest that the variation in degree of coordination reflects the dyad's effort to optimize dyadic functioning. Dyadic functioning involves maintaining connection to others in order to accomplish a socially mediated task. Just as the attainment and maintenance of connection to others drives much social behavior (e.g., Burgoon et al., 1995; Cappella, 1996; Goffman, 1967), it also appears, more specifically, to drive nonverbal behavior associated with rapport. Research on the automatic functions of simple forms of behavioral mimicry (e.g., face touching or foot shaking) suggests that individuals mimic and respond to mimicry in order to affiliate with one another (Lakin et al., 2003). Many factors (including subliminal priming and recent failure to affiliate satisfactorily with another person) that stimulate affiliation and affiliation goals induce mimicry and associated feelings of liking (Lakin & Chartrand, 2003).

CONTEXT AND DIMENSIONALITY IN THE NONVERBAL BEHAVIOR OF THE RAPPORT ECOSYSTEM

This overview of the recent research on rapport demonstrates that the behavioral components of prosocial or positive expressivity, interpersonal coordination, and an attentive engagement combine in function to initiate, produce, indicate, and sustain rapport. These behavioral components of rapport emerge in relation (a) to challenges in the context of interaction, including challenges to effective communication, connection, and relationship and (b) to achieving other beneficial dyadic outcomes. There is moderation, or a slight degree of "looseness," in the intensity and structure of behavior when individuals experience rapport. Relatively low or high levels of intensity in the behavioral components of rapport may indicate that individuals are either not connecting or attempting to do so in conditions that are challenging for preserving the interpersonal connection required to achieve beneficial dyadic outcomes.

Outcome goals and process subgoals operate simultaneously and interactively during interpersonal interaction (Austin & Vancouver, 1996; Dijksterhuis & Bargh, 2001) and shape the physical, spatial, and temporal structure of interaction. With respect to rapport, relevant outcome goals include affiliation, enjoyment, and the accomplishment of an interpersonal task (e.g., getting a child to eat, completing a project on deadline, or facilitating student learning). Relevant process subgoals include communicating internal states, enabling partner responses, and showing agreement and cooperation.

There may be, at times, a simpler goal structure, that is, fewer goals and more integrated or congruent goals, in contexts that support rapport than in contexts that do not. Under a simple goal structure, behavioral positivity, coordination, and attentiveness may covary with one another in a relatively stable fashion across the interaction, all being correlated positively with rapport. A complex goal structure may occur in contexts that do not support rapport. Individuals may express negativity, poor responsiveness, and inattention, and mix or alternate these signals with others that indicate their intention to attempt to establish or restore rapport. In these situations, there may be more than one dimension in the correlational structure of behavior and the experience of rapport.

The most direct support for this idea of uni- versus multidimensionality to the correlational structure of behavior and experienced rapport comes from studies of different interpersonal tasks. Bernieri et al. (1996) and Puccinelli et al. (2003, 2004) had each of their participating dyads perform two tasks: one in which the purpose was to communicate important personal information via face-to-face conversation, and another one, in which the purpose was to solve a problem using props and physical objects creatively in an object-focused task.

Bernieri et al. (1996) compared an adversarial debate with a cooperative trip-planning task. They found more behavioral elements to be associated with the dyad members' experienced rapport during the debate than during the trip-planning task. In addition, the behavioral elements indicative of rapport during the debate were less intercorrelated—that is, more multidimensional—compared with those elements indicative of rapport during the trip-planning task, which were more intercorrelated—that is, more unidimensional. In the debate task, behaviors associated with rapport included those involved in expressing and connecting, such as synchrony, proximity, and to a small degree expressivity, as well as those involved in conversing effectively face to face, such as the back-channel responses of head nodding and "uh hmms," eye contact, and talkativeness. In the trip-planning task, on the other hand, individuals were active and expressive or were relatively quiet and nonexpressive, and if they were active and expressive they had higher rapport. Furthermore, observers were able to detect the rapport experienced by the participants more accurately from the more simple configuration of behavior encoded during the trip-planning task than from the more complex configuration encoded during the debate.

In a similar vein, Puccinelli et al. (2003, 2004) compared conversations about daily life activities and aspirations with behaviors during a puzzle construction task. In contrast with Bernieri et al. (1996), who measured much of the dyads' nonverbal behavior at a molecular level (e.g., coded amount of eye contact), Puccinelli et al. (2003, 2004) measured nonverbal behavior at a more molar level (e.g., raters' judgments of degree of attentive behavior). Despite this difference in methods, Puccinelli et al.'s findings were similar to those of Bernieri et al. (1996), in that there was a higher degree of rapport-relevant behavior in the conversation than puzzle task, yet observers were more sensitive to dyads' experience of rapport in the puzzle task.

Bernieri et al. (1996) and Puccinelli et al. (2003, 2004) made sense of their findings by suggesting that their conversation tasks were more difficult interpersonally than their object-focused tasks. Individuals had to be expressive and talkative to accomplish the purposes of the conversations successfully regardless of how much rapport they felt. The verbal content during these tasks would be more likely to expose partners' differences in intention, attitude, and affect (and thus threaten rapport). Nevertheless, the social context required behavior to be supportive and accepting implicitly. Actual feelings may have been encoded less clearly under these circumstances, and a high degree of social skill was required. The object-focused tasks of trip planning and puzzle construction, on the other hand, did not require as much talking or negotiation of personal or intimate territory for success. Thus, there was little possibility of the partners finding themselves at odds with one another, and self-presentation was of little concern. Success was determined clearly, simply, and impersonally by using up the money for the trip or by making a puzzle design that matched a model. There would be little need to hide feelings in this context and, thus, less social skill required than in the conversation tasks. It is not surprising, then, that in the object-focused tasks, nonverbal expressivity held a direct association with rapport, and was

decoded accurately by observers as indicative of felt rapport.

A set of studies (Dunkerley, Tickle-Degnen, & Coster, 1997; Tickle-Degnen & Coster, 1995) of occupational therapy sessions in a pediatric clinic demonstrated similar findings to those of Bernieri et al. (1996) and Puccinelli et al. (2003, 2004). Two periods within a session were studied: The beginning minutes of the session, when therapists and their child clients undertook light and easy warm-up sensory-motor tasks, and the middle minutes, when the dyads worked on more challenging tasks. In these studies, experienced rapport was not assessed. Rather, the degree of dyadic rapport in the videotaped sessions was judged by pediatric therapists.

In the less-challenging beginning minutes, rated child behaviors showed a unidimensional association with the dyad's judged rapport. Rapport was judged to be higher as children showed a uniformly enjoyable, less anxious, and successful performance, and judged to be lower as children showed a more uniformly negative, more anxious, and unsuccessful performance. In the middle minutes, the children appeared to be a bit overchallenged relative to their ability levels, and the associations between child behaviors and judged rapport showed a more complex pattern than that shown in the easier, beginning minutes. The pattern involved two dimensions: positivity and anxious effort. Dyadic rapport was judged as higher in children who showed enjoyment and success, but the children also showed a slight edge of anxiety, considerable physical effort, and more help seeking. Rapport was judged as lower when children showed less enjoyment, success, anxiety, and effort.

Together these findings suggest that the goals and procedures of interpersonal tasks create challenges that constrain and shape the physical, spatial, and temporal structure of nonverbal behavior indicative of rapport. Specifically, linearity, dynamics, and dimensionality in the correlational structure of experienced rapport and nonverbal behavior appear to vary according to task goals and procedures. To understand better the role of nonverbal behavior in rapport, there is a need for research that systematically relates task attributes and other contextual factors to the *complexity* of patterns of behavior.

◆ Nonverbal Behavior in the Regulation of Rapport During Interpersonal Tasks

A model developed by Csikszentmihalyi and his colleague (Csikszentmihalyi, 1990; Csikszentmihalyi & Csikszentmihalyi, 1988) may be useful for guiding future investigations in this area. The model explains optimal experience as emerging from individuals' skill levels and as interactive with the challenges of the tasks they are performing. Although the model does not address nonverbal behavior directly, its framework is general and flexible enough to include nonverbal behavior. It serves as an exemplar for how task parameters and other contextual factors might operate with respect to nonverbal behavior and rapport.

Csikszentmihalyi and colleague (Csikszentmihalyi, 1990; Csikszentmihalyi & Csikszentmihalyi, 1988) have shown that activities evoking an optimal experience are ones that are challenging, but not too challenging, for one's skill level. As applied to dyads, tasks that challenge dyads at their level of interactive capacity or skill intellectually, physically, emotionally, or socially are most likely to generate an optimal level of rapport. In addition to the match of task challenge with skill, activities that evoke an optimal experience are ones in which there are clear goals and clearly marked steps in the

incremental progress toward goal achievement. Optimal experience is found more frequently in structured than unstructured tasks, and in work than nonwork activities, where task goals and progress are often overt and systematically monitored (Csikszentmihalyi & LeFevre, 1989; Massimini, Csikszentmihalyi, & Delle Fave, 1988).

The optimal experience has both emotional and cognitive dimensions. A deeply enjoyable activity is one in which individuals' attention becomes absorbed in the doing of an activity. Activity and awareness merge as attention is focused on the task at hand. Individuals have feelings of competence. Worries, hassles, distractions, and self-consciousness fade, and although there is engaged intention, the experience is one of ease, enjoyment, and harmony. In Csikszentmihalyi's (1990) words, there is a feeling of being in *flow*. Suboptimal experiences result from task conditions that fail to support challenging and skillful interaction with the environment. According to this model, boredom is the result of tasks and activities that offer too little challenge relative to skill and that have little overt structure, purpose, and interactive feedback. Anxiety, on the other hand, occurs when tasks and activities offer too great a challenge relative to skill and that have complicated structure, ambiguous goals, and little feedback enabling successful performance.

Optimal experience has been shown to be associated with dyadic rapport experience and nonverbal behavior. Puccinelli and Tickle-Degnen (2004) measured the experience of rapport from items that ask dyad members to assess how much they and their partner felt attentive, positive, and coordinated, and measured the experience of flow from items developed by Csikszentmihalyi and Csikszentmihalyi (1988). As self-reported rapport in dyads increased, so did shared feelings of enjoyment and having the capacity to meet the challenges of the situation. At the same time, self-consciousness declined. Similarly, in studies of therapist-child interactions (Dunkerley et al., 1997; Tickle-Degnen & Coster, 1995), as behavioral attentiveness, positivity, and coordination increased so did the match between the challenge of therapeutic tasks and the child's demonstrated ability level increasingly. On the other hand, these behavioral correlates of rapport showed very little relationship to the task challenge as measured independently of the child's ability, which indicates that task challenge alone did not moderate this behavior. Rather, nonverbal behavior was associated with the child's own capacities in interaction with the context of action.

Table 20.1 shows the distinctions between optimal and suboptimal rapport experiences based on Csikszentmihalyi's (1990) model, which I have modified for the purposes of understanding the rapport ecosystem. When conditions provide the just-right challenge (i.e., not over- and not underchallenging) to a dyad's skill level, the dyad's nonverbal behavior would clearly and simply express the rapport experience. When conditions are overchallenging to dyad skill, the behavior would show signs of effort and nervousness and, perhaps, more behavioral elements or more intense behavior indicative of attempts to establish or recover rapport. When underchallenging, there would be very little purposeful interpersonal behavior, unless there are other implicit contextual pressures to establish rapport.

◆ *Individual and Group Differences in the Rapport Ecosystem*

The nonverbal correlates of rapport are shaped by many contextual features and pressures besides task challenge and dyad skill. A complete research agenda requires that additional features and pressures, such as those related to individual and group differences, be investigated systematically as well. For example, the individual in the dyad who has the highest level of trait expressivity drives rapport (Sullins, 1991; Tickle-Degnen & Puccinelli, 1999). Relative to individuals who are less accurate in interpreting others' inner states from nonverbal behavior, individuals who are more accurate have rapport experiences that are more reactive or sensitive to the other's emotional traits (Puccinelli & Tickle-Degnen, 2004). Similarly, individuals who have strong social motives, such as a need to belong or a tendency toward high self-monitoring, are more attentive to nonverbal behavior and respond with greater empathic accuracy (Pickett, Gardner, & Knowles, 2004) and behavioral mimicry (Cheng & Chartrand, 2003).

Emotional expressivity, nonverbal sensitivity, and social motives vary according to gender, health conditions, and age as well. Females are more emotionally expressive generally, their own emotions are more responsive to the behavior of others (Fischer, 2000), and their interactions are driven more by mutual participation goals (Strough & Berg, 2000) compared with males. Some health conditions, such as the movement disorder of Parkinson's disease, prevent individuals from expressing their inner states with clarity and responding to others' states in a coordinated manner. Observers often have negative impressions and presume social apathy or negative social motives, such as deceptiveness, inaccurately in these individuals, leading to stigmatization processes that prevent or erode rapport (Lyons & Tickle-Degnen, 2003; Tickle-Degnen & Lyons, 2004). Interestingly, the movement disorder of Parkinson's disease mimics the expressive behavior of the very old (Singer, 1974) and can occur in younger and older adults who, otherwise, are

Table 20.1   Optimal Experience and Nonverbal Behavior in Rapport

Sub-optimal Experience: Bored	Optimal Experience: Calm and Energized	Sub-optimal Experience: Anxious
Task conditions		
Too little of a challenge for dyad members	Task challenge matches dyad members' skills	Overly challenging for dyad members
Unstructured	Structured	Complicated structure
Purposeless	Clear goals	Ambiguous goals
Feedback irrelevant	Ongoing feedback about success in achieving goals	Little feedback about success in achieving goals
Thoughts and feelings		
One's competence is irrelevant	Competent	Incompetent
Negative: bored	Positive: calm and energized	Negative: anxious
No concern, no interest	Absorbed in interaction	Overriding concern about self
Partner is irrelevant	Partner accepts one's attitudes, intentions, and feelings	Partner may not be accepting of and responding to self
Emptiness	Harmony, flow, in rapport	Disharmony, disorder
Nonverbal behavior		
Unfocused	Absorbed attention	Vigilant attention
Inactive, perhaps prosocial intentions	Expressive, prosocial affect and intentions	Disregulated affect, perhaps prosocial intentions
No effort	Engaged but relaxed	Effortful, intense
Lethargic, off-task behavior	Calm, socially clear behavior	Nervous or socially ambiguous behavior
Hypo-responsivity to partner's behavior	Moderate responsivity to partner's behavior	Excessive responsivity to partner's behavior
Rapport ecosystem		
Unengaged	Resilient, secure bond	Insecure bond
Failure to develop or maintain bond. There may be attempts to create or restore bond.	Ease in sustaining interaction toward goal achievement	Difficulty effectively interacting toward goal achievement. Failure to develop or maintain bond. There may be attempts to create or restore bond.

NOTE: Table influenced by Csikszentmihalyi (1990).

developmentally normal. Research in this area can inform the role of aging on the nonverbal correlates of rapport.

In addition, cultural contexts influence the properties of nonverbal behavior related to rapport. In Asian cultures, moderation of emotion and expression are seen as central to achieving harmonious relationships with others, an achievement highly valued within the Confucian tradition and collectivistic culture (Chang & Holt, 1994). This emphasis on moderation contrasts to the emphasis on personal expression in individualistic cultures. For example, Asians compared with North Americans show more control of facial expressivity in response to emotionally evocative stimuli (Okazaki, Liu, Longworth, & Minn, 2002).

♦ Implications for Future Research

People experience rapport with their family members, friends, physicians, teachers, and coworkers as they engage in tasks that vary in how challenging, structured, comfortable, or intimate they are. In contrast to the variety of task conditions found in natural social life, the laboratory, in which most research on rapport is conducted, manipulates or represents only a limited array of conditions. It presents specialized and unique sets of task constraints that influence patterns of nonverbal behavior and their functional associations with outcomes (Grahe & Sherman, 2005; Tamir et al., 2004). Experimental interaction tasks involve unacquainted or mildly acquainted participants typically, and implicit norms require pleasantness and appropriate modulation of emotion. Research on rapport and nonverbal communication must take into account these constraints operating on behavior. We should also consider how laboratory task constraints related to interpersonal expressivity and coordination are similar to or deviate from the everyday situations of participants outside the laboratory. Finally, how individual and group differences interact with task constraints as nonverbal behavior mediates and responds

to the rapport experience is far from understood and requires more research.

Despite the call in this chapter to integrate an understanding of rapport with optimal experience, rapport has been studied rarely in contexts in which conditions are favorable for such experience. Yet social enjoyment is one of the primary types of satisfaction that individuals experience and seek out (Csikszentmihalyi & LeFevre, 1989). To further understand the implications of this contention, more research is needed on describing people's tasks when they have optimal social experience and what their behavior looks like under these optimal conditions. Specifically, the review of the literature on rapport and nonverbal behavior suggests the following hypothesis: *When contextual factors support rapport, nonverbal behavior will show a clear and simple relationship to experienced rapport. On the others hand, when contextual factors threaten or undermine rapport, nonverbal behavior will show a complex or ambiguous relationship to experienced rapport.* To test this hypothesis, we need to clarify what is meant by "simple" or "complex" relationship, and the following constructs require more careful development and operationalization: linearity, loose versus tight coordination, and dimensionality in the association of nonverbal behavior with rapport.

The experience of rapport also requires more careful elaboration from a temporal or dynamic perspective (see Cappella & Schreiber, this volume). Individuals may fluctuate in the strength of their rapport over time, yet they may have strong motives to retain rapport. At times, they may not feel in rapport with one another, but their behavior demonstrates features that are somewhat congruent with what would be demonstrated if their rapport experience were stronger. Tracking the development, waning, and restoration of rapport across time in enduring relationships will shed light on these differences in rapport experiences. Finally, there is a need for measures that assess not only *being in rapport* but also *desire to be in rapport*.

Together, this work will enable a theoretically more coherent approach to studying the nonverbal correlates of rapport and interpreting the results. Models such as that of Csikszentmihalyi (Csikszentmihalyi, 1990; Csikszentmihalyi & Csikszentmihalyi, 1988) are helpful in guiding this work forward. They illustrate how optimal experiences, such as rapport, emerge in the context of accomplishing interpersonal tasks to meet personal, dyadic, and group needs. These models can be used to organize the systematic investigation of how nonverbal behavior functions in context to initiate, produce, indicate, and sustain rapport.

◆ References

Ambady, N., Bernieri, F. J., & Richeson, J. A. (2000). Toward a histology of social behavior: Judgmental accuracy from thin slices of the behavioral stream. *Advances in Experimental Social Psychology, 32,* 201–271.

Austin, J. T., & Vancouver, J. B. (1996). Goal constructs in psychology: Structure, process, and content. *Psychological Bulletin, 120,* 338–375.

Bem, D. J. (1972). Self-perception theory. In L. Berkowitz (Ed.), *Advances in experimental social psychology* (Vol. 6, pp. 1–62). New York: Academic Press.

Bernieri, F. (1988). Coordinated movement and rapport in teacher-student interactions. *Journal of Nonverbal Behavior, 12,* 120–138.

Bernieri, F. J., Gillis, J. S., Davis, J. M., & Grahe, J. E. (1996). Dyad rapport and the accuracy of its judgments across situations: A lens model analysis. *Journal of Personality and Social Psychology, 71,* 110–129.

Bernieri, F. J., Reznick, J. S., & Rosenthal, R. (1988). Synchrony, pseudosynchrony, and dissynchrony: Measuring the entrainment process in mother-infant interactions. *Journal*

of *Personality and Social Psychology, 54,* 243–253.

Bernieri, F. J., & Rosenthal, R. (1991). Interpersonal coordination: Behavior matching and interactional synchrony. In R. Feldman & R. Rime (Eds.), *Fundamentals of nonverbal behavior* (pp. 401–432). Cambridge, UK: Cambridge University Press.

Boone, T., & Buck, R. (2003). Emotional expressivity and trustworthiness: The role of nonverbal behavior in the evolution of cooperation. *Journal of Nonverbal Behavior, 27,* 163–182.

Brunswik, E. (1955). Representative design and probabilistic theory. *Psychological Review, 62,* 193–217.

Burgoon, J. K, Stern, L. A., & Dillman, L. (1995). *Interpersonal adaptation: Dyadic interaction patterns.* Cambridge, UK: Cambridge University Press.

Butler, E. A., Egloff, B., Wilhelm, F. H., Smith, N. C., Erickson, A., & Gross, J. J. (2003). The social consequence of expression suppression. *Emotion, 3,* 48–67.

Cappella, J. N. (1996). Dynamic coordination of vocal and kinesic behavior in dyadic interaction: Methods, problems, and interpersonal outcomes. In J. H. Watt & C. A. VanLear (Eds.), *Dynamic patterns in communication processes* (pp. 353–386). Thousand Oaks, CA: Sage.

Chang, H-C, & Holt, G. R. (1994). A Chinese perspective on face as inter-relational concern. In S. Ting-Toomey (Ed.), *The challenge of facework: Cross-cultural and interpersonal issues* (pp. 95–132). Albany: State University of New York Press.

Chartrand, T. L., & Bargh, J. A. (1999). The chameleon effect: The perception-behavior link and social interaction. *Journal of Personality and Social Psychology, 76,* 893–910.

Cheng, C. M., & Chartrand, T. L. (2003). Self-monitoring without awareness: Using mimicry as a nonconscious affiliation strategy. *Journal of Personality and Social Psychology, 85,* 1170–1179.

Compact Oxford English dictionary. (2005). Oxford, UK: Oxford University Press. Retrieved May 5, 2005, from www .askoxford.com

Crown, C. L., Feldstein, S., Jasnow, M. D., Beebe, B., & Jaffe, J. (2001). The cross-modal coordination of interpersonal timing: Six-week-old infants' gaze with adults' vocal behavior. *Journal of Psycholinguistic Research, 30,* 1–23.

Csikszentmihalyi, M. (1990). *Flow: The psychology of optimal experience.* New York: HarperCollins.

Csikszentmihalyi, M., & Csikszentmihalyi, I. S. (1988). *Optimal experience: Psychological studies of flow in consciousness.* Cambridge,UK: Cambridge University Press.

Csikszentmihalyi, M., & LeFevre, J. (1989). Optimal experience in work and leisure. *Journal of Personality and Social Psychology, 56,* 815–822.

DePaulo, B. M. (1992). Nonverbal behavior and self-presentation. *Psychological Bulletin, 111,* 203–243.

Dijksterhuis, A., & Bargh, J. A. (2001). The perception-behavior expressway: Automatic effects of social perception on social behavior. In M. Zanna (Ed.), *Advances in experimental social psychology* (Vol. 33, pp. 1–40). San Diego, CA: Academic Press.

Dunkerley, E., Tickle-Degnen, L., & Coster, W. (1997). Therapist-child interaction in the middle minutes of sensory integration treatment. *American Journal of Occupational Therapy, 51,* 799–805.

Ekman, P., & Keltner, D. (1997). Universal facial expressions of emotion: An old controversy and new findings. In U. Segerstråle & P. Molnár (Eds.), *Nonverbal communication: Where nature meets culture* (pp. 27–46). Mahwah, NJ: Erlbaum.

Elfenbein, H. A., & Ambady, N. (2002). Predicting workplace outcomes from the ability to eavesdrop on feelings. *Journal of Applied Psychology, 87,* 963–971.

Fischer, A. H. (Ed.). (2000). *Gender and emotion: Social psychological perspectives.* Paris: Cambridge University Press.

Freud, S. (1924). On the history of the psychoanalytic movement. In J. Riviere (Trans.) & E. Jones (Ed.), *Collected papers* (Vol. I, pp. 287–359). London: Hogarth. (Original work published 1914)

Fridlund, A. J. (1997). The new ethology of human facial expression. In J. A. Russell &

J. M. Fernandez-Dols (Eds.), *The psychology of facial expression* (pp. 103–129). Paris: Cambridge University Press.

Gibson, J. J. (1986). *The ecological approach to visual perception.* Hillsdale, NJ: Erlbaum. (Original work published 1979).

Giles, H., & Coupland, N. (1991). *Language: Contexts and consequences.* Pacific Grove, CA: Brooks/Cole.

Goffman, E. (1967). *Interaction ritual: Essays on face-to-face behavior.* New York: Pantheon.

Gottman, J. M. (1994). *What predicts divorce? The relationship between marital processes and marital outcomes.* Hillsdale, NJ: Erlbaum.

Grahe, J. E., & Bernieri, F. J. (2002). Self-awareness of judgment policies of rapport. *Personality and Social Psychology Bulletin, 28,* 1407–1418.

Grahe, J. E., & Sherman, R. A. (2005). *An ecological examination of rapport using a dyadic puzzle task.* Unpublished manuscript.

Grammer, K. Kruck, K. B., & Magnusson, M. S. (1998). The courtship dance: Patterns of nonverbal synchronization in opposite-sex encounters. *Journal of Nonverbal Behavior, 22,* 3–29.

Hatfield, E., Cacioppo, J. T., & Rapson, R. L. (1994). *Emotional contagion.* Paris: Cambridge University Press.

Heft, H. (2003). Affordances, dynamic experience, and the challenge of reification. *Ecological Psychology, 15,* 149–180.

Izard, C. (1994). Innate and universal facial expressions: Evidence from developmental cross-cultural research. *Psychological Bulletin, 115,* 288–299.

Jaffe, J., Beebe, B., Feldstein, S., Crown, C. L., & Jasnow, M. D. (2001). Rhythms of dialogue in infancy: Coordinated timing in development. *Monographs of the Society for Research in Child Development, 66*(2), vi-131.

James, W. (1890). *Principles of psychology.* New York: Holt.

Kendon, A. (1970). Movement coordination in social interaction: Some examples described. *Acta Psychologica, 32,* 100–125.

Kritzer, R., & Valenti, S. S. (1990, March). *Rapport in therapist-client interactions:*

An ecological analysis of the effects of nonverbal sensitivity and interactional synchrony. Paper presented at the 61st annual meeting of the Eastern Psychological Association, Philadelphia.

LaFrance, M. (1979). Nonverbal synchrony and rapport: Analysis by the cross-lag panel technique. *Social Psychology Quarterly, 42,* 66–70.

LaFrance, M. (1990). The trouble with rapport. *Psychological Inquiry, 1,* 318–320.

LaFrance, M., & Broadbent, M. (1976). Group rapport: Posture sharing as nonverbal indicator. *Group and Organization Studies, 1,* 328–333.

LaFrance, M., & Ickes, W. (1981). Posture mirroring and interactional involvement: Sex and sex typing effects. *Journal of Nonverbal Behavior, 5,* 139–154.

Lakin, J. L., & Chartrand, T. L. (2003). Using nonconscious behavioral mimicry to create affiliation and rapport. *Psychological Science, 14,* 334–339.

Lakin, J. L., Jefferis, A. E., Cheng, C. M., & Chartrand, T. L. (2003). The chameleon effect as social glue: Evidence for the evolutionary significance of nonconscious mimicry. *Journal of Nonverbal Behavior, 27,* 145–162.

Lichtenberg, J. W., Wettersten, K. B., Mull, H., Moberly, R. L., Merkley, K. B., & Corey, A. T. (1998). Relationship formation and relational control as correlates of psychotherapy quality and outcome. *Journal of Counseling Psychology, 45,* 322–337.

Lyons, K. D., & Tickle-Degnen, L. (2003). Dramaturgical challenges of Parkinson's disease. *Occupational Therapy Journal of Research: Occupation, Participation, and Health, 23,* 27–34.

Massimini, F., Csikszentmihalyi, M., & Delle Fave, A. (1988). Flow and biocultural evolution. In M. Csikszentmihalyi & I. S. Csikszentmihalyi (Eds.), *Optimal experience: Psychological studies of flow in consciousness* (pp. 60–81). Cambridge, UK: Cambridge University Press.

McArthur, L. Z., & Baron, R. M. (1983). Toward an ecological theory of social perception. *Psychological Review, 90,* 215–238.

Niederhoffer, K. G., & Pennebaker, J. W. (2002). Linguistic style matching in social interaction. *Journal of Language and Social Psychology, 21,* 337–360.

Okazaki, S., Liu, J. F., Longworth, S. L., & Minn, J. Y. (2002). Asian American-White American differences in expressions of social anxiety: A replication and extension. *Cultural Diversity and Ethnic Minority Psychology, 8,* 234–247.

Papoušek, H., & Papoušek, M. (1997). Preverbal communication in humans and the genesis of culture. In U. Segerstråle & P. Molnár (Eds.), *Nonverbal communication: Where nature meets culture* (pp. 87–108). Mahwah, NJ: Erlbaum.

Park, R. E., & Burgess, E. W. (1924). *Introduction to the science of sociology.* Chicago: University of Chicago Press.

Patterson, M. L. (1994). Strategic functions of nonverbal behavior. In J. A. Daly & J. M. Wiemann (Eds.), *Strategic interpersonal communication* (pp. 273–293). Hillsdale, NJ: Erlbaum.

Patterson, M. L. (1999). The evolution of a parallel process model of nonverbal communication. In P. Philippot, R. S. Feldman, & E. J. Coats (Eds.), *The social context of nonverbal behavior* (pp. 317–347). Paris: Cambridge University Press.

Patterson, M. L. (2003). Evolution and nonverbal behavior: Functions and mediating processes. *Journal of Nonverbal Behavior, 27,* 201–207.

Pickett, C. L., Gardner, W. L., & Knowles, M. (2004). Getting a cue: The need to belong and enhanced sensitivity to social cues. *Personality and Social Psychology Bulletin, 30,* 1095–1107.

Puccinelli, N. M., & Tickle-Degnen, L. (2004). Knowing too much about others: Moderators of the relationship between eavesdropping and rapport in social interaction. *Journal of Nonverbal Behavior, 28,* 223–243.

Puccinelli, N. M., Tickle-Degnen, L., & Rosenthal, R. (2003). Effect of dyadic context on judgments of rapport: Dyad task and partner presence. *Journal of Nonverbal Behavior, 27,* 211–236.

Puccinelli, N. M., Tickle-Degnen, L., & Rosenthal, R. (2004). Effect of target position and target task on judge sensitivity to felt rapport. *Journal of Nonverbal Behavior, 28,* 211–220.

Renfro, S., & Rauh, C. (2005, May). *Video delay effects on emotions, communication outcomes, and involvement.* Paper presented at the 55th annual conference of the International Communication Association, New York.

Riggio, H. R., & Riggio, R. E. (2002). Emotional expressiveness, extraversion, and neuroticism: A meta-analysis. *Journal of Nonverbal Behavior, 26,* 195–218.

Rosenthal, R. (1982). Conducting judgment studies. In K. R. Scherer & P. Ekman (Eds.), *Handbook of methods in nonverbal behavior research* (pp. 287–361). New York: Cambridge University Press.

Singer, E. (1974). Premature social aging: The social-psychological consequences of a chronic illness. *Social Science & Medicine, 8,* 143–151.

Strack, F., & Deutsch, R. (2004). Reflective and impulsive determinants of social behavior. *Personality and Social Psychology Review, 8,* 220–247.

Strough, J., & Berg, C. A. (2000). Goals as a mediator of gender differences in high-affiliation dyadic conversations. *Developmental Psychology, 36,* 117–125.

Sullins, E. S. (1991). Emotional contagion revisited: Effects of social comparison and expressive style on mood convergence. *Personality and Social Psychology Bulletin, 17,* 166–174.

Tamir, M., Robinson, M. D., Clore, G. L., Martin, L. L., & Whitaker, D. J. (2004). Are we puppets on a string? The contextual meaning of unconscious expressive cues. *Personality and Social Psychology Bulletin, 30,* 237–249.

Tickle-Degnen, L., & Coster, W. (1995). Therapeutic interaction and the management of challenge during the beginning minutes of sensory integration treatment. *Occupational Therapy Journal of Research, 15,* 122–141.

Tickle-Degnen, L., & Gavett, E. (2003). Changes in nonverbal behavior during the development of therapeutic relationships. In P. Philippot, R. S. Feldman, & E. J. Coats (Eds.), *Nonverbal behavior in clinical settings* (pp. 75–110). Oxford, UK: Oxford University Press.

Tickle-Degnen, L., & Lyons, K. D. (2004). Practitioners' impressions of patients with Parkinson's disease: The social ecology of the expressive mask. *Social Science & Medicine, 58,* 603–614.

Tickle-Degnen, L., & Puccinelli, N. (1999). The nonverbal expression of negative emotions: Peer and supervisor responses to occupational therapy students' emotional attributes. *Occupational Therapy Journal of Research, 19,* 18–39.

Tickle-Degnen, L., & Rosenthal, R. (1987). Group rapport and nonverbal behavior. In C. Hendrick (Ed.), *Review of personality and social psychology: Volume 9, Group processes and intergroup relations* (pp. 113–136). Newbury Park, CA: Sage.

Tickle-Degnen, L., & Rosenthal, R. (1990). The nature of rapport and its nonverbal correlates. *Psychological Inquiry, 1,* 285–293.

van Baaren, R. B., Holland, R. W., Kawakami, K., & van Knippenberg, A. (2004). Mimicry and prosocial behavior. *Psychological Science, 15,* 71–74.

Warner, R. M. (1992). Speaker, partner and observer evaluations of affect during social interaction as a function of interaction tempo. *Journal of Language and Social Psychology, 11,* 253–266.

Warner, R. M., Malloy, D., Schneider, K., Knoth, R., & Wilder, B. (1987). Rhythmic organization of social interaction and observer ratings of positive affect and involvement. *Journal of Nonverbal Behavior, 11,* 57–74.

Watzlawick, P., Beavin, J., & Jackson, D. D. (1967). *Pragmatics of human communication: A study of interactional patterns, pathologies, and paradoxes.* New York: Norton.

Zebrowitz, L. A., & Collins, M. A. (1997). Accurate social perception at zero acquaintance: The affordances of a Gibsonian approach. *Personality and Social Psychology Review, 1,* 204–223.

PART IV

CONTEXTS AND CONSEQUENCES

21

NONVERBAL COMMUNICATION IN CLOSE RELATIONSHIPS

◆ Patricia Noller
University of Queensland

The importance of communication in close relationships may be seen in Wood's (1995) claim that "communication is not only a central, generative process of intimacy, but is actually what we experience *as relationships*" ([italics added] p. 125). Whereas communication can be both verbal and nonverbal, evidence suggests that the nonverbal channels may be particularly crucial to relationship processes and outcomes (Gottman, Markman, & Notarius, 1977; Noller, 1984; Nowicki & Duke, 2001). The communicative potential of nonverbal cues contributes to their importance in relationships. As Manusov (2002) points out, "One of the most intriguing aspects of nonverbal communication is its ability to be interpreted in myriad ways" (p. 15).

Nowhere is this fact more evident, or more problematic, than in close relationships, in which nonverbal communication performs two important functions: the *expression of emotions* (expressing one's feelings about the self, the partner, or some other person or thing) and the *display of relational messages* (indicating the type of relationship, e.g., close vs. distant; Manusov, 2002). In particular, their ability to "signal how participants regard each other, their relationship, and themselves in the relationship" (Burgoon & Dillman, 1995, p. 63) makes nonverbal cues particularly pertinent to relationships. In Noller's (1995) study, for example, the most frequent way in which negative messages were sent to partners, irrespective of gender or relationship satisfaction, was with a smile accompanied by negative words or tone of voice. This set of behaviors can be interpreted in terms of spouses wishing to get their complaint across to the partner but wishing to send a positive message about the relationship at the same time.

In addition to (and perhaps because of) their ability to be interpreted in an array of ways, nonverbal cues are also particularly able to be misunderstood. Misunderstandings may occur either because the message was not sent clearly (an encoding error) or because the message, although sent clearly, was not decoded accurately (a decoding error; Noller, 1984; for a general discussion of encoding and decoding skills, see Riggio, this volume). Friedman (2001) notes that the success of nonverbal communication depends on factors related to the communicator and factors relating to the perceiver. The factors that he specifies as relevant to encoding include that person's communication skills and his or her motivation to be accurate or not in conveying the message, the situational context (e.g., an argument or an intimate conversation, public or private), and the communicator's current emotional state (such as angry or excited). For the perceiver, decoding is affected by factors such as personality, the extent to which he or she is paying attention or is distracted, and the motivation to understand what the partner is seeking to communicate.

The possibility for errors—and what may contribute to more successful encoding and decoding of nonverbal cues—is perhaps most germane for looking at the consequentiality of nonverbal communication in relationships. For this reason, it provides the primary focus of the present chapter. In this chapter, my goal is to review the literature on nonverbal communication in close relationships from both an empirical and a theoretical perspective. I focus first on *interpersonal sensitivity*, or the success in decoding nonverbal communication, in close relationships. I follow this with discussion of *nonverbal expressiveness*, or the encoding of nonverbal communication in close relationships. I then discuss what is known about the role of nonverbal communication in courtship. Finally, I focus on nonverbal communication in the context of two other influential theories of close relationships: attachment theory and attribution theory.

◆ Decoding Sensitivity

Interpersonal sensitivity concerns the ability to decode others' nonverbal communication accurately and thus be sensitive to the emotional material they are expressing through the nonverbal channel. Friedman (2001) notes that there are several paradoxes with regard to interpersonal sensitivity: "In various situations it appears that a tremendous amount of important interpersonal knowledge is being rapidly communicated, mostly nonverbally" (p. 351). Nevertheless, or perhaps precisely because so much information is being transmitted, "there is a great deal of mis-information and misunderstanding in face-to-face human relations" (Friedman, 2001, p. 351).

According to Zebrowitz (2001), increasing our understanding of the processes involved in decoding nonverbal behavior is important because decoding sensitivity predicts more effective social functioning in general (Losoya & Eisenberg, 2001; Noller, 2001; Nowicki & Duke, 2001). Losoya and Eisenberg (2001) focus on *affective empathy*, which is the ability to recognize a person's emotion and also feel that emotion with the person. The authors review studies concerned with empathy-related responding (or responding in a way that lets the other person know that one empathizes with their situation), including those studies involving the assessment of facial and gestural cues of young children (e.g., Miller, Eisenberg, Fabes, & Shell, 1996; Zahn-Waxler, Radke-Yarrow, Wagner, & Chapman, 1992; Zahn-Waxler, Robinson, & Emde, 1992).

Using actual facial expressions of emotion in research studies to assess people's empathy can help deal with the problem of social desirability affecting self-report responses and the tendency, particularly of older children and adults, to react in socially expected ways in more constrained research paradigms. Losoya and Eisenberg (2001) show that affective empathy can be distinguished from sympathy (which does not involve feeling the person's distress), however, and that affective empathy is correlated with the overall quality of social functioning.

Besides individual skill in affective empathy, there is also some evidence for a "closeness of relationship effect" on decoding sensitivity, with close relationship partners' greater knowledge about each other's lives leading to greater accuracy at decoding nonverbal behavior. For example, romantic partners (Noller & Ruzzene, 1991) and friends (Fleming, Darley, Hilton, & Kojetin, 1990; Stinson & Ickes, 1992) are generally better at decoding one another's nonverbal cues than are strangers. More specifically, Sternglanz and DePaulo (2004) compared the accuracy of friends and strangers at decoding nonverbal cues to emotion and found that, overall, friends were more accurate than strangers at decoding cues to emotion, and close friends were more accurate at decoding clearly expressed negative emotions. For some negative emotions in their study, however,

less close friends were more accurate than close friends, particularly if the senders had been asked to conceal the negative emotion (making the message more ambiguous). These researchers suggest that close friends may have more to lose than do less close friends if they perceive concealed negativity accurately. These friends may believe that if the negative message is ignored, the issue will go away.

Another relational feature is overall satisfaction, and it too may be related to sensitivity. In support of this suggestion, Noller (1984, 2001), using the standard-content paradigm (a research procedure that involves the use of ambiguous words to ensure that decoders are focusing on the nonverbal cues; see Noller, 2005a), found a relation between decoding accuracy and relationship satisfaction: Those who were happy in their marriages, and particularly husbands, were more accurate at decoding their spouses than those who were unhappy in their marriages. The study also showed that satisfied spouses were more accurate at decoding their spouses than they were at decoding strangers, whereas those who were unhappy with their marriages were more accurate at decoding strangers than they were at decoding their spouses. In addition, Noller and Ruzzene (1991) showed that happy couples were more accurate than unhappy couples at identifying the type of affect being experienced by their partners and were also better able to identify their partners' goals and intentions in an interaction.

In a later study involving newlyweds, and also using the standard-content paradigm, Noller and Feeney (1998) reported that nonverbal accuracy increased over time for all three message types: positive, neutral, and negative. This finding suggests that couples may become better at understanding each other's nonverbal behavior over time, although practice effects, while unlikely, cannot be ruled out (see Noller & Feeney, 1994, for more discussion of this issue). We also found that wife-to-husband communications were decoded more accurately than were husband-to-wife communications, particularly if the messages were positive. This finding is similar to that in the earlier study where the effect was a function of the more accurate encoding of positive messages by wives. Husbands' accuracy at decoding positive messages from their wives was associated with their current marital satisfaction, and husbands' earlier satisfaction predicted their later accuracy at decoding their wives' communications across all three types of messages. It seems likely that these husbands' decoding was more accurate because their ability was not affected by negative perceptions of the relationship with the partner.

MOTIVATED INACCURACY

Ickes and Simpson (1997, 2001) have proposed an empathic accuracy model that may help to explain some of the findings just discussed. They suggested that there are times when those in close relationships are actually motivated to be *inaccurate* in terms of their decoding of one another's nonverbal behavior. The authors argue that this motivated inaccuracy can be explained in terms of the threatening versus nonthreatening nature of the discussion in which the partners are engaged. They proposed a positive relation between accuracy and relationship satisfaction when the material being discussed is relatively nonthreatening and a negative relation when the discussion is contentious, conflicted, and threatening to the relationship.

Simpson, Ickes, and their colleagues have carried out several studies to test this model. For example, Simpson, Ickes, and Blackstone (1995) showed, in a sample of dating couples, that empathic accuracy was

affected negatively in relationships characterized by high levels of interdependence, high levels of insecurity, and consequent concerns about the vulnerability of the relationship. On the other hand, Simpson, Ickes, and Grich (1999) found that anxiously attached women became hypervigilant and hence *more* accurate when the relationship was under threat. This latter finding suggests that a complex model is needed to account for the role of cognitive biases in explaining decoding in close relationships.

Simpson, Orina, and Ickes (2003) tested their empathic accuracy model further in a sample of married couples and found support for their predictions. Feelings of closeness decreased for those who were more empathically accurate when their partners reported relationship-threatening thoughts and feelings, and feelings of closeness increased for those accurate decoders whose partners reported nonthreatening thoughts and feelings. Similar results were found when outsiders rated the level of threat contained in the partners' thoughts and feelings. There was also evidence in these data that an individual's own perception of relationship vulnerability, and not just his or her perception of the partner's sense of relationship vulnerability, affected the sense of closeness with the partner. As before, these findings fit with those of Sternglanz and DePaulo (2004), who found some evidence for motivated inaccuracy in the decoding of close friends.

BIAS IN DECODING

The decoding of nonverbal cues may be biased in various ways, particularly by cognitive processes that make individuals prone to distortions of perception in a negative direction. For example, although Noller (1984) did not find an expected bias related to marital satisfaction, the study did reveal a bias related to gender. Wives tended to make errors in a positive direction, decoding negative messages as neutral and neutral messages as positive, whereas husbands tended to make them in a negative direction, decoding positive messages as neutral and neutral messages as negative. Gaelick, Bodenhausen, and Wyer (1985) found a similar bias: Spouses reciprocated the emotion they thought their partner was expressing, but because they were less accurate at decoding partners' expressions of love, only hostility tended to be reciprocated.

Downey and Feldman (1996) have explored the construct of *rejection sensitivity* as leading to bias in the decoding of nonverbal behavior. They argued that rejection-sensitive individuals are prone, because of their heightened anxiety and sensitivity, to perceive ambiguous nonverbal cues as indications of dislike and rejection. Rejection sensitivity tends to be maladaptive for relationships (Downey, Freitas, Michaelis, & Khouri, 1998), because rejection-sensitive individuals tend to focus on any potential negativity in a message and ignore or fail to perceive positivity. Likewise, Pickett, Gardner, and Knowles (2004) argue that individuals who are chronically high in the need to belong are likely to be hypervigilant in scanning the social environment for indications of acceptance or rejection, especially if they are lonely or have experienced rejection continually (Gardner, Jefferis, Knowles, & Pickett, 2003; Gardner, Pickett & Brewer, 2000).

Need to belong and rejection sensitivity are likely to be related in terms of their effects on nonverbal decoding. Pickett et al. (2004) explored the association between the need to belong and accuracy in the identification of facial expression and vocal tone. They found that accuracy in identifying both facial expressions and vocal tone was positively correlated with scores on a measure of need to belong. The authors also reported that this relationship was maintained irrespective of the valence of the stimuli. In a more complex empathic accuracy task, these researchers were also able to show an effect of need to belong on individuals' sensitivity to the thoughts and feelings of another. Thus, those with a strong need to belong are likely to be highly sensitive to close others' nonverbal communication. In a study assessing the extent to which need to belong and rejection sensitivity could predict accuracy on the social perception task, known as The Diagnostic Analysis of Nonverbal Accuracy 2 (Nowicki & Duke, 1994), however, Pickett et al. (2004) found that accuracy was predicted by the need to belong, but it was *not* predicted by rejection sensitivity. They explain this difference in terms of the nature of the task, arguing that rejection sensitivity is likely to be more influential in a task involving ambiguous stimuli that could be interpreted as rejecting.

SUMMARY

Overall, decoding accuracy tends to be affected by the closeness of the relationship, although accuracy may be lower in very close relationships when communications are perceived as threatening the stability of the relationship. The quality of the relationship also influences decoding accuracy, at least in some studies. There is also evidence that decoding accuracy can be affected by gender and by such cognitive processes as rejection sensitivity and the need to belong. As shall be discussed in a later section of this chapter, decoding accuracy may also be affected by attachment insecurity.

◆ Nonverbal Expressiveness

Accurate expression of emotion (or intention, according to Fridlund, 1994; Fridlund

& Russell, this volume) is important in close relationships. Much of the time, each partner needs to know how the other is feeling so that those feelings can be taken into account in their attempts to solve problems and make decisions. It is also important for partners to let one another know when they are feeling sad or disappointed so that the appropriate level of social support can be provided. Nevertheless, individuals differ in their willingness to express their feelings, and this willingness can be affected by gender, by their ambivalence about the value of communicating feelings, by the type of relationship in which they are involved, and by the quality of their relationship.

Specifically, nonverbal behaviors are central to the expression of love in close relationships. A study by Gonzaga, Keltner, Londahl, and Smith (2001) indicated that behaviors, such as head nods, forward leans, and Duchenne (felt as opposed to contrived) smiles were central to the expression of love. In addition, nonverbal behaviors that create closeness, such as gaze, close distance, body orientation, touch, and smiling, are important in the nonverbal expression of love (Andersen, 1985). These behaviors (often termed *immediacy behaviors*) are seen as signaling warmth, communicating availability, decreasing distance, and promoting involvement in interactions (see Andersen, Guerrero, & Jones, this volume).

Because social support is important for relationship satisfaction (Coyne & Smith, 1994; Pasch & Bradbury, 1998), it often needs to be expressed clearly, as does the supportive response. As Neff and Karney (2005) have pointed out, the timing of such a response may be critical. These researchers found that husbands and wives provided equal proportions of supportive behaviors, but wives tended to provide the most support when the husbands' levels of stress were highest, whereas husbands provided the least support (in fact the most

negative behavior) when wives were most stressed. Neff and Karney argue, on the basis of these data, that husbands and wives are equally capable of providing support to their partners, but that wives seem able to provide that support *when it is most needed*. It may be that husbands do not recognize the cues indicating their wives' greater levels of stress or that they believe support will be more effective if offered in "calmer" moments. Alternatively, husbands more than wives may resent the expectation that they will support their wives at times of distress and become negative in response. A further possibility is that husbands, because of their greater emphasis on autonomy and independence, are less sympathetic to those who need to seek support (MacGeorge, 2003).

Willingness to express feelings depends, at least to some extent, on the individuals' "ambivalence about emotional expression" (King & Emmons, 1990, p. 864), which has been defined as experiencing a conflict between "the competing goals of wanting to show how one is feeling yet fearing the consequences of such self-expression" (Mongrain & Vettese, 2003, p. 545). Mongrain and Vettese found that women's self-reported ambivalence over the expression of emotion was related to their reports of suppressed anger toward their boyfriends. In other words, "ambivalent" women reported that they were not prepared to express the anger that they felt about the behavior of their boyfriends. In addition, when these highly ambivalent (about emotional expression) women were observed in a conflict resolution task, they were less congruent in their communication (i.e., there was a mismatch between their verbal and nonverbal channels). Furthermore, when mood and personality constructs were controlled for, they displayed more overt submissiveness toward their boyfriends than did women who were low in ambivalence. These findings suggest that women are likely to tolerate bad behavior from their boyfriends and even be submissive toward them in such circumstances. The chances of these couples having healthy, egalitarian, and respectful relationships seem bleak.

Guerrero (1997) explored whether *type* of relationship affects encoding. She explored nonverbal behavior using a partial round-robin design, so that an individual's behavior could be compared across relationships: with a same-sex friend, an opposite-sex friend, and a romantic partner. She found that romantic relationships could be distinguished from other types of relationships by the closer proximity and higher levels of touch and gaze in those relationships. In addition, there were more silences, longer response latencies, and less fluency in romantic relationships. Nodding and vocal interest were more common in friendships than in romantic relationships, and there was more evidence of postural congruence in same-sex than in opposite-sex dyads.

Particular patterns of nonverbal expression are also linked to relationship quality or satisfaction. Unhappy couples display more negative nonverbal behaviors and less positive emotion than more satisfied couples (Burgoon, Buller, & Woodall, 1996). Specifically, Gottman (1994) has argued that happy couples tend to display five positive behaviors for every negative behavior, whereas unhappy couples have a much lower ratio of positive to negative behaviors and may even display more negative behaviors than positive. Thus, if we think of this issue in terms of a bank account model, these couples would not have any positive resources to draw on in terms of expressing their feelings about their relationships.

In recent years, there has been an increased interest in comparing married couples with different histories of cohabitation. In one study, Kline et al. (2004) assessed the association between the timing of cohabitation and couple interaction before and after marriage. Using self-reports

of negative danger signs, such as invalidation, escalation, and withdrawal, these researchers found that those who cohabited before engagement reported more danger signs both before and after marriage than did those who cohabited only after engagement or marriage.

Cohan and Kleinbaum (2002) proposed that cohabiters treat each other less positively than other couples and that this tendency to less positive behavior carries over into the marriage and may contribute to the higher divorce rate among those who cohabit before marriage (see, also, Heaton, 2002; Kieran, 2002). In the study by Kline et al. (2004), those who had cohabited before their engagement were coded as more negative than those who cohabited only after engagement or after marriage. Those who cohabited before marriage were also coded as less positive than those who cohabited only after marriage, and those who cohabited after engagement were also coded as less positive than those who cohabited after marriage. These differences in the positivity of communication were found *before* marriage and were also in evidence *after* the marriage. These findings also fit with those of Cohan and Kleinbaum (2002): that married couples who had cohabited before marriage tended to treat each other less positively than those who had not.

Other research has explored the associations between emotional expression and marital satisfaction in couples. Waldinger, Schulz, Hauser, Allen, and Crowell (2004), for example, used naive coders' observational data based on conflict interactions to assess four factors of emotional expression: hostility, empathy, affection, and distress. The researchers found that men who were part of satisfied couples expressed more empathy and personal distress, such as sadness and anxiety, less hostility, and marginally more affection than did less satisfied men. Women in satisfied couples expressed greater empathy in their marital interactions, and marginally more affection, than did less satisfied women. These results were similar whether the marriage qualities were assessed using spouse self-report or an interview-based assessment. The researchers also explored the association between emotional expression and relationship dissolution (within 5 years). Using the four emotion scales scores in a logistic regression, the researchers were able to identify correctly 85% of those whose relationships had remained intact, and overall relationship status at follow-up was predicted with 83% accuracy using the women's emotional expression and 81% accuracy using the men's emotional expression.

The encoding of nonverbal behavior also involves the expression of both power and intimacy. Burgoon and Dillman (1995), for example, have argued that knowing who wields power and how that power is expressed through nonverbal communication is central to understanding the dynamics of any relationship (see also Burgoon & Dunbar, this volume). Nonverbal behaviors, such as touch, gaze, body movements, and spacing, can be used to express power and control (Edinger & Patterson, 1983; Guerrero, Andersen, & Afifi, 2001). A study comparing violent couples with distressed nonviolent and nondistressed nonviolent couples found that distressed couples engaged in lower levels of mutual gaze than did other couples, although the violent couples seemed to be maintaining gaze with different affect (e.g., the angry stare; Gottman, Driver, Yashimoto, & Rushe, 2002). Violent couples also rated their interaction less positively than did either of the nonviolent groups.

One behavior generally seen as problematic in couple relationships is withdrawal from conflict. Because the likely consequences of withdrawal from conflict are that issues are not resolved and resentment may increase, withdrawal is generally seen as having a negative impact on relationships.

Holtzworth-Munroe, Smutzler, and Stuart (1998) have also suggested that withdrawal can lead to ongoing power struggles and "a pattern of coercive efforts can gradually develop, creating a rigid pattern of negative polarized interaction" (p. 72) (see also Gottman et al., 2002).

Researchers have pointed to a gendered pattern in the use of withdrawal in marriage, particularly with regard to the demand-withdraw pattern of conflict interaction. Females are more likely to be in the role of demander and males in the role of withdrawer, although whose issue is being discussed is also important (Christensen & Heavey, 1990). For example, Noller, Feeney, Roberts, and Christensen (2005) reported an observational study of the nonverbal concomitants of withdrawal in married couples engaged in conflict interactions. They were interested in whether the nonverbal behavior related to withdrawal would be affected by gender and whose issue was being discussed. They found that the clearest pattern of nonverbal behavior related to withdrawal was for husbands during discussion of their wives' issues. Husbands' withdrawal was indicated by a lack of gaze and open gestures and by head down and head turn. These behaviors may reflect avoidance and a lack of immediacy, with husbands seeming to avoid any eye contact with their wives. Wives' withdrawal was indicated by a lack of open or neutral gestures and head down. Interestingly, and as would be expected, highly satisfied spouses tended to be more open and less withdrawn in their conflict interactions with partners than did spouses low in satisfaction.

SUMMARY

Overall, nonverbal communication is important for the expression of love, for the expression of support, and to indicate the need for support. Individuals differ in their willingness to express their feelings, with women often not prepared to express their anger in romantic relationships. Gender also affects the extent to which individuals are able to express support to their partners and express that support when it is needed most. In addition, researchers have found a pattern of men's nonverbal withdrawal when issues raised by their wives are being discussed. There is also evidence of effects related to the type and quality of relationships including the following: (1) negativity is particularly marked in low-quality relationships, (2) empathy and lack of hostility are especially noticeable in high-quality relationships, and (3) nonverbal behaviors indicating withdrawal are less evident in the conflict interactions of satisfied couples.

◆ Nonverbal Behavior and Courtship

The research on decoding and encoding just reviewed has centered largely on ongoing relationships, such as marriage and friendship. In addition to nonverbal cues in established relationships, courtship, or the potential *establishment* of romantic relationships, is also an area where nonverbal behavior is critical. Expressions of interest in specific members of the opposite sex are often nonverbal (Renninger, Wade, & Grammer, 2004). In addition, although males tend to be seen as the initiators of courtship, they may seek nonverbal signs that females are interested before making any approaches (Grammer, Kruck, Juette, & Fink, 2000). Because nonverbal signals of interest are likely to be somewhat ambiguous, there is a strong possibility that misunderstandings can occur, both in terms of the level of interest expressed and in terms of the desired level of involvement. Misunderstandings about the levels of

involvement desired are particularly likely to be problematic, especially if the female is signaling interest in "getting to know you," and the male decodes that message as interest in sexual activity.

Studies of nonverbal courtship behavior, however, have generally failed to find a specific list of behaviors that could be considered as signs of interest in pursuing a relationship. Moore (1985), for example, catalogued 52 behaviors that occurred in a singles bar; however, because of the large amount of variability between participants, he was unable to identify specific behaviors that could be classified as courtship behaviors. Grammer, Honda, Juette, and Schmitt (1999), in their study of initial interactions between opposite-sex strangers in two cultures (Germany and Japan), were unable to identify behaviors that could be consistently classified as courtship behaviors. They did find, however, that when female interest was high, mutual gaze was initiated and partners made a similar number of comments. They also found that women were more nonverbally involved and open in their interactions than were men during initial conversations. Argyle (1988) also identified a number of courtship behaviors including high levels of mutual gaze, touch, movement, smiling, erect and open posture, and proximity.

Differences between males and females have been found, at least within heterosexual courtship displays. Analysis of courtship interactions by Grammer et al. (2000), for example, showed that unless males received nonverbal indicators of interest, such as eye contact, they were less likely to approach females. But females may rely on males' signals in deciding whether to encourage the approach of a male. In support of this, Renninger et al. (2004) observed the nonverbal behaviors of males in a bar and found that those who made contact with females successfully tended to engage in more glancing behaviors, more space-maximization movements (generally seen as signs of dominance), more intrasexual touching (generally seen as indicating social power), and fewer closed body movements (suggesting that they are more interpersonally oriented). Renninger et al. note that, commonly, females need to show enough interest to elicit courtship behavior from males, whereas males need to display such qualities as their status, health, and strength to attract female attention.

Henningsen (2004) focused his attention on the decoding of flirting behaviors, or behaviors that indicate interest in a cross-sex target and are likely to promote contact with that target. These behaviors are typically nonverbal. He found that men attributed different motivations to flirting behaviors than did women, with men tending to interpret flirting behaviors as indicating sexual interest to a greater extent than did women. Abbey (1982) discovered likewise that males tended to see the same nonverbal cues as more "seductive" that female observers rated as "friendly." Whereas there is evidence that flirting is often associated with a desire for sexual contact (Greer & Buss, 1994; Simpson, Gangestad, & Biek, 1993), there is also evidence that not all flirting is motivated by sexual desire or interest (Guerrero et al., 2001). These findings suggest that there is considerable room for miscommunication between the sexes because males are likely to believe that women who flirt are more interested in sexual contact than they may actually be.

◆ *Attachment and Nonverbal Communication*

Several different theoretical perspectives have been used to explain the role of communication in developing and sustaining relationships. For instance, Tucker and Anders (1998) discuss the possibility of

problematic communication in couples where at least one partner is insecure in attachment. They claim that

> it is possible that the feelings of discomfort or ambivalence over closeness that are experienced by insecure individuals, coupled with the negative affect they feel within the relationship, are communicated to their partners through nonverbal behaviors. The communication of these feelings, in turn, should be associated with lower relationship satisfaction for both partners. (p. 112)

Attachment security or insecurity can be seen as working like a filter in the communication process, blocking sensitivity to certain nonverbal messages and also discouraging the expression of particular nonverbal signals (Noller, 2005b). In other words, both the encoding and the decoding of those who are insecure in attachment are likely to be affected by their working models of attachment. Those categorized as anxious in terms of attachment, for example, are likely to have problems decoding positive messages from a close other because of their negative views of themselves (Bartholomew, 1990) and to have difficulty decoding negative messages, as such messages would serve to increase their already potent fears about being rejected.

As Mikulincer and Shaver (2003) have suggested, anxious individuals' tendency to focus on their own needs and vulnerabilities and to be concerned excessively about rejection may make it difficult for them to be sensitive to their partner's nonverbal signals and to respond appropriately. Because of their tendency to distrust the good will of relational partners and to strive to maintain independence and emotional distance from them, those high in avoidance are also likely to be impaired in terms of their nonverbal sensitivity. As Schachner, Shaver, and

Mikulnicer (2005) note, anxious individuals are likely to have difficulty decoding negative messages that arouse unwanted attachment needs and positive messages that promote intimacy and closeness.

In studying the association between attachment security and the decoding of nonverbal messages by young married couples (Noller & Feeney, 1994), my colleague and I found that decoding accuracy was affected by both gender and attachment security. Husbands' attachment anxiety was associated with low levels of accuracy in decoding wives' messages, irrespective of whether the messages were positive, neutral, or negative, suggesting a general decoding deficit related to anxiety. For wives, however, anxiety did not affect decoding of husbands' messages, but avoidance was associated with low levels of accuracy in decoding neutral and negative messages only. Thus, highly anxious husbands were less accurate decoders overall, and wives who were high in comfort with closeness tended to be more accurate for neutral and negative messages. Also, attachment security after a year of marriage predicted decoding accuracy after almost 2 years, following the same pattern as reported above for husbands and wives.

Attachment security or insecurity is also likely to influence people's willingness to express their feelings to a partner. The behaviors most likely to be affected are those related to expressing discomfort and distress and to seeking support and comfort. Moreover, because of problems with decoding, people may assume incorrectly that their partner does not care about their distress. Thus, "insecures" (i.e., people categorized as having an insecure form of attachment) may struggle in their close relationships, not because their partner does not care about their distress, but because the filter of their attachment insecurity distorts their perception in such a way that it is difficult for them to believe that their partner cares. A similar filter can make it difficult for individuals to express their feelings. Specifically, "avoidant" individuals were less expressive in interactions with their partners (Fraley & Shaver, 2000; Guerrero, 1996; Le Poire, Sheppard, & Duggan, 1999; Tucker & Anders, 1998), perhaps because of their lack of trust in others. Alternatively, expressivity may be perceived as involving the type of intimacy likely to threaten their autonomy and independence.

Tucker and Anders also assessed the encoding of nonverbal behavior in dating couples and related expressions of nonverbal closeness to attachment style. They found that individuals with a secure attachment style were rated as less tense, as more nonverbally expressive, and as seeming to enjoy the conversation more than other individuals. Their interactions with their partners tended to involve more laughing, touching, gazing, and smiling than was true for insecure individuals. In contrast, the interactions of "preoccupied" individuals were rated as less nonverbally expressive, and these individuals were rated as experiencing less enjoyment of the conversation. Both avoidants and preoccupieds tended to smile and gaze less than secures. It is interesting to note, however, that preoccupieds were *not* seen as engaging in more clingy behaviors, as may have been expected.

Noller et al. (2005) report a study of attachment and emotional reactions in a partner-distant interaction (where a partner or a confederate was asked to act distant with his or her partner). For females, comfort with closeness was related to low levels of negative affect (both hostile and worried affects), and anxiety over abandonment was related to high levels of avoidance (turning the head or body away from the partner or resisting contact) and low levels of touch (hugging, hand holding, etc.). For males, comfort with closeness predicted high levels of touch and low levels of avoidance, and anxiety over abandonment was unrelated to nonverbal behavior. Highly anxious males did, however, engage in negative verbal behavior in response to their partner's distancing.

Overall, attachment security seems to act as a filter and affect both the encoding and the decoding of nonverbal behavior in close relationships. Highly anxious individuals, especially males, seem to have a general decoding deficit, to be less nonverbally expressive than other partners, and to engage in more avoidance. Thus, highly anxious individuals are likely to have difficulty in maintaining close relationships. But it is important to keep in mind that attachment theory is not the only theory relevant to nonverbal behavior in close relationships. Attributions for nonverbal behavior are also important, particularly for understanding where communication differences may arise.

◆ Attributions for Nonverbal Behavior

Attributions are the explanations we construct to explain our own and others' behavior. Because of the ambiguity of nonverbal cues noted earlier, it is particularly important in the context of close relationships to understand the attributions that those in intimate relationships make for one another's nonverbal behavior (Abbey, 1982; Manusov, Floyd, & Kerssen-Griep, 1997). In support of this proposition, Solomon (2001) notes that the interplay among affect, attributions, and communication is particularly important in the context of close relationships. In this section, I will focus on Manusov's work, which has explored (1) the kinds of attributions partners in romantic relationships make for partners' nonverbal behaviors and (2) the effect of the attribution on the attributors' own nonverbal response.

Manusov (1990) laid out a set of principles detailing the ways in which attribution theories applied to the meanings people give to nonverbal cues. Following work by other relational scholars who used attribution theories to predict couples' sense-making for other behaviors such as conflict (e.g., Fincham & Bradbury, 1992), she argued that couples make attributions to explain why the partner acted as he or she did (i.e., sat closer, sighed, avoided eye contact). Furthermore, these attributions are linked to marital satisfaction, such that more satisfied couples interpret the same behaviors differently than less satisfied couples.

In a follow-up study, Manusov et al. (1997) again looked to see if those in satisfying relationships make more "spouse-enhancing attributions" and those in unhappy relationships make more "distress-maintaining attributions," as tends to occur for other marital events (Fincham, Beach, & Baucom, 1987; Fincham & Bradbury, 1992). Spouse-enhancing attributions tend to involve internal and stable attributions for positive behaviors and external and unstable attributions for negative behavior. Distress-maintaining attributions, on the other hand, tend to involve external and unstable attributions for positive behavior and internal and stable attributions for negative behavior.

As with previous research, Manusov et al. (1997) found that, in general, couples were more likely to notice (and hence report) negative behavior than positive behavior, although relationship satisfaction tended to increase the likelihood of noticing positive behavior, particularly for males. In addition, those in satisfying relationships were more likely to adopt a spouse-enhancing attribution pattern by attributing similar causes to their own and their spouse's behavior. In contrast, those who were more dissatisfied were more likely to attribute negative causes to their spouse's behavior than to their own behavior. In spite of this tendency, however, all couples reported more benign attributions for their own behavior than their partner gave for the same behavior. Overall relationship satisfaction was not as clearly tied to relationship-enhancing and distress-maintaining attributions as has been the case in previous research. Perhaps, the inherent ambiguity of many nonverbal behaviors is again relevant here.

Looking beyond attributions, Manusov (2002) focused on the effect of one member's attributions for the partner's behavior *on his or her responses to that behavior*. In other words, what was the association between individuals' attributions for their partner's behavior and their own nonverbal behavior? She found a positive association between attributions that were relationship enhancing and a response involving positive facial and vocal behavior. The pattern for distress-maintaining attributions was not as clear, but there was still evidence of an association between distress-maintaining attributions for partner behavior and the negativity of one's own nonverbal behavior, behavior indicative of personal discomfort. Apparently, then, relationship satisfaction affects the attributions made for a partner's nonverbal behavior, with those in satisfying relationships more likely to adopt a spouse-enhancing attribution pattern. Attributions influence the decoding of nonverbal behavior, with a spouse-enhancing attribution pattern increasing the likelihood that partners would respond positively to the partner's behavior.

◆ Conclusion

As noted at the outset of this chapter, it is important to keep in mind the essential ambiguity of nonverbal behavior, making it prone to misinterpretation within close relationships. This ambiguity may be particularly critical in courtship situations where a female's interest in getting to know a male may be misinterpreted as an indication of interest in sexual activity. Although researchers have been unsuccessful in their attempts to find a specific list of behaviors related to the early stages of courtship, there is evidence that both males and females rely on nonverbal behavior in deciding whether to approach and whether to encourage approach. Because nonverbal behavior can be ambiguous, however, accuracy in decoding and clarity in encoding are particularly important in developing close relationships.

The quality of the relationship affects decoding consistently, with those in satisfying relationships generally more accurate than those in unhappy relationships, and those in unhappy relationships even less accurate at decoding their partners' messages than they are at decoding the messages of strangers. There is also evidence that couples become more accurate at decoding one another's messages over time. Decoding sensitivity can be affected by the closeness of the relationship, with those in very close relationships likely to ignore negativity in partners' communications, particularly if the negativity is concealed. This unwillingness to process negative messages has been termed *motivated inaccuracy* and is an issue particularly where the content of messages is seen as threatening and therefore best ignored. Other biases in decoding are related to gender, rejection sensitivity, need to belong, and attachment insecurity.

An important aspect of understanding decoding sensitivity is exploring the attributions couples make for their partner's nonverbal behavior. These attributions can be either more spouse enhancing or more distress maintaining. Spouse-enhancing attributions tend to be made by those in satisfying relationships, whereas distress-maintaining attributions tend to be made by those in distressed relationships.

Moreover, there appear to be "self-spouse" differences in the ways attributions are made. All these differences point toward the complexity of meaning for nonverbal cues in relationships.

Nonverbal behaviors are, however, important to the expression of love and of social support in relationships (Trees, 2000). Yet individuals differ in their willingness to express their feelings, with gender, ambivalence about the value of communicating feelings, and the type and quality of the relationship in which they are involved all affecting willingness to express feelings. For example, there is an interesting contrast in the circumstances of husbands and wives expressing support. Wives express the most support when husbands are experiencing the most stress, whereas husbands provide the least support when wives are experiencing the most stress.

Satisfaction and nonverbal cues also seem to be linked in important ways. Unhappy couples tend to display more negative and less positive nonverbal behavior. Those who have cohabited before marriage tend to be more negative than other couples, particularly if they have cohabited before engagement. In addition, men in satisfying relationships express more empathy and personal distress, and less hostility, than those in less satisfying relationships. There is also evidence that emotional expression is a good predictor of relationship stability. High-satisfaction spouses tend to be more open and less withdrawn in their conflict interactions. A clear pattern of withdrawal is reflected in avoidance and a lack of immediacy by husbands during discussion of issues raised by their wives.

Attachment insecurity also affects both the encoding and the decoding of nonverbal behavior, blocking sensitivity to certain nonverbal messages and discouraging the expression of particular nonverbal signals. Insecure individuals may have difficulty interpreting positive messages because of their negative views of themselves, and difficulty decoding negative messages because these messages arouse unwanted attachment needs. Secure individuals, on the other hand, are likely to be more nonverbally expressive and more comfortable in interaction situations.

Whereas there is no doubt that all communication is critical to the development and maintenance of relationships, it seems that nonverbal cues, because of their modifying effect on words and the overall interpretation of the message and its tie to affect, may be the more important "side" of that communication. Those who seek to help couples communicate more constructively need to ensure that they focus on what is happening in the nonverbal channels; helping individuals to understand the rather trite saying, "It's not what you say but the way that you say it," may have the strongest impact in—and the most important consequences for—a close relationship.

◆ References

Abbey, A. (1982). Sex differences in attributions for friendly behavior: Do males misperceive females' friendliness? *Journal of Personality and Social Psychology, 42*, 830–838.

Andersen, P. A. (1985). Nonverbal immediacy in interpersonal communication. In A. W. Siegman & S. Feldstein (Eds.), *Multichannel integrations of nonverbal behavior* (pp. 1–36). Hillsdale, NJ: Erlbaum.

Argyle, M. (1988). *Bodily communication* (2nd ed.). London: Methuen.

Bartholomew, K. (1990). Avoidance of intimacy: An attachment perspective. *Journal of Social and Personal Relationships, 7*, 147–178.

Burgoon, J. K., Buller, D. B., & Woodall, W. G. (1996). *Nonverbal communication: The unspoken dialogue* (2nd ed.). New York: McGraw-Hill.

Burgoon, J. K., & Dillman, L. (1995). Gender, immediacy, and nonverbal communication. In P. J. Kalbfleisch & M. J. Cody (Eds.), *Gender, power and communication in human relationships* (pp. 63–81). Hillsdale, NJ: Erlbaum.

Christensen, A., & Heavey, C. L. (1990). Gender and social structure in the demand/withdraw pattern of marital conflict. *Journal of Personality and Social Psychology, 59,* 73–81.

Cohan, C., & Kleinbaum, S. (2002). Toward a greater understanding of the cohabitation effect: Premarital cohabitation and subsequent marital stability. *Journal of Marriage and the Family, 64,* 180–192.

Coyne, J. C., & Smith, D. A. F. (1994). Couples coping with a myocardial infarction: Contextual perspective on patient self-efficacy. *Journal of Family Psychology, 8,* 43–54.

Downey, G., & Feldman, S. (1996). Implications of rejection sensitivity for intimate relationships. *Journal of Personality and Social Psychology, 70,* 1327–1343.

Downey, G., Freitas, A. L., Michaelis, B., & Khouri, H. (1998). The self-fulfilling prophecy in close relationships: Do rejection-sensitive women get rejected by romantic partners? *Journal of Personality and Social Psychology, 75,* 545–560.

Edinger, J. A., & Patterson, M. L. (1983). Nonverbal involvement and social control. *Psychological Bulletin, 93,* 30–56.

Fincham, F. D., Beach, S. R. H., & Baucom, D. H. (1987). Attribution processing in distressed and nondistressed couples: 4. Self-partner attribution differences. *Journal of Personality and Social Psychology, 52,* 739–748.

Fincham, F. D., & Bradbury, T. N. (1992). Assessing attributions in marriage: The relationship attribution measure. *Journal of Personality and Social Psychology, 62,* 457–468.

Fleming, J. H., Darley, J. M., Hilton, J. L., & Kojetin, B. A. (1990). Multiple audience problem: A strategic communication perception on social perception. *Journal of Personality and Social Psychology, 58,* 593–609.

Fraley, R. C., & Shaver, P. R. (2000). Adult romantic attachment: Theoretical developments, emerging controversies, and unanswered questions. *Review of General Psychology, 4,* 132–154.

Fridlund, A. J. (1994). *Human facial expression: An evolutionary view.* San Diego, CA: Academic Press.

Friedman, H. S. (2001). Paradoxes of nonverbal detection, expression and responding: Points to ponder. In J. A. Hall & F. J. Bernieri (Eds.), *Interpersonal sensitivity: Theory and measurement* (pp. 351–362). Mahwah, NJ: Erlbaum.

Gaelick, L., Bodenhausen, G. V., & Wyer, R. (1985). Emotional communication in close relationships. *Journal of Personality and Social Psychology, 49,* 1246–1265.

Gardner, W. L., Jefferis, V., Knowles, M. L., & Pickett, C. L. (2003). *Loneliness and selective memory: A general bias for remembering social events.* Unpublished manuscript.

Gardner, W. L., Pickett, C. L., & Brewer, M. B. (2000). Social exclusion and selective memory: How the need to belong influences memory for social events. *Personality and Social Psychology Bulletin, 26,* 486–496.

Gonzaga, G. C., Keltner, D., Londahl, E. A., & Smith, M. D. (2001). Love and the commitment problems in romantic relations and friendship. *Journal of Personality and Social Psychology, 81,* 247–262.

Gottman, J. M. (1994). *What predicts divorce: The relationship between marital processes and marital outcomes.* Hillsdale, NJ: Erlbaum.

Gottman, J. M., Driver, J., Yoshimoto, D., & Rushe, R. (2002). Approaches to the study of power in violent and nonviolent marriages, and in gay male and lesbian cohabiting relationships. In P. Noller & J. A. Feeney (Eds.), *Understanding marriage: Developments in the study of couple interaction* (pp. 323–347). New York: Cambridge University Press.

Gottman, J. M., Markman, H. J., & Notarius, C. I. (1977). The topography of marital conflict: A sequential analysis of verbal and nonverbal behavior. *Journal of Marriage and the Family, 39,* 461–477.

Grammer, K., Honda, M., Juette, A., & Schmitt, A. (1999). Fuzziness of nonverbal courtship communication unblurred by motion energy detection. *Journal of Personality and Social Psychology, 77,* 487–508.

Grammer, K., Kruck, K., Juette, A., & Fink, B. (2000). Nonverbal behavior as courtship signals: The role of control and choice in selecting partners. *Evolution and Human Behavior, 21,* 371–390.

Greer, A. E., & Buss, D. M. (1994). Tactics for promoting sexual encounters. *Journal of Sex Research, 31,* 185–201.

Guerrero, L. K. (1996). Attachment-style differences in intimacy and involvement: A test of the four-category model. *Communication Monographs, 63,* 269–292.

Guerrero, L. K. (1997). Nonverbal involvement across interactions with same-sex friends, opposite-sex friends and romantic partners: Consistency or change? *Journal of Social and Personal Relationships, 14,* 31–58.

Guerrero, L. K., Andersen, P. A., & Afifi, W. A. (2001). *Close encounters: Communicating in relationships.* Mountain View, CA: Mayfield.

Heaton, T. B. (2002). Factors contributing to increasing marital stability in the U. S. *Journal of Family Issues, 23,* 392–409.

Henningsen, D. D. (2004). Flirting with meaning: An examination of miscommunication in flirting interactions. *Sex Roles, 50,* 481–489.

Holtzworth-Munroe, A., Smutzler, N., & Stuart, G. L. (1998). Demand and withdraw communication among couples experiencing husband violence. *Journal of Consulting and Clinical Psychology, 66,* 731–743.

Ickes, W., & Simpson, J. A. (1997). Managing empathic accuracy in close relationships. In W. Ickes (Ed.), *Empathic accuracy* (pp. 218–250). New York: Guilford Press.

Ickes, W., & Simpson, J. A. (2001). Motivational aspects of empathic accuracy. In G. J. O. Fletcher & M. Clark (Eds.), *The Blackwell handbook of social psychology: Interpersonal processes* (pp. 229–249). Oxford, UK: Blackwell.

Kieran, K. (2002). Cohabitation in Western Europe: Trends, issues and implications. In A. Booth & A. Crouter (Eds.), *Just living together: Implications of cohabitation for families, children and social policy* (pp. 3–32). Mahwah, NJ: Erlbaum.

King, L. A., & Emmons, R. A. (1990). Conflict over emotional expression: Psychological and physical correlates. *Journal of Personality and Social Psychology, 58,* 864–877.

Kline, G. H., Stanley, S. M., Markman, H. J., Olmos-Gallo, P. A., St Peters, M., Whitton, S. W., et al. (2004). Timing is everything: Pre-engagement cohabitation and increased risk for poor marital outcomes. *Journal of Family Psychology, 18,* 311–318.

Le Poire, B. A., Sheppard, C., & Duggan, A. (1999). Nonverbal involvement, expressiveness, and pleasantness as predicted by parental and partner attachment style. *Communication Monographs, 66,* 293–311.

Losoya, S. H., & Eisenberg, N. (2001). Affective empathy. In J. A. Hall & F. J. Bernieri (Eds.), *Interpersonal sensitivity: Theory and measurement* (pp. 21–43). Mahwah, NJ: Erlbaum.

MacGeorge, E. L. (2003). Gender differences in attributions and emotions in helping contexts. *Sex Roles, 48,* 175–182.

Manusov, V. (1990). An application of attribution principles to nonverbal behavior in romantic dyads. *Communication Monographs, 57,* 104–118.

Manusov, V. (2002). Thought and action: Connecting attributions to behaviors in married couples' interactions. In P. Noller & J. A. Feeney (Eds.), *Understanding marriage: Developments in the study of marital interaction* (pp. 14–31). New York: Cambridge University Press.

Manusov, V., Floyd, K., & Kerssen-Griep, J. (1997). Yours, mine, and ours: Mutual attributions for nonverbal behavior in couples' interactions. *Communication Research, 24,* 234–260.

Mikulincer, M., & Shaver, P. R. (2003). The attachment behavioral system in adulthood: Activation, psychodynamics, and interpersonal processes. In M. P. Zanna (Ed.), *Advances in experimental social psychology* (Vol. 35). New York: Academic Press.

Miller, P. A., Eisenberg, N., Fabes, R. A., & Shell, R. (1996). Relations of moral reasoning and vicarious emotion to young children's prosocial behavior towards peers and adults. *Developmental Psychology, 32*, 210–219.

Mongrain, M., & Vettese, L. C. (2003). Conflict over emotional expression: Implications for interpersonal communication. *Personality and Social Psychology Bulletin, 29*, 545–555.

Moore, M. (1985). Nonverbal courtship patterns in women: Context and consequences. *Ethology and Sociobiology, 6*, 237–247.

Neff, L. A., & Karney, B. R. (2005). Gender differences in social support: A question of skill or responsiveness. *Journal of Personality and Social Psychology, 88*, 79–90.

Noller, P. (1984). *Nonverbal communication and marital interaction.* Oxford, UK: Pergamon.

Noller, P. (1995). Parent-adolescent relationships. In M. A. Fitzpatrick & A. L. Vangelisti (Eds.), *Explaining family interactions* (pp. 77–111). Thousand Oaks, CA: Sage.

Noller, P. (2001). Using standard content methodology to assess nonverbal sensitivity in dyads. In J. A. Hall & F. J. Bernieri (Eds.), *Interpersonal sensitivity: Theory and measurement* (pp. 243–264). Mahwah, NJ: Erlbaum.

Noller, P. (2005a). Standard content methodology: Controlling the verbal channel. In V. Manusov (Ed.), *The sourcebook of nonverbal measures: Going beyond words* (pp. 417–430). Mahwah, NJ: Erlbaum.

Noller, P. (2005b). Attachment insecurity as a filter in the encoding and decoding of nonverbal behavior in close relationships. *Journal of Nonverbal Behavior, 29*, 171–176.

Noller, P., & Feeney, J. A. (1994). Relationship satisfaction, attachment, and nonverbal accuracy in early marriage. *Journal of Nonverbal Behavior, 18*, 199–221.

Noller, P., & Feeney, J. A. (1998). Communication in early marriage: Responses to conflict, nonverbal accuracy and conversational patterns. In T. N. Bradbury (Ed.), *The developmental course of marital dysfunc-tion* (pp. 11–43). New York: Cambridge University Press.

Noller, P., Feeney, J. A., Roberts, N., & Christensen, A. (2005). Withdrawal in couple interactions: Exploring the causes and consequences. In R. E. Riggio & R. S. Feldman (Eds.), *Applications of nonverbal communication* (pp. 195–213). Mahwah, NJ: Erlbaum.

Noller, P., & Ruzzene, M. (1991). Communication in marriage: The influence of affect and cognition. In G. J. O. Fletcher & F. D. Fincham (Eds.), *Cognition in close relationships* (pp. 203–233). Hillsdale, NJ: Erlbaum.

Nowicki, S., & Duke, M. P. (1994). Individual differences in the nonverbal communication of affect: The Diagnostic Analysis of Nonverbal Accuracy scale. *Journal of Nonverbal Behavior, 18*, 9–35.

Nowicki, S., & Duke, M. P. (2001). Nonverbal receptivity: The Diagnostic Analysis of Nonverbal Accuracy (DANVA). In J. A. Hall & F. J. Bernieri (Eds.), *Interpersonal sensitivity: Theory and measurement* (pp. 183–198). Mahwah, NJ: Erlbaum.

Pasch, L. A, & Bradbury, T. N. (1998). Social support, conflict, and the development of marital dysfunction. *Journal of Consulting and Clinical Psychology, 66*, 219–230.

Pickett, C. L., Gardner, W. L., & Knowles, M. (2004). Getting a cue: The need to belong and enhanced sensitivity to social cues. *Personality and Social Psychology Bulletin, 30*, 1095–1107.

Renninger, L. A., Wade, J. T., & Grammer, K. (2004). Getting that female glance: Patterns and consequences of male nonverbal behavior in courtship contexts. *Evolution and Human Behavior, 25*, 416–431.

Schachner, D. A., Shaver, P. R., & Mikulincer, M. (2005). Patterns of nonverbal behavior and sensitivity in the context of attachment relationships. *Journal of Nonverbal Behavior, 29*, 141–169.

Simpson, J. A., Gangestad, S. W., & Biek, M. (1993). Personality and nonverbal social behavior: An ethological perspective of relationship initiation. *Journal of Experimental Social Psychology, 29*, 434–461.

Simpson, J. A., Ickes, W., & Blackstone, T. (1995). When the head protects the heart: Empathic accuracy in dating relationships. *Journal of Personality and Social Psychology, 69,* 629–641.

Simpson, J. A., Ickes, W., & Grich, J. (1999). When accuracy hurts: Reactions of anxious, uncertain individuals to a relationship-threatening situation. *Journal of Personality and Social Psychology, 76,* 754–769.

Simpson, J. A., Orina, M. M., & Ickes, W. (2003). When accuracy hurts, and when it helps: A test of the empathic accuracy model in marital interactions. *Journal of Personality and Social Psychology, 85,* 881–893.

Solomon, D. H. (2001). Affect, attribution, and communication: Uniting interaction episodes and global relationship judgments. In V. Manusov & J. H. Harvey (Eds.), *Attribution, communication behavior, and close relationships* (pp. 79–90). Cambridge, UK: Cambridge University Press.

Sternglanz, R. W., & DePaulo, B. M. (2004). Reading nonverbal cues to emotions: The advantages and liabilities of relationship closeness. *Journal of Nonverbal Behavior, 28,* 245–266.

Stinson, L., & Ickes, W. (1992). Empathic accuracy in the interactions of male friends versus male strangers. *Journal of Personality and Social Psychology, 62,* 787–797.

Trees, A. R. (2000). Nonverbal communication and the support process: Interactional sensitivity in interactions between mothers and young adult children. *Communication Monographs, 67,* 239–261.

Tucker, J. S., & Anders, S. L. (1998). Adult attachment style and nonverbal closeness in dating couples. *Journal of Nonverbal Behavior, 22,* 109–124.

Waldinger, R. J., Schulz, M. S., Hauser, S. T., Allen, J. P., & Crowell, J. A. (2004). Reading others' emotions: The role of intuitive judgments in predicting marital satisfaction, quality and stability. *Journal of Family Psychology, 18,* 58–71.

Wood, J. T. (1995). *Relational communication: Continuity and change in personal relationships.* Belmont, CA: Wadsworth.

Zahn-Waxler, C., Radke-Yarrow, M., Wagner, E., & Chapman, M. (1992). Development of concern for others. *Developmental Psychology, 28,* 126–136.

Zahn-Waxler, C., Robinson, J., & Emde, R. N. (1992). The development of empathy in twins. *Developmental Psychology, 28,* 1038–1047.

Zebrowitz, L. A. (2001). Groping for the elephant of nonverbal sensitivity. In J. A. Hall & F. J. Bernieri (Eds.), *Interpersonal sensitivity: Theory and measurement* (pp. 333–350). Mahwah, NJ: Erlbaum.

22

NONVERBAL COMMUNICATION IN INSTRUCTIONAL CONTEXTS

◆ James C. McCroskey and
Virginia P. Richmond
University of West Virginia

◆ Linda L. McCroskey
California State University, Long Beach

Instructional communication is the area of communication theory and research that centers attention on the role of communication in teaching and training contexts. It focuses on communication in the instructional environment and assesses its effects on cognitive, affective, and psychomotor learning of students and trainees. Instructional communication examines applications of general theories of communication to the instructional environment as well as generates theory applicable specifically to the instructional environment. Whereas this area considers applications of instructional communication theory in any content area, it is also concerned with applications of instructional communication to instruction *in* communication (commonly referred to as "speech education" or "communication education").

This chapter focuses on the relationship between nonverbal communication research and instructional communication research. In the beginning, we provide an historical perspective of how the relationships between these two areas of scholarship in communication evolved. Then we examine several choices that early researchers made in their studies of nonverbal behavior in the instructional context. In doing so, we direct attention to nonverbal constructs, including both categorical constructs and collective constructs, that have been prominent in instructional research. Finally, we examine briefly some of the implications of this research, highlighting ways in which the research can work to increase teacher effectiveness.

◆ An Historical Account

The origins of research on nonverbal behavior and on instructional behavior have a great deal in common. Both began prior to the 20th century as a wide array of unrelated studies, none of which was driven by a theoretical understanding of human communication. They also both appeared as research in disciplines other than Communication: Nonverbal behavior was studied originally in a wide range of the social sciences and humanities but primarily in Psychology, whereas instructional behavior was researched in Education predominantly. For a thorough discussion of this early work, see Andersen (1978, pp. 60-90).

In 1970, the first author taught what may have been the first graduate seminar in nonverbal communication. The bibliography of nonverbal research developed by the graduate students in that seminar (in response to the unavailability of any textbook on nonverbal communication) identified hundreds of published (in over 25 disciplines) and unpublished works (theses and dissertations) that dealt with nonverbal behavior. Quite a few of these works on nonverbal behavior provided information that could be interpreted as relating to communication, but they were not presented as research on nonverbal "communication."

In 1973, the first author received permission from the administration at West Virginia University to initiate a new graduate course to be designed for in-service elementary and secondary teachers, "Communication in the Classroom." This class led ultimately to the development of a full program leading to an M.A. degree in Instructional Communication. As had been the case with nonverbal communication previously, there was no book available on instructional communication or communication in instruction. Not surprisingly, given that one of the faculty members and a doctoral student involved in the program were students in the first author's previously described nonverbal communication seminar, nonverbal communication was deemed to be a critical element of communication in instruction. Hence, it was included in the first course on communication in the classroom.

When Janis Andersen was beginning to develop the idea for her doctoral dissertation (Andersen, 1978), she undertook the assignment of finding out what educational research had determined what good teachers do that poor teachers do not do. Her literature review identified many published and unpublished works that related to effective teaching. After categorizing these works to find commonalities, she concluded that a large number of these works dealt with nonverbal communication behaviors and appeared to be associated with Albert Mehrabian's (1971) concept of *immediacy*, particularly nonverbal immediacy. The results of her dissertation confirmed some of these links and stimulated the research that followed and that established the currently strong theoretical association between nonverbal communication and instructional communication. It is to this research, and the directions it has taken, that we now turn.

◆ Choices Made and Why

Over the course of years, researchers in any area make many choices. Some of these are well thought out in advance; others are recognized as "choices" only long after they were actually made. Instructional/nonverbal researchers have made four important choices: (1) to focus on but reframe the focus of the "immediacy principle," (2) to focus on affective outcomes, (3) to focus on short-term outcomes, and (4) to focus on the forest rather than the trees. Within this discussion we assess the implications of these choices for past, current, and future research.

REFRAMING THE IMMEDIACY PRINCIPLE

Immediacy is defined as the degree of perceived physical or psychological closeness between two (or more) people (Mehrabian, 1971; see Andersen, Guerrero, & Jones, this volume). Immediacy behaviors (verbal and nonverbal) are those that result in people perceiving others to be closer or more distant interactionally. Whereas Mehrabian (1971) suggested that there were both verbal and nonverbal elements related to immediacy, communication research has dealt primarily with nonverbal immediacy. This may be in part because development of measures of verbal immediacy has proven to be problematic. Although there is no extant valid measure of verbal immediacy (for a critique of existing measures, see Robinson & Richmond, 1995), research reported by Mottet and Richmond (1998) suggests there are 10 verbal strategies (approach messages) that are likely to increase perceptions of immediacy, and there are 8 verbal strategies (avoidance messages) that are likely to decrease perceptions of immediacy. All of these strategies are likely to be employed simultaneously with compatible nonverbal behaviors to produce increased or decreased perceptions of immediacy.

To help make sense of the influence that immediacy may have, Mehrabian (1971) advanced what he called *the principle of immediacy*. He suggested that "people are drawn toward persons and things they like, evaluate highly, and prefer; they avoid or move away from things they dislike, evaluate negatively, or do not prefer" (p. 1). This principle advances immediacy as a marker for how people feel about other people, which can be considered a psychological perspective. Even though many credit Mehrabian's writings as the foundation for their work, communication scholars have moved away from this psychological orientation and assumed that the causal path was the reverse of what Mehrabian assumed. He argued that orientation toward another produces one's immediacy choices, whereas communication scholars suggest that one's immediacy choices produce others' orientations.

Richmond and McCroskey (2000b) formalized this "production" approach recently in their *principle of immediate communication*. As they put it, "The more communicators employ immediate behaviors, the more others will like, evaluate highly, and prefer such communicators; and the less communicators employ immediate behaviors, the more others will dislike, evaluate negatively, and reject such communicators" (p. 212). Immediate or nonimmediate communication behaviors are seen as causes of communication outcomes, reflecting what can be called a communication orientation. This view is consistent with a larger perspective of communication researchers, particularly those interested in social influence: that communicative messages produce outcomes (e.g., McCroskey, 1988).

Whereas these two conceptualizations of immediacy may appear to be the opposite of one another, it is not asserted (at least in published papers) that one is correct and the other is incorrect. Research in Psychology, for example, has provided strong support for the principle of immediacy (e.g., Mehrabian,

1971), and research in several areas of Communication has provided strong support for the principle of immediate communication (e.g., Richmond, Lane, & McCroskey, 2006). Indeed, organizational research results suggest that, rather than being at odds with one another, psychological and communicative approaches to immediacy may well coexist and together produce a cyclical process leading to both higher or lower immediacy and higher or lower liking between individuals over time (Richmond & McCroskey, 2000a). Such research suggests that the immediacy behaviors of either a supervisor or a subordinate tend to produce reciprocal immediacy on the part of the other person and are associated with more subordinate job satisfaction. This result is likely to transfer to instructional contexts.

FOCUS ON AFFECTIVE LEARNING OUTCOMES

In addition to a focus on immediacy, instructional communication researchers have been concerned with learning outcomes associated with communication behaviors, including immediacy. The traditional view of learning advanced in Educational Psychology posits three distinct types of learning: cognitive, psychomotor, and affective (Bloom, 1956; Krathwohl, Bloom, & Masia, 1964). From the earliest reported instructional research involving nonverbal communication (Andersen, 1978), instructional communication researchers have embraced this conceptualization. Most of this work has sought to determine relationships between various communication variables and cognitive and/or affective learning (e.g., Richmond et al., 2006). Little work has been directed toward psychomotor learning, but some studies have examined affect toward behaviors learned instead (e.g., Andersen, 1978).

Whereas considerable research has examined both cognitive and affective learning outcomes, that which has centered on nonverbal communication generally has focused most attention on affective learning. This focus has been chosen for two reasons: (1) the belief that verbal communication has its largest impact on cognitive learning and nonverbal communication has its largest impact on affective learning, and (2) measuring cognitive learning has been confronted with the numerous challenges that have not yet been overcome to everyone's satisfaction. These two areas are reviewed here.

Although verbal and nonverbal messages are both present in the vast majority of instructional environments, it has been argued that they perform different functions in those environments. More specifically, researchers assert that the verbal messages stimulate primarily cognitive meanings in receivers (what the students learn about the subject matter), whereas the nonverbal messages stimulate affective meanings in receivers (i.e., the feelings and attitudes toward the content as well as feelings and attitudes toward the teacher) (McCroskey, Richmond, & McCroskey, 2006; Richmond & McCroskey, 2000b). From this perspective, subject competence of the instructor is said to be the critical element in cognitive learning, whereas behavior, particularly nonverbal communication, produces a relational impact on the student attitudes and feelings. Although this view cannot be said to be scientifically proven, virtually all the available research results are consistent with it (see Mottet & Beebe, 2006).

Besides a theoretical push toward affective learning, scholars may focus less on cognitive learning for methodological reasons. Specifically, the development of measures, or even approaches to the measurement, of cognitive learning has frustrated instructional communication researchers consistently. No approach to measuring cognitive learning, much less a specific measuring instrument, has met with acceptance by a majority of scholars (for a discussion of this issue, see Richmond et al., 2006). This is also true of scholars in Education, who have been working on this problem far longer than have Communication scholars.

An analysis of these issues, discussed in Richmond et al. (2006), concludes that measuring the impact of nonverbal communication behaviors (such as immediacy) on students' cognitive learning outside the carefully controlled experimental environment is very difficult. Some approaches have been found to be successful and valid in controlled experiments, including methods developed by instructional communication researchers (e.g., Chesebro & McCroskey, 2000). The use of these measures in typical classroom environments has yet to be validated to the point that they are accepted by some scholars.

Given that nonverbal communication behaviors likely have their greatest impact on affective learning, and given that some scholars are not willing to accept the validity of the cognitive learning measures that are available currently, nonverbal communication in instruction has therefore been concerned with affective learning primarily. Instructional researchers have studied both verbal and nonverbal aspects of instructional communication. One of the most extensive programs of research in instructional communication focused on the verbal messages that teachers use to influence students. This "power in the classroom" series of studies determined that use of different categories of verbal influence messages produced marked differences in the effectiveness of instruction (McCroskey, Richmond, Plax, & Kearney, 1985; Richmond, 1990). When both verbal and nonverbal variables were considered, however, the nonverbal variables proved to have considerably more influence (Plax, Kearney, McCroskey, & Richmond, 1986).

Whereas more research is needed before a firm conclusion can be drawn, the instructional research to date suggests that nonverbal factors may have a much stronger impact on learning in the classroom than do verbal factors. This is particularly true for affective learning. The available results have led to an increased focus on nonverbal immediacy in the instructional arena, as well as in organizational and health contexts (see, Robinson, this volume for more discussion of immediacy in health contexts).

SHORT- VERSUS LONG-TERM LEARNING

The concern with learning outcomes forces another choice that researchers must make in the area of nonverbal communication and instruction: whether to assess short- or long-term learning outcomes. The overwhelming majority of instructional communication research, including that focused on nonverbal communication, has centered on short-term learning effects (Richmond et al., 2006). It is most likely that this is the case because studying long-term effects is so difficult. This assumption is bolstered by the fact that many of the researchers, when reporting short-term effects, note the need for more long-term research.

It can also be argued, however, that affective learning has its primary impact on long-term, not short-term, cognitive learning. If students learn to like a teacher and/or a subject matter, it is likely they will choose to take another class from that teacher and/or in that subject matter. Hence, these students will have greater opportunities for cognitive learning than will students who do not develop this positive affect toward the teacher or the subject matter. Students who study a subject longer learn more than students who don't. Given this view, affective learning probably should be the primary focus for scholars interested in the role of nonverbal communication in learning environments. As noted, this decision is reflected in much of the current research being published in this area.

A theoretical view advanced by some instructional communication researchers (including the present authors) is that long-term learning is the most important form of learning (McCroskey, 1998). This view holds that schools are created primarily to acculturate young people and prepare them for success in the surrounding culture. Whereas schools are seen as teaching the content of many disciplines, as well as the values and attitudes of the people in that culture, their primary function is, arguably, to teach the students the differences between right and wrong (as seen by their culture), and prepare them with lifelong learning skills. Much of this socialization deals with matters of affect, such as developing positive affect for learning and the norms and values of the culture. Given that nonverbal communication has been found to have a major impact on the development of affect (Richmond et al., 2006), it may well be the critical element producing the desired (as well that which is not desired) outcomes of educational institutions. The long-term impact of nonverbal communication, therefore, should be a major focus of future instructional and nonverbal communication researchers.

STUDYING THE TREES OR THE FOREST

In addition to choices made regarding *what* is to be the focus of research and at what point the focus is captured, scholars also make choices as to the perspective from which to approach the topics. From the beginning of formal communication research relating to nonverbal

communication, and in textbooks concerned with nonverbal communication, communication scholars have chosen to take two different approaches, which we refer to as the "trees" or the "forest." The "tree" approach (also referred to as the "categorical" approach; Knapp, 1972; Malandro & Barker, 1983) separates the elements into categories and centers on how each of these elements affects communication outcomes across contexts. The "forest" approach, also referred to as the "functional" approach (Burgoon & Saine, 1978), centers on how multiple elements of nonverbal behavior influence communication outcomes collectively in specific contexts. Most researchers have chosen one or the other of these to organize or frame their work on nonverbal communication. Some textbook authors also have followed this pattern, whereas others have chosen to include both approaches in their works (e.g., Hickson & Stacks, 1985; Richmond & McCroskey, 2004).

Instructional communication researchers, for the most part, have taken the "forest" approach, and their emphasis on nonverbal immediacy is representative of this choice. They recognize that single nonverbal behaviors rarely manifest alone (e.g., Hickson & Stacks, 1985) and that, typically, there are many nonverbal messages transmitted simultaneously in instructional communication by both teachers/trainers and students. Whereas single nonverbal behaviors may have a direct impact in this context, it is most likely that outcomes are also influenced by multiple nonverbal behaviors interacting with one another. This impact of both single nonverbal behaviors and the interaction of nonverbal behaviors has been demonstrated in experimental research (e.g., Kelley & Gorham, 1988).

Yet, because most of the nonverbal categories were conceptualized by nonverbal communication researchers prior to the onset of the blending of nonverbal behaviors within instructional research, we will first examine the "tree" approach. This conceptualization involves the categorization or classification of the types of nonverbal behaviors that are available to instructional communicators. Subsequently, we will examine the "forest": collections of multiple nonverbal behaviors that are the foundations of larger conceptualizations that have been studied in the instructional context.

Categories of Nonverbal Behaviors: The "Tree" Approach

Researchers have identified 10 primary categories of nonverbal elements: physical appearance, gesture, bodily movement, face, eye, touch, vocal, space, environment, and time. Each of these exists within most instructional settings (mediated instruction prevents some of these from influencing communication), at least within the context of the general North American culture. Given that culture often has a dramatic influence on nonverbal behaviors and interpretation of nonverbal behaviors (see Matsumoto, this volume), our discussion should not be assumed to be generalizable to other cultures. Much of the information for the following material is drawn from summaries provided by Richmond (1997) and Richmond and McCroskey (2000a, b). Rather than citing all of the sources they provide and the description in that review, readers interested in more detail and references to research can find such information in those sources.

The nonverbal message received first when people meet is, in most cases, that of the *physical appearance* of the other person. Responses may be triggered instantly by such messages: Some of these cognitive and affective reactions will stimulate the person to be attracted to the other; some

will produce the opposite response. Whereas nonverbal messages associated with physical appearance may have a strong initial impact, even to the point that one or both people determine not to communicate any further with the other. In the instructional environment, it is presumed that this process will function in much the same manner that it does in other contexts. Available research suggests that teachers or students who are deemed physically attractive will be chosen for more positive future communication and other positive treatment than will those perceived as less attractive (Richmond, 1997).

In addition to the many cues involved in physical appearance, there are many nonverbal behaviors that are included in the classification of *gesture*. Any movements of the hands and/or arms qualify as gestures, although not all these movements are received as meaningful. Research on gestures in the instructional context has been limited, but some work has found, for example, that teachers vary in the amount of gesture in which they engage, and students report that they learn more from teachers who gesture more (Richmond, Gorham, & McCroskey, 1987). Gestures are part of a larger category of *body movement*. This class of nonverbal behaviors references the actual movement of a teacher within the classroom (e.g., walking and leaning). Students report that they learn more when teachers walk around in the classroom, and learn less when they teach while seated or standing behind a podium (Richmond et al., 1987). Experimental research indicates that teachers who lean toward the students have students who learn more than teachers who lean away from the students (Kelley & Gorham, 1988).

Another subset of body movements are those that occur on the face. There are many potential *facial expressions* that teachers may express in the classroom. Most of these are yet to be researched.

Research has indicated, however, that students report greater learning from teachers who smile frequently in the classroom than from those who do not (Richmond et al., 1987). Similarly, *eye behavior* has been studied in the classroom. Research on gaze has found that teachers may be looking anywhere in a classroom at any given time. But students report that they learn more from those teachers who look at the students most of the time (establishing eye contact), and less from those teachers who look at the board or their notes more frequently (Richmond et al., 1987). Another potentially important eye behavior for teachers is the "teacher stare," which is often used to help manage students' classroom behavior. Research has not yet confirmed this behavior to be effective, however.

Touch can also be considered a subset of body movements, and it has been alleged that in the general North American culture, touch is the most powerful nonverbal message one can send (Richmond & McCroskey, 2000a, b). Touch also is the most suspect of all the nonverbal behaviors in which people in this culture can be engaged. When we teach material on nonverbal communication to groups of adults working in organizational environments, we commonly ask them what is the most important rule that their organization demands. Their answers consistently rate "Don't touch" as Number 1. This response is also the number one answer given by teachers, particularly male teachers, in educational organizations. Touch is another area that instructional researchers have rarely studied. Research indicates, however, that even college students who report that their teachers touch students report a higher level of learning from those teachers than from those who touch less or not at all (Richmond et al., 1987).

In addition to movement, vocal communication accompanies verbal communication under most circumstances (occasionally vocal communication is produced without the use of verbal language). This nonverbal behavior has been referred to as *vocalics* or *paralanguage*. Among the many elements of vocalic behavior is variety in vocal use. Students report that vocal variety is the nonverbal behavior that is most positively associated with their learning. In contrast, the use of a vocal monotone is reported to be the behavior that is most negatively associated with learning (Richmond et al., 1987). Another vocalic element is the accent of the spoken language. All speakers have an accent, but some are clearer to student listeners than are others. In her research, Linda McCroskey (2003) determined that clarity of a teacher was an extremely strong predictor of the evaluation of the teacher, students' affect toward the subject matter, and both cognitive and affective learning in U.S. classrooms. This was found for both domestic and foreign teachers.

Quite a different subset of nonverbal cues in the classroom concerns the use of *space*. The two primary components of space in research are territory and interpersonal space. Particularly in the lower grades, territoriality of students is a major concern, and it is the number one cause of students' physical conflicts (Richmond, 1997). Whereas adults often have learned to control their territorial instinct, young children usually have not. The nonverbal behavior of violating another's space often results in strong verbal responses, and it is not unusual to find these conflicts to result in physical attacks and subsequent retaliations. Although little kids (often referred to as "space invaders") usually don't know any better, older students (often referred to as "bullies") do understand what they are doing, and do it on purpose. This is an area of research in Education; instructional communication researchers have shown little interest in this nonverbal behavior problem, however.

Many factors of the *environment* either send constant messages to people or control the communication that exists within the environment directly. These effects occur in educational environments. Considerable research on instructional environments has been conducted, but virtually none by instructional communication researchers. Such research has been reported in fields such as Architecture, Education, Psychology, and Sociology. What little research that has been reported by instructional communication researchers, however, indicates that even the arrangement of seating in a classroom can have an important impact on student communication behavior and student learning (e.g., McCroskey & McVetta, 1978).

The use of time, also known as *chronemics*, can be highly communicative in the classroom. How people react to time will vary greatly based on the culture in which they were born or in which they have been enculturated. Not only do large national cultures have a system of time, but individual organizations have a culture as well that addresses the time rules for its members. Schools, at least within the general North American culture, are examples of the most rigid ways of dealing with time. Everything within a given day usually is timed down to the minute. One of the major concerns in most elementary schools is teaching the system of time required by its rules to young children who have not already been taught the system enforced in their culture. Time imposes rules for communicating (or not communicating). It determines when students can talk, how long they can talk, where they can talk, and what they can talk about. Penalties that can be very severe are imposed on students who do not follow the communication time rules. This is an area that instructional communication researchers have generally ignored up until this time.

Summary. As we have noted above, there are very many different kinds of nonverbal behaviors that may individually affect instruction. Each has the potential to enhance or impede communication in this context. This concludes our discussion of the specific categories of nonverbal behaviors. Now we turn our attention to collections of these variables.

Collective Nonverbal Constructs: The "Forest" Approach

As noted, it is rare that a single nonverbal variable will exist alone in an instructional environment. Whereas many nonverbal cues function within and affect most instructional contexts, their collective impact may be of much greater theoretical and practical importance. Hence, instructional researchers have sought to develop or adopt constructs that can explain the general effects of the combined forces of multiple nonverbal behaviors (i.e., the nonverbal "forest"). The collective nonverbal constructs we focus on here are immediacy, clarity, and sociocommunicative style.

As noted, immediacy is the degree of perceived physical or psychological closeness between people (Mehrabian, 1971), and it may be reflected in or a result of immediacy behaviors. Nonverbal *immediacy* research has determined that it has a powerful impact on instructional outcomes. These outcomes include (1) increased affinity for the teacher, (2) increased affective learning (affect for the content of the subject matter), (3) increased student perceptions of their own cognitive learning, and (4) the granting of increased referent power to teachers by students. Each of these will be discussed in turn.

The *affinity* construct was first explored by interpersonal communication researchers (Bell & Daly, 1984; McCroskey & Wheeless, 1976) who argued that development of affinity is the "first function of communication" (McCroskey & Wheeless, 1976, pp. 21–22). Having affinity for another person essentially means liking that other person. Nonverbal immediacy is considered one of the main means one person can use to get another person to like him or her. This "liking" is believed to include a number of positive affects—for example, having increased interpersonal attraction (social and/or task) for the other person, having increased respect for the other person, seeing the other person as more credible (competence, caring, and/or trustworthiness), being more responsive to the other person, and so on (McCroskey & Wheeless, 1976). Instructional communication research has observed that teachers employ nonverbal immediacy consciously to increase students' affinity for them (McCroskey & McCroskey, 1986). It also has produced consistent results showing that teachers' increased nonverbal immediacy is associated with similar increases in students' evaluations of the teacher, both in the United States and in other cultures (e.g., McCroskey, Richmond, Sallinen, Fayer, & Barraclough, 1995; McCroskey, Valencic, & Richmond, 2004).

As noted earlier in this chapter, the construct of affective learning was advanced in educational psychology (Krathwohl et al., 1964). It refers to students' development of positive (or negative) affect toward the subject matter taught. Many studies have produced results indicating a strong, positive relationship (in the United States and other cultures) between the nonverbal immediacy of teachers and the affective learning of their students (e.g., Christophel, 1990; McCroskey, Fayer, Richmond, Sallinen, & Barraclough, 1996; McCroskey et al., 2004; Richmond, 1990). Cognitive learning was also advanced in educational psychology (Bloom, 1956). Whereas the measurement of cognitive learning has been controversial, nonverbal immediacy has been found to be

associated with both actual content learned (Kelley & Gorham, 1988) and students' perceptions of their own learning (e.g., Christophel, 1990; McCroskey et al., 2004; McCroskey, Sallinen, Fayer, Richmond, & Barraclough, 1996; Richmond, 1990; Richmond et al., 1987). Actual learning (measured via a content test) and student perceived learning have been found to be correlated substantially ($r = .50$; Chesebro & McCroskey, 2000). Collectively, the research evidence suggests a strong positive association between teacher nonverbal immediacy and cognitive learning of their students.

The final factor involved with immediacy to be discussed here that can have a strong impact on students is the teacher's referent power. French and Raven (1959) conceptualized five types of power. Referent power is one of those, the one that has been found to produce the most positive influence on students when used by teachers (Richmond & McCroskey, 1984). Opinion leaders, mentors, and others who are seen as positive models and/or people whom others wish to emulate are said to have referent power. These individuals are seen to be both credible and task attractive. Teachers who are nonverbally immediate have been found to be perceived as both more credible and task attractive than are teachers who are less nonverbally immediate (McCroskey et al., 2004; Thweatt & McCroskey, 1998). Overall, then, nonverbally immediate teachers tend to produce substantially more positive instructional outcomes. Students have more affinity for immediate teachers, they have more affective learning, they have more cognitive learning, and they grant the teacher more referent power in the instructional environment.

Another collective construct implicating nonverbal cues is *clarity*. Clarity has long been believed to be an important factor in effective instruction. Considerable research on teacher clarity conducted by Education scholars indicates a strong relationship between teacher clarity and both student achievement and satisfaction (Hines, Cruickshank, & Kennedy, 1985). Most of this work has centered on organizational and verbal factors. Some researchers, however, have linked a lack of clarity to nonverbal factors (McCroskey, 2003). For example, vocal monotony and vocalized pauses have been identified as factors which students identify as interfering with clarity. A possibly very important nonverbal component, the teacher's accent, has been discussed widely by people concerned with teachers who teach in their second language, or any language other than their first, or teach students whose language is the same as the teacher's but employ a different accent of that language (e.g., a Texan teaching in Maine).

Recent research (Sidelinger & McCroskey, 1997) has found that clarity is correlated highly with teacher evaluation and affective learning. This research also found that both teacher nonverbal immediacy and teacher sociocommunicative style are highly related with both clarity and both of these instructional outcomes. Chesebro and McCroskey (1998, 2001) also found that nonverbal immediacy was associated positively with clarity. They also determined that both increased clarity and nonverbal immediacy were associated with reductions in students' receiver apprehension. In addition, increased clarity was associated with both increased affective learning and increased cognitive learning. These research results suggest a strong association between clarity and positive instructional outcomes. That association, however, may be influenced by nonverbal immediacy and sociocommunicative style as well. There are indications that these constructs are interwoven and all are critical nonverbal aspects of effective instruction.

The final collective nonverbal construct to be discussed here, *sociocommunicative style*, is a blend of both verbal and nonverbal components. It is also correlated with both immediacy and clarity. This construct was developed primarily by researchers interested in interpersonal communication (McCroskey & Richmond, 1996; Richmond & Martin, 1998; Richmond & McCroskey, 1990) but was discovered to be important in instructional communication as well (Richmond, 2002). The sociocommunicative style and orientation constructs are based on earlier variables related to communicator style (Norton, 1983), social style (Merrill & Reid, 1981), and androgyny (Bem, 1974).

Sociocommunicative *style* is conceptualized as the way the receiver perceives the style of the source. Sociocommunicative *orientation* is defined as the way people perceive their own style of communication. These constructs are seen as highly related to communication competence across communication contexts. Three components are argued to be common to both of these constructs: assertiveness, responsiveness, and versatility (or flexibility) (McCroskey & Richmond, 1996). Because of the difficulty in developing a measure of versatility (one that would be independent of the other two components), however, most of the research in this area has focused on only assertiveness and responsiveness.

Assertiveness is seen as communication behavior that reflects individuals' ability to stand up for themselves and prevent others from taking advantage of them, while not aggressing against the other person. These individuals are likely to make requests, express their feelings, and manage conversations in ways consistent with their communicative goals. Bem (1974) has argued that this type of communication behavior is stereotypically characteristic of males in the general North American culture (and many other cultures). Assertive communication is viewed as a positive characteristic for both females and males, however, and necessary for attaining communication competence for members of both sexes.

Likewise, responsiveness is seen as other-oriented communication behavior that reflects an individual's ability to recognize the needs of others without being submissive to the others. Communicators who are responsive are sensitive to others, consider others' feelings, and listen carefully to their communication. Bem (1974) has argued that this type of communication behavior is stereotypically characteristic of females in the general North American culture (and many other cultures). As is the case with assertive communication, however, responsive communication is viewed as a positive characteristic of both males and females, one that is often necessary for attaining communication competence for members of both sexes.

Whereas both assertiveness and responsiveness are seen as characteristic traits of an individual's behavior, versatility is seen as an individual's ability to be flexible and adaptable with regard to his or her use of either or both assertiveness and responsiveness. Competent communicators, then, are seen as being assertive when it is needed and responsive when it is needed as well as reducing their assertiveness and/or responsiveness when that would be appropriate. In the instructional environment, for example, a teacher who is teaching a mass lecture class might need to be more assertive, whereas that teacher, when teaching an interactive class such as a seminar, might need to be more responsive. Teachers who are highly assertive or highly responsive, and not versatile, might be more effective in one type of class and less effective in another type of class.

In support of this, research has indicated that, in general, teachers who are more assertive and more responsive produce more positive instructional outcomes: more positive student affect, more affective learning, more cognitive learning, more motivated students, more student trust for the teacher, and so on (e.g., Kearney & McCroskey, 1980; McCroskey et al., 2004; Thomas, 1994; Wanzer & McCroskey, 1998; Wooten & McCroskey, 1996). Those who are less assertive and/or responsive are less effective. As was the case with teacher clarity, teacher immediacy is correlated with teacher assertiveness and responsiveness. Although teacher assertiveness and teacher responsiveness have been found not to be statistically or meaningfully correlated with each other, they have been found to be correlated consistently with nonverbal immediacy (McCroskey et al., 2004; Thomas, Richmond, & McCroskey, 1994).

Summary. Based on the research reported up to this time, it is clear that nonverbal communication has a major impact on teachers' effectiveness in the classroom. In particular, nonverbal immediacy, clarity, and sociocommunicative style all are important factors in that success or failure. Recent research indicates that immediacy and two components of sociocommunication style, responsiveness and assertiveness, have a strong genetic base (McCroskey, Heisel, & Richmond, 2001); however, no research of this type related to clarity has been reported.

◆ Implications

The research choices reviewed in this chapter, and the subsequent findings of that research, help us understand much of what nonverbal behaviors do in instructional contexts. This research is important to those who study instructional communication and nonverbal communication. It is also important to those who may use nonverbal cues in the instructional context. We close this chapter with a discussion of some recent research that focuses specifically on the importance of teacher effectiveness in multi-cultural classrooms.

Two studies reported by Linda McCroskey (2002, 2003) have provided considerable assistance in determining what nonverbal constructs are particularly important to the effectiveness of teachers in the instructional environment. In these two studies, McCroskey sought to determine whether, and, if so, why, foreign instructors are evaluated less positively than are domestic instructors. The first study (McCroskey, 2002) examined student ethnocentrism and several student communication traits (e.g., intercultural communication apprehension, willingness to communicate). The student participants were asked to respond to two of their current teachers: one a domestic teacher and the other a foreign teacher.

Her results confirmed the expected difference between students' reactions to domestic and foreign teachers. The mean differences between the two groups were significant and large. The results also indicated that student ethnocentrism had a low but significant relationship with the various outcome variables (perceived effectiveness of the teacher, willingness to initiate communication with the teacher, student motivation to work with the teacher, affective learning, perceived cognitive learning). The student trait predictors produced correlations that were trivial (average $r = .11$) and nonsignificant. The "bottom line" in this study was that although the students perceived very large differences between the foreign and domestic teachers, neither ethnocentrism nor the student communication traits could predict a large amount of this variation between domestic and foreign teachers.

The second study (McCroskey, 2003) was designed to examine the predictability of teacher nonverbal communication

constructs as predictors of the differences between student perceptions of domestic and foreign teachers as well as their predictability in predicting the outcomes within the two teacher groups separately. The specific constructs she employed were the ones discussed in the previous section: immediacy, clarity, and sociocommunicative style. Student ethnocentrism was also included as a predictor of the outcome variables (affect toward instructor, instructor evaluation, affective learning, and perceived cognitive learning). This study employed a more reliable and valid measure of ethnocentrism than the one used in the first study. The results of the research replicated the results of the first study with regard to ethnocentrism. The correlations of ethnocentrism with all the outcome variables were trivial ($r = .04$ to .11) and nonsignificant. Ethnocentrism could not predict students' varying responses to foreign and domestic instructors.

The students' responses to each of the outcomes were substantially different when they were responding to a domestic or a foreign instructor. *All the mean differences strongly favored the domestic teachers.* It is important to note, however, that approximately 30% of the students responded more positively to their foreign teacher than their domestic teacher. Where the teacher came from was not a consistent indicator of student preferences. In contrast, *each of the communication variables served individually as a significant predictor of all the outcome variables.* The multiple correlations of just assertiveness and responsiveness with each of the outcome variables were extremely strong, ranging from .54 to .72. The multiple correlations involving immediacy and clarity predicting the outcome variables were equally strong, ranging from $r = .52$ to .81. The results of this research suggest that effective instruction is based on such teacher behaviors as are collectively included in the constructs of nonverbal immediacy, clarity, and sociocommunicative style, all of which include at their base nonverbal communication.

◆ Conclusion

Effective teaching is dependent upon "appropriate" nonverbal communication of teachers. In our opinion, certification of teachers without substantial instruction in nonverbal communication concepts and skills would be pure folly. The success of teachers at all levels depends on how they communicate nonverbally. It may be that some teachers are genetically programmed to be more effective, whereas others are equally programmed to fail. Individuals considering teaching as a profession need to be aware that these nonverbal behaviors are expected of them, at least in the U.S. culture, and measure that in their decision. Similarly, administrators of teacher education and teacher/trainer selection should consider these communication abilities (or lack of) in their decisions to admit or hire people for their programs.

◆ References

Andersen, J. A. (1978). *The relationship between teacher immediacy and teaching effectiveness.* Unpublished doctoral dissertation, West Virginia University, Morgantown.

Bell, R., & Daly, J. A. (1984). The affinity-seeking function of communication. *Communication Monographs, 51,* 91–115.

Bem, S. L. (1974). The measurement of psychological androgyny. *Journal of Consulting and Clinical Psychology, 47,* 155–162.

Bloom, B. S. (1956). *Taxonomy of educational objectives (Handbook I: Cognitive domain).* New York: McKay.

Burgoon, J. K., & Saine, T. J. (1978). *The unspoken dialogue: An introduction to nonverbal communication.* Boston, MA: Houghton Mifflin.

Chesebro, J. L., & McCroskey, J. C. (1998). The relationship of teacher clarity and teacher immediacy with students' experiences of state receiver apprehension. *Communication Quarterly, 46,* 446–456.

Chesebro, J. L., & McCroskey, J. C. (2000). The relationship between students' reports of learning and their actual recall of lecture material: A validity test. *Communication Education, 49,* 297–301.

Chesebro, J. L., & McCroskey, J. C. (2001). The relationship of teacher clarity and immediacy with student state receiver apprehension, affect, and cognitive learning. *Communication Education, 50,* 59–68.

Christophel, D. M. (1990). The relationships among teacher immediacy behaviors, student motivation, and learning. *Communication Education, 39,* 323–340.

French, J. R. P., & Raven, B. (1959). The bases of social power. In D. Cartwright (Ed.), *Studies in social power* (pp. 150–167). Ann Arbor, MI: Institute for Social Research.

Hickson, M. L., III, & Stacks, D. W. (1985). *Nonverbal communication: Studies and applications.* Dubuque, IA: Wm. C. Brown.

Hines, C., Cruickshank, D., & Kennedy, J. (1985). Teacher clarity and its relationship to student achievement and satisfaction. *American Educational Research Journal, 22,* 87–99.

Kearney, P., & McCroskey, J. C. (1980). Relationships among teacher communication style, trait and state communication apprehension, and teacher effectiveness. *Communication Yearbook, 4,* 533–551.

Kelley, D. H., & Gorham, J. (1988). Effects of immediacy on recall of information. *Communication Education, 37,* 198–207.

Knapp, M. L. (1972). *Nonverbal communication in human interaction.* New York: Holt, Rinehart, and Winston.

Krathwohl, D. R., Bloom, B. S., & Masia, B. B. (1964). *Taxonomy of educational objectives (Handbook II: Affective domain).* New York: McKay.

Malandro, L. A., & Barker, L. (1983). *Nonverbal communication.* Reading, MA: Addison-Wesley.

McCroskey, J. C. (1998). *An introduction to communication in the classroom* (2nd ed.). Acton, MA: Tapestry Press.

McCroskey, J. C., Fayer, J. M., Richmond, V. P., Sallinen, A., & Barraclough, R. A. (1996). A multi-cultural examination of the relationship between nonverbal immediacy and affective learning. *Communication Quarterly, 44,* 297–307.

McCroskey, J. C., Heisel, A. D., & Richmond, V. P. (2001). Eysenck's BIG THREE and communication traits: Three correlational studies. *Communication Monographs, 68,* 360–366.

McCroskey, J. C., & McCroskey, L. L. (1986). The affinity-seeking of classroom teachers. *Communication Research Reports, 3,* 158–167.

McCroskey, J. C., & McVetta, R. W. (1978). Classroom seating arrangements: Instructional communication theory versus student preferences. *Communication Education, 27,* 99–111.

McCroskey, J. C., & Richmond, V. P. (1996). *Fundamentals of human communication.* Prospect Heights, IL: Waveland.

McCroskey, J. C., Richmond, V. P., & McCroskey, L. L. (2006). *An introduction to communication in the classroom: The role of communication in teaching and training.* Boston, MA: Allyn & Bacon.

McCroskey, J. C., Richmond, V. P., Plax, T. G., & Kearney, P. (1985). Power in the classroom V: Behavior alteration techniques, communication training, and learning. *Communication Education, 34,* 214–226.

McCroskey, J. C., Richmond, V. P., Sallinen, A., Fayer, J. M., & Barraclough, R. A. (1995). A cross-cultural and multi-behavioral analysis of the relationship between nonverbal immediacy and teacher evaluation. *Communication Education, 44,* 281–290.

McCroskey, J. C. Sallinen, A., Fayer, J. M., Richmond, V. P., & Barraclough, R. A. (1996). Nonverbal immediacy and cognitive learning: A cross-cultural investigation. *Communication Education, 45,* 200–211.

McCroskey, J. C., Valencic, K. M., & Richmond, V. P. (2004). Toward a general model of instructional communication. *Communication Quarterly, 53,* 197–210.

McCroskey, J. C., & Wheeless, L. R. (1976). *Introduction to human communication.* Boston, MA: Allyn & Bacon.

McCroskey, L. L. (2002). Domestic and international college instructors: An examination of perceived differences and their correlates. *Journal of Intercultural Communication Research, 31,* 63–83.

McCroskey, L. L. (2003). Relationships of instructional communication styles of domestic and foreign instructors with instructional outcomes. *Journal of Intercultural Communication Research, 32,* 75–96.

Mehrabian, A. (1971). *Silent messages.* Belmont, CA: Wadsworth.

Merrill, D. W., & Reid, R. H. (1981). *Personal styles and effective performance: Make your style work for you.* Radnor, PA: Chilton Book.

Mottet, T. P., & Beebe, S. A. (2006). Foundations of instructional communication. In T. P. Mottet, V. P. Richmond, & J. C. McCroskey (Eds.), *The handbook of instructional communication: Rhetorical and relational perspectives* (pp. 3–32). Boston, MA: Allyn & Bacon.

Mottet, T., & Richmond, V. P. (1998). Verbal approach and avoidance items. *Communication Quarterly, 46,* 25–40.

Norton, R. (1983). *Communicator style: Theory, applications, and measures.* Beverly Hills, CA: Sage.

Plax, T. G., Kearney, P., McCroskey, J. C., & Richmond, V. P. (1986). Power in the classroom VI: Verbal control strategies, nonverbal immediacy, and affective learning. *Communication Education, 35,* 43–55.

Richmond, V. P. (1990). Communication in the classroom: Power and motivation. *Communication Education, 39,* 181–195.

Richmond, V. P. (1997). *Nonverbal communication in the classroom.* Acton, MA: Tapestry Press.

Richmond, V. P. (2002). Socio-communicative style and orientation in instruction. In J. L. Chesebro & J. C. McCroskey (Eds.),

Communication for teachers (pp. 104–115). Boston, MA: Allyn & Bacon.

Richmond, V. P., Gorham, J. S., & McCroskey, J. C. (1987). The relationship between selected immediacy behaviors and cognitive learning. *Communication Yearbook, 10,* 574–590.

Richmond, V. P., Lane, D. R., & McCroskey, J. C. (2006). Teacher immediacy and the teacher–student relationship. In T. P. Mottet, V. P. Richmond, & J. C. McCroskey (Eds.), *Handbook of instructional communication: Rhetorical and relational perspectives.* Boston, MA: Allyn & Bacon.

Richmond, V. P., & Martin, M. M. (1998). Socio-communicative style and socio-communicative orientation. In J. C. McCroskey, J. A. Daly, M. M. Martin, & M. J. Beatty (Eds.), *Communication and personality: Trait perspectives* (pp. 133–148). Cresskill, NJ: Hampton Press.

Richmond, V. P., & McCroskey, J. C. (1984). Power in the classroom II: Power and learning. *Communication Education, 33,* 125–136.

Richmond, V. P., & McCroskey, J. C. (1990). Reliability and separation of factors on the assertiveness–responsiveness measure. *Psychological Reports, 67,* 449–450.

Richmond, V. P., & McCroskey, J. C. (2000a). The impact of supervisor and subordinate immediacy on relational and organizational outcomes. *Communication Monographs, 66,* 85–95.

Richmond, V. P., & McCroskey, J. C. (2000b). *Nonverbal behavior in interpersonal relations* (5th ed.). Boston, MA: Allyn & Bacon.

Richmond, V.P., & McCroskey, J.C. (2004). *Nonverbal behavior in interpersonal relations* (5th ed.). Boston, MA: Allyn & Bacon.

Robinson, R. Y., & Richmond, V. P. (1995). Validity of the verbal immediacy scale. *Communication Research Reports, 12,* 80–84.

Sidelinger, R. J., & McCroskey, J. C. (1997). Communication correlates of teacher clarity in the college classroom. *Communication Research Reports, 14,* 1–10.

Thomas, C. E. (1994). *An analysis of teacher socio-communicative style as a predictor of classroom communication behaviors, student liking, motivation, and learning.* Unpublished doctoral dissertation, West Virginia University, Morgantown.

Thomas, C. E., Richmond, V. P., & McCroskey, J. C. (1994). Is immediacy anything more than just being nice? The association between immediacy and socio-communicative style. *Communication Research Reports, 11,* 107–115.

Thweatt, K. S., & McCroskey, J. C. (1998). The impact of teacher immediacy and misbehaviors on teacher credibility. *Communication Education, 47,* 348–358.

Wanzer, M. B., & McCroskey, J. C. (1998). Teacher socio-communicative style as a correlated of student affect toward teacher and course material. *Communication Education, 47,* 43–52.

Wooten, A. G., & McCroskey, J. C. (1996). Student trust of teacher as a function of socio-communicative style of teacher and socio-communicative orientation of student. *Communication Research Reports, 13,* 94–100.

NONVERBAL COMMUNICATION AND PHYSICIAN-PATIENT INTERACTION

Review and New Directions

◆ Jeffrey D. Robinson
Rutgers University

O nce considered to be an intangible aspect of "bedside manner," the scientific study of nonverbal communication during visits between patients and medical physicians is now well documented. Research suggests that physicians' nonverbal behavior shapes participants' visit communication (e.g., patients' self-disclosure); ratings of physicians' rapport, dominance, and medical-technical skills; patients' satisfaction with physicians; patients' understanding and recall of visit information; and patients' adherence to physicians' medical recommendations. Physicians' nonverbal behavior is consequential in other ways as well. For example, both the accreditation of residency programs and the certification of physicians require assessment of physicians' competence in "interpersonal skills," which involve "inherently relational"

Author's Note: The author thanks James Dillard, Jenny Mandelbaum, Valerie Manusov, and Richard Street for comments on earlier drafts.

and "humanistic" aspects of nonverbal and verbal communication (Duffy, Gordon, Whelan, Cole-Kelly, & Frankel, 2004). There is also some evidence that training in nonverbal communication skills aids success in the American Board of Surgery's oral-certification exam, which is designed primarily to test candidates' medical-technical skills or their "clinical reasoning, problem solving ability, and clinical judgment" (Rowland-Morin, Burchard, Garb, & Coe, 1991, p. 655).

This chapter begins by providing a rationale for studying nonverbal communication between medical physicians and their patients,[1] reviews findings related to individual nonverbal behaviors or variables, and discusses new directions for nonverbal research. The premise of the final section is that the social meaning of individual nonverbal behaviors—and thus their production, understanding, and effects—is shaped fundamentally and irremediably by, and must be studied relative to, their situation within a variety of aspects of *interactional context*. This context includes other modalities of communication (e.g., other nonverbal and verbal behaviors), as well as norms and rules that structure the interaction itself, such as those dealing with turn taking, social action, and sequences of action.

◆ Rationale for Studying Nonverbal Communication

Patients do not abide strictly by a rational-consumer model of medicine. That is, they seldom select and retain physicians, nor do they evaluate physicians and their medical care or competence, based solely on physicians' medical-technical skills and patients' health outcomes (Glassman & Glassman, 1981). Akin to organizational communication generally (Farace, Monge, & Russell, 1977), physicians' and patients'

communication has at least two underlying dimensions: medical-technical (i.e., instrumental) and affective-relational. The affective-relational dimension appears to be particularly salient to patients. At the point when physical medical problems drive patients to seek professional medical help, such problems may create uncertainty, anxiety, and feelings of fear, frustration, and vulnerability in patients, who (1) must disclose private (and sometimes socially delicate, embarrassing, illegal, etc.) information (e.g., sexual history, drug use) to physicians who are relative strangers and (2) are largely dependent on physicians, who are relatively knowledgeable experts and legitimate brokers of treatment (Mishel, 1988).

Patients can discriminate between medical-technical and affective-relational dimensions of physicians' communication (Bensing & Dronkers, 1992) and, within the latter set of messages, they are able to distinguish between "positive" and "negative" nonverbal affective-relational styles, such as those communicating "attention or concern" rather than "inattention or distance" (Aruguete & Roberts, 2002). Whereas patients base their evaluations of physicians' communicative competence on both dimensions (Cegala, McNeilis, McGee, & Jonas, 1995), and although patients' evaluations of these dimensions are positively correlated such that an increase in one tends to result in an increase in the other (Ben-Sira, 1982; Street & Buller, 1987), there is an accumulation of evidence suggesting that *patients' evaluations of the quality of physicians and their medical care are influenced more heavily by the affective-relational (vs. medical-technical) dimension of physicians' communication* (Ben-Sira, 1982; Griffith, Wilson, Langer, & Haist, 2003; Mechanic & Meyer, 2000).

This evidence leads to the conclusion that successful medical treatment involves physicians' competent management of the affective-relational dimension of communicative action. For example, practices of interaction that address the affective-relational dimension "positively" (e.g., reassurance) have been associated with decreases in patients' requests for postoperative narcotics (Egbert, Battit, Welch, & Bartlett, 1964; Langer, Janis, & Wolfer, 1975) and increases in patients' levels of physical functioning, such as their levels of blood glucose and diastolic blood pressure (Kaplan, Greenfield, & Ware, 1989). Although the affective-relational dimension of communication (including empathy and rapport) is managed partially through verbal behavior, such management involves nonverbal behavior primarily (Ekman & Friesen, 1969; Harrigan & Rosenthal, 1986).

The next section reviews associations between a variety of communicative, social, and psychological outcomes and the following nonverbal behaviors: gaze orientation, head nodding, and body orientation (including proximity). Space prevents an exhaustive review of all nonverbal variables, including smiling, touch, tone of voice, physical appearance, and skill at encoding and decoding emotion (for more on the latter, see Riggio, this volume). Given the concern in this section of the *Handbook* with the implications of our work, the variables reviewed here are relatively more "controllable" by, and thus "teachable" to, physicians.

◆ *Findings Related to Individual Nonverbal Behaviors*

PHYSICIANS' GAZE ORIENTATION

Gaze orientation communicates one's current attention to, availability for, and participation with others' actions (or lack thereof; Goodwin, 1981; Kendon, 1990) as well as who one is addressing when

speaking (Goodwin, 1981; Sacks, Schegloff, & Jefferson, 1974). Research on gaze in physician-patient interaction has focused on its effects on both verbal communication and visit or medical outcomes. Concerning verbal communication, Verhaak (1988) and Bensing, Kerrsens, and van der Pasch (1995) examined physicians' gaze toward patients, and Van Dulmen, Verhaak, and Bilo (1997) examined the amount of time physicians gazed directly at patients' faces, and these studies showed that physicians' gaze orientation was associated positively with the amount of psychosocial (rather than somatic) information given by patients. Along similar lines, Duggan and Parrott (2001) found physicians' lack of direct facial orientation toward patients to be negatively associated with patients' self-disclosure (e.g., about life beyond symptoms). Some results are non-intuitive and beg further investigation. For example, Van Dulmen et al. (1997), found the amount of time that physicians gazed directly at patients' faces was negatively associated with the amount of agreements given by patients and the amount of reassurance, orientation, and medical counseling given by physicians.

A somewhat inconsistent picture emerges when the research focus concerns visits or medical outcomes. For instance, Larsen and Smith (1981) discerned that physicians' direct facial orientation toward patients was negatively associated with patients' post-visit satisfaction with medical care. Relatedly, Harrigan, Oxman, and Rosenthal (1985) found physicians' increased and decreased mutual gaze with patients to be negatively and positively associated with external raters' evaluations of physicians' rapport, respectively.[2] These research studies suggest that gaze and face orientation toward patients may increase disclosure but decrease patients' satisfaction. In possible contradiction to these findings, however, Smith, Polis, and Hadac (1981) showed that physicians' time spent reading patients' medical records, which was also physicians' time spent gazing away from patients, was *negatively* associated with patients' post-visit satisfaction and understanding of medical information. Furthermore, Bensing (1991) showed that physicians' gaze toward patients was positively associated with external physician-raters' evaluations of the quality of participant-physicians' psychosocial care.

One explanation of this possible contradiction lies in an analysis of where physicians are gazing—and what physicians are doing—while patients are talking. For example, Harrigan et al. (1985) also found that, compared with low-rapport physicians, high-rapport physicians gazed at (i.e., read) patients' medical records more often when not gazing at patients, but they were more likely to continue to gaze at patients when patients were talking. In support of this, Giron, Manjon-Arce, Puerto-Barber, Sanchez-Garcia, and Gomez-Beneyto (1998) revealed that physicians' eye contact *while patients spoke* was positively associated with physicians' psychodiagnostic abilities.

In sum, physicians' gaze toward (rather than away from) patients appears to be positively associated with patients' giving of psychosocial information, which may explain the concomitant positive associations with physicians' psychodiagnostic abilities and patients' positive evaluations of at least the affective-relational dimension of physicians' communication. These findings are confounded by a lack of control for what physicians and patients are *doing* while gazing, however, as well as where patients are gazing (e.g., toward or away from physicians). A particularly salient issue seems to be whether physicians and patients are talking generally and, specifically, *what social actions are getting accomplished through such talk* (e.g., instructing patients to sit on the examination table vs.

delivering bad medical news). The analytic "payoff" of looking at the larger interaction, rather than discrete variables, will be discussed later in this chapter.

PHYSICIANS' HEAD NODDING

When people gaze at speakers, especially when speakers are producing multi-unit turns (e.g., when patients produce illness narratives or when physicians explain treatments), gazers nod their head frequently, which, at a minimum, communicates attention (Schegloff, 1982). Hall, Irish, Roter, Ehrlich, and Miller (1994) found that, compared with male physicians, female physicians nod more overall and they nod more to female patients. Harrigan and Rosenthal (1983) discovered external raters' evaluations of physicians' nodding to be positively associated with raters' perceptions of physicians' rapport. In a later study, however, Harrigan et al. (1985) found no association between nodding and rapport. Nodding is, however, more commonly studied in association with other variables than as an isolated cue, and the findings when nodding is viewed as part of a larger communicative function are more robust. For example, Weinberger, Greene, and Mamlin (1981) found physicians' nonverbal *encouragement*—operationalized in terms of nodding and gesture—was positively associated with patients' post-visit satisfaction. Duggan and Parrott (2001) showed likewise that physicians' facial *reinforcement*—operationalized in terms of nodding and facial animation—was positively associated with patients' self-disclosure (e.g., about life beyond symptoms).

PHYSICIANS' BODY ORIENTATION

Although head movement and gaze orientation communicate persons' *current* engagement, the front of a person's body communicates a frame of dominant orientation: a frame of space wherein long-term and dominant social actions are most likely to be focused (Goodwin, 1981; Kendon, 1990; Schegloff, 1998). The orientation of persons' bodies communicates their availability or nonavailability for collaborative action. When two persons bring each other into (or remove the other from) their frame of dominant orientation, they establish (or dismantle) a *participation framework* (Goodwin, 1981).

This orientation appears to have a number of outcomes. Larsen and Smith (1981) found that the amount of time physicians spend with their bodies oriented toward patients was positively associated with patients' post-visit satisfaction and understanding. Street and Buller (1987) showed that physicians' indirect body orientation (i.e., away from patients) was positively associated with patients' perceptions of physicians' dominance. Harrigan et al. (1985) reported that physicians' body orientation away from patients was negatively associated with external raters' evaluations of physicians' rapport. In a different vein, Giron et al. (1998) found physicians' open face-to-face posture while patients spoke to be positively associated with physicians' psychodiagnostic abilities. A range of studies has also found positive relationships between physicians' proximity to and lean toward patients and outcomes such as patients' post-visit understanding (Larsen & Smith, 1981; Smith, Polis, & Hadac, 1981) and external raters' evaluations of physicians' rapport (Harrigan & Rosenthal, 1983; Harrigan et al., 1985).

Overall, this work shows that physicians' body orientation toward (and physical proximity to) patients appears to be positively and negatively associated with ratings of physicians' rapport and dominance, respectively, and this may partially explain the positive association between physicians'

body orientation and patients' satisfaction with physicians. As with gaze, however, these findings may be confounded by a lack of control for what physicians and patients are doing.

SUMMARY

A variety of individual nonverbal behaviors have been associated with communicative, social, and psychological outcomes. The majority of these outcomes relate to the affective-relational (vs. medical-technical) dimension of communication, such as ratings of physicians' dominance, rapport, and likeability, and to psychosocial (vs. somatic) aspects of care, such as patients' self-disclosure of lifeworld events and physicians' psychodiagnostic abilities. Together, they suggest the important role that nonverbal cues may play in physician-patient interactions.

Despite the overall strength of their conclusions, the findings just reviewed can be extended in a number of ways that highlight new directions for research on nonverbal communication. Put generally, to understand the process more completely—that is, *how* these behaviors come to have the consequences that they do—research needs to be situated within a larger framework for understanding communication per se. Whereas communication simultaneously involves multiple, mutually influential modalities of meaning (nonverbal, verbal, artifactual) and is interactive inherently, much of the research done in the medical context focuses in isolation on one modality of behavior (i.e., nonverbal) produced by one participant (i.e., the physician). To make its largest contribution—to help understand how communication in the medical context comes to work as it does—research on physician-patient communication needs to be situated within (i.e., needs to control for) aspects of *interactional context* that have been shown to shape how nonverbal behavior is produced and understood. The following section suggests how this may be done.

◆ New Directions for Research Dealing With Interactional Context

Street (2003) proposed an ecological model of communication that recognizes that "visit communication" and its outcomes are organized by reference to organizational, political, media, cultural, and interpersonal contexts. This section of the chapter extends Street's model generally, and his *interpersonal context* specifically (which includes verbal and nonverbal communication), by recognizing the organizing effects of interactional context. That is, in addition to traditional conceptions of context, interaction has its own, independent orders of social organization (Goffman, 1983) that can affect both the production and the understanding of nonverbal communication. Over the past 30 years, three of the most robust "interaction orders" involve turn taking, social action, and sequences of talk and action. Before addressing these issues, however, this section begins with a discussion of the inseparability of nonverbal and verbal behavior.

THE INSEPARABILITY OF NONVERBAL AND VERBAL BEHAVIOR

Almost 15 years ago, Streeck and Knapp (1992) asserted that "the classification of communicative behavior as either 'verbal' or 'nonverbal' is misleading and obsolete" (p. 3). Although this position is not new, and has continued to be a mantra of research reform (see Bavelas & Chovil, this volume), its implications often go ignored. There are at least two different ways of conceptualizing the relationship between verbal and nonverbal behavior that focus on their co-occurrence in social meaning. The first conceptualization is that verbal behavior and nonverbal behavior constitute two distinct channels of communication that are attended to and processed separately by receivers (e.g., Ekman & Friesen, 1969). Researchers adopt this position tacitly whenever they examine phenomena whose functions entail both verbal and nonverbal communication (e.g., dominance) yet analyze such phenomena exclusively in terms of one channel, or modality, of meaning.

The second, alternative, conceptualization (which this chapter adopts) is that the meaning of communicative events is shaped by, and thus *depends* on, the "context" in which it is situated and that verbal and nonverbal behavior *are each forms of context* (Goodwin, 1995; Sanders, 1987). From this perspective, the relationship between verbal and nonverbal behavior is neither additive nor multiplicative, in the sense that each constitutes a separate yet combinable factor of meaning. Rather, their relationship is holistic and metamorphic, with a multitude of modalities (e.g., verbal, nonverbal, artifactual) working together to convey a single meaning (for more on this, see McNeill, Cassell, & McCullough, 1994).

This second conceptualization shifts analytic attention away from the function of individual nonverbal behaviors to how they achieve their social meanings in and through interaction—that is, to the multimodal array of communication practices that participants rely on to accomplish certain meanings (Sanders, 1987). This conceptualization is in line with Burgoon's (1994) message perspective and Stamp and Knapp's (1990) interaction perspective on the nature of nonverbal communication, and Robinson and Stivers (2001) supported the validity of a multimodal perspective in physician-patient interaction specifically.

From this multimodal perspective, the first conceptualization (stated above) is statistically *reified* (rather than supported) by physician-patient studies showing that, when controlling for verbal variables, nonverbal variables retain independent significance (e.g., Bensing, 1991; Griffith, Wilson, Langer, & Haist, 2003).

THREE ASPECTS OF INTERACTIONAL CONTEXT

Taking into account the multimodal conceptualization, and because in face-to-face interaction, nonverbal behavior is produced and understood largely by reference to talk, researchers studying nonverbal communication need to account for the organizing effects of at least three aspects of interactional context: (1) turn taking, (2) social action, and (3) sequences of talk and action. Furthermore, researchers need to account for the fact that (4) individual nonverbal behaviors are (almost always) produced and understood by reference to each other. These four issues are discussed in order.

Turn Taking

Buller and Street (1992) noted that traditional measures of nonverbal behavior "do not account for how communicators *qualitatively* interpret the behaviors being *quantified*" (p. 135, emphasis in original). The underlying issue in their statement is whether operationalizations of nonverbal behavior are ecologically valid (i.e., relevant to participants). An integral component of operationalizing talk is *unitization*. In studies of physician-patient communication, nonverbal behavior has been unitized historically in terms of its duration and frequency (e.g., in seconds) across (sometimes randomly selected) segments of (or entire) visits. Contrary to this, *physicians and patients organize much of their nonverbal behavior relative to talk, and organize their talk according to turn-taking rules for ordinary conversation* (Sacks, Schegloff, & Jefferson, 1974; for a review, see Robinson, 2001a).[3]

One example occurs with gaze orientation. Because gaze can communicate that one is "listening," interactants orient to the general rule that recipients (e.g., physicians) should gaze at speakers (e.g., patients) when being spoken to (Goodwin, 1981). Turns of talk have consequential "positions," such as beginnings, middles, and endings (Schegloff, 1996), and Goodwin (1981) showed that recipients' gaze toward speakers is particularly salient at turn beginnings. For instance, in Extract 1, when the physician begins to ask his question (Line 1), he is gazing at the computer screen (see Figure 23.1, which corresponds positionally to the "1" in the transcript). Precisely at the completion of his question—that is, just as he is about to become a recipient of the patient's talk—the physician shifts his gaze to the patient (Figure 23.2; commas "," symbolize movement of the physician's head, the "X" symbolizes the point at which the physician's gaze reaches the patient, and brackets "[ ]" symbolize simultaneous behavior).

```
Extract 1 [MC:12:03]

              1                                    2

01  DOC:  What's wrong=with your ea:r[s. (.)]

02  DOC:                              [,,,,,X]

03  PAT:  I think they're both infected.
```

Figure 23.1

Figure 23.2

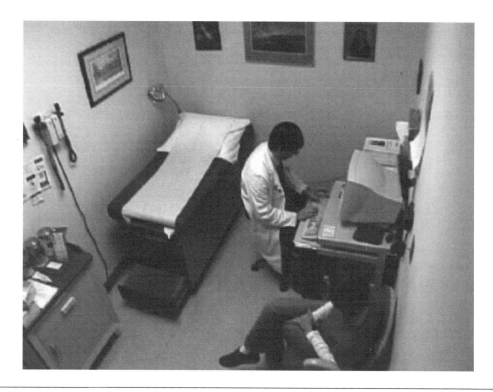

Figure 23.3

Due to the rules of gaze orientation in ordinary conversation (Goodwin, 1981), if speakers (e.g., patients) do not secure recipients' (e.g., physicians') gaze at the beginning of their turns, speakers use vocal hitches and perturbations—such as pauses, cutoffs, and other marked prosodic patterns—to secure recipients' gaze prior to beginning or completing their turns. This is equally true in physician-patient interaction (Heath, 1986; Ruusuvuori, 2001). In Extract 1, the patient *does* secure the physician's gaze prior to beginning her turn, and she produces a fluent response (Line 3). This, however, is *not* the case in Extract 2. When the physician completes his question "What's up." (Line 1), he is gazing down at the computer keyboard (Figure 23.3).

At the outset of her response (Line 2), the patient attempts to secure the physician's gaze by pausing briefly (i.e., breathing in, symbolized by ".h") and further delaying her answer with "Uh:m." In this case, the patient does not succeed in securing the physician's gaze, and she continues to produce a self-diagnosis: "I believe I have a sinus infection." (Line 2).[4] Research shows, however, that although recipients' gaze is particularly salient at the beginning of speakers' turns, it is relevant *throughout* speakers' turns, and speakers continue frequently to work to secure recipients' gaze (e.g., Goodwin, 1981; Heath, 1986). When the patient in Extract 2 continues to produce more talk (Line 3), she again attempts to secure the physician's gaze by cutting herself off (symbolized by the hyphen, "a-") and pausing for three tenths of a second (each tenth is symbolized by a dash, "(—)"). This time, she succeeds—that is, immediately after her cutoff and two tenths of a second of silence, the physician shifts his gaze toward the patient (Figure 23.4). The patient begins to speak again precisely as the physician's gaze arrives.

```
Extract 2 [MC:20:02]

                    3

01   DOC:   What's up.

02   PAT:   .h Uh:m I believe I have a sinus infection.

03          I've had=a- (- - [-) c]o:ld yyou know [stuf]fy nose
            fer about a week

04   DOC:                  [,,,X]                    [,,,O]

                            4                         5

05   PAT:   an' then Saturday (0.2) it's: kinda stayed

06          ri:ght, (- [-)] in thee  e:ye e:a[r ]

07   DOC:          [,,X]                  [Y:]eah.

                    6
```

Recipients' gaze is relevant not merely once (i.e., fleetingly) but throughout speakers' turns (Goodwin, 1981), and speakers may work to recover recipients' lost gaze. For example, in Extract 2, as the patient describes her "stuffy nose" (Line 3), the physician removes his gaze back to the computer screen (Figure 23.5). The patient, however, is not finished speaking. Instead, as the patient describes (and gestures with her right hand toward) the location of her problem (Lines 5–6), she markedly stretches and inflects "ri:ght," (symbolized by the colon and the comma, respectively) and pauses for three tenths of a second, which succeeds in resecuring the physician's gaze (Figure 23.6).

Extract 2 raises an additional issue dealing with unitization. Physician-patient talk has been coded historically in terms of vaguely operationalized "thought units" or "utterances." However, turns (1) are constructed from particular types of *turn-constructional units*, (2) can contain more than one turn-constructional unit, and (3) are produced and understood in terms of turn-constructional units (Sacks et al., 1974). In Extract 2, it can be argued that the patient's turn includes three turn-constructional units ("I believe I have a sinus infection.", "I've had a cold you know stuffy nose fer about a week", and "an' then Saturday it's kinda stayed right in the eye ear") and that the patient orients to the relevance of the physician's gaze in (and before the completion of) each unit.

In sum, gaze orientation is organized largely by reference to turn construction. Not only have there been specific calls for understanding physicians' and patients' gaze orientation in terms of turn taking (Irish, 1997), but there is preliminary evidence that doing so can produce analytic payoff. For example, Harrigan et al. (1985) found that high (vs. low) rapport physicians are more likely to gaze at patients when patients are speaking. Giron et al. (1998) measured both physicians' gaze and body orientation toward patients separately depending on whether physicians or patients were speaking and found these variables to be positively associated with

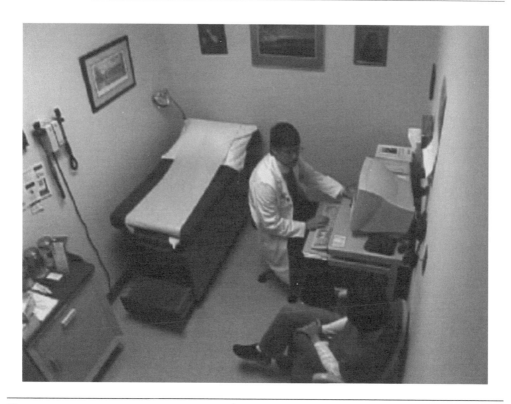

Figure 23.4

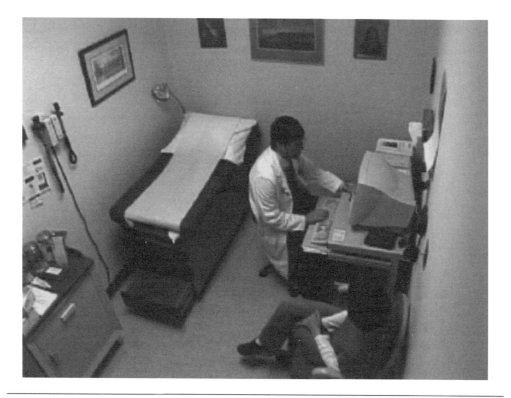

Figure 23.5

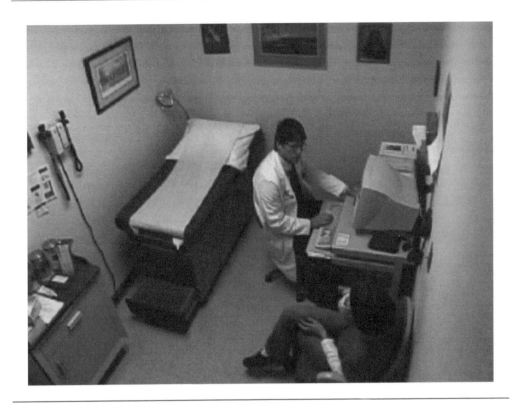

Figure 23.6

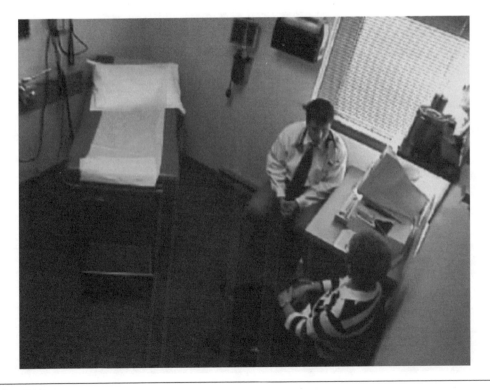

Figure 23.7

physicians' psychodiagnostic abilities only when patients were speaking.

Other nonverbal behaviors, such as head nodding, also appear to be organized by reference to turn construction. For example, across Extract 3, the physician maintains his gaze and body orientation toward the patient (Figure 23.7). In the transcript, "/" and "\" symbolize the upward and downward nodding of the physician's head, respectively.

Extract 3 [MC:11:02]

```
01   DOC:  When=did that sta:rt. (.) la- °°e-=uh-°° beginning

02         a last week? .hhhhhhhh thuh co[:ld? ]

03   PAT:                              [Y:eah] might even

04         sta:rted duh week be[fore a little bit. an' the:n] (.)

05   DOC:                     [             /\/              ]

06   PAT:  la:st week w's- thuh sore throat [ca:me an'- (.)] no:w

07   DOC:                                   [      /\      ]

08         thuh si:nus. [(--)]

09   DOC:              [ \/ ]

10   DOC:  °Okay.°
```

The physician's three instances of nodding (Lines 5, 7, and 9) map finely onto places where the patient's turn-constructional units (in this case, sentences) are possibly (or projectably) complete. The first nod begins as the patient is saying "before" (Line 4), which is a possible sentence ending (i.e., "might even started duh week before"); the second nod begins after "throat" (Line 6), which is a possible sentence ending (i.e., "An' then last week w's thuh sore throat"); and the third nod occurs in the two tenths of a second of silence after "si:nus." (Line 8), which is a possible sentence ending (i.e., "An' now thuh sinus.").

Like gaze, nodding has been coded historically in terms of gross frequency. If nodding is organized relative to turn-constructional units, however, then it may have different meanings depending on its position within turn-constructional units, such as being positioned before or after they are possibly complete. Importantly, the relationship between nonverbal behavior and turn taking does not stop at gaze orientation and head nodding. For example, Harrigan (1985) found that physicians and patients self-touched more at the beginning and middle (vs. the end) of utterances. In line with evidence from ordinary conversation (e.g., Streeck, 1993), a variety of physicians' and patients' nonverbal behaviors are organized by reference to turn construction, such as touching, gesturing, and smiling (Beach & LeBaron, 2002; Haakana, 2002).

Social Action

Once nonverbal and verbal communication are reunited, researchers must recognize that (1) persons produce and understand all communication primarily in terms of the action(s) it performs (e.g., explaining, advising, informing; Schegloff, 1995); (2) actions are organized by social rules that transcend individual actors (Heritage, 1984); and (3) different social rules—for example, the rules for (or practices of) providing good (vs. bad) diagnostic news (e.g., Maynard, 2003)—shape at least verbal behavior differentially (Heritage, 1984).

Although the claim that the social organization of action structures nonverbal behavior is in need of further support, it is buttressed by a variety of findings. Harrigan (1985) found that patients self-touched more when *answering* questions than when being asked questions and concluded that "the semantic context of an utterance may be expected to exert the strongest influence on the expression of self touching" (p. 1164), which "is more complex than a simple cue of anxiety" (p. 1167). Certain actions, such as apologizing for causing emotional pain (Beach & LeBaron, 2002), may make physicians' touching of patients more normative relative to other actions and thus affect patients' evaluations of physicians' touch.

In line with Goffman's (1963) notion of *civil inattention*, while patients engage in a variety of private actions such as undressing (Heath, 1986), it may be more normative for physicians to avert their gaze, even if engaged in conversation. The action of "remembering" publicly is associated commonly with gazing away from interlocutors (Beach & LeBaron, 2002; Goodwin, 1987). When patients discuss personally

sensitive or embarrassing events (Beach & LeBaron, 2002; Heath, 1986, 1988), or when they receive bad medical news (e.g., cancer diagnoses; Maynard, 2003), they sometimes look away from their interlocutors or cover their faces. One systematic finding, then, is that while physicians engage in physical examination, patients tend to adopt a *middle distance* gaze orientation "away from the doctor yet at no particular object within the local environment" (Heath, 1988, p. 149).

The possibility that the social organization of different verbal actions structures nonverbal behavior differently has direct implications for the types of outcomes discussed earlier. For example, it has already been documented that physicians' nonverbal behavior affects raters' evaluations of the affective-relational dimension of communication. Such evaluations are, however, also affected by physicians' verbal behaviors, which shape outcomes. For example, when physicians are more verbally empathetic (e.g., provide more reassurance), patients are more satisfied and adherent to medical recommendations and less willing to sue for malpractice (for a review, see Frankel, 1995). When providers are less verbally domineering or controlling (e.g., less directive), patients are more assertive, expressive, and disclose more information (Street, 1992b); are more satisfied (Street, 1992a); and experience better physical-health outcomes (e.g., metabolic control; Street et al., 1993). Researchers need to determine if these types of verbal behaviors structure nonverbal behavior in particular ways, and they need to analyze nonverbal behaviors in conjunction with them.

If researchers are going to link nonverbal behavior to talk in interaction, in this case physical-patient interaction, and if different social organizations of verbal action structure nonverbal behavior differentially, then, at the very least, researchers need to refine extant coding schemata to better control for social action. The bulk of most coding schemata categorize talk *not* in terms of social action but rather in terms of a combination of grammatical form and topical content. These limitations have been addressed partially by narrowing analyses to, and developing new coding schemata around, particular (classes of) social actions, such as patients' requests for medical services (Kravitz, Bell, & Franz, 1999).[5]

Sequencing

One of the most fundamental interactional contexts organizing social action is the adjacency-pair sequence (Schegloff & Sacks 1973). In its basic form, the adjacency-pair sequence is composed of two turns of talk: a first-pair part, produced by one speaker, which initiates a course of action, and a second-pair part, produced by a different speaker, which responds to the initiated action. Space limitations prohibit full explication of the adjacency-pair sequence, and only two points are made here.

First, first-pair parts affect second-pair parts by normatively obligating, and constraining what counts as, relevant responses. For example, "Yes"/"No"-formatted questions constrain initial responses to versions of "Yes" or "No" (Raymond, 2003), and such constraints can have implications for patient participation (Heritage & Robinson, 2006; Robinson, 2001a). Second, first-pair parts establish frameworks for understanding second-pair parts, and thus the meaning of communicative behavior is heavily influenced by its sequential positioning (Schegloff & Sacks, 1973). For example, in Extract 3, the physicians' first two head nods (Lines 5 and 7) are produced after the patient's response and are understood as acknowledging the patient's talk and as encouragement to continue (Schegloff, 1982). Evidence for this claim is that in each case, the patient continues to produce a new turn-constructional unit. In contrast, in Extract 4, the physician's head nod (Line 4) is produced *as a response* to the patient's request for confirmation (Line 1); because of its sequential positioning, it gets understood differently as a confirmation.

Extract 4 [MC:14:02]

```
01   PAT: That takes effect right away? ((gazing at doctor))
02        (1.2)
03   PAT: Thuh [flu shot.]
04   DOC:      [      /\[/
05   DOC:              [°Mm hm,°
06   PAT: ((Shifts gaze from doctor to computer))
```

Research attempting to discover variables that affect physicians' and patients' communication has been criticized for (1)

not accounting for "the two-way and contingent (i.e., sequential) nature of physician-patient interaction" (Hall, Harrigan, &

Rosenthal, 1995, p. 25) and (2) implying claims about causation while using the correlation statistic (for other critiques, see Buller & Street, 1992; Street & Buller, 1987). Because correlations do not reveal the direction of causality, because much of social action is organized by the adjacency-pair sequence, and because first-pair parts affect second-pair parts, if sequencing is not accounted for, then significant correlations are constantly in danger of being sequentially spurious.

It also appears that nonverbal behavior can be sequenced independent of verbal adjacency-pair sequences (although nonverbal sequences are still often organized by reference to talk). That is, there is preliminary evidence that physicians' and patients' nonverbal behaviors are nonrandom, patterned, and synchronized. For instance, Street and Buller (1987) provided evidence that physicians and patients "matched" gaze orientation, body orientation, and illustrative gestures, and Street and Buller (1988) demonstrated physician-patient reciprocation or convergence regarding body orientation. Koss and Rosenthal (1997) found external raters' evaluations of physician-patient nonverbal synchrony to be positively associated with raters' evaluations of physician-patient rapport. Several reviews (Kiesler & Auerbach, 2003; Lepper, Martin, & DiMatteo, 1995) have suggested that the presence or absence of physicians' and patients' nonverbal synchrony (or exchange) plays a role in a variety of participants' affective-relational attributions, such as affiliation and dominance, respectively (for more on synchrony, see Tickle-Degnen, this volume).

The above correlational research is supported by focused studies of interaction. For example, in line with the observation that gaze communicates persons' current focus of attention, Heath (1988) showed that a physician's gaze shift to a female patient's chest can lead directly to the patient gazing at her own chest. Similarly, Heath (1986) showed that physicians' gaze shifts to objects of discussion, such as X rays, can lead directly to patients' gazing at the same objects. In the same way that patients can use vocal hitches and perturbations to solicit physicians' gaze (see above), patients can use nonverbal behaviors—such as gaze shifts toward physicians, hand gestures, torso shifts, and leg movements—to solicit both physicians' gaze and talk (Heath, 1986). For example, patients sometimes seek physicians' gaze nonvocally for purposes of exhibiting embodied characteristics of their suffering (Beach & LeBaron, 2002; Heath, 1986, 2002). In Figure 23.6, in addition to using vocal hitches and perturbations to solicit the physician's gaze, the patient additionally gestures with her right hand to locate the position of her symptoms (i.e., her "e:ye e:ar"). Although more research is necessary, Heath (1986) noted that some of these nonverbal sequences operate in a fashion similar to verbal summons-answer sequences (Schegloff, 1968).

The Inseparability of Nonverbal Behaviors From Themselves

In addition to turn taking, social action, and sequences, nonverbal behavior embodies its *own* interactional context. That is, the social meaning of individual nonverbal behaviors can be altered when they are employed simultaneously. For example, Harrigan and Rosenthal (1983) found external raters' evaluations of physicians' rapport to be associated with interactions between physicians' torso position (i.e., forward or backward lean), head nodding, and leg position (i.e., crossed or uncrossed). Based on these types of findings, Harrigan and Rosenthal (1986) later asserted,

Nonverbal units of behavior are difficult, if not impossible, to study in total isolation from one another. While the head is nodding, the trunk may be angled forward or back, the limbs may be still or moving, the face expressionless or animated, and the gaze steady, averted, or darting. Each unit of nonverbal behavior is interrelated in that each is capable of influencing the evaluation of another behavior. (p. 45)

Studies have not often tested for interaction effects between individual nonverbal behaviors. In fact, such interactions are obscured when individual nonverbal behaviors are collapsed into larger-order variables, such as immediacy, which has been operationalized in terms of decreased physical proximity and increased touch, forward lean, gaze, and body orientation (Larsen & Smith, 1981; see also the section on head nodding). This is not to suggest that the aggregation of individual nonverbal behaviors is completely unprincipled. For instance, researchers often evaluate their coherence with statistical techniques, such as factor analysis. Aggregation is less principled, however, when it is motivated by professional demands involving acceptable levels of interrater reliability or significance, statistical demands involving cell size, and so on. Aggregation does, however, obscure the effects of individual nonverbal behaviors, as well as the fact that individual nonverbal behaviors do interact.

One of the most well-documented interrelationships is between gaze and body orientation (Mehrabian, 1967). Although different segments of the body (e.g., the head, torso, and legs) can be oriented in different directions (Kendon, 1990), there remains a socially understood body-segment hierarchy in terms of persons' levels of attention and engagement. Specifically, even though gaze orientation communicates persons' current foci of attention, relative to upper-body segments (e.g., the head), lower-body segments (e.g., the legs) more strongly communicate persons' frames of dominant orientation (Kendon, 1990).

For example, in Figure 23.5, the physician's head, torso, and legs are in alignment and face the desk or computer; the patient is gazing at the physician. When physicians arrange their body segments to have divergent orientations—for example, in Figure 23.6 (compared with Figure 23.5), when the physician keeps his torso and legs oriented toward the desk or computer yet rotates his head 30° to the right of his body to gaze at the patient—they may communicate (1) postural instability (e.g., of their head relative to their body); (2) potential resolutions to such instability by reference to the more stable segments of the body (e.g., returning their head into alignment with their body); (3) an orientation to multiple courses of action (e.g., one by their head, such as engaging the patient to ask them a question, and another by their body, such as documenting the patient's answer in the medical records); and (4) a ranking of these multiple courses of action in terms of level of orientation (e.g., the action of documenting is more primary and long term than that of engaging the patient in talk; Robinson, 1998).

The interrelated social organizations of gaze and body orientation can affect raters' attributions. For example, in a nonmedical context, Mehrabian (1967) found the amount of time senders maintained head orientation toward receivers to be positively associated with external raters' evaluations of senders' positive attitudes toward receivers, but only when senders' bodies were also oriented toward receivers. In a medical context, Ruusuvuori (2001) examined patients' responses to physicians' opening questions (e.g., "What can I do for you today?") and showed that when physicians removed their gaze from patients prior to patients having completed their responses, patients tended to produce disfluencies to (re)solicit physicians' gaze. Ruusuvuori found that patients produced fewer disfluencies when physicians' bodies were oriented toward (vs. away) from patients (e.g., Figure 23.7 compared with Figure 23.6). Ruusuvuori's findings suggest that in terms of physicians' levels of engagement with patients (i.e., attention to patient's responses), patients understand the absence or removal of physicians' gaze differently depending on the orientation of physicians' bodies.

The interrelationship between gaze and body orientation can be complicated by other nonverbal behaviors. For example, in a nonmedical context, Goodwin (1981) suggested that recipients' lack of attention communicated by shifting their gaze away from speakers can be partially offset by recipients nodding during and after their gaze removal. To further complicate matters, because gaze and body orientation are used primarily to communicate (dis)engagement, their understanding cannot be separated from that of the objects being (dis)engaged. Patients can differentiate between physicians' gaze at patients' eyes versus other body parts (e.g., legs, breasts, backs), versus medical records, with different interactional and attributional implications (Heath, 1986, 1988; Robinson, 1998).

◆ *Conclusion*

This chapter reviews findings related to nonverbal behavior and physician-patient interaction and shows that physicians' nonverbal behavior—which is integral to the construction and management of empathy, rapport, and generally a "positive" affective-relational communication style—has wide-ranging effects (direct and indirect) on patients' communicative, social, psychological, and physiological health outcomes. Despite these empirical strides, research on nonverbal communication can be improved. The bulk of prior research has focused exclusively on individual nonverbal behaviors (e.g., body orientation) or coherent aggregates of nonverbal behaviors (e.g., reinforcement). This chapter argues that the social meaning of nonverbal behavior—and thus its production, understanding, and effects—is fundamentally and irremediably shaped by, and thus must be studied relative to, its situation within a variety of aspects of interactional context. This is not to say that the effects of nonverbal behavior are relative. Rather, nonverbal behavior is organized systematically and finely by reference to both talk and other nonverbal behavior.

This chapter demonstrates that physicians' production of individual nonverbal cues (e.g., gaze, body orientation, head nodding), and patients' understandings of such cues, is organized by rules associated with turn taking, the construction of particular social actions, the sequencing of actions, and the organization of other nonverbal behaviors (e.g., the interorganization of gaze and body orientation). Not taking these aspects of interactional context into account obscures our understanding of the cause-effect relationships between nonverbal (as well as verbal) communication variables and their outcomes.

Relative to research on nonverbal communication between 1965 and 1995, research over the last 10 years has languished. New directions in research point toward developing new ways of classifying—that is, conceptualizing and measuring—nonverbal communication. On the one hand, "without classification, there could be no advanced conceptualization, reasoning, language, data analysis or, for that matter, social science research" (Bailey, 1994, p. 1). Traditional methodologies for coding interaction will always (for a variety of statistical and other reasons) be blunt to the ecological validity of interaction (Mishler, 1984). As such, advances in research will require large-scale partnerships between multiple teams of researchers representing multiple methodological and ontological perspectives. Largely qualitative research on the interorganizational relationships between multiple modes of communication (e.g., verbal, nonverbal, artifactual) must proceed both simultaneously and in conjunction with largely quantitative, effects-based research, preferably without too many analytic compromises on either side.

◆ Notes

1. Because of space limitations, this chapter excludes research on patient-nurse and patient-psychotherapist interaction (for a review, see Caris-Verhallen, Kerkstra, & Bensing, 1999, and Hall, Harrigan, & Rosenthal, 1995, respectively).

2. Compared with self-report measures of emotional expressiveness, those that are based on external raters' observations of concrete behaviors are more conservative and thus more appropriate for isolating nonverbal "predictors" of behavior (Riggio & Riggio, 2002).

3. Overall, researchers seldom measure physicians' and patients' turns. For an exception, see Street and Buller (1988), who found physicians' turns to be longer than those of patients and older patients' turns to be longer than those of younger patients.

4. The fact that the patient's ".h Uh:m" does not secure the physician's gaze in this particular instance does not invalidate it as being a member of a class of practices designed to do so (Goodwin, 1981; Heath, 1986; Ruusuvuori,

2001). As this section goes on to discuss, this extract demonstrates both the interrelated and the negotiated character of verbal and nonverbal communication.

5. The argument concerning social action can be extended to *social activity*. In physician-patient communication, medical action is frequently produced within specific medical phases or activities. For instance, primary-care acute visits have roughly six phases: opening, problem presentation, information gathering such as history taking and physical examination, diagnosis, treatment, and closing (Robinson, 2003). These phases can have their own forms of social organization that can shape the production and understanding of their constituent actions, as does opening (Robinson, 1998), problem-presentation (Robinson & Heritage, 2005), and closing (Robinson, 2001b). Along these lines, a number of studies of nonverbal communication have controlled for medical phase (e.g., Duggan & Parrott, 2001; Harrigan, Oxman, & Rosenthal, 1985; Larsen & Smith, 1981; Street & Buller, 1987).

◆ References

Aruguete, M. S., & Roberts, C. A. (2002). Participants' ratings of male physicians who vary in race and communication style. *Psychological Reports, 91,* 793–806.

Bailey, K. D. (1994). *Typologies and taxonomies: An introduction to classification techniques.* Thousand Oaks, CA: Sage.

Beach, W. A., & LeBaron, C. D. (2002). Body disclosures: Attending to personal problems and reported sexual abuse during a medical encounter. *Journal of Communication, 52,* 617–639.

Bensing, J. M. (1991). Doctor-patient communication and the quality of care. *Social Science & Medicine, 32,* 1301–1310.

Bensing, J. M., & Dronkers, J. (1992). Instrumental and affective aspects of physician behavior. *Medical Care, 30,* 283–298.

Bensing, J. M., Kerssens, J. J., & van der Pasch, M. (1995). Patient-directed gaze as a tool for discovering and handling psychosocial problems in general practice. *Journal of Nonverbal Behavior, 19,* 223–242.

Ben-Sira, Z. (1982). Stress potential and esotericity of health problems: The significance of the physician's affective behavior. *Medical Care, 20,* 414–424.

Buller, D. B., & Street, R. L., Jr. (1992). Physician-patient relationships. In R. S. Feldman (Ed.), *Applications of nonverbal behavior theories and research* (pp. 119–141). Hillsdale, NJ: Erlbaum.

Burgoon, J. K. (1994). Nonverbal signals. In M. L. Knapp & G. R. Miller (Eds.), *Handbook of interpersonal communication* (2nd ed., pp. 229–285). Thousand Oaks, CA: Sage.

Caris-Verhallen, W. M., Kerkstra, A., & Bensing, J. M. (1999). Non-verbal behaviour in nurse-elderly patient communication. *Journal of Advanced Nursing, 29,* 808–818.

Cegala, D. J., McNeilis, K. S., McGee, D. S., & Jonas, A. P. (1995). A study of doctors' and patients' perceptions of information processing and communication competence during the medical interview. *Health Communication, 7,* 179–203.

Duffy, F. D., Gordon, G. H., Whelan, G., Cole-Kelly, K., & Frankel, R. (2004). Assessing competence in communication and interpersonal skills: The Kalamazoo II Report. *Academic Medicine, 79,* 495–507.

Duggan, A. P., & Parrott, R. L. (2001). Physicians' nonverbal rapport building and patients' talk about the subjective component of illness. *Human Communication Research, 27,* 299–311.

Egbert, L. D., Battit, G. E., Welch, C. E., & Bartlett, M. K. (1964). Reduction of postoperative pain by encouragement and instruction of patients: A study of doctor-patient rapport. *New England Journal of Medicine, 270,* 825.

Ekman, P., & Friesen, W. V. (1969). The repertoire of nonverbal behavior: Categories, origins, usage, and coding. *Semiotica, 1,* 49–98.

Farace, R. V., Monge, P. R., & Russell, M. (1977). *Communicating in organizations.* Reading, MA: Addison-Wesley.

Frankel, R. M. (1995). Emotion and the physician-patient relationship. *Motivation & Emotion, 19,* 163–173.

Giron, M., Manjon-Arce, P., Puerto-Barber, J., Sanchez-Garcia, E., & Gomez-Beneyto (1998). Clinical interview skills and identification of emotional disorders in primary care. *American Journal of Psychiatry, 155,* 530–535.

Glassman, M., & Glassman, N. (1981). A marketing analysis of physician selection and patient satisfaction. *Journal of Health Care Marketing, 1,* 25–31.

Goffman, E. (1963). *Behavior in public places.* New York: Free Press.

Goffman, E. (1983). The interaction order. *American Sociological Review, 48,* 1–17.

Goodwin, C. (1981). *Conversational organization: Interaction between speakers and hearers.* New York: Academic Press.

Goodwin, C. (1987). Forgetfulness as an interactive resource. *Social Psychology Quarterly, 50,* 115–131.

Goodwin, C. (1995). Seeing in depth. *Social Studies of Science, 25,* 237–274.

Griffith, C. H., Wilson, J. F., Langer, S., & Haist, S. A. (2003). House staff nonverbal communication skills and standardized patient satisfaction. *Journal of General Internal Medicine, 18,* 170–174.

Haakana, M. (2002). Laughter in medical interaction: From quantification to analysis, and back. *Journal of Sociolinguistics, 6,* 207–235.

Hall, J. A., Harrigan, J. A., & Rosenthal, R. (1995). Nonverbal behavior in clinician-patient interaction. *Applied and Preventive Psychology, 4,* 21–37.

Hall, J. A., Irish, J. T., Roter, D. L., Ehrlich, C. M., & Miller, L. H. (1994). Gender in medical encounters: An analysis of physician and patient communication in a primary care setting. *Health Psychology, 13,* 384–392.

Harrigan, J. A. (1985). Self-touching as an indicator of underlying affect and language processes. *Social Science & Medicine, 20,* 1161–1168.

Harrigan, J. A., Oxman, T. E., & Rosenthal, R. (1985). Rapport expressed through nonverbal behavior. *Journal of Nonverbal Behavior, 9,* 95–110.

Harrigan, J. A., & Rosenthal, R. (1983). Physicians' head and body positions as determinants of perceived rapport. *Journal of Applied Social Psychology, 13,* 496–509.

Harrigan, J. A., & Rosenthal, R. (1986). Nonverbal aspects of empathy and rapport in physician-patient interaction. In P. D. Blanck, R. Buck, & R. Rosenthal (Eds.), *Nonverbal communication in the clinical context* (pp. 36–73). University Park: The Pennsylvania State University Press.

Heath, C. (1986). *Body movement and speech in medical interaction.* Cambridge, UK: Cambridge University Press.

Heath, C. (1988). Embarrassment and interactional organization. In P. Drew & A. Wootton (Eds.), *Erving Goffman: Exploring the interaction order* (pp. 136–160). Boston, MA: Northeastern University Press.

Heath, C. (2002). Demonstrative suffering: The gestural (re)embodiment of symptoms. *Journal of Communication, 52,* 597–616.

Heritage, J. C. (1984). *Garfinkel and ethnomethodology.* New York: Polity Press.

Heritage, J., & Robinson, J. D. (2006). The structure of patients' presenting concerns: Physicians' opening questions. *Health Communication, 19,* 89–102.

Irish, J. T. (1997). Deciphering the physician-older patient interaction. *International Journal of Psychiatry in Medicine, 27,* 251–267.

Kaplan, S. H., Greenfield, S., & Ware, J. E. (1989). Impact of the doctor-patient relationship on the outcomes of chronic disease. In M. Stewart & D. Roter (Eds.), *Communicating with medical patients* (pp. 228–245). Newbury Park, CA: Sage.

Kendon, A. (1990). *Conducting interaction: Patterns of behavior in focused encounters.* Cambridge, UK: Cambridge University Press.

Kiesler, D. J., & Auerbach, S. M. (2003). Integrating measurement of control and affiliation in studies of physician-patient

interaction: The interpersonal circumplex. *Social Science & Medicine, 57,* 1707–1722.

Koss, T., & Rosenthal, R. (1997). Interactional synchrony, positivity, and patient satisfaction in the physician-patient relationship. *Medical Care, 35,* 1158–1163.

Kravitz, R. L., Bell, R. A., & Franz, C. E. (1999). A taxonomy of requests by patients (TORP): A new system for understanding clinical negotiation in office practice. *Journal of Family Practice, 48,* 872–878.

Langer, E. J., Janis, I. L., & Wolfer, J. A. (1975). Reduction of psychological stress in surgical patients. *Journal of Experimental Social Psychology, 11,* 155.

Larsen, K. M., & Smith, C. K. (1981). Assessment of nonverbal communication in the patient-physician interview. *The Journal of Family Practice, 12,* 481–488.

Lepper, H. S., Martin, L. R., & DiMatteo, M. R. (1995). A model of nonverbal exchange in physician-patient expectations for patient involvement. *Journal of Nonverbal Behavior, 19,* 207–222.

Maynard, D. W. (2003). *Bad news, good news: Conversational order in everyday talk and clinical settings.* Chicago: University of Chicago Press.

McNeill, D., Cassell, J., & McCullough, K. (1994). Communicative effects of speech-mismatched gestures. *Research on Language and Social Interaction, 27,* 223–237.

Mechanic, D., & Meyer, S. (2000). Concepts of trust among patients with serious illness. *Social Science & Medicine, 51,* 657–668.

Mehrabian, A. (1967). Orientation behaviors and nonverbal attitude communication. *Journal of Communication, 17,* 324–332.

Mishel, M. H. (1988). Uncertainty in illness. *Image: Journal of Nursing Scholarship, 20,* 225–232.

Mishler, E. (1984). *The discourse of medicine: Dialectics of medical interviews.* Norwood, NJ: Ablex.

Raymond, G. (2003). Grammar and social organization: Yes/no interrogatives and the structure of responding. *American Sociological Review, 68,* 939–967.

Riggio, H. R., & Riggio, R. E. (2002). Emotional expressiveness, extraversion, and neuroticism: A meta-analysis. *Journal of Nonverbal Behavior, 26,* 195–218.

Robinson, J. D. (1998). Getting down to business: Talk, gaze, and body orientation during openings of doctor-patient consultations. *Human Communication Research, 25,* 98–124.

Robinson, J. D. (2001a). Asymmetry in action: Sequential resources in the negotiation of a prescription request. *Text, 21,* 19–54.

Robinson, J. D. (2001b). Closing medical encounters: Two physician practices and their implications for the expression of patients' unstated concerns. *Social Science & Medicine, 53,* 639–656.

Robinson, J. D. (2003). An interactional structure of medical activities during acute visits and its implications for patients' participation. *Health Communication, 15,* 27–59.

Robinson, J. D., & Heritage, J. (2005). The structure of patients' presenting concerns: The completion relevance of current symptoms. *Social Science and Medicine, 61,* 481–493.

Robinson, J. D., & Stivers, T. (2001). Achieving activity transitions in primary-care consultations: From history taking to physical examination. *Human Communication Research, 27,* 253–298.

Rowland-Morin, P. A., Burchard, K. W., Garb, J. L., & Coe, N. P. W. (2002). Influence of effective communication by surgery students on their oral examination scores. *Academic Medicine, 66,* 169–171.

Ruusuvuori, J. (2001). Looking means listening: Coordinating displays of engagement in doctor-patient interaction. *Social Science & Medicine, 52,* 1093–1108.

Sacks, H., Schegloff, E. A., & Jefferson, G. (1974). A simplest systematics for the organization of turn-taking for conversation. *Language, 50,* 696–735.

Sanders, R. E. (1987). The interconnection of utterances and nonverbal displays. *Research on Language and Social Interaction, 20,* 141–170.

Schegloff, E. A. (1968). Sequencing in conversational openings. *American Anthropologist, 70,* 1075–1095.

Schegloff, E. A. (1982). Discourse as an interactional achievement: Some uses of "uh-huh" and other things that come between sentences. In D. Tannen (Ed.), *Analyzing discourse: Text and talk* (pp. 71–93). Washington, DC: Georgetown University Press.

Schegloff, E. A. (1995). Discourse as an interactional achievement III: The omnirelevance of action. *Research on Language and Social Interaction, 28,* 185–211.

Schegloff, E. A. (1996). Turn organization: One intersection of grammar and interaction. In E. Ochs, E. Schegloff, & S. Thompson (Eds.), *Interaction and grammar* (pp. 52–133). Cambridge, UK: Cambridge University Press.

Schegloff, E. A. (1998). Body torque. *Social Research, 65,* 535–596.

Schegloff, E. A., & Sacks, H. (1973). Opening up closings. *Semiotica, 7,* 289–327.

Smith, C. K., Polis, E., & Hadac, R. R. (1981). Characteristics of the initial medical interview associated with patient satisfaction and understanding. *Journal of Family Practice, 12,* 283–288.

Stamp, G. H., & Knapp, M. L. (1990). The construct of intent in interpersonal communication. *Quarterly Journal of Speech, 76,* 282–299.

Streeck, J. (1993). Gesture as communication I: Its coordination with gaze and speech. *Communication Monographs, 60,* 275–299.

Streeck, J., & Knapp, M. (2002). Culture, meaning, and interpersonal communication. In M. L. Knapp & J. A. Daly (Eds.), *Handbook of interpersonal communication* (pp. 286–319). Thousand Oaks, CA: Sage.

Street, R. L., Jr. (1992a). Analyzing communication in medical consultations: Do behavioral measures correspond to patients' perceptions? *Medical Care, 30,* 976–988.

Street, R. L., Jr. (1992b). Communicative styles and adaptations in physician-parent consultations. *Social Science & Medicine, 34,* 1155–1163.

Street, R. L. Jr. (2003). Communication in medical encounters: An ecological perspective. In T. Thompson, A. M. Dorsey, K. I. Miller, & R. Parrott (Eds.), *Handbook of health communication* (pp. 63–89). Mahwah, NJ: Erlbaum.

Street, R. L., Jr., & Buller, D. B. (1987). Nonverbal response patterns in physician-patient interactions: A functional analysis. *Journal of Nonverbal Behavior, 11,* 234–253.

Street, R. L., Jr., & Buller, D. B. (1988). Patients' characteristics affecting physician-patient nonverbal communication. *Human Communication Research, 15,* 60–90.

Street, R. L., Jr., Piziak, V. K., Carpentier, W. S., Herzog, J., Hejl, J., Skinnner, G., et al. (1993). Provider-patient communication and metabolic control. *Diabetes Care, 16,* 714–721.

Van Dulmen, A. M., Verhaak, P. F. M., & Bilo, H. J. G. (1997). Shifts in doctor-patient communication during a series of outpatient consultations in non-insulin-dependent diabetes mellitus. *Patient Education & Counselling, 30,* 227–237.

Verhaak, P. F. M. (1988). Detection of psychological complaints by general practitioners. *Medical Care, 26,* 1009–1020.

Weinberger, M., Greene, J. Y., & Mamlin, J. J. (1981). The impact of clinical encounter events on patient and physician satisfaction. *Social Science & Medicine, 15E,* 239–244.

24

NONVERBAL DYNAMICS IN COMPUTER-MEDIATED COMMUNICATION, OR :(AND THE NET :('S WITH YOU, :) AND YOU :) ALONE

◆ Joseph B. Walther
Michigan State University

I t may seem ironic, at first glance, to review research on nonverbal communication in the realm of computer-mediated communication (CMC). A considerable history of theory and research suggests that CMC differs from face-to-face (FtF) communication precisely on account of the *lack* of nonverbal cues in the new medium, and, that as a result, CMC offers meager social meaning and limited value. As is known to the blind and deaf, who cannot use all the cues that those with sight and hearing can use, or to distant lovers, who depend on written letters to express their love, however, this chapter will show that there are indeed a variety of cues and adaptations for affective and comprehensible communication when a larger set of cues is unavailable, even in the textually oriented mode of CMC. Specifically, some nonverbal cues—those involving chronemics— traverse CMC and are quite potent. As well, textual symbols—emoticons— that are presumed to work as surrogates for nonverbal cues are widely known and easily recognized although their utility is questionable.

The limited research on extant nonverbal cues or their substitutes, as well as emerging research on specific reintroductions of nonverbal features through avatars, videoconferencing, and virtual reality systems is leading to a more functionally oriented perspective on mediated human communication. Newer research is focusing on what people communicate, and the variety of means by which to do so, some of which means were considered previously the exclusive domain of nonverbal cues. As a result, a major consequence of contemporary CMC research is to help us learn more about communication symbol systems and their functions in general, by observing both their absence and their systematic replacement.

This chapter reviews the major theories and their research traditions on CMC and the similarities and differences among them with respect to how the relative absence of nonverbal cues may affect communication and social perceptions. As will be argued, most of these approaches have relegated nonverbal communication to a "black box," in a kind of all-or-nothing fashion, assuming that all nonverbal cues lead to a variety of functions, and that the cues and functions are isomorphic (i.e., that nonverbal cues are tied directly and exclusively to communicative social functions, such that the absence of such cues precludes functional effects from occurring).

The chapter then discusses the potency of chronemics in CMC (e.g., alternative temporal scales, time pressure, and the implicit and explicit effects of timing cues on interpersonal judgments online). It turns next to a variety of ways in which users or technology designers attempt to reintroduce nonverbal cues into CMC or other electronic communication systems. Finally, considering exemplary approaches to online deception and some research employing virtual reality systems, we see that future

theoretical and technological development requires more exacting research on nonverbal communication in an area once thought to be devoid of such features.

◆ Hypothesizing About the "Lack" of Nonverbal Cues in Early CMC Theories

SOCIAL PRESENCE THEORY

The earliest predictions applied to CMC stressed the depersonalizing, predominantly negative effects of communication without nonverbal cues. The first of these theories was social presence theory (Short, Williams, & Christie, 1976), the original treatment of which is noteworthy for its comprehensive treatment of the role of nonverbal cues in communication. Originally focused on video- and audioconferencing, its theoretical specifications have also been applied to text-only communication (Hiltz, Johnson, & Agle, 1978; Rice, 1984; Rice & Case, 1983). The theory deals with decrements in interpersonal affect as communication systems incrementally reduce the cue systems that users may employ. Thus, as communicators shift from FtF to videoconferencing, many proxemic, as well as haptic, cues are unavailable. Moving to audioconferencing, kinesics and any remaining proxemic cues are also removed. Short et al. (1976) equate the uses or absence of these cue systems with the degree of "social presence" that communicators may experience, positing that social presence declines as the number of cue systems declines. Social presence, in turn, is conceptualized as the communicator's involvement with the target of the conversation, and it is associated with warmth and friendliness. Many studies have supported the premises of social presence theory (for review, see Walther & Parks,

2002), although it has also received much criticism insofar as its application to CMC is concerned (e.g., Lea, 1991; Walther, 1992).

THE LACK OF SOCIAL CONTEXT CUES HYPOTHESIS

A similar perspective to social presence theory is the lack of social context cues hypothesis (Kiesler, 1987; Kiesler, Siegel, & McGuire, 1984; Siegel, Dubrovsky, Kiesler, & McGuire, 1986; Sproull & Kiesler, 1986). This position argues that nonverbal cues in FtF settings establish the social context of interaction, and with the awareness of social context, participants infer and perform normative behavior. Without social context cues, participants are deindividuated and thus behave aberrantly, including being self- rather than other-focused, task-oriented, and disinhibited. These states lead not only to colder and more task-oriented communication, it is argued, but also to engage in "flaming" (name-calling, swearing, or other uninhibited expressions) online and more attitude polarization. This position, like social presence theory, suggests that the absence of nonverbal cues is the causal factor distinguishing FtF and online interaction.

MEDIA RICHNESS

A third theory also regards the differences among media and their effects due to the range of nonverbal cue systems media carry, although media richness theory (Daft & Lengel, 1984, 1986) differs from the previous positions in three important respects. First, although the number of cue systems supported is a primary difference among communication media in this theory, cue systems are joined by three other elements in differentiating media capacity: the ability to personalize messages (i.e., to tailor messages for a specific recipient), the capacity to use natural and varied language, and the extent to which message exchanges offer immediate feedback (i.e., sender and receiver exchanges are bidirectional, or they are asynchronous and responses are delayed). Together, these dimensions define "media richness."

The second important difference between this theory and the others is the specification regarding the predicted effectiveness and efficiency of richer versus leaner media when considering the degree of equivocality and uncertainty involved in the communication task. Thus, for highly equivocal tasks, richer media are posited to be more efficient, whereas for simpler tasks, although a rich or lean medium might be equally as effective, a leaner medium may be more efficient (Daft & Lengel, 1984). For instance, to ask a colleague what time a meeting is scheduled to take place, one may go down the hallway FtF, but a phone call or e-mail would work as well, possibly more quickly, and with less effort.

The third difference is that, whereas this theory, like others, places a premium on nonverbal and other aspects of communicative flexibility, it stresses the role of multiple cues as sources to facilitate the *comprehension* of information rather than as a source of individuation, social presence, or social context. In media richness theory, the availability of nonverbal cues (without differentiation) and other communication system attributes are expected to help make media, and messages, richer, leading to the reduction of equivocality in shorter periods of time. Although interpersonal effects have been imputed as derivatives of this theory (Markus, 1994), the original formulation of the theory makes no such claim.

OVERVIEW AND SUMMARY

As a group, all three of these theories suggest a "black box" approach to the role of nonverbal cues in communication. They each seem to assume that if the capacity to exhibit and detect the use of nonverbal codes is supported by alternative media, users will be or must be using these codes and attending to them, without privileging one code over another. They also presume, as some critiques have suggested (Culnan & Markus, 1987), that there is a one-to-one correspondence between nonverbal codes and the social functions with which they are associated (e.g., increases in close proximity, gaze, and touch always mean intimacy and never mean threat). Moreover, there appears to be an assumption that nonverbal codes have a monotonic, additive association with those functions (i.e., the more codes that may be used, or the more codes that will be used, the more warm or understandable a given communication episode will be). The perspectives do not consider that the more cue systems available, or by the use of text alone, for that matter, the better communicators may be able to reach *intended* or *desired* levels of affect, even if those targets are homeostasis (Danchak, Walther, & Swan, 2001) or, as later CMC research has shown, disaffiliation and psychological distance from others (Douglas & McGarty, 2001; Markus, 1994; O'Sullivan, 2000; Walther, Loh, & Granka, 2005; Walther, Slovacek, & Tidwell, 2001). Other models do, however, consider the potential for cues of all kinds—multimodal or text alone—to affect relationships differentially.

◆ Adaptation Theories

SOCIAL IDENTIFICATION MODEL OF DEINDIVIDUATION EFFECTS

The next theory discussed is not associated traditionally with the above cues-filtered-out perspective, because it specifies socially oriented responses to the lack of nonverbal cues in CMC. But it relies on an assumption that nonverbal cues, and therefore their individuating identification functions, are occluded by electronic text systems. SIDE, or the social identification model of deindividuation effects (see for review Postmes, Spears, Lea, & Reicher, 2000) is derived from the social identification/self-categorization theory (see Hogg & Abrams, 1988), which holds that people often identify on the basis of common group membership, or ingroup and outgroup identifications, and that certain contextual factors encourage or discourage these forms of identification.

SIDE theorists argue that the process of CMC interaction often facilitates group identification: There may be a salient group or social category associated with an online interaction event, and, most important with respect to nonverbal cues, communicators operate under visual anonymity and are therefore deindividuated. Because they do not see that they differ from one another idiosyncratically, as would be apparent FtF, they are more likely to experience their partners and interpret others' behavior as reflecting group norms, which they value and to which they themselves then adhere. Both SIDE and the lack of social context cues approaches argue that the reintroduction of visual cues ameliorates deindividuation.

The SIDE model is more specific with respect to visual cues than are other traditions. SIDE research has looked at both *between*-media and *within*-media variations. That is, not only have SIDE dynamics been supported in comparisons between CMC and FtF conditions, but they have also been found between CMC alone and CMC in a room where people can see one another (Lea & Spears, 1992), CMC with only text compared with CMC with a photo of one's partners (see Postmes, Spears, & Lea, 1998), and CMC alone versus CMC plus videoconferencing (Lea, Spears, & de Groot, 2001). With respect to nonverbal cues, however, SIDE treats all visual cues the same theoretically. No differentiation is made on the basis of whether visual cues are dynamic (as in videoconferencing) or static (as in photographs). Within SIDE, the function of visual information is to cue individuating identifications, whereas its absence can promote immersion in group identity. Like the previous positions reviewed, SIDE treats text-based CMC as bereft of cues about the individuals using it and asserts that without visual information, users do not identify with one another as individuals. From this perspective, it is only possible to achieve interpersonal relationships online by introducing visual, individuating nonverbal cues such as photographs or video (Rogers & Lea, 2004). In contrast to previous theories, according to SIDE, the outcome of the deindividuated, nonvisual state may be prosocial (raising attraction and evaluations of partners relative to FtF interaction), or it can increase bias and intergroup denigration (Douglas & McGarty, 2001; Lea et al., 2001; Postmes et al., 1998; Postmes & Spears, 2002).

HYPERPERSONAL CMC

One additional model of CMC interaction also places the absence of physical cues as a causal factor in explaining the differences between CMC and FtF communication. The hyperpersonal model of CMC strived originally to explain how CMC interactions may lead to levels of intimacy and social orientation exceeding those of FtF interactions in parallel social contexts (Walther, 1996), but it has been expanded to predict both hyperpositive and hypernegative outcomes (Walther et al., 2001). Like the SIDE model, the hyperpersonal

framework acknowledges that receivers stereotype and idealize their partners when they receive messages without the information about the partner's idiosyncratic characteristics (although the hyperpersonal model does not dictate group- or categorical-level stereotypes; Walther, 1997). The hyperpersonal model also considers the idealizing potential of CMC that eliminates potentially undesirable *dynamic* nonverbal behavior, such as interruptions and other distracting vocalizations, unconventional gaze patterns, and unattractive physical appearance characteristics (Walther & Parks, 2002), although these particular elements have not yet been tested.

Beyond perceptions of partners, however, the reduction of nonverbal cues in CMC is pivotal in other specifications of hyperpersonal interaction. One is that senders, in the process of message construction, engage in selective self-presentation to a degree not afforded in FtF interaction. Because many nonverbal cues are more difficult to control (from body shape and other physical appearance features, vocalic attributes, to kinesic behaviors that are less consciously controlled) compared with verbal behaviors, CMC users can create more intentional messages and avoid unintentional cues. The ability to edit text messages enhances this effect (Walther, in press). Finally, as the CMC process frees users from needing to attend to one's own nonverbal behavior, as well as attending to partners' nonverbal affect, information, or conversation management cues, CMC users recapture cognitive resources that would normally be allocated to those processes and apply them instead to message creation, allowing for further expressive selectivity.

Empirical investigations have supported several aspects of this model. In a test of self-presentation, CMC dyads exchanged more self-disclosure and more intimate personal questions in an online "get-to-know-you" session than did FtF partners, who relied to a greater extent on environmental characteristics, physical attributes, and kinesic behaviors to reduce uncertainty about their partners (Tidwell & Walther, 2002). In a direct test of the impact of facial photographs as a benefit or detriment to hyperpersonal online relationship formation, Walther et al. (2001) employed groups, half of which had interacted via CMC over several tasks, whereas members of the other half were unknown to one another. In each of these conditions, half of them experienced the presence or absence of photographs of their partners' faces immediately prior to a chat. Results showed that those who came to know one another online and did *not* see each other's pictures rated their partners as more affectionate and socially attractive, but the introduction of photos reduced attraction among those who were familiar with each other only online. Only among strangers, a photo enhanced affection and social attraction relative to no photo. Moreover, interesting correlations emerged between participants' self-reported impression management efforts and ratings of their physical attractiveness by partners. When there was no photo, physical attractiveness ratings were positively correlated with self-presentation efforts, but when pictures were shown, self-presentation effort and physical attractiveness were negatively correlated. When one's photo shows, the more one tries to enhance one's impression, the worse it seems to get (Walther et al., 2001).

The hyperpersonal perspective may be the most specific CMC framework with respect to the role of nonverbal communication and its functions in FtF interaction, and how they are transformed online. Not all dimensions of the model have been tested directly, and the model is less specific about the kinds of partners for which hyperpersonal processes should be expected to adhere, drawing on other theories to create contexts in which these dynamics emerge.

SOCIAL INFORMATION PROCESSING

A final theoretical model of CMC employs a different perspective on the relationship between nonverbal cues offline and text-only CMC. The social information processing theory (SIP; Walther, 1992) argues that impression-bearing and relational functions, for which communicators rely on nonverbal cues FtF, are translated into verbal content, linguistic, stylistic, and chronemic cues in the CMC environment. Given that all functions—task, social, and otherwise—must be conveyed through the single conduit of text, it may take more messages, over a longer time, to imbue exchanges with sufficient information for participants to decode and aggregate in order to construct impressions and manage relationships. Add to this slowdown that CMC messages may be exchanged in fits and spurts intermittently (as in e-mail) and even further retardation of evolving social dynamics is expected relative to FtF processes. Central to SIP, however, is the premise that all other things being equal, CMC is as capable as FtF communication of sharing impressions and managing relational communication, based on the substitutability of verbal and nonverbal cues in the service of social functions.

This premise is disconcerting to those who hold that there is unique value to nonverbal cues that cannot be replaced. Indeed, Jones and LeBaron's (2002) review of nonverbal communication literature concluded that it has been assumed that "verbal and nonverbal behaviors are generally different kinds of messages with rather different meanings and potential functions" (p. 501). SIP, on the other hand, argues that information is information and that it can be expressed through a variety of modalities. Like media richness theory (Daft & Lengel, 1984), SIP acknowledges that written cues alone may be less efficient within a given time interval compared with a simultaneously multimodal (i.e., kinesic, vocalic, and verbal) exchange, but given sufficient time and exchange, the two systems may be functionally equivalent, and CMC users make these adaptations fluidly.

The SIP theory has been supported in several empirical studies (for review, see Walther & Parks, 2002). For instance, Liu, Ginther, and Zelhart (2002) found that impression development in CMC was sensitive to both the length of e-mail messages and the frequency of e-mail messages from a partner over time, and Walther and Burgoon (1992) found that relational communication levels changed more or less in parallel between CMC and FtF groups in response to time accrual rather than to the differences between communication conditions (see also Chidambaram & Bostrom, 1993). These studies lend credence to the model's causal factors and predicted effects; they did not examine the microprocesses implicated by the theory—that is, the substitution of verbal cues in the service of functions for which nonverbal cues are employed offline.

A recent study addressed this gap by assessing the specific behaviors in alternative channels that express affinity. Walther et al.'s (2005) experiment employed decision-making dyads meeting FtF or via synchronous computer chat. One member was prompted to enact greater or lesser levels of liking toward his or her partner after an initial interaction period, by whatever way he or she chose to display the affect. The other dyad partner rated the ad hoc confederates' performance on perceived immediacy and affection. Coders rated kinesic cues from videotapes of the FtF confederates and independently rated the vocalic performances as heard through a content-filtering device. Additional coders analyzed both FtF

and CMC transcripts for verbal indications of affinity. Regression analyses of the cues in both conditions were used to identify the variations in cues and channels that most strongly predicted the variations in partner ratings of affect. As expected, that FtF partners expressed affinity through nonverbal cues primarily, with vocalic cues (pleasantness, vocal sharpness, vocal condescension, and timber) predominating over kinesics; verbal cues were not significantly associated with FtF liking in comparison with these nonverbal variations. In CMC conversations, however, an equivalent proportion of the variance in liking was accomplished through verbal behaviors (explicit verbal statements of affection, changing the subject, and various forms of disagreement), demonstrating comparability and substitutability of verbal cues in CMC for vocalic and kinesic cues in FtF interaction.

SUMMARY

The major theories of CMC each portray significant effects of the reduction of nonverbal cues online. Positions range from the austere, early formulations, where nonverbal cues were isomorphic with certain communicative functions, to the more adaptive models of hyperpersonal CMC and SIP, in which users exploit or work through the relative lack of nonverbal cues. Cutting across these models, other research has focused on specific cues—natural or stylized—and the degree to which CMC users adapt affective meaning to their usage.

◆ The Cues That Remain: Chronemics

Whereas physical behavior, voice, space, and appearance cues are indeed absent in text-based CMC, the chronemic cue system remains, although it is frequently over-looked in descriptions of CMC's nonverbal capacity. Hesse, Werner, and Altman (1988) were among the first to recognize the potential for temporal dynamics and cues to play a significant role in CMC, noting potential departures from traditional interaction patterns in terms of temporal scale (the temporal scope and duration of events and relationships), the sequencing of actions, the pace, and the salience of past, present, or future issues in ongoing CMC interactions. Although several studies can now be said to address some of these issues, few of them have noted Hesse et al.'s original thinking.

Among those studies examining temporal factors in CMC, chronemic dynamics are potent forces in the experience of CMC users. As Kalman and Rafaeli (2005) observed, for example, "One of the unknowns of emailing is the time it will take the receiver to form and post a reply. Response times vary considerably, and the chronemics of email are an important non-verbal cue which can convey meaning" (p. 1). According to Rice (1990), e-mail users attend to the time stamps that are placed on messages automatically, inferring from them when a message was sent and how much latency occurred before one of their own messages received a reply.

Temporal dynamics affect virtual groups in a variety of ways, although specific chronemic cues may or may not play a role in these effects. Orlikowski and Yates (2002) found that virtual groups' activity cycles became oriented more toward critical events, such as the occasional exchange of collaborative documents, than toward the influence of predetermined deadlines. In a field study of organizational CMC, Steinfield (1986) found that CMC becomes more task oriented and less socially oriented as collaborators get closer to project deadlines. In a closer inspection of time pressure and CMC, Reid and colleagues

(Reid, Ball, Morley, & Evans, 1997; Reid, Malinek, Stott, & Evans, 1996) determined that the relational tone of CMC is more sensitive to time scarcity than is FtF interaction: In CMC groups, more than in FtF groups, discourse became less rational, and less affective content appeared, as pressure increased with shorter time limits. Conversely, it appears that a *long* duration of time spent in CMC with a partner is inferred as a token of relational intimacy (Henderson & Gilding, 2004).

Response latencies are another familiar chronemic characteristic, and their effects have been studied in several CMC contexts. Members make biased attributions for response delays, assuming personal rather than situational causes for lags by distant team members (Cramton, 2001). Failure to get responses may erode initial levels of trust in virtual groups (Jarvenpaa, Knoll, & Leidner, 1998), and frequent messaging is noted consistently as a critical factor in virtual group trust, affective relations, and effectiveness (Walther & Bunz, 2005), especially with regard to partners' replies to an individual's conversational initiations or requests (Iacono & Weisband, 1997). Latencies also have mixed effects in dyadic, synchronous CMC. In organizational settings where members use Instant Messenger, a query that goes without a response is frequently attributed to one's partner being busy (Nardi, Whittaker, & Bradner, 2000). In social chatting, however, individuals who find themselves waiting for replies grow increasingly frustrated if not hostile (Rintel & Pittam, 1997; see also Feenberg, 1989).

One study tested the interpersonal impressions affected by variations in e-mail response latency, as well as whether messages were sent at night or during the day (Walther & Tidwell, 1995). Researchers created several pairs of e-mail message facsimiles featuring an initial message and a reply that appeared to be initiated by a vice president and replied to by a manager who were separated geographically within a corporation. The time stamps on these e-mail facsimiles made one pair appear to have been sent shortly after 10 a.m. and another pair after 10 p.m. This factor was crossed by the apparent response lag. In some pairs, the reply seemed to occur several minutes after the initial message; alternatively, 24 hours and several minutes appeared to have elapsed. The time stamps were further crossed over two kinds of message exchanges, a task-oriented request versus social banter.

Ratings of these various stimuli confirmed chronemics-based hypotheses. When task messages were sent at night the sender was rated highest on dominance compared with the same message sent during the day. The pattern was opposite for social messages, which signaled more dominance by day than at night. The amount of affection ascribed to a sender's message was affected by an interaction between day and night, the promptness of the reply, and the thematic content. The most affection accorded to task exchanges occurred when there was a quick reply to a daytime request, and the least affection was associated with a prompt response to a nighttime message. As for social messages, more affection was perceived in a slower reply to a daytime message than a fast reply, but a fast reply at night showed more affection than a slow one. Consistent with Hall's (1959) observations about FtF speech lags, it appears that expectations of quick e-mail replies are relaxed within established social relationships, although reactions to response latency are quite different within impersonal relations, both online and offline.

♦ **Reintroducing Cues**

Whereas chronemic cues have always been available, thus countering the ideas that nonverbal cues are lacking from CMC, new

and emerging technologies selectively reintroduce additional cues into communicative exchanges among people who do not meet FtF. Whether executed by users or technology designers, these developments and their impacts inform nonverbal communication principles.

CUE SURROGATES: EMOTICONS

A considerable amount of attention has been devoted to the use of "emoticons" in CMC. Emoticons are the presentation of keyboard symbols used in such manner as to resemble facial expressions. They are assumed widely to express emotion and are frequently described as emotional surrogates in CMC for facial expressions and other nonverbal cues to emotion. "Because the use of e-mail eliminates visual cues such as head nodding, facial expressions, posture, and eye contact found in FtF communication, CMC users often incorporate emoticons as visual cues to augment the meaning of textual electronic messages" (Rezabek & Cochenour, 1998, pp. 201–202). The use of emoticons in CMC dates back at least as far the early 1980s, and for many years "smiley dictionaries" circulated in the Internet, containing hundreds of variations and the verbal labels of their alleged emotional equivalents (e.g., Godin, 1993; Sanderson, 1993). The best known of these symbols are "a smile, wink, and frown, respectively: :-) ;-) :-(" (Danet, Ruedenberg-Wright, & Rosenbaum-Tamari, 1997, n.p.). These symbols are well recognized within the CMC-using community. Among one college student sample, basic emoticons were interpreted more reliably than were photos of human facial expressions of emotion: Whereas Ekman and Friesen (1975) report percentages of agreement about the association of facial photos depicting basic human emotions from 97% for happiness to 67% for anger, Walther and D'Addario

(2001) found that the :) and :(emoticons achieved 98% consensus for happiness and sadness, respectively, and associations of other emoticons with anger, disgust, and fear ranged from 88% to 85%.

Although the literature on emoticons asserts frequently that they function as nonverbal (facial) expressions, very little research has examined the functional impact of these symbols. Most of the research on emoticons has analyzed patterns of their use based on demographic factors: Females use them more frequently than do males (Witmer & Katzman, 1997) and their usage even depends on which part of the United States e-mail users reside (Rezabek & Cochenour, 1998). Walther and D'Addario (2001) explored their functional dynamics. Reviewing the facial affect literature, they derived hypotheses predicting relationships between emoticons and accompanying verbal messages on affective message interpretation. These relationships included a variety of additive effects, by which the emotional valence of the emoticon would be added to the emotional valence of a verbal message, leading to supplementation (for a positive emoticon plus a positive verbal message, a negative emoticon plus a negative verbal message) or modification (a positive element plus a negative "canceling out" or neutralizing overall affect). Alternatively, visual primacy was posited: An emoticon's valence might override that of the verbal statement. The combination of positive and negative messages, among emoticon and verbal statements, might also result in an interpretation of sarcasm, as might the iconic ;) or "winkie."

In a 4 by 2 experimental procedure, :) ;) :(or no emoticon were inserted alternately in simulated e-mail message mock-ups that contained either a positive or a negative verbal statement about a college course. Participants viewed one of these mock-ups and then rated the supposed message

sender's affective state and attitude about the course. There was very little effect of emoticons on attitude and interpretation; what impact they did exhibit was not in accord with the hypotheses from facial expression research. Specifically, *smiley* emoticons had no effect on message interpretation whatsoever. *Frown* emoticons reduced the positivity of a positive verbal message, but frowns did not affect interpretations of negative verbal messages—that is, did not make them even more negative. Overall, there appeared to be a negativity effect: When any negative message element appeared, whether it was an emoticon or a verbal statement, the interpretation was negative. Additionally, the combination of verbal statements and their opposite emoticon were not significantly different in sarcasm from other combinations; only a positive verbal message with a ;) emoticon was rated higher in sarcasm than other combinations, suggesting that the wink symbol has some iconic value in CMC but that a negative verbal statement may override the emoticon effect. Given that only the frown emoticon affected meaning, it appears to be the case that :(and the net :('s with you, but :) and you :) alone.

AVATARS AND VIDEO

In addition to stylized affective cues such as emoticons, developers and users explore the utility of reintroducing certain visual cues into distributed interaction. This has been done primarily through the use of avatars, icons, and videoconferencing.

Avatars. Avatars are two-dimensional representations on a computer screen that chat users can select and move around the screen during online interaction. Avatars are used frequently in various multiplayer computer games such as Everquest and the

SimsOnline, although they have a somewhat longer history in multiuser chat spaces such as the *Palace* (www.thepalace.com/; see Suler, 1999). In most environments, one selects an avatar initially from among a stock of available figures. Avatars are often cartoonish and range from very generic with few distinguishing features to rather elaborate in design. It is also possible to create an individual avatar using graphics software or to craft an avatar from a photograph and upload it to the interaction space. During interaction, dialogue often appears as text, as though emanating from an avatar like the conversational bubbles that appear in comic strips. Advocates of these systems argue that they help orient players and that they reduce the impersonal nature of text-based systems. Much of the research employing avatars focuses on the psychoanalytic dimensions of avatar selection and usage, such as how an avatar both reflects aspects of the user's personalities as it also shapes the online persona through social interaction (Suler, 1999). In some online multiplayer games, avatars are used to duel or fight, although users socialize through text to a large extent alongside the avatar battles (Peña & Hancock, 2006).

Two avatar studies bear immediate relevance to nonverbal communication research. Nowak and Biocca (2003) examined avatars varying in anthropomorphic appearance, representing conversational partners. The more anthropomorphic representations depicted 3-D drawings of heads and faces, whereas less anthropomorphic versions featured disembodied, cartoonish pairs of eyes and lips. Contrary to hypotheses, the less anthropomorphic the avatar, the greater the participants' responses on various measures of presence. The authors concluded that the more realistic but imperfect human resemblances frustrated users' expectations, whereas the more abstract images drew greater interest

(see also Bengtsson, Burgoon, Cederberg, Bonito, & Lundberg, 1999).

Krikorian, Lee, and Chock (2000) examined proxemic responses using avatars. Within a *Palace* chat space, participants engaged in a get-to-know-you conversation online, exchanging text and manipulating the positions of their respective avatars. Researchers captured the video images and developed an automated system for measuring the dynamic distance between avatars based on the pixels in the center of the avatars and the relative distances between them. Results showed relatively even proportions among the pairs of participants who moved their avatars closer, farther, or not at all over the course of the conversation. Among those who moved farther apart, there was also an increase in avatar expressive movement— as if being too close inhibited other kinesics—which was accompanied by self-reports of greater conversational appropriateness and conversational involvement among participants. There was also a curvilinear trend on other ratings, however. In general, the correspondence of participants' social attraction ratings and avatar distances mapped onto the predictions of nonverbal expectancy violations theory (Burgoon & Hale, 1988), in that attraction was greater when avatars interacted either at relatively close or far distances rather than at median ranges.

Anthropomorphic Icons. A less manipulable form of avatars is anthropomorphic graphics, or icons, accompanying CMC messages or appearing fixed on a screen during chat. Icons have the capacity to influence receiver's interpretations of messages, even if receivers are aware that the icon does not necessarily represent the characteristics of the actual message sender. Isotalus (2003) found that receivers' responses to news stories delivered to handheld computers differed based on the apparent gender of an icon accompanying the story. Participants paid more attention when the icon appeared to be female. Furthermore, males found the news more credible when accompanied by a male icon, whereas females' credibility assessments were higher for female icons; evaluations of the stories' entertainment followed an opposite pattern. Lee (2005) also used gendered icons to accompany spontaneous, dyadic CMC chat messages, but the participants were aware that the gendered icon had been randomly assigned to users; that is, there was an even chance that the gender of the icon and the user were mismatched. Despite this awareness, participants (especially female participants) attributed the gender of the chat partner on the basis of the icon's gender. This over-interpretation of gender based on a simple physical appearance representation suggests, as previous perspectives have argued, that CMC plus a little nonverbal representation leads to potentially exaggerated perceptions.

Videoconferencing. Research exploring videoconferencing to enhance social presence and improve remote collaborations predates the Internet and digital technology considerably (see for review Chapanis, Ochsman, Parrish, & Weeks, 1972). Most videoconferencing arrangements and studies involve real-time visual conveyance of participants' faces to remote partners, accompanied by their voices. The results of this research have been generally disappointing. Whereas users report greater subjective presence when video is available, their communication effectiveness and task output tends to be no better, and sometimes worse, than non-visual interfaces provide (Gale, 1991; Storck & Sproull, 1995). Similarly, a recent study comparing *asynchronous* videoconferencing with synchronous video, text-only systems, and FtF

conditions obtained few differences on task performance quality or interpersonal perceptions due to main effects of the interfaces (Nowak, Watt, & Walther, 2005). There was greater perceived involvement with others group members in those conditions with *fewer* visual cues, which, in turn, led to increases in social attraction and credibility ratings of partners.

Interestingly, by focusing video on the *objects* that collaborators discuss rather than on facial displays (but including participants' voices) seems to be superior to face-oriented videoconferencing in many cases (Brittan, 1992). This may be due to the communication efficiency with which humans process multimodal messages, when one level of content traverses the vocal-to-auditory channel, leaving vision free to focus on a common object. When videoconferencing depicts the communicators rather than the objects they are discussing, the objects and the image of partners compete for visual attention, leading to decrements in efficiency and performance.

Fussell and colleagues (Fussell, Kraut, & Siegel, 2000; Gergle, Kraut, & Fussell, 2004; Kraut, Fussell, & Siegel, 2003) have employed audio/videoconferencing with the visual field aimed at an object that one partner manipulates but both can see. In one study (Kraut et al., 2003) a head-mounted camera focused on a bicycle that one partner repaired while an expert helper elsewhere viewed the bicycle (and the repairer's manipulations of it) via video, and instructed the repairer via audio while both looked at the bike. In another study (Gergle et al., 2004), both partners viewed puzzle pieces on an electronic video display, while one partner guided the other via voice toward the puzzle's completion. Compared with other video foci, or no video, participants performed more accurately and quickly at the tasks that were employed in these studies. In the scenarios, the face's physical appearances and expressive dynamics are less useful, and, instead of distracting users with these irrelevant data, their visual attention is directed to objects providing what Clark and Brennan (1991) conceptualize as "communicative grounding."

As promising as this line of research on the role of video appears to be, its promise is limited to those collaborative activities in which physical objects are the focus of the conversation. There are many conversations, however, where the focus is not on tangible items but rather on abstract issues that reside in the thoughts and feelings of communicators. A conversational efficiency framework—that complementary receptors such as the ears and the eyes are well suited to multimodal presentations of voice and visual data—can be extended to the realm of subjective data. *Object-oriented conversation* can be distinguished from *person-oriented conversation,* however, with the latter referring to conversation about persons' ideas, attitudes, and feelings. The most useful and efficient combination of verbal, vocal, and visual cues in person-oriented videoconferencing would be, quite traditionally, verbal content accompanied by vocalic and facial/kinesic cues supplementing the verbiage with affective information. There is little novelty in this proposition, except that in the present argument we may advance that these combinations are most useful and efficient for person-oriented conversations, and not for object-oriented discussions. In the case of mediated interaction with video, more advanced research should explore whether the focus of video on objects or faces interacts with the orientation of the conversation in predicting conversational effectiveness.

Moreover, in many conversations, participants switch between object orientation and person orientation ad hoc and often, and technological systems need to adapt or

simultaneously facilitate both. As designers advance systems that can support these conversations, it would be useful for designers to recall who, in FtF interaction, gets to choose the view. In contemporary videoconferencing systems, the message sender is often the party who chooses where to point the camera; the *sender* chooses the *receiver's* field of vision. In FtF interaction, however, the receiver chooses what he or she sees; the receiver chooses the receiver's visual field. Advancing new telecommunication systems that replace nonverbal cues in electronic form will do well to attend to, and build into new systems, these fundamentals of opportunistic visual choice.

◆ Critique and Consequences

A variety of consequences for further theoretical and system development may be inferred from current research trends, and as new technologies develop, we may predict that the need for conceptual and empirical specificity about nonverbal cues, their functions, and their re-representations will become even more consequential. As the Internet becomes a permanent fixture in contemporary life, notions about CMC are applied to other domain-specific theories. Such applications often revert to the premises of some of the older theories reviewed above, regardless of the current state of support for those theories.

It is not uncommon, for instance, for researchers to assume that without nonverbal cues, communicators cannot accomplish certain functions that they do in full-cue environments, and to apply this assumption to other communication theories. In persuasion, for example, it has been suggested that the lack of nonverbal cues in CMC prevents receivers from forming liking assessments of the online persuader, reducing the likelihood of "peripheral processing" and promoting instead attention to persuasive arguments (Guadagno & Cialdini, 2005). When such claims are accompanied by supporting data, such findings often obtain in experiments employing CMC in relatively compressed time periods. Such conclusions are untenable from the perspective of the SIP model, which would qualify such findings as occurring when participants lack sufficient motivation and/or online experience with one another to have formed impressions. Indeed, in many such studies reflecting the dampening of affect, influence, or sociability of the medium, the *incapacity* of CMC to allow normal performance is often unquestioned, even though these effects might disappear if CMC-using subjects had ample time. More attention to the corpus of CMC research may prevent theoretical and empirical missteps as people examine CMC in new functional domains. In the future, more specific consideration of nonverbal cues, those missing and those that are replaceable, will be critical to the development of more sophisticated theories and better interfaces.

One exception to the undifferentiated approach to nonverbal cues in CMC appears in recent studies on interpersonal deception theory (IDT; Buller & Burgoon, 1996) applied to the CMC context (Carlson, George, Burgoon, Adkins, & White, 2004). Most commentary on CMC and deception suggests that the absence of nonverbal cues should make deception less likely to detect, due to an assumed connection between the availability of kinesic and vocalic indicators of deception and receivers' deception detection success (see, e.g., Hollingshead, 2000). IDT, however, recognizes the transactional nature of deception. Because *receivers* nonverbally signal suspicion and incredulity to deceivers in FtF settings, *deceivers* monitor and learn to accommodate to these suspiciousness cues, leading to relatively effective (undetected) deception. Thus, when CMC masks *receivers'* feedback cues, *deceivers* do not have these guideposts with which to adjust their performances. Their unfolding deceptive performance is less tailored to the receiver's suspicions, and ultimately, the deception is performed more poorly in CMC, with more frequent deception detection in CMC rather than less. Related research has varied and measured the cues available in FtF conditions, whereas CMC conditions have been varied with regard to synchrony and interactivity, and both have been examined with respect to the effects of receiver suspiciousness and sender motivation to remain undetected (Burgoon, Stoner, Bonito, & Dunbar, 2003; George, Marrett, & Tilley, 2004; Woodworth, Hancock, & Goorha, 2005), all of which tell us about the *functional* aspect of cues absent in CMC, and the combinations of factors that alter interpersonal deception online.

The importance of precise conceptual and empirical specifications of nonverbal cues is also seen in research employing virtual reality (VR) systems to facilitate distributed interaction. When any nonverbal behavior can be detected and represented virtually (see Biocca & Delaney, 1995), it is critical to represent it in meaningful ways in order to elicit particular responses. The development of remote haptic capabilities, for instance, has dealt with measuring and conveying subjects' exertion, and resistance by objects, formulating the "collision point" at which an actor's representation meets and object's, to provide proprioceptive feedback (Kim et al., 2004). In representing people, a study revisiting Argyle and Dean's (1965) equilibrium theoretic predictions was conducted using varied levels of eye contact by virtual projections in an immersive 3-D environment. Bailenson, Blascovich, Beall, and Loomis (2001) had research participants don head-mounted VR eyewear and interact with a virtual man who varied his gaze at precise intervals, including eyes shut, to persistent gaze, to gaze with head turns, to gaze with pupil dilation when the subject approached. As predicted, there were correlations between the levels of gaze exhibited by the virtual man and the distances to him adopted by human participants.

This study not only demonstrates the robustness of equilibrium theory but also contrasts the icon and avatar studies in finding that more is more (rather than less is more) by isolating an aspect of nonverbal behavior rooted in theoretical understanding. It illustrates the means to test extant theories and apply them to new settings, and to employ methods to create effective interfaces through careful attention to defined, controlled reintroduction of specific nonverbal elements through communication technology. It will be imperative for designers of new electronic communication systems to know what nonverbal, behavioral cues precisely affect particular functions, if new systems will be successful at representing those signals through alternative symbols such as text, time, icons, video, or VR representations.

◆ References

Argyle, M., & Dean, J. (1965). Eye-contact, distance and affiliation. *Sociometry, 28,* 289–304.

Bailenson, J. N., Blascovich, J., Beall, A. C., & Loomis, J. M. (2001). Equilibrium theory revisited: Mutual gaze and personal space in virtual environments. *Presence, 10,* 583–598.

Bengtsson, B., Burgoon, J. K., Cederberg, C., Bonito, J., & Lundberg, M. (1999). *The impact of anthropomorphic interfaces on influence, understanding, and credibility.* Proceedings of the 32nd Annual Hawaii International Conference on Systems Science. Retrieved July 30, 2005 from http://ieeexplore.ieee.org/search/wrapper.jsp?arnumber=772736

Biocca, F., & Delaney, B. (1995). Immersive virtual reality technology. In F. Biocca & M. R. Levy (Eds.), *Communication in the age of virtual reality* (pp. 57–124). Hillsdale, NJ: Erlbaum.

Brittan, D. (1992). Being there: The promise of multimedia communications. *Technology Review, 95*(4), 42–50.

Buller, D. B., & Burgoon, J. K. (1996). Interpersonal deception theory. *Communication Theory, 6,* 203–242.

Burgoon, J. K., & Hale, J. L. (1988). Nonverbal expectancy violations: Model elaboration and application to immediacy behaviors. *Communication Monographs, 55,* 58–79.

Burgoon, J. K., Stoner, G. M., Bonito, J. A., & Dunbar, N. E. (2003). *Trust and deception in mediated communication.* Proceedings of the 36th Annual Hawaii International Conference on Systems Sciences. Retrieved July 30, 2005 from http://ieeexplore.ieee.org/search/wrapper.jsp?arnumber=1173792

Carlson, J. R., George, J. F., Burgoon, J. K., Adkins, M., & White, C. (2004). Deception in computer-mediated communication. *Group Decision and Negotiation, 13,* 5–28.

Chapanis, A., Ochsman, R. B., Parrish, R. N., & Weeks, G. D. (1972). Studies in interactive communication: I. The effects of four communication modes on the behavior of teams during cooperative problem-solving. *Human Factors, 14,* 487–509.

Chidambaram, L., & Bostrom, R. P. (1993). Evolution of group performance over time: A repeated measures study of GDSS effects. *Journal of Organizational Computing, 3,* 443–469.

Clark, H. H., & Brennan, S. E. (1991). Grounding in communication. In L. B. Resnick, R. M. Levine, & S. D. Teasley (Eds.), *Perspectives on socially shared cognition* (pp. 127–149). Washington DC: American Psychological Association.

Cramton, C. D. (2001). The mutual knowledge problem and its consequences for dispersed collaboration. *Organization Science, 12,* 346–371.

Culnan, M. J., & Markus, M. L. (1987). Information technologies. In F. M. Jablin, L. L. Putnam, K. H. Roberts, & L. W. Porter (Eds.), *Handbook of organizational communication: An interdisciplinary perspective* (pp. 420–443). Newbury Park, CA: Sage.

Daft, R. L., & Lengel, R. H. (1984). Information richness: A new approach to managerial behavior and organization design. In B. M. Staw & L. L. Cummings (Eds.), *Research in organizational behavior* (pp. 191–233). Greenwich, CT: JAI Press.

Daft, R. L., & Lengel, R. H. (1986). Organizational information requirements, media richness, and structural determinants. *Management Science, 32,* 554–571.

Danchak, M. M., Walther, J. B., & Swan, K. P. (2001, November). *Presence in mediated instruction: Bandwidth, behavior, and expectancy violations.* Paper presented at the conference on Asynchronous Learning Networks, Orlando, FL.

Danet, B., Ruedenberg-Wright, L., & Rosenbaum-Tamari, Y. (1997). "HMMM . . . WHERE'S THAT SMOKE COMING FROM?" Writing, play and performance on Internet Relay Chat. *Journal of Computer-Mediated Communication, 2.* Retrieved March 15, 2005, from http://jcmc .indiana.edu/vol2/issue4/danet.html

Douglas, K. M., & McGarty, C. (2001). Identifiability and self-presentation: Computer-mediated communication and intergroup interaction. *British Journal of Social Psychology, 40,* 399–416.

Ekman, P., & Friesen, W. V. (1975). *Unmasking the face: A guide to recognizing emotions from facial cues.* Englewood Cliffs, NJ: Prentice Hall.

Feenberg, A. (1989). A user's guide to the pragmatics of computer mediated communication. *Semiotica, 75,* 257–278.

Fussell, S. R., Kraut, R. E., & Siegel, J. (2000). Coordination of communication: Effects of shared visual context on collaborative work. In *Proceedings of CSCW 2000* (pp. 21–30). New York: ACM Press.

Retrieved January 30, 2005, from http://www.cs.cmu.edu/~sfussell/pubs/Man us cripts/p21-fussell.pdf

Gale, S. (1991). Adding audio and video to an office environment. In J. M. Bowers & S. D. Benford (Eds.), *Studies in computer-supported collaborative work* (pp. 49–62). North-Holland: Elsevier Science.

George, J. F., Marrett, K., & Tilley, P. (2004). Deception detection under varying electronic media and warning conditions. *Proceedings of the 34th Annual Hawaii International Conference on System Sciences.* Retrieved July 30, 2005 from http://ieeexplore.ieee.org/ie15/8934/28293/ 01265080.pdf?tp=&arnumber=1265080 &isnumber=28293

Gergle, D., Kraut, R. E., & Fussell, S. R. (2004). Language efficiency and visual technology: Minimizing collaborative effort with visual information. *Journal of Language and Social Psychology, 23,* 491–517.

Godin, S. (1993). *The smiley dictionary.* Berkeley, CA: Peachpit Press.

Guadagno, R. E., & Cialdini, R. B. (2005). Online persuasion and compliance: Social influence on the Internet and beyond. In Y. Amichai-Hamburger (Ed.), *The social net: The social psychology of the Internet* (pp. 91–113). New York: Oxford University Press.

Hall, E. T. (1959). *The silent language.* New York: Anchor Books.

Henderson, S., & Gilding, M. (2004). "I've never clicked this much with anyone in my life": Trust and hyperpersonal communication in online friendships. *New Media & Society, 6,* 487–506.

Hesse, B. W., Werner, C. M., & Altman, I. (1988). Temporal aspects of computer-mediated communication. *Computers in Human Behavior, 4,* 147–165.

Hiltz, S. R., Johnson, K., & Agle, G. (1978). *Replicating Bales' problem solving experiments on a computerized conference: A pilot study* (Research report no. 8). Newark: New Jersey Institute of Technology, Computerized Conferencing and Communications Center.

Hogg, M. A., & Abrams, D. (1988). *Social identifications: A social psychology of intergroup relations and group processes.* London: Routledge.

Hollingshead, A. B. (2000). Truth and lying in computer-mediated groups. In M. A. Neale, E. A. Mannix, & T. Griffith (Eds.), *Research in managing groups and teams* (Vol. 3: Technology and teams, pp. 157–173). Greenwich, CT: JAI Press.

Iacono, C. S., & Weisband, S. (1997). *Developing trust in virtual teams.* Proceedings of the 30th Annual Hawaii International Conference on System Sciences. Retrieved July 30, 2005, from http://ieeexplore.ieee.org/search/wrapper .jsp?arnumber=665615

Isotalus, P. (2003, November). *Gender and interface agents in the on-line news.* Paper presented at the annual meeting of the National Communication Association, Miami Beach, FL.

Jarvenpaa, S. L., Knoll, K., & Leidner, D. E. (1998). Is anybody out there? The implications of trust in global virtual teams. *Journal of Management Information Systems, 14,* 29–64.

Jones, S. E., & LeBaron, C. D. (2002). Guest editors' introduction. *Journal of Communication, 52,* 499–521.

Kalman, Y. M., & Rafaeli, S. (2005). *Email chronemics: Unobtrusive profiling of response times.* Proceedings of the 38th Annual Hawaii International Conference on System Sciences. Retrieved July 30, 2005, from http://ieeexplore.ieee.org/search/ wrapper. jsp?arnumber =1385456

Kiesler, S. (1987). Social aspects of computer environments. *Social Science, 72,* 23–28.

Kiesler, S., Siegel, J., & McGuire, T. W. (1984). Social psychological aspects of computer-mediated communication. *American Psychologist, 39,* 1123–1134.

Kim, J., Kim, H., Tay, B. K., Muniyandi, M., Srinivasan, M. A., Jordan, J., et al. (2004). Transatlantic touch: A study of haptic collaboration over long distance. *Presence, 13,* 328–337.

Kraut, R. E., Fussell, S. R., & Siegel, J. (2003). Visual information as a conversational resource in collaborative physical tasks. *Human-Computer Interaction, 18,* 13–49.

Krikorian, D. H., Lee, J., & Chock, T. M. (2000). Isn't that spatial? Distance and communication in a 2D virtual environment. *Journal of Computer-Mediated Communication, 5.* Retrieved March 7, 2006, from http://www.jcmc.indiana.edu/ vol5/issue4/krikorian.html

Lea, M. (1991). Rationalist assumptions in cross-media comparisons of computer-mediated communication. *Behaviour & Information Technology, 10,* 153–172.

Lea, M., & Spears, R. (1992). Paralanguage and social perception in computer-mediated communication. *Journal of Organizational Computing, 2,* 321–341.

Lea, M., Spears, R., & de Groot, D. (2001). Knowing me, knowing you: Anonymity effects on social identity processes within groups. *Personality and Social Psychology Bulletin, 27,* 526–537.

Lee, E. (2005). Effects of the influence agent's sex and self-confidence on informational social influence in computer-mediated communication: Quantitative versus qualitative presentation. *Communication Research, 32,* 29–58.

Liu, Y. L., Ginther, D., & Zelhart, P. (2002). An exploratory study of the effects of frequency and duration of messaging on impression development in computer-mediated communication. *Social Science Computer Review, 20,* 73–80.

Markus, M. L. (1994). Finding a happy medium: Explaining the negative effects of electronic communication on social life at work. *ACM Transactions on Information Systems, 12,* 119–149.

Nardi, B., Whittaker, S., & Bradner, E. (2000). Interaction and outeraction: Instant messaging in action. In *Proceedings of the 2000 ACM Conference on Computer Supported Cooperative Work* (pp. 79–88). New York: ACM Press. Retrieved March 1, 2006, from http://www.dis.shef.ac.uk/stevewhittaker/ outeraction_cscw2000.pdf

Nowak, K. L., & Biocca, F. (2003). The effect of the agency and anthropomorphism on users' sense of telepresence, copresence, and social presence in virtual environments. *Presence, 12,* 481–494.

Nowak, K., Watt, J. H., & Walther, J. (2005). The influence of synchrony and sensory modality on the person perception process in computer mediated groups. *Journal of Computer-Mediated Communication, 10*(3), article 3. Retrieved July 1, 2005, from http://jcmc.indiana.edu/vol10/issue3/nowak.html

Orlikowski, W. J., & Yates, J. (2002). It's about time: Temporal structuring in organizations. *Organization Science, 13,* 684–700.

O'Sullivan, P. B. (2000). What you don't know won't hurt me: Impression management functions of communication channels in relationships. *Human Communication Research, 26,* 403–431.

Pen, J., & Hancock, J. T. (2006). An analysis of socioemotional and task communication in online multiplayer videogames. *Communication Research, 33,* 92–109.

Postmes, T., & Spears, R. (2002). Contextual moderators of gender differences and stereotyping in computer-mediated group discussions. *Personality and Social Psychology Bulletin, 28,* 1073–1083.

Postmes, T., Spears, R., & Lea, M. (1998). Breaching or building social boundaries? SIDE-effects of computer-mediated communication. *Communication Research, 25,* 689–715.

Postmes, T., Spears, R., Lea, M., & Reicher, S. D. (2000). *SIDE issues centre stage: Recent developments in studies of deindividuation in groups.* Amsterdam: Royal Netherlands Academy of Arts and Sciences.

Reid, F. J. M., Ball, L. J., Morley, A. M., & Evans, J. S. B. T. (1997). Styles of group discussion in computer-mediated decision making. *British Journal of Social Psychology, 36,* 241–262.

Reid, F. J. M., Malinek, V., Stott, C., & Evans, J. S. B. T. (1996). The messaging threshold in computer-mediated communication. *Ergonomics, 39,* 1017–1037.

Rezabek, L. L., & Cochenour, J. J. (1998). Visual cues in computer-mediated communication: Supplementing text with emoticons. *Journal of Visual Literacy, 18,* 210–215.

Rice, R. E. (1984). Mediated group communication. In R. E. Rice & Associates (Eds.), *The new media: Communication, research, and technology* (pp. 129–156). Beverly Hills, CA: Sage.

Rice, R. E. (1990). Computer-mediated communication system network data: Theoretical concerns and empirical examples. *International Journal of Man-Machine Studies, 32,* 627–647.

Rice, R. E., & Case, D. (1983). Electronic message systems in the university: A description of use and utility. *Journal of Communication, 33,* 131–154.

Rintel, E. S., & Pittam, J. (1997). Strangers in a strange land: Interaction management on Internet Relay Chat. *Human Communication Research, 23,* 507–534.

Rogers, P., & Lea, M. (2004). Cohesion in online groups. In K. Morgan, C. A. Sanchez, C. A. Brebbia, & A. Vioskounsky (Eds.), *Human perspectives on the Internet society: Culture, psychology and gender* (pp. 115–124). Southampton, England: WIT Press.

Sanderson, D. (1993). *Smileys.* Sebastopol, CA: O'Reilly & Associates.

Short, J., Williams, E., & Christie, B. (1976). *The social psychology of telecommunications.* London: Wiley.

Siegel, J., Dubrovsky, V., Kiesler, S., & McGuire, T. W. (1986). Group processes in computer-mediated communication. *Organizational Behavior and Human Decision Processes, 37,* 157–187.

Sproull, L., & Kiesler, S. (1986). Reducing social context cues: Electronic mail in organizational communication. *Management Science, 32,* 1492–1512.

Steinfield, C. W. (1986). Computer-mediated communication in an organizational setting: Explaining task-related and socioemotional uses. In M. L. McLaughlin (Ed.), *Communication yearbook 9* (pp. 777–804). Beverly Hills, CA: Sage.

Storck, J., & Sproull, L. (1995). Through a glass darkly: What do people learn in videoconferences? *Human Communication Research, 22,* 197–219.

Suler, J. (1999). *The psychology of avatars and graphical space in multimedia chat communities, or, how I learned to stop worrying and love my Palace props.* Retrieved March 6, 2005, from http://www.rider.edu/~suler/psycyber/psyav.html

Tidwell, L. C., & Walther, J. B. (2002). Computer-mediated communication effects on disclosure, impressions, and interpersonal evaluations: Getting to know one another a bit at a time. *Human Communication Research, 28,* 317–348.

Walther, J. B. (1992). Interpersonal effects in computer-mediated interaction: A relational perspective. *Communication Research, 19,* 52–90.

Walther, J. B. (1996). Computer-mediated communication: Impersonal, interpersonal, and hyperpersonal interaction. *Communication Research, 23,* 3–43.

Walther, J. B. (1997). Group and interpersonal effects in international computer-mediated collaboration. *Human Communication Research, 23,* 342–369.

Walther, J. B. (in press). Selective self-presentation in computer-mediated communication: Hyperpersonal dimensions of technology, language, and cognition. *Computers in Human Behavior.*

Walther, J. B., & Bunz, U. (2005). The rules of virtual groups: Trust, liking, and performance in computer-mediated communication. *Journal of Communication, 55,* 828–846.

Walther, J. B., & Burgoon, J. K. (1992). Relational communication in computer-mediated interaction. *Human Communication Research, 19,* 50–88.

Walther, J. B., & D'Addario, K. P. (2001). The impacts of emoticons on message interpretation in computer-mediated communication. *Social Science Computer Review, 19,* 323–345.

Walther, J. B., Loh, T., & Granka, L. (2005). Let me count the ways: The interchange of verbal and nonverbal cues in computer-mediated and face-to-face affinity. *Journal of Language and Social Psychology, 24,* 36–65.

Walther, J. B., & Parks, M. R. (2002). Cues filtered out, cues filtered in: Computer-mediated communication and relationships. In M. L. Knapp & J. A. Daly (Eds.), *Handbook of interpersonal communication* (3rd ed., pp. 529–563). Thousand Oaks, CA: Sage.

Walther, J. B., Slovacek, C., & Tidwell, L. C. (2001). Is a picture worth a thousand words? Photographic images in long term and short term virtual teams. *Communication Research, 28,* 105–134.

Walther, J. B., & Tidwell, L. C. (1995). Nonverbal cues in computer-mediated communication, and the effect of chronemics on relational communication. *Journal of Organizational Computing, 5,* 355–378.

Witmer, D., & Katzman, S. (1997). On-line smiles: Does gender make a difference in the use of graphic accents? *Journal of Computer-Mediated Communication, 2*(4). Retrieved March 16, 2006, from http://www.jcmc.indiana.edu/vol2/issue4/witmer1.html

Woodworth, M. T., Hancock, J. T., & Goorha, S. (2005). *The motivational enhancement effect: Implications for our chosen modes of communication in the 21st century.* Proceedings of the 38th Annual Hawaii International Conference on System Sciences. Retrieved July 30, 2005, from http://ieeexplore.ieee.org/search/wrapper.jsp?arnumber=1385273

25

NONVERBAL COMMUNICATION, RACE, AND INTERGROUP INTERACTION

◆ John F. Dovidio
University of Connecticut

◆ Michelle Hebl
Rice University

◆ Jennifer A. Richeson
Northwestern University

◆ J. Nicole Shelton
Princeton University

P erceiving others and oneself in terms of group identity influences the way people interact with others. When group memberships are salient, interactions are often guided by social roles (Eagly & Wood, 1999). To the extent that people rely on category-based, rather than individual-based, processing in their interaction, their perceptions will be influenced by group stereotypes and attitudes that can be activated automatically and without full awareness. When people think of themselves as members of a group, they view themselves not only as a representative of that group but also as the embodiment of that group's values, beliefs, and interests (Turner, Hogg, Oakes, Reicher, & Wetherell, 1987). Thus, interpersonal interactions under these conditions become, in essence, intergroup encounters. Because of the importance of social identity in everyday activity (Tajfel & Turner, 1979), and the need to manage the complexity and demands of social functioning (Fiske, Lin, & Neuberg, 1999), such intergroup interactions are common.

This chapter examines nonverbal behavior in an intergroup context. We begin by considering how members of different groups, defined by majority and minority status, may differ systematically in their *intra*group nonverbal behavior. Next, we focus on the dynamics of interactions between members of different groups, identifying important elements that can influence nonverbal behavior. We present a general model of "mixed social interaction" and explore the role of nonverbal behavior in these interactions, considering the causes and consequences of these nonverbal behaviors. We conclude with a discussion of the importance of understanding the reciprocal relationship between interpersonal and intergroup interaction and the fundamental importance of nonverbal behavior in these interactions.

Although we examine a range of intergroup contexts in this chapter, we illustrate the relationship between intergroup relations and nonverbal behavior mainly within the context of Black-White relations and primarily within the cultural context of the United States. Even though there has been substantial recognition of the importance of culture (see Matsumoto, this volume) and gender (see Hall, this volume) for nonverbal behavior, the literature on nonverbal behavior and intergroup relations is relatively sparse. Focusing on Black-White relations thus helps provide a coherent test, within a defined context, of the hypothesized dynamics of intergroup identity and nonverbal behavior.

◆ Group Differences in Nonverbal Behavior: Status and Race

In this section of the chapter, we provide an overview of theoretical perspectives that suggest why and how members of majority and minority groups in general may differ in the types of nonverbal behaviors they display regularly. The focus, thus, is on systematic group differences in nonverbal behavior during *intra*group interaction. We summarize the empirical literature building on Halberstadt's (1985) comprehensive review of racial differences in nonverbal behavior by drawing on more recent work.

Because of personal and group motivations for esteem and social dominance, *status* is a fundamental dimension of intergroup encounters (see Burgoon & Dunbar, this volume). Power and status are relational concepts that are often determined contextually. For instance, a college senior may be high status in an interaction with a college freshman but low status in a meeting with a professor. In general, high-status individuals may have more freedom of movement and thus may be more open in their postures and approach others more closely than do low-status individuals (Ellyson & Dovidio, 1985). Low-status individuals may be more inhibited in their actions and monitor their partners more closely than do high-status individuals. Keltner, Gruenfeld, and Anderson (2003) hypothesize that high power and status are associated with a general approach orientation, whereas lower power and status are related to inhibition.

Consistent with this view, individual status has been found to exert a strong influence on nonverbal behavior between people (see Hall, Coats, & Smith LeBeau, 2005).

In a comprehensive meta-analytic review of the literature, Judith Hall and her colleagues found that people who have higher status or social power showed greater facial expressiveness, held more open postures (with arms and legs), interacted with others at closer distances, and interrupted others more often than did those with lower status or power. Whereas Hall and her colleagues did not find systematic differences for touch, gesturing, postural relaxation, or visual contact, it is possible that such behaviors can be tied to status but that the relationship is more complex. For instance, in the case of visual contact, lower status people look *more* while listening but *less* while speaking than do higher status people (Dovidio & Ellyson, 1985).

Because societies are structured strongly in terms of group hierarchy, group identities also can produce relatively stable core experiences of status. For example, in the United States, men have had higher status and greater social power traditionally than have women, and Whites have had higher status and greater social power than Blacks. These chronic differences in status have been hypothesized to produce consistent differences in the nonverbal behavior of minority- and majority-group members. The oppression hypothesis (Henley, 1977; LaFrance & Henley, 1994) posits that the chronic stigmatization of certain groups produces adaptations that lead members of oppressed groups to exhibit systematic nonverbal skills and behaviors that differ from those of members of dominant groups and that are functional for coping with their low status. In particular, members of chronically oppressed groups are hypothesized to be more sensitive and attentive to their social environment, making them better at decoding others' nonverbal behaviors and leading to higher levels of visual contact in social interaction; they also tend to be more vigilant and guarded, making them more inhibited in their emotional expression and nonverbal behaviors (Frable, Blackstone, & Sherbaum, 1990).

When socially meaningful and enduring groups, such as racial groups, are involved, cultural differences also need to be considered to understand intergroup relations and nonverbal behavior. Jones (1986), for example, observed that Black culture is composed of both reactive and evolutionary components. The *reactive* component refers to the collective adjustments U.S. Blacks have made to cope with oppression; the *evolutionary* component refers to aspects of Black culture that represent "the unfolding of a cultural core laid in an African past and characterized in function, if not form, across the cultures of the African Diaspora" (Jones, 1986, p. 294). In particular, Jones identified key elements of many Blacks' cultural orientation, reflected in five dimensions: time, rhythm, improvisation, oral expression, and spirituality. These cultural values guide a range of social behaviors, including nonverbal behaviors. E. T. Hall (1966) emphasized the importance of culture in understanding racial differences in nonverbal behavior, hypothesizing that Black culture, relative to that of Whites, reflects a closer and more "sensorially involved" orientation. These ideas can be organized theoretically as the *cultural hypothesis*. Both the oppression hypothesis and the cultural hypothesis suggest different patterns of racial differences in nonverbal behavior.

Systematic patterns of behavior in intergroup relations can influence nonverbal behavior and produce chronic racial differences in nonverbal skill and behavior. In terms of skill at decoding other's nonverbal behavior, Halberstadt's (1985) meta-analysis of racial differences revealed that although Black children (ages 4–11) showed equivalent or slightly lower levels of decoding accuracy relative to Whites, Black college students showed a higher level of accuracy than did White college students. Halberstadt interpreted these results as consistent with the oppression hypothesis. In general, though, Whites and Blacks are more accurate in decoding the nonverbal behavior of members of their own race than they are of other races (Bailey, Nowicki, & Cole, 1998; Weathers et al., 2004). Greater intragroup than intergroup accuracy is a function of greater familiarity and more experience with in-group members than with out-group members (Elfenbein & Ambady, 2002).

Racial differences in nonverbal behaviors have been studied most commonly in terms of proxemics (interpersonal distance and body orientation), touch, and visual contact (gaze). Halberstadt's (1985) review of studies on interpersonal distances maintained between Blacks and between Whites showed no overall racial differences. Age was an important moderating factor, however. Halberstadt's review revealed that Black children maintained closer interpersonal distances than did White children, but Black adults maintained *greater* interpersonal distance than did White adults. Reid, Tate, and Berman (1989), however, found that Black children do not always maintain closer distances than White children. They found that Black children (ages 4–7) stood *farther* away from an infant of the same race than did White children.

Across the eight studies of body orientation reviewed by Halberstadt (1985), Blacks exhibited a less direct body orientation than did Whites when interacting with others, and this difference tended to increase with age. With respect to touch, Halberstadt's review of eight studies revealed that Blacks touched one another during their interactions more often than Whites did. Finally, with respect to visual contact, both the oppression hypothesis and E. T. Hall's (1966) cultural hypothesis predict that Blacks will exhibit higher levels of eye gaze than will Whites. The results of Halberstadt's (1985) analysis of eight visual contact studies, however, are inconsistent with both positions. In

same-race interactions, Blacks displayed significantly lower levels of visual contact than did Whites. In addition, other studies of adults (Smith, 1983) and children (Reid et al., 1989), beyond the literature Halberstadt (1985) reviewed, have also shown that Blacks display lower levels of visual contact than do Whites.

In summary, the results of studies that examined racial differences in nonverbal behavior have revealed systematic differences in spatial behavior, touch, and visual contact. The pattern of findings does not provide clear support for either the oppression hypothesis or Hall's (1966) cultural hypothesis, however. In particular, the findings for spatial behavior (i.e., greater interpersonal distance among Black than White adults) are more consistent with oppression than with the cultural hypothesis, the results for touch (more touching by Blacks than Whites) are more consistent with the cultural hypothesis, and the findings for visual behaviors (less eye contact by Blacks than by Whites) are inconsistent with both positions. Although racial differences in nonverbal behavior do not conform uniformly to predictions derived from the oppression hypothesis or the cultural hypothesis, it is important to recognize that nonverbal behavior is highly sensitive to social context. Racial differences may therefore be more pronounced, apparent, and consistent in situations in which social identity is salient, such as in dyadic interactions between members of different social identity groups.

◆ Social Identity and Nonverbal Behavior in Intergroup Interaction

One of the most influential theories of group influences on intergroup interaction and nonverbal behavior is expectation states theory (Berger, Wagner, & Zelditch, 1985; Correll & Ridgeway, 2003). According to this sociological framework, interactions between members of different groups are accompanied by differential expectations about the status of the interactants in cases in which group membership is associated systematically with prestige and status in everyday life. Berger et al. (1985) referred to characteristics of individuals that give rise to differential status expectations as "diffuse status characteristics." These expectations, in turn, can generalize to a broad range of situations and, through a process of behavioral confirmation of expectancies similar to the self-fulfilling prophecy, affect power-related behavior and perceptions across a variety of social contexts. Expectation states theory has received substantial empirical support with respect to interaction between women and men, and it has received some support in the realm of interracial behavior (see Berger et al., 1985; Correll & Ridgeway, 2003).

Whereas expectation states theory views the effect of group membership on interpersonal interaction as a relatively rational, albeit not necessarily conscious, process of evaluating the relative contributions of interactants in creating social organization, psychological perspectives have posited a much more pervasive and fundamental influence of group membership and identity. Social identity theory (Tajfel & Turner, 1979) and self-categorization theory (Turner et al., 1987) view the distinction between personal identity and social identity as critical. According to these theories, when personal identity is salient, a person's individual needs, standards, beliefs, and motives determine behavior. In contrast, when social identity is salient, "people come to perceive themselves as more interchangeable exemplars of a social category than as unique personalities defined by their individual differences from others" (Turner et al., 1987, p. 50). Under these

latter conditions, collective needs, goals, and standards are primary.

Social categorization and social identity can influence the nature of communication, and thus nonverbal behavior, through a broad range of cognitive, affective, and motivational mechanisms. Social categorization activates, often without awareness or control, stereotypic associations that can influence expectations of the encounter and online attributions of the behavior of the other person in the interaction (see Lakin, this volume). In addition, the general evaluative biases that accompany recognition of different group memberships can produce general approach or avoidance tendencies that are systematically reflected in nonverbal behaviors. These prejudices may be blatant or subtle (Gaertner & Dovidio, 1986), and people who have explicitly nonprejudiced attitudes may still harbor implicit intergroup biases (Dovidio & Gaertner, 2004).

Recognition of different group memberships in the interaction also typically arouses intergroup anxiety (Stephan & Stephan, 1985, 2000). Part of this anxiety may be due to uncertainty about how to behave in this intergroup context, and part may be a function of feelings of real or symbolic threat. In addition to anxiety, intergroup interactions can arouse a number of different motivations. For members of majority groups, for instance, intergroup interactions can arouse dominance orientations (Sidanius & Pratto, 1999) or the desire to appear nonprejudiced (Gaertner & Dovidio, 1986). For members of minority groups, the desire to detect and potentially compensate for anticipated discrimination by majority-group interaction partners may be activated (Miller & Myers, 1998; Shelton, Richeson, & Salvatore, 2005).

In general, these positions suggest that majority-group members would be likely to display nonverbal behaviors associated with lower levels of liking or attraction and with higher levels of social dominance or power than would minority-group members in intergroup interaction. Minority-group members would be expected to show nonverbal behaviors associated with greater vigilance (e.g., greater sensitivity to nonverbal cues) and defensiveness or inhibition (e.g., less direct orientation) more strongly than would majority-group members.

Overall, there is some support for these expectations. For instance, young and middle-aged adults have been shown to patronize older adults by speaking in a higher pitch and modified register similar to that used to address babies and pets (Caporael, 1981; Caporael & Culbertson, 1983; Kemper, Vandeputte, Rice, Cheung, & Gubarchuk, 1995). Similarly, Whites show less intimate, attentive, and involved nonverbal behaviors with Blacks than with Whites (Feldman, 1985; Weitz, 1972; Word, Zanna, & Cooper, 1974). In addition, Blacks tend to show heightened attentiveness and sensitivity to nonverbal cues of prejudice (Richeson & Shelton, 2005; Rollman, 1978). Nevertheless, because of the complexity of intergroup interaction, generalizations about differences in the behavior of members of majority and minority groups in intergroup interaction may obscure important dynamics and reciprocal relationships in intergroup communication. Thus, in the next section we present a model of interactions between majority- and minority-group members that incorporates nonverbal communication as part of a general interaction process.

◆ Interaction in an Intergroup Context: A Model of Mixed Social Interaction

One of the first comprehensive models to articulate the components of nonverbal interaction was Patterson's (1982) Sequential Functional Model of Nonverbal Exchange.

In this model, Patterson explained and predicted changes in the levels of nonverbal involvement that social interactants display toward each other. More specifically, Patterson proposed that people approach each other with preexisting orientations (antecedent conditions), such as *personal factors, experiential factors, and relational or situational factors*, that can influence whether and how they interact. These antecedent conditions trigger preinteraction variables in the context, such as *cognitions and affective reactions, levels of arousal, and behavioral propensities to act*, that mediate the effect of these preexisting orientations and determine whether an individual will engage in interaction. Once individuals decide to interact, they make functional judgments about an interaction and determine the extent to which they should become behaviorally involved. In this stage, interactants also determine whether their expressed level and their partner's expressed level of involvement match their expectations, which in turn influence future cognitions and affect and can produce stable or unstable exchanges. Ultimately, these interaction variables determine whether interactants will terminate or continue the interaction.

Hebl and Dovidio (2005) broadened the scope of Patterson's (1982) model to address the uniquely complex interactions that occur between majority- and minority-group interactants. This model is depicted in Figure 25.1. The shaded areas represent the extensions by Hebl and Dovidio (2005) from Patterson's (1982) model to address key elements of an intergroup interaction. In the remainder of the chapter, we review each component of the model (i.e., antecedents, preinteraction mediators, and interaction phase), addressing within each component both majority and minority interactants' perspectives. Where the data exist, we discuss how each of the components influences or is influenced by nonverbal behaviors.

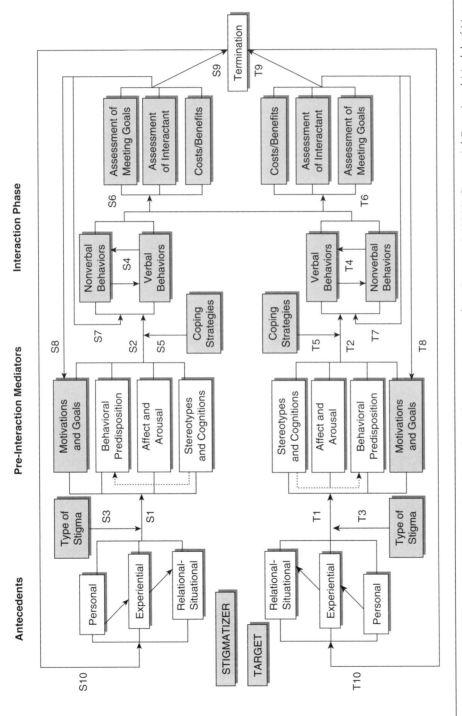

Figure 25.1 Hebl and Dovidio's (2005) Model of Mixed Social Interactions Based on Patterson's (1982) Sequential Functional Model of Nonverbal Exchange

♦ 487

ANTECEDENTS

Majority- and minority-group interactants bring different resources and background experiences to social interactions. Three critical factors described by Patterson (1982) are (a) *personal*, (b) *experiential*, and (c) *relational-situational*. The fourth factor, *type of stigma*, was identified by Hebl and Dovidio (2005). These four factors lay the groundwork for creating an ideology that individuals use to express themselves verbally and nonverbally in interactions.

Personal variables include differences in attitudes or ideologies that predispose people to act in particular ways during an interaction. For example, Whites who are more prejudiced toward Blacks will be more predisposed to behave more negatively toward Blacks in the interaction (Dovidio, Kawakami, & Gaertner, 2002). Similarly, Blacks with more in-group-favoring attitudes are more likely to avoid contact with Whites (Ashburn-Nardo, Knowles, & Monteith, 2003; Patchen, 1983). Furthermore, individual differences in racial identity may predispose Blacks to perceive the prejudice and discrimination displayed toward them as well as to shape their affective and coping responses (Sellers & Shelton, 2003).

Experiential variables also serve as antecedent conditions predicting nonverbal involvement. People who have more intergroup contact tend to have more positive intergroup attitudes and display less anxiety in intergroup interaction (Pettigrew & Tropp, 2000). In addition, Whites with more previous interracial contact showed less cardiovascular evidence of threat during interracial interactions (Blascovich, Mendes, Hunter, Lickel, & Kowai-Bell, 2001).

Relational-situational variables, such as the social domain, the type of relationship, and power balances, are also critical considerations when examining the way in which interracial interactions unfold. Social norms and legal requirements differ across situations (Crandall & Eshleman, 2003), and thus they produce very different patterns of nonverbal expression and interaction outcomes. In general, Whites' discrimination against Blacks is less pronounced in situations with stronger and clearer normative expectations (see Dovidio & Gaertner, 2004). Thus, Whites tend to experience greater discomfort and invest more effort in consciously regulating their behavior in interracial interactions that are less structured or in which they receive feedback that they may be responding in a biased and inappropriate fashion (Richeson & Trawalter, 2005).

Individuals' power in the interaction also influences their nonverbal displays. People in power show less restraint from taking action (Galinsky, Gruenfeld, & Magee, 2003), are more likely to express anger (Tiedens, 2000), and show greater variability in their interactive behaviors than do less powerful people (Guinote, Judd, & Brauer, 2002). Low power, by contrast, produces a tendency to inhibit responses (Keltner et al., 2003). Furthermore, when members of dominant groups are in a high-power position, implicit biases toward lower status partners become activated (Richeson & Ambady, 2003) and are expressed openly (e.g., explicit bias in verbal evaluation) or more subtly (e.g., standoffish nonverbal behavior; Dovidio, Kawakami, Johnson, Johnson, & Howard, 1997).

What makes power even more influential in relationships is the finding that interactants tend to assume complementarity in behavioral interactions (Tiedens & Fragale, 2003). That is, individuals exposed to dominant, powerful individuals tend to react in very submissive ways, which reinforces the power imbalance. Similarly, individuals exposed to submissive behavioral displays tend to react by assuming more dominant stances. Such complementarity, which may be present in some situations more than in others, serves to reinforce the power differentials that exist in mixed interactions (Dovidio, Brown, Keating, Heltman, & Ellyson, 1988).

In addition to personal, experiential, and relational or situational factors, the nature of intergroup biases and relations differs substantially as a function of the *types of stigma* attached to people (i.e., obesity, facial disfigurement, devalued racial group; Hebl & Dovidio, 2005). Whereas Whites' attitudes toward Blacks are characterized by both negative attitudes and status differentials, sexism involves strong subordinate role prescriptions for women but not antipathy toward women generally (Eagly & Karau, 2002). In addition, some types of intergroup biases have a stronger emotional component than others (Stangor, Sullivan, & Ford, 1991), and some biases (e.g., racism) are inhibited more strongly by social norms than are others (e.g., heterosexism; Crandall & Eshleman, 2003). Thus, the type of stigma can be an important antecedent factor that may determine whether and how members of these different groups will interact.

PREINTERACTION MEDIATORS

Antecedent conditions influence the preinteraction states with which Whites and ethnic minorities enter into interracial interaction (see paths labeled S1 and T1 in Figure 25.1). These states include stereotypes and prejudices, affective reactions and arousal levels, behavioral predispositions and propensities to act, and motivations and goals (Hebl & Dovidio, 2005). Although these interaction elements often work together and cannot always be

disentangled from each other clearly, we discuss them separately to maximize the readers' understanding of each component's potential contribution to nonverbal behavior during intergroup interactions.

Much of past research on the dynamics of interracial interaction can be captured within the *stereotypes and cognitions* component of the model. A vast amount is known about how Whites' attitudes, expectations, stereotypes, and prejudices regarding racial minorities influence their behavior during interracial interactions. Overall, this literature largely finds that Whites often react negatively to Black interaction partners; however, Whites' responses are not necessarily simple and direct. For instance, people's unconscious (implicit) attitudes, which are often measured with response latency techniques (Fazio & Olson, 2003), and their overt (explicit) expressions of bias, which are measured with self-reports, frequently diverge (Dovidio et al., 2002).

In addition, interactants in intergroup encounters not only possess stereotypes of members of other groups but also possess beliefs about how the members of other groups will perceive them. Whites anticipating interracial interaction often express concerns that they will be viewed as prejudiced (Vorauer, Main, & O'Connell, 1998). Similarly, Blacks anticipating interracial interactions often express concerns that they will be stereotyped by Whites (Pinel, 1999). These beliefs about how they will be perceived can alter the behavior that individuals display during intergroup interactions (Shelton et al., 2005; Vorauer & Turpie, 2004).

There is considerable evidence that *affect and arousal*, such as feelings of threat and anxiety, are also significant factors in mixed interaction (Hebl, Tickle, & Heatherton, 2000; Stephan & Stephan, 2000). Negative affect may be particularly likely to translate into the display of nonverbal behaviors in an interaction (see path S2 of Figure 25.1). Individuals may be able to monitor their cognitions (e.g., explicit attitudes and verbal behaviors) relatively easily, but they may be less skilled at monitoring and controlling their affective reactions. Instead, affective reactions may "leak out" through nonverbal and paraverbal channels (Ekman, Friesen, & O'Sullivan, 1988). Affective reactions may arise from different processing modes than those that trigger cognitive reactions, such that affective reactions may be more experiential or immediate, whereas cognitive reactions may be more rational and deliberative.

Whereas Whites' anxiety may relate to increased cognitive demand associated with not wanting to appear biased (Dovidio & Gaertner, 2004; Richeson & Shelton, 2003; Richeson & Trawalter, 2005; Shelton, 2003), Blacks' anxiety and arousal may be related to ways of coping with potential prejudice and discrimination, which may involve greater vigilance and mindfulness than would otherwise occur (Hyers & Swim, 1998). Consistent with this possibility, Ickes (1984) found that Blacks were particularly anxious during interactions with White partners who generally avoid interracial contact. In addition, Tropp (2003) found that ethnic minorities who had reason to believe their White interaction partners were prejudiced against their group experienced considerable anxiety in anticipation of the interaction. Similarly, Shelton (2003) found that Blacks who were led to believe that their interaction partners might be prejudiced fidgeted more during the interaction than Blacks who were not given the prejudice expectancy.

Both Blacks' and Whites' interaction outcomes are influenced by the propensities, the intentions, and the past ways in which they have responded. That is, the antecedent conditions combine to create *behavioral tendencies or predispositions*, which can influence verbal and nonverbal communication within an interaction (see path S2 of Figure 25.1). These behavioral predispositions may be activated automatically and without awareness in response to racial categorization. Chen and Bargh (1997), for instance, demonstrated that White participants who were primed subliminally with photographs of Blacks, compared with those primed with photographs of Whites and those in a no-photograph control condition, behaved with more hostility in a subsequent interaction with another White participant and elicited more hostile behavior from the partner in return.

Both context-dependent, as well as chronic, *motivations and goals* shape individuals' responses to each other during intergroup interactions. For example, Whites' motivation to appear nonprejudiced in interracial interaction may be internally driven, based on personal standards of behavior, as well as externally oriented, rooted in a concern with social norms and sanctions (Plant & Devine, 1998). The motivation to appear nonprejudiced can influence Whites' nonverbal behavior in interracial interactions (Shelton, 2003). Blacks, in contrast, are often motivated to avoid the stigmatization process altogether: Targets do *not* want to be the target of stereotypes typically or to be devalued across social interaction contexts or be the recipient of interpersonal rejection, social discrimination, and financial disadvantage. Research suggests, however, that concern about being the target of prejudice can sometimes facilitate smooth interactions between Whites and Blacks. Specifically, Whites experienced less negative affect and enjoyed interactions more with Black individuals who had been primed to expect prejudice compared with Black individuals who were not primed to expect prejudice (Shelton et al., 2005).

INITIAL INTERACTION PHASE

According to Hebl and Dovidio's (2005) model, the preinteraction mediators just discussed influence the expression of verbal and nonverbal behaviors within a social interaction (see paths S2 and T2 in Figure 25.1). As discussed earlier, intergroup attitudes and stereotypes, because of the negative feelings and assumptions of status differences embedded in them, influence both *verbal and nonverbal behaviors* in intergroup interaction. Weitz (1972), for example, demonstrated that Whites use colder voice tones for interactions with Blacks than with Whites. Word et al. (1974) found that Whites terminated interactions sooner with Blacks than with other Whites, and they exhibited greater physical distance during the interactions. Similarly, Fugita, Wexley, and Hillery (1974) reported that Whites maintained less eye contact and shorter glances with Black interviewers than with White interviewers. Feldman (1985) likewise reported that both White and Black teachers behaved more positively with members of their own race than with members of the other race. Consistent with the status differences associated with race, Turkstra, Ciccia, and Seaton (2003) found that Whites tended to take the floor more often, whereas Blacks tended to answer more questions in intergroup conversations.

Antecedent factors and preinteraction mediators can not only influence the expression of verbal and nonverbal behaviors in intergroup interaction but may also affect the correspondence between these behaviors. Although many Whites report that they are nonprejudiced on self-report measures, and presumably believe that they are not prejudiced at a conscious level, they commonly harbor negative feelings and beliefs at an unconscious, implicit level (Dovidio, Kawakami, & Beach, 2001).

These explicit and implicit attitudes are dissociated frequently.

Moreover, implicit and explicit attitudes are hypothesized to influence behavior in different ways. Dovidio et al. (1997) proposed that explicit attitudes primarily predict deliberative forms of behavior, which people have the ability to formulate carefully, monitor, and control. Dovidio et al. argued further that implicit attitudes, in contrast, predict spontaneous behaviors, which people have little or no ability to control and which typically occur without awareness or reflection. Consistent with this hypothesis, Dovidio et al. (1997) found that explicit (i.e., self-reported) prejudice predicted overt bias in how Whites judged and evaluated Blacks, but implicit prejudice primarily predicted their nonverbal behaviors reflecting anxiety (rate of blinking) and dislike (gaze aversion) in interactions with Blacks. McConnell and Leibold (2001) also reported that Whites' implicit racial attitudes—but not their explicit racial attitudes—predicted Whites' speaking time, speech errors, and speech hesitations, and the attitudes tended to correlate with how much the Whites leaned away from their partner and seating distance during interracial interactions.

Hebl, Foster, Mannix, and Dovidio (2002) found parallel results, with more evidence of bias for subtle and spontaneous behaviors than for overt and formal actions, for another type of intergroup bias, the prejudice of potential employers toward gay men and lesbians. In this study, employers did not discriminate against confederates portrayed as homosexual on formal employment behaviors, such as permission to complete a job application and callbacks for further consideration. Bias was expressed more subtly in employers' interaction behaviors, however. Employers spent less time and used fewer words when interacting with the stigmatized applicants than with the nonstigmatized applicants.

Systematic differences in communication are also evident in other important types of intergroup encounters. Johnson, Roter, Powe, and Cooper (2004), for example, found that physicians displayed greater verbal dominance, less positive affect, and less patient-centered communication with Black patients than with White patients. It is perhaps because of such differences in communication orientation that same-race interactions between physicians and patients (Cooper et al., 2003), and same-race interactions between teachers and students (Feldman & Donohoe, 1978) are experienced more positively than cross-race interactions.

Importantly, subtle differences in these types of interaction behaviors can exert significant impact on the nature and outcomes of intergroup interactions. Specifically, nonverbal behavior is an important mechanism in self-fulfilling prophecies. Word et al. (1974) demonstrated that Whites exhibited less immediate, more negative nonverbal behaviors when interviewing Black relative to White confederates. In addition, they showed that participants with interviewers who showed low-immediacy behaviors (behaviors mirroring Whites' interactions with Blacks), compared with participants with interviewers who displayed high-immediacy behaviors, responded in a less favorable and responsive way during the interaction and were judged by independent raters as less suitable for the position. Thus, the nonverbal behaviors of the interviewers, which reflected the differences displayed in interactions with Blacks and Whites, elicited complementary verbal and nonverbal responses from the interviewees. This study illustrates the powerful role of nonverbal behavior in perpetuating racial disparities.

Whereas researchers have amassed a great many insights regarding the perspective of majority-group members, the less frequent research conducted on minority-group members suggests that they, too, behave in ways that influence intergroup interaction. In particular, minority-group members attempt to act in strategic ways to manage intergroup interactions. These behaviors may take a number of different forms, but they are characterized generally as ways to cope with actual or anticipated discrimination. Majority and minority members engage in coping strategies in intergroup interactions. They are adjusting to different types of threats, however, and thus the methods and consequences of coping are quite different. As suggested by Gaertner and Dovidio (1986) (see also Dovidio & Gaertner, 2004), Whites commonly find interracial interaction to be anxiety arousing and, thus, they may avoid interracial interactions when possible. When they cannot avoid these interactions, they may become focused on not acting inappropriately, particularly in ways that can be attributed to racism.

Preoccupation with behaving in a non-prejudiced manner can further contribute to inconsistencies in Whites' verbal and nonverbal behaviors in interracial interaction. Hebl and Dovidio (2005) found in their review that across a range of different types of interactions, stigmatizers' (i.e., members of majority or socially dominant groups) display of negative nonverbal behaviors was frequently at odds with their verbal behaviors (see paths S4 and T4 in Figure 25.1). In general, stigmatizers often report feeling positively toward targets, whereas their nonverbal and paraverbal behaviors indicate more negative reactions. This divergence between self-reported favorable orientations and negative nonverbal behaviors is typically observed for Whites in interracial interactions (see Crosby, Bromley, & Saxe, 1980). Because Whites may be concerned about acting in a prejudiced or otherwise inappropriate way in interracial interactions

(Gaertner & Dovidio, 1986), they may focus the majority of their attention on managing their verbal behaviors, which can be easier to monitor and control than nonverbal behaviors. Moreover, to the extent that monitoring and controlling of verbal responses involve high cognitive demand, these activities may actually facilitate the expression of more spontaneous responses (see also Patterson, 1995). As a consequence, Whites (and other types of stigmatizers) may be less adept at managing affect-driven behaviors that occur in interactions spontaneously and without time for deliberation.

Vorauer and Turpie (2004) found similar effects in interactions between Canadian majority- (White) and minority- (First Nations) group members. Whereas higher evaluative concerns reduced bias in intimacy-building behaviors (e.g., eye contact, self-disclosure) among high-prejudiced Whites, higher evaluative concerns interfered with intimacy-building behaviors among low-prejudiced Whites. Vorauer and Turpie interpreted these results as low-prejudiced Whites "choking" under the pressure of high evaluative concerns.

Blacks' coping strategies in interracial interaction are directed generally at coping with actual, perceived, or anticipated bias. Like Whites, Blacks may also avoid interracial interactions when possible (Patchen, 1983), but when avoidance is not an option, they can make use of several coping strategies, including disengagement, vigilance, and compensation. *Disengagement* involves limiting the extent to which feelings of self-worth are dependent on feedback within the interaction. If Blacks disengage, they do not allow the biases of Whites to influence them in substantially negative, or at least direct, ways. As a consequence, Blacks may be less responsive to feedback, either positive or negative, from Whites than are Whites in interactions (Major, Quinton, & McCoy, 2002).

Repeated disengagement may lead to a more long-term strategy of *disidentification*, in which Black individuals disengage permanently from the domain of evaluation. Disengagement may be one reason why Blacks tend to be less emotionally expressive in interracial interaction than are Whites (Ickes, 1984).

Alternatively, minority-group members, such as U.S. Blacks, often cope with anticipated discrimination by either being particularly *vigilant* to cues of bias or *compensating* for potential bias. With respect to ethnic minority/White relations, daily encounters with potential discrimination may lead ethnic minorities to interpretations that confirm and reconfirm that prejudice exists and to label ambiguous behaviors as discriminatory (Sellers & Shelton, 2003). Instead of monitoring for bias that is occurring, minorities can also compensate for potential bias before it has the opportunity to affect the interracial interactions in which they engage (Miller & Myers, 1998). Specifically, when they are concerned about the potential bias of their White interaction partners, ethnic minority participants often engage in compensatory strategies, such as smiling and talking more, to ward off potentially negative outcomes (Shelton et al., 2005). Thus, coping styles can influence the assessment processes identified in the secondary process phase systematically (see Figure 25.1).

SECONDARY INTERACTION PHASE

After individuals have exchanged verbal and nonverbal behaviors, they are likely to assess the interaction in an attempt to continue or terminate it. In deciding which course to pursue, both individuals often engage in an assessment of their goals, the other interactant, and their outcomes. In terms of *assessing one's goals*, interactants, for example, might examine their social goals (e.g., did they make a good impression on their interaction partner?) or their task-oriented goals (e.g., did they get the job or other outcome they sought?). In terms of *assessing the interactant*, interactants both evaluate and judge each other actively during the interaction (e.g., what does the other person think of me and my contributions?).

The dissociation of majority-group members' explicit and implicit attitudes and their consequent effect on verbal and nonverbal behavior can produce a significant divergence in their self-assessments and how they are evaluated by their interaction partners. Dovidio et al. (2002) showed that Whites' *explicit* attitudes and *verbal* behaviors were related, whereas their *implicit* attitudes and *nonverbal* behaviors were related. Specifically, Whites' explicit racial attitudes predicted the positivity of their verbal communications with Black interaction partners, but their implicit racial attitudes predicted the positivity of their nonverbal communication. In addition, Whites based their impressions of how friendly they behaved during their interracial interactions on the attitudes that were accessible (i.e., their explicit attitudes) and the behaviors that they could readily monitor (i.e., their verbal behaviors). Because most of the Whites in the study perceived themselves as nonprejudiced, they generally believed that they behaved in a friendly and unbiased manner toward their Black partners.

Blacks, in contrast, relied on their White interaction partners' nonverbal behavior in making their assessments of how friendly their partners behaved. Because Whites' nonverbal behavior was correlated with their implicit attitudes that were, on average, negative, Blacks often left the interaction with a negative perception of their White partners. Thus, Whites' and Blacks' assessments of how the White person

behaved in the interaction were essentially uncorrelated. Other researchers have shown similarly that Whites' implicit intergroup attitudes and stereotypes, of which they have limited awareness, predict the impressions that ethnic minorities form of them during interactions (Fazio, Jackson, Dunton, & Williams, 1995; McConnell & Leibold, 2001; Sekaquaptewa, Espinoza, Thompson, Vargas, & von Hippel, 2003).

Because of heightened awareness and anticipated rejection in interracial interactions, Whites tend to overestimate the extent to which racial minorities will perceive their behavior as friendly (Vorauer & Sakamoto, 2005). Furthermore, both Whites and Blacks often misinterpret anxiety-related behaviors, such a shorter gaze durations and more frequent self-touching, as signals of unfriendliness more frequently in interracial than in intraracial encounters (Devine & Vasquez, 1998; Dovidio & Johnson, 2005). This vigilance may produce more accurate sensitivity to racial bias among Blacks, however (Rollman, 1978). Richeson and Shelton (2005) found, for instance, that Black judges (college student participants) were, on average, better able to detect both the explicit and the implicit racial bias levels of White individuals from 20 seconds of their nonverbal behavior during interracial interactions than were White judges. Specifically, Black judges' ratings of how positively a sample of White targets behaved during an interracial interaction were more highly correlated (albeit negatively) with those targets' automatic racial bias scores than were the ratings made by White judges. Furthermore, Black judges' ratings of the White targets' prejudice levels were more highly correlated with those targets' explicit prejudice scores than were the same ratings made by White judges.

In addition to assessing their goals and their interaction partner, individuals engage in ongoing assessment of the *costs and benefits* of the interaction (see Figure 25.1). This assessment can be very conscious and deliberative, but it can also involve the use of relatively nonconscious global impressions. The assessment of costs and benefits involves not only the likelihood of gaining (or losing) tangible outcomes or resources but also the cost of self-presentation. In addition, as we noted earlier, whereas the assessment of majority-group members may be based on the more overt aspects of the exchange, minority-group members may weigh more subtle behaviors in their evaluation of the costs and benefits of continuing the interaction. If the ratio indicates net personal gains for the interactant, he or she may choose to continue the interaction, whereas the accumulation of personal losses may lead to interaction termination.

◆ Interaction Continuation or Termination

Majority- and minority-group interaction partners decide ultimately, either unilaterally or consensually, whether to continue or to terminate the interaction. This critical decision is based largely on the verbal and nonverbal behaviors that have been displayed during the interaction and individuals' assessments of themselves, of their partners, and of the costs and benefits of the interaction. The continuation of an interaction is a negotiation in which both interactants contribute. Disparities may exist, however; for instance, one interactant's strong desire to continue the interaction may overwhelm the other interactant's weak desire to end the interaction. In addition, because higher status people often exert more control over conversation and interaction, they may be more influential in determining the length of the interaction.

◆ Implications of the Model for Intergroup Interaction Outcomes

In this chapter, we made use of Hebl and Dovidio's (2005) model of mixed social interactions to explore how nonverbal behavior may be expressed and interpreted during intergroup interactions. Our examination of each phase of the interaction reveals how susceptible intergroup interactions are to misunderstandings, if not categorically negative outcomes. Nonverbal behavior thus can be a critical element of interpersonal relations that reflects and reinforces intergroup relations.

With respect to race relations, in particular, as our analysis has revealed, Whites' self-consciousness in interracial interaction may lead them to focus primarily on the controllable aspects of their behavior, such as the verbal content of their speech, but to increase the signs of discomfort and other negative states they exhibit nonverbally. Because they interpret their behavior based on the behaviors they can monitor most easily, Whites tend to overestimate how favorably they are appearing. In contrast, Blacks, because of their self-consciousness, may be particularly vigilant to cues of Whites' bias in these interactions. As a result, they may rely on nonverbal behavior primarily, largely discounting the verbal content, in forming impressions of Whites and the interaction. Given their vigilance to cues of bias, Blacks are likely to attribute their White partners' negative nonverbal behavior to racial bias (Dovidio & Johnson, 2005; Richeson & Shelton, 2005). Thus, racial distrust influences how Blacks interpret Whites' nonverbal behavior, and the discrepancy between Whites' overt expressions and their nonverbal behavior reinforces this distrust.

Furthermore, the different reliance on verbal and nonverbal behavior by Whites and

Blacks in forming their impressions can lead to vastly divergent views not only about their interpersonal relations but also ultimately to race relations in general. These dynamics provide insight into why Blacks and Whites view race relations so differently. For instance, in the United States, whereas most (69%) of Whites perceive that Blacks are treated "the same as Whites", the majority of Blacks (59%) report that Blacks are treated worse than Whites (Gallup Organization, 2002). Understanding the role of nonverbal behavior in interaction can thus provide fundamental insights for understanding and improving intergroup relations.

◆ Conclusion

Despite its obvious practical importance and theoretical value, nonverbal behavior in intergroup contexts is a curiously understudied topic. In 1985, Halberstadt observed specifically that "the first research on race and socioeconomic differences in nonverbal communication was conducted in the 1930s . . . , but interest in these issues was not sustained until the early 1970s" (p. 228). Our review of the literature reveals that the interest in race and nonverbal communication peaked in the 1970s; research activity on this topic has waned since then. The bulk of this seminal work on nonverbal behavior, race, and intergroup interaction focuses on the contention that majority- and minority-group members, perhaps because of differences in status, social power, and stigmatization, are likely to develop different styles of communication, reflected in nonverbal and verbal behaviors. The data, however, are suggestive but not yet conclusive.

We propose that a comprehensive understanding of nonverbal behavior requires a consideration of the complex processes involved in intergroup as well as intragroup interactions. Building on Patterson's (1982) Sequential Functional Model of Nonverbal Exchange, we presented a model of mixed social interaction (Hebl & Dovidio, 2005) that outlines key elements in the dynamics of communication in an intergroup context. Thus, although nonverbal behavior can be studied in terms of separate encoding and decoding processes, the dynamic nature of nonverbal communication can best be studied during interactions. Unfortunately, studies of actual intergroup interaction, including measures of verbal and nonverbal behavior, remain all too rare. Yet we believe that this type of research, along with appropriate theoretical development, is crucial to understanding the important role of nonverbal behavior in intergroup communication and ultimately intergroup relations.

◆ References

Ashburn-Nardo, L., Knowles, M. L., & Monteith, M. J. (2003). Black Americans' implicit racial associations and their implications for intergroup judgment. *Social Cognition, 21,* 61–87.

Bailey, W., Nowicki, S., Cole, S. P. (1998). The ability to decode nonverbal information in African American, African, and Afro-Caribbean and European American adults. *Journal of Black Psychology, 24,* 418–431.

Berger, J., Wagner, D. G., & Zelditch, M. (1985). Introduction: Expectation states theory. In J. Berger & M. Zelditch Jr. (Eds.), *Status, rewards, and influence* (pp. 1–71). San Francisco: Jossey-Bass.

Blascovich, J., Mendes, W. B., Hunter, S. B., Lickel, B., & Kowai-Bell, N. (2001). Perceiver threat in social interactions with stigmatized individuals. *Journal of Personality and Social Psychology, 80,* 253–267.

Caporael, L. R. (1981). The paralanguage of caregiving: Baby talk to the institutionalized aged. *Journal of Personality and Social Psychology, 40*, 876–884.

Caporael, L. R., & Culbertson, G. H. (1983). Verbal response modes of baby talk and other speech at institutions for the aged. *Language and Communication, 6*, 99–112.

Chen, M., & Bargh, J. A. (1997). Nonconscious behavioral processes: The self-fulfilling consequences of automatic stereotype activation. *Journal of Experimental Social Psychology, 33*, 541–560.

Cooper, L. A., Roter, D. L., Johnson, R. L., Forde, D. E., Steinwachs, D. M., & Powe, N. R. (2003). Patient-centered communication, ratings of care, and concordance of patient and physician race. *Annals of Internal Medicine, 139*, 907–915.

Correll, S. J., & Ridgeway, C. L. (2003). Expectation states theory. In J. Delamater (Ed.), *Handbook of social psychology* (pp. 29–51). New York: Kluwer Academic/Plenum.

Crandall, C. S., & Eshleman, A. (2003). A justification suppression model of the expression and experience of prejudice. *Psychological Bulletin, 129*, 414–446.

Crosby, F., Bromley, S., & Saxe, L. (1980). Recent unobtrusive studies of black and white discrimination and prejudice: A literature review. *Psychological Bulletin, 87*, 546–563.

Devine, P. G., & Vasquez, K. A. (1998). The rocky road to positive intergroup relations. In J. L. Eberhardt & S. T. Fiske (Eds.), *Confronting racism: The problem and the response* (pp. 234–262). Thousand Oaks, CA: Sage.

Dovidio, J. F., Brown, C. E., Keating, C. F., Heltman, K., & Ellyson, S. L. (1988). Power displays between women and men in discussions of gender-linked tasks: A multi-channel study. *Journal of Personality and Social Psychology, 55*, 580–587.

Dovidio, J. F., & Ellyson, S. L. (1985). Visual dominance behavior in humans. In S. L. Ellyson & J. F. Dovidio (Eds.), *Power, dominance, and nonverbal behavior* (pp. 129–149). New York: Springer-Verlag.

Dovidio, J. F., & Gaertner, S. L. (2004). Aversive racism. In M. P. Zanna (Ed.), *Advances in experimental social psychology* (Vol. 36, pp. 1–51). San Diego, CA: Academic Press.

Dovidio, J. F., & Johnson, J. (2005). *Racial bias in interpreting cues of anxiety*. Unpublished data, University of Connecticut, Storrs.

Dovidio, J. F., Kawakami, K., & Beach, K. (2001). Implicit and explicit attitudes: Examination of the relationship between measures of intergroup bias. In R. Brown & S. L. Gaertner (Eds.), *Blackwell handbook of social psychology, Vol. 4: Intergroup relations* (pp. 175–197). Oxford, UK: Blackwell.

Dovidio, J. F., Kawakami, K., & Gaertner, S. L. (2002). Implicit and explicit prejudice and interracial interaction. *Journal of Personality and Social Psychology, 82*, 62–68.

Dovidio, J. F., Kawakami, K., Johnson, C., Johnson, B., & Howard, A. (1997). On the nature of prejudice: Automatic and controlled process. *Journal of Experimental Social Psychology, 33*, 510–540.

Eagly, A. H., & Karau, S. J. (2002). Role congruity theory of prejudice toward female leaders. *Psychological Review, 109*, 573–598.

Eagly, A. H., & Wood, W. (1999). The origins of sex differences in human behavior: Evolved dispositions versus social roles. *American Psychologist, 54*, 408–423.

Ekman, P., Friesen, W. V., & O'Sullivan, M. (1988). Smiles when lying. *Journal of Personality and Social Psychology, 54*, 414–420.

Elfenbein, H. A., & Ambady, N. (2002). On the universality and cultural specificity of emotion recognition: A meta-analysis. *Psychological Bulletin, 128*, 203–235.

Ellyson, S. L., & Dovidio, J. F. (1985). Power, dominance, and nonverbal behavior: Basic concepts and issues. In S. L. Ellyson & J. F. Dovidio (Eds.), *Power, dominance, and nonverbal behavior* (pp. 1–27). New York: Springer-Verlag.

Fazio, R. H., Jackson, J. R., Dunton, B. C., & Williams, C. J. (1995). Variability in automatic activation as an unobtrusive measure of racial attitudes: A bona fide pipeline? *Journal of Personality and Social Psychology, 69*, 1013–1027.

Fazio, R. H., & Olson, M. A. (2003). Implicit measures in social cognition research: Their meaning and uses. *Annual Review of Psychology, 54,* 297–327.

Feldman, R. S. (1985). Nonverbal behavior, race, and the classroom teacher. *Theory Into Practice, 24,* 45–49.

Feldman, R. S., & Donohoe, L. F. (1978). Nonverbal communication of affect in interracial dyads. *Journal of Educational Psychology, 70,* 979–987.

Fiske, S. T., Lin, M., & Neuberg, S. L. (1999). The continuum model: Ten years later. In S. Chaiken & Y. Trope (Eds.), *Dual process theories in social psychology* (pp. 231–254). New York: Guilford.

Frable, D. E. S., Blackstone, T., & Scherbaum, C. (1990). Marginal and mindful deviants in social interactions. *Journal of Personality and Social Psychology, 59,* 140–149.

Fugita, S. S., Wexley, K. N., & Hillery, J. M. (1974). Black–white differences in nonverbal behavior in an interview setting. *Journal of Applied Social Psychology, 4,* 343–350.

Gaertner, S. L., & Dovidio, J. F. (1986). The aversive form of racism. In J. F. Dovidio & S. L. Gaertner (Eds.), *Prejudice, discrimination, and racism* (pp. 61–89). Orlando, FL: Academic Press.

Galinsky, A. D., Gruenfeld, D. H., & Magee, J. C. (2003). From power to action. *Journal of Personality and Social Psychology, 85,* 453–466.

Gallup Organization. (2002). *Poll topics & trends: Race relations.* Washington, DC: Author. Retrieved October 3, 2004, from http://www.gallup.com/poll/topics/race.asp

Guinote, A., Judd, C. M., & Brauer, M. (2002). Effects of power on perceived and objective group variability: Evidence that more powerful groups are more variable. *Journal of Personality and Social Psychology, 82,* 708–721.

Halberstadt, A. G. (1985). Race, socioeconomic status, and nonverbal behavior. In A. W. Siegman & S. Feldstein (Eds.), *Multichannel integrations of nonverbal behavior* (pp. 227–266). Hillsdale, NJ: Erlbaum.

Hall, E. T. (1966). *The hidden dimension.* New York: Doubleday.

Hall, J. A., Coats, E. J., & Smith LeBeau, L. (2005). Nonverbal behavior and the vertical dimension of social relations: A meta-analysis. *Psychological Bulletin, 131,* 898–924.

Hebl, M. R., & Dovidio, J. F. (2005). Promoting the "social" in the examination of social stigmas. *Personality and Social Psychology Review, 9,* 156–182.

Hebl, M. R., Foster, J., Mannix, L. M., & Dovidio, J. F. (2002). Formal and interpersonal discrimination: A field study understanding of applicant bias. *Personality and Social Psychological Bulletin, 28,* 815–825.

Hebl, M., Tickle, J., & Heatherton, T. F. (2000). Awkward moments in interactions between nonstigmatized and stigmatized individuals. In T. F. Heatherton, R. E. Kleck, M. R. Hebl, & J. G. Hull (Eds.), *Stigma: Social psychological perspectives* (pp. 273–306). New York: Guilford Press.

Henley, N. M. (1977). *Body politics: Power, sex, and nonverbal communication.* Englewood Cliffs, NJ: Prentice Hall.

Hyers, L. L., & Swim, J. K. (1998). A comparison of experiences of dominant and minority group members during an intergroup encounter. *Group Processes and Intergroup Relations, 12,* 143–163.

Ickes, W. (1984). Compositions in black and white: Determinants of interaction in interracial dyads. *Journal of Personality and Social Psychology, 47,* 330–341.

Johnson, R. L., Roter, D., Powe, N. R., & Cooper, L. A. (2004). Patient race/ethnicity and quality of patient–physician communication during medical visits. *American Journal of Public Health, 94,* 2084–2090.

Jones, J. M. (1986). Racism: A cultural analysis of the problem. In J. F. Dovidio & S. L. Gaertner (Eds.), *Prejudice, discrimination, and racism* (pp. 279–314). Orlando, FL: Academic Press.

Keltner, D., Gruenfeld, D. H., & Anderson, C. (2003). Power, approach, and inhibition. *Psychological Review, 110,* 265–284.

Kemper, S., Vandeputte, D., Rice, K., Cheung, H., & Gubarchuk, J. (1995). Spontaneous adoption of elderspeak during referential communication tasks. *Journal of Language and Social Psychology, 14,* 40–59.

LaFrance, M., & Henley, N. M. (1994). On oppressing hypotheses: Or differences in nonverbal sensitivity revisited. In H. L. Radtke & H. J. Stam (Eds.), *Power/gender: Social relations theory and practice* (pp. 287–311). London: Sage.

Major, B., Quinton, W., & McCoy, S. (2002). Antecedents and consequences of attributions to discrimination: Theoretical and empirical advances. In M. P. Zanna (Ed.), *Advances of Experimental Social Psychology* (Vol. 34, pp. 251–330). New York: Academic Press.

McConnell, A. R., & Leibold, J. M. (2001). Relations among the Implicit Association Test, discriminatory behavior, and explicit measures of racial attitudes. *Journal of Experimental Social Psychology, 37,* 435–442.

Miller, C. T., & Myers, A. M. (1998). Compensating for prejudice: How heavyweight people (and others) control outcomes despite prejudice. In J. K. Swim & C. Stangor (Eds.), *Prejudice: The target's perspective* (pp. 191–218). San Diego, CA: Academic Press.

Patchen, M. (1983). Students' own racial attitudes and those of peers of both races, as related to interracial behaviors. *Sociology and Social Research, 68,* 59–77.

Patterson, M. L. (1982). A sequential functional model of nonverbal exchange. *Psychological Review, 89,* 231–249.

Patterson, M. L. (1995). Invited article: A parallel process model of nonverbal communication. *Journal of Nonverbal Behavior, 19,* 3–29.

Pettigrew, T. F., & Tropp, L. R. (2000). Does intergroup contact reduce prejudice? Recent meta-analytic findings. In S. Oskamp (Ed.), *Reducing prejudice and discrimination* (pp. 93–114). Hillsdale, NJ: Erlbaum.

Pinel, E. C. (1999). Stigma consciousness: The psychological legacy of social stereotypes. *Journal of Personality and Social Psychology, 76,* 114–128.

Plant, E. A., & Devine, P. G. (1998). Internal and external motivation to respond without prejudice. *Journal of Personality and Social Psychology, 75,* 811–832.

Reid, P. T., Tate, C. S., & Berman, P. W. (1989). Preschool children's self-presentations in situations with infants: Effects of race and sex. *Child Development, 60,* 710–714.

Richeson, J. A., & Ambady, N. (2003). Effects of situational power on automatic racial prejudice. *Journal of Experimental Social Psychology, 39,* 177–183.

Richeson, J. A., & Shelton, J. N. (2003). When prejudice does not pay: Effects of interracial contact on executive function. *Psychological Science, 14,* 287–290.

Richeson, J. A., & Shelton, J. N. (2005). Thin slices of racial bias. *Journal of Nonverbal Behavior, 29,* 75–86.

Richeson, J. A., & Trawalter, S. (2005). Why do interracial interactions impair executive function? A resource depletion account. *Journal of Personality and Social Psychology, 88,* 934–947.

Rollman, S. A. (1978). The sensitivity of Black and White Americans to nonverbal cues of prejudice. *Journal of Social Psychology, 105,* 73–77.

Sekaquaptewa, D., Espinoza, P., Thompson, M., Vargas, P., & von Hippel, W. (2003). Stereotypic explanatory bias: Implicit stereotyping as a predictor of discrimination. *Journal of Experimental Social Psychology, 39,* 75–82.

Sellers, R. M., & Shelton, J. N. (2003). The role of racial identity in perceived racial discrimination. *Journal of Personality and Social Psychology, 84,* 1079–1092.

Shelton, J. N. (2003). Interpersonal concerns in social encounters between majority and minority group members. *Group Processes & Intergroup Relations, 6,* 171–185.

Shelton, J. N., Richeson, J. A., & Salvatore, J. (2005). Expecting to be the target of prejudice. Implications for interethnic interactions. *Personality and Social Psychology Bulletin, 39,* 1189–1202.

Sidanius, J., & Pratto, F. (1999). *Social dominance: An intergroup theory of social hierarchy and oppression.* New York: Cambridge University Press.

Smith, A. (1983). Nonverbal communication among Black female dyads: An assessment of intimacy and race. *Journal of Social Issues, 39,* 55–67.

Stangor, C., Sullivan, L. A, & Ford, T. E. (1991). Affective and cognitive determinants of prejudice. *Social Cognition, 9,* 359–380.

Stephan, W., & Stephan, C. W. (1985). Intergroup anxiety. *Journal of Social Issues, 41,* 157–175.

Stephan, W. G., & Stephan, C. W. (2000). An integrated threat theory of prejudice. In S. Oskamp (Ed.), *Reducing prejudice and discrimination: The Claremont Symposium on Applied Psychology* (pp. 23–45). Mahwah, NJ: Erlbaum.

Tajfel, H., & Turner, J. C. (1979). An integrative theory of intergroup conflict. In W. G. Austin & S. Worchel (Eds.), *The social psychology of intergroup relations* (pp. 33–48). Monterey, CA: Brooks/Cole.

Tiedens, L. Z. (2000). Powerful emotions: The vicious cycle of social status positions and emotions. In N. Ashkanasy, W. Zerbe, & C. Hartel (Eds.), *Emotions in the workplace: Research, theory, and practice* (pp. 71–81). Westport, CT: Quorum Books.

Tiedens, L. Z., & Fragale, A. R. (2003). Power moves: Complementarity in dominant and submissive nonverbal behavior. *Journal of Personality and Social Psychology, 3,* 558–568.

Tropp, L. R. (2003). The psychological impact of prejudice: Implications for intergroup contact. *Group Processes and Intergroup Relations, 6,* 131–149.

Turkstra, L., Ciccia, A., & Seaton, C. (2003). Interactive behaviors in adolescent conversation dyads. *Language, Speech, and Hearing Services in Schools, 34,* 117–127.

Turner, J. C., Hogg, M. A., Oakes, P. J., Reicher, S. D., & Wetherell, M. S. (1987). *Rediscovering the social group: A self-categorization theory.* Oxford, UK: Basil Blackwell.

Vorauer, J., Main, K. J., & O'Connell, G. B. (1998). How do individuals expect to be viewed by members of lower status groups? Content and implications of meta-stereotypes. *Journal of Personality and Social Psychology, 75,* 917–937.

Vorauer, J. D., & Sakamoto, Y. (2005). *I thought we could be friends, but . . . . Systematic miscommunication and defensive distancing as obstacles to cross-group friendship formation.* Unpublished manuscript.

Vorauer, J. D., & Turpie, C. (2004). Disruptive effects of vigilance on dominant group members' treatment of outgroup members: Choking versus shining under pressure. *Journal of Personality and Social Psychology, 27,* 706–709.

Weathers, M. D., Kitsantas, P., Lever, T., O'Brien, P., Campbell, S., & Rastatter, M. (2004). Recognition accuracy and reaction time of vocal expressions of emotion by African-American and Euro-American college women. *Perceptual and Motor Skills, 99,* 662–668.

Weitz, S. (1972). Attitude, voice, and behavior: A repressed affect model of interracial interaction. *Journal of Personality and Social Psychology, 24,* 14–21.

Word, C. O., Zanna, M. P., & Cooper, J. (1974). The nonverbal mediation of self-fulfilling prophecies in interracial interaction. *Journal of Experimental Social Psychology, 10,* 109–120.

26

USES AND CONSEQUENCES OF NONVERBAL COMMUNICATION IN THE CONTEXT OF ORGANIZATIONAL LIFE

◆ Martin S. Remland
West Chester University

Nonverbal communication is a vital part of our personal and professional lives. As the chapters in this section show, nonverbal cues affect various measures of success in personal relationships, education, health care, computer-mediated interactions, and intergroup relations. It is no less important in the context of organizational life, where face-to-face interaction with superiors, subordinates, and peers consumes much of our time and energy. Some features of these routine interactions—status differences, chain of command, division of labor, measurable performance objectives—are unique to the organizational context and create special communication challenges for the members of any organization.

Many of these challenges arise from the natural intersection of context and function. For example, one of the *primary functions* of nonverbal communication is signaling one's identity (Patterson, 1983; Remland, 2004). In the context of work life, people learn to manage the tension that exists between expressing their individuality or their membership in some

◆ 501

group (e.g., unique styles of dress) and indicating their affiliation with the organization (e.g., dressing like everyone else). People also confront and cope with discriminatory practices based on a person's race, sex, age, and so forth.

In this chapter, I discuss those challenges about which there is sufficient empirical research of use to scholars and practitioners. The first major set of challenges, which stems most directly from the *identification* and *relationship* functions of nonverbal communication, is how to manage the displays of status that are such an integral part of organizational life. The second major set of challenges deals with the *emotion* function and focuses on the impact of emotional exchanges on task performance. The third major set of challenges addresses the *delivery* function, which involves the coordination and integration of verbal and nonverbal channels of communication. Table 26.1 offers one view of how these communication challenges emerge from the interplay of context and function. The table also serves to identify and organize much of the research that has been done on the uses and consequences of nonverbal communication in organizations.

◆ Managing Nonverbal Displays of Status

Research suggests that the nonverbal communication of high-status persons differs in fundamental ways from that of lower-status persons (Andersen & Bowman, 1990; Burgoon & Dunbar, this volume; Edinger & Patterson, 1983; Hall, 2005). These nonverbal displays of status serve a useful function: They clarify and reinforce the role relationships that exist in an organization, helping to sustain the organization's hierarchy. But unlike verbal reminders of status

(e.g., "I'm telling you to do this"), the greater ambiguity of nonverbal displays carries the potential to produce unintended consequences that interfere with the goals of an organization. Moreover, because we are generally less aware of these "below the radar" signals, the consequences may be especially difficult to avoid. The section below addresses three possible consequences of status cues: dysfunctional leadership, sexual harassment, and workplace discrimination.

STATUS DISPLAYS AND DYSFUNCTIONAL LEADERSHIP

Social exchange theory provides a useful framework for appreciating how status differentials between leaders and followers can result in a leader's loss of power (Blau, 1964; Jacobs, 1970; see also Burgoon & Dunbar, this volume). Based on social exchange theory principles, a leader can lose influence over subordinates when subordinates begin to assess their relationship with a leader as more costly than rewarding— that is, in a state of disequilibrium. A social exchange view of leadership emphasizes the interactive or transactional nature of the leadership process. In each superior-subordinate interaction, an exchange of resources is negotiated in a way that is perceived as equitable by both parties. *Effective communication allows the leader to keep the exchange in a state of equilibrium.* Jacobs (1970) suggests, for example, that supervisors avoid interactions "that make evident power or status differentials" (p. 237).

The interactive nature of social exchange theory suggests that the nonverbal communication of both superior and subordinate should shape perceptions of leadership, as the status displays of either person can steer the relationship into a state of disequilibrium (Remland, 1981). Whereas there is no

Table 26.1 A Functional View of Nonverbal Communication Research in Organizations

Function	Definition	Communication Challenges	Outcomes
Identification	Identification of self as individual or group member	Overcoming stereotypes	Workplace discrimination
		Balancing desire for individuality and need for conformity	
Relationship	Creation and maintenance of relations based on control and intimacy	Managing displays of status and power	Leadership perceptions
		Negotiating relational expectations (friend, boss, coworker, romantic partner)	Organizational climate
			Job satisfaction
			Sexual harassment
Emotion	Expression and recognition of emotions	Managing emotional displays (e.g., emotional contagion, emotional labor)	Job stress
			Job satisfaction
			Burnout
			Motivation
			Productivity
		Accurately inferring emotional states	Rapport
Delivery	Coordination and integration of verbal and nonverbal channels	Developing speaking and listening competencies (expectancy effects; mixed messages; involvement behavior)	Performance assessments
			Credibility judgments
			Leadership perceptions
			Productivity

lack of research on the effects of a leader's nonverbal cues (e.g., Heintzman, Leathers, Parrott, & Cairns, 1993; Remland, 1984; Richmond & McCroskey, 2000), there is little regarding the impact of a subordinate's nonverbal behavior. In one study,

however, Remland (1984) produced four videotapes of the same two male actors, role-playing a scene in which a superior reprimands his subordinate. Although the script was the same in each role play, the actors altered their nonverbal cues so that each had a high-status and a low-status performance. In the high-status (HS) performance, they used a relaxed posture, indirect body orientation, loud voice, inattentive behavior, and an act of spatial invasion. In the low-status (LS) performance, they used a tense posture, direct body orientation, soft and hesitating speech, and attentive gaze.

Not surprisingly, judges rated the superior as more considerate when he used LS behaviors than when he used HS behaviors. But they also rated him as more considerate when the subordinate he interacted with used HS behaviors rather than LS behaviors. This finding suggests that observers may perceive a male leader as more considerate when status differentials are reduced, either from a reduction in the leader's displays of status, or an increase in the subordinate's. Perhaps the leader receives some "credit" for allowing or encouraging subordinates to behave in a high-status manner, empowering them in the process. Unfortunately, however, the results of this experiment do not permit any inferences about how *subordinates* judge such interactions with their superiors, a central component in the social exchange hypothesis.

Some research indicates that the nonverbal communication of leaders frequently includes a mix of high- and low-status cues that reduces the differential that exists between them and their subordinates. In one study, Hall and Friedman (1999) found that higher-status persons spoke more, used more hand gestures, and leaned forward less than did lower-status persons. But the higher-status persons also nodded more frequently. Unlike the first set of behaviors, all of which signal higher status, head nodding, which implies attentiveness, agreement, or the desire for approval, tends to signal lower status.

One especially interesting finding in the study was that the greater the disparity was between the high-status person and the low-status person, the *less* the high-status person spoke. As the researchers point out, "this seemingly paradoxical pattern is understandable if the [high-status] person is motivated to downplay his or her own status in the service of comfortable social interaction by (as one example) encouraging the partner to speak more" (Hall & Friedman, 1999, p. 1088). But, despite the benefit of minimizing status differentials, some research suggests that leaders often prefer asymmetrical relations. For example, Yukl (2002) reports studies showing a positive correlation between ingratiation by subordinates and leaders' liking for those subordinates. Moreover, a recent study found that persons in low-status positions often choose low-status behavior, which may be more "comfortable" for them, when interacting with higher-status persons in task-oriented encounters (Tiedens & Fragale, 2003).

The maintenance of status differentials is not just about exchange, however. It is also a cultural artifact. Hofstede (1982) maintains that cultures classified as high in "power distance" tend to embrace authoritarian values and encourage actions that perpetuate status distinctions. For example, Kowner and Wiseman (2003) asked Japanese and American participants to imagine various interactions between high-status and lower-status individuals. Although there was considerable agreement on the specific behaviors differentiating high- from low-status persons, the magnitude of the differences varied, with Japanese, a more hierarchical, collectivistic, and high-context people, reporting greater differences than did Americans, representing a more egalitarian, individualistic, and lower context society. Thus, what seems "excessive" in one culture may seem quite ordinary in another.

The challenge of managing displays of status is complicated further by the effects of sex-role stereotyping and the corresponding claim that sex constitutes a diffuse status characteristic, with women viewed as lower in status (Lockheed & Hall, 1976). A sizeable body of research shows how status takes root in the communication behavior of men and women. Specifically, and although contested in the larger literature, research shows that women's nonverbal communication differs to some degree from that of men's along the dimension of status and power (Hall, 1984, this volume; Henley, 1995). But researchers also find that many of these differences disappear when women assume positions of leadership or possess levels of power equal to those of men. That is, the influence of authority and power on nonverbal communication may be greater than that of gender (Johnson, 1994; Dovidio, Ellyson, Keating, Heltman, & Brown, 1988). In addition, women's nonverbal cues become more "powerful" than men's when men and women work together on "feminine" tasks (Dovidio, Brown, Heltman, Ellyson, & Keating, 1988). Research also shows that women use more assertive (high status) nonverbal communication, such as a more confident tone of voice, when they interact with superiors and subordinates compared with their interactions with peers (Steckler & Rosenthal, 1985).

But women in leadership positions may still face the challenge of overcoming sex-role expectations. Carli, LaFleur, and Loeber (1995) compared the effectiveness of a task style of nonverbal communication (competent) with that of a dominant style, a submissive style, and a social style (friendly and competent). They prepared videotapes of a male or female speaker using one of the four styles to deliver the same persuasive message to a seated listener. The judges who watched the tapes were persuaded most by male and female speakers when those speakers used the task and social styles.

Contrary to expectations, female speakers were not penalized more than male speakers were for using a dominant (i.e., masculine) style: Male and female speakers using this style were equally ineffective. But female speakers who used a task style were judged as less effective by males than were male speakers who used the same task style. Moreover, when female speakers injected some warmth and friendliness into their presentations (a social style) they were more persuasive with male judges than when they used the "cooler" task style; this was not true for the male speakers. The male judges also rated female speakers using the task style as less likeable and more threatening than the male speakers who used the same style. Although the results of this study show that women were, in this case, better off using a task-oriented style than one that highlights feminine (submissive) or masculine (dominant) traits, it still reveals the presence of a double standard: For the same performance, women apparently get less credit from men than do their male counterparts.

Almost certainly there is some link between nonverbal displays of status and leadership success. Social exchange theory raises one possibility for this link: Dysfunctional leadership results from asymmetrical patterns of nonverbal communication in superior-subordinate interactions that favor the superior or the subordinate to excess, creating a state of disequilibrium. Yet despite the intuitive nature of this proposition, it has not yet been adequately tested. Research on gender differences in nonverbal communication suggests another possibility: that female leaders may be judged more harshly than their male counterparts for using the same displays of status. But researchers are still a long way from identifying systematically the conditions under which organizational members are most likely to impose such double standards.

STATUS DISPLAYS AND SEXUAL HARASSMENT

Another potential workplace problem involving nonverbal displays of status is sexual harassment. Although many cases of harassment involve the deliberate abuse of authority and power, other cases likely occur because one person misses or misreads the signals of another. For example, a recent experiment by Woodzicka and LaFrance (2005) demonstrates how a smile in response to sexually provocative questions, *which do at times occur in the workplace*, has the potential for prompting inappropriate sexual conduct. Based on the idea that women use social smiles for a variety of reasons, they discovered that female job applicants were more likely to use "masking" smiles (concealing negative feelings) in response to questions such as "Do you have a boyfriend?" than in response to questions such as, "Do you have a best friend?" Interestingly, these smiling responses (coded by the researchers as unfelt or "non-Duchenne" smiles) were correlated with perceptions of the interviewer as sexist and sexually harassing. What is more, men were less able to read these uncomfortable smiles *correctly* than women were, and men who scored higher on an instrument that measures likelihood to sexually harass were most likely to interpret the smiles as flirtatious.

Explanations of sexual harassment usually refer to the actions of both the perpetrator and the victim: inappropriate sexual behavior by the perpetrator alongside some form of resistance, or at least disapproval, by the victim. Studies show that judgments of whether an individual is guilty of sexual harassment depend on the actions of both parties (e.g., Jones & Remland, 1997). The more people view a behavior as inappropriate, and the more unwelcome the behavior is, the more likely those people are to define it as a case of sexual harassment. But studies also show that men and women often don't agree on what actions constitute sexual harassment. In general, men are less likely than women to see the same actions as sexually harassing, particularly when

there is some degree of ambiguity in the actions of either party (Jones & Remland, 1997; for an application to courtship contexts, see Noller, this volume).

The danger of being misunderstood is particularly acute in asymmetrical relationships, where a nonverbal display of status can take on sexual connotations. A superior's use of immediacy behaviors—touching, staring, and getting close, for example—has long been the prerogative of higher-status individuals. But because these actions are subject to multiple interpretations (e.g., friendliness, intimidation, sexual interest), there is always the chance of misreading the signals (Le Poire, Burgoon, & Parrot, 1992). In addition, a subordinate's use of submissive or low-status behaviors, such as smiling, head nodding, silence, eye contact, and direct body orientation, can make it equally difficult to tell whether the subordinate welcomes the superior's advances or is behaving like a subordinate is expected to behave. Moreover, the ambiguity of nonverbal signals makes it possible for harassers to deny the charges against them ("I didn't mean anything by it").

Nonverbal displays of status may also reveal whether someone is prone to engage in sexual harassment. Studies on the attitudes, beliefs, and perceptions of persons likely to sexually harass show that such persons tend to describe themselves in ways that emphasize social and sexual dominance (Pryor, 1987). Some research indicates that nonverbal displays of status may be *symptomatic* of persons likely to sexually harass. In one study, participants viewed silent clips of videotaped interviews of men being interviewed by an attractive female subordinate (who could not be seen by the viewers). Only observing the men's nonverbal behavior, the participants were able to predict which men scored high on a test that measured likelihood to sexually harass and which men scored low (Driscoll, Kelly, & Henderson, 1998).

In a follow-up study to Driscoll et al. (1998), male undergraduate participants, classified as high or low on likelihood to sexually harass, were interviewed individually by a female confederate posing as a high school senior (Murphy, Driscoll, & Kelly, 1999). To put the men in a more powerful position relative to the interviewer, the researchers told them they would be evaluating the performance of the female interviewer following the interview. Men classified as more likely to sexually harass expressed greater dominance through their nonverbal behavior (e.g., less time in the interview, less forward leaning, more indirect body orientation, and more direct eye contact) compared with those less likely to sexually harass. Underscoring the idea that sexual harassment is more about power and control than it is about sexual attraction, the researchers found no differences between the two groups in any nonverbal signals of sexual interest (e.g., smiles, sexual glances).

STATUS DISPLAYS AND WORKPLACE DISCRIMINATION

In addition to dysfunctional leadership and sexual harassment, nonverbal displays of status can lead to a form of differential treatment that often escapes the awareness of organizational members. This "invisible" discrimination stems from the tendency to think less of someone whose appearance or actions are indicative of low status. For example, an employer might not reject a job applicant consciously because the applicant is short in stature or has a high-pitched voice. Yet these cues may still influence the employer's perception of the applicant (e.g., "He isn't very mature," "She doesn't seem very confident").

Some studies suggest a bias in the workplace that downgrades individuals who, in some way, communicate a low status identity. In particular, evidence is available that

"powerless stereotypes"—being seen as weak, incompetent, unreliable, lower class, and so on—afflict people who share certain physical and behavioral attributes. Much of this research focuses on a person's physical appearance. For instance, numerous studies document a beauty bias in the workplace that affords attractive individuals greater opportunities for success when compared with less attractive persons, including greater compensation (French, 2002; Hammermesh & Biddle, 1994) and more job offers (Marlowe, Schneider, & Nelson, 1996). Studies also confirm discriminatory practices against individuals who are obese (Cawley, 2004), short (Loh, 1993), and baby faced (Zebrowitz, 1997). Other studies show differential treatment of light-skinned relative to darker-skinned Blacks. For example, using interview data from Black adults as well as data obtained from a national survey of Black (U.S.) Americans, Kieth and Herring (1991) reported an association between socioeconomic status and skin-tone variations. Complexion was a stronger predictor of occupation and income than factors such as family background, thus providing support for the view that darker Americans are less likely to elevate their status than are those with lighter complexions in the United States.

Much less research is available on the existence of a bias in the workplace against behaviors defined as low status. Whereas numerous studies show discrimination against persons with certain nonstandard accents and dialects (Bradac, 1990), for example, these studies do not extend to any discernable pattern of job discrimination in terms of pay, promotion, or other such practices. One intriguing study, however, points to the possibility of a demeanor bias against persons who exhibit signs of negative affectivity typical of many bullying victims (e.g., anxiety, sadness, defensiveness, insecurity). In their study of city government employees, Aquino and Bradfield

(2000) discovered that negative affectivity correlated with the reporting of indirect rather than direct forms of victimization (e.g., sabotaging work). They suggest that displays of negative affect are more likely to elicit acts of contempt than of anger or aggression, making persons who exhibit such behavior "appear as vulnerable targets for exploitation, gossip, and other less obtrusive forms of mistreatment" (Aquino & Bradfield, 2000, p. 533).

The research reviewed in this section supports a connection between nonverbal communication and various organizational outcomes originating from the identification and relationship functions of nonverbal communication. In the context of organizational life, nonverbal displays of status include an array of behaviors that symbolize one person's power over another. These displays not only reinforce the role relationships that exist in an organization, but they also can create conditions that can lead to dysfunctional leadership, sexual harassment, and workplace discrimination.

◆ Managing Nonverbal Displays of Emotion

The preceding discussion addressed the uses and consequences of nonverbal communication in the service of an organization's hierarchy: maintaining the social order. In this section, I direct attention to how nonverbal displays of emotion may affect the routine performances of organizational members. The subject of emotions in organizations is worthy of serious investigation (Fineman, 1993), and a great deal of interest has been shown specifically in the development of "emotional intelligence" in the workplace, as advocated fervently by Goleman (1998), Goleman, Boyatzis, and McKee (2002), and Dulewicz and Higgs (2003). Along

with this surge of interest in emotions generally has come a focused examination of nonverbal communication in three particular areas: emotional contagion, emotional labor, and emotion recognition.

EMOTIONAL CONTAGION

Emotional contagion refers to a phenomenon in which emotions spread from person to person. Primitive emotional contagion theory maintains that we "catch" others' emotions by means of automatic mimicry of emotional expressions and the subsequent feedback that results from our emotional displays (Hatfield, Cacioppo, & Rapson, 1994). Laboratory experiments show that mere exposure to a facial expression is sufficient to produce muscle contractions in observers that mirror the expression they see (Dimberg & Ohman, 1996). In addition, studies confirm the facial feedback hypothesis: that an individual's facial expression of an emotion can influence the person's experience of that emotion directly and immediately (McIntosh, 1996).

The implications of facial feedback for organizations has not escaped the attention of scholars, such as Goleman et al. (2002), who consider it a ubiquitous process that leaders should harness for the good of the organization. Among the studies they cite in their review is one where researchers observed 70 work teams across diverse industries and found that members who sat in meetings together ended up sharing moods in a relatively short period of time (Bartel & Saavedra, 2000). Goleman et al. (2002) claim that the more cohesive a work group is, the more contagious the emotional displays will be. Furthermore, they argue that leaders are most likely to control the contagion that takes place because group members generally see the leader's emotional reaction as the most valid response, and therefore, members tend to model their own reactions on the leader's, particularly in emotionally ambiguous situations. They also suggest that a leader's ability to spread emotions depends on his or her capacity to convey those emotions. That is, a leader with a highly expressive face, voice, and body is more likely to activate the emotional contagion process than is a leader who is much less expressive.

Emotional contagion may occur wherever individuals work together in face-to-face groups, or meet directly with the public. But does it affect task performance? Some research suggests that the spread of *positive* emotions can boost the performance of work groups (Barsade, 2002), predict job satisfaction among employees (Fisher, 2000), increase cooperation and minimize conflict (Barsade, 2002), improve sales performance, and increase customer satisfaction (Homburg & Stock, 2004; Verbeke, 1997). Researchers have also discovered, however, that the spread of *negative* emotions is a contributing factor to stress and burnout among physicians (Bakker, Schaufeli, Sixma, & Bosveld, 2001), nurses (Omdahl & O'Donnel, 1999), teachers (Bakker & Schaufeli, 2000), and sales personnel (Verbeke, 1997). Thus, studies show that emotional contagion may have positive and negative effects on the health and well-being of an organization.

EMOTIONAL LABOR

The contagion process depends on the genuine (i.e., spontaneous) expression of emotions. But the workplace often also demands that individuals engage in various kinds of emotional dissimulation, pretending to be cheerful when really annoyed or frustrated, for instance. Expressing an unfelt emotion, exaggerating a felt emotion,

and suppressing a felt emotion are acts of emotional labor in the workplace, which Hochschild (1983) defined as "the management of feeling to create a publicly observable facial and bodily display [that] is sold for a wage [and] therefore has exchange value" (p. 7). The management of emotions, according to Hochschild, requires a worker to engage in either surface acting or deep acting. Whereas surface acting only requires the actor to display an emotion with no attendant feelings, deep acting requires the actor to elicit the corresponding emotion in some way, as a method actor might do to prepare for an emotionally charged scene. Curiously, whereas the short-term effort involved in deep acting may surpass that needed for surface acting, the long-term effort required for the latter appears to take a heavier toll (Grandey, 2003; Totterdell & Holman, 2003).

In her early research, Hochschild (1983) estimated that "roughly one-third of American workers have jobs that subject them to substantial demands for emotional labor" (p. 11). Mann (1999) surveyed 12 U.K. companies and found moderate levels of emotional labor in almost two thirds of the communications reported by respondents and high levels in about one third of the reported communications. More than half of the participants reported that they laughed or frowned, not because they wanted to but because they were expected to. Sixty percent of the reported communications involved suppressing an emotion, mostly anger. In addition, those higher up in the organization reported less emotional labor than did those lower in the chain of command, supporting Van Maanen and Kunda's (1989) astute observation that "only the dominant and the dormant have relative freedom from emotional constraints in organizational life" (p. 55).

Early qualitative studies of flight attendants, nurses, cashiers, and others led to a conception of emotional labor as a multidimensional construct consisting of (1) the frequency, duration, and intensity of emotional displays; (2) the variety of emotions displayed; (3) attentiveness to display rules; and (4) the discrepancy between the felt and the displayed emotion, referred to as *emotional dissonance* (Mann, 1999; Morris & Feldman, 1996). Subsequent surveys have identified emotional dissonance consistently as a strong predictor of job dissatisfaction, emotional exhaustion, depersonalization, and other factors contributing to job burnout (Diefendorff & Richard, 2003; Lee & Ashforth, 1996; Pugliesi, 1999). There is also evidence that emotional dissonance, particularly the suppression of negative emotions, can produce health consequences related to prolonged stress (Maslach, 1982). But the research also points to factors that moderate the impact of these negative consequences, such as job autonomy and social support (Morris & Feldman, 1996; Wharton, 1996).

Although most of the research on emotional labor highlights negative effects, some work identifies benefits that arise under certain conditions. For example, the use of "deep acting" and the regular display of positive emotions can result in decreased dissonance, improved performance, and increased satisfaction (Diefendorff & Richard, 2003; Grandey, 2003; Totterdell & Holman, 2003). Other researchers contend that *any* requirement to display positive emotions leads ultimately to improved performance (e.g., increased sales) and a heightened sense of accomplishment (Rafaeli & Sutton, 1987). In a qualitative study of sales workers, for example, Abiala (1999) found that emotional labor was most likely to produce positive effects when interacting with customers was a small part of the workers' day, there were few rules to follow, the intent to sell was not concealed, and the workers were hired for their training and experience rather than their looks or demeanor.

EMOTION RECOGNITION

Whereas the research on emotional contagion and emotional labor generally focuses on the expression and regulation of emotion, other studies have examined the recognition of emotion. The ability to recognize emotions in others is a mainstay in the research on interpersonal sensitivity, which Riggio (2001, this volume) contends is necessary for leadership success, personnel functions of hiring and performance appraisal, the development and functioning of work teams, and successful customer service. Emotion recognition is also the most reliably valid component of emotional intelligence (Elfenbein & Ambady, 2002). Early research on nonverbal decoding ability using the profile of nonverbal sensitivity (PONS) reported positive correlations between PONS scores and measures of job effectiveness of foreign service officers, leadership skills of school principals, and job ratings of human service workers (Rosenthal, Hall, DiMatteo, Rogers, & Archer, 1979). More recently, it has been linked to effective leadership in organizations (Goleman et al., 2002).

But recent studies have also begun to raise questions about the benefits of emotion recognition, finding support for the counterintuitive claim that "people reading" has a downside. Using the diagnostic analysis of nonverbal accuracy (DANVA), Elfenbein and Ambady (2002) found that the ability to read negative emotions conveyed through the voice rather than the face damaged workplace evaluations received from peers and supervisors. The ability to pick up emotions from less controllable nonverbal communication channels, which the researchers call "eavesdropping," may burden individuals with difficult or unpleasant information that was not meant to be shared. Similarly, Puccinelli and Tickle-Degnen (2004), using the PONS, found a negative correlation between emotional eavesdropping (increased ability to read body cues and decreased ability to read facial cues) and ratings of rapport from an interaction partner.

Scholarly interest in the emotional domain of the workplace includes studies of emotional contagion, emotional labor, and emotion recognition. Whereas systematic studies in these areas lag behind the promise of improved organizational performance, research confirms the short-term benefits of spreading positive emotions and the likely costs of spreading negative emotions, the potentially negative consequences of emotional labor, and, with the possible exception of emotional eavesdropping, the advantage of recognizing emotions in others. The next section highlights research on the delivery of verbal messages in organizations—that is, the ability to coordinate and integrate multiple channels of communication.

◆ Managing the Delivery of Verbal Messages

Increasingly, organizational life seems to involve less rather than more time in face-to-face interactions, as technology offers greater options for long distance communications. Yet despite these advances, text messages are not likely to replace the much richer, multichanneled communication environment afforded by face-to-face exchanges (see Walther, this volume). The challenge in multichannel communication lies in being able to *deliver* messages with the desired effects. In the organizational context, studies focusing on the delivery of messages

confirm the importance of expectancy effects, mixed messages, and nonverbal involvement behaviors.

EXPECTANCY EFFECTS

Rosenthal (1966) showed how an experimenter's nonverbal communication could unwittingly prod human subjects into behaving the way the experimenter hoped they would rather than the way they might in the absence of the experimenter's influence, a finding that demonstrated how a researcher's nonverbal communication can damage the validity of a scientific experiment. Turning their attention to the classroom, Rosenthal and Jacobsen (1968) discovered that a teacher's nonverbal cues could produce a similar kind of self-fulfilling prophecy. Studies confirm that teachers' nonverbal cues influence the performance of students in ways that confirm the teachers' expectations, assisting some students and penalizing others (Babad, 1992). Expectancies are probably present in a variety of workplace contexts (Eden, 2003; Rosenthal, 1994). For example, judges often get the verdicts they expect after signaling their expectations to members of the jury (Blanck & Rosenthal, 1992). In job interviews, employers have been found to elicit, inadvertently, the undesirable behavior they expect to see from a job applicant (Word, Zanna, & Cooper, 1974).

Although there may be some deleterious effects from expectancies (e.g., groupthink), overall, research confirms that workplace performances improve in response to positive expectancies, although these results seem to apply more to military personnel than to business organizations, to male workers than to females, and to workers for whom low expectations are initially held (McNatt, 2000). According to Rosenthal (1994), efforts to cope with expectancy effects should focus more on getting authority figures to raise their expectations than on the more difficult task of having them monitor and control their nonverbal cues. Some research shows, however, that training managers to hold higher expectations for their subordinates, as well as to convey those expectations to the subordinates, is difficult at best (Eden et al., 2000; White & Locke, 2000).

MIXED MESSAGES

One of the properties of communication is the potential for sending mixed messages, where a message conveyed across one channel (e.g., facial) may not be consistent with messages conveyed across one or more other channels (e.g., vocal, verbal). Early experiments revealed that message receivers may use a "weighted sum" method of inferring the attitudes of a speaker, placing more weight on facial and vocal expression than on words (Mehrabian & Wiener, 1967). In the workplace, Newcombe and Ashkanasy (2000) reported that perceptions of a leader delivering feedback to subordinates were affected more by the leader's facial expressions than by the verbal content of the message. Negative facial expressions elicited the most unfavorable judgments of the leader. Other studies show that receivers weigh verbal and nonverbal messages when making inferences about politeness (LaPlante & Ambady, 2003; Trees & Manusov, 1998) and sexual harassment (Remland & Jones, 1985).

The uses and consequences of mixed messages may be related to status and gender. LaPlante (2001) found status differences in the delivery of mixed messages. When delivering news, low-status persons were more likely than higher-status persons to use nonverbal communication that was consistent with their verbal content; but when making requests, lower-status persons were more likely to use positive nonverbal cues, regardless of verbal content. Apparently, low status prompts individuals to follow a distinct set of rules that emphasize clarity when delivering news, and politeness when making requests.

In their study of gender and mixed messages, LaPlante and Ambady (2002) varied the performance feedback of a supervisor in terms of content and delivery (tone of voice). They found that male supervisors were most successful when the content was negative and their tone of voice was positive. In contrast, female supervisors were most successful with feedback that included positive content paired with a negative tone of voice. Overall, however, a positive tone of voice was only more effective in the male dyads. The results for verbal content are consistent with sex-role expectations: People are more likely to expect compliments from women and criticism from men. The difference in tone of voice seems to suggest that a negative tone adds seriousness to the female supervisor's feedback, reinforcing her legitimate authority, whereas the positive tone softens the impact of criticism given to male subordinates, making it less threatening.

NONVERBAL INVOLVEMENT BEHAVIOR

Most research findings on the uses and consequences of nonverbal communication in formal workplace interactions, such as customer service transactions, interviews, and oral presentations, converge on the construct of nonverbal involvement behavior. Gaze, body orientation, facial expressiveness, gesticulation, head nods, vocal animation, and more indicate the degree to which a person is overtly involved in an interaction (Coker & Burgoon, 1987; Edinger & Patterson, 1983; see also Andersen, Guerrero, & Jones, this volume).

Generally, research shows that nonverbal involvement behavior leads to positive outcomes. Richmond and McCroskey (2000) found that perceptions of a supervisor's nonverbal immediacy behavior were associated with favorable evaluations of the supervisor, subordinate motivation, and job satisfaction. In customer service transactions, studies generally show that the use of touch and eye contact generates more positive reactions from patrons (Crusco & Wetzel, 1984; Kaufman & Mahoney, 1999). Information gathering interviews also tend to benefit from involvement cues. Certain forms of touching and making eye contact with a person increase the likelihood that the person will comply with a request to participate in a survey (Hornik & Ellis, 1988). Even apprehensive respondents will talk more and like their interviewer more when the interviewer uses high levels of nonverbal involvement—direct body orientation, forward lean, head nods, backchannels, and gazing while listening—as opposed to much lower levels (Remland & Jones, 1989).

In the employment interview, research confirms the positive impact of an applicant's nonverbal involvement behavior (Gifford, Cheuk, & Wilkinson, 1985; McGovern & Tinsley, 1978; Young & Beier, 1977). Instances of such behavior may even predict subsequent job performance evaluations (DeGroot & Motowidlo, 1999). The importance of nonverbal communication notwithstanding, some research suggests that what applicants say, the verbal content, influences hiring decisions more than how they say it (Riggio & Throckmorton, 1988). In addition, because social skills are more important for some types of jobs than others, the impact of nonverbal communication may depend on the skills needed for a particular job (DePaulo, 1992).

Research also recommends the use of nonverbal involvement behaviors in oral presentations. One study found that professional buyers rated a salesperson as more believable when he used a steady gaze, and more interesting and persuasive when he avoided speech hesitations (Leigh & Summers, 2002). Awamleh and Gardner (1999) manipulated the speech delivery of a bogus CEO and found, not surprisingly, that the CEO's presentation was more effective with eye contact, fluency, smiles, and dynamic gestures. They also found that delivery was a more important predictor of performance than either the leader's vision or the organizational performance of the leader's company. Howell and Frost (1989) reported higher levels of task performance and satisfaction when a leader's delivery included vocal variety, eye contact, relaxed gestures, and animated facial expressions. Holladay and Coombs (1993, 1994) found that a leader's nonverbal cues were more predictive of charisma than was the "visionary content" of the leader's message. Furthermore, Kirkpatrick and Locke (1996) documented that delivery boosted perceptions of a leader's charisma, but it did not help the performance of subordinates.

This section reviewed the research on the delivery function of nonverbal communication, which refers to the coordination and integration of verbal and nonverbal messages. In the context of organizational life, researchers have been interested chiefly in outcomes associated with expectancy effects, mixed messages, and various nonverbal involvement behaviors. In this regard, there is strong support for the claim that a speaker's nonverbal cues are often more important than the speaker's words (see also Giles & Le Poire, this volume). Specifically, through nonverbal channels, a speaker can signal positive or negative expectations, modify the meaning of a verbal message, and influence the reactions and judgments of listeners. Studies show that in each of these ways, a speaker's delivery can have a powerful impact on various measures of organizational performance.

◆ Conclusion

Research on the uses and consequences of nonverbal communication in the context of organizational life addresses in a limited way each of the four primary functions of nonverbal communication (see Table 26.1). As this chapter shows, studies focusing on the identification and relationship functions indicate that when mismanaged or misread, nonverbal displays of status can create conditions leading to dysfunctional leadership, sexual harassment, and workplace discrimination. Recent studies focusing on the emotion function confirm the potential benefits and costs of emotional contagion, emotional labor, and emotion recognition. Lastly, studies concerned with the delivery function (i.e., the coordination and integration of verbal and nonverbal messages) show that expectancy effects, mixed messages and nonverbal involvement behaviors can strengthen or weaken the impact of workplace communications.

Although the research reviewed in this chapter clearly points to the importance of nonverbal communication in the workplace, the organizational environment continues to be somewhat neglected by social scientists whose interest centers on nonverbal cues. Riggio (2005) cites several reasons for this neglect, among them the fact that organizations are reluctant to grant researchers access to naturally occurring interactions for observation and analysis and the equally important fact that nonverbal researchers themselves are guilty of not paying enough attention to business and organizational applications. Regrettably, when researchers turn their attention to the study of nonverbal communication, instead of observing

behaviors in context, they frequently rely on laboratory methods that fall short of meeting the highest standards of ecological validity.

Given the powerful consequences of nonverbal cues in organizations, particularly those that promote some people and not others, create unhealthy environments, and the like, more work is needed, despite these very real challenges to doing research in organizations. As well, much of the research reviewed in this chapter assesses only short-term outcomes, such as immediate reactions to a prerecorded oral performance. Longitudinal studies in particular would provide much needed data about the consequences for team leaders and work groups of elusive phenomena such as status differentials, emotional contagion, expectancy effects, and nonverbal involvement behavior. Long-term study would also yield critical insights into the organization-wide consequences of nonverbal cues responsible for sexual harassment, workplace discrimination, and emotional labor, with respect to law suits, lost productivity, absenteeism, turnover, job burnout, and so forth.

In recent years, researchers have demonstrated that the nonverbal cues contained in "thin slices" (Ambady & Rosenthal, 1992; see Gray & Ambady, this volume) of naturally occurring social interactions (e.g., 30-second segments) can predict long-term outcomes, as evidenced in studies of marital interactions that predict divorce (Carrere & Gottman, 1999) and teacher-student interactions that predict end-of-term evaluations (Ambady & Rosenthal, 1993). In his hugely popular book, *Blink: The Power of Thinking Without Thinking*, Malcolm Gladwell (2005) has succeeded in bringing a mass audience to the subject of thin slices. Perhaps organizations in the future will be more receptive to researchers who are interested in studying the impact of nonverbal communication where a brief episode may predict a big consequence.

◆ References

Abiala, K. (1999). Customer orientation and sales situations: Variations in interactive service work. *Acta Sociologica, 42,* 207–222.

Ambady, N., & Rosenthal, R. (1992). Thin slices of expressive behavior as predictors of interpersonal consequences: A meta-analysis. *Psychological Bulletin, 111,* 256–274.

Ambady, N., & Rosenthal, R. (1993). Half a minute: Predicting teacher evaluations from thin slices of nonverbal behavior and physical attractiveness. *Journal of Personality and Social Psychology, 64,* 431–441.

Andersen, P. A., & Bowman, L. (1990). Positions of power: Nonverbal influence in organizational communication. In J. A. DeVito & M. L. Hecht (Eds.), *The nonverbal communication reader* (pp. 391–411). Prospect Heights, IL: Waveland.

Aquino, K., & Bradfield, M. (2000). Perceived victimization in the workplace: The role of situational factors and victim characteristics. *Organization Science, 11,* 525–537.

Awamleh, R., & Gardner, W.L. (1999). Perceptions of leader charisma and effectiveness: The effects of vision content, delivery, and organizational performance. *Leadership Quarterly, 10,* 345–373.

Babad, E. (1992). Teacher expectancies and nonverbal behavior. In R. S. Feldman (Ed.), *Applications of nonverbal behavioral theories and research* (pp. 167–190). Hillsdale, NJ: Erlbaum.

Bakker, A. B., & Schaufeli, W. B. (2000). Burnout contagion processes among teachers. *Journal of Applied Social Psychology, 30,* 2289–2309.

Bakker, A. B., Schaufeli, W. B., Sixma, H. J., & Bosveld, W. (2001). Burnout contagion among general practitioners. *Journal of Social and Clinical Psychology, 20,* 82–98.

Barsade, S. G. (2002). The ripple effect: Emotional contagion and its influence on group behavior. *Administrative Science Quarterly, 47,* 644–675.

Bartel, C. A., & Saavedra, R. (2000). The collective construction of work group moods. *Administrative Science Quarterly, 45,* 197–242.

Blanck, P. J., & Rosenthal, R. (1992). Nonverbal behavior in the courtroom. In R. S. Feldman (Ed.), *Applications of nonverbal behavioral theories* (pp. 167–190). Hillsdale, NJ: Erlbaum.

Blau, P. M. (1964). *Exchange and power in social life.* New York: Wiley.

Bradac, J. J. (1990). Language attitudes and impression formation. In H. Giles (Ed.), *Handbook of language and social psychology* (pp. 387–412). Oxford, England: Wiley.

Carrere, S., & Gottman, J. (1999). Predicting divorce among newlyweds from the first three minutes of a marital conflict discussion. *Family Process, 38,* 293–301.

Carli, L. L., LaFleur, S. J., & Loeber, C. C. (1995). Nonverbal behavior, gender, and influence. *Journal of Personality and Social Psychology, 68,* 1030–1041.

Cawley, J. (2004). The impact of obesity on wages. *Journal of Human Resources, 39,* 451–475.

Coker, D. A., & Burgoon, J. K. (1987). The nature of conversational involvement and nonverbal encoding patterns. *Human Communication Research, 13,* 463–494.

Crusco, A. H., & Wetzel, C. G. (1984). The Midas touch: The effects of interpersonal touch on restaurant tipping. *Personality and Social Psychology Bulletin, 10,* 512–517.

DeGroot, T., & Motowidlo, S. J. (1999). Why visual and vocal interview cues can affect interviewers' judgments and predict job performance. *Journal of Applied Psychology, 84,* 986–993.

DePaulo, P. J. (1992). Applications of nonverbal behavior research in marketing and management. In R. S. Feldman (Ed.), *Applications of nonverbal behavioral theories and research* (pp. 63–87). Hillsdale, NJ: Erlbaum.

Diefendorff, J. M., & Richard, E. M. (2003). Antecedents and consequences of emotional display rule perceptions. *Journal of Applied Psychology, 88,* 284–294.

Dimberg, U., & Ohman, A. (1996). Behold the wrath: Psychophysiological responses to facial stimuli. *Motivation and Emotion, 20,* 149–182.

Dovidio, J. F., Brown, C. E., Heltman, K., Ellyson, S. L., & Keating, C. F. (1988).

Power displays between women and men in discussions of gender-linked tasks: A multi-channel study. *Journal of Personality and Social Psychology, 55*, 580–587.

Dovidio, J. F., Ellyson, S. L., Keating, C. F., Heltman, K., & Brown, C. E. (1988). The relationship between social power and visual displays of dominance between men and women. *Journal of Personality and Social Psychology, 54*, 233–242.

Driscoll, D. M., Kelly, J. R., & Henderson, W. M. (1998). Can perceivers identify likelihood to sexually harass? *Sex Roles, 38*, 557–588.

Dulewicz, V., & Higgs, M. (2003). Leadership at the top: The need for emotional intelligence in organizations. *The International Journal of Organizational Analysis, 11*, 193–210.

Eden, D. (2003). Self-fulfilling prophecies in organizations. In J. Greenberg (Ed.), *Organizational behavior: The state of the science* (pp. 91–122). Mahwah, NJ: Erlbaum.

Eden, D., Geller, D., Gerwirtz, A., Gordon-Terner, R., Inbar, I., Liberman, M., et al. (2000). Implanting Pygmalion leadership style through workshop training: Seven field experiments. *Leadership Quarterly, 11*, 171–210.

Edinger, J. A., & Patterson, M. L. (1983). Nonverbal involvement and social control. *Psychological Bulletin, 93*, 30–56.

Elfenbein, H. A., & Ambady, N. (2002). Predicting workplace outcomes from the ability to eavesdrop on feelings. *Journal of Applied Psychology, 87*, 963–971.

Fineman, S. (1993). *Emotion in organizations.* Newbury Park, CA: Sage.

Fisher, C. D. (2000). Mood and emotions while working: Missing pieces of job satisfaction? *Journal of Organizational Behavior, 21*, 185–202.

French, M. T. (2002). Physical appearance and earnings: Further evidence. *Applied Economics, 34*, 569–572.

Gifford, R., Cheuk, F. N., Wilkinson, M. (1985). Nonverbal cues in the employment interview: Links between applicant qualities and interviewer judgments. *Journal of Applied Psychology, 4*, 729–736.

Gladwell, M. (2005). *Blink: The power of thinking without thinking.* New York: Little, Brown.

Goleman, D. (1998). *Working with emotional intelligence.* New York: Bantam.

Goleman, D., Boyatzis, R., & McKee, A. (2002). *Primal leadership.* Boston, MA: Harvard Business School Press.

Grandey, A. A. (2003). When "the show must go on": Surface acting and deep acting as determinants of emotional exhaustion and peer-rated service delivery. *Academy of Management Journal, 46*, 86–96.

Hall, J. A. (1984). *Nonverbal sex differences: Communication accuracy and expressive style.* Baltimore, MD: Johns Hopkins University Press.

Hall, J. A. (2005). Meta-analysis of nonverbal behavior. In V. Manusov (Ed.), *The sourcebook of nonverbal measures* (pp. 483–492). Mahwah, NJ: Erlbaum.

Hall, J. A., & Friedman, G. (1999). Status, gender, and nonverbal behavior: A study of structured interactions between employers of a company. *Personality and Social Psychology Bulletin, 25*, 1082–1091.

Hammermesh, D., & Biddle, J.E. (1994). Beauty and the labor market. *American Economic Review, 84*, 1174–1194.

Hatfield, E., Cacioppo, J. T., & Rapson, R. (1994). *Emotional contagion.* Cambridge, UK: Cambridge University Press.

Heintzman, M., Leathers, D. G., Parrott, R. L., & Cairns, A. B. (1993). Nonverbal rapport-building behaviors' effects on perceptions of a supervisor. *Management Communication Quarterly, 7*, 181–209.

Henley, N. M. (1995). Body politics revisited: What do we know today? In P. J. Kalbfleisch & M. J. Cody (Eds.), *Gender, power, and communication in human relationships* (pp. 27–62). Hillsdale, NJ: Erlbaum.

Hochschild, A. (1983). *The managed heart: Commercialization of human feeling.* Berkeley: University of California Press.

Hofstede, G. (1982). *Culture's consequences* (abridged ed.). Beverly Hills, CA: Sage.

Holladay, S. J., & Coombs, W. T. (1993). Communicating visions: An exploration of the role of delivery in the creation of leader charisma. *Management Communication Quarterly, 6,* 405–427.

Holladay, S. J., & Coombs, W. T. (1994). Speaking of visions and visions being spoken: An exploration of the effects of content and delivery on perceptions of leader charisma. *Management Communication Quarterly, 8,* 165–189.

Homburg, D., & Stock, R. M. (2004). The link between salespeople's job satisfaction and customer satisfaction in a business-to-business context: A dyadic analysis. *Journal of the Academy of Marketing Science, 32,* 144–159.

Hornik, J., & Ellis, S. (1988). Strategies to secure compliance for a mall intercept interview. *Public Opinion Quarterly, 52,* 539–551.

Howell, J. M., & Frost, P. J. (1989). A laboratory study of charismatic leadership. *Organizational Behavior and Human Decision Processes, 43,* 243–269.

Jacobs, T. O. (1970). *Leadership and exchange in formal organizations.* Alexandria, VA: Human Resources Research Organization.

Johnson, C. (1994). Gender, legitimate authority, and leader-subordinate conversations. *American Sociological Review, 59,* 122–135.

Jones, T. S., & Remland, M. S. (1997). An ounce of prevention: Suggestions for training to prevent sexual harassment. In C. D. Brown, C. Snedeker, & B. Sykes (Eds.), *Conflict and diversity* (pp. 251–266). Cresskill, NJ: Hampton Press.

Kaufman, D., & Mahoney, J. M. (1999). The effect of waitresses' touch on alcohol consumption in dyads. *Journal of Social Psychology, 139,* 261–267.

Kieth, V. M., & Herring, C. (1991). Skin tone and stratification in the black community. *American Journal of Sociology, 97,* 760–779.

Kirkpatrick, S. A., & Locke, E. A. (1996). Direct and indirect effects of three core charismatic leadership components on performance and attitudes. *Journal of Applied Psychology, 81,* 36–51.

Kowner, R., & Wiseman, R. (2003). Culture and status-related behavior: Japanese and American perceptions of interaction in asymmetric dyads. *Cross-Cultural Research, 37,* 178–210.

LaPlante, D. A. (2001). Mixing up politeness theory: Channel consistency and conflict in the expression of politeness. (Doctoral dissertation, Harvard University, 2001). *Dissertation Abstracts International, 62* (4-B), 2113.

LaPlante, D. A., & Ambady, N. (2002). Saying it like it isn't: Mixed messages from men and women in the workplace. *Journal of Applied Social Psychology, 32,* 2435–2457.

LaPlante, D. A., & Ambady, N. (2003). On how things are said: Voice tone, voice intensity, verbal content, and perceptions of politeness. *Journal of Language and Social Psychology, 22,* 434–441.

Lee, R. T., & Ashforth, B. E. (1996). A meta-analytic examination of three dimensions of job burnout. *Journal of Applied Psychology, 81,* 123–133.

Leigh, T. W., & Summers, J. O. (2002). An initial evaluation of industrial buyers' impressions of salespersons' nonverbal cues. *Journal of Personal Selling and Sales Management, 22,* 41–53.

Le Poire, B. A., Burgoon, J. K., & Parrott, R. (1992). Status and privacy restoring communication in the workplace. *Journal of Applied Communication Research, 20,* 419–436.

Lockheed, M. E., & Hall, K. P. (1976). Conceptualizing sex as a status characteristic: Applications to leadership training strategies. *Journal of Social Issues, 32,* 111–125.

Loh, E. S. (1993). The economic effects of physical appearance. *Social Science Quarterly, 74,* 420–438.

Mann, S. (1999). Emotion at work: To what extent are we expressing, suppressing, or faking it? *European Journal of Work and Organizational Psychology, 8,* 347–369.

Marlowe, C. M., Schneider, S. L., & Nelson, C. E. (1996). Gender and attractiveness biases in hiring decisions: Are more experienced managers less biased? *Journal of Applied Psychology, 81,* 11–21.

Maslach, C. (1982). *Burnout: The cost of caring.* Englewood Cliffs, NJ: Prentice Hall.

McGovern, T. V., & Tinsley, H. E. A. (1978). Interviewer evaluations of interviewee nonverbal behavior. *Journal of Vocational Behavior, 13,* 163–171.

McIntosh, D. N. (1996). Facial feedback hypotheses: Evidence, implications, and directions. *Motivation and Emotion, 20,* 121–147.

McNatt, D. B. (2000). Ancient Pygmalion joins contemporary management: A meta-analysis of the result. *Journal of Applied Psychology, 85,* 314–322.

Mehrabian, A., & Wiener, M. (1967). Decoding of inconsistent communications. *Journal of Personality and Social Psychology, 6,* 108–114.

Morris, J. A., & Feldman, D. C. (1996). The dimensions, antecedents, and consequences of emotional labor. *Academy of Management Review, 21,* 986–1010.

Murphy, J. D., Driscoll, D. M., & Kelly, J. R. (1999). Differences in the nonverbal behavior of men who vary in the likelihood to sexually harass. *Journal of Social Behavior and Personality, 14,* 113–128.

Newcombe, M. J., & Ashkanasy, N. M. (2002). The role of affect and affective congruence in perceptions of leaders: An experimental study. *Leadership Quarterly, 13,* 601–615.

Omdahl, B. L., & O'Donnel, C. (1999). Emotional contagion, empathic concern, and communicative responsiveness as variables affecting nurses' stress and occupational commitment. *Journal of Advanced Nursing, 29,* 1351–1360.

Patterson, M. L. (1983). *Nonverbal behavior: A functional perspective.* New York: Springer-Verlag.

Pryor, J. B. (1987). Sexual harassment proclivities in men. *Sex Roles, 17,* 269–290.

Puccinelli, N. M., & Tickle-Degnen, L. (2004). Knowing too much about others: Moderators of the relationship between eavesdropping and rapport in social interaction. *Journal of Nonverbal Behavior, 28,* 223–243.

Pugliesi, K. (1999). The consequences of emotional labor: Effects on work stress, job satisfaction, and well-being. *Motivation and Emotion, 23,* 125–154.

Rafaeli, A., & Sutton, R. I. (1987). Expression of emotion as part of the work role. *Academy of Management Review, 12,* 23–37.

Remland, M. S. (1981). Developing leadership skills in nonverbal communication: A situational perspective. *Journal of Business Communication, 18,* 17–29.

Remland, M. S. (1984). Leadership impressions and nonverbal communication in a superior-subordinate interaction. *Communication Quarterly, 32,* 41–48.

Remland, M. S. (2004). *Nonverbal communication in everyday life* (2nd ed.). Boston: Houghton Mifflin.

Remland, M. S., & Jones, T. S. (1985). Sex differences, communication consistency and judgments of sexual harassment in a performance appraisal interview. *Southern Speech Communication Journal, 50,* 156–176.

Remland, M. S., & Jones, T. S. (1989). The effect of nonverbal involvement and communication apprehension on state anxiety, interpersonal attraction, and speech duration. *Communication Quarterly, 37,* 170–183.

Richmond, V. P., & McCroskey, J. C. (2000). The impact of supervisor and subordinate immediacy on relational and organizational outcomes. *Communication Monographs, 67,* 85–95.

Riggio, R. E. (2001). Interpersonal sensitivity and organizational psychology: Theoretical and methodological applications. In J. A. Hall & F. J. Bernieri (Eds.), *Interpersonal sensitivity: Theory and measurement* (pp. 305–318). Mahwah, NJ: Erlbaum.

Riggio, R. E. (2005). Business applications of nonverbal communication. In R. E. Riggio & R. S. Feldman (Eds.), *Applications of nonverbal communication* (pp. 121–138). Mahwah, NJ: Erlbaum.

Riggio, R. E., & Throckmorton, B. (1988). The relative effects of verbal and nonverbal behavior, appearance, and social skills in evaluations made in hiring interviews. *Journal of Applied Social Psychology, 18,* 331–348.

Rosenthal, R. (1966). *Experimenter effects in behavioral research.* New York: Appleton-Century-Crofts.

Rosenthal, R. (1994). Interpersonal expectancy effects: A 30-year perspective. *Current Directions in Psychological Science, 3,* 176–179.

Rosenthal, R., Hall, J. A., DiMatteo, M. R., Rogers, P. L, & Archer, D. (1979). *Sensitivity in nonverbal communication: The PONS test.* Baltimore: Johns Hopkins University Press.

Rosenthal, R., & Jacobson, L. (1968). *Pygmalion in the classroom.* New York: Holt, Rinehart & Winston.

Steckler, N. A., & Rosenthal, R. (1985). Sex differences in nonverbal and verbal communication with bosses, peers, and subordinates. *Journal of Applied Psychology, 70,* 157–163.

Tiedens, L. Z., & Fragale, A. R. (2003). Power moves: Complementarity in dominant and submissive nonverbal behavior. *Journal of Personality and Social Psychology, 84,* 558–568.

Totterdell, P., & Holman, D. (2003). Emotion regulation in customer service roles: Testing a model of emotional labor. *Journal of Occupational Health Psychology, 8,* 55–73.

Trees, A. R., & Manusov, V. (1998). Managing face concerns in criticism: Integrating nonverbal behaviors as a dimension of politeness in female friendship dyads. *Human Communication Research, 24,* 564–582.

Van Maanen, J., & Kunda, G. (1989). Real feelings: Emotional expression and organizational culture. In L. L. Cummings & B. M. Staw (Eds.), *Research in organizational behavior* (Vol. 11, pp. 43–103). Greenwich, CT: JAI.

Verbeke, W. (1997). Individual differences in emotional contagion of salespersons: Its effect on performance and burnout. *Psychology and Marketing, 14,* 617–637.

Wharton, A. S. (1996). Service with a smile: Understanding the consequences of emotional labor. In C. L. McDonald & C. Sirianni (Eds.), *Working in the service society* (pp. 91–112). Philadelphia: Temple University Press.

White, S. S., & Locke, E. A. (2000). Problems with the Pygmalian effect and some proposed solutions. *Leadership Quarterly, 11,* 389–415.

Woodzicka, J. A., & LaFrance, M. (2005). Working on a smile: Responding to sexual provocation in the workplace. In R. E. Riggio & R. S. Feldman (Eds.), *Applications of nonverbal communication* (pp. 141–155). Mahwah, NJ: Erlbaum.

Word, C. O., Zanna, M. P., & Cooper, J. (1974). The nonverbal mediation of self-fulfilling prophecies in interracial interaction. *Journal of Experimental Social Psychology, 10,* 109–120.

Young, D. M., & Beier, E. G. (1977). The role of applicant nonverbal communication in the employment interview. *Journal of Employment Counseling, 14,* 154–165.

Yukl, G. (2002). *Leadership in organizations.* Upper Saddle River, NJ: Prentice Hall.

Zebrowitz, L. A. (1997). *Reading faces: Window to the soul?* Boulder, CO: Westview Press.

PART V

FINAL THOUGHTS

NONVERBAL COMMUNICATION

Basic Issues and Future Prospects

◆ Miles L. Patterson
University of Missouri, St. Louis

◆ Valerie Manusov
University of Washington

The chapters in this *Handbook* reflect the breadth and vitality of research on nonverbal communication. Looking across these chapters, we see a range of sophisticated arguments regarding the communicative potential of nonverbal behavior. Because the authors have done a commendable job representing the field, it is neither our intention in this chapter, nor do we feel it desirable, to attempt a general commentary on the chapters in this volume. Rather, we focus attention on a select set of issues important for understanding the field today and for anticipating its future direction. To appreciate where we are and where we may be headed, however, it is useful to consider from whence we came. So, first, we consider, in very broad strokes, how the field has changed in the last 50 years.

♦ Emerging Trends

There are many threads shaping the current status of research and theory on nonverbal communication (see Knapp, this volume). Nevertheless, widespread and systematic research on nonverbal communication can be traced back to the period from the mid-1950s to the early 1960s with work on spatial behavior (Sommer, 1959), gaze (Exline, 1963), facial expressions (Ekman, 1965), and vocal cues (Mahl, 1956). Not surprisingly, most of the early research focused on a single behavior at a time, providing a "channel" approach to nonverbal communication. Thus, researchers who studied interpersonal distance did not also measure gaze patterns, and those who studied gaze patterns were not interested typically in facial expressions. As a result, the field was structured nominally around behaviors rather than issues or processes in nonverbal communication. This is still reflected in the organization of some textbooks and scholarly volumes. In such books, there may be a chapter on spatial behavior, one on gaze, another on touch, then vocal cues, and so on.

It is not surprising that this kind of organization has been dominant in the study of nonverbal behavior. It is difficult to describe and analyze a complicated system of communication without segmenting the content by behavior. But there are also some problems with this approach. Although certain components of this system can be relatively well represented by a single metric, others are much more complex. For example, distance can be operationalized in terms of feet or meters, gaze in terms of duration, and lean and body orientation in angular changes. This is not the case with highly complex and multidimensional behaviors such as gestures, tone of voice, and, especially, facial expressions.

More important perhaps, focusing attention on one, isolated behavior may come at the expense of a broader appreciation of the complexity and subtlety of the larger system of communication. This cue-based focus may have contributed to the popularity of the decoding strategy in studying nonverbal communication (see Gray & Ambady, this volume, who talk about methods for assessing particular stimulus displays that might be photographed or videotaped). Later, *judgments of the displays* (e.g., overall affect, vocal comfort) would inform researchers of the meaning and impact of specific nonverbal behaviors.

In contrast, the actual measurement of nonverbal patterns, reflected in an encoding strategy, was typically more complicated. This was the case, not only because the nonverbal system is a multidimensional one, but also because the instrumentation was much more limited as the field was first developing. In the 1950s and 1960s, for example, videotaping equipment was expensive and relatively cumbersome. Although video cameras then might have been on rollers, they were hardly portable. Without such formidable and expensive pieces of equipment, the study of interactive behavior required one or more observers counting, estimating, or timing the relevant behaviors from behind an observation window. Although it was possible to measure more than one fluid behavior at time, it was not a simple endeavor. The various options employed in the decoding and encoding strategies are discussed in Gray and Ambady's chapter in this volume (see also the set of assessments in Manusov, 2005).

There were, however, important exceptions to the channel approach in the way that nonverbal communication was conceptualized. For example, Argyle and Dean's (1965) nonverbal "intimacy" and Mehrabian's (1969) "immediacy" both emphasized the *multivariate nature of non-verbal communication in a coordinated set of behaviors*. Conceptual recognition of the multidimensional nature of nonverbal communication was not, however, the same as actually measuring it. Even with the advances in videotaping and sophisticated techniques of computerized recording and analysis, multivariate studies of nonverbal communication are still complicated and time-consuming. Nevertheless, conceptualizing nonverbal communication as multivariate in nature set the stage for two important developments in the field: (1) the formulation of theories of interactive behavior (see Patterson, this volume) and (2) emphasis on the various functions of nonverbal communication (Argyle, 1972; Patterson, 1983; see chapters in Part III of this volume).

Consistent with these two developments, the focus of research also changed as the field matured. In the 1970s and 1980s, research moved away from the study of specific channels as isolated aspects of subtle communication to a greater focus on the processes mediating nonverbal communication and the consequences and applications of nonverbal communication (see the chapters in Part IV of this volume). Furthermore, there was increased attention to the way in which the moderating variables of culture, sex or gender, age, and personality affected nonverbal communication (see the chapters in Part II of this volume).

The focus on various determinants facilitated an appreciation of nonverbal behavior as part of a larger set of communicative practices shaped and constrained by the cultural context or code in which they occur. Thus, for many researchers, understanding the communicative value of non-verbal communication depends on its integration with language (see Bavelas & Chovil, this volume). For others, the non-verbal behaviors can be understood only when seen within a framework of gender rules and power (see chapters by Hall and by Remland, this volume), expectations for normative behavior (see Robinson, this volume), and an awareness of what a particular speech community values or stigmatizes (see Manusov & Jaworksi, this volume).

Ethnographic work on nonverbal behavior is one way to reveal more qualitatively how some of these issues work themselves out in interaction. One exemplar by Donal Carbaugh (1999) provided a discussion of the functions of silence among members of the Blackfeet, a confederacy of three independent Indian tribes presently living in Montana and Alberta, Canada. In his analysis, Carbaugh described the process of "listening" (i.e., being silent, usually in sacred spaces) as both a mode of learning and a reflection of cultural values. This practice does not occur—at least not in the same form—in other cultural groups, and it can only be understood by reference to the values of that group. In providing this description, Carbaugh was able to show effectively how certain rules for and interpretation of nonverbal behaviors can only be understood when the larger communicative context is also understood.

Although these issues—mediating processes, applications, and moderating variables—continue to affect the contemporary study of nonverbal communication, another emerging development from the mid-1980s through the present day changed the way that researchers viewed nonverbal communication. Specifically, and in some ways inconsistent with the more relativistic perspectives of studies that look at differences across groups, there was a growing recognition of the importance of evolution in shaping nonverbal communication (see the Floyd and Buck & Renfro Powers chapters, this volume). Basic elements of everyday life, particularly those related to survival, reproduction, and care of offspring were linked to natural selection. Thus, there is an increased appreciation of hardwired reactions predisposing people to behave and to make judgments in a fashion promoting survival of the species. As noted, other factors, such as culture (see Matsumoto, this volume), individual differences (see Gifford, this volume), and social norms (see Dovidio, Hebl, Richeson, & Shelton, this volume) can moderate this hardwiring. There is also the predictable disagreement over the *relative* impact of these hardwired predispositions, but it is clear that the biological bases of nonverbal communication cannot be ignored.

At the risk of oversimplifying the field in its contemporary form, what do these developments suggest about the nature of nonverbal communication? First, nonverbal communication is best represented as *a system comprising interdependent components* (see chapters by Bavelas & Chovil and Patterson, this volume) and not a haphazard collection of unrelated cues and behaviors. We cannot attend to all the pieces in any single study, but we can recognize that any specific focus is part of a larger system of communication, embedded within a larger set of communicative practices. Second, social judgments and behavior are pragmatic, serving a variety of different functions and having important social, personal, and relational consequences (see Part IV of this volume). These consequences can be valuable (as in the case of developing close relationships) or harmful (as in the case of unwarranted affection). The reflection of functions in goals can even be activated outside of awareness (Bargh, 1997). That is, particular situations, such as an interview or a social gathering, may be sufficient to prime a specific goal and activate adaptive social judgment and behavioral processes, all outside of awareness (see chapters by Lakin and Patterson, this volume).

Third, individuals are not simply reactive in their social environments, as the early interactive theories suggested. They are also active agents, initiating behavior and testing preliminary judgments in social settings. Fourth, although people possess some adaptive flexibility in relating to others, and some more than others (e.g., high self-monitors), we are constrained substantially in our social judgments and behavior. That is, the residual effects of biology, culture, gender, and personality constitute the "baggage" that limits the range of our judgments and behavior (for more on this, see Part II of this volume), while also providing a rich set of interpretive practices that reflect those forces.

So from this basic foundation, where are we headed and what merits special attention in the years to come? In the remainder of this chapter, we highlight a few issues that may shape the direction of research and theory in the future. Specifically, we discuss the automaticity of much nonverbal communication, advances in methods for assessing nonverbal communication, and some ways in which new technologies may work to extend how we conceptualize and what we attend to in the study of nonverbal communication.

◆ A Glimpse at Future Issues

AUTOMATIC PROCESSES

A growing body of research and theory points to the dominance of automatic processes in the sending and receiving of nonverbal communication (see Bargh, 1997; Lakin, this volume). Although we may prefer to see ourselves as rational and deliberate in our social contacts, automatic processes seem to be the "default setting" in relating to others. In many cases, neither judgments nor behaviors can wait for a logical assessment of alternatives before some decision or action is required. Even when individuals have the luxury of adequate time, they are biased toward the quick and easy solutions. That is, people are inclined to be "cognitive misers," avoiding unnecessary (and sometimes, necessary) cognitive effort (Fiske & Taylor, 1995).

It is clear that receivers' automatic judgments are typically neither arbitrary nor maladaptive (Bargh, 1997). Perceivers make relatively accurate judgments of others quickly on the basis of limited appearance and behavioral information (Ambady & Rosenthal, 1992). Greater accuracy might be expected in practical, affordance judgments dealing with how we relate to others than in more abstract trait judgments (McArthur & Baron, 1983; Swann, 1984; Zebrowitz & Collins, 1997). Of course, automatic judgments are sometimes wrong (e.g., the fundamental attribution error). Correcting such errors requires not only the availability of cognitive resources, but it also necessitates the motivation to apply those resources in resolving inconsistencies (Gilbert & Malone, 1995). Thus, without the necessary cognitive resources and motivation, initial, automatic judgments will dominate. On the other hand, because the automatic judgments are relatively accurate, more is *not* necessarily better when it comes to applying cognitive resources to our judgments. Thinking too much about initially automatic judgments can actually decrease accuracy (Patterson & Stockbridge, 1998; Wilson & Schooler, 1991).

So there is something of a dilemma here. Automatic judgments, particularly affordance judgments, are generally accurate. But when they are not, cognitive effort must be applied to correct the judgments. Without independent evidence, however, we do not usually know when our judgments are inaccurate. Occasionally, such mistakes catch up with us, as problems arise in relationships or bank accounts are drained, but by then the damage is done. Documenting that automatic judgments are more accurate than chance still leaves a lot of room for knowing when we can be confident in the accuracy of our judgments. This is especially the case when confidence in judgments does not predict their accuracy (DePaulo, Charlton, Cooper, Lindsay, & Muhlenbruck, 1997; Patterson, Foster, & Bellmer, 2001). Future research might well consider the circumstances related to accuracy in judgments, especially automatic judgments. There is research documenting individual differences in judgment accuracy, but different measures of decoding accuracy are not highly correlated (see Riggio, this volume).

So is there a simple, general dimension underlying decoding accuracy? What are the particular circumstances that contribute to increased accuracy in judgments? Are some specific pieces of appearance and behavioral information especially diagnostic or is the overall gestalt, even in very brief glimpses of others, more important? In everyday experience, are we more attuned to reading the emotions of others or to reading their behavioral intentions (see Fridlund & Russell, this volume)? To what extent can training improve accuracy in judgments, and if training makes us more aware, what does that do to the automaticity of judgments? These are just a few of the questions that may merit attention in future research.

Recent research on encoding nonverbal communication has also emphasized the primacy of automatic processes for a wide range of behaviors. Like social judgment, it is possible to initiate controlled, deliberate patterns of behavior. But individuals must be motivated enough to expend the effort and have the necessary cognitive resources to monitor and manage the behavior. Nevertheless, thinking more about managing one's behavior is not necessarily desirable, especially with behavioral routines that are otherwise automatic. Vallacher and Wegner (1987) make this point in their action identification theory. Specifically, when actions are well learned or automatic, people tend to conceptualize them in general terms, focused primarily on the goals or consequences of actions. For example, deciding to go to the supermarket to get milk and bread is sufficient to get into the car and drive 3 miles to the store. A person does not have to think about the specific elements of driving a car, including the coordinated movements involved with a stick shift. If attention is directed to the particular components' actions (e.g., the timing of applying the clutch, shifting the gear, and accelerating), the efficiency of the sequence may suffer. This is similar to Bargh's (1997) *goal-dependent automaticity.* For Bargh, individuals are aware of particular goals, but once they decide to pursue them, the instrumental behaviors frequently run on automatic.

In addition, when goals are commonly pursued in a particular setting, the context itself may be sufficient to activate goals and goal-directed behavior. A common form of automaticity in social settings is *behavioral mimicry.* Individuals mimic speech patterns, facial expressions, posture, and movement in interactions routinely and automatically (Lakin, Jefferis, Cheng, & Chartrand, 2003; see also chapters by Cappella & Schreiber and Tickle-Degnen, this volume). Behavioral mimicry is clearly adaptive, not only facilitating the immediate interaction but also increasing liking and interdependence between partners. One suggestion for how mimicry happens so quickly and smoothly is that there is a direct perception-behavior link selected over the course of evolution because it was critical for our survival (Dijksterhuis & Bargh, 2001). That is, because social animals depend on others for affiliation and

support, automatic mimicry provided an efficient and adaptive way to increase the social bonds.

Although it is convenient to discuss the social judgment and behavioral "sides" of interaction as isolated processes, they are interdependent elements in a larger system of communication (see Patterson, this volume). In social settings, specific goals activate adaptive judgments and behavior simultaneously. Much of this process is initiated automatically and often proceeds to conclusion without any reflection. But unexpected or unusual behavior from others can prompt attention and effort in forming judgments, just as our own awkward behavior can prompt attempts at behavior management. It seems likely that once awareness and effort are applied in one process, they are likely to spread to the complementary process.

For example, if a friend behaves in an unusual fashion, controlled processes are activated to determine just what this means. At the same time, our own behavior may be more deliberately managed to facilitate an accurate judgment. In a similar fashion, the realization of one's own behavioral faux pas directs attention to correcting the mistake and, simultaneously, focuses attention on the reactions of those around us. Following these kinds of events, it may take some time before automaticity becomes the norm again. Although automatic processes generally constitute the "default" setting for social judgments and behavior, as circumstances change, more controlled processes can be activated. Of course, individuals have to be sufficiently motivated and have adequate cognitive resources to apply in evaluating their judgments or managing their behavior. Nevertheless, more is not necessarily better when it comes to thinking about our judgments and managing our behavior. Automaticity is there for a reason.

NEW METHODS

Over the last 50 years, our knowledge of nonverbal communication has increased dramatically. *How* we study this system of communication has also changed. In this section, we highlight a few newer methods that offer considerable promise for understanding the subtleties of nonverbal communication. First, the recent advances in the biology of nonverbal communication (see Buck & Renfro Powers, this volume) are likely to continue and provide new insights into how this system works. Particularly important here are brain-imaging techniques that relate the understanding (social judgment) and execution (behavior) of actions to particular patterns of neural activity. In recent years, there is even evidence at the neurological level that "mirror neurons" may provide the mechanism underlying the direct perception-behavior link involved in mimicry (Rizzolatti & Craighero, 2004; see also Cappella & Schreiber, this volume). Specifically, the same neurons seem to be activated when individuals view a particular behavior as when they actually initiate the same behavior. The close link between perceiving and behaving is also consistent with the view of nonverbal communication as an integrated system of parallel processes operating in the service of particular interpersonal goals (see Patterson, this volume). In the future, it may even be possible to map the circuitry of such a system as people engage in coordinated, goal-oriented social judgments and behavior.

A second technological advance is the development of immersive virtual environments for studying interactive behavior. One form, collaborative virtual environments (CVEs), allows researchers to study continuous patterns of behavior from interactants in remote physical locations. That is, the verbal and nonverbal behavior of interactants in different locations is rendered onto representations of individuals in virtual reality (avatars) as it actually occurs (Blascovich et al., 2002; see Walther, this volume). Furthermore, because these are digital signals, they can be transformed and experimentally manipulated to examine the effects of precise changes in the avatar's behavior on the reactions of another person.

In a recent study, for example, evidence was found for the effects of subtle behavioral mimicry initiated by an embodied agent (humanlike digital representation under computer control) on subsequent persuasion and impressions (Bailenson & Yee, 2005). Specifically, when the agent mimicked the participant's head movements with a 4-second delay, compared with nonmatching head movements, the agent was more persuasive and was rated more positively. It is impressive that even under the artificial circumstances of interacting with a virtual person, the influence of mimicry is evident.

One ingenious study combined a brain-imaging measure, functional magnetic resonance imaging (fMRI), with a manipulation on a virtual reality apparatus. When participants received a 1-second glance from an approaching agent, compared with gaze avoidance, brain activity increased dramatically in the right hemisphere superior temporal sulcus (Pelphrey, Viola, & McCarthy, 2004). The superior temporal sulcus is apparently involved in deriving social meaning from facial and bodily movement (Kolb & Whishaw, 2003, p. 375). The elaborate instrumentation involved in brain imaging and virtual reality provides impressive, new alternatives for researchers. Nevertheless, these high-tech devices are expensive and not easily accessible to most investigators. In addition, the control and precision of these measures comes with another cost: decreased external validity or representativeness.

There is also reason to consider the potential for low-tech alternatives in studying subtle behavioral changes in public settings. This is really a suggestion to reemphasize the study of unfocused interactions (Goffman, 1963, pp. 83–88) in a new and systematic fashion with field experiments. Unfocused interactions are social settings where people simply share a common presence without any expectation of having a conversation. They are "interactions" because the behavior of one person affects others in close proximity. For example, as we share a ride on an elevator, stand in line at the grocery store, or choose a seat in our physician's waiting room, we make subtle adjustments to the close presence of others. These settings are important because individuals necessarily negotiate their relationships to others through their nonverbal behavior.

A particularly interesting example of unfocused interactions is the simple experience of passing another pedestrian as we walk down the sidewalk. By employing confederates and observers walking behind the confederates, these microinteractions can be reliably studied in the real-world settings where they normally occur (Patterson, 2005). In fact, people are sensitive to the gender and level of recognition (avoid, look, or smile) from a pedestrian as they approach and pass the person (Patterson & Tubbs, 2005; Patterson, Webb, & Schwartz, 2002). In the 1 to 2 seconds it takes for people to cover a "passing zone" of 10 to 12 feet, they make rapid adjustments to an approaching stranger.

The utility of this kind of field-experiment technique extends well beyond simply discovering norms for pedestrian passings. Because many of our contacts with outgroup members take this form, the subtle adjustments that individuals make in these microinteractions may also serve as an unobtrusive measure of out-group attitudes. In addition, there is also evidence for cultural differences in the way that people manage these common events (Patterson, Iizuka, Tubbs, Ansel, & Anson, 2006). There are countless opportunities for studying nonverbal communication in the unfocused interactions that all of us experience in everyday life. This field experiment approach, maximizing external validity, provides a useful complement to precise and controlled methods such as brain imagery and virtual reality techniques.

NEW MEDIA

Not only are new technologies important for expanding our options in managing and exchanging information, but they also bear on the understanding of what nonverbal communication entails. As Walther (this volume) points out, much of the scholarship on computer-mediated communication (CMC) started with the premise that this technology was largely, if not entirely, devoid of nonverbal communication. This "cues-filtered-out" perspective suggested that CMC was different inherently from face-to-face interaction specifically because it was less rich communicatively. The "lack" of nonverbal cues meant, for many, a deficit to communicating online.

But this scholarship has shown us a more complicated picture. First, it reveals that people will work to make up for certain nonverbal cues not being available. The quick rise of user-created emoticons to reflect facial expressions or intentions provided a way of reducing the potential ambiguity of verbal messages. Users also began writing in capital letters to reflect particular vocal cues their conversational partners could not hear online. Not long after these user-generated practices emerged, technologies were created for replicating them. Now, for example, smiley faces are built into word processing programs directly. These examples highlight our reliance on nonverbal communication and its integration with language (Bavelas & Chovil, this volume). They also reflect the degree to which people can use an array of behaviors to communicate the same messages or perform the same functions: When one cue is not available, others take its place.

Second, an exploration of online communicating reveals the importance of nonverbal cues to an array of vital social issues (see chapters in Part IV of this volume). Specifically, research on CMC has revealed the extent to which we rely on nonverbal cues to display—and constrain—identity. When our physical attractiveness, cues to gender, race, and age, and physical abilities are absent from the interaction, as occurs in many but not all online interactions, we get a chance to see the ways in which the nonverbal cues of identification sometimes limit, and certainly configure, our face-to-face interactions. So, for example, research reveals the extent to which we require nonverbal cues to personalize another; without them, people may categorize others vaguely as "out-group" members and be less likely to treat them fairly (Postmes, Spears, Lea, & Reicher, 2000; see also, Dovidio et al., this volume).

At the same time, the absence of certain nonverbal cues that work typically to categorize a person into a stigmatized group (e.g., skin color, body size) may allow for enhancement of certain peoples' identities when they can minimize the influence of the cue. Furthermore, as Walther (this volume) notes, CMC allows for selective identity presentation in a way that face-to-face communication does not. For example, people can take more time to think through what they want to say, they may choose to send a photograph of themselves that is particularly flattering (or several years old), or they may state that their age or sex is other than what it actually is.

Third, research on CMC reveals the importance of certain nonverbal cues that

have not received much attention in research (for a notable exception, see Levine, 1997). Specifically, Walther argues that chronemics make up an important set of cues in CMC and are available without any technological advances. For example, how quickly people respond to one another's messages can send important communicative messages of relationships, importance, and communicative skill (see Riggio, the volume). Yet chronemic cues have been neglected as relevant in the CMC context.

Closer attention to the new technologies may provide a new perspective on how nonverbal communication works and what is most central in our research endeavors. Many of the assumptions that we hold (including the automaticity of our cue use) can be reinvestigated when nonverbal communication takes on a more strategic form. Finally, although the new technologies advance the range and efficiency of interpersonal communication, there may also be unwanted side effects. As people spend more time online, talking on cell phones, and text messaging, what happens to the important social benefits possible only in face-to-face interactions? Some scholars suggest that the impersonal nature of our new technologies reduces our sense of belonging and affects the social fabric adversely (see Bugeja, 2005). The effect of technologically mediated communication on the frequency and quality of face-to-face interactions is an important issue for future research.

◆ Conclusion

The study of nonverbal communication has changed dramatically over the last 50 years. Conceptual and methodological advances have facilitated a growing appreciation of the influence of nonverbal communication in our social world. We now have a better understanding of how biology, culture, gender, and personality help shape the course of nonverbal communication. In face-to-face interactions, there is a growing appreciation for the interdependence of parallel processes of sending and receiving information in the service of specific goals. Furthermore, this system of communication operates primarily on automatic, but it can shift to more controlled processes as corrections and adjustments are required in interactions. New methods, such as brain imaging and virtual reality techniques, provide us with interesting and powerful alternatives for studying nonverbal communication. There is, however, still much to learn from careful research in mundane public settings where nonverbal communication is *the* means of negotiating unfocused interactions. New media and computer technologies also enlist nonverbal elements, but not in the fashion we have seen in the past. Thus, as some issues seem closer to resolution, new questions will keep us busy in the future.

◆ References

Ambady, N., & Rosenthal, R. (1992). Thin slices of behavior as predictors of interpersonal consequences: A meta-analysis. *Psychological Bulletin, 111*, 256–274.

Argyle, M. (1972). *The psychology of interpersonal behavior* (2nd ed.). London: Penguin.

Argyle, M., & Dean, J. (1965). Eye-contact, distance, and affiliation. *Sociometry, 28*, 289–304.

Bailenson, J. N., & Yee, N. (2005). Digital chameleons: Automatic assimilation of nonverbal gestures in immersive virtual environments. *Psychological Science, 16*, 814–819.

Bargh, J. A. (1997). The automaticity of everyday life. In R. S. Wyer Jr. (Ed.), *Advances in social cognition* (Vol. 10, pp. 1–61). Mahwah, NJ: Erlbaum.

Blascovich, J., Loomis, J., Beall, A., Swinth, K., Hoyt, C., & Bailenson, J. N. (2002). Immersive virtual environment technology as a methodological tool for social psychology. *Psychological Inquiry, 13*, 103–124.

Bugeja, M. (2005). *Interpersonal divide.* Oxford, UK: Oxford University Press.

Carbaugh, D. (1999). "Just listen": "Listening" and landscape among the Blackfeet. *Western Journal of Communication, 63*, 250–270.

DePaulo, B. M., Charlton, C., Cooper, H., Lindsay, J. J., & Muhlenbruck, L. (1997). The accuracy-confidence correlation in the detection of deception. *Personality and Social Psychology Review, 1*, 346–357.

Dijksterhuis, A., & Bargh, J. A. (2001). The perception-behavior expressway: Automatic effects of social perception on social behavior. In M. P. Zanna (Ed.), *Advances in experimental social psychology* (Vol. 33, pp. 1–46). San Diego, CA: Academic Press.

Ekman, P. (1965). Differential communication of affect by head and body cues. *Journal of Personality and Social Psychology, 2*, 726–735.

Exline, R. V. (1963). Explorations in the process of person perception: Visual interaction in relation to competition, sex, and need for affiliation. *Journal of Personality, 31*, 1–20.

Fiske, S. T., & Taylor, S. E. (1995). *Social cognition* (2nd ed.). New York: McGraw-Hill.

Gilbert, D. T., & Malone, P. S. (1995). The correspondence bias. *Psychological Bulletin, 117*, 21–38.

Goffman, E. (1963). *Behavior in public places.* New York: Free Press.

Kolb, B., & Whishaw, I. Q. (2003). *Fundamentals of human neuropsychology* (5th ed.). New York: Worth.

Lakin, J. L., Jefferis, V. E., Cheng, C. M., & Chartrand, T. L. (2003). The chameleon effect as social glue: Evidence for the evolutionary significance of nonconscious mimicry. *Journal of Nonverbal Behavior, 27*, 145–162.

Levine, R. (1997). *A geography of time.* New York: Basic Books.

Mahl, G. F. (1956). Disturbances and silences in the patient's speech in psychotherapy.

Journal of Abnormal and Social Psychology, 53, 1–15.

Manusov, V. (2005). (Ed.). *The sourcebook of nonverbal measures: Going beyond words.* Mahwah, NJ: Erlbaum.

McArthur, L. Z., & Baron, R. (1983). Toward an ecological theory of social perception. *Psychological Review, 90,* 215–238.

Mehrabian, A. (1969). Significance of posture and position in the communication of attitude and status relationships. *Psychological Bulletin, 71,* 359–372.

Patterson, M. L. (1983). *Nonverbal behavior: A functional perspective.* New York: Springer-Verlag.

Patterson, M. L. (2005). The passing encounters paradigm: Monitoring microinteractions between pedestrians. In V. Manusov (Ed.), *The sourcebook of nonverbal measures: Going beyond words* (pp. 431–440). Mahwah NJ: Erlbaum.

Patterson, M. L., Foster, J. L., & Bellmer, C. D. (2001). Another look at accuracy and confidence in social judgments. *Journal of Nonverbal Behavior, 25,* 207–219.

Patterson, M. L., Iizuka, Y., Tubbs, M., Ansel, J., & Anson, J. (2006, January). *Passing encounters East and West: A comparison of Japanese and American pedestrian interactions.* Poster presented at the annual convention of the Society of Personality and Social Psychology, Palm Springs, CA.

Patterson, M. L., & Stockbridge, E. (1998). Effects of cognitive demand and judgment strategy on person perception accuracy. *Journal of Nonverbal Behavior, 22,* 253–263.

Patterson, M. L., & Tubbs, M. E. (2005). Through a glass darkly: Effects of smiling and visibility on recognition and avoidance in passing encounters. *Western Journal of Communication, 69,* 219–231.

Patterson, M. L., Webb, A., & Schwartz, W. (2002). Passing encounters: Patterns of recognition and avoidance in pedestrians. *Basic and Applied Social Psychology, 24,* 57–66.

Pelphrey, K. A., Viola, R. J., & McCarthy, G. (2004). When strangers pass: Processing of mutual and averted gaze in the superior temporal sulcus. *Psychological Science, 15,* 598–603.

Postmes, T., Spears, R., Lea, M., & Reicher, S. D. (2000). *SIDE issues centre stage: Recent developments in studies of deindividuation in groups.* Amsterdam: Royal Netherlands Academy of Arts and Sciences.

Rizzolatti, G., & Craighero, L. (2004). The mirror-neuron system. *Annual Review of Neuroscience, 27,* 169–192.

Sommer, R. (1959). Studies in personal space. *Sociometry, 22,* 247–260.

Swann, W. B., Jr. (1984). Quest for accuracy in person perception: A matter of pragmatics. *Psychological Review, 91,* 457–477.

Vallacher, R. R., & Wegner, D. M. (1987). What do people think they're doing? Action identification and human behavior. *Psychological Review, 94,* 3–15.

Wilson, T. D., & Schooler, J. W. (1991). Thinking too much: Introspection can reduce the quality of preferences and decisions. *Journal of Personality and Social Psychology, 60,* 181–192.

Zebrowitz, L. A., & Collins, M. A. (1997). Accurate social perception at zero acquaintance: The affordances of a Gibsonian approach. *Personality and Social Psychology Review, 1,* 204–223.

AUTHOR INDEX

SUBJECT INDEX

ABOUT THE EDITORS

Valerie Manusov is Professor in the Department of Communication at the University of Washington. She has published two previous edited volumes: *Communication, Attribution, and Close Relationships* with John Harvey (2001) and *The Sourcebook of Nonverbal Measures: Going Beyond Words* (2005). She has been Associate Chair of her department and Associate Editor of the *Journal of Social and Personal Relationships*. Her work focuses primarily on patterns of nonverbal behavior and the meanings given to nonverbal cues at a relational and cultural level. She also serves as Leadership Fellow for the College of Arts & Sciences at the University of Washington and teaches courses in nonverbal communication, interpersonal communication, intercultural communication, and research methods. One of her favorite achievements is completing the Avon 3-Day Walk for breast cancer prevention and research. She received her PhD from the University of Southern California in 1989 and worked for 4 years after that at Rutgers University.

Miles L. Patterson is Professor and former Chairperson of the Psychology Department at the University of Missouri at St. Louis (UMSL). He is the author of two books and more than 70 chapters and articles, mostly on nonverbal communication. Some of this research was supported by grants from the National Institute of Mental Health. He was the editor of the *Journal of Nonverbal Behavior* from 1986 to 1992 and has been on the editorial boards of several other journals in psychology, communication, and sociology. He was the 1990 recipient of the UMSL Chancellor's Award for Research and Creativity and is a fellow of both the American Psychological Association and the American Psychological Society. His current research interests focus primarily on theory in nonverbal communication, social behavior in public settings, and the role of nonverbal communication in interpersonal influence. His teaching interests include social psychology, nonverbal communication, and environmental psychology. He has also appeared on St. Louis radio and television a number of times as an expert commentator on communication and politics. In his spare time, he is an avid jogger, with over 24,000 miles run, and a golfer, always with high hopes for the next round. He received his PhD from Northwestern University in 1968 and has been at UMSL since 1969.

ABOUT THE CONTRIBUTORS

Nalini Ambady is Associate Professor at Tufts University. Before joining the Tufts faculty in the spring of 2004, she taught at Holy Cross College and in 1994 joined the faculty at Harvard. Her research interests include examining the accuracy of social, emotional, and perceptual judgments; how personal and social identities affect cognition and performance; dyadic interactions, especially those involving status differentiated dyads; and nonverbal communication. She is particularly interested in applying innovative and integrative methods to examine these phenomena from multiple perspectives, ranging from the biological to the sociocultural. She received her PhD in social psychology from Harvard University in 1991.

Peter A. Andersen, Professor of Communication at San Diego State University, has authored five books and more than 150 book chapters, research papers, and journal articles. His four most recent books are *The Handbook of Communication and Emotion* (1998), *Nonverbal Communication: Forms and Functions* (1999), *Close Encounters: Communicating in Relationships* (2001), and *The Complete Idiot's Guide to Body Language* (2004). He has recently published papers on communication and emotion, nonverbal communication, interpersonal relationships, risk communication, helmet safety, health communication, homeland security, and communication and technology. He has served as the President of the Western Communication Association, as Editor of the *Western Journal of Communication*, and as Director of Research for the Japan-U.S. Telecommunications Research Institute. He won the Robert Kibler Award for personal and professional excellence from the National Communication Association in 2003. He is a co-investigator on six federal grants in health communication and disaster preparedness. He received his PhD from Florida State University in 1975.

Janet Beavin Bavelas is the author of *Pragmatics of Human Communication* (with Watzlawick & Jackson) and *Equivocal Communication* (with Chovil, Black, & Mullett) and has published about 60 research articles or chapters, primarily on interpersonal communication. As of 2005, she is Professor Emeritus of Psychology at the University of Victoria, where she leads a research team doing experimental, microanalytic studies of the unique features of face-to-face dialogue, with an emphasis on speech-related nonverbal acts (hand and facial gestures) and on collaboration in dyadic interaction. Her applied research includes microanalysis of communication in psychotherapeutic, medical, and electronic interactions and in texts related to social justice issues. Her AB (psychology), AM (communication research), and PhD (psychology) are from Stanford University, and she is a fellow of the International Communication Association, the Canadian Psychological Association, and the Royal Society of Canada.

Ross Buck is Professor of Communication Sciences and Psychology at the University of Connecticut, Storrs. His books include *Human Motivation and Emotion* and *The Communication of Emotion*, and he is the author of over 100 other publications. He has received grants from the National Institute of Mental Health, the Harry Frank Guggenheim Foundation, the EJLB Foundation, and the Russell Sage Foundation, and his research has been featured on *ABC News, 20–20,* and FUJI-TV, Japan. He is Organizer and Charter Chair of the Nonverbal Communication Division of the National Communication Association. His present work centers on emotional experience, expression, and communication in human cooperation and competition, trustworthiness, and altruism; brain mechanisms of emotional communication; emotion in persuasion, including safe-sex communication; cross-cultural studies of social and moral emotion; emotional communication in clinical samples; emotional factors in maintaining drug regimens; and higher-level social, cognitive, and moral emotions as aspects of self-organizing dynamic systems emerging effortlessly from experience in social interaction.

Judee K. Burgoon is Professor of Communication, Professor of Family Studies and Human Development, Director of Human Communication Research for the Center for the Management of Information, and Associate Director of the Media Interface Network Design Lab at the University of Arizona. She is also a Visiting Professor of Communication at Michigan State University. She has authored or coauthored seven books and monographs and over 240 articles, chapters, and reviews related to deception, nonverbal and relational communication, dyadic interaction patterns, and computer-mediated communication. Her current research on interpersonal communication and deception detection has been funded by several federal agencies. She is a former Chairperson of the National Communication Association's Interpersonal Communication Division; a recipient of NCA's Distinguished Scholar, Golden Monographs, and Charles E. Woolbert awards; and an elected fellow of the International Communication Association. She received her EdD from West Virginia University.

Joseph N. Cappella is Professor of Communication and holds the Gerald R. Miller Chair at the Annenberg School for Communication at the University of Pennsylvania. His research has produced more than 90 articles and book chapters and three coauthored books focusing on political communication, health, social interaction, media effects, and statistical methods. His research has been supported by grants from the National Institutes of Mental Health, the National Institute on Drug Abuse, the National Science Foundation, the National Cancer Institute, the Twentieth Century Fund, and the Markle, Ford, Carnegie, Pew, and Robert Wood Johnson foundations. He has served on the editorial boards of 15 different journals. He is a Fellow of the International Communication Association, a Distinguished Scholar of the National Communication Association, a Past President of ICA, and a recipient of the B. Aubrey Fisher Mentorship Award. He received his PhD in 1974 from Michigan State University.

Nicole Chovil is an author of *Equivocal Communication* (with Bavelas, Black, & Mullett), plus 15 articles and chapters on equivocal communication, hand and facial displays in dialogue, and motor mimicry. She conducted the first systematic experimental studies of nonemotional functions of facial displays in face-to-face dialogue. She was also co-investigator and collaborator on a project using discourse analysis to study the language characterizing sexualized assault in legal judgments. She has a BA, with honors (psychology), from the University of Victoria; an MA (psychology) from Simon Fraser University; and a PhD (psychology) from the University of Victoria. In 2006, she left her position as Director of Education for the British Columbia Schizophrenia Society to become an independent research and education consultant specializing in mental illness.

John F. Dovidio is Professor of Psychology at the University of Connecticut. He is currently Editor of the *Journal of Personality and Social Psychology—Interpersonal Relations and Group Processes* and has previously been Editor of *Personality and Social Psychology Bulletin*. His research interests are in intergroup relation, nonverbal communication, and prosocial behavior. He received SPSSI's Kurt Lewin Award in 2004 (with S. L. Gaertner) for his career contributions to the study of prejudice and discrimination. He received the Gordon Allport Intergroup Relations Prize in 1985, 1998, and 2001 for his research on intergroup relations. He has an MA and PhD from the University of Delaware.

Norah E. Dunbar is Associate Professor of Communication Studies at California State University Long Beach. Her research interests are in relational conflict, deception, power and dominance, and nonverbal communication. Currently, she is working on several projects, including a study on the nonverbal expressions of dominance in close relationships. Her work can be found in journals such as the *Journal of Social and Personal Relationships* and the *Journal of Family Communication*. She teaches undergraduate and graduate classes in interpersonal communication, persuasion, nonverbal communication, research methods, and communication theory. She received her PhD in 2000 from the University of Arizona.

Robert S. Feldman is Associate Dean for Faculty and Student Development and Professor of Psychology at the University of Massachusetts at Amherst. A winner of the College Distinguished Teacher award, he is a fellow of the American Psychological Association and the American Psychological Society. He is a winner of a Fulbright Senior Research Scholar and Lecturer award, and he has written more than 100 books, book chapters, and scientific articles. His research has been supported by grants from the National Institute of Mental Health and the National Institute on Disabilities and Rehabilitation Research. His research interests include the development of nonverbal behavior in impression management and honesty and deception.

Kory Floyd is Associate Professor of Human Communication and Director of the Communication Sciences Laboratory at Arizona State University. His research focuses on the communication of affection in personal relationships and on the interplay between communication, physiology, and health. Currently, he is studying the ability of affectionate behavior to reduce the hormonal, cardiovascular, and hematological effects of stress. He has written or edited five books, including *Communicating Affection: Interpersonal Behavior and Social Context* (in press), and has published nearly 70 journal articles and book chapters on the topics of affection, family communication, nonverbal behavior, and physiology. He is currently Chair of the Family Communication Division of the National Communication Association and Editor of the *Journal of Family Communication*. He received his PhD from the University of Arizona.

Alan J. Fridlund is Associate Professor at the University of California, Santa Barbara. He is a social and clinical psychologist whose interests lie in human ethology (especially nonverbal communication), neuroethology, psychopathology, and sexology. He won the Distinguished Early Career Contribution Award of the Society for Psychophysiological Research and was a member of the Faculty in Experimental Psychopathology at the University of Pennsylvania. He is the author of *Human Facial Expression: An Evolutionary View* (1994) and has coauthored with Dan Reisberg (Reed College) and Henry Gleitman (U. Penn.) the introductory text *Psychology* (2003, 6th ed.).

Robert Gifford was born near where the gold rush began in northern California but almost 100 years too late to join in. He migrated up the coast to British Columbia in the late 1960s. After teaching at both ends

and in the middle of Canada, he is now Professor of Psychology at the University of Victoria. He is a fellow of the American and the Canadian Psychological Associations, the author of three editions of *Environmental Psychology: Principles and Practice*, and Editor of the *Journal of Environmental Psychology*. His current research includes studies of nonverbal behavior in relationships, a theory of social evaluation, cooperation in resource dilemmas, and the habitability of the International Space Station. He thinks everyone should have a grocery store within a 10-minute walk.

Howard Giles is Professor of Communication at the University of California, Santa Barbara, where he is also Assistant Dean of Undergraduate Studies, Director of the Center for Police Practices and Community, and Affiliated Professor in Psychology and Linguistics. Although his current interests relate to diverse areas of intergroup communication, he has sustained a long-standing interest in nonverbal communication by studying the social consequences of social dialects.

Heather M. Gray is a doctoral candidate in the Department of Psychology at Harvard University. As an undergraduate, she became interested in the manner in which transient fluctuations in mood state influence social information processing. Recently, she has been exploring the potential effects of mood state on the ability to make accurate inferences about others on the basis of minimal information. Together with Nalini Ambady, she has investigated the effects of sadness on social acuity in a number of domains, including the thin-slice paradigm, computer-based social sensitivity tasks, and more naturalistic social interactions. In a second line of research, she is exploring the manner in which relevance to the self influences the allocation of attentional resources to incoming stimuli. She has turned recently to psychophysiological techniques to more precisely investigate how self-relevance affects the early stages of social information processing.

Laura K. Guerrero is Professor in the Hugh Downs School of Human Communication, where she specializes in relational and nonverbal communication. She has published over 60 articles and chapters in these areas. Her work in nonverbal communication has focused on tactile behavior and other nonverbal immediacy cues, particularly in the context of romantic relationships and friendships. Her book credits include *The Handbook of Communication and Emotion* (coedited with Peter Andersen) and *Nonverbal Communication in Close Relationships* (coauthored with Kory Floyd). She was awarded the Gerald R. Miller Early Achievement Award from the International Association for Relationship Research in 2001 and twice received the Dickens Best Article Award from the Western States Communication Association. She received her PhD in 1994 from the University of Arizona.

Judith A. Hall is a professor in the Department of Psychology at Northeastern University. She held positions at Johns Hopkins University and the Harvard Medical School before coming to Northeastern in 1986. Her interests are in nonverbal communication, gender differences and gender roles, and physician-patient communication, with special focus on interpersonal sensitivity and the impact of hierarchical roles on nonverbal behavior and communication. Her books include *Nonverbal Sex Differences; Nonverbal Communication in Human Interaction* (coauthored with Mark Knapp), *Doctors Talking With Patients/Patients Talking With Doctors* (coauthored with Debra Roter), and *Interpersonal Sensitivity:*

Theory and Measurement (coedited with Frank Bernieri). She earned her doctorate at Harvard University.

Michelle "Mikki" Hebl is Associate Professor of Psychology at Rice University. She joined the Rice faculty in 1998, was named the Radoslav Tsanoff Assistant Professor of Psychology in 2001, and was promoted to Associate Professor in 2004. She is part of the industrial/organizational program at Rice University, and her research examines issues related to diversity and discrimination. She is particularly interested in identifying remediation strategies available to both individuals and organizations in addressing discrimination in the workplace and other settings. She received her bachelor's degree from Smith College in 1991 and her doctorate from Dartmouth College in 1997.

Adam Jaworski is Professor at the Centre for Language and Communication Research, Cardiff University. His latest books are *Metalanguage: Social and Ideological Perspectives* (2004, with Nikolas Coupland and Dariusz Galasiński) and *Discourse, Communication and Tourism* (2005, with Annette Pritchard). His research interests include discourse analysis, visual communication, and nonverbal communication. He coedits the book series *Oxford Studies in Sociolinguistics* (with Nik Coupland).

Susanne M. Jones is Assistant Professor in the Department of Communication Studies at the University of Minnesota, Twin Cities. She examines nonverbal and verbal comforting and emotional support behaviors, as well as the communication of emotion. Her work has been published in *Communication Monographs, Human Communication Research, Communication Research*, and *Sex Roles*. She received her PhD in 2000 from Arizona State University.

Caroline F. Keating is Professor of Psychology at Colgate University. She studies the nonverbal skills and physical appearances associated with social dominance, leadership, and charisma in children and adults. Together with collaborators, she has demonstrated that humans convey dominance through facial expressions akin to those of other primates, facial features that make people appear powerful also make them seem untrustworthy, people who are socially powerful have unusually good acting skills, and persuasive performances begin with kidding oneself. She also studies the charismatic processes by which groups inspire a following. Her studies of dominance, leadership, and deception (funded by the Harry Frank Guggenheim Foundation) have been featured in the print media, on radio talk shows, and on television. At Colgate, she teaches in specialty seminars on leadership, social bonds, and cross-cultural psychology. She received her PhD from Syracuse University.

Mark L. Knapp is the Jesse H. Jones Centennial Professor in Communication and Distinguished Teaching Professor at the University of Texas at Austin. His publications include *Nonverbal Communication in Human Interaction* (with J. A. Hall), *Interpersonal Communication and Human Relationships* (with A. L. Vangelisti), and *Handbook of Interpersonal Communication* (coedited with John A. Daly). He is a Past President of the International Communication Association and the National Communication Association, a fellow of the International Communication Association, and a Distinguished Scholar in the National Communication Association. He has served as Editor of *Human Communication Research*, and he developed and edited the Sage Series in Interpersonal Communication.

Jessica L. Lakin is Assistant Professor of Psychology at Drew University in Madison, New Jersey. Her main research interest is nonverbal behavior, specifically nonconscious behavioral mimicry, and its relationship to affiliation and the development of liking and rapport. Her other research interests include automatic processes, more generally, the self, and motivated social cognition. Her work has appeared in *Psychological Science*, the *Journal of Nonverbal Behavior*, and *Personality and Social Psychology Bulletin*, as well as in several edited volumes. She received her BA in psychology from Butler University in 1998 and her PhD in social psychology from Ohio State University in 2003.

David Matsumoto is Professor of Psychology and Director of the Culture and Emotion Research Laboratory at San Francisco State University. He has studied culture, emotion, social interaction, and communication for 20 years. His books include well-known titles such as *Culture and Psychology: People Around the World* (translated into Dutch and Japanese), *The Handbook of Culture and Psychology* (translated into Russian), and *The New Japan* (translated into Chinese). He is the recipient of many awards and honors in the field of psychology, including being named a G. Stanley Hall lecturer by the American Psychological Association. He is the series editor for *Culture, Cognition, and Behavior* for Oxford University Press. He is also Associate Editor for the *Journal of Cross-Cultural Psychology* and is on the editorial boards of the *Asian Journal of Social Psychology, Asian Psychologist*, the *Journal of Nonverbal Behavior, Motivation and Emotion, Cognition and Emotion*, and *Human Communication*.

James C. McCroskey is Professor of Communication Studies at West Virginia

University. He has authored or coauthored over 50 books and 250 journal articles and book chapters. He coauthored the first book on instructional communication in the field and taught one of the first graduate courses in nonverbal communication in the field. His research, writing, and teaching have focused on instructional communication, interpersonal communication, nonverbal communication, organizational communication, intercultural communication, communication traits, social influence, and communibiology. He has received numerous awards for his teaching and research from his university and a wide variety of national and international professional associations in communication, teacher education, and pharmacy education. He has been recognized as the most prolific published scholar in the history of the field of communication.

Linda L. McCroskey is Associate Professor of Communication Studies at California State University, Long Beach. Her research, writing, and teaching have focused on intercultural communication, organizational communication, business communication, instructional communication, communication traits, and communication theory. She has published in several leading journals in the field of communication, including *Communication Quarterly, Communication Research Reports*, and the *Journal of Intercultural Communication Research*. She is a coauthor of books on instructional communication and organizational communication and a forthcoming book on business communication. She is an active member of the International Communication Association, the National Communication Association, the Eastern Communication Association, and the Western States Communication Association. She also has employed her education in business,

organizational communication, and intercultural communication to launch and manage her own private business for 5 years and to serve as a consultant for a major international business organization.

Beth A. Le Poire is currently Associate Professor of Communication at California Lutheran University. She has authored over 45 research papers in the areas of family and interpersonal communication and specializes in nonverbal communication research. She recently published in the text *Family Communication* (Sage, 2006) and is in the process of completing an edited volume on interpersonal, socially meaningful research with Rene Dailey at the University of Texas at Austin. She was a professor at the University of California at Santa Barbara when she completed this introductory chapter with Howard Giles.

Patricia Noller is currently Emeritus Professor of Psychology at the University of Queensland. For 7 years, she was Director of the University of Queensland Family Centre. She has published extensively in the area of marital and family relationships, including 12 books and over 100 journal articles and book chapters. She is a fellow of the Academy of the Social Sciences in Australia and of the National Council on Family Relationships in the United States. She has served on a number of editorial boards and was appointed as Foundation Editor of *Personal Relationships: Journal of the International Society for the Study of Personal Relationships*, a position she held from 1993 to 1997. She was President of that society from 1998 to 2000.

Stacie Renfro Powers is a third-year doctoral student in communication sciences at the University of Connecticut. She is the recipient of a University of Connecticut Outstanding Scholars predoctoral fellowship and has worked as a research assistant on projects relating to the communication of trustworthiness (funded by the Russell Sage Foundation), the communication of emotion in Huntington's Disease patients and caregivers (funded by the University of Connecticut Health Center Huntington's Disease Program), and brain mechanisms of empathic ability (funded by the Olin Neuropsychiatry Center of the Hartford Hospital Institute of Living). She is certified in the Facial Action Coding System (FACS) and has received training in functional brain imaging (fMRI) study design and data analysis. Her main research interests are in facial expressivity, empathic ability, interpersonal coordination, and sex differences in emotion communication.

Martin S. Remland is Associate Professor of Communication Studies at West Chester University of Pennsylvania. His research interests include nonverbal displays of status and power and cross-cultural differences in nonverbal involvement behaviors. He is the author of *Nonverbal Communication in Everyday Life* (Houghton Mifflin, 2004) and coauthor of *Interpersonal Communication Through the Lifespan* (Houghton Mifflin, in press). His work has appeared in numerous journals in the fields of communication and psychology. He received his BA from Western Illinois University, his MA from Central Michigan University, and his PhD from Southern Illinois University.

Jennifer A. Richeson is Associate Professor in the Department of Psychology and Faculty Fellow at the Institute for Policy Research, both at Northwestern University. Her research is in the areas of prejudice, stereotyping, and intergroup relations. Her work considers the ways in which social group memberships such as race and gender influence the way people think, feel, and behave. More specifically, her research investigates multiple dynamics of prejudice and stereotyping from the perspectives of members of both traditionally stigmatized and dominant social groups. She is currently working on three primary lines of research: the dynamics and consequences of interracial contact, detecting and controlling racial bias, and racial categorization and identity. She earned her BS in psychology from Brown University in 1994 and her PhD in social psychology from Harvard University in 2000.

Virginia P. Richmond is Professor of Communication Studies at West Virginia University. She has authored or coauthored over 25 books and 150 journal articles and book chapters. Her book on nonverbal communication, *Nonverbal Behavior in Interpersonal Relations* (coauthored with J. C. McCroskey), is now in its fifth edition (2004). Her research, writing, and teaching have focused on nonverbal communication, instructional communication, interpersonal communication, organizational communication, communication traits, social influence, and training and development. She has received numerous awards for her teaching and research from her university and a wide variety of national professional associations in communication, teacher education, and pharmacy education. She has been recognized as one of the top five prolific published scholars in the history of the field of communication.

Ronald E. Riggio is the Henry R. Kravis Professor of Leadership and Organizational Psychology and Director of the Kravis Leadership Institute at Claremont McKenna College. He is the author of over 100 books, book chapters, and research articles in the areas of leadership, assessment centers, organizational psychology, and social psychology. His research work has included studies on the role of social skills and emotions in leadership potential and success, empathy, social intelligence, emotional skill, and charisma. He is Associate Editor of *The Leadership Quarterly* and is on the editorial boards of *Leadership* and the *Journal of Nonverbal Behavior*. His recent books are *Multiple Intelligences and Leadership* and *The Future of Leadership Development* (coedited with Susan Murphy, 2002, 2003), *Improving Leadership in Nonprofit Organizations* (coedited with Sarah Smith Orr, 2004), *Applications of Nonverbal Behavior* (coedited with Robert S. Feldman, 2005), and *Transformational Leadership* (2nd ed., coauthored with Bernard M. Bass, 2006).

Jeffrey D. Robinson is Associate Professor in the Department of Communication at Rutgers University. He is broadly interested in interpersonal communication, health communication, and language and social interaction. He specializes in conversation analysis and physician-patient interaction. He received his BA (communication) from the University of California, Santa Barbara, his MA (communication), from the University of Southern California, and his PhD (sociology) from the University of California at Los Angeles.

James A. Russell is Professor and Chair in the Psychology Department at Boston College. He spent most of his academic career at the University of British Columbia. An initial interest in the emotional impact of large-scale physical environments led to studies on the language of emotion, taxonomies of emotion, facial expressions of emotion, cultural differences in emotion, the developmental course of emotion knowledge, and theories of emotion. This research was brought together in a model called the psychological construction of emotion. He is a fellow of the APA and the APS. He received his PhD from the University of California at Los Angeles in 1974.

Darren M. Schreiber is Assistant Professor of Political Science at the University of California at San Diego. His research centers on emergence and complexity in political systems. He studied politics, philosophy, and economics as an undergraduate at Claremont McKenna College, later attending the U.C. Davis School of Law, where he focused on civil rights litigation. He then specialized in federal litigation at the law firm of Neumiller and Beardslee. His dissertation research used functional brain imaging (fMRI) to study the neural substrates of political cognition and affect. He has shown that ideological sophisticates differ from political novices in their heightened use of the posterior cingulate, a brain region associated with automatic social evaluation. His goal is to integrate agent-based models of macropolitical dynamics with his computational model of political cognition in individuals in order to illuminate the emergence of political ideology in the mass public. He served as Research Director at the Center of Excellence in Cancer Communication Research at the Annenberg School of Communication, University of Pennsylvania, during 2004 to 2005. He earned his PhD in political science at the University of California at Los Angeles in 2005.

J. Nicole Shelton is Associate Professor of Psychology at Princeton University. She was a postdoctoral fellow at the University of Michigan from 1998 to 2000. Her primary research, which has been funded by the National Institute of Mental Health and the National Science Foundation, focuses on how whites and ethnic minorities navigate issues of prejudice in interracial interactions. Specifically, she is interested in how whites' concerns with appearing prejudiced and ethnic minorities' concerns with being the target of prejudice influence affective, cognitive, and behavioral outcomes during interracial interactions. Her secondary line of research focuses on the consequences of confronting perpetrators of prejudice. Specifically, she is interested in the interpersonal consequences of confronting perpetrators and the intrapersonal consequences of not confronting perpetrators of prejudice. She earned her BA in psychology from the College of William and Mary in 1993 and her PhD in psychology from the University of Virginia in 1998.

Linda Tickle-Degnen is Associate Professor of Occupational Therapy in Sargent College of Health & Rehabilitation Sciences at Boston University. Her research is directed toward understanding the social-psychological implications of Parkinson's disease and other chronic health conditions, specifically as related to cross-cultural health care interactions, interpersonal rapport, and quality of life. Her research is funded by the National Institute of Neurological Disorders and Stroke and the National Institute of Aging at the National Institutes of Health. She received her doctorate in experimental social psychology from Harvard University, her master's degree in occupational therapy from the University of Southern California, and her bachelor's degree in anthropology from Stanford University.

James M. Tyler is an Assistant Professor in the Department of Communication at Purdue University. He was recently awarded an American Psychological Association Dissertation Research Award and he has written nearly 20 journal articles and book chapters. His research, which focuses on the social aspects of the

self in the context of the self-regulation and self-presentation of interpersonal behavior, examines how people's behaviors and emotions are influenced by their concerns about others' impressions and acceptance of them. His current projects range from examining the relationship between the self's regulatory resources and the capacity to monitor the social environment for relational value cues to the influence that threatening social circumstances exert on people's self-presentation efforts. He received his PhD in social psychology from the University of Massachusetts Amherst in 2006.

Aldert Vrij is Professor of Applied Social Psychology at the University of Portsmouth. His main research interest is deception, particularly nonverbal aspects of deception (e.g., how liars behave), verbal aspects of deception (e.g., what they say), people's ability to detect deceit, and ways to improve this ability. He has published almost 300 articles and book chapters and six books to date, the majority of which are related to deception. He currently holds research grants from the Economic and Social Research Council (ESRC), the British Academy, and the Nuffield Foundation, and in the past he has held grants from the ESRC, the Nuffield Foundation, the Leverhulme Trust, and the Dutch Ministry of Justice. All these research grants were related to deception. He is the Editor of *Legal and Criminological Psychology* and sits on the editorial boards of *Law and Human Behavior*, *Human Communication Research*, and the *Journal of Nonverbal Behavior*.

Joseph B. Walther is Professor in the Department of Communication and the Department of Telecommunication, Information Studies, and Media at Michigan State University. His research focuses on the interpersonal dynamics of communication via computers in personal relationships, work groups, and educational settings. He has held regular or visiting appointments in psychology, information technology, education and social policy at universities in the US and UK. He was Chair of the Organizational Communication and Information Systems division of the Academy of Management and the Communication and Technology division of the International Communication Association. His professional honors include the National Communication Association's 2002 Woolbert Award for an article that has stood the test of time and influenced thinking in the discipline for more than 10 years. He received his PhD from the University of Arizona in 1990.